ADVANCES IN BUSINESS
FINANCIAL MANAGEMENT

A Collection of Readings

ADVANCES IN BUSINESS FINANCIAL MANAGEMENT

A Collection of Readings

Edited by
Philip L. Cooley
Trinity University

The Dryden Press
Chicago   Fort Worth   San Francisco   Philadelphia
Montreal   Toronto   London   Sydney   Tokyo

Acquisitions Editor: Ann Heath
Project Editor: Susan Jansen
Design Manager: Alan Wendt
Production Manager: Barb Bahnsen
Permissions Editor: Cindy Lombardo
Director of Editing, Design, and Production: Jane Perkins

Text and Cover Designer: C.J. Petlick
Copy Editor: Karen Vertovec
Compositor: TCSystems, Inc.
Text Type: 10/12 Times Roman

Library of Congress Cataloging-in-Publication Data
Advances in business financial management.
    Includes bibliographies.
    1. Corporations—Finance. I. Cooley, Philip L.
HG4026.A34 1990   658.1′5   88-33602
ISBN 0-03-009943-9

Address orders:
The Dryden Press
Orlando, FL 32887

Address editorial correspondence:
The Dryden Press
908 N. Elm Street
Hinsdale, IL 60521

The Dryden Press
Holt, Rinehart and Winston
Saunders College Publishing

To
Miss Esther Berry

The Dryden Press Series in Finance

Berry and Young
Managing Investments: A Case Approach

Boyet
Security Analysis for Investment Decisions

Brigham
Fundamentals of Financial Management
Fifth Edition

Brigham, Aberwald, and Ball
Finance with Lotus 1-2-3®: Text, Cases, and Models

Brigham and Gapenski
Cases in Financial Management

Brigham and Gapenski
Financial Management: Theory and Practice
Fifth Edition

Brigham and Gapenski
Intermediate Financial Management
Third Edition

Campsey and Brigham
Introduction to Financial Management
Second Edition

Chance
An Introduction to Options and Futures

Clayton and Spivey
The Time Value of Money

Cooley
Advances in Business Financial Management: A Collection of Readings

Cooley and Roden
Business Financial Management

Crum and Brigham
Cases in Managerial Finance
Sixth Edition with 1986 Tax Law Changes

Fama and Miller
The Theory of Finance

Gardner and Mills
Managing Financial Institutions: An Asset/Liability Approach

Gitman and Joehnk
Personal Financial Planning
Fifth Edition

Goldstein Software, Inc.
Joe Spreadsheet

Harrington
Case Studies in Financial Decision Making
Second Edition

Johnson
Issues and Readings in Managerial Finance
Third Edition

Johnson and Johnson
Commercial Bank Management

Kidwell and Peterson
Financial Institutions, Markets, and Money
Fourth Edition

Koch
Bank Management

Martin, Cox, and MacMinn
The Theory of Finance: Evidence and Applications

Mayo
Investments: An Introduction
Second Edition

Myers
Modern Developments in Financial Management

Pettijohn
PROFIT+

Reilly
Investment Analysis and Portfolio Management
Third Edition

Reilly
Investments
Second Edition

Seitz
Capital Budgeting and Long-Term Financing Decisions

Siegel and Siegel
Futures Markets

Smith and Weston
PC Self-Study Manual for Finance

Tallman and Neal
Financial Analysis and Planning Package

Turnbull
Option Valuation

Weston and Brigham
Essentials of Managerial Finance
Ninth Edition

Weston and Copeland
Managerial Finance
Eighth Edition with Tax Update

PREFACE

New ideas in business financial management appear in journals published in diverse locations by professional groups, government agencies, universities, and corporations. Staying abreast of the ideas in these far-flung publications is a formidable task even for dedicated scholars. This collection of 48 finance articles from 26 different sources eases the task and provides a convenient way of learning about the advances in business financial management.

The intended readers of this collection include undergraduate and graduate students taking their first or second course in finance. Each article lies within the intellectual grasp of these students. Complicated mathematics and statistics will not be found in any of the articles. The focus is on the ideas of finance, not on methodology.

This book of readings can be used to supplement textbooks and casebooks on business financial management. Its contents add depth to the materials covered in such books, offering a perspective that they cannot provide. Standard texts are necessarily limited in their depth of coverage because of the need for breadth. Selected finance articles greatly enrich the educational process by taking students beyond conventional wisdom and closer to the leading edge of knowledge.

Organization of the Book

The book contains seven parts covering the major topics of business financial management. Sequencing of the parts and the articles within them approximately follows the progression of ideas found in many finance textbooks. The parts and the articles can be rearranged to suit the purposes of the reader. Understanding an individual article does not depend on the particulars of preceding articles.

In brief, the following titles and subtitles describe the subject matter of the parts and the content of the articles:

Part 1. Business Financial Management and Its Environment
Corporate goals, the nature of corporations, and executive compensation.

Part 2. Valuation and Cost of Capital
Security valuation, the efficient market hypothesis, historical rates of return, estimating beta, corporate debt levels, and capital structure.

Part 3. Capital Budgeting
Corporate practice, strategy, theory, and behavioral applications.

Part 4. Managing Working Capital
Corporate practice, repurchase agreements, commercial paper, hedging, factoring, credit terms, inventory control, bank loans, and interest rate swaps.

Part 5. Analyzing and Planning Financial Performance
Corporate practice, bankruptcy, analytical procedures, financial ratios, and break-even analysis.

Part 6. Institutional Features of Long-Term Financing
Junk bonds, preferred stock, financial innovations, dividend policy, and stock repurchases.

Part 7. Special Topics
Term loans, leases, mergers and acquisitions, foreign exchange markets, and Japanese finance.

About the Articles

In order to be included in this collection of readings, an article must meet a complex mixture of criteria. Overriding these criteria, however, are two requirements: (1) The article must be accessible to students taking their first course in finance, and (2) the article must add to the understanding of ideas that are usually presented in introductory finance courses. Most of the articles have explicit implications for improving financial decision making, and several of them report on financial practices in the business world.

Because the focus of this text is on the advances in business financial management, the articles are of recent vintage. Thirty of them were published in 1985 or later; only two were published prior to 1980. As a result, the collection represents the up-to-date thinking of scholars in the finance discipline.

The articles in this book have survived the winnowing of hundreds of candidate articles. Dozens of academic and professional journals in finance, economics, accounting, management science, and general business were thoroughly searched to identify articles meeting the criteria for inclusion. In addition, many professors of finance shared their ideas on candidates for the collection. The result is 48 articles that were originally published in the following sources:

Business Conditions	*Economic Perspectives*
Business Horizons	*Financial Analysts Journal*
Business Review	*Financial Executive*
Credit & Financial Management	*Financial Management*

Financial Review

Harvard Business Review

Interfaces

Journal of Accountancy

Journal of Cash Management

Journal of Commercial Bank Lending

Journal of Economics and Business

Journal of Finance

Journal of Financial Education

Journal of Financial Research

Journal of Financial and Quantitative Analysis

Journal of Portfolio Management

Management Accounting

Midland Corporate Finance Journal Review

Securities Industry Review

Sloan Management Review

Vital Speeches of the Day

Special Feature

Several discussion questions are included at the conclusion of each article to enhance its learning value. In total, the book contains more than 250 such questions. After reading an article, students can use the questions to test themselves for comprehension. Instructors may wish to assign the questions for written responses, or they may use them to structure classroom discussion. Experience shows that students greatly appreciate the guidance provided by these questions.

Acknowledgments

A readings book owes its life to the authors of the original works. Their insights, new twists, and clarity of thought are valuable commodities. I am grateful to these authors for their intellectual contributions and for their permission to reprint their work. My gratitude also extends to the publishers of the original works for their permission to reprint the material.

The staff of The Dryden Press has a well-earned reputation for publishing finance books. Authors and editors know well the importance of working with a competent and caring publishing staff. I thank Ann Heath for signing this project and Susan Jansen and Karen Vertovec for guiding the project to its completion.

My former assistant Yvonne Cortright cheerfully helped with the beginning of this project. I feel gratitude for her dedication and wish her success in her new endeavors. My current assistant Aurora Molina is a great finisher. I truly appreciate her commitment to meeting deadlines.

To my colleagues who suggested articles for this collection of readings, a resounding thank you. Their suggestions and encouragement greatly improved the finished product:

Raj Aggarwal
John Carroll University

James S. Ang
Florida State University

Christopher B. Barry
Texas Christian University

William L. Beedles
University of Kansas

Helen M. Bowers
University of Notre Dame

Dallas Brozik
Marshall University

Andrew H. Chen
Southern Methodist University

It-Keong Chew
University of Kentucky

Lal C. Chugh
University of Massachusetts

Ronnie J. Clayton
University of Central Florida

Larry A. Cox
University of Georgia

Wallace N. Davidson III
Louisiana Tech University

Steve Dawson
University of Hawaii

John Dobson
University of Minnesota-Duluth

Mary E. Ellis
Bryant College

David C. Ewert
Georgia State University

Joseph E. Finnerty
University of Illinois

J. Stephen Gaske
Trinity University

James A. Gentry
University of Illinois

Diana R. Harrington
University of Virginia

George W. Hettenhouse
Indiana University

Andrea J. Heuson
University of Miami

Carl M. Hubbard
Trinity University

William C. Hunter
Emory University

Michael D. Joehnk
Arizona State University

O. Maurice Joy
University of Kansas

William R. Lane
Louisiana State University

Ronald C. Lease
Tulane University

C. F. Lee
Rutgers University

Daniel E. McCarty
Florida Atlantic University

Pamela P. Peterson
Florida State University

Rodney L. Roenfeldt
University of South Carolina

Frederick P. Schadler
East Carolina University

Daniel L. Schneid
Central Michigan University

Ernest W. Swift
Georgia State University

Robert A. Taggart
Boston University

John M. Wachowicz
University of Tennessee

Daniel T. Walz
Trinity University

James W. Wansley
Louisiana State University

Daniel T. Winkler
University of North Carolina-Greensboro

A Concluding Note

You, the reader, are the final judge of this readings book. It is my hope that the authors' insights will light up the eyes of students with excitement. Personally, I will judge the book a success if both students and instructors share the magic of enlightenment from its use. I invite your suggestions for articles to include in the next edition.

Philip L. Cooley
San Antonio, Texas
August 1989

CONTENTS

PART I
BUSINESS FINANCIAL MANAGEMENT AND ITS ENVIRONMENT

1

The Financial Objective in the Widely Held Corporation

Jack L. Treynor

In the widely held corporation, the split between ownership and control is often virtually complete. Should those in control of the corporation share that traditional financial objective of those who own it—the maximization of share value?

Chester Barnard has argued that a corporation owes its existence to the consent of a number of factions. When a customer ceases to buy or the worker refuses to work, for example, the result is usually a crisis for management. Edward Banfield calls the ability of the executive to elicit cooperation "power," or "influence," and views executive action in terms of trading in power. Banfield's remarks about management's exercise of power apply a fortiori *to financial power. The key to management's power to spend is the willingness of its creditors to continue lending. Management has unused financial power whenever the corporation's creditors consider that existing loans have not exhausted their security.*

Since, in a rational market, the aggregate value of the corporate common stock equals the economic value of the corporation less the outstanding claims of creditors, the untapped borrowing power of the corporation—hence management's power to spend—is measured by the aggregate market value of the common stock. It is doubtful whether other factions with a financial stake in the corporation will be best served by a policy of merely "satisficing" with respect to the shareholder. Those who regard share value maximization as irrelevant or immoral are forgetting that the stockholder is not merely the beneficiary of the corporation's financial success, but also the referee who determines management's financial power.

The split between ownership and control in the widely held corporation is often virtually complete, with ownership vested in a large and

Jack L. Treynor, "The Financial Objective in the Widely Held Corporation," *Financial Analysts Journal* (March/April 1981): 68–71. Reprinted with permission.

At the time of this writing, Jack L. Treynor was the editor of the *Financial Analysts Journal*.

diverse population of stockholders and control wielded by a small group of professional managers. For this kind of corporation, it is no longer realistic to regard management as the hired hand of the owner.[1] Management will have its own interests, which may diverge significantly from the owners'. In particular, some argue, those in control of the corporation may no longer share that traditional financial objective of those who own it—the maximization of share value.

Professor Gordon Donaldson of the Harvard Business School has argued that the interest of management "quite naturally relates to the specifics of near-term movements in cash inflow and outflow, with all their inevitable irregularities from one period to another." The administration of cash flows, chiefly through mundane business operations, rarely involves the corporate shareholder. As Donaldson sees it, the stockholder's contribution is limited to providing management with continuity in office and, when needed, new equity capital. Furthermore, "for the large and mature corporation, the second of these may not be a vital consideration. Many such companies do not give serious consideration to stock issues as a source of cash for growth, finding that internally generated funds, net of the customary dividends, very adequately supply the needed growth in the equity base." In other words, management asks of ownership only to be left alone to do its job free of "harassments from individual champions of the stockholder interest" and free of the threat of "raids that would unseat existing management."[2]

If the stockholder's contribution to the corporation is largely passive, why then should management take seriously the objective of maximizing the per share value of the common stock? According to Edward S. Mason (former Dean of the Graduate School of Public Administration, Harvard University), "If ownership is completely divorced from control, it becomes hard to see why stockholders are entitled to more than an interest payment, plus a premium for risks that are substantially smaller for large than for small firms. If there are no legally enforceable responsibilities of management . . . to owners . . . it becomes doubtful whether over time these responsibilities will be recognized." He quotes Lord Keynes, who pointed out that when "the stockholders are almost entirely disassociated from management . . . the direct personal interest of the latter in the making of great profit becomes quite secondary. When this stage is reached, the general stability and reputation of the institution are more considered by the management than the maximum profit for the stockholders."[3]

Professor Robert N. Anthony of the Harvard Business School describes a management point of view toward financial objectives in the widely held corporation that is probably not far from typical: "Many companies formed to achieve some specific short-run objective (e.g., a real estate syndicate, a stock promotion) undoubtedly fit the profit maximization pattern. So do speculators in both securities and commodities. So do various types of fly-by-night operators and get-rich-quick artists. But I know of no study of general business practice that supports the profit maximization premise . . . . Although we find leaders of the business community stressing the importance of a *satisfactory* profit, we also find them discussing business responsibilities, the need for a fair division of income among the parties involved in the business and other subjects that are *incompatible with the profit maximization goal."* Anthony concludes that profit maximization is not only too difficult to achieve, but also immoral.[4]

In this writer's view, any management—no matter how powerful and independent—that flouts the financial objective of maximizing share value does so at its peril.

Management Ends

Chester Barnard has argued that a corporation owes its continued existence to the consent of any number of factions—the customer, the stockholder, the banker, the supplier, the worker, the voter.[5] When one or more of these factions suspends cooperation, the result is usually a crisis for the corporation—and for its management. Consider what happens, for example, when a customer ceases to buy or the worker refuses to work.

Edward Banfield calls the ability of the executive to elicit cooperation "power," or "influence," and views executive action in terms of exercising, and trading in, power. The executive "may have a sizable inventory [of power] and many accounts receivable." The goodwill of the customer constitutes a stock of corporate power, as does the confidence of the banker. "This power is like capital; [the executive] can either 'consume' it or 'invest' it." But, "it goes without saying," Banfield continues, "that if he is to stay in business very long [he] . . . must like any trader maintain his capital and support himself while doing so."

The executive must, in other words, "employ the incentives at his disposal so as to (a) secure the cooperation he needs to accomplish his immediate purposes and (b) replenish the supply of incentives (and if possible increase it) so that he can accomplish other purposes on future occasions . . . . On any particular occasion [he] . . . might indulge himself in the luxury of 'consuming' rather than 'investing' influence, i.e., of using it for present purposes without regard to its replenishment, but if he consumed it for very long he would be out of business."[6]

Since it will usually be hard to determine whether management seeks power for its own sake, to fulfill a social responsibility to the community, or out of practical recognition of the vital need for continued cooperation from the factions on which the corporation depends, the morality of management's drive to develop and maintain its stock of power is necessarily ambiguous.

Management Means

Banfield's remarks about management's exercise of power apply *a fortiori* to financial power, since the corporation has a financial relationship with each of the factions on which its continued existence depends. The customer wants a high-quality product at a competitive price. The worker wants decent working conditions at the highest possible wage. The concerns of the stockholder, banker and supplier are obviously financial. No matter how much the worker likes management, he will stop working soon after the payroll stops. No matter how much the customer likes the corporation's product, he will stop buying when the price ceases to be competitive. When the corporation ceases to fulfill its financial obligations, the stock of goodwill residing in the several factions is exhausted fairly quickly.

In most cases, the financial claims of the several factions must be met with cash, or cash equivalents, and they must be met when they fall due. Otherwise the various factions lose confidence in the corporation and withdraw their support. Cash is truly the lifeblood of the corporation; without it, the corporation sickens and dies very quickly. Although the power to distribute cash at a point in time is only one of the forms the stock of corporate power takes, it is an important form.

The financial objective of the corporation is to conserve, and when possible enhance, the corporation's power to distribute cash.

Financial Power

The corporation's financial power cannot be measured by toting up its cash balances. The amount of cash and near cash on hand in excess of the cash inventory required for operating purposes may understate or overstate the corporation's power to distribute cash. It will understate if the corporation has unused borrowing power and overstate if the corporation has liabilities that rely in part on the cash in question for security. (As a practical matter, a corporation is unlikely to have simultaneously a large inventory of "surplus" cash and large debts unless it has a seasonal cash need.)

A corporation can put its creditors, hence its financial power, in jeopardy while maintaining a cash flow from operations entirely adequate to service its debt obligations. For example, a commodity processing company that neglects to hedge its position in the commodities market — either long or short — may find the security for its creditors jeopardized by a sudden fluctuation in the market, even though its processing margins, hence its operating cash flows, are virtually unaffected.

Prospects for future cash flows from operations will have a certain present value, but if this value — together with the value of the company's other assets — is not sufficient to cover its liabilities, creditors are no longer fully protected. The fact that cash flows from operations may ultimately return to creditors the dollar value of their claims does not constitute full compensation, since creditors must incur in the interim equity risk that results in an irreplaceable loss in the present value of their claims.

On the other hand, a rapidly growing company may be absorbing more cash into plant and working capital than it can currently generate from operations. If rapid expansion promises to be profitable, the company can usually find creditors — very often the original creditors — willing to step in and provide additional funds. Inability to generate the cash needed to service outstanding debt without further borrowing is not in itself a disaster — either for management or for creditors.

The willingness of the corporation's creditors to continue lending is in fact the key to the corporation's power to distribute cash. The corporation has unused power whenever creditors consider that existing loans have not exhausted their security.[7]

Although most creditors will insist on some margin of safety, the rough measure of the borrowing power of the corporation at a point in time is the amount by which the gross market value of the corporation exceeds its existing liabilities. Whatever increases the margin tends to increase the amount of cash the corporation can generate at a point in time, hence the financial power of the corporation. Whatever reduces the margin tends to reduce the financial power of the corporation.

Under most circumstances of practical interest, the financial objective in the widely held corporation is to conserve, and when possible increase, the margin between the gross market value of the corporation and its liabilities.

Stocks, Not Flows

Our interpretation of the corporate financial objective would be of largely academic interest were it not for the fact that, in a rational market, the aggregate value of the corporate common stock equals the gross market value of the corporation less the outstanding claims of creditors. It follows immediately that, except for some margin of safety for the creditors, the untapped borrowing power of the corporation — hence management's financial power — is measured by the market value of the outstanding common stock.

Financial power will fluctuate from day to day with fluctuations in the value of the common stock.[8] Uncertainty surrounding these fluctuations, rather than uncertainty surrounding the flow of cash from operations, is the fundamental financial risk for management. If corporate managements are really preoccupied with "near-term movements in cash inflow and outflow" and their "irregularities from one period to another," they are wasting a lot of valuable time.

Share Value Maximization Is Management's Objective

The financial objective is, of course, only one among a number of corporate objectives and, as such, is not necessarily controlling in any specific decision. Even when the financial objective is subordinated to other corporate objectives, however, management will be well advised to measure the cost of a decision in terms of financial power. This means, in terms of our interpretation, measuring its effect on the value of the corporate common shares.[9]

The other parties with a stake in the corporation—the worker, the customer, the supplier, the banker and certainly management itself—are hardly likely to be preoccupied with stockholder interests. Yet it is doubtful whether any of these parties will be best served by a policy of merely "satisficing" with respect to the value of corporate shares. Those who criticize the goal of share value maximization are forgetting that stockholders are not merely the beneficiaries of a corporation's financial success, but also the referees who determine management's financial power.

Footnotes

1. See Berle and Means, *The Modern Corporation and Private Property* (New York: The Macmillan Company, 1933).

2. G. Donaldson, *Corporate Debt Capacity* (Boston, MA: Division of Research, Graduate School of Business Administration, Harvard University, 1961).

3. E.S. Mason, *The Corporation in Modern Society* (Cambridge, MA: Harvard University Press, 1959).

4. R.N. Anthony, "The Trouble with Profit Maximization," *Harvard Business Review,* 1960.

5. C. Barnard, *Executive Action,* 30th Anniversary Ed. (Cambridge, MA: Harvard University Press, 1968).

6. E. Banfield, *Political Influence* (New York: The Free Press, 1963).

7. It is sometimes supposed that creditors look primarily to the liquidation value of corporate assets for security. Secured lenders are obviously interested in the liquidation value of those corporate assets on which they have a lien. But liquidation value is a limited measure of corporate borrowing power, for several reasons. Investments in research and market development, for example, are likely to have little or no value in liquidation. In some cases, even plant and equipment are so specialized that they have little value apart from the current operation. Even when assets can be assigned a market value, it is likely to fluctuate as widely or more widely than the value of the corporation itself, since the assets depend for their true value on the same economic uncertainties underlying the aggregate corporate earning power.

8. Some will argue that because market value fluctuates constantly, no meaning can be attached to it. Nothing could be further from the truth. In a celebrated 1965 paper, Professor Paul Samuelson argued that "properly anticipated prices fluctuate randomly." If temporary vicissitudes of buying and selling pressures

were the primary cause of fluctuations, share prices would not exhibit their familiar random walk.

9. This leads naturally to present value techniques as the appropriate means of evaluation and to the conclusion that the proper discount rates to use are the rates the capital markets will use. If a discount rate is adjusted for risk, therefore, it is risk to investors that is relevant. It follows that the decision-maker's personal utility function has no relevance in the choice of the discount rate.

Questions

1. What is the difference between a widely held corporation and a closely held corporation?

2. Who are the stakeholders in a widely held corporation? What is the stake of each stakeholder?

3. Define the terms *profit* and *share value*. Are there any differences between the goal of maximizing profit and the goal of maximizing share value? Explain.

4. Berle and Means wrote a famous book entitled *The Modern Corporation and Private Property,* which is referenced in the first footnote of this article. In their book, the authors observe a "centripetal force on economic power but a centrifugal force on ownership" among U.S. corporations. Explain the meaning of this quotation.

2

Is Profit Maximization vs. Value Maximization Also Economics vs. Finance?

Richard B. Coffman

Introduction

Many financial management texts include a section on profit maximization vs. value maximization as decision criteria for the firm. Presumably many instructors cover the same topic in lecture. The purpose of this treatment is to introduce students to the central financial concept of value maximization, and at the same time, to explain why simple profit maximization is not deemed appropriate as a decision criterion in finance. Unless handled carefully, however, the coverage of this topic may have the unintended side effect of leaving students with the impression that microeconomics, which uses profit maximization, is analytically primitive and inferior to finance, which uses value maximization. In fact, the wording of some texts would make it difficult for students not to reach that conclusion. Perhaps the most striking wording is in *Basic Financial Management,* by Petty *et al* (1982).

> *While profit maximization is frequently used as the goal of the firm in microeconomics courses, it is not adequate for finance . . . . It assumes away . . . many of the complexities of the real world that we will try to address in our decisions. In being too simplistic, the goal of profit maximization is insufficient . . . .In beginning microeconomics courses uncertainty or risk is simply ignored . . . . While it may be used in microeconomics courses, its applicability to real-world complexities renders it useless for our purposes . . . (pp. 5,6).*

Perhaps Petty *et al* do not actually intend to attack microeconomics but the wording used is quite strong and reasonably can be read as antagonistic. Even where the wording in text and lecture is less strong,

Richard B. Coffman, "Is Profit Maximization vs. Value Maximization Also Economics vs. Finance?", *Journal of Financial Education,* Vol. 12, (Fall 1983): 37–40. Reprinted with permission from the *Journal of Financial Education.*

At the time of this writing, Richard B. Coffman was affiliated with the University of Idaho.

the very success of financial management in using value maximization to deal with practical, real world problems of business management may confirm in the minds of predisposed students that microeconomics is hopelessly impractical, abstract, and ivory tower. Can a field which ignores risk and the time value of money be anything else?

It would, of course, be highly unfortunate if finance courses turned students against microeconomics, for the disciplines clearly are closely allied. In the weak view ". . . financial management is closely related to other areas of business decision-making, particularly accounting and economics" (Moyer *et al*, 1980, p. 14). In a stronger view ". . . *finance can be very appropriately considered as economics extended into the dimensions of time and uncertainty*" (Boudreaux and Long, 1977, p. 4). And, ". . . we continue to view financial management as applied microeconomics in a business policy context" (Solomon and Pringle, 1980, p. viii).

Whether finance is a subpart of economics or an independent discipline drawing on economics among other fields is not at issue here. All can agree that finance makes frequent use of economic concepts (marginal logic, opportunity costs, fixed vs. variable costs, breakeven analysis, efficient markets, etc.). All can agree that economists have contributed to the development of financial theory, and that there are many research interfaces and crossovers between the two fields. Finance students need and do receive heavy exposure to economics, and financial managers who expect to keep up with developments in their field need familiarity with formal economics. According to Boudreaux and Long:

To develop expertise in corporate financial affairs requires that large amounts of time and effort be expended in studying detailed descriptions of corporations' financial environment and decision making within that environment. These efforts, however, are little more than shallow exercises without a firm appreciation of the basic economic ideas of corporate finance.

The institutional characteristics of corporate finance can and do change rapidly. New techniques for optimal decision making also appear with encouraging regularity. The chances of successfully comprehending and profitably using these are enhanced immeasurably by understanding their stable economic underpinnings (p. 375).

The Conflict

Given the above, it is of some interest to ask whether financial management's rejection of profit maximization does, in any sense, constitute a rejection of the microeconomic theory of the firm as well. This can be accomplished by examining the standard criticisms of profit maximization. These are that profit maximization (1) ignores the timing of returns, and thus the time value of money, (2) ignores risk, and (3) is ambiguous due to accounting ambiguities.

Timing of Returns

This criticism is expressed a number of ways. Sometimes it is said profit maximization focuses on the short run to the exclusion of the long run. Other times it is said profit maximization provides no guidance in weighing off short vs. long considerations. Sometimes it is said profit maximization ignores the time value of money. These criticisms are fairly wide of the mark when directed at microeconomic theory.

The standard, comparative statics theory of the firm discusses and identifies both short and long run equilibria. There is no particular emphasis on the short run over the long run. Also, there is no conflict between maximizing profits in the short run and maximizing them in the long run. The analytical distinction between short and long runs is in the number of factors which are variable. As each factor moves from fixed to variable the profit maximizing equilibrium output changes, and the firm can leave one equilibrium state for another, gradually moving from the short to the long run. Could this analysis be better conducted by using market value of owners' equity as a decision criterion? Not according to leading financial theorists Fama and Miller:

The market value of the owner's equity in the firm, in particular, is rarely, if ever, mentioned in the ordinary theory of the firm, most of which is expounded in terms of flow concepts, such as profits and profit maximization. It is important to emphasize, therefore, that properly interpreted there is no conflict between the stock and the flow form of the criterion. When we speak of maximizing profits in ordinary static price theory, we really mean profits in every unit of time; we raise the value of the firm, which is essentially just a weighted sum of the returns per period. Lack of exact correspondence between the two criteria arises only when we deal with particular problems in which increases in returns for some periods involve reductions in other periods; and when this is so, the correct solution requires falling back on the more cumbersome, but universally applicable, market value criterion (The Theory of Finance, p. 74).

In other words, ordinary microeconomics addresses a set of general problems for which the profit maximization assumption is not only appropriate, but actually superior to value maximization in that it is less cumbersome. Finance, on the other hand, takes as central a set of "particular problems in which increases in returns for some periods involve reductions in other periods." Value maximization is the more useful criterion for these problems.

Has economics been guilty of misapplying profit maximization in situations where value maximization is more appropriate? Fama and Miller seem more inclined to question the sophistication of critics of economic theory:

Failure to realize that the simple flow criterion is not adequate in problems in which the timing of the returns is of the essence has been responsible for much unnecessary confusion, such as the frequently heard argument that the profit maximization criterion and hence, most of

*the economic theory, does not apply to the business world as we know it,
because most large firms could certainly raise prices and profits in the
short run (pp. 74–75).*

Further, it is of interest to note that the standard theory of the firm
has been reworked to frame cost and production decisions in present
value, wealth-maximization terms (Alchian, 1959; De Alessi, 1967), but
that this formulation has proven cumbersome and is little used in
microeconomics texts: even managerial economics texts which adopt
value maximization as an overall objective fall back on conventional
profit maximization in their exposition of cost and production theory
(Brigham and Pappas, 1976; McGuigan and Moyer, 1979).

Risk

In the earlier quotation from Petty *et al* it was asserted that ". . . in
beginning microeconomics courses uncertainty or risk is simply ignored."
The implication is, of course, misleading. Elementary economics is not
deficient because it "ignores" uncertainty and risk. All theory must, by
definition, abstract from the real world. Elementary microeconomics
abstracts by, among other things, assuming a world of certainty. That
assumption contributes to the simplicity and analytical power of the
theory.

The success of elementary microeconomics is implicitly recognized
by Boudreaux and Long in their MBA-level text, *The Basic Theory of
Corporate Finance,* when they indicate that finance uses shareholder
wealth maximization as a decision criterion because it ". . . is comparable to the profit-maximization assumption made by economists when
they describe a company in microeconomic theory." The basis of
comparability is "that economic profit maximization is, for a single-time-
point world *under conditions of certainty,* the equivalent of our shareholder wealth maximization" (p. 160, italics added).

Advanced microeconomics, of course, deals extensively with risk
and uncertainty, and the theoretical work done there on expected utility,
state preference theory, risk aversion, and so forth underlies important
portions of financial theory. (See Fama and Miller, 1972, Part II,
Uncertainty Models, for development of these topics.)

Ambiguities of Profit Maximization

It is true that generally accepted accounting principles are slippery
enough to render the concept of profit ambiguous in the real world. The
notion that this makes suspect profit maximization in economics can be
immediately dismissed: The firm in economics does not maximize accounting profit; it maximizes economic profit. (See Benston, 1982,
especially Section B, for a detailed discussion of differences between
economic and accounting values.)

Suggestions

As the above analysis has shown, the profit vs. value maximization issue does not imply any serious conflict between economics and finance. This basic conclusion should be explicitly stated by both textbook writers and classroom teachers. Passages from Fama and Miller and Boudreaux and Long, cited earlier in this article, provide a useful basis for such statements. Further, it would be helpful to have students exposed to positive statements indicating the close links between the two fields. Finally, discussions of the criterion choice problem could usefully focus on the issue of an operational criterion—maximization of accounting profits vs. maximization of shareholders' wealth rather than on economics vs. finance. In this operational context, as shown by Solomon (*The Theory of Financial Management,* 1963, pp. 19–20), all the standard objections to profit maximization apply, and value maximization is revealed as a superior criterion for actual decisions.

References

1. Alchian, Armen A., "Costs and Outputs," in *The Allocation of Economic Resources,* Stanford University Press, 1959, pp. 23–40, reprinted in W. Breit and H.M. Hochman, *Readings in Microeconomics,* 2nd edition, Holt, Rinehart, and Winston, 1971, pp. 159–171.

2. Benston, George J., "Accounting Numbers and Economic Values," *The Antitrust Bulletin,* Vol. XXVII, Number 1, Spring 1982, pp. 161–215.

3. Boudreaux, Kenneth J. and Hugh W. Long, *The Basic Theory of Corporate Finance,* Prentice-Hall, 1977.

4. Brigham, Eugene F. and James L. Pappas, *Managerial Economics,* 2nd edition, The Dryden Press, 1976.

5. De Alessi, Louis, "The Short Run Revisited," *American Economic Review,* June 1967, pp. 450–461, reprinted in W. Breit and H.M. Hochman, *Readings in Microeconomics,* Holt, Rinehart, and Winston, 1971, pp. 149–158.

6. Fama, Eugene F. and Merton H. Miller, *The Theory of Finance,* Holt, Rinehart, and Winston, 1972.

7. McGuigan, James R. and R. Charles Moyer, *Managerial Economics,* 2nd edition, West Publishing Co., 1979.

8. Moyer, R. Charles, James R. McGuigan, and William J. Kretlow, *Contemporary Financial Management,* West Publishing Company, 1981.

9. Petty, J. William, Arthur J. Keown, David F. Scott, Jr., and John D. Martin, *Basic Financial Management,* 2nd edition, Prentice-Hall, 1982.

10. Solomon, Ezra and John J. Pringle, *An Introduction to Financial Management,* Goodyear, 1980.

11. Solomon, Ezra, *The Theory of Financial Management,* Columbia University Press, 1963.

Questions

1. Identify the corporate goal assumed in microeconomics. Identify the corporate goal assumed in finance.

2. Traditional arguments against the goal of profit maximization declare the following: (1) It ignores the timing of returns. (2) It ignores risk. (3) It is ambiguous.

    Present a defense for using profit maximization as a goal in microeconomics.

3. What is the difference between accounting profit and economic profit?

4. "Economics is the mother discipline of finance." In your opinion, is this a true statement? Explain.

3
Reflections on the Corporation as a Social Invention

William H. Meckling and
Michael C. Jensen

At least until the 1940s, modern business enterprise grew in spite of public and government opposition. Many Americans — probably a majority — looked on large scale enterprise with suspicion . . . the coming of modern business enterprise in its several forms brought strong political and legislative action. The control and regulation of the railroads, of the three types of mass retailers — department stores, mail order houses, and the chains — and of the large industrial enterprise, became major political issues. In the first decade of the twentieth century, the control of the large corporation was, in fact, the paramount political question of the day.

— Alfred Chandler, The Visible Hand

Big business has never suffered from a dearth of critics. The language employed by these critics, the tactics and the rationale they advance for their hostility perpetually change, but condemnation seems immutable. Recently, big business has been cast in the role of villain by various activist groups — anti-war protesters, consumer advocates, environmentalists, and the like.[1] Since most "big businesses" are organized

William H. Meckling and Michael C. Jensen, "Reflections on the Corporation as a Social Invention," *Midland Corporate Finance Journal* (Fall 1983): 6–15. Reprinted with permission.

At the time of this writing, Michael C. Jensen was professor of Economics, Finance, and Organization Theory and director of the Managerial Economics Research Center at the Graduate School of Management, University of Rochester. William H. Meckling was Dean Emeritus and James E. Gleason Distinguished Research Scholar in Management and Government Policy of the University of Rochester's Graduate School of Management.

[1] William R. Allen, an economist, notes that ". . . those who wish to use the power of the state to pervert the corporate arrangement are not confined to the intellectually unwashed among politicians, social activists, and Hollywood stars: astonishingly, they include some representatives of major corporations." *Midnight Economist: Broadcast Essays IV*, Original Paper/38, July 1982, International Institute for Economic Research, p. 40.

as corporations, the corporation as an institutional form has become the major focus of the hostility.[2]

Separation of Ownership and Control

Nowadays, the attack on the corporation is comprised of two distinctly different themes. One of these themes—concern over the so-called "separation of ownership from control" which characterizes large corporations—has been around at least since 1776, when Adam Smith denounced joint-stock companies on those grounds. In Smith's day, of course, joint-stock companies were the exception rather than the rule: individual proprietorships dominated the conduct of business.

Use of the corporate form of organization grew throughout the 19th century, but early 19th-century corporations tended to be "closely held" rather than "publicly held." During the latter part of the 19th century in the United States, sizable businesses which had been owned and managed by a single entrepreneur, or by a closely-knit entrepreneurial cadre (sometimes all members of one family), began to be transformed into the large publicly held corporations which dominate the business scene today—corporations in which no single stockholder or small group of stockholders have anything like a controlling interest.[3] Because responsibility for operation of these firms has devolved into the hands of professional managers, "ownership" is said to have been separated from "control." As a result of this separation, management is alleged to be insensitive to the welfare of investors. Corporate management, so the story goes, possesses vast discretionary power which it uses to operate firms to suit itself.

Corporate Social Responsibility

A second line of attack against the corporation—one that in an important sense is contradictory to the first—charges corporations with anti-social behavior on a broad front. Corporations pollute the environment, bribe foreign officials, ignore the impact of plant relocations on local communities, discriminate against the handicapped, minorities, women and the

---

[2] It is worth noting that there are many "big businesses" operated by governments, e.g., the U.S. Post Office, state universities, metropolitan school systems, the TVA and other power authorities, municipal airports, metropolitan mass transit systems, metropolitan sanitary and waste disposal services, metropolitan water systems, and the New York Port Authority. Government big businesses are not without their critics, but the criticism is of an entirely different sort. Government managers, such as school superintendents and postal administrators, for example, are seldom depicted in the media as ruthless and power hungry.

[3] See Alfred Chandler, *The Visible Hand—The Managerial Revolution in American Business* (Boston: Belknap Press, 1977). Chandler documents the history of this transformation, and refers to the new organizational form as "managerial capitalism."

elderly in hiring and promotion, support and help elect dictatorial governments in developing countries, and so on. It is this kind of charge that has led to the popular prescription that corporations be "socially responsible."[4]

It is important to distinguish these two lines of attack. Indictment of the corporation on grounds that management is not responsible to investors is one thing; indictment on grounds that management behaves anti-socially is an entirely different affair. The first purports to defend investors from usurping managers; the second effectively attacks investors on behalf of a usurping community.

Concern over whether, or to what extent, management in the modern corporation is controlled by investors implicitly assumes that management *ought* to behave in the interest of investors. In technical language it implies acceptance of investor welfare as "the objective function" of the firm.[5] Thus, it is consistent with conventional views regarding corporate "purposes" — in particular, the view that investors are willing to hold wealth in the form of claims on such organizations because (or to the extent that) management acts on their behalf.

The second line of attack on the corporation, the charge that corporations display anti-social behavior, does not stem from any concern, real or professed, about the welfare of investors. Indeed, the charges levied often implicitly or explicitly presume that the corporation behaves badly in pursuing profits, that is, when it behaves in the interest of investors. More importantly, the antidotes for corporate anti-social behavior prescribed by these critics generally imply wealth transfers from investors to other groups in society.[6]

Those who contend that management has too much discretion can (and do) prescribe policies which will make investors worse off rather than better off. This raises the question of whether the charge of "separation of ownership from control" is not simply a guise used to discredit the corporation rather than an expression of concern over investors' well-being. When individuals and organizations attack the corporation for failure to serve the interest of its stockholders and, at the same time, prescribe policies which transfer wealth from investors to

[4] The more politic interest groups avoid specifically indicting corporations while nonetheless maintaining that corporations have an obligation to do more good, i.e., be more socially responsible.

[5] Behaving in the interest of investors is, under a very broad range of circumstances, equivalent to maximizing the value of the firm, i.e., maximizing the net present value of future cash flows.

[6] It is not uncommon for policies which purport to deal with anti-social behavior by some corporations to end up bestowing benefits on investors in other corporations. Investors in firms producing water or air purification equipment are likely to be delighted with strict air and water pollution statutes. Wealth transfers from one group of investors to another, however, are usually incidental to larger transfers from investors (and others, particularly consumers) to noninvestor interest groups. Firms likely to benefit from coerced social responsibility, i.e., statutory decrees which require firms to engage in wealth transfers, will often be members of the interest group lobbying for enactment of such laws.

others, one is led to suspect that the appearance of concern for investor welfare is a pretense.

What constitutes either "anti-social" behavior or its converse, "socially responsible" behavior, depends of course on how "anti-social" and "socially responsible" are defined. These terms cannot be defined except by appeal to some value or set of values—some specification of what is "good" and what is "bad." Social responsibility is a normative catch-all, something which each of us is likely to define very differently. The allegation that investors are the victims of management expropriation or neglect differs from the charge of anti-social behavior in this respect. Whether, or to what extent, managers act in the interest of investors is an empirical question, a question of fact. Because the motive for holding claims on corporations is indisputably to receive the earnings therefrom (including appreciation in value), investors' welfare is something we can define and measure. Research can provide evidence about the extent to which modern corporate management behaves in the interest of investors. By contrast, any particular measure of social responsibility is bound to be highly subjective and thus arbitrary. In attempting to assess the social value of a firm's behavior, how do we decide what weights to assign to Community Chest contributions vs. support of higher education, or to the employment of minorities vs. employment of the disabled or aged?

Serious examination of the notion of social responsibility suggests that the popularity it enjoys stems more from what it conceals than from what it adds. Since "social" responsibility is a "good" (as distinct from a "bad"), the term arouses the right sentiments on the side of whatever cause is being pressed. At the same time, "social" is a word vague enough to encompass any cause. Most importantly, the term "social responsibility" has the advantage, from the standpoint of its proponents, that it disguises what they really have in mind: namely, that managers should deliberately take actions which adversely affect investors in order to bestow benefits on other individuals. While various advocate groups would disagree about what constitutes socially responsible behavior, they will all agree that investor welfare must be rejected as *the* corporate objective.[7] Otherwise, why introduce the notion of "social responsibility"?

Vulnerability of the Corporation

Calling attention to the arbitrary nature of "social responsibility" is not mere semantic quibbling. The case against the corporation is not being brought, nor will it be decided, on the basis of scientific analysis and

---

[7] Professor James W. Evans of San Diego State University puts the point very directly: ". . . corporate social responsibility means simply that business firms have an obligation to act for the social good even if this might lower their economic profits." University of San Diego Newsletter, Autumn 1982, Vol. 6, No. 1.

research. The corporation is on trial in the political and public opinion arenas. In those arenas, choice of language is a critically important aspect of the trial. Unfortunately, the jury is uninformed and will likely remain so; it will not pay the individual citizen to invest much in understanding the issues surrounding the corporation controversy. If he is at all realistic he will understand that he is virtually powerless to do anything to affect the outcome. His attitude regarding corporations is likely to depend heavily on the language used by the media. He is not likely to undertake careful analysis of the arguments or painstaking collection of the facts.

Politicians and bureaucrats, on the other hand, have a powerful incentive to join forces with corporate critics. Corporations control substantial accumulations of wealth. Politicians and bureaucrats can expand their own role if they can transfer rights to determine the use of that wealth from the corporation to government. The right to decide how corporate assets will be used is a form of power, and politicians and bureaucrats have strong incentives to accumulate power in government. It is not surprising, given these circumstances, that public discussion of the corporation is fraught with semantic ambushes.

The Corporation and the Organizational Test of Survival

Critics of the corporation are confronted by a striking historical phenomenon not readily reconciled with their views. The corporation has come to dominate production and commerce, not only in the United States, but in all of the world's highly developed nations. If the corporation is such a defective institution, how do we explain its chronicle of success? Freedom to choose among forms of organization provides an "organizational" test of survival just as markets provide a survival test for individual firms.[8] There are no private rights in organizational ideas. Organizational innovations cannot be copyrighted or patented. Entrepreneurs and promoters are free both to replicate and innovate organizational forms. In such an environment, more costly organizational forms will tend to be replaced by less costly forms because cost-reducing modifications to organizations will yield rents (over the short run) to those innovators and entrepreneurs. Eventually, such rents will be eliminated by competition, and the organizational forms that survive and prosper will be those that satisfy consumer demands at lowest cost.

[8] The unconditional proposition that "the fittest survive," of course, is not testable. But the notion of "survival processes" is not scientifically useless. The concept of survival provides a vehicle for structuring scientific inquiry. It focuses attention on the factors which determine "fitness."

Moreover, survival propositions which specify the criterion that serves as a basis for selection are testable, so long as the criterion itself is observable. Statutes which increase (or decrease) the costs of using particular organizational forms, for example, provide what amounts to an experiment from which we can glean evidence regarding the importance of costs to organizational survival.

Moreover, it is investors, not managers, who ultimately choose among competing organizational forms. Managers who choose forms which yield subnormal rates of return to investors will find themselves without investors. Capital markets thus discipline managers in the choice of organization.

Wherever competition among organizational forms is open and unfettered, the large corporation has demonstrated its strength and durability. It has not, however, won the survival race in all arenas. Non-profit forms dominate in certain service areas, such as museums and private education at the undergraduate and graduate levels in the United States. In the legal, accounting, and consulting businesses, professional partnerships dominate. In retailing, proprietorships coexist with private corporations; and in the financial industry, private corporations and mutuals coexist. In capital-intensive industries, such as manufacturing, private corporations with wide-spread stock ownership have swept the field.[9] The role the corporation has come to play in society during the last 150 years suggests that, far from being a social menace, the corporation is an enormously productive social invention.

What the Corporation Is

Understanding the success of the corporation involves understanding what the corporation *is* and what it *is not*. Stripped to its essentials, the corporation is simply a legal fiction which serves as a nexus of contracts. Individuals and organizations — employees (including managers), investors, suppliers, customers — contract with each other in the name of a fictional entity, the corporation.

Two points about the development of the corporation are worth noting here. First, it is misleading and inaccurate to view the corporate organizational form as a *static* institution. The corporation is the product of hundreds of years of individual human ingenuity — hundreds of years during which individuals have fashioned a complex network of contractual relations to serve more effectively the objectives of the parties to the legal fiction. Corporate financial officers, financial consultants, potential investors, *et al,* have spawned a remarkably diverse set of corporate financial claims (contracts). Moreover, the development of the claims themselves has been accompanied by an equally remarkable development of markets in which the claims are traded. Contracts between the corporation and its employees, customers, and suppliers reflect a similar history of ingenuity and diversity.

---

[9] See Eugene F. Fama and Michael C. Jensen, "Separation of Ownership and Control," *Journal of Law and Economics,* Vol. 26, June 1983; and Eugene F. Fama and Michael C. Jensen, "Agency Problems and Residual Claims," *Journal of Law and Economics,* Vol. 26, June 1983.

The second point is that the corporation is *neither* the creature of the state *nor* the object of special privileges extended by the state. The corporation did not draw its first breath of life from either minister of state or civil servant. More importantly, the corporation requires for its existence only freedom of contract. Corporate vitality is in no way dependent on *special* dispensation from the authorities.[10] Limited liability, for example, is not unique to corporations. Non-profit organizations, partnerships, mutuals and cooperatives, for example, all exhibit limited liability. And, even if private corporations were the only organizations which invoked limited liability, that would not constitute a special privilege. Freedom of contract surely encompasses the right of parties to prescribe limits to liability in contracts. When the state requires those who wish to organize and operate in the corporate form to be chartered or licensed, they do not thereby extend a special privilege to promoters or stockholders. In fact, such requirements abridge the freedom of individuals to contract. The truth is, the corporation has survived and prospered despite unfavorable treatment by the state — despite unfavorable taxation and despite costly legal restrictions that have not bound its competitors.

What the Corporation Is Not

A corporation is an artificial being, invisible, intangible, and existing only in comtemplation of law.

Chief Justice Marshall, 1819
—Dartmouth College v. Woodward

The disposition to treat corporations as if they were individuals has venerable roots in both law and economics. In the legal arena this practice serves a function which is of great practical importance: it provides a focus for legal actions. Suits can be brought in the name of the "corporation," and the "corporation" can serve as the object of legal action.

Economists have found it convenient to treat the corporation as if it were a wealth-maximizing individual in explaining how market systems function. For many purposes, assuming that corporations choose and maximize like an individual simplifies our analysis without seriously impairing the usefulness of the theory. More generally, of course, ascribing human characteristics to the corporation is often a useful linguistic expedient.

This anthropomorphic practice, however, has not been an unmixed blessing. Until very recently, at least, it has distracted social scientists away from the study of the corporation as an organizational form. More importantly, it has distorted both popular and academic understanding of

---

[10] See Robert Hessen, *In Defense of the Corporation* (Stanford: Hoover Institution Press, 1979).

the corporation by obfuscating analysis and public discussion of the effects of government policies when those policies operate *through* the corporation. The source of this obfuscation is the illusion that the impact of such policies falls *on* the corporation.

The corporation is not an individual. It does not feel; it does not choose; it cannot bear the burden of taxes; it cannot bear the costs of regulation; it cannot benefit from tariffs or subsidies. All such actions, of course, can and generally do benefit or harm *individuals* who have some relationship with the corporation, such as investors, employees or customers. But it is literal nonsense to say that the *corporation* is benefited or is harmed. The viability of the corporation as an organizational form depends on the cost of doing business as a corporation. Government policies which impose costs on firms who do business as a corporation will discourage the use of that organizational form. But those costs cannot be borne by the corporation; costs are borne only by individuals.

More to the point, the corporation cannot be socially (or otherwise) responsible! However we end up defining it, the notion of "being responsible" is a normative concept relevant only to human beings. A corporation can no more be responsible than can a lump of coal.

Corporate Democracy and Federal Chartering

One of the captions which has become the vogue in more recent proposals for rehabilitating the corporation is "corporate democracy." Those who argue for "corporate democracy" have again chosen a label that evokes favorable "vibes." Who could oppose "corporate democracy"? When we look at the embodiment of corporate democracy in the Corporate Democracy Act, however, we find that it means limiting freedom of contract to work for, buy from, sell to, lend to, or own stock in a corporation that does not:

- meet certain rules regarding membership on its board of directors.
- disclose certain kinds of information.
- include certain contractual guarantees against the disciplining and firing of employees.[11]

It is difficult to see what the word "democracy" has to do with any of the provisions of this Act. Ralph Nader and the other authors of this Act either misunderstand the essential nature of the proposed Act or are deliberately deceiving the unsuspecting public. In their book, *Taming the Giant Corporation,* they quote the following provision in Delaware's 1899 Incorporation Act—a provision perfectly consistent with the notion of freedom of contract:

[11] In addition, Title V of the "Corporate Democracy Act" provides for various penalties and sanctions to be imposed on corporations and their executives for violating federal or state law.

The certification of incorporation may also contain any provision which the incorporators may choose to insert for the management of the business and for the conduct of the affairs of the corporation, and any provision creating, defining, limiting, and regulating the powers of the corporation, the directors and stockholders; provided, such provisions are not contrary to the laws of this State.

Nader *et al* then go on to the comment on this provision:

These sanguine little words literally turned corporate law inside out. The first hundred years of the corporation's history in the United States had established one rule above all else: The business corporation could only exercise power explicitly provided or necessarily implied in its charter with the state. Delaware's "self-determination" provision allowed the corporation to be a lawmaker itself. The corporation could conduct business in any way it chose as long as the state did not explicitly prohibit it.[12]

Using the term "lawmaker" to describe the corporation under the 1899 Delaware Incorporation Act is either deliberate deception or gross ignorance. The provisions of the Act did not turn over the lawmaking powers of the state to the corporation.[13] The language is clear. The Act simply allows individuals voluntarily to agree to whatever contractual provisions they choose in organizing a corporation so long as they do not contravene state laws.

"Our Largest Corporations Are Governments"

The *piece de resistance* of the anti-corporation rhetoric is the charge that corporations have become governments in their own right.[14] This assertion is simply the extreme version of the cliche that corporations have "too much" power. It is a confusion to claim that corporations have become governments. The distinguishing feature of government is its role as the locus of the police powers or, to put it more directly, its legal monopoly over the use of physical violence. Be they democratic or otherwise, governments are governments in precisely this sense. Corporations do not fit this bill; they do not have the legal right to use physical violence or coercion.

Corporate managers are delegated rights to decide many questions — how corporate assets will be used, what contracts will be executed

---

[12] Ralph Nader, Mark Green, and Joel Seligman, *Taming the Giant Corporation* (New York: W.W. Norton & Co., 1976), p. 52.

[13] Robert Hessen, in his article "Credible Crusader? An Assessment of Ralph Nader's Scholarship" in *Controlling the Giant Corporation, A Symposium* (Rochester: Center for Research in Government Policy and Business, 1983), points out that the first two sentences of the paragraph are factually incorrect since versions of the policy existed in earlier New Jersey and Connecticut statutes, going back in the latter case as far as 1837. Hessen goes on to document numerous errors and inadequacies in the documentation for the one chapter of the book he examined.

[14] Mark Green, "The Case for Corporate Democracy." *Regulation* (May/June, 1980), p. 21.

in the name of the corporation, who will be hired, who will be fired, where plants will be located, etc. But they cannot decide what the law will be, nor can they enforce the law. Managers can and do attempt to influence what the law is and how it is enforced.[15] Moreover, they have the right to resort to the courts and the police where the corporation's rights are infringed. In that respect, however, they are not different from any other citizen. The government has an obligation to protect the rights of private citizens. That is why the police powers exist and are lodged in government. That obligation, incidentally, extends to the protection of the rights of private citizens, even if it happens that those citizens are acting through a legal fiction like the corporation.

Fiat Labeled Democracy

The specific measures which promoters of corporate democracy wish to impose by law — such as what the composition of boards of directors will be, how discretion over employment is to be limited, or what information is to be supplied to the public — are all measures that the parties to the corporate nexus could voluntarily put into effect if they chose to do so. The fact that all of the contracts between the "corporation" and other individuals are voluntary is a persuasive reason for adopting a skeptical attitude toward those who promote corporate democracy. Barring intervention by the state, corporate organizers could choose whatever board make-up they like. If it were truly in the interest of investors to deny membership on boards of directors to management, we would expect to observe that stipulation written into articles of incorporation. Corporate organizers or reorganizers adopting such a policy would thereby be able to market shares in the organization at higher prices, reflecting the higher value investors attach to their increased welfare. Since we do not observe corporations which explicitly deny its top managers membership on the board of directors, we must presume that it is not in the interest of investors to do so.

Similarly, there is nothing to prevent corporations from guaranteeing tenure in contracts with employees. Indeed, it is clear that if employees value tenure or security enough to trade off salary reductions large enough to cover the costs of increased security, the corporation can make investors better off by offering it. The same argument applies with respect to the provision of information to customers, creditors, suppliers, or investors.

---

[15] One recent success of the anti-corporation forces designed to curb the political influence of corporations is the constraints which have been imposed on corporate contributions to political campaigns.

The Alleged Failure of State Chartering

Proponents of corporate democracy contend that state chartering has failed. They allege that the revenue generated by having corporations chartered in the various states leads to competition among states to enact chartering statutes allowing managers to exploit stockholders. The corporations themselves then engage in a "movement towards the least common denominator" or a "race for the bottom," seeking charters in those states with the most lax statutes.[16] The prescription advocated to protect shareholders from exploitation by management is the imposition of federal minimum standards on corporate charters.

Delaware is generally regarded as the most pro-management charterer, which explains why corporations are chartered there in such disproportionate numbers. The charge, however, that corporations choose Delaware as their state of charter in order to exploit stockholders is not based on any scientific study of the effects of corporate chartering on shareholders' welfare.

In fact, a careful study of the effects on shareholder wealth of 140 changes in the state of incorporation during the period 1928–1967 has been performed (126 of these changes were to Delaware). Peter Dodd and Richard Leftwich, the authors of the study, find that in the 25 months prior to and including the month of the switch, stockholders of firms which switched the state of incorporation earned a positive abnormal return (after adjusting for market-wide effects and risk) of slightly over 30 percent. For a period up to five years after the switch, the abnormal stockholder returns are insignificantly different from zero.

The Dodd/Leftwich evidence is inconsistent with the hypothesis that the switch enables management to exploit stockholders. It is consistent with the converse proposition, however, that management is switching the state of incorporation for the benefit of stockholders. As the news of the intended switch becomes available in investment markets, even before the switch is actually effected, investors revise upward their evaluation of the firm's prospects. That revaluation leads to an increase in the price of the shares, which in turn generates the abnormal returns to shareholders. Professors Dodd and Leftwich conclude:

The evidence presented here lends no support to the arguments that stockholders are harmed by management's choice of a state of incorporation. Stockholders do not earn negative abnormal returns when managements initiate a change in the state of incorporation to a state which is supposedly more pro-management (such as Delaware). Indeed, the change follows a period of abnormal positive returns. Subsequent to the

---

[16] See, for example, W.L. Carey, "Federalism and Corporate Laws: Reflections Upon Delaware." *Yale Law Journal,* Vol. 83, No. 4 (March 1974), pp. 663–707.

*change, stockholders earn normal returns, contrary to the basic argu-
ments of the proponents of federal chartering regulation.*[17]

Control of Managerial Behavior:
Analysis and Evidence

The charge that management exploits investors, as pointed out earlier, is
a testable proposition. In recent years, scholars have devoted substantial
effort to assessing the validity of that charge. The result is a growing body
of analysis and evidence bearing on the question of how managerial
behavior is controlled. The study of corporate chartering cited above is
only one example. Much of this research has focused on what has come to
be called the "market for corporate control."

The charge that managers can disregard the wishes of investors is
deduced from a very simple model of the factors controlling managerial
behavior. It begins with the proposition that ownership of stock in large
corporations tends to be widely dispersed.[18] Individual stockholders
therefore, it is said, have little influence on (or even interest in) the
election of directors. This, in turn, allows management to control
membership on boards of directors, arranging even to be elected themselves. Boards of directors are therefore captives of management rather
than watchdogs protecting investors. This is why managers can disregard
the welfare of investors and run corporations to suit themselves.

This chain of logic is incomplete in one very important respect. It
ignores the market for corporate control. Whenever management exploits
stockholders, whether through laziness, incompetence or outright depre-
dation, such behavior creates a profit opportunity. Anyone who can
replace management and eliminate this exploitation can increase the value
of the firm. There is no shortage of individuals and organizations,
including other firms, constantly searching for such opportunities.
Moreover, it is not necessary to enlist the support of a majority of current
stockholders to take over the corporate managerial reins. Control can be
shifted to newcomers in a variety of ways, the most common of which is
through tender offers or mergers.

The market for control of corporations differs from the market for
control in the political sector in one important respect. Voters do not have

---

[17] Peter Dodd and Richard Leftwich, "The Market for Corporate Charters: 'Unhealthy
Competition' Versus Federal Regulation," *Journal of Business,* Vol. 53, No. 3, Part 1 (July
1980), p. 261.

[18] The extent of dispersion of stock ownership itself has been challenged. See Harold
Demsetz. "The Structure of Ownership and the Theory of the Firm," *Journal of Law and
Economics,* 26 (June 1983).

the right to sell their political vote in an open market.[19] Since voting rights almost universally follow title to common shares, corporate votes *are* for sale. Therefore, corporate control is always for sale, and in a market to which there is ready access. Contenders for control can also avail themselves of the proxy fight to effect takeovers.

How effectively managerial behavior is controlled depends on how costly it is to exploit the profit opportunities created by management's exploitation of shareholders. Specifically, it depends on (1) the cost of gathering information about managerial performance and (2) the cost of exercising the various options for acquiring control. If it is relatively costless to assess managerial performance, and if it is relatively costless for control to be transferred, managers will have very limited opportunity to exploit investors.

Study of the operation of the market for corporate control is still in its infancy. (A bibliography of scientific research on this market is contained at the end of this article.) Nonetheless, certain facts about the performance of the market for corporate control are apparent. There is convincing evidence that stockholders of acquired firms earn, on average, large positive returns on their shares in the course of a successful takeover. The size of the abnormal return to the acquired firm's shareholders is not independent of the form of the takeover — that is, whether it is a merger, tender offer, or proxy fight. But in all three cases, the abnormal return is significantly positive. Evidently, management is not so well entrenched and so indifferent to stockholder welfare that it simply rebuffs every takeover opportunity.

Even when management does ward off potential suitors, there is at best mixed evidence that stockholders suffer. Management sponsorship of anti-takeover charter amendments, for example, is not necessarily evidence of managerial actions inimical to shareholders.[20] Anti-takeover provisions can enhance the price target shareholders are finally paid in a subsequent takeover. "Targeted buybacks" and "standstill" agreements are the only instances where it appears that management of targeted firms acts in its own behalf at the expense of shareholders. A targeted buyback occurs when management, using corporate funds, buys out the interest of a specific large shareholder at a premium. This shareholder is typically a

---

[19] This does not mean there is no vote-buying in the political arena, but it does mean that such buying takes other forms. Interest groups contribute to political candidates' campaigns, and successful candidates repay by taking legislative and/or administrative actions which bestow benefits on their financiers.

[20] Such amendments can impose supra-majority provisions for approval of mergers, staggered election of members of the board of directors, and fair price provisions. See Harry DeAngelo and Edward M. Rice, "Anti-takeover Charter Amendments and Stockholder Wealth," *Journal of Financial Economics,* Vol. 11, April 1983; and Scott C. Linn and John J. McConnell, "An Empirical Investigation of the Impact of 'Anti-takeover' Amendments on Common Stock Prices," *Journal of Financial Economics,* Vol. 11, April 1983.

potential or actual participant in a takeover attempt. When such buyback transactions take place, the selling shareholder often agrees to limit his holding of shares for some period into the future. The latter is referred to as a "standstill" agreement. Shareholders on average suffer abnormal negative returns as a result of targeted buybacks and standstill agreements.[21] This is perhaps the single most direct piece of evidence in the market for corporate control literature supporting the proposition that management behaves, at least on occasion, in ways inimical to shareholders.

Whether the shareholders of acquiring firms are made better or worse off as a result of acquisition activity remains an open question. Some research shows acquisitions leading to positive abnormal returns to shareholders of acquiring firms; other research leads to the opposite conclusion—that acquiring shareholder returns are negative. While the jury is still out on the precise fate of acquiring firm shareholders, it would be surprising if future research concluded that acquisitions led either to very large benefits or very large losses.

The surge of interest in corporate control research that has occurred in recent years suggests that a much more detailed and authentic assessment of managerial performance will be available. Such an assessment is not yet possible.

Will the Corporation Survive?

The private corporation has been an enormously productive social invention, but it is on the way to being destroyed. Large corporations will become more like Conrail, Amtrak and the Post Office. One scenario seems clear. It begins with the creation of a crisis by the politicians and the media. In some cases the crisis will be blamed on the "bad" things corporations do or might do, e.g., the multi-nationals. In any case the remedy will be more and more controls on the corporations (something like what is happening in the transportation and oil industries). When the controls endanger the financial structure of the corporations they will be subsidized by the public sector at the cost of more controls. When the controls bring the industry to the brink of collapse the government will take over. The details of the scenario will no doubt vary. Moreover, some firms will simply be driven out of business because of regulatory costs and the inability to raise capital.

---

[21] See Larry Y. Dann and Harry DeAngelo, "Standstill Agreements, Privately Negotiated Stock Repurchases, and the Market for Corporate Control," *Journal of Financial Economics*, Vol. 11, April 1983; and Michael Bradley and L. Macdonald Wakeman, "The Wealth Effects of Targeted Share Repurchases," *Journal of Financial Economics*, Vol. 11, April 1983.

These words were written by the authors in 1976, in an article entitled "Can the Corporation Survive?"[22] Little has transpired since that time that suggests we ought to change our prediction. Since the mid-1960s the stock market has performed remarkably poorly. The real value of the Dow Jones stocks fell by 62 percent over the 18-year period from December 1964 to the end of 1982. The *real* (after inflation) rate of return on all common stocks on the NYSE in the 40 year period from 1926 to 1965 was about 8.6 percent per year.[23] If stocks included in the Dow Jones Index had provided that same 8.6 percent inflation-adjusted rate of return over the period 1965–1982, the Index would have been about 5,600 on January 1, 1983 — instead of 1,047.

Despite its record of success (or perhaps because of it), the large corporation is a highly vulnerable organizational form. The viability of the corporation critically depends on respect for the rights of the parties to the corporate contract — especially the rights of stockholders, who hold the residual claims on net cash flows. Over the years, the right of managers to use corporate assets in the interest of stockholders has gradually been eroded. Special interest groups of various sorts have joined forces with politicians to limit severely managerial decision rights. The special interest groups thereby transfer wealth from parties to the corporate contract to themselves, and politicians enhance their role in society by transfering decision rights to the government. Investors, on the other hand, will not long continue to turn over their wealth to organizations from which it will, with high probability, be expropriated. We believe the attack on the corporation lies behind the poor performance of the stock market during the last 18 years. It is hard to imagine any change in the political process in Western democracies that would reverse this trend.

References

Bradley, M., "Interfirm Tender Offers and the Market for Corporate Control," *The Journal of Business,* Vol. 54, No. 4, October 1980, pp. 345–376.

Dodd, P., "Merger Proposals, Management Discretion and Stockholder Wealth," *Journal of Financial Economics,* Vol. 8, No. 2, June 1980, pp. 105–137.

Jarrell, G.A., and Bradley, M., "The Economic Effects of Federal and State Regulations of Cash Tender Offers," *Journal of Law and Economics,* V. 23, No. 2, October 1980, pp. 371–376.

Manne, H.G., "Mergers and the Market for Corporate Control," *Journal of Political Economy,* 73, April 1965, pp. 110–120.

[22] Michael C. Jensen and William H. Meckling, "Can the Corporation Survive?," Public Policy Working Paper Series, PPS-76-4, Center for Research in Government Policy and Business, University of Rochester (May 1976); reprinted in the *Financial Analysts Journal* (January/February 1978) and the International Institute for Economic Research (July 1977).

[23] Calculated from data given in R.G. Ibbotson and R.A. Sinquefield, "Stocks, Bonds, Bills and Inflation: Updates." *Financial Analysts Journal* (July/August 1979).

The remainder of the articles cited appeared in a recent volume of the *Journal of Financial Economics:* Vol. 11, April 1983, a symposium on the "Market for Corporate Control":

Jensen, Michael C. and Richard S. Ruback, "The Market for Corporate Control: The Scientific Evidence";

Asquith, Paul, "Merger Bids, Uncertainty, and Stockholder Returns";

Schipper, Katherine and Rex Thompson, "Evidence on the Capitalized Value of Merger Activity for Acquiring Firms";

Asquith, Paul, Robert F. Bruner, and David W. Mullins, Jr., "The Gains to Bidding Firms from Merger";

Ruback, Richard S., "Assessing Competition in the Market for Corporate Acquisitions";

Malatesta, Paul H., "The Wealth Effect of Merger Activity and the Objective Functions of Merging Firms";

Bradley, Michael, Anand Desai, and E. Han Kim, "The Rationale Behind Interfirm Tender Offers: Information or Synergy?";

Wier, Peggy G., "The Costs of Antimerger Lawsuits: Evidence from the Stock Market";

Stillman, Robert, "Examining Antitrust Policy Toward Horizontal Mergers";

Eckbo, Bjorn Espen, "Horizontal Mergers, Collusion, and Stockholder Wealth";

Dann, Larry Y., and Harry DeAngelo, "Standstill Agreements, Privately Negotiated Stock Repurchases, and the Market for Corporate Control";

Bradley, Michael, and L. Macdonald Wakeman, "The Wealth Effects of Targeted Share Repurchases";

DeAngelo, Harry, and Edward M. Rice, "Anti-takeover Charter Amendments and Stockholder Wealth";

Linn, Scott C. and John J. McConnell, "An Empirical Investigation of the Impact of 'Anti-takeover' Amendments on Common Stock Prices";

Dodd, Peter R. and Jerold B. Warner, "On Corporate Governance: A Study of Proxy Contests";

Lease, Ronald C., John J. McConnell, and Wayne H. Mikkelson, "The Market Value of Control in Publicly Traded Corporations."

Questions

1. According to Meckling and Jensen, in what ways is the corporation being attacked?

2. "Stripped to its essentials, the corporation is simply a legal fiction which serves as a nexus of contracts." In what sense is the corporation a legal fiction? How does the corporation serve as "a nexus of contracts?"

3. *Personification:* Representation of a thing or abstraction as a person.
    Anthropomorphism: An interpretation of what is not human or personal in terms of human or personal characteristics.
    To which of the following statements do the preceding two definitions apply? Explain your answer.
    a. "A corporation is an artificial being, invisible, intangible, and existing only in the contemplation of law."
    b. "Multinational corporations act irresponsibly in Central America."
    c. "Corporations attempt to maximize shareholder wealth."
    d. "Managers who fail to maximize stock price may find themselves looking for another job."

4. In what sense do corporations pay taxes? In what sense do corporations *not* pay taxes?

5. Buying votes in the political arena is unethical and illegal. Is the purchase of votes in the corporate arena unethical and/or illegal? Explain.

6. According to Meckling and Jensen, the future success of the corporation depends on what factors?

4

Top Executives Are Worth Every Nickel They Get

Kevin J. Murphy

Each spring, critics, journalists, and special-interest groups devour hundreds of corporate proxy statements in a race to determine which executive gets the most for allegedly doing the least. They're running the wrong race.

The "excessive" compensation paid these greedy types, we are told, gouges the nation's 30 million shareholders. Their salaries are arbitrarily set at outrageous levels without regard to either profitability or performance. Moreover, the six- and seven-digit base salaries are just the tip of the compensation iceberg — executives fatten their already sizable paychecks several-fold through bonuses, stock options, and other short- and long-term incentive plans. As a result, the public view prevails that executives are paid too much for what they do and that compensation policies are irrational and ignore the needs of shareholders.

Simply put, the public view is wrong and based on fundamental misconceptions about the managerial labor market. One reason for these misconceptions is that executive compensation is an emotional issue. And because critics become wound up in their emotions, they rely on a blend of opinion, intuition, and carefully selected anecdotes to prove their points.[1] Of course, such anecdotal evidence is not useless and may even be valuable in identifying abuses in the compensation system when carefully interpreted. Critics cannot use such evidence, however, to show compensation trends or to support across-the-board condemnations of compensation policies.

I have devised a better way to test the validity of the complaints about executive pay by subjecting each proposition to a series of logical

Reprinted by permission of the *Harvard Business Review*. "Top Executives Are Worth Every Nickel They Get" by Kevin J. Murphy (March/April 1986): 125–132. Copyright © 1986 by the President and Fellows of Harvard College; all rights reserved.

At the time of this writing, Kevin J. Murphy was an assistant professor at the Graduate School of Management of the University of Rochester.

Author's note: I am indebted to Michael Jensen and Jerold Zimmerman for their help. I gratefully acknowledge financial support from the Managerial Economics Research Center.

and statistical tests. My data are drawn, in part, from an examination of the compensation policies of almost 1,200 large U.S. corporations over ten years and are supplemented by the findings of a 1984 University of Rochester symposium, "Managerial Compensation and the Managerial Labor Market."[2] My results paint a very different picture of executive compensation by showing that

- The pay and performance of top executives are strongly and positively related. Even without a direct link between pay and performance, executives' incomes are tied to their companies' performance through stock options, long-term performance plans, and, most important, stock ownership.

- Compensation proposals like short- and long-term incentive plans and golden parachutes actually benefit rather than harm share-holders.

- Changes in SEC reporting requirements and a shift toward compen-sation based on long-term performance explain most of the apparent compensation "explosion." This shift links compensation closely to shareholder wealth and motivates managers to look beyond next quarter's results.

Of course, some executives are overpaid or underpaid or paid in a way unrelated to performance. But, on average, I have found that compensation policies encourage executives to act on behalf of their shareholders and to put in the best managerial performance they can.

Exhibit I   Relationship between Rate of Return on Common Stock and Percentage Changes in Executive Salary and Bonus, 1975–1984

| Annual Rate of Return on Common Stock | 1975–1984 | |
	Number of Executive-Years in Sample	Average Annual Change in Salary and Bonus
Entire sample	6,523	7.8%
Less than −20%	639	0.4%
−20% to 0%	1,734	5.3%
0% to 20%	1,917	8.3%
20% to 40%	1,212	9.6%
More than 40%	1,021	13.8%

Note: Rates of return and percentage pay increases have been adjusted for inflation. As an example of how the rate of return is calculated, suppose that a share of stock worth $10 at the beginning of the year had increased in price to $12 by the end of the year and that the company paid cash dividends of $1 per share during the year. The holder of a share of the company's common stock would have realized a return of $3, or 30% for the year. Salary and bonus data were constructed from *Forbes* annual compensation surveys from 1975 to 1984. The sample consists of 1,948 executives in 1,191 corporations.

Pay and Performance

Because shareholders are the owners of the corporation, it makes sense to analyze the executive compensation controversy from their perspective. One way to motivate managers is to structure compensation policies that reward them for taking actions that benefit their shareholders and punish them for taking actions that harm their shareholders. Shareholders measure corporations in terms of stock price and dividend performance. Thus a sensible compensation policy would push an executive's pay up with good price performance and down with poor performance.

A common criticism of compensation policies is that they encourage executives to focus on short-term profits rather than on long-term performance. Assuming efficient capital markets, current stock price reflects all available information about a company, thus making its stock market performance the appropriate measure of its long-term potential. My analysis (shown in Exhibits I and II) indicates that compensation gives executives the incentive to focus on the long term since it is implicitly or explicitly linked to their companies' stock market performance.

The statistics in Exhibit I compare the rate of return on common stock (including price appreciation and dividends) with percentage changes in top executives' salaries and bonuses over ten years. I have grouped the data, which represent sample averages, by the companies' stock price performance, but experiments with alternative measures like sales growth and return on equity yield similar qualitative results.

1975–1979		1980–1984	
Number of Executive-Years in Sample	Average Annual Change in Salary and Bonus	Number of Executive-Years in Sample	Average Annual Change in Salary and Bonus
3,314	6.9%	3,209	8.8%
257	0.5%	382	0.4%
1,002	5.5%	732	4.9%
989	7.5%	928	9.2%
538	7.1%	674	11.6%
528	11.1%	493	16.6%

Exhibit II   **Average Increase in Executive Salary and Bonus Corresponding to Each Additional 10% Rate of Return on Common Stock, 1975–1984**

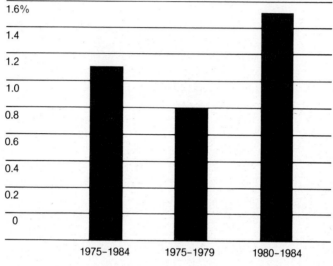

Note: The percentage changes are estimated coefficients from regressions of percentage changes in salary and bonus on shareholder return. All estimates are statistically significant at confidence levels exceeding 99.99%.

Throughout the ten-year period, executives received inflation-adjusted average annual increases in salary and bonus of 7.8%; more important is the positive relationship shown between the rate of return on common stock and average percentage changes in salary and bonus. When returns were less than −20%, executives received pay increases of only .4%; when performance exceeded 40%, pay increases averaged 13.8%.

As Exhibit I shows, the relationship between pay and performance has remained positive over time and has actually become stronger in recent years. Chief executives in companies with returns greater than 40% received inflation-adjusted average annual increases in salary and bonus of 11.1% from 1975 to 1979 and 16.6% from 1980 to 1984.

You can also use statistical regression techniques to estimate changes in executives' salaries and bonuses corresponding to each additional 10% of shareholder return. A company realizing a 10% return on its common stock will boost executive pay by some percentage, and you can use an estimate of the average pay increase to measure the magnitude of the relationship between pay and performance. By dividing the sample into subperiods, you can see if the relationship between pay and performance strengthens or weakens over time.

Exhibit II shows the results of the regression analysis. For every 10% rise in a company's stock price over the ten-year sample, the top executive's salary and bonus rose an average of 1.1%. Moreover, the relationship was stronger in the last half of the decade than in the first half. For each 10% shareholder return, annual salaries and bonuses increased by .8% from 1975 to 1979 and by 1.5% from 1980 to 1984.

As measured by the rate of return on common stock, a strong, positive statistical relationship exists between executive pay and company performance. These results are sharply at odds with recent studies that compare pay levels with measures of profitability and conclude that compensation is independent of performance.[3] The problem with such studies is that they look at the level of executive compensation across companies at a particular time instead of considering the extent to which compensation varies with companies' performance *over time*. This is an important distinction. Whether a company has well-paid—or low-paid— executives tells us nothing about the sensitivity of pay to performance.

To illustrate, consider two well-documented relationships—the positive relationship between company size and executive compensation and the negative one between company size and the average rate of return realized by shareholders.[4] From these it follows that a large company would have low rates of return and well-paid executives, while a small company would have high rates of return and low-paid executives. You'd conclude that pay and performance didn't correlate, and you'd be right if you took this kind of snapshot of the relationships. But if you took a moving picture—that is, looked at the results over time—you'd see that the pay of individual executives and the performance of their companies are strongly and positively related.

It is better to study how executive pay varies from year to year in a given company. Exhibit I and Exhibit II show that changes in executive pay mirror changes in shareholders' wealth. Two studies presented at the Rochester symposium corroborate this result. The first was based on a sample of 461 executives in 72 manufacturing companies over 18 years; in it I examined salary, bonus, stock options, deferred compensation, total compensation, and stock ownership. It shows that executive compensation parallels corporate performance as measured by the rate of return on common stock.[5]

Another study of 249 executives from as many companies from 1978 to 1980 reaches the same conclusion. It found a strong, positive correlation between changes in executive compensation and stock-price performance (adjusted for marketwide price changes). Ranking companies on the basis of their stock-price performance, it suggests that those in the top 10% will raise their executives' compensation by an inflation-adjusted 5.5% and those in the bottom 10% will lower pay by 4%. In addition, the study finds that chief executives in the bottom 10% of the performance ranking are almost three times more likely to leave their companies than executives in the top 10%.[6]

The Expanded Compensation Package

Suppose that I had not found a positive relationship between cash compensation and performance. Could I then conclude that executives do not act on behalf of their shareholders? The point is not moot; although I've shown a positive relationship between cash compensation and performance, I could easily find some companies where the relationship does not exist. So it is important to determine whether *total* compensation policies are doing the best job possible.

To do so requires that you look at more than just salary and bonus. Most studies in the financial press consider *only* salary and bonus and ignore potentially crucial variables like restricted stock, stock options, and long-term performance plans. In fact, these plans have become increasingly important. By their very nature, these plans tie executives' ultimate compensation directly to their companies' performance.

Executives' holdings of their companies' common stock constitute a large part of their wealth. The value of these stock holdings obviously goes up in good years and down in bad ones, quite independently of any relationship between performance and base pay. Suppose an executive with $4 million of stock sees the share price drop 25%. Because of his company's poor performance in the securities market, he has lost a million dollars—a loss that trivializes anything a board of directors might do to his base pay.

To assess the importance of inside stock ownership, I collected a 20-year time series of chief executive officer data from the proxy statements of 73 *Fortune* "500" manufacturing companies. Executives in this sample, which covered fiscal years 1964 through 1983, held an average (in 1984 constant dollars) of almost $7 million in their companies' common stock. Although this sample does not include shares held by family members and outside trusts, it does include a few executives with extraordinary stock holdings; the median stock holding for executives in this 20-year period is $1.5 million. That is, 50% of the chief executives in the 73 sample companies held more than $1.5 million in their companies' common stock.

Exhibit III depicts the relationships among company performance, salary and bonus, and changes in the value of executives' stock holdings for all chief executives in the 73 companies from 1964 to 1983. The point is clear; year-to-year changes in the value of executives' individual stock holdings often exceed their cash compensation. In companies with returns of less than −20%, executives lost an average of $2.9 million each on their stock holdings (compared with an average salary and bonus of $506,700); the median executive lost $643,800. In companies with returns greater than 40%, executives saw their stock holdings go up by an average

Exhibit III   **Relationships among Rate of Return on Common Stock, Executive Salary and Bonus, and Change in Value of Inside Stock Holdings, 1964–1983**

Annual Rate of Return on Common Stock	Number of Executive-Years in Sample	Average Annual Salary and Bonus	Average Annual Change in Value of Inside Stock Holdings	Median Annual Change in Value of Inside Stock Holdings
Entire sample	1,394	$541,700	$ 270,900	$ 27,600
Less than −20%	243	$506,700	−$2,914,200	−$643,800
−20% to 0%	361	$559,900	−$ 883,200	−$ 93,000
0% to 20%	360	$574,400	$ 560,600	$125,500
20% to 40%	223	$541,700	$2,260,700	$464,300
More than 40%	207	$494,300	$3,594,500	$635,600

Note: All variables have been adjusted for inflation (1984 constant dollars). Rate of return on common stock includes price appreciation and dividends. Inside stock holdings include only shares held directly and do not include shares held by family members or trusts. The change in the value of inside stock holdings is calculated by multiplying the value of each executive's share holdings (at the beginning of the fiscal year) by the rate of return on common stock. Data were constructed from proxy statements for 213 chief executives in 73 *Fortune* "500" manufacturing corporations from 1964 to 1983. Data were unavailable for 66 of the 1,460 possible executive-years.

of $3.6 million each (the median figure was $635,600) compared with an average salary and bonus of $494, 300.[7]

Does Generosity Backfire?

Executive employment contracts are determined by the board of directors, which in turn is elected by shareholders. A cooperative relationship between executives and their directors is usually required for corporate success, and some have incorrectly interpreted this fact as evidence that executives can set their own salaries by pushing their compensation plans past "captive" directors. A friendly relationship between executives and their boards does not mean that the executives are free of contraints; rather, constraints usually operate in subtle yet powerful ways.

For example, some corporations have adopted short- and long-term compensation plans that pay off only if the executives meet a certain performance standard. Golden parachutes, which compensate executives if they leave their company after a takeover, have also grown in popularity. If, as some critics contend, these plans benefit executives and harm shareholders, you would expect stock prices to fall at the announcement of the plan. Likewise, if these plans benefit shareholders, you would expect prices to rise.

Three symposium studies examined market reaction. One found that average stock prices rise by about 11% when companies make the first public announcement of bonus and other plans that reward short-term performance.[8] Another concluded that shareholders realize a 2% return when companies adopt long-term compensation plans.[9] A third study found that, on average, stock prices increase by 3% when companies announce the adoption of a golden parachute provision.[10] This favorable reaction supports the contention that golden parachutes benefit shareholders by removing managers' incentives to block economically efficient takeovers. The price increase may also indicate that takeovers are more likely when golden parachutes are adopted but does not indicate that these provisions harm shareholders.

In each study, stock values not only increase when companies announce compensation plans but also continue to trade at the new, higher levels. The studies thus support the idea that such plans help align the interests of executives and shareholders and signal "good times ahead" to the market. They refute the view that executives "overreach" when they adopt lucrative compensation schemes.

On average, executives do not harm shareholders when they alter employment-contract provisions nor do they arbitrarily set their own salaries. If executives were truly able to set their salaries, why wouldn't they make them comparable with those of rock stars like Michael Jackson, whose income is many times that of even the highest paid executive? The only way the "set-their-own-salaries" argument works is if you assume that these salaries are somehow within some reasonable range of the competition — what other executives in similar industries are paid.

What's Out of Hand?

"Top management pay increases have gotten out of hand," warns Arch Patton, citing an apparent "explosion in top management compensation."[11] Indeed, a casual (but careless) look at compensation totals published in the business press seems to justify such concern. Exhibit IV shows the total compensation received by the nation's best paid executives from 1974 to 1984 using *Forbes* data (unadjusted for inflation). Before 1977, the fattest paycheck hovered around $1 million but then jumped to $3.4 million in 1978, $5.2 million in 1979, and $7.9 million in 1980. Warner Communications' Steven Ross shattered the eight-digit barrier with a total compensation of $22.6 million in 1981; in 1982, Frederick Smith of Federal Express received a total package of $51.5 million. The figure "plummeted" in 1983 to the mere $13.2 million received by NCR's retiring William Anderson but rebounded in 1984 to the $23 million received by Mesa's T. Boone Pickens, Jr.

A closer look at the data reveals that the apparent increase stems, in part, from a shift in the structure of compensation and has been exaggerated by changes in SEC reporting requirements. Moreover, the increase does not indicate that the conflict of interest between executives and their shareholders has worsened. Rather, the trend reflects a growing reliance on stock options and other long-term performance plans designed

Exhibit IV   Total Compensation Received by the Nation's Highest-Paid Executives, 1974–1984

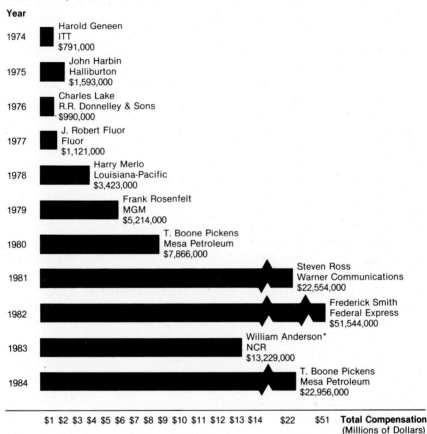

Year

1974 — Harold Geneen
ITT
$791,000

1975 — John Harbin
Halliburton
$1,593,000

1976 — Charles Lake
R.R. Donnelley & Sons
$990,000

1977 — J. Robert Fluor
Fluor
$1,121,000

1978 — Harry Merlo
Louisiana-Pacific
$3,423,000

1979 — Frank Rosenfelt
MGM
$5,214,000

1980 — T. Boone Pickens
Mesa Petroleum
$7,866,000

1981 — Steven Ross
Warner Communications
$22,554,000

1982 — Frederick Smith
Federal Express
$51,544,000

1983 — William Anderson*
NCR
$13,229,000

1984 — T. Boone Pickens
Mesa Petroleum
$22,956,000

$1 $2 $3 $4 $5 $6 $7 $8 $9 $10 $11 $12 $13 $14 $22 $51   **Total Compensation**
(Millions of Dollars)

* Forbes does not include Anderson in its 1984 compensation survey since he retired just prior to the end of the 1983 fiscal year.

Note: Data are not adjusted for inflation. Total compensation before 1978 does not include gains from exercise of stock options.

Source: *Forbes,* various issues.

to link compensation more closely with shareholder wealth. The often spectacular payoffs are a once-in-a-lifetime experience.

For example, Frederick Smith's 1982 salary and bonus of $413,600 accounted for less than 1% of his $51.5 million total compensation; if the ranking had been based on salary and bonus alone, he wouldn't have made the top 300. NCR's William Anderson received only 8% of his 1983 compensation in the form of salary and bonus; his salary and bonus of $1,075,000 was only the nation's thirty-seventh highest. (Mr. Pickens's 1984 salary and bonus of $4.2 million was indeed the nation's highest but included $3 million for services provided in 1982 and 1983 when bonuses were not awarded.) In any given year, only a small percentage of executives enjoy big gains from stock options or other performance plans. The overwhelming majority get most of their compensation in the form of salaries and cash bonuses.

Even so, the great popularity of stock options and other long-term performance plans has several implications. First, an executive's pay in any given year reflects amounts actually accrued or earned over several years and tends to increase the maximum compensation observed, just as a switch from weekly to monthly pay periods will increase the maximum compensation observed in any given week (for example, the last week of the month).

Second, long-term performance plans give high rewards for excellent performance but are neutral toward poor or mediocre performance. It's the same as designing a state lottery with one grand prize of $1 million rather than a hundred prizes of $10,000 each; you increase the amount paid to the winner but not the total amount awarded. If the chief executives of ten different companies were each awarded stock options at the beginning of the year, their value at the date of grant might be similar. By the end of the option period, however, only a few would be worth a great deal of money; the others would be worthless.

Third, most long-term performance plans are based on stock prices. The stock market boom produced high payoffs from 1981 to 1983, while the market decline in the 1970s produced low or zero payoffs. Thus an executive awarded an equal number of stock options or performance plan units each year would have realized zero gains during the stock market decline and large gains during the boom; cyclical movements produced increases in the dollar amounts realized even though the amounts granted under these plans remained relatively constant.

Finally, before 1978, the payoffs from stock options and other long-term plans were reported in a somewhat incomprehensible table at the back of corporate proxy statements. Changes in SEC reporting rules have moved these payoffs to the front of the statement, where they are much more accessible to the media. Compensation totals published in *Forbes* (see Exhibit IV) and other business periodicals before 1978 exclude option realizations; data published after 1978 include them. The editors of these compensation surveys warn against making year-to-year comparisons when the definitions have changed. Unfortunately, critics have often ignored these warnings.

Why Such Controversy?

The recent attacks on executive compensation come mainly from a few individuals and special-interest groups who use the controversy to further their own agendas. In 1984, for example, former U.S. Trade Representative William Brock assailed "excessive" auto executive bonuses to argue against Japanese import quotas. Labor unions have used the executive pay issue to bolster demands for higher wages for their members. Mark Green's condemnation of "over-reaching" executives continues the general Nader-Green attack on the corporation. In each case, the executive compensation question is virtually unrelated to the ultimate objectives of the attackers.

Such highly publicized assaults cause confusion about executive compensation, a confusion exacerbated by the second-rate research conducted and reported by most media commentators. How compensation is determined is complex; current performance is only one of the many factors that affect executive pay. Thus performance cannot explain all or even most of an individual's compensation even though the relationship between pay and performance is strong, positive, and statistically significant. In any case, estimating the relationship between pay and performance is tricky and cannot be done by making simple cross-sectional comparisons.

Another source of confusion is the use of isolated examples and anecdotal evidence. The quoted numbers are usually taken out of context and fail to tell the whole story. Single examples purporting to show no relationship between pay and performance mislead since they often include big long-term payoffs but never changes in the value of the executive's stock holdings.

Some executives are undoubtedly abusing the compensation system, and anecdotal evidence may help identify and eliminate these excesses. I believe, however, that the true excesses are not made by the million-dollar executives, who are, by and large, rewarded for a history of superior performance in behalf of shareholders. Real abuses are more likely found among lower paid executives whose pay is both unrelated to performance and out of line with the pay of their peers in similar companies. Even if the critics were to identify real excesses, it is unfortunate that their isolated examples would help justify a blanket condemnation.

The nation's shareholders need not fear that they are being swindled by greedy executives. Compensation policies normally make a great deal of sense. Companies are, moreover, adopting compensation plans that benefit shareholders by creating better managerial incentives.

My evidence cannot prove that all or even most boards of directors are doing the best possible job of tying executive pay to company performance. Some executives are undoubtedly being overpaid, while others are being underpaid or paid in a way unrelated to performance. But even so, the evidence does indicate that executive compensation in U.S. corporations is characterized not by madness but by basic corporate common sense.

References

[1] See, for example, Joseph E. Muckley, " 'Dear Fellow Shareowner'," HBR March-April 1984, p. 46; Mark Green and Bonnie Tenneriello, "From Pay to

Perks to Parachutes: The Trouble with Executive Compensation," Democracy Project Report No. 8, March 1984.

[2] Papers presented at the symposium are published in the *Journal of Accounting and Economics,* April 1985.

[3] See, for example, Carol Loomis, "The Madness of Executive Compensation," *Fortune,* July 1982, p. 42.

[4] The relationship between compensation and sales is reported by Harland Fox, *Top Executive Compensation,* Report No. 854 (New York: Conference Board, 1985). Evidence relating company size and shareholder return appears in the Symposium on Size and Stock Returns, published in the *Journal of Financial Economics,* June 1983.

[5] Kevin J. Murphy, "Corporate Performance and Managerial Remuneration: An Empirical Analysis," *Journal of Accounting and Economics,* April 1985, p. 11.

[6] Anne T. Coughlan and Ronald M. Schmidt, "Executive Compensation, Management Turnover, and Firm Performance: An Empirical Investigation," *Journal of Accounting and Economics,* April 1985, p. 43.

[7] For more evidence on the importance of executive stock holdings, see George J. Benston, "The Self-Serving Management Hypothesis: Some Evidence," *Journal of Accounting and Economics,* April 1985, p. 67.

[8] Hassan Tehranian and James Waegelein, "Market Reaction to Short-Term Executive Compensation Plan Adoption," *Journal of Accounting and Economics,* April 1985, p. 131.

[9] James Brickley, Sanjai Bhagat, and Ronald C. Lease, "The Impact of Long-Range Managerial Compensation Plans on Shareholder Wealth," *Journal of Accounting and Economics,* April 1985, p. 113.

[10] Richard A. Lambert and David F. Larcker, "Golden Parachutes, Executive Decision Making, and Shareholder Wealth," *Journal of Accounting and Economics,* April 1985, p. 179.

[11] Arch Patton, "Those Million-Dollar-A-Year Executives," HBR January-February 1985, p. 56.

Questions

1. Describe the evidence that supports a positive relationship between executive compensation and corporate performance.

2. Why do critics (e.g., Ralph Nader and Mark Green) charge that executive compensation is excessive?

3. Why should owners of common stock be concerned about the relationship between changes in executive compensation and changes in stock price?

4. Assume that the president of General Motors Corporation owns less than one percent of GM's common stock. Does it follow that GM's president will be relatively unmotivated by self interest to maximize GM's stock price?

5.   When heavyweight champion Michael Tyson fought challenger Michael Spinks, Tyson earned more than $20 million; Spinks earned "only" $13 million. Tyson knocked out Spinks only 91 seconds into the fight. How is it possible for Tyson and Spinks to earn more money for one boxing match than most top executives earn for several years of work?

PART II
VALUATION AND COST OF CAPITAL

5
An Explanation of Large Share Price Changes
Steven M. Dawson

Introduction

In December 1985 the Singapore Stock Exchange was closed by the authorities for three days because of uncertainties caused by the financial collapse of Pan-Electric Industries. When the market reopened prices plunged: the Straits Times Industrial Index lost 12 percent of its value while declines for certain shares were even greater. Numerous reports in the foreign press noted Singapore's reputation as a volatile market, a description supported by academic research,[1] and hence a market for serious investors to avoid. The *Far Eastern Economic Review* called it the "dramatic crash"[2] following a market closure that "had no precedent in any major stock market in the world."[3] Reacting to the situation, the *Wall Street Journal* editorialized that "By getting itself into so dramatic a fix, the city-state looks less attractive to the markets. On the margin, money men will be a bit more likely to look to Seoul or Milan or Sydney and, above all, deregulating Tokyo."[4]

Steven M. Dawson, "An Explanation of Large Share Price Changes," *Securities Industry Review*, Vol. 12, No. 1 (April 1986): 9–17. Reprinted with permission.

At the time of this writing, Steven M. Dawson was a professor of finance in the Department of Finance at the University of Hawaii.

[1] For example, Iain Allan, "Returns and Risk in International Capital Markets," *Columbia Journal of World Business*, Summer, 1982; James S. Ang and Randolph A. Pohlman, "A Note on the Price Behavior of Far Eastern Stocks," *Journal of International Business Studies*, Volume 9, Number 1, Spring, Summer, 1978; Charles A. D'Ambrosio, "Distributions of Pacific Basin Common Stock Returns," *Singapore Stock Exchange Journal*, Volume 9, Number 6, June, 1981; and Herbert L. Jensen, "Rates of Return from the Stock Exchange of Singapore," *Singapore Stock Exchange Journal*, Volume 12, Number 10, October, 1984.

[2] Paul Sillitoe, "Markets Blow a Fuse," *Far Eastern Economic Review*, December 19, 1985.

[3] Anthony Rowley, "Lull Before the Storm," *Far Eastern Economic Review*, December 19, 1985.

[4] "Suspended in Singapore," *The Wall Street Journal*, December 6, 1985.

The objective of this article is to demonstrate the ease with which large share price changes can occur. Relatively small changes in the principal factors which determine prices can lead to surprisingly large changes in the value of the shares. Provided the market is responding to real changes, large price fluctuations, which do not overreact to developments in the fundamental economic forces affecting value, can be a sign of well-functioning market, not a market which should be unattractive to investors. We begin by asking what gives value to shares issued by a company.

Determinants of Share Value

Appraisers often note that they need only three facts to calculate the financial value of any asset, real or financial. They are (1) the size of future cash flows to be received from the asset, (2) the time when the cash flows will be received, and (3) the annual rate of return the owner or investor requires. Investors who own common shares normally receive two types of cash flows, dividends as long as the shares are held and the market price of the shares when they are sold. Thus the value of a share is simply the future cash inflows, both dividends and the sale price, discounted by the investor's required rate of return. In the special cases of bankruptcy or acquisition, the sale price is replaced by the final liquidating payout, if any, or the cash and/or securities paid by the acquirer.

If we assume that an investor plans to hold an investment for one year, the value of the shares is the present value of the dividends plus the present value of the market price one year from now, as follows:

$$\textbf{(1)} \quad P_0 = \frac{E(D_1)}{(1 + r)^1} + \frac{E(P_1)}{(1 + r)^1}$$

where
$P_0 = $ the value of the shares as of today,
$E(D_1) = $ the expected cash dividend in the first period
$E(P_1) = $ the expected market price at the end of one period, and
$r = $ the investor's expected return for investments with this level of risk.

For convenience we will assume the dividend is paid annually and at the end of the period. The investor's expected rate of return (r) is influenced by both the yield on alternative investments and the level of risk associated with this particular security: the greater the perceived risk the higher the expected return. When we divide the future payments of dividends and the future market price by $(1 + r)^n$, with n equal to the number of periods until the cash flow is received, we obtain the present value of the future payments. Discounting the future amounts to find their value today is just the reverse of future or compound value, which begins with an amount today and asks what it will become at some future time if it is invested to earn a return of (r) per period. Thus an investor who pays the price of P_0 for the shares will receive a return of (r) if the shares pay the expected dividend and are sold for the expected market price.

We can extend equation (1) from a one-period model to a model for several periods as follows:

$$(2) \qquad P_0 = \frac{E(D_1)}{(1 + r)^1} + \frac{E(D_2)}{(1 + r)^2} + \cdots + \frac{E(P_n)}{(1 + r)^n}$$

Dividends are received as long as the shares are held and when the shares are sold in period n, the market price (P_n) is received.

Since the future market price at which the shares can be sold (P_n) is also the present value of future dividends received beyond that point, the estimated sales price can be replaced with another series of dividends stretching further into the future and the value of the shares becomes simply the present value of all future dividends. If we assume that the dividends grow at a constant rate of growth, the present value of all future dividends can be simplified to:

$$(3) \qquad P_0 = \frac{E(D_1)}{r - g}$$

where $E(D_1)$ is the expected dividend in year one and g is the constant dividend growth rate which increased D_0 to D_1.[5] This simple model is known to investment analysts variously as the dividend capitalization model, the Gordon dividend model, and the dividend growth model. It works as long as we can assume a more or less constant rate of growth for all future dividends. A more general form of the dividend capitalization model is:

$$(4) \qquad P_n = \frac{E(D_{n+1})}{r - g}$$

which says that the value of the shares at any time (n) is the present value of all dividends received after time (n).

Of course dividends paid by many companies do not grow at a constant rate. Keeping in mind that the value of a share is the present value of the future dividends, the dividend capitalization model can be revised for variable growth rates as follows:

$$(5) \qquad P_0 = \sum_{t = 1}^{n} \frac{E(D_t)}{(1 + r)^t} + \frac{E(D_{n+1})}{r - g} \left(\frac{1}{(1 + r)^n}\right)$$

This rather complicated formula merely says that the expected value of the share (P_0) is the sum of the present values of the dividends which grow at a non-constant rate for n periods, plus the present value of the dividends after we can assume a constant rate of growth begins.[6] The

---

[5] The dividend capitalization model is described in most books on investment analysis and corporate financial management. This theory was first developed in detail in John B. Williams, *The Theory of Investment Value,* Cambridge: Harvard University Press, 1938.

[6] For the development of this model see Burton Malkiel, "Equity Yields, Growth, and the Structure of Share Prices," *American Economic Review,* Volume 53, December, 1963.

second term in equation (5), which is the same as equation (4), gives the expected market value as of time n and this amount is then discounted back to the present.

Let us work two examples to show how the dividend capitalization model can be used. First, using figures which could be expected for shares on the Stock Exchange of Singapore, let us assume that the current dividend is \$.20, it is expected to grow at a constant annual growth of 10 percent, and the investor expects to receive a return of 15 percent.[7] The estimated value of this share is \$4.40, as follows using equation (4):

$$P_0 = \frac{E(D_1)}{r - g} = \frac{\$.22}{.15 - .10} = \$4.40$$

Next let us assume that the dividends grow at 20 percent for the first three years and they then drop down to a 10 percent constant rate of growth in year 4. The value of the shares is now \$5.66 determined as follows with equation (5):

$$P_0 = \frac{\$.24}{(1.15)^1} + \frac{\$.29}{(1.15)^2} + \frac{\$.35}{(1.15)^3} + \frac{\$7.60}{(1.15)^3} = \$5.66$$

Although infrequently seen in security analyses published by brokerage firms,[8] the dividend capitalization model is the basis for most, if not all, share valuation models used by investors and analysts. For example, price earnings ratios, which tell an investor how much the shares are worth given their earnings per share, are a shortcut version of the complete dividend capitalization model.[9] Instead of saying a share with a given dividend, dividend payout percentage, growth rate, and required return is worth \$4.40, for instance, the price earnings model will say shares with this outlook for growth should have a price earnings ratio which gives a price of \$4.40. Just as higher growth shares have a higher price earnings ratio and hence a higher market price, high growth shares using the dividend capitalization model also have high market prices.

Careful observers will also note that the dividend capitalization model uses dividends, not earnings. There are two reasons for this. First, it is clear that the value of the stock should equal the present value of future payments and it is dividends, not earnings, that investors receive. After all, a stock which guarantees it will never have a cash dividend, or a liquidating or acquisition dividend, will not have a value, regardless of its earnings, unless it is associated with the "bigger fool" theory. Companies which do not pay dividends now can still have a value if investors expect they will pay dividends later. Often it is good financial management to

[7] Jensen reports a value weighted annual return of 15.48 percent for all Stock Exchange of Singapore shares during the period from June 1973 to December 1981. Jensen, *op. cit.*

[8] For a good discussion of why the dividend capitalization model is not used directly more often in practice, see Tang Wee Loke, "Security Analysis," *Singapore Stock Exchange Journal,* Volume 3, Number 10, October, 1975.

[9] See Douglas A. Hayes and W. Scott Bauman, *Investments: Analysis and Management,* MacMillan, 1976, and Williams, *op. cit.,* pp. 82–83 for a mathematical proof.

retain earnings, reinvest in profitable projects, so that the company grows and then can pay much bigger dividends. The second reason dividends are used rather than earnings is that earnings involve double counting. If we value earnings now, but part of the earnings are retained in the business to create higher earnings later, the part of today's earnings which is not paid out will be counted twice.

Effect of Changing Expectations

The value of a share of stock is determined by the size of the dividend, its expected rate of growth, and the rate of return required by investors. A change in any of these variables will change the value of the shares. Earlier we determined that a share with a $.20 dividend, an expected dividend growth rate of 10 percent, and a required return by investors of 15 percent, would be priced at $4.40. We can use this example to determine the change in value that will occur if there is a change in the growth rate, which will change future dividends, or if there is a change in the required return.

A change in the expected rate of growth can occur quite easily. It can be caused by changes in the general economic outlook for all companies, by changes for one particular company or industry, or even by a change in the mood of investors. The Pan-Electric situation was generally interpreted as a negative development for both the Singapore economy and more specifically for companies with links to Pan-Electric. We can use the dividend capitalization model to calculate what would be the change in the value of the share for a given change in investor's expected rate of growth. These changes in value for a sample of possible growth rates are in Table 1. A mere 1 percent decline in the growth rate, from 10 percent to 9 percent, decreases the value of the shares by 17.5 percent. Further decreases in expected growth lower the value even further. When we recall that the Straits Times Index fell by 12 percent when trading opened after the suspension, we can see how small a change in growth rates expected by investors was needed to produce that change. With a 15 percent required return and a starting growth rate of 10 percent, a 0.65 percent decrease in the expected growth rate to 9.35 percent would produce a 12 percent fall in the share value.[10]

Changes in the investor's required rate of return (r) also can occur quite easily and have an equally noticeable effect upon value. Common causes of changes in the required return are changes in the general level of returns available to investors on other securities or changes in the perceived risk associated with the individual company. Table 2 is similar to Table 1 except that the expected rate of growth for dividends is now held constant and (r) is gradually increased from 15 percent to 20 percent.

[10] $.2187/(.15 − .0935) = $3.87, which is 12 percent less than $4.40.

Table 1   **Share Value Change for a Given Change in the Expected Dividend Growth Rate**

Expected Dividend Growth	First-Year Dividend	Required Return	Share Price	Percent Change
+10%	$.220	.15	$4.40	—
+ 9%	$.218	.15	$3.63	−17.5%
+ 8%	$.216	.15	$3.09	−29.8%
+ 7%	$.214	.15	$2.67	−39.3%
+ 6%	$.212	.15	$2.36	−46.4%
+ 5%	$.210	.15	$2.10	−52.3%

As occurred in Table 1, the decrease in the share price caused by a small change in the required return is relatively large. A mere one percent increase in the required return causes the price to fall by 16.6 percent. A five percent increase in the required return lowers the market price by 50 percent.

Events such as the Pan-Electric situation can change both the expected rate of growth and the required return and the two changes combined have an even larger effect upon the price. For example, a one percent decrease to 9 percent in the expected dividend growth rate in our example, combined with a 1 percent increase in the required return to 16 percent, leads to a decrease in value of 29.3 percent. The effect on value of other combinations of expected dividend growth and required return can be found using equation (4), and a sample of results is contained in Table 3.

Thus far we have assumed a constant rate of growth for all future dividends. If we instead assume a temporary decrease for a limited period of time, and then a return to a constant expected rate of growth, the effect on the value is less, although still significant. In Table 4, for example, we assume that the lower rate of growth for the dividend continues for 3 years, and then the dividend growth rate returns to the previous constant rate of 10 percent per year. Table 4 shows that if we assume dividend

Table 2   **Share Value Change for a Given Change in the Investor's Required Return**

Expected Dividend Growth	First-Year Dividend	Required Return	Share Price	Percent Change
+10%	$.22	.15	$4.40	—
+10%	$.22	.16	$3.67	−16.6%
+10%	$.22	.17	$3.14	−28.6%
+10%	$.22	.18	$2.75	−37.5%
+10%	$.22	.19	$2.44	−44.5%
+10%	$.22	.20	$2.20	−50.0%

Table 3   **Share Value Change Caused by a Combined Change in Dividend Growth and Required Return**

Expected Dividend Growth	Level of Required Return					
	15%	16%	17%	18%	19%	20%
+10%	0%	−16.7%	−28.6%	−37.5%	−44.5%	−50.0%
+ 9%	−17.5%	−29.3%	−38.0%	−45.0%	−50.5%	−55.0%
+ 8%	−29.8%	−38.6%	−45.5%	−51.8%	−55.5%	−59.1%
+ 7%	−39.1%	−45.9%	−51.4%	−55.7%	−59.5%	−62.5%
+ 6%	−46.4%	−51.8%	−56.1%	−59.8%	−63.0%	−65.7%
+ 5%	−52.3%	−56.6%	−60.2%	−63.2%	−65.9%	−68.2%

growth decreases temporarily to 6 percent for 3 years, and then returns to its expected constant growth of 10 percent, and there is no change in the investors' required return, the decline in value is 12.9 percent, close to the Straits Times Index decrease. Of course, periods of non-constant growth other than 3 years, additional changes in growth rates, and higher or lower growth rates not in Table 3, can also be used in the calculations.

In Table 5 we combine changes in the dividend growth rate for the next three years with increases in the required rate of return from 15 percent to 20 percent. The results of this combined change are greater than the decrease in value caused by a single change. For example, if a 2 percent dividend growth rate decline for three years is combined with an increase in the required return by 3 percent to 18 percent, the value falls by 41.6 percent.

Concluding Observations

Based on the analysis in this paper we should not be surprised that large stock price changes occasionally occur, but rather the surprise is that the price changes are not even larger. Using the dividend capitalization model

Table 4   **Share Value Change Caused by a Temporary Three-Year Change in Dividend Growth**

3-Year Dividend Growth*	Required Return	Share Price	Percent Change
+10%	15%	$4.40	—
+ 9%	15%	$4.21	− 4.3%
+ 8%	15%	$4.11	− 6.0%
+ 7%	15%	$3.97	− 9.6%
+ 6%	15%	$3.83	−12.9%
+ 5%	15%	$3.70	−15.9%

* Normal growth assumed to be 10 percent starting in year 4.

Table 5   **Share Value Change Caused by a Combined Change in
Dividend Growth for Three Years and Required Return**

Expected Dividend Growth*	Level of Required Return					
	15%	16%	17%	18%	19%	20%
+10%	0%	−16.7%	−28.6%	−37.5%	−44.5%	−50.0%
+ 9%	− 4.3%	−19.3%	−31.1%	−39.5%	−46.2%	−51.6%
+ 8%	− 6.6%	−22.3%	−33.2%	−41.6%	−48.2%	−53.2%
+ 7%	− 9.8%	−24.8%	−35.7%	−43.4%	−49.5%	−54.5%
+ 6%	−12.9%	−27.3%	−37.7%	−45.2%	−51.1%	−56.1%
+ 5%	−15.9%	−29.8%	−39.7%	−47.0%	−53.0%	−57.5%

* Normal growth assumed to be 10 percent starting in year 4.

commonly used by economists and market analysts to explain changes in share values, relatively small changes in the investors' required rate of return and in the expected growth rate for dividends can cause much larger changes in the share values. The emphasis in the article is on decreases in value, but as every investor knows, it is also possible for market prices to rise dramatically. When changes occur in the fundamental factors determining value we should expect the market adjustment to be both rapid and reasonably accurate. Thus volatility on the Singapore Stock Exchange can possibly be a sign of market responses to significant economic changes and thus the sign of a healthy market.[11] Only if a market consistently overreacts are large price changes a negative sign.

Although the dividend capitalization model presented in this study shows the relationship between the principal economic determinants of share values and changes in share values, it is less effective in determining precise values of individual shares. For the purpose of the study it was sufficient to determine the change in share values for a given change in growth or the required return. For the model to be used by investors to predict actual prices it is necessary first to forecast the dividend growth rate, to determine whether they are constant or variable, and to arrive at the required return expected for investments of the same level of risk. Although there is widespread agreement about what determines share values, and hence about what investors must estimate or forecast, being able to make the necessary estimates and forecasts with superior skill remains elusive. This is the province of the security analyst.

Questions

1.   What are the three basic determinants of the financial value of an asset?

[11] Whether the Singapore market price changes are greater than justified by future dividends has not been studied. For the U.S. market see Robert J. Shiller, "Do Stock Prices Move Too Much to be Justified by Subsequent Changes in Dividends," *American Economic Review*, Volume 7, June, 1981.

2. Explain why you might observe large swings in the price of a share of common stock.

3. Estimate the value of a share of common stock given the following information:
    - Expected cash dividend at the end of the year: $2.
    - Expected price per share at the end of the year: $50.
    - Expected (required) rate of return: 15 percent per year.

4. Use the dividend growth model to estimate the value per share of SMD's common stock. Investors expect SMD to pay a cash dividend of $1.50 one year from now. Investors expect dividends to grow 10 percent per year over the foreseeable future, and they require a 15 percent annual return on the stock.

5. If you buy 100 shares of SMD's common stock (described in Question 4), then how much money do you lose when the expected growth rate declines to 5 percent annually?

6. Assume that you wish to buy one share of SIR's common stock. Investors expect SIR to pay cash dividends per share as follows: $2 one year from now and $3 two years from now. Thereafter, they expect dividends per share to grow 4 percent annually. If investors require a 12 percent annual return on this stock, then what is its market price per share?

7. If you buy 100 shares of SIR's common stock (described in Question 6), then how much money do you gain when the expected growth rate increases to 6 percent annually?

6

The Great Bull Markets 1924–29 and 1982–87: Speculative Bubbles or Economic Fundamentals?

G.J. Santoni

Every so often, it seems, humankind almost en masse *has a compulsion to speculate, and it yields to that compulsion with abandon.*
　　　　—Robert T. Patterson, *The Great Boom and Panic*, p. xiii.

Many people attribute the bull market of 1924–29 and the subsequent collapse in stock prices to a "speculative bubble."[1] According to this view, the crash was inevitable because it was only a matter of time until the bubble burst (see the boxed item entitled "Some Popular Notions Regarding the Cause of the 1929 Crash").

The same theory of stock price formation is used to describe the bull market of 1982–87. Recent discussions have characterized this bull market as the product of "unexpected insanity," subject to "trading fads and frenzies rather than economic fundamentals" and "out of control."[2] Comparisons between the 1920s and 1980s like the one summarized in Chart 1 have appeared recently in the press.[3] Table 1, which plots quarterly data on the levels of the Dow Jones Industrial Index over the two periods, shows that the behavior of stock prices in both periods is similar.[4] Both bull markets began in the second quarter of the year; each lasted 21 quarters; each hit its peak in the third quarter with the timing of the peaks separated by only a few days (September 3, 1929, and August

G.J. Santoni, "The Great Bull Markets 1924–29 and 1982–87: Speculative Bubbles or Economic Fundamentals? *Review* (Federal Reserve Bank of St. Louis, November 1987): 16–29.

At the time of this writing, G.J. Santoni was a senior economist at the Federal Reserve Bank of St. Louis. Thomas A. Pollmann provided research assistance.

[1] See the boxed item on page 62 and Kindleberger (1978), p. 17.

[2] "Abreast of the Market" (1987) and Jonas and Farrell (1986).

[3] See, for example, Koepp (1987), Powell (1987), Schwartz and Tsiantar (1987) and *Wall Street Journal* (1987).

[4] Scale (1982–87) = 8 × scale (1924–29).

Some Popular Notions Regarding the Cause of the 1929 Crash

"Gambling in stock has become a national disease . . . Neither assets nor earnings, large as the earnings have been in many instances, warrant the market values of hundreds of stock issues. There has been an inflation (in stock prices) not free from the charge of criminality, . . . It was inevitable that a day of reckoning would come and the billions would be lost as the water and hot air were eliminated from hundreds of stock issues." Senator King, *New York Times* (October 25, 1929).

"The bull market was created by phenomenal profits in a few leading shares. Even in these shares there were not sufficient profits to justify the prices which prevailed before October 1928." Niebuhr (1930), p. 25.

"This growth (in stock prices) was matched by widespread, intense optimism which in the end deteriorated into lack of perspective and discipline. This optimism went so far in places that people began to believe that there was such a thing as 'permanent prosperity' and that economic crises could be eliminated." Roepke (1936).

"As already so often emphasized, the collapse in the stock market in the autumn of 1929 was implicit in the speculation that went before." Galbraith (1955), p. 174.

"The most common explanation of the Crash to this day is that the market was overpriced because of speculation . . ." Wanniski (1978), p. 125.

"In the end, fright may have been what turned retreat into rout. And that fright may have been partly motivated by the perception of absurdly high stock prices . . ." Schumpeter (1939), p. 876.

"Among the immediate or precipitating causes (of the crash) were the unjustifiably high prices of common stocks . . ." Patterson (1965), p. 215.

"The breakdown of 1929 was as nearly the result of willful mismanagement and violation of every principle of sound finance as such occurrence has ever been. It was the outcome of vulgar grasping for gain at the expense of the community." Willis (1930).

"It may be legitimately said that the boom and slump were caused by the alternate domination of greed and fear, and that the one was bound to resign sooner or later in favor of the other, . . ." Hodson (1933).

"Never a boom and high prosperity without an outbreak of speculation. Never such an outbreak that has not ended in a financial crisis." Snyder (1940).

"Might one still suppose that this kind of stock market crash (in 1929) was a rational mistake, a forecast error that rational people might make? This paper . . . implies that the answer is no." Shiller (1981), p. 422.

Chart 1   **The Bull Markets of the 1920s and 1980s**[1]
Dow Jones Industrial Index (Nominal Values)

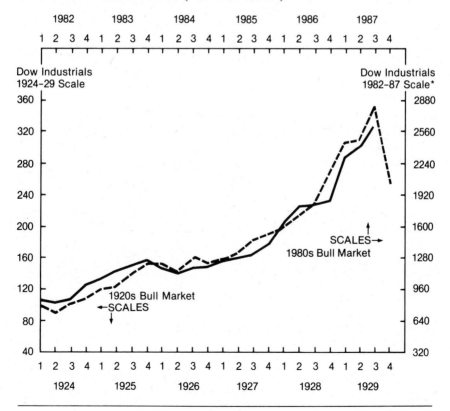

[1] Sources: Moore (1961), pp. 109, 145, and *Economic Report of the President,* various years.
* Scale 1982–87 = 8x Scale 1924–29.

Table 1   **Growth Rates in Stock Prices (Annual Average Growth Rates)**[1]

Panel A: II/1924–III/1929

Period	Dow Industrials
II/1924–IV/1924	32.8%
IV/1924–IV/1925	34.6
IV/1925–IV/1926	1.5
IV/1926–IV/1927	21.5
IV/1927–IV/1928	32.7
IV/1928–III/1929	37.7
Average II/1924–III/1929[2]	25.7%

Panel B: II/1982–III/1987

Period	Dow Industrials
II/1982–IV/1982	40.1%
IV/1982–IV/1983	20.9
IV/1983–IV/1984	–4.4
IV/1984–IV/1985	17.8
IV/1985–IV/1986	26.8
IV/1986–III/1987	31.5
Average II/1982–III/1987[2]	20.0%

[1] Computed from quarterly averages of seasonally adjusted data. See Moore (1961), pp. 106–09.

[2] In computing this average, the growth rates for each period are weighted by the length of the period.

25, 1987); in each case, 54 days elapsed between the peak and the crash; and each crash stripped slightly more than 20 percent from the stock market averages.

The belief that speculative bubbles might cause a persistent deviation in stock prices from the price consistent with the fundamentals is important. At the time of the 1929 crash, it spawned legislative proposals that would curb credit for speculation, amend the National Banking and Federal Reserve acts, impose an excise tax on stock sales and regulate the activities of stock exchanges and investment trusts.[5] Furthermore, if stock price bubbles exist, economic policymakers face a difficult problem because bubbles suggest that plans to save and invest may be based on irrational criteria and subject to erratic change.[6]

[5] *New York Times* (October 25, 1929).

[6] Keynes (1935), p. 159. Keynes discussed erratic shifts in the investment schedule caused by changes in the "state of confidence" (pp. 153–55) and "speculation" (p. 161). He argues that a

. . . *boom which is destined to end in a slump is caused, therefore, by the combination of a rate of interest, which in a correct state of expectation would be too high for full employment, with a misguided state of expectation which, so long as it lasts, prevents this rate of interest from being in fact deterrent. A boom is a situation in which over-optimism triumphs over a rate of interest which, in a cooler light, would be seen to be excessive (p. 322).*

See, as well, Gordon (1952), p. 378, and Varian (1979).

The purpose of this paper is to compare the implications of a theory of stock prices based on fundamentals to one that allows for bubbles, then to examine evidence from the 1920s and the 1980s to determine which set of implications is supported by the data. The behavior of stock prices during these two periods is particularly useful in testing asset prices for the presence of speculative bubbles. The 1924–29 experience is one of the most significant bull markets in U.S. history in both its duration and rate of advance. Though not quite as dramatic, the behavior of stock prices in the 1980s has been similar. If stock price bubbles exist, these are likely places to look for them.

The Fundamentals of Stock Prices

People value common stocks for their expected return. Since investors may choose among broad categories of stock, the expected return on any particular stock must be equal to the expected return on other stocks of similar risk. For example, if a particular stock is expected to yield a relatively low return, investors will shun it, causing its price to fall. This raises its expected return. The reverse holds for any stock with an expected return that is higher than other stocks of similar risk. An equilibrium exists when the expected returns are equal across equally risky stocks. Economists call this equilibrium return the required discount rate. Equation 1 calculates the expected return from holding a stock for one year assuming dividends are paid at year-end.[7]

(1)   Expected rate of return $= \dfrac{\text{Forecast of price at year end} + \text{Forecast of dividend} - \text{Current price}}{\text{Current price}}$

Equation 2 solves equation 1 for the current price by noting that the expected return is equal to the required discount rate in equilibrium.

(2)   Current price $= \dfrac{\text{Forecast of price at year-end} + \text{Forecast of dividend}}{(1 + \text{Required discount rate})}$

The Price Depends on Forecasts of Future Outcomes

The important thing to note in equation 2 is that the current price depends on forecasts of *future* outcomes which, of course, are subject to change as new information becomes available. The price does not depend on dividends that are observed in the present as Senator King and others have implied in their comments on the behavior of stock prices during the 1920s (see boxed item on page 62). The current price may change even though observed dividends do not and conversely.

---

[7] See Brealey (1983), pp. 67–72, and Brealey and Meyers (1984), pp. 43–58.

How Far Ahead?

The discussion so far indicates that investors must forecast the price of the stock next period. What are the fundamentals for this future price? In principle, the future price depends on the stream of dividends and the required discount rate investors expect to prevail over the life of the firm. Typically this requires forecasts that extend into the distant future and suggests that the job of analyzing stock prices is formidable. It is sometimes possible to simplify the calculation, however. If dividends are expected to grow at a constant rate and the discount rate is constant, the calculation can be simplified as shown in equation 3.[8]

(3)   Current price = $\dfrac{\text{Forecast of dividend}}{\substack{\text{Required discount rate} - \\ \text{Expected growth rate of dividends}}}$

The Price Fundamentals

Restating the solution for the current price as in equation 3 is particularly useful for the purposes of this paper. Equation 3 is a list of the price fundamentals: the forecast of the dividend next period, the required discount rate, and the expected (forecast) growth rate of dividends. The solution for the current price in equation 3 is called the fundamentals price. Furthermore, the equation can be used to show how relatively small changes in forecasts can account for relatively large changes in the fundamentals price. For example, suppose investors forecast a year-end dividend of $.60 per share, an annual dividend growth rate of 6 percent and the required discount rate is 8 percent. Equation 3 indicates that the fundamentals price is $30 per share [= .6/(.08 − .06)]. Now suppose that new information leads investors to lower the forecast of dividend growth to 5 percent. This is a decline of about 17 percent in expected growth [= (.01/.06)100]. The fundamentals price, however, declines to $20 [= .6/(0.8 − .05)], or more than 30 percent. Notice that a large decline in price may occur even though observed dividend payments do not change. It is even possible for the price to decline when observed dividends rise.

Stock Prices and Measures of the Fundamentals

Table 1 shows annual average growth rates of the Dow Jones Industrial Index in each year during the two bull markets.[9] The index rose rapidly during the initial phases of the bull markets, slowed down considerably in

---

[8] Brealey (1983), p. 69. The current price is defined by equation 3 only if the expected growth rate in dividends is less than the required discount rate.

[9] The data on stock prices used in this paper are daily closing levels of the Dow Jones Industrial Index. Daily closing levels of this index are available on a consistent basis from January 1915. See Pierce (1982). When possible, the statistical results obtained with this data were checked against results using daily closing levels of the Standard and Poor's Composite Index. In no case were any qualitative differences observed.

1926 and 1984, then rose rapidly through the third quarters of 1929 and 1987.

A rapid advance in stock prices is not surprising if it results from changes in the fundamentals. The investigator, however, seldom has the luxury of direct observation of the fundamentals. Instead, other variables (proxies) that are believed to provide information about the behavior of the unobserved fundamentals must be used. For example, credit market interest rates and actual dividend payments have been used to proxy the required discount rate and the expected stream of future dividends. It is important to recognize that, at best, the behavior of these (or other) proxies may give only a rough approximation of the behavior of the fundamentals and, on occasion, they may be entirely misleading. The 1920s may be an example of the latter case.

Long-term rates were roughly constant from 1924–29.[10] Data on actual per share dividends are very sketchy for this period. One estimate, however, indicates that actual dividends increased at an annual rate of about 8.8 percent from 1924–29.[11] While this is a fairly rapid rate of increase, it is far less than the growth observed in stock values. (See boxed item on page 68 for a more precise estimate of the relationship between stock prices and these proxy variables.) When the market crashed, people like Senator King pointed to these proxy variables and claimed that stock prices before October 1929 contained "water and hot air." An alternative explanation is that the proxies give a misleading impression of the behavior of the fundamentals.

Fundamentals, Fools and Bubbles

In order to evaluate the notion that stock prices in the 1920s and 1980s were driven by psychological factors extraneous to the fundamentals, it is necessary to be clearer about the implications that can be observed by the investigator. This paper considers three different theories that potentially explain stock prices: the efficient market hypothesis, the greater fool theory and the theory of rational bubbles.

Efficient Markets and Fundamentals

A long-standing proposition in both economics and finance is that stock prices are formed in efficient markets.[12] This means that all of the relevant information currently known about interest rates, dividends and the future prospects for firms is contained in current stock prices. Stock prices change only when new information regarding the fundamentals is

---

[10] See Friedman and Schwartz (1982), table 4.8, and Homer (1977), p. 352.

[11] See Cowles (1938), p. 389.

[12] See Brealey and Meyers (1984), pp. 266–81; Malkiel (1981), pp. 171–79; Brealey (1983), pp. 15–18; Leroy (1982); and Fama (1970).

The Relationship between Growth in Stock Prices, Dividends per Share and the Interest Rate: 1872–1930

The following regression estimate relates first differences in the natural log of the Cowles Commission index of stock prices, ΔLnP, to first differences in the natural logs of the Cowles Commission estimate of per share dividend payments, ΔLnD, and the interest rate on long-term bonds, ΔLnR. The data are annual and span the period 1872–1930. The regression estimate is intended to illustrate the results that are obtained when observed values of dividends and credit market interest rates are used to proxy expected dividends and the required discount rate.

$$\Delta LnP \;=\; .16 + .49\Delta LnD - 1.26\Delta LnR.$$
$$ (.11) \quad (4.54) \qquad (4.07)$$

Rho $\;=\;$ .03
 (.23)

RSQ $\;=\;$ .39

SE $\;\;=\;\;$ 10.40

The estimated coefficients of these proxy variables are significantly different from zero and the qualitative relationship between stock prices and these proxies is the same as that expected for their theoretical counterparts. There is a considerable amount of "noise" in the estimate, however, in the sense that variation in the proxy variables explains a relatively small amount (about 40 percent) of the variation in stock prices.

More importantly, the estimated equation performs very poorly in 1929 and 1930. For example, the percentage change in stock prices predicted by the regression estimate for 1929 is −1.24 percent. Stock prices actually rose in 1929 by 23.86 percent. This deviation of the actual from the predicted value is 25.10 percent. This deviation exceeds two standard errors of the estimate, indicating that such a large deviation is not likely to result from chance. In short, it suggests that the large increase in stock prices in 1929 was unrelated to movements in the proxy variables. In the case of 1930, the actual decline in stock prices exceeds the predicted decline by more than two standard errors. This pattern — a significantly larger percentage increase in stock prices than predicted for 1929 and a significantly larger decrease in stock prices than predicted for 1930 — appears to be consistent with the notion that a speculative bubble was responsible for a boom in prices and a crash when the bubble burst.

obtained by someone. New information, by definition, cannot be predicted ahead of its arrival; because the news is just as likely to be good as it is to be bad, jumps in stock prices cannot be predicted in advance.

Many present-day stock market analysts are skeptical of the efficient markets hypothesis.[13] Similarly, traders in the 1920s generally did not subscribe to it (see boxed item on page 70). But that is not important. If the behavior of stock prices is consistent with the implications of the theory, the hypothesis helps both to understand how stock markets work and to evaluate the claim that the bull markets were products of price bubbles.

If the efficient markets hypothesis is correct, past price changes contain no useful information about future price changes. With some added assumptions, this can be translated into useful empirical propositions. If the expected return to holding stock is constant and the volatility of stock prices does not change during the time period examined, the efficient market hypothesis implies that observed *changes* in stock prices should be uncorrelated and that price changes should not exhibit long sequences of successive changes that are greater or less than the median change for the sample.

The above propositions should hold even if the *level* of stock prices appears to drift upward or downward. These propositions concern the relationship between the sequence of price changes, not the average change over some specific period. Clearly, stock prices drifted upward during both bull markets; but that does not necessarily mean that price changes were correlated or that there were long runs of positive changes that exceeded the median change for these periods. Put differently, it does not necessarily mean that market participants were able to predict future changes in stock prices by observing the past.

Greater Fools

The notion that self-feeding speculative bubbles, on occasion, can drive stock prices is known as the "greater fool theory." According to this theory, people regard the fundamentals as irrelevant. Rather, they buy stock on the belief that some (bigger?) fool will buy the shares from them at a higher price in the future. People maintain this belief because they think "that market values will rise—as they did yesterday or last week—and a profit can be made."[14] Once the speculation begins, stock prices continue rising because people, seeing the rise in the previous period, demand additional shares in the belief that prices will continue to rise. This pushes prices still higher.

The greater fool theory is based on the presumption that there are times when past movements in stock prices matter. According to this

[13] See Malkiel (1981), pp. 126–79.
[14] Galbraith (1955), p. 23. See, as well, Malkiel (1981), pp. 31–49.

What Some Big Plungers Thought of Efficient Markets[a]

William C. Durant

Durant had been acquiring a large interest in American Smelters and its share price had risen from $119 to $140. One day during this period a friend burst into his office and exclaimed, "Now look here, Billy, what are you doing with Smelters? You know it's not worth $140." "Possibly not," Durant said, "but take my advice and don't sell me any more of it, because it's going much higher." The stock went to $390 on a split share basis.

Jesse Livermore

"A gambler is a man who doesn't know the market. He goes to a broker and says, "What can I do to make a thousand dollars?" He is only an incident. The speculative investor buys or sells against future conditions on his knowledge of what has happened in the past under a similar set of conditions."

Louis W. Zimmerman

"Zimmerman employed a team of experts to study the market constantly. He never purchased a stock until he received a final report from the analysts concerning the condition of the company.

Arthur W. Cutten

"Yes, I have taken my bit out of the market. Oh, quite a bit. But I would advise other men to stay away from it. If I had a son I wouldn't let him touch it with a ten-foot pole.

There are two many wrecks down there in the pit. People call them brokers. They are only part of that—the broke part."

The efficient markets hypothesis (EMH) suggests that Durant was lucky. He could not have known that the price of American Smelters would rise. Livermore's evaluation of the "gambler's" strategy vs. the "investor's" contradicts the implication of EMH that the strategy of each is just as likely to succeed (or fail). Similarly, EMH suggests that hiring teams of experts, as Zimmerman did, is not expected to result in raising the return from stock purchases above a normal return. This applies to Cutten's comment regarding brokers who, according to EMH, are expected to earn a normal return on their stock trades, not a negative return as suggested by Cutten.

[a] See Sparling (1930), various pages.

theory, during the "fooling" periods, there should be positive correlation in the past sequence of price changes and long runs of positive changes that exceed the median change for the sample period.

Rational Bubbles

Recently, some economists have discussed the possibility that stock prices may contain "rational" bubbles.[15] The theory of rational price bubbles is based on the belief that some asset prices (for example, stock, gold and foreign currency prices) are too variable to be justified by variation in the fundamentals.[16] Briefly, the theory says that there may be occasions when stock prices deviate from the price that is consistent with the fundamentals. The deviation is called a bubble.

Bubbles must possess certain characteristics if they are to have economic significance:

Bubbles must be persistent so that a forecast of stock prices based solely on the fundamentals is biased. This means that forecast errors (actual price minus forecast price) will tend to have the same sign and not average out. The persistence of one-sided errors is important because random variation in the data generally will cause the actual price to differ from any well-constructed forecast of the price even though a bubble is not present. If bubbles were only a name used to describe random variation in the data, they would not be very interesting.

Bubbles must be explosive in the sense that they must grow at a rate that compensates the stock purchaser for the additional amount invested in the stock due to the bubble. In addition, there may be a risk premium to compensate stockholders for the additional risk that the bubble may burst.[17] This characteristic causes the price to deviate further and further from the fundamentals for as long as the bubble lasts.

Bubbles cannot be negative. A negative bubble means that stock prices are less than implied by the fundamentals. The explosive characteristic of bubbles means that the prices implode with some chance that stock prices will be negative at some future date.[18] Negative stock prices, however, are impossible; they are inconsistent with the liability rules associated with common stock which limit potential losses to the extent of the initial investment.

[15] See Flood and Garber (1980 and 1982), Blanchard and Watson (1982), West (1986), and Diba and Grossman (1985 and 1986).

[16] See, for example, Shiller (1981) and Mankiw, Romer and Shapiro (1985).

[17] See Diba and Grossman (1985 and 1986), Blanchard and Watson (1982), Flood and Garber (1980), and West (1986).

[18] See Diba and Grossman (1985 and 1986) and Blanchard and Watson (1982).

Rational Bubbles and Stock Price Behavior

The theory of rational bubbles has implications for the behavior of stock prices that are different than the theory of efficient markets.[19] This is shown in Table 2, which makes use of the fundamentals theory of stock price determination discussed above. One important assumption of this example is that, at each moment in time, investors expect dividends to grow at a constant rate over the future. To keep things simple, the example assumes that subsequent events conform to the expectations of investors (perfect foresight, an extreme version of rational expectations) and that the dividend is initially expected to be $2. The expected dividend is constant in panel A (expected growth rate is zero) but grows in panel B at an expected annual rate of 2 percent. The required discount rate is 10 percent, and a bubble of $1 occurs in period zero.

Column 3 of panel A computes the fundamentals price, P_t^f. This is simply the expected dividend, $E_t(D_{t+1}) = \$2$, (assumed constant in panel A) divided by the difference between the required discount rate, $r = .10$, and the expected growth rate in dividends, $g = 0$. The fundamentals price is $20 each period.

The fourth column computes the bubble component of the price. As discussed above, the bubble expands over time at the required discount rate, r. The observed price, P_t, is the sum of the fundamentals price and the bubble as in column 5.

Column 6 calculates the percentage changes in the price. These are positive. More importantly, the numbers in column 6 rise over time indicating that this bubble produces a time series of observed price changes that are positively correlated. The observed price does not follow a random walk. Of course, the real world is never so neat. Changes in the fundamentals — $r, g, E_t(D_{t+1})$ — may cause the observed price to change in a way that masks the bubble. If that occurs, however, it is not clear that the bubble is very important since an investor's behavior under the theory of rational bubbles depends on his ability to detect the presence of bubbles.

The example in panel B is similar to the example in panel A except that dividends are expected to grow at a 2 percent annual rate. Notice that this does not change the qualitative result with respect to the observed price changes. These rise over time and will be positively correlated. The only difference between the two examples is that the fundamentals price in panel B rises (drifts upward) over time at a constant 2 percent rate (see column 7). This results from the growth in dividends. While the fundamentals price drifts upward at a constant rate of 2 percent, the sequence of changes in the fundamentals price are uncorrelated. The fundamentals price will follow a random walk with drift.

---

[19] See Diba and Grossman (1985).

Table 2   Fundamentals vs. Bubbles: An Example

Panel A: Expected growth of dividends is zero

Years	$E_t(D_{t+1})$	P_t^f	$B_t=(1+r)^t B_0$	$P_t=P_t^f+B_t$	$\%\Delta P_t$	$\%\Delta P_t^f$
0	$2.00	$20.00	$1.00	$21.00		
1	2.00	20.00	1.10	21.10	.48%	0.0%
2	2.00	20.00	1.21	21.21	.52	0.0
3	2.00	20.00	1.33	21.33	.57	0.0
4	2.00	20.00	1.46	21.46	.61	0.0
5	2.00	20.00	1.61	21.61	.70	0.0

Panel B: Expected growth of dividends is 2 percent

Years	$E_t(D_{t+1})$	P_t^f	$B_t=(1+r)^t B_0$	$P_t=P_t^f+B_t$	$\%\Delta P_t$	$\%\Delta P_t^f$
0	$2.00	$25.00	$1.00	$26.00		
1	2.04	25.50	1.10	26.60	2.31%	2.00%
2	2.08	26.01	1.21	27.22	2.33	2.00
3	2.12	26.53	1.33	27.86	2.35	2.00
4	2.17	27.06	1.46	28.52	2.37	2.00
5	2.21	27.60	1.61	29.21	2.42	2.00

Where: $E_t(D_{t+1})$ = the expected dividend next period

P_t^f = the fundamentals price in period t

B_t = the bubble in period t and B_0 is the initial bubble

r = the required discount rate

P_t = the observed price in period t

g = the expected growth rate in dividends

$$P_t = P_t^f + B_t = \frac{E_t(D_{t+1})}{r - g} + B_t$$

An important thing to note is that both the greater fool theory and the theory of price bubbles discussed in this paper imply that stock prices behave similarly. Both reject the efficient markets hypothesis, which implies that stock prices follow a random walk.

Some Problems with Bubbles

The notion that stock prices are influenced by bubbles is troublesome because it is not based on a well-specified theory. A complete theory of bubbles should identify the cause of bubbles in terms of some phenomenon *that can be observed separately* from bubbles themselves. On those occasions when the cause is observed, a bubble should also be observed and conversely. This allows a direct test of the theory and explains why bubbles may be observed on some occasions but not others.

In contrast, the greater fool and rational bubble theories do not suggest a cause of bubbles that can be observed separately. Rather, unusual price behavior (the bubble) is attributed to "intense optimism," "a compulsion to speculate" and "manias." These do not identify the cause of the bubble; they merely give the bubble a different name.[20]

These criticisms suggest that attributing crashes in stock prices to bursting bubbles adds nothing to our understanding of why crashes occur or how to prevent similar occurrences in the future. To illustrate, Wesley Clair Mitchell (a noted student of business cycles) wrote that

By a combination of various agencies such as public regulation of the prospectuses of new companies, legislation supported by efficient administration against fraudulent promotion, more rigid requirements on the part of stock exchanges concerning the securities admitted to official lists, more efficient agencies for giving investors information, and more conservative policy on the part of the banks toward speculative booms, we have learned to avoid certain of the rashest errors committed by earlier generations.[21]

Mitchell made this statement in 1913 in reference to the legislative and regulatory precautions instituted after the Panic of 1907. Like the crash in 1929, the 1907 crash had been attributed to a speculative bubble.

Efficient Markets vs. Price Bubbles: Some Evidence

The efficient markets hypothesis suggests that stock prices follow a random walk. The hypothesis has no implication for the drift in stock prices. Prices may be higher or lower at the end of the period being examined. Neither of these events is necessarily inconsistent with the hypothesis. Rather, the hypothesis implies that the sequence of price changes are unrelated; they behave as random variables. In contrast, the greater fool theory and the theory of rational bubbles discussed here imply that changes in stock prices are not random but are positively related. Which explanation is better supported by the evidence for the 1924–29 and 1982–87 bull markets?

To evaluate these theories, data on the level of the Dow Jones Industrial Index are used. Two periods are examined. One extends from January 3, 1928, through September 3, 1929. The second runs from January 2, 1986, through August 25, 1987. The data are first differences of the log of the Dow's daily closing level multiplied by 100 and are

[20] Brunner and Meltzer (1987) note that
Some further reflections on bubbles and sunspots equilibria should make us doubt their contribution to a useful reconciliation of analysis with critical observations. The bubble term refers neither directly nor indirectly to any observable entities. It is fundamentally inconsistent with any rational exploitation of information invoked by the same analysis (p. 2).
See, as well, Singleton (1987), pp. 28–30. Sirkin (1975) and Schwartz (1981), p. 25, question the bubble hypothesis as an explanation of the 1929 crash.
[21] Mitchell (1950), p. 172.

Table 3   **Autocorrelation Coefficients and Box-Pierce Statistics (First Differences of Logs of Dow Industrial Index)**

January 3, 1928–September 3, 1929

To Lag	Autocorrelation Coefficient	Box-Pierce Statistic
1	.0196	.18
2	−.0325	.70
3	−.0494	1.91
6	.0200	10.41
12	.0069	16.43
18	−.0521	21.65
24	.0213	29.58

Means of series = .128[a]
t-score   = 2.57

January 2, 1986–August 25, 1987

To Lag	Autocorrelation Coefficient	Box-Pierce Statistic
1	.0553	1.28
2	−.0140	1.36
3	−.0095	1.40
6	−.0151	4.66
12	−.0076	7.86
18	−.0044	13.14
24	.0024	14.24

Mean of series = .136[a]
t-score   = 2.83

[a] Statistically significant at the 5 percent level.

approximately equal to the daily percentage change in the index. Each sample contains more than 400 observations. Stock prices advanced very rapidly in these periods. If bubbles were present, they should be apparent in these data.

Were Stock Prices a Random Walk?

Table 3 presents the results of a test (called a Box-Pierce test) based on the estimated autocorrelations of percentage changes in the Dow Jones Industrial Index. This test is designed to determine whether there is significant autocorrelation in the data, that is, whether current changes in the index are related to past changes. Recall that the efficient markets hypothesis implies that past changes in stock prices are unrelated to (contain no information about) current or future changes. An empirical counterpart of this proposition is that changes in the index are not correlated. Conversely, if the hypothesis that stock prices were influenced by self-feeding bubbles is correct, percentage changes in the index should be positively correlated.

Table 3 shows tests results for the two periods discussed above. None of the test statistics indicate significant correlation at conventional confidence levels.[22] Stock prices followed a random walk, which is consistent with the efficient markets hypothesis.

Table 3 also shows the mean change for each period. The means are positive and significantly different from zero in a statistical sense. Today, the upward drift in stock prices during these time periods is obvious. At that time, however, the upward drift is not something that investors could have bet on with any confidence.

Runs Test

A run is the number of sequential observations that are greater or less than the sample median (the middle value of the sample). If a series of observations exhibits too few runs relative to what is expected for independent observations, the data are positively correlated or drawn from different populations.

The efficient markets hypothesis suggests that observed changes in stock prices are uncorrelated, that is, the changes are independent of one another. This means, for example, that there is no tendency for a large positive change to be followed by another large positive change. Consequently, the sequence of observed changes will move back and forth across the median change for the sample fairly frequently as shown in panel A of Chart 2. If changes in stock prices are correlated as implied by the bubble hypothesis, however, a plot of the observations in the order that they appear will indicate some tracking as shown in panel B. This plot crosses the sample median infrequently. The example exhibits relatively long and, consequently, fewer runs than expected of independent observations.[23]

Table 4 presents the results of a runs test for the bull markets of the 1920s and 1980s. The third column of the table shows the number of runs observed for daily percentage changes in the Dow Jones Industrial Index during each period of rapidly increasing stock prices. Column 4 gives the number of runs expected for a series of (495 and 417) independent observations and column 5 gives the variance of this series. Since the observed number of runs is not much different than expected, the hypothesis that percentage changes in the Dow Index behaved randomly during the sample periods is not rejected by this data.

---

[22] Daily data between October 22, 1929, and March 31, 1930, show significant autocorrelation at various lags. This is likely a statistical artifact produced by a substantial increase in the variance of the data at the time of the crash in October and November that appears to taper off over time. Consequently, the significant correlations do not suggest the presence of a bubble. Furthermore, stock prices were declining at this time and bubbles cannot be negative.

[23] See Wonnacott and Wonnacott (1977), pp. 486–88.

Chart 2   **An Illustration of a Random Sequence vs. Correlated Observations**[1]

Panel A: Random Sequence

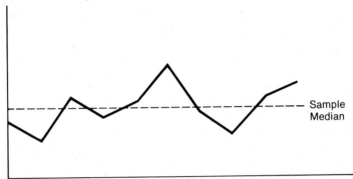

Panel B: Correlated Observations

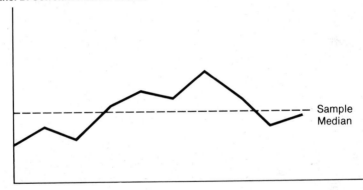

[1] See Wonnacott and Wonnacott (1977), p. 487.

Table 4   **Runs Test**

Sample Period	Number of Observations	Observed Number of Runs	Expected Number of Runs	Variance
Jan. 3, 1928– Sept. 3, 1929	495	233	248.0	123.50
Jan. 2, 1986– Aug. 25, 1987	417	220	209.0	104.00

Expected number of runs = (Number of observations + 1)/2

Variance = (Number of observations − 1)/4

The evidence on the behavior of stock prices (as characterized by the Dow Index) is not consistent with the notion that stock prices were driven by self-feeding speculative bubbles during the 1920s and 1980s.

Conclusion

Many people attribute the stock market crashes of 1929 and 1987 to bursting speculative bubbles. The perception that stock prices may be driven by bubbles presents economic policymakers with an important problem because such bubbles suggest that plans to save and invest may be based on irrational criteria and subject to erratic behavior.

This paper has examined data on stock prices around the time of the Coolidge and Reagan bull markets. The paper provides evidence contrary to the notion that the crashes were the result of bursting speculative bubbles. No evidence was found that changes in stock prices were autocorrelated or that the data contained long runs. Rather, the data suggest that stock prices followed a random walk. This evidence is consistent with the efficient markets hypothesis, which is based on the proposition that all relevant and ascertainable information regarding stock price fundamentals (interest rates, dividends, future prospects, etc.) is contained in current stock prices.

References

"Abreast of the Market," *Wall Street Journal,* January 26, 1987.

Blanchard, Oliver J., and Mark W. Watson. "Bubbles, Rational Expectations, and Financial Markets," in Paul Wachtel, ed., *Crises in the Economic and Financial Structure* (Lexington Books, 1982), pp. 295–315.

Brealey, R.A. *An Introduction to Risk and Return from Common Stocks* (The MIT Press, 1983).

Brealey, Richard, and Stewart Meyers. *Principles of Corporate Finance* (McGraw-Hill, 1984).

Brunner, Karl. "Epilogue: Understanding the Great Depression," in Karl Brunner, ed., *The Great Depression Revisited* (Martinus Nijhoff, 1981), pp. 316–58.

Brunner, Karl, and Allan H. Meltzer. "Bubbles and Other Essays," *Carnegie-Rochester Conference Series on Public Policy* (Spring 1987), pp. 1–8.

Cowles, Alfred III, and Associates. *Common-Stock Indexes, 1871–1937* (Principia Press, 1938).

Diba, Behzad T., and Herschel I. Gros sman. "Rational Bubbles in Stock Prices?" (National Bureau of Economic Research, Working Paper 1779, 1985).

———."On the Inception of Rational Bubbles in Stock Prices," (National Bureau of Economic Research, Working Paper 1990, 1986).

Fama, Eugene F. "Efficient Capital Markets: A Review of Theory and Empirical Work," *Journal of Finance Papers and Proceedings* (May 1970), pp. 383–417.

Flood, Robert P., and Peter M. Garber. "Bubbles, Runs, and Gold Monetization," in Paul Wachtel, ed., *Crises in the Economic and Financial Structure* (Lexington Books, 1982), pp. 275–93.

———."Market Fundamentals versus Price-Level Bubbles: The First Tests," *Journal of Political Economy* (August 1980), pp. 745–70.

Friedman, Milton, and Anna J. Schwartz. *Monetary Trends in the United States and United Kingdom, 1867–1975* (Chicago University Press, 1982).

———. *A Monetary History of the United States, 1867–1960* (Princeton University Press, 1963).

Galbraith, John Kenneth. *The Great Crash* (Houghton Mifflin, 1955).

Gordon, Robert A. *Business Fluctuations* (Harper and Brothers, 1952).

Hodson, H.V. *Economics of a Changing World* (Harrison Smith and Robert Haas, 1933), p. 164.

Homer, Sidney. *A History of Interest Rates* (Rutgers University Press, 1977).

Jonas, Norman, and Christopher Farrell. "Program Trading: Let the Little Guy In," *Business Week* (September 29, 1986), p. 100.

Keynes, John Maynard. *The General Theory of Employment, Interest and Money* (Harcourt, Brace and Company, 1935).

Kindleberger, Charles P. *Manias, Panics and Crashes* (Basic Books, 1978).

Koepp, Stephen. "How Ripe for a Crash?" *Time* (October 5, 1987), pp. 44–46.

Leroy, Stephen F. "Expectations Models of Asset Prices: A Survey of Theory," *Journal of Finance* (March 1982), pp. 185–217.

Malkiel, Burton G. *A Random Walk Down Wall Street* (W.W. Norton and Company, 1981).

Mankiw, N. Gregory, David Romer, and Matthew D. Shapiro. "An Unbiased Reexamination of Stock Market Volatility," *Journal of Finance* (July 1985), pp. 677–87.

Mitchell, Wesley Clair. *Business Cycles and Their Causes* (University of California Press, 1950).

Moore, Geoffrey H. *Business Cycle Indicators,* vol. 2 (Princeton University Press, 1961).

New York Times (September 6, October 24, and 25, 1929).

Niebuhr, Reinhold. "The Speculation Mania," *The World of Tomorrow* (January 1930), pp. 25–27.

Patterson, Robert T. *The Great Boom and Panic* (Henry Regnery Company, 1965).

Peters, William S., and George W. Summers. *Statistical Analysis for Business Decisions* (Prentice-Hall, Inc., 1968).

Powell, Bill. "The Prophets of Gloom '87," *Newsweek* (September 14, 1987), p. 56.

Pierce, Phyllis S. *The Dow Jones Averages 1885–1980* (Dow Jones-Irwin, 1982).

Roepke, William. *Crises and Cycles* (William Hodge and Company, Ltd., 1936), pp. 51–52.

Schumpeter, Joseph A. *Business Cycles* (McGraw-Hill, 1939), vol. 2.

Schwartz, Anna J. "Understanding 1929–1933," in Karl Brunner, ed., *The Great Depression Revisited* (Martinus Nijhoff, 1981), pp. 5–48.

Schwartz, John, and Dody Tsiantar. "The Market's Latest Bull Run," *Newsweek* (August 24, 1987), p. 32.

Shiller, Robert J. "Do Stock Prices Move Too Much to be Justified by Subsequent Changes in Dividends?" *American Economic Review* (June 1981), pp. 421–36.

Singleton, Kenneth. "Speculation and the Volatility of Foreign Currency Exchange Rates," *Carnegie-Rochester Conference Series on Public Policy* (Spring 1987), pp. 9–56.

Sirkin, Gerald. "The Stock Market of 1929 Revisited: A Note," *Business History Review* (Summer, 1975), pp. 223–31.

Snyder, Carl. *Capitalism the Creator* (The Macmillan Company, 1940), p. 229.

Sparling, Earl. *Mystery Men of Wall Street* (Blue Ribbon Books, 1930).

Varian, Hal R. "Catastrophe Theory and the Business Cycle," *Economic Inquiry* (January 1979), pp. 14–28.

Wall Street Journal. October 26, 1987.

Wanniski, Jude. *The Way the World Works* (Basic Books, 1978), pp. 116–48.

West, Kenneth D. "Dividend Innovations and Stock Price Volatility," Discussion Paper 113 (Princeton University Working Paper, July 1986).

Willis, Parker H. "Who Caused the Panic of 1929?" *North American Review* (February 1930), p. 183.

Wonnacott, Thomas H., and Ronald J. Wonnacott. *Introductory Statistics for Business and Economics* (John Wiley and Sons, 1977).

Questions

1. Define the following terms: bull market, efficient market, Dow Jones Industrial Average, speculative bubble, and greater fool theory.

2. Say that you buy 100 shares of common stock for $20 per share. After one year passes, you sell the stock for $24 per share. Just before you sell the stock, however, you receive a $1 dividend per share. What is your rate of return?

3. Identify the effect of each of the following changes (taken one at a time) on the price per share of ABC Corporation's common stock: (a) the expected growth rate of dividends increases, (b) the required discount rate increases, and (c) the forecast of next year's dividend increases.

4. "The efficient market hypothesis suggests that stock prices follow a random walk." Another example of a random walk is the motion of a drunk placed in the middle of an empty field. If you wish to locate the drunk some time later, where should you begin your search? According to the random walk hypothesis, you should begin at the middle of the field because that location is an unbiased estimate of the drunk's future location. Presumably, the drunk will wander

aimlessly, with the possible direction of each step being equally probable. Explain the analogy between the drunk and the price of a share of common stock.

5.   According to the evidence, does knowledge of past stock prices help you estimate future stock prices? Explain.

6.   Do you believe that graphing IBM's stock price over time is helpful in deciding whether or not to invest in IBM's stock? Explain.

Hunting the Stock Market Snark

O. Maurice Joy

"Just the place for a Snark!" the Bellman cried,
As he landed his crew with care;
Supporting each man on the top of the tide
By a finger entwined in his hair.

"Just the place for a Snark! I have said it twice:
That alone should encourage the crew.
Just the place for a Snark! I have said it thrice:
What I tell you three times is true."

—Lewis Carroll
The Hunting of the Snark

This article, much like Lewis Carroll's poem, recounts a tale of hunting; only the tale that is about to unfold describes the ancient, persistent search for stock market inefficiencies.

Efficiency means different things to different people. Sometimes the word is used in its economic allocative sense, referring to a condition where resources have been distributed in some best way. Sometimes the word is used in an engineering sense of minimum cost of operations. To those interested in the stock market, efficiency means you cannot "beat" the market. In other words, the market, the entire accumulation of investors, is so smart in its collective totality, that you cannot get rich, except accidentally or illegally, from trading profits. Competition for information about stocks is so keen and widespread that the market correctly prices stocks, on average. More formally, the stock market is efficient if it is impossible to make an abnormal profit—a profit too large given the riskiness of the stock—by using a given information set.

O. Maurice Joy, 'Hunting the Stock Market Snark,'' *Sloan Management Review* (Spring 1987: 17–24.

At the time of this writing, O. Maurice Joy was the Joyce C. Hall Distinguished Professor of Business Administration at the University of Kansas.

Contrariwise, a market *inefficiency* occurs when it can be shown that some "beat-the-market" scheme works.

The Stock Market Snark

"But oh, beamish nephew, beware of the day,
If your Snark be a Boojum! For then
You will softly and suddenly vanish away,
And never be met with again!"

The snark is a mysterious and rarely seen beast. We are never told exactly what it is or what it looks like. We are never sure if the elusive snark exists until the very end of the poem. And even then, its existence is only dimly revealed through indirect evidence. Nonetheless, the hunting expedition is launched with a colorful cast of characters. Stock market inefficiencies are also mysterious, rare, and dimly seen, and the hunting crew is equally colorful, ranging from Joe Granville to computer-wielding academicians.

There is another striking similarity. If a snark were a member of the species boojum, the hunter would *vanish* when snark and hunter met. The stock market analogy seems clear here, at least up to a point. If a stock market snark—a market inefficiency—is encountered, and it is a boojum, it too should vanish. Exactly how it vanishes is debatable. In one interpretation, the market may be thought of as becoming more efficient with the passage of time, or seasoning, so that abnormal trading profits vanish under natural competitive pressures. In a second interpretation, the stock market snark may disappear because new evidence may convince us that what appeared to be a market inefficiency was illusory. Many articles refuting market inefficiency findings are of this latter kind.

To complete the analogy one should consider what becomes of the financial researcher, our hunter, when stock market snarks, boojum or otherwise, are encountered. Actually, the analogy is badly strained here. No researchers have been reported missing, although any hunter who found a truly lucrative inefficiency might prefer to vanish into the land of private profit making. And, while it is tempting to argue that one's manuscript or academic respectability vanishes when the snark turns out to be a boojum, that, too, is pushing the comparison too far. In any event we will now go hunting the stock market snark. We should not forget that determining whether snarks are boojums is of great importance to the hunting story.

Predicting the Future: Preparations for the Journey

"He had bought a large map representing the sea,
Without the least vestige of land:
And the crew were much pleased when they found it to be
A map they could all understand."

Prediction of future events is an important task of many disciplines, and this is particularly true of the stock market. Two points can be made about predicting stock market returns. First, it is difficult to do successfully. Second, it is relatively easy to *claim* success. These two points are important individually, but taken together they spotlight a vexing problem. Apart from religion, macroeconomics, and foreign policy, it is hard to find fields of human endeavor that rival security analysis for its mixture of large stakes and unsubstantiated claims of prediction expertise. Claims of predictive success abound in the stock market arena, both on the professional side and in the academic literature. Such claims, nonetheless, cry out for verification or, more scientifically, falsification tests.

Only in the past quarter-century has the finance discipline been able to test predictive stock market claims in a scientific fashion. One may ask why it has taken so long to address properly this issue. There are three reasons.

First, although we have long possessed financial data, only since the 1960s have we begun to collect systematically large bodies of data that are, in any sense, accurate. The advent of the COMPUSTAT and Center for Research in Security Prices (CRSP) data tapes has opened doors for a variety of stock market research studies. The second reason is the capacity growth in computers in the middle years of this century. Prior to that growth, lack of data-handling facilities severely limited our ability to analyze large data collections. Finally, it has only been in the past three decades that the finance area developed the theoretical and statistical expertise necessary to perform reliable predictive tests. The change in tenor of the academic finance literature since the 1950s has been startling, and was a requisite development of that testing.

Three Versions of Market Efficiency

"Come, listen, my men, while I tell you again
The five unmistakable marks
By which you may know, wheresoever you go,
The warranted genuine Snarks."

Earlier, an efficient market was defined as one where securities are "properly" priced based on a given information set. This assertion, known as the *efficient market hypothesis* (EMH), is predicated on a particular information set. There are three versions of the EMH, one for each proposed base or set of information:

- *Weak form efficiency:* the information base is the collection of past stock prices (or rates of return).
- *Semistrong form efficiency:* the information base is any publicly available source of data.
- *Strong form efficiency:* the information base is insider information.

While this structure is somewhat awkward—for example, semi-strong efficiency subsumes weak form efficiency—it has two admirable features. First, this ordering structure allows us to compartmentalize where inefficiencies are found. More important, each of the three information sets can be linked directly to a major stock market evaluation philosophy. The links, which can be used to push our hunt along, are

- weak form efficiency—*technical analysis,*
- semistrong form efficiency—*fundamental analysis,* and
- strong form efficiency—*insider trading.*

Hunting the Snark with Technical Analysis

"We have sailed many months, we have sailed many weeks,
(Four weeks to the month you may mark),
But never as yet ('tis your Captain who speaks)
Have we caught the least glimpse of a Snark!"

In its most common form, technical analysis involves examining historical records of stock price behavior, identifying recognizable patterns that precede price movements, and then watching for repetitions of these patterns. The underlying rationale is that history repeats itself, and a careful student of history can profit from that fact.

The original Dow Theory is the forerunner of modern technical analysis. In several *Wall Street Journal* editorials written between 1900 and 1902, Charles Dow argued that stock market activity could be thought of as three-phased: primary movements, secondary movements, and daily fluctuations. He analyzed charts of industrial and railroad stock price averages to identify primary and secondary phases. Modern technical analysis techniques that use price or price and volume patterns are direct descendants of the Dow Theory. Other approaches to technical analysis have appeared in recent years. These include use of advance/decline lines, short sales, and odd lot ratios. All of these techniques share the underlying premise of the existence of a recognizable historical rhythm.

One of the first instances of a scientific test of market efficiency was Louis Bachelier's 1900 doctoral dissertation, *Theory of Speculation.* Bachelier developed a sophisticated mathematical theory of stock price behavior based on the notion that price changes (rates of return) are independent over time. The rate-of-return series, if this thesis were true, would have no memory: tomorrow's price change would not be related to today's price change. This proposal never fails to startle stock market students on first encounter, and it has an important implication for hunting snarks with technical analysis: history repeats itself only accidentally and not in a predictable way. Bachelier's work was mainly theoretical in nature, but he did some rough testing of the idea on the French bond market that seemed to verify the theory. Unfortunately, because Bachelier's work was in French, the English-speaking investment community was never aware of it until it was translated over half a century later. The English version is reprinted in Cootner.[1]

The decades of the 1930s, 1940s, and 1950s marked the beginning of sophisticated testing of the EMH. These early tests were statistical explorations of dependencies of changes in price indices rather than of individual stocks. Tests were performed on both commodity and stock market series. Most of them supported the conclusion that price changes, or rates of return, were independent over time; however, a subset of results seemed to indicate statistical dependencies strong enough to violate the EMH.

While there was some evidence that hinted of snarks, it was soon found that averaging across stocks' rates of return, which is inherent in price indices, can introduce false correlations. On reexamination, the early work on indices were examples of just such a phenomenon. The conclusion was that, if these indices were snarks, they were boojums because they disappeared. In the 1950s' terminology, academic researchers were frequently describing stock market price movements as resembling a "random walk," which, by definition, is unpredictable. A broad collection of these studies was compiled by Cootner.[2]

Another influential article appeared at the end of the 1950s. Harry Roberts, a University of Chicago statistician, made the previous statistical criticism of technical analysis understandable to all parties by directly confronting "charting." Roberts suggested that charted price patterns may be only statistical artifacts that have no historical rhythm, and therefore no predictive capability.[3] To illustrate his point, Roberts generated purely random price patterns, pictorially compared them to actual price patterns, and found the two sets to be indistinguishable. His moral is quite clear: we often see a snark where none exists.

The 1960s was a crucial decade for testing technical analysis. Two main lines were pursued: one involved "derivative statistical" properties of rate-of-return series; the other looked at the profitability of "trading rules" using technical analysis techniques. Foremost among the former kind of research were two articles by Eugene Fama of the University of Chicago.[4] Fama properly focused on individual securities rather than on indices. He collected an impressive assembly of data and performed many sophisticated computer tests. He concluded that stock price changes were independent over time, which is consistent with the EMH.

At the same time work progressed on the trading rules front. "Filter rules" were used to identify stocks that were over- or under-valued. A filter rule is merely a mechanical trading rule. For an investor using an X% filter, the trading rule would go like this: if the price of a stock increases by at least X%, buy the stock and hold it until its price declines by at least X% from a subsequent high price, at which time simultaneously sell the stock and go short. This process is repeated over time. Price changes of less than X% are ignored.

Filter rule tests have two advantages over the kind of derivative statistical property work conducted by Fama. First, the rules tested were more like the techniques that technical analysts actually use. Thus, these investigations more nearly corresponded to tests of security analysis as practiced by stock market technicians. Second, these tests raised the notion of economic significance of the results rather than just statistical significance. The variable of interest in these tests was profitability, which provided a clearer interpretation of the results and their practical implications.

Some of the first filter results looked very promising for technical analysis. In particular "small X" filter rules appeared to uncover some very large snarks. But after these results were analyzed more closely— with more attention given to some important details that originally were not accounted for—several shortcomings were uncovered. The main one concerned transaction costs, including broker fees, clearinghouse fees, and transfer taxes. To overcome the EMH, the filter rule must generate profits large enough to completely cover these unavoidable trading costs. This is particularly important in small X filter rules where many trades are triggered by the low value of X. Researchers found that when transaction costs were included in the analysis, filter rules could not generate sufficient profits to cover these costs.[5] Once again, if these were snarks, they were boojums.

With the close of the 1960s two things became clear: technical analysis was discredited academically; several dozen technical analysts were employed on Wall Street. Since that time, little academic research has been done in the technical analysis area: it is considered a dead subject academically. Today, it still seems clear: technical analysis is discredited academically; several dozen technical analysts are still employed on Wall Street.

Why technical analysis still thrives today in the face of all the evidence that it does not work is an interesting question. One answer may be that Wall Street does not pay much attention to academic research. But that is, at best, only partly true. We know Wall Street does pay attention to academic research. For example, many of the tenets of modern portfolio management have become widely accepted and practiced by the professional investment community.

Perhaps the answer is that technical analysis tests are not very good. Yet the research papers that are most damaging to technical analysis are of an exacting and careful nature. It is an impressive and compelling set of tests. The only apparent weakness in this body of empirical literature is that perhaps the tests have not been directed enough to specific technical analysis schemes that are actually practiced. That is, academicians may have inferred too much from the tests. Few research papers, for instance, have investigated the companion role that trading volume plays in conjunction with price movements. Yet that role is central to many technical analysis schemes.

Of course, another explanation for the continued use of technical analysis is closely akin to that expressed by Julian Huxley in a similar context: "Mythology, religion, and superstition all flourish when men must make decisions about matters over which they have no control."

Hunting the Snark with Fundamental Analysis

"It's a Snark" was the sound that first came to their ears,
And seemed almost too good to be true.
Then followed a torrent of laughter and cheers:
Then the ominous words "It's a Boo—"

Fundamental analysis refers to analyzing the underlying economic factors that determine stock price movements. Security analysts who are fundamentalists attempt to search out information that reflects future cash flow prospects for companies and how those prospects will be viewed (capitalized) by the marketplace. Historically, this is the oldest and most respectable form of evaluation. It has been for many years, and is today, the dominant form of security analysis.

One of the most influential proponents of fundamental analysis in this century was the late Benjamin Graham. His research output spanned the decades from the 1930s to the 1960s: several editions of his books were primers for generations of security analysts.[6] Because most of Graham's writing preceded the use of computers in security research, his work has not received much attention in the empirical literature. Yet many of the statistical tests performed in recent years have been related to his earlier writings.[7] A direct test of his approach is described below.

An early stock market research pioneer who began his work in the precomputer days was J.W. Meader, who approached the valuation topic using regression analysis.[8] Using a valuation formula that involved volume, book value, net working capital, earnings, and dividends, Meader developed a regression model that appeared to explain stock prices very well. This, in turn, offered the possibility of identifying misvalued securities.

As Meader repeated his work from 1930 to 1940, a curious result occurred. In any one year, Meader could "explain" the structure of stock prices quite well using his collection of variables. The model, however, proved incapable of "predicting" stock price changes, which was, of course, what Meader was interested in doing. He was discouraged by the results of his work.

Another, much simpler, type of research began to appear in the 1960s. Graham argued for years that investors should not buy stocks with high price-to-earnings (P/E) ratios. Using annual earnings to form P/E ratios, researchers found that stocks with low P/E ratios outperformed stocks with high P/E ratios. These studies appeared to offer clear sightings of snarks. This was surprising not only to academicians, who believed the semistrong version of the EMH, but also to many market professionals, who, while they believed in inefficiencies, viewed the P/E ratio strategy as too naive to be useful.

Empirical studies are inherently fragile, as their results are wholly dependent on the skill with which the data has been collected and explored. The early P/E studies were flawed in two important ways. One of the main tenets of finance is that risk and return are closely related. Therefore, the finding that low P/E stocks offer higher returns than high P/E stocks is not sufficient by itself to demonstrate market inefficiency. It may mean merely that low P/E stocks are riskier than high P/E stocks, and the extra return on the low P/E stocks is fair compensation only for the extra risk. This simple, but important, point is crucial to understanding fully what the snark hunt is all about: We found a market inefficiency only when we uncovered a stock selection scheme that offered a rate of return in excess of the rate of return from an equally risky investment alternative. In other words, we must find a scheme that offers excess rates of return on a fully risk-adjusted basis. The early P/E studies failed to adequately satisfy that requirement.

A second major criticism relates to data integrity. Often the data was collected in ways that introduced biases toward inefficiency in the results. Some studies, for example, were not careful in noting earnings announcement dates. Therefore, some earnings used in P/E studies had not been announced publicly. This introduced an insider trading profit unrelated to P/E trading rules based on publicly available data. Consequently, it was difficult to determine if the reported results were representative of real-world circumstances.

P/E ratio work continued to progress in the 1970s. Researchers began to use more timely earnings, namely, the quarterly earnings announced in unaudited interim earnings reports. Some attention focused on *changes* in quarterly earnings.[9] The results from these studies looked very interesting, pointing to market inefficiencies. By now, however, the academic community had learned to scrutinize any claims of success in snark hunting.

In the past, when attention was given to test refinement, the apparent inefficiencies always disappeared. Similar expectations were held here, at least in the academic community, as empirical work intensified in the 1970s. As the problems of the earnings studies were reexamined in later work, however, the anomalous findings remained.

One of the most prestigious academic finance journals, and the one most skeptical of snarks, the *Journal of Financial Economics,* dedicated a double issue (June/September 1978) to the "anomalous evidence regarding market efficiency." For the most part, the issue recounted snark sightings that were pervasive and difficult to dismiss. In June 1983, the journal elaborated on a similar issue that emphasized the surprising finding that stocks of small firms seemed to offer excessively large risk-adjusted rates of return. Today, this finding is referred to as the "size" or "small cap" effect.

Today, snark sightings abound. Besides the size effect, among the techniques that appear to offer uncommonly high risk-adjusted rates of return are stocks with low P/E ratios[10] and stocks with unexpectedly large announced earnings.[11] In a similar vein Graham's investment advice recently has been tested. Over the years Graham consistently recommended stocks with relatively modest P/E ratios and debt levels that were not excessive and that were of reasonable size with good industry positions. The results of this test confirmed Graham's advice.[12] Warren Buffet offers updated testimony to Graham's wisdom.[13]

Results like these are hardly surprising to Wall Street. For years professional analysts have claimed that research on the EMH has overstated the case for efficiency. Therefore, recent findings have vindicated the long-standing Wall Street view that expertise in fundamental analysis is rewarded.

What about the other side of this issue? What do proponents of the efficient market theory have to say about the recent spate of apparently successful snark hunts? Three main criticisms are raised.

The first criticism, which is an old one, concerns transaction costs. Narrowly defined, transaction costs refer to the costs of buying and selling stocks. Several market inefficiency studies have incorporated these cost estimates. However, in a beat-the-market strategy there may be other kinds of transaction costs involved as well, such as opportunity costs for time spent on administering the scheme, computer usage costs, and differential bid/ask spreads on stocks. These are difficult to measure accurately. Even the more careful recent studies have not accounted fully for all such costs.

The second major objection to snark sightings is that today's easy access to computers and data tapes has led to extensive "data mining," where researchers repeatedly dig through the same data until they find their snark. Uncovered empirical oddities may be sample-specific and have no predictive success outside of those samples.

Perhaps the most compelling argument, however, is one raised by Ray Ball.[14] He correctly notes that any test of the EMH is predicated on an expectations model of stock price behavior. Consequently, any such test is unavoidably a joint test of market efficiency *and* the validity of the underlying expectations model. Ball interprets the results of the various tests not as indications of inefficiencies, but as evidence that the current widely used expectations model, which is based on market betas, is flawed.

Ball's criticism cuts across all forms of snark sightings, including P/E ratios, size, earnings surprises, and Graham's procedures. The simplest version of the model misspecification that Ball suspects involves risk. If extant models understate risk for certain types of stocks (e.g., low P/E stocks), then observed risk-adjusted returns are overstated for those stocks.

Ball's analysis is a good example of Kuhn's theory of what happens during a breakdown of a major research paradigm within a scientific discipline.[15] Inference becomes more difficult than in normal times, and beliefs are diffused. One may not agree with all aspects of Ball's criticism, but he has raised debatable points that are central to further investigation in this area. To claim market inefficiencies today requires a reconciliation of Ball's issues.

In summarizing the evidence on fundamental analysis, three points seem clear:

- Snarks have been reported, and not all have been shown yet to be boojums. Several anomalies have yet to be explained.
- Wall Street believes in snarks.
- The majority of the academic community does not believe in the existence of snarks. The final line of defense is Ball's model mis-specification criticism.

Hunting the Snark with Insider Information

("That's exactly the method," the Bellman bold
In a hasty parenthesis cried,
"That's exactly the way I have always been told
That the capture of Snarks should be tried!")

The last version of the EMH is concerned with insider information. Can someone with insider information beat the market? This is the "strong form" of the EMH.

This issue always strikes market professionals as ludicrous. Who could not beat the market if one possessed insider information? Does anyone think Ivan Boesky didn't? Actually, this version of the EMH was never intended to be a hypothesis in the sense that the weak and semistrong versions were. No one, including the staunchest proponent of market efficiency, ever believed that insiders could not beat the market. Rather, this version was intended to provide a benchmark of where market efficiency broke down. In other words, this insider trading case could provide a contrast to the technical and fundamental analysis cases, where insider information was not available.

While the results are not as voluminous as they are in the preceding two cases, they are about what was expected. Corporate officers, who presumably have access to privy information, have traded with excess economic profits. Some merger studies have reflected the same phenom-enon. However, insider trading is, by definition, illegal. Therefore, while it is profitable, this game is illicit, perilous, and not available to the average investor.

Perhaps the most important part of this EMH version is the work that shows who does not get insider information. Over the years there has been a series of tests concerning mutual fund performance. These are important because mutual funds supposedly employ sophisticated ana-lysts and may, because of their connections, have access to insider information.

Tests have shown that mutual funds do not outperform the market by more than the expenses charged to their customers. That is, mutual funds apparently can beat the market in a risk-adjusted return sense without considering transaction costs to the mutual fund investors. But once the investors' transaction costs, mutual fund management fees, and load costs are considered, the funds do not outperform the market.[16] These results are, of course, fully consistent with the EMH. This does not imply, however, that mutual funds are a bad investment: the valuable service they *do* provide is broad diversification.

So What Is a Snark?

"They sought it with thimbles, they sought it with care;
They pursued it with forks and hope;
They threatened its life with a railway-share;
They charmed it with smiles and soap."

Apparently, Lewis Carroll himself did not know what a snark was, so snark hunting has been a murky business from the very beginning. However, two things seem clear today about the stock market version of the snark:

- While acceptance of the possibility of snarks seems to have increased within the academic community, most academics have never seen snarks and never expect to. Moreover, if ever there were such a thing as snarks, academicians would view them as boojums.

- The professional investment community, on the other hand, believes that snarks are everywhere, and those that are boojums are always those found by the other guy.

Why does this difference in attitudes and beliefs exist? Academicians are, by training, skeptical, and rightly so. Tests finding market inefficiencies are flawed in various ways. The attitude that tighter proof of snark finds is required is consistent with conservative scientific principles regarding hypothesis testing. At this point, the burden of proof is on the snark hunters to provide more illuminating pictures of their quarry.

It is also worth remembering that while the practice of finance may be ancient, the science of financial theory is in its infancy. Moreover, communication between theory and practice is sometimes limited. Given that the EMH is reasonably correct, the trickle down of that idea from theory to practice will take a long time. We have seen only the first phase of this movement.

Finally, we should never expect academic and professional attitudes to correspond perfectly in stock market research. Every profession has its optimistic and pessimistic groups, and in investments, the professional community will always be, by nature, more optimistic than the academic community about beating the market. Indeed, one of the primary reasons the market is relatively efficient today is that professional investors are keen to beat the market.

Attitudes within the two camps will no doubt change in the future. On the academic side, the theory will be improved to the point that even more snarks will be identified as boojums. However, academic opinion probably will be more attuned to the possibility of *temporary* market inefficiencies than they are today. Programmed trading is one such instance. On the professional side, Wall Street will rediscover the EMH. The basic idea of market efficiency will be elevated from that of a theoretical curiosity to a more fundamental and lasting common belief that serves as a powerful standard of comparison against which security analysts and portfolio managers must measure up. We are, in fact, already seeing that today in the increased use of index comparisons. Of course, Wall Street *always* will believe in snarks.

In the interim, what does all this mean for investors from a practical standpoint? First, according to the EMH, get-rich schemes are almost always fraudulent: Joe Granville and friends notwithstanding, it is hard to beat the market. Second, don't churn your account. Trading schemes that involve high portfolio turnover rates are doomed to failure because of transaction costs. Third, more adventuresome investors may wish to consider the relatively conservative segment of the snark literature. Benjamin Graham's strategies, low P/E strategies, and the like are anomalous and do not require churning. An investment strategy that prudently uses such elements can possibly enhance investment performance. But we should never forget that today's snark is likely to be tomorrow's boojum.

References

[1] P. Cootner, *The Random Character of Stock Market Prices* (Cambridge: MIT Press, 1967).

[2] Ibid.

[3] H. Roberts, "Stock Market Patterns and Financial Analysis: Methodological Suggestions," *Journal of Finance,* March 1959.

[4] E.F. Fama, "The Behavior of Stock-Market Prices," *Journal of Business,* January 1965, pp. 34–105; E.F. Fama, "Tomorrow on the New York Stock Exchange," *Journal of Business,* July 1965, pp. 285–299.

[5] E.F. Fama and M.E. Blume, "Filter Rules and Stock-Market Trading," *Journal of Business,* January 1966, pp. 226–241.

[6] B. Graham, *The Intelligent Investor* (New York: Harper & Row, 4th ed., 1973).

[7] B. Graham, D. Dodd, and S. Cottle, *Security Analysis* (New York: McGraw-Hill, 4th ed., 1961).

[8] J.W. Meader, "A Formula for Determining Basic Values Underlying Common Stock Prices," *The Analyst,* 29 November 1935.

[9] O.M. Joy, R.H. Litzenberger, and R.W. McEnally, "The Adjustment of Stock Prices to Announcements of Unanticipated Changes in Quarterly Earnings," *Journal of Accounting Research* 15 (1977): 207–225.

[10] S. Basu, "The Relationship between Earnings' Yield, Market Value, and Return for NYSE Common Stocks: Further Evidence," *Journal of Financial Economics* 12 (1983): 129–156.

[11] R.J. Rendleman, Jr., C.P. Jones, and H.A. Latané, "Empirical Anomalies Based on Unexpected Earnings and the Importance of Risk Adjustments," *Journal of Financial Economics* 10 (1982): 269–287.

[12] H.R. Oppenheimer and G.G. Schlarbaum, "Investing with Ben Graham: An *Ex Ante* Test of the Efficient Market Hypothesis," *Journal of Financial and Quantitative Analysis,* September 1981, pp. 341–360.

[13] W. Buffett, "Up the Inefficient Market: Graham & Dodd Is Alive and Well on Wall Street," *Barron's,* 25 February 1985.

[14] R. Ball, "Anomalies in Relationships between Securities' Yields and Yield-Surrogates," *Journal of Financial Economics* 6 (June/September 1978): 106–126.

[15] T.S. Kuhn, *The Structure of Scientific Revolutions* (Chicago: University of Chicago Press, 1969).

[16] N. Mains, "Risk, the Pricing of Capital Assets, and the Evaluation of Investment Portfolios: Comment," *Journal of Business*, July 1977.

Questions

1.   What is "the stock market snark"?

2.   When a stock market is operationally efficient, does it necessarily follow that stock prices will reflect fundamental (true) values? Explain.

3.   Describe the three versions of the efficient market hypothesis.

4.   Compare and contrast technical analysis with fundamental analysis.

5.   Some researchers using fundamental analysis claim to have discovered "snarks" in the stock market. Describe these snarks.

6.   "But we should never forget that today's snark is likely to be tomorrow's boojum." What does this statement mean?

Stocks, Bonds, Paper, and Inflation: 1870–1985

Charles P. Jones and Jack W. Wilson

Although the Ibbotson–Sinquefield (IS) data covering the returns on major financial assets—common stocks, government and corporate bonds, Treasury bills—and inflation begin in 1926 and are updated on an annual, quarterly, and monthly basis, the entire record of the returns of financial assets dates back nearly sixty years farther. We can almost double the history of returns for major asset classes, resulting in a "complete" record of 115 years covering the period 1871–1985.

The construction of such a record can offer new insights into the wealth accumulation power of equity securities as well as information on a consistently constructed corporate bond series. Furthermore, we can provide a look at the long-term performance of short-term interest rates in an alternative form to the IS Treasury bill data. After all, the first Treasury bills were issued only in December 1929 and were used sparingly until World War II. Finally, if heretofore unavailable data on the Consumer Price Index can be constructed and analyzed, we can evaluate the complete record described above on both a nominal and an inflation-adjusted basis.

This article presents the entire 115-year performance record—December 31, 1870–December 31, 1985—for a composite index of common stock returns, a corporate bond series, and commercial paper. We also construct and present new CPI data for the earlier period in order to be able to examine for the first time inflation-adjusted returns similar to those that IS provide. The additional information of this complete record should be helpful in analyzing long-term price cycles and movements, and

Charles P. Jones and Jack W. Wilson, "Stock, Bonds, Paper, and Inflation: 1870–1985," *Journal of Portfolio Management* (Fall 1987): 20–24. Reprinted with permission.

At the time of this writing, Charles P. Jones was Professor of Economics and Finance and Jack W. Wilson was Associate Professor of Economics and Business at North Carolina State University in Raleigh. The authors are deeply indebted to Peter Bernstein for his very substantive comments and suggestions on an earlier draft of this paper. His suggestions stimulated them to more fully develop both their data and their methodology, and his arguments led to insights that had been overlooked.

in documenting the well-known power of compounding over very long periods of time. Comparisons between the early period and the IS period — two periods of roughly equal length — are useful in substantiating both the absolute and relative relationships found in the IS data.

Construction of the Data

The choice of 1926 as a starting point for the IS data is arbitrary, particularly with regard to common stock data.[1] Comparable data of high quality are available in printed form from the reconstruction of stock prices and dividends in *Common Stock Indexes,* published in 1939 by the Cowles Commission for Research in Economics. This Commission was an outgrowth of Alfred Cowles's interest in such matters as stock market forecasting following the Great Crash of 1929. The membership reads, as Kenneth Boulding notes, "like an international 'Who's Who' of economics" (1953–1954, p. 150).

The Standard Statistical Service, which merged with Poor's in 1941 to become Standard & Poor's, published a value-weighted index starting in 1926, with an extension back to 1918. The Cowles Commission chose this form of stock index and extended it back to the beginning of 1871. Except for adjustments for new listings, delistings, and mergers, this index is supposedly identical to the current value-weighted formula used for the S&P index.[2] We have constructed and examined the entire file of 659 monthly total returns, capital appreciation, and income returns from the original Cowles Commission records for the period January 1871 through December 1925.[3]

We calculated our corporate bond series by using monthly interest rates from Moody's data for Aaa corporate bonds for the period 1919–1985 and from Macaulay's (1938) railroad bond yields for the period 1870–1919.[4] The methodology for calculating monthly returns was based on the assumption of a $100 par, 4% coupon bond making semi-annual payments. We used a standard formula to calculate the price of the bond based on the current yield to maturity.[5]

The sources for the monthly commercial paper rates are the same as those used for corporate bonds. We used Macaulay's rates until January 1919, when the Moody's series became available in the Federal Reserve's *Banking and Monetary Statistics* and *Annual Statistical Digest.* The rates are for high-quality paper quoted in New York City.[6] The calculation of monthly returns parallels the calculation for corporate bonds.[7]

Methodology

Ibbotson and Sinquefield calculate and report stock return data based on the assumption that dividends are reinvested monthly. They then form annual calendar returns by compounding the monthly returns or, alterna-

---

[1] Footnotes appear at the end of the article.

tively, by using year-end index values where the wealth index is initialized as of December 31, 1925, as 1.00. The Cowles Commission provides a similar cumulative wealth index based on monthly reinvestment, making it possible to construct a nominal wealth index series from 1871 through 1985 by linking together the earlier series with the IS data.

Such a series provides the complete record for a composite of common stocks.[8] We present the results in the form of a cumulative relative wealth index (exactly identical in nature to the wealth index presented by IS), with year-end 1870 initialized at 1.00.

Ibbotson and Sinquefield state that "historical data suggest that . . . returns have been related to inflation rates" (1986, p. 33). They use the Consumer Price Index to measure inflation. Monthly inflation-adjusted returns are estimated as the difference between the nominal return and the estimate of inflation.[9]

December values of the CPI are necessary for deflating the calendar returns, but monthly surveys by the Bureau of Labor Statistics (BLS) were not instituted until the 1940s. In 1986, the BLS issued releases of a monthly series from January 1913 that appear to be a reconstruction of the year-end, semi-annual, and occasional quarterly data collected from their original city averages. We use the December values from the BLS releases from 1913 forward.[10]

In order to examine inflation-adjusted returns on a basis comparable to IS for the entire early period, using the assumption of monthly reinvestment, we had to construct some new CPI data. Our results permit, for the first time, the adjustment of the entire Cowles data series to an inflation-adjusted basis comparable to that of IS. They also enabled us to construct a complete corporate bond and commercial paper return series on a real basis.

Prior to 1913, BLS and the Department of Commerce seem to rely on the work of Ethel Hoover (1961) and Albert Rees (1961), who individually constructed Laspeyres-type indexes on an annual average basis for earlier years.[11] In order to go back to 1871, we spliced the Hoover and Rees series for annual average CPI values, calculated the mean of the adjacent year index values (so as to be centered in December), spliced these to the December 1913 value of the BLS reconstruction, and calculated the inflation rates from December to December from 1870 through 1925.

Results

Table 1 shows the complete annual record of cumulative wealth for the three series for the period 1871–1985. Year-end 1870 is initialized at 1.00.

The common stock cumulative wealth series shows that an initial $1.00 invested on December 31, 1870, grew to $47.52 by December 31, 1925. For the IS data, $1.00 invested at the beginning of 1926 would have grown to $279.00 by the end of 1985. For the entire period 1871–1985, $1.00 invested in a composite of common stocks with dividends rein-

Table 1   **Nominal and Real Cumulative Wealth, with Monthly Reinvestment, from Common Stocks, Aaa Corporate Bonds, and Four- to Six-Month Commercial Paper, with the Consumer Price Index, December Values from 1870–1985**

	Nominal Cumulative Wealth				Real Cumulative Wealth		
Year	Stocks	Bonds	Paper	CPI	Stocks	Bonds	Paper
1870	$1.00	$1.000	$1.000	1.000	$1.00	$1.00	$1.00
1871	1.12	1.106	1.070	.958	1.17	1.15	1.12
1872	1.26	1.203	1.167	.937	1.35	1.28	1.24
1873	1.16	1.271	1.308	.931	1.25	1.37	1.41
1874	1.28	1.478	1.415	.910	1.41	1.63	1.56
1875	1.31	1.685	1.493	.875	1.50	1.93	1.71
1876	1.15	1.855	1.579	.840	1.37	2.21	1.88
1877	1.11	2.012	1.668	.823	1.35	2.45	2.03
1878	1.24	2.213	1.758	.795	1.56	2.78	2.21
1879	1.87	2.494	1.845	.760	2.46	3.28	2.43
1880	2.33	2.873	1.947	.757	3.08	3.80	2.57
1881	2.51	3.029	2.053	.767	3.28	3.95	2.67
1882	2.57	3.198	2.180	.774	3.32	4.13	2.82
1883	2.49	3.405	2.315	.760	3.28	4.48	3.04
1884	2.21	3.617	2.448	.733	3.02	4.94	3.34
1885	2.79	4.023	2.558	.715	3.90	5.62	3.58
1886	3.14	4.293	2.670	.708	4.43	6.06	3.77
1887	3.06	4.430	2.835	.708	4.32	6.25	4.00
1888	3.11	4.751	2.995	.715	4.35	6.64	4.19
1889	3.35	5.016	3.135	.722	4.64	6.94	4.34
1890	3.01	5.086	3.305	.719	4.19	7.08	4.60
1891	3.71	5.416	3.533	.715	5.19	7.57	4.94
1892	3.93	5.734	3.691	.715	5.50	8.02	5.16
1893	3.31	6.018	3.994	.711	4.65	8.46	5.61
1894	3.37	6.524	4.135	.692	4.87	9.43	5.98
1895	3.54	6.848	4.260	.668	5.30	10.25	6.38
1896	3.61	7.159	4.545	.660	5.46	10.84	6.88
1897	4.24	7.744	4.718	.656	6.45	11.80	7.19
1898	5.22	8.199	4.915	.652	8.00	12.57	7.53
1899	5.77	8.474	5.068	.652	8.85	12.99	7.77
1900	6.87	8.977	5.329	.656	10.46	13.68	8.12
1901	8.26	9.359	5.565	.664	12.44	14.09	8.38
1902	8.69	9.596	5.828	.672	12.93	14.28	8.67
1903	7.42	9.838	6.173	.684	10.84	14.39	9.03
1904	9.73	10.446	6.490	.696	13.99	15.02	9.33
1905	11.70	10.864	6.747	.696	16.81	15.62	9.70
1906	12.54	11.116	7.143	.700	17.93	15.89	10.21
1907	8.80	10.957	7.578	.723	12.16	15.15	10.48
1908	12.73	12.089	8.065	.731	17.41	16.54	11.03
1909	15.27	12.551	8.357	.719	21.23	17.45	11.62
1910	14.04	12.982	8.819	.731	19.21	17.76	12.06
1911	14.86	13.537	9.195	.747	19.90	18.13	12.31
1912	16.09	13.956	9.599	.755	21.32	18.50	12.72
1913	14.60	14.130	10.185	.770	18.96	18.34	13.22
1914	14.06	14.550	10.764	.778	18.08	18.70	13.84
1915	19.08	15.614	11.213	.793	24.05	19.68	14.13
1916	21.03	16.469	11.574	.885	23.75	18.60	13.07
1917	15.89	15.500	12.071	1.049	15.15	14.77	11.50
1918	19.94	16.975	12.812	1.264	15.77	13.43	10.13

Year	Nominal Cumulative Wealth			CPI	Real Cumulative Wealth		
	Stocks	Bonds	Paper		Stocks	Bonds	Paper
1919	23.87	16.678	13.535	1.451	16.45	11.49	9.33
1920	19.38	16.580	14.526	1.484	13.06	11.17	9.79
1921	22.19	19.374	15.738	1.326	16.74	14.61	11.87
1922	28.22	21.528	16.513	1.292	21.84	16.66	12.78
1923	29.22	22.626	17.405	1.326	22.04	17.07	13.13
1924	36.75	24.225	18.224	1.323	27.78	18.31	13.77
1925	47.52	25.770	18.939	1.374	34.58	18.75	13.78
1926	$53.03	$27.631	$19.795	1.354	$39.17	$20.41	$14.62
1927	72.95	29.784	20.691	1.326	55.03	22.47	15.61
1928	104.74	30.546	21.632	1.313	79.78	23.27	16.48
1929	95.90	31.765	23.017	1.315	72.90	24.15	17.50
1930	72.04	33.912	24.083	1.236	58.28	27.44	19.48
1931	40.82	31.942	24.646	1.118	36.50	28.56	22.04
1932	37.49	36.965	25.600	1.003	37.38	36.85	25.52
1933	57.69	39.127	26.032	1.008	57.22	38.80	25.82
1934	56.88	44.782	26.369	1.029	55.29	43.53	25.63
1935	83.97	48.867	26.586	1.059	79.26	46.12	25.09
1936	112.48	52.794	26.790	1.072	104.90	49.24	24.98
1937	73.09	53.856	27.020	1.106	66.11	48.71	24.44
1938	95.80	56.633	27.282	1.075	89.13	52.69	25.38
1939	95.42	59.617	27.453	1.070	89.20	55.73	25.66
1940	86.11	63.112	27.610	1.080	79.73	58.44	25.57
1941	76.13	63.783	27.759	1.185	64.25	53.83	23.43
1942	91.57	65.893	27.932	1.295	70.72	50.89	21.57
1943	115.33	68.399	28.129	1.336	86.34	51.20	21.06
1944	138.10	70.693	28.333	1.364	101.24	51.83	20.77
1945	188.42	73.622	28.550	1.395	135.10	52.79	20.47
1946	173.22	75.507	28.759	1.648	105.10	45.82	17.45
1947	183.10	74.674	29.035	1.797	101.92	41.57	16.16
1948	193.17	77.689	29.427	1.845	104.69	42.10	15.95
1949	229.48	82.222	29.907	1.812	126.65	45.38	16.51
1950	302.24	83.323	30.300	1.917	157.68	43.47	15.81
1951	374.85	81.337	30.905	2.029	184.71	40.08	15.23
1952	443.66	84.374	31.660	2.047	216.70	41.21	15.46
1953	439.29	85.410	32.493	2.060	213.24	41.46	15.77
1954	670.43	90.578	33.128	2.050	327.06	44.19	16.16
1955	882.04	90.146	33.647	2.058	428.69	43.81	16.35
1956	939.88	85.399	34.720	2.116	444.09	40.35	16.41
1957	838.56	89.513	36.093	2.180	384.59	41.05	16.55
1958	1202.19	88.489	37.090	2.219	541.83	39.88	16.72
1959	1345.90	86.421	38.407	2.252	597.64	38.37	17.05
1960	1352.22	93.260	40.249	2.285	591.70	40.81	17.61
1961	1715.80	96.226	41.461	2.301	745.79	41.83	18.02
1962	1566.06	103.352	42.850	2.329	672.47	44.38	18.40
1963	1923.14	105.823	44.331	2.367	812.41	44.70	18.73
1964	2240.11	109.690	46.134	2.395	935.19	45.79	19.26
1965	2519.01	110.510	48.171	2.441	1031.78	45.26	19.73
1966	2265.53	106.265	50.758	2.523	897.84	42.11	20.12
1967	2808.70	100.909	53.602	2.600	1080.24	38.81	20.62
1968	3119.39	103.536	56.826	2.723	1145.61	38.02	20.87
1969	2854.08	94.979	61.023	2.889	987.82	32.87	21.12
1970	2968.42	106.925	66.990	3.048	973.91	35.08	21.98
1971	3393.31	118.942	70.870	3.150	1077.14	37.76	22.50
1972	4037.22	129.640	74.155	3.258	1239.26	39.79	22.76

continued

Table 1

	Nominal Cumulative Wealth				Real Cumulative Wealth		
Year	Stocks	Bonds	Paper	CPI	Stocks	Bonds	Paper
1973	3445.29	129.762	79.604	3.544	972.04	36.61	22.46
1974	2533.41	123.782	88.294	3.977	637.03	31.13	22.20
1975	3475.90	137.833	95.519	4.256	816.74	32.39	22.44
1976	4304.67	164.252	101.469	4.461	965.05	36.82	22.75
1977	3995.40	170.525	106.663	4.763	838.92	35.81	22.40
1978	4257.53	166.691	114.083	5.192	819.94	32.10	21.97
1979	5042.58	155.404	126.649	5.883	857.08	26.41	21.53
1980	6677.36	144.624	142.977	6.613	1009.76	21.87	21.62
1981	6349.56	146.798	169.243	7.204	881.40	20.38	23.49
1982	7708.95	210.366	195.327	7.483	1030.21	28.11	26.10
1983	9444.57	221.275	213.473	7.767	1215.99	28.49	27.48
1984	10036.40	263.015	238.734	8.074	1243.04	32.58	29.57
1985	13263.91	361.442	260.181	8.379	1583.07	43.14	31.05

vested monthly would have produced a final wealth accumulation figure of $13,264.00, the result of starting the compounding process in 1926 at $47.52 instead of $1.00.[12] Thus, although the growth of a $1 investment in common stocks at the beginning of 1926 would have produced an ending wealth of $279 by year-end 1985, a less-than-doubling of the time period magnifies the ending wealth accumulation by a factor of 47.5. Such is the power of compound interest over very long periods of time!

The annual average compound rate of return (geometric mean) of this common stock wealth series for the 115-year period is 8.60%. This return is below the comparable figure for the IS data of 9.84% because of a lower growth rate of 7.27% in the earlier period. Investors can take comfort in the long-term performance of common stocks, but the superior performance of stocks has not been a consistent feature of the long-run history. On a nominal basis, the cumulative wealth of bonds exceeded that of stocks through 1904, and bonds regained a slight advantage in 1914. By 1932, common stocks on a cumulative wealth basis exceeded only slightly the comparable figure for bonds. The outstanding performance of stocks is a post-World War II phenomenon.

The results for corporate bonds and commercial paper pale by comparison to common stocks. The ending cumulative wealth figure for corporate bonds is $361.44; for commercial paper it is $260.18. The geometric mean returns for the two series for the entire period 1871–1985 were 5.26% and 4.95%, respectively. The geometric means in the 1926–1985 period were 4.50% and 4.46%, respectively, but with standard deviations of 8.25% and 3.75%. Thus, the ex-post average annual maturity premium between long and short non-riskless fixed-income securities over the IS period has been virtually nil.

The second part of Table 1 restates the nominal results in real terms. The cumulative CPI of 8.38 for the entire period is an interesting contrast to the final value of 6.10 for the IS period. The latter part of the nineteenth century was a period of no inflation or deflation, while the early years of the twentieth century showed either no inflation or low inflation until 1916, but the inflation rate for the next four years — 13.8% a year — was an all-time high for the entire 115-year period. Given the low inflation rates of the mid-1980s, analyses of the pre-1926 data are particularly appropriate.

The inflation-adjusted series show that for common stocks, on a real basis, $1.00 invested on December 31, 1870, would have accumulated to $34.58 by year-end 1925, while the comparable IS data indicate that $1.00 invested at the beginning of 1926 would have accumulated to $45.16 by the end of 1985. For the entire time period, $1.00 would have accumulated to $1,583.07 by the end of 1985.

For the early period, the geometric mean and standard deviation are 6.65% and 18.30%, while for the later period they are 6.58% and 23.17%. For the entire period, they were 6.62% and 20.85%. Thus, on an inflation-adjusted basis, the average results for these two periods of roughly equal length have been remarkably similar, but with greater variability in the latter period. Common stocks have returned over the entire 115 years approximately a 6.6% annual average inflation-adjusted total return.

On a cumulative wealth basis, the ending figures for corporate bonds and commercial paper are $43.14 and $31.05, respectively. Respective geometric mean annual returns are 3.33% and 3.03% for the entire period, and 1.40% and 1.36% for the latter period (1926–1985).

Figure 1 shows the performance of the three asset classes on a nominal basis together with the CPI for the entire 115-year period. The vertical scale of this figure is logarithmic; therefore, equal distances represent equal percentage changes anywhere along the axis. These figures are directly comparable to Exhibit 1 in the Ibbotson-Sinquefield 1986 *Yearbook* (1986, p. 9) and almost double the number of years heretofore presented.

Summary

This article presents the complete record — 115 years — of returns for major financial assets in the United States, including a cumulative wealth index based on monthly reinvestment for common stocks, corporate bonds, and commercial paper. The Consumer Price Index, previously unavailable for the earlier period, is calculated and used to present inflation-adjusted returns back to 1871.

On a wealth index basis, common stocks have increased by a factor of 13,264 from the 1870 base of $1, while bonds and commercial paper have grown by factors of 361 and 260, respectively. On an inflation-adjusted basis, comparable figures for the three series are 1583, 43, and 31, respectively. For the entire 115-year period, annual average geometric means are 8.60%, 5.26%, and 4.95%, respectively, on a nominal basis, and 6.62%, 3.33%, and 3.03%, respectively, on an inflation-adjusted basis.

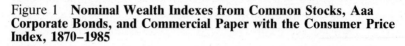

Figure 1   **Nominal Wealth Indexes from Common Stocks, Aaa
Corporate Bonds, and Commercial Paper with the Consumer Price
Index, 1870–1985**

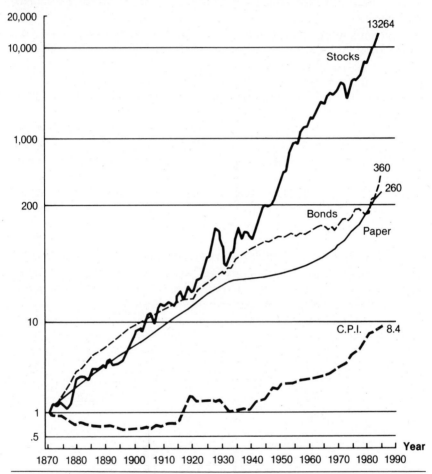

This paper offers a look at a non-riskless short-term instrument, commercial paper, as a contrast to the Treasury bill series typically presented. Although corporate bonds have outperformed commercial paper for the entire period, as expected, the difference is small. In the IS period — 1926–1985 — the annual average geometric means (nominal) are 4.50% for corporates and 4.46% for commercial paper.

[1] IS start their series in 1926 as Fisher and Lorie did in their studies of stock returns. The latter felt that the files should begin "at least a full business cycle before the 1929 stock-market crash" (1977, p. 7).

[2] Because of data limitations, the Cowles data were based on tables of monthly highs and lows published for each stock quoted in the *Commercial and Financial*

Chronicle. The monthly prices were the arithmetic mean of the high and low price for that month, adjusted for ex-dividends and rights.

[3] We discovered that in ten months the income returns were negative, requiring us to make adjustments to correct for these discrepancies.

[4] The two series were spliced together in June 1919, using the overlap ratio of 1.0384455 to inflate the Macaulay series. From December 1870 until 1934, the interest rates were average rates for the month. From 1934 through 1985, the interest rates are the values for the last week of the month. Several changes in definition in the Moody's coverage occurred between 1919 and 1985.

[5] Let P = the price of the bond and r = yield to maturity. Then:

$$P = (2/0.5r) [1 - (1 + 0.5r)^{-m}] + 100 [(1 + 0.5r)^{-m}].$$

For each month an acquisition price (A) was calculated with m = 40, and a sale price (S) was calculated with m = 39 ⅚.

[6] From 1870 until 1934, the rates are averages for the month; for the latter period they are the averages for the last week in the month. For most of the series, the rates are for four- to six-month paper, and since 1970 the rates are for six-month paper.

[7] Monthly price is calculated using the bank discount rate formula:

$$P = 100 - [100r / (360/d)],$$

where d is days to maturity. We assumed that the paper was five-month paper with d = 152.1875 at acquisition, and after one month d = 121.75. For each month an acquisition price was calculated (A) along with a sale price (S). The monthly return was calculated as S(t) divided by A(t − 1).

[8] The IS data are for the S&P 500 Composite Index, which prior to March 1957 consisted of the stocks of 90 corporations. The number of stocks covered by the Cowles Commission expanded steadily during the period, from 48 at the beginning of 1871 to 258 by the end of 1925.

[9] Although it is common practice to subtract the inflation rate from the nominal rate to obtain the real return, proper adjustment requires converting the nominal return rate and the inflation rate into (1 + r) terms and dividing the nominal rate by inflation.

[10] The inflation rates calculated from this series matched those reported by IS from 1926.

[11] Rees's index (1914 = 100) was constructed for the years 1890 through 1914. Hoover's index (1890 = 100) was constructed from 1851 through 1880, with a rough extension annually through 1890 to match with Rees's index.

[12] Dividing the 1985 figure of 13263.908 by the year-end 1925 figure of 47.5213 produces 279.115, which exactly matches the IS wealth index figure for 1985 (1986, Exhibit 6).

References

Boulding, Kenneth. "Economic Theory and Measurement." *Kyklos,* Vol. 6, Fasc. 2, (1953–1954), pp. 149–152.

Cowles, Alfred III, and Associates. *Common-Stock Indexes,* 2nd Edition, Cowles Commission Monograph No. 3. Bloomington, Ind.: Principia Press, Inc., 1939.

Fisher, Lawrence, and James H. Lorie. *A Half Century of Returns on Stocks and Bonds: Rates of Return on Investments in Common Stocks and on U.S. Treasury Securities.* Chicago: University of Chicago Graduate School of Business, 1977.

Hoover, Ethel D. "Retail Prices after 1850," in *Trends in the American Economy in the Nineteenth Century.* National Bureau of Economic Research, General Series, Studies in Income and Wealth, Vol. 24. Comment by John Kendrick, pp. 141–190. Princeton: Princeton University Press, 1961.

Ibbotson Associates. *Stocks, Bonds, Bills, and Inflation: 1986 Yearbook.* Chicago: Ibbotson Associates, 1986.

Macaulay, Frederick R. *Some Theoretical Problems Suggested by the Movements of Interest Rates, Bond Yields, and Stock Prices in the United States Since 1856.* National Bureau of Economic Research, 1938.

Rees, Albert. *Real Wages in Manufacturing 1890–1914.* National Bureau of Economic Research, General Series, No. 70. Princeton: Princeton University Press, 1961.

U.S. Department of Labor, Bureau of Labor Statistics. *1941 Handbook of Labor Statistics.* Washington, D.C.: U.S. Government Printing Office, 1942.

———. *Interim Adjustment of the Consumer Price Index.* Bulletin No. 1039. Washington, D.C.: U.S. Government Printing Office, 1951.

———. Consumer Price Index, All Urban Consumers. U.S. City Average, All Items. Release dated May 21, 1986.

Williams, Faith M., and Stella Stewart, *Changes in Cost of Living in the United States 1913–41.* Bulletin 699, U.S. Department of Labor, Bureau of Labor Statistics. Washington, D.C.: U.S. Government Printing Office, 1941.

Questions

1. On a nominal basis, what was the annual average compound rate of return on common stock during the 115-year period? Answer the same question for corporate bonds and commercial paper.

2. On a real basis, what was the annual average compound rate of return on common stock during the 115-year period? Answer the same question for corporate bonds and commercial paper.

3. An initial investment of $1.00 in common stock on December 31, 1870, grew to $47.52 by December 31, 1925. An initial investment of $1.00 in common stock on December 31, 1925, grew to $279.00 by December 31, 1985. Explain how the relatively small dollar figures $47.52 and $279.00 are consistent with the following fact: An initial investment of $1.00 in common stock on December 31, 1870, grew to $13,264.00 by December 31, 1985.

4. "The outstanding performance of stocks is a post–World War II phenomenon." Describe the evidence supporting this statement.

5. Identify the periods of U.S. history during which inflation appears to be a significant economic factor.

9
Whose Beta Is Best?
Diana R. Harrington

A cursory examination of the betas provided by different investment services reveals that these betas vary greatly, even when they are calculated on the basis of historical returns. How can one determine which beta is best? Using a mean square error test, the author evaluates betas from various commercial sources in terms of their accuracy in predicting subsequent betas and in predicting subsequent returns.

In general, the longer the horizon and the larger the portfolio, the better the forecast accuracy of any beta. On the other hand, all the methods tested left the possibility for over- and underestimations of troubling magnitudes.

More specifically, in terms of predicting ensuing betas, the Value Line forecasts exhibited the lowest mean square errors for a sample of utility stocks, but a naive forecast (assuming betas would equal one) performed almost as well. The Rosenberg long-term fundamental beta proved superior in forecasting the betas of a sample of industrial stocks. Performance in predicting return varied greatly, depending on the model parameters for market return and risk-free rate. A naive model performed best for the utility sample, but no one beta proved best in the case of the industrial sample.

Beta! It's hard to keep track of the number of articles that have been written about what it is and isn't, how to calculate, adjust, refine it (or find a better one), or why it is a concept whose time has passed. Some people suggest the beta is being kept alive by "hype" alone.

Is another article about beta like a discussion about the Edsel— historically interesting but of little practical value? I think not, and for several reasons. The primary reason is that beta, while under increasing scrutiny, is, at the same time, becoming more widely used to solve practical problems.

Diana R. Harrington, "Whose Beta Is Best?," *Financial Analysts Journal* (July/August 1983): 67–73. Reprinted with permission.

At the time of this writing, Diana Harrington was Associate Professor at the Colgate Darden Graduate School of Business Administration of the University of Virginia.

As investment analysts, portfolio managers and corporate planners and financial staff have increased their use of beta, several organizations have started to provide beta forecasts for a large number of common stocks. These forecasts, derived in a variety of ways, are revised and published monthly or quarterly, and beta users have begun to ask: "How good are these forecasts?"

That question led to this article. In order to provide some perspective on the quality of commerically available betas, I tested the accuracy of these beta forecasts and of forecasts that could be made by using several other methods available to the practitioner.

Beta Use and Users

The following description of how betas are being used in evaluating stocks, optimizing portfolios and evaluating performance will demonstrate the importance of good beta forecasts.

Essentially, beta is used two ways. First, it is used as a part of the Capital Asset Pricing Model (CAPM) to forecast the returns from a stock or portfolio.[1] The forecasts are then used by

. . . analysts in public utility rate-relief proceedings to estimate the expected return on equity for a given public utility; this return — the cost of equity — when combined with the costs of other capital, becomes part of the expenses allowed the public utility when establishing the rates charged customers . . . (This use of the CAPM, infrequent in the past, has increased considerably since 1975.[2])

. . . corporate managers, in search of ways to estimate corporate or divisional hurdle rates; they have used and are using the CAPM to estimate costs of equity.

Beta by itself has been used by practitioners even more extensively, and perhaps more creatively, than the CAPM. Beta has been used to estimate the "risk class" of a given stock so that

. . . rate analysts in public utility proceedings can choose a group of comparable-risk, nonutility companies against which to test the "fairness" of the return on equity for a particular utility . . .

. . . security analysts and portfolio managers can identify over- and undervalued stocks . . .

. . . portfolio managers can design portfolios with particular risk characteristics. (Portfolio optimization models often require the manager to set a level of risk — beta — that will be tolerated in the portfolio.)

The increased use of beta has increased the need for beta forecasts. The practitioner has two primary methods for obtaining the necessary beta estimates — calculate betas from historical data or use beta estimates made by one of the investment advisory services. In either case, the user must be aware of the difficulty of obtaining a useful beta estimate.

---

[1] Footnotes appear at end of article.

Unfortunately, there is no single best method of estimating a beta. Even beta estimates based on the same historical returns may vary depending on such things as the time period over which the beta is calculated and the index chosen as a proxy for the market. The beta services use various methods for deriving their estimates. Some of the betas rest solely on the historical data. Others are adapted for problems such as the mean regression tendency of beta that were identified and recognized by the academic community.[3] Still others have created fundamental beta estimates from multivariate regressions of time-series, firm-fundamental characteristics.[4]

To have some idea of the difficulties encountered in choosing between beta estimates, one need only look at the differences between the betas estimated by the popular services. All the betas shown in Table I (except two of those provided by Barr Rosenberg) were taken from services that calculate betas from historical returns. The table vividly demonstrates just how different beta estimates can be when made by different services, for different stocks, and at different points in time.

Choosing a beta, then, is no simple task. If the user recognizes the substantive differences that can occur between betas from commercially published services, she or he has no way, other than intuition, of choosing among the offerings. It may be, however, that more information about some of these commercially available betas would allow a more informed choice.

To provide information to beta users, I examined the estimated betas of stocks in two sample groups — public utility stocks and industrials. Public utilities, whose betas are usually below the market average of 1.0, have had, over time, the most stable and significant betas; the stocks of industrial firms typically have betas near or above 1.0. I gathered, for each stock, eight beta forecasts from five commercial beta producers. In addition, I calculated two other betas from historical returns; these are the kind of betas that practitioners might calculate themselves. Those two betas, plus two very simple, naive, forecasts, were included for comparison. Table II describes each of the 12 betas included in the study.

Beta Estimates as Predictors of Beta

The best test of beta forecast accuracy is one that measures the size of the errors that could be made if one were to use the forecast to predict. Thus each forecast was used to predict the actual, ensuing, beta and the difference between the predicted and actual betas was measured. (The actual betas were ordinary least-squares betas calculated using monthly total rates of return for each stock and the Standard & Poor's (S&P) 500.[5]) These forecast errors were squared, then averaged, and the mean square error for each stock was averaged for each of the two samples.[6]

This mean square error (MSE) test is especially useful since it can be used to determine the differences in accuracy of the beta forecasts. It can

Table I Betas Calculated by Investment Services for Selected Stocks

	Merrill Lynch (Adjusted)		Market Model (Adjusted)	
January 1974				
American Airlines	2.04	(1.69)	2.11	(1.01)
American Cyanamid	0.99	(1.00)	0.97	(0.98)
Houston Industries	1.08	(1.05)	1.12	(1.00)
San Diego Gas and Electric	0.99	(0.99)	0.98	(0.99)
Southern California Edison	1.33	(1.22)	1.33	(1.02)
December 1972				
American Airlines	1.53	(1.35)	1.15	(0.77)
American Cyanamid	1.04	(0.84)	0.84	(0.76)
Houston Industries	1.00	(1.00)	0.69	(0.73)
San Diego Gas and Electric	0.61	(0.74)	0.48	(0.66)
Southern California Edison	0.72	(0.81)	0.52	(0.67)

Source: D.R. Harrington, "Predicting Betas and Returns Using Commercially Available Beta Forecasts" (Darden School Working Paper, Darden Graduate School of Business, University of Virginia, Charlottesville, 1982).

Table II Characteristics of the Beta Predictors

Source	Method	Time Period
Merrill Lynch (ML1)	OLS[a]	5 years
Merrill Lynch (ML2)	OLS/Bayesian-adjusted[a]	5 years
Value Line (Value Line)	OLS[a]	5 years
Drexel Burnham Lambert (Drexel)	OLS/Bayesian-adjusted[a]	8 cycles
Wilshire Associates (Wilshire)	Fundamental	—
Barr Rosenberg & Assoc. (RF1)	OLS[a]	5 years
Barr Rosenberg & Assoc. (RF2)	Fundamental[b]	—
Barr Rosenberg & Assoc. (RF3)	Fundamental[b]	—
Ordinary Least Squares (OLS)	OLS[a]	5 years
Adjusted Ordinary Least Squares (OLSB)	OLS/Bayesian-adjusted[a]	5 years
Naive (Naive 2)	β = mean of the sample (utilities or industrials)	5 years
Naive (Naive 1)	$\beta = 1$	5 years

N/A = not applicable

[a] A simple linear regression of historical returns from the stock and the market (usually proxied by the S&P 500):

$$R_j = \alpha_j + \beta_j(R_m) + \epsilon_j,$$

where:

R_j = the total returns on a particular security or portfolio,

R_m = the return on the market,

α_j = the intercept from the regression,

ϵ_j = the residuals, or errors, and

β_j = the slope of the regression line.

[b] A Rosenberg Assoc. spokesman stated that this particular fundamental prediction process is not good for utility stocks. Another method designed to provide better betas for utilities is being developed by them.

| | Barr Rosenberg | | |
Historical	Short-Term Fundamental	Long-Term Fundamental	Value Line
	January 1974		
2.12	2.35	2.22	2.26
0.98	1.01	1.03	1.08
1.21	1.12	1.10	0.77
1.03	0.87	0.90	0.73
1.32	0.99	0.99	0.98
	December 1972		
1.41	1.67	1.60	1.45
0.95	0.95	0.98	1.05
1.05	1.08	0.98	0.90
0.65	0.82	0.88	0.70
0.72	0.82	0.84	0.80

Interval	Index	Special Notes	Available From
monthly	S&P 500	price relatives only	1972
monthly	S&P 500	price relatives only	1972
weekly	NYSE Composite	price relatives only	1972
8 cycles as defined by Drexel	S&P 500	Sample: 28 utilities, 16 industrials	10/1974
quarterly	—		1971–77
monthly	S&P 500	compound returns	1974
—	—	—	1974
—	—	—	1974
monthly	S&P 500	compound returns	N/A
monthly	S&P 500	compound returns	N/A
monthly	S&P 500	compound returns	N/A
N/A	N/A	N/A	N/A

Table III   **MSE and Mean Forecast Beta Using Naive 1 Beta Forecast**

| | Utility Sample | | |
| | | | |
Horizon	MSE	Mean Beta	MSE as % of Mean
1 year	0.1617	0.6795	24%
2 years	0.1092	0.6669	16
3 years	0.0866	0.6348	14
4 years	0.0630	0.5854	11

also be used to evaluate three potential sources of error — a consistent over- or underprediction (bias), an error that is linked to the size of the beta (inefficiency), or random error. Since some beta services purport to reduce one of these sources of error, such an analysis is useful.[7]

Time Horizon and Portfolio Effects

In executing the study, I attempted to approximate the way a practitioner might use these beta forecasts. Investors with a buy-and-hold strategy should be interested in longer horizons (four years was the longest from the available data), whereas those who trade more frequently would be interested in the accuracy of beta forecasts over shorter horizons. While shorter actual betas would be more difficult to forecast accurately because of the limited actual data, horizons of one, two, three and four years were included. In addition, because earlier tests showed that errors were significantly reduced when individual stocks were placed in portfolios, I tested beta forecasts for portfolios of five, 10 and 15 randomly chosen stocks from each of the two samples.[8]

Table III shows the results of using the Naive 1 estimate of beta (all beta forecasts equal to 1.0) to forecast betas over various time horizons. The forecasts made using betas from other sources yielded similar results.[9]

Several things are immediately apparent. First, as we might have anticipated, the longer the forecast horizon, the smaller the MSE (the random-error portion dropping most dramatically). Second, the MSEs for the utility sample were smaller than those for the industrials. Because the average beta for a utility is smaller than that for the average industrial, however, the real magnitude of the errors can only be seen in comparison with the average beta forecast. The table shows that the MSEs of the utility forecast were smaller in both an absolute and relative sense: Utility betas are more accurately forecast.

Table IV shows the results of using the Merrill Lynch unadjusted beta forecast in a portfolio context. The accuracy of the forecast improved as the size of the portfolio increased — that is, the MSE dropped, the reduction stemming from reductions in random error. The

	Industrial Sample	
MSE	**Mean Beta**	**MSE as % of Mean**
0.4176	1.1304	37%
0.1092	1.1103	23
0.0866	1.0707	18
0.0630	0.9943	17

industrial sample MSE for the unadjusted Merrill Lynch beta five-stock portfolio was 0.2013; for the 15-stock portfolios, the MSE was 0.0600.

For the practitioner, these findings underline old lessons. First, the longer the horizon, the better the forecast, as the short-term errors cancel out. Second, better forecasts come when portfolios, rather than single securities, are being forecast; once again, errors cancel out.

Ranking the Forecasting Methods

The rankings by MSE of the various methods of forecasting beta were relatively stable over different horizons, particularly in the case of the utility sample. Table V shows that, for the utility sample, the Value Line forecast had the smallest MSE over each horizon. What is somewhat surprising is that the Naive 1 beta (all beta forecasts equal to 1.0) had the next lowest MSE for three of the four horizons. This beta is the simplest forecast that could be made. Note that, while the MSE differences were not large, the forecasts with the lowest MSEs had errors that were of very similar magnitude. Thus, from an economic point of view, when the errors are similar, the cheapest beta may be the best.

Typically, the beta forecasts for the utility sample overestimated the actual betas. Because the betas for this sample are generally small, this result suggests inefficiency in the beta forecasts. An inefficient forecast will result in positive errors at low betas and negative errors at high betas.

The results for the utility sample suggest several conclusions. First, sizable errors can be made. If, for instance, your horizon was three years

Table IV   **Portfolio Effect Using Merrill Lynch Unadjusted Forecast and One-Year Horizon**

Portfolio Size	MSE, Utility Sample	MSE, Industrial Sample
5 stocks	0.0874	0.2013
10 stocks	0.0733	0.0728
15 stocks	0.0723	0.0600

Table V   **MSE Results for the Utility Sample**

Horizon	Smallest MSE (source)	Next Smallest MSE (source)	Mean MSE	Maximum MSE
1 year	0.1560 (V. Line)	0.1617 (Naive 1)	0.2062	0.2857
2 years	0.1005 (V. Line)	0.1071 (OLSB)	0.1324	0.2503
3 years	0.0799 (V. Line)	0.0866 (Naive 1)	0.1166	0.2271
4 years	0.0584 (V. Line)	0.0630 (Naive 1)	0.1098	0.1972

and you were using Value Line betas to forecast the beta for an average utility over this period, the average error you could have made would have been 0.28. Since the mean beta forecast for Value Line was only 0.7241, the error potential was sizable. Second, for the utilities, almost every method studied overestimated the actual beta. And third, when the direction as well as the magnitude of the error is taken into account (mean difference), the OLS forecast was better than the Value Line forecast for the utility sample. That is because the OLS beta forecasts both over- and underestimated actual betas. The offsetting errors yielded a better on-average forecast, a result the MSE test alone does not show.

For the industrial sample, the results, shown in Table VI, are somewhat different. The Rosenberg long-term fundamental beta (RF3) proved superior for each horizon being forecast. Again, however, the errors are sizable: For the three-year horizon, the mean error was 0.37, compared with the mean beta forecast of 1.228.

The implications of these findings for the beta user can be summarized as follows. (1) Longer forecast horizons provided more accurate forecasts than shorter ones. (2) Betas for larger portfolios were more accurately forecast than those for smaller portfolios. (3) The smaller MSEs were associated with the utility sample. (4) Some forecast methods consistently resulted in smaller MSEs. (5) All methods left the possibility of over- and underestimations of troubling magnitude. (6) Different forecasting methods reduced inefficiency more than they reduced the bias or random-error portion of the MSE.

Table VI   **MSE Results for the Industrial Sample**

Horizon	Smallest MSE (source)	Next Smallest MSE (source)	Mean MSE	Maximum MSE
1 year	0.3572 (RF3)	0.3624 (RF2)	0.4028	0.5644
2 years	0.1879 (RF3)	0.1962 (RF2)	0.2521	0.3941
3 years	0.1399 (RF3)	0.1434 (V. Line)	0.1975	0.3337
4 years	0.1239 (RF3)	0.1323 (V. Line)	0.1098	0.3180

Table VII   **Risk-Free Rate and Market Return Proxies**

Model	Risk-Free Rate	Market Return*
Perfect Foresight	actual return on 90-day Treasury bills over period being forecast	Actual return on S&P 500 over period being forecast
1	the rate on 90-day Treasury bills	S&P 500 average compound return (1926 to forecast date)
2	the rate on 7-year Treasury bonds	S&P 500 average compound return (1926 to forecast date)
3	the rate on 90-day Treasury bills	S&P 500 average compound return (1950 to forecast date)
4	the rate on 7-year Treasury bonds	S&P 500 average compound return (1950 to forecast date)

*Several investment management organizations have started to provide forecasts for the market return. Although these forecasts were not available for the full period studied, a forecast for the market return from May 1975 to December 1979 provided by Wells Fargo Investment Advisors was tested. The results were similar to the results given by the four basic models for the same period, but the MSEs for all the models tested over this period were smaller. Thus the period over which forecasts are made seems to be more important than how the forecasts are made, in determining the magnitude of the error.

Beta Estimates as Predictors of Return

Practitioners have been using beta, not only to predict beta, but to forecast expected returns. Thus a test of beta to predict beta does not fully resolve the problem facing practitioners. To test returns-forecasting accuracy, beta predictions must be turned into forecast returns and then tested against actual returns garnered by each security over the ensuing one, two, three or four years.

The CAPM was used to turn beta forecasts into forecasts of returns. The difficulty with this approach is that CAPM theory does not provide specific directions for implementation, and academics and practitioners disagree on the proper proxies for the risk-free rate and market return. I therefore used five different combinations of various possible risk-free rate and market return proxies to forecast returns using the given beta forecasts.[10] Table VII details the combinations.

Table VIII   **Minimum MSE Estimate by Model (three-year horizon)**

	Utility Sample		Industrial Sample	
Model	MSE* (source)	Mean Forecast	MSE (source)	Mean Forecast
PF	0.0080 (OLS)	0.0880	0.0231 (Naive 2)	0.0797
1	0.0104 (Naive 2)	0.0896	0.0251 (RF3)	0.0956
2	0.0105 (Naive 2)	0.0896	0.0252 (RF1)	0.0934
3	0.0098 (Naive 2)	0.1026	0.0255 (OLSB)	0.0936
4	0.0098 (Naive 2)	0.1026	0.0256 (OLS)	0.1036

*The Drexel beta, based on a more limited sample, outperformed all other forecasting methods on the basis of smaller, matched samples.

The "perfect foresight" forecast was included to provide a benchmark for evaluating those models requiring forecasts for all three factors. To create the perfect foresight forecast, I assumed that one could accurately forecast the actual return on Treasury bills and the S&P 500 over the horizons of one, two, three and four years.[11]

Results

Table VIII provides the basic results for the five models. For the utility sample, the largest errors occurred with Models 1 and 2, which used a market return from 1926. Unexpectedly, for the more volatile industrials, the use of the longer market return resulted in a slightly smaller MSE. More importantly, it appeared to make little difference whether the rate of return from a short or longer-term Treasury security was used for the risk-free rate.

Note that perfect foresight did improve the results, especially for the utility sample. Even this improvement did little to yield good forecasts, however. Using perfect foresight, the utility mean error was 0.0894, with a mean forecast return of 0.0880. Even though the size of the error varies from stock to stock, the potential exists for a major misforecast. The same is true for the industrial sample, where the mean forecast, using perfect foresight, was 0.0797, with a mean error of 0.1520.

Finally, the accuracy of the forecast depended on the time over which it was tested (a fact of which investment professionals are all too aware), the size of the portfolio, and the length of the horizon. Again, longer periods and larger portfolios yielded the smallest errors.

Conclusion

Forecast accuracy seems to depend more on stability of the equity markets during the time period over which one is forecasting than on any elegantly refined forecast. Using a beta to forecast returns compounds forecasting difficulty but, at least in some cases, reaps the benefits of offsetting errors.

The test has provided discouraging results: No method is very accurate. If we cannot develop an accurate beta forecast from history, is beta as a concept practically useless? No, for it is possible that history is a poor proxy for the future, and it is possible that no one has yet forecast beta with the required level of skill. Since the concept is economically logical, and the uses alluring, the arena is open for new and innovative artists. Meanwhile, Caveat Emptor.

Footnotes

[1] The CAPM is:

$$\bar{R}_j = \bar{R}_j + \bar{\beta}_j(\bar{R}_m - \bar{R}_f),$$

where:
$\tilde{R}_j$ = the expected return for the asset, security or portfolio,
$\tilde{R}_f$ = the expected return on a risk-free asset,
$\tilde{R}_m$ = the expected average return on all risky assets, and
$\tilde{\beta}_j$ = a measure of risk—the expected volatility of the asset's or portfolio's returns over time, relative to returns of R_m.

[2] See D.R. Harrington, "The Changing Use of Capital Asset Pricing Model in Utility Regulation," *Public Utilities Fortnightly*, 14 February 1980, pp. 28–30 and "Trends in Capital Asset Pricing Model Use," *Public Utilities Fortnightly*, 13 August 1981, pp. 27–31.

[3] See M. Blume, "Betas and Their Regression Tendencies," *Journal of Finance*, June 1975, pp. 785–796.

[4] Barr Rosenberg Associates, *Fundamental Risk Measurement Service* (Berkeley, CA: Barr Rosenberg Associates, Inc., *Capital Equilibrium Statistics* (Santa Monica, CA: Wilshire Associates, Inc., June 30, 1978).

[5] The actual betas are estimated as described in Table II and were not adjusted in any way. I was not attempting to form better forecasts from historical data, but to represent the actual relative volatility of the stocks' returns over the period being forecast.

[6] The richest version of mean square error is calculated as follows:

$$MSE = \frac{1}{n} \sum_{j=1}^{n} (A_j - P_j)^2,$$

where:
n = the number of predictions,
j = the particular stock or portfolio,
A = the actual beta for the security or portfolio, and
P = the predicted beta for the security or portfolio;
or:

$$MSE = (\bar{A} - \bar{P})^2 + (1 - \beta_1)^2 S_P^2 + (1 - \gamma_{AP}^2) S_A^2,$$

where:

$(\bar{A} - \bar{P})^2$ = bias, to indicate whether the average prediction (P) is over or under the average realization (A),
$(1 - \beta_1)^2 S_P^2$ = inefficiency, the tendency for errors to be negative for high beta forecasts and positive for low beta forecasts. Where β_1 is the slope coefficient of A regressed on P and S_P^2 is the variance of P, and
$(1 - \gamma_{AP}^2) S_A^2$ = random error, where γ_{AP}^2 is the coefficient of determination for the regression of A on P, and S_A^2 is the variance of A on P.

To estimate the one-year MSE, the beta forecast for each stock was compared with its actual beta for the next 12 months. Since forecasts were typically updated monthly, the reported MSE for a stock is the average of the squared errors for each of the 60 forecast dates. The MSE for the sample was the average of the average MSEs for each stock in the sample.

[7] Other methods of testing forecast accuracy are reported in G. Hawawini and A. Vora, "Investment Horizon, Diversification and the Efficiency of Alternative Beta Forecasts."

[8] M. Blume, "On the Assessment of Risk," *Journal of Finance*, March 1971, pp. 1–10 and R.C. Klemkosky and J.D. Martin, "The Adjustment of Beta Forecasts," *Journal of Finance*, September 1975, pp. 1123–1128.

[9] The full results are provided in D.R. Harrington, "Predicting Betas and Returns Using Commercially Available Beta Forecasts" (Darden School Working Paper, Darden Graduate School of Business, University of Virginia, Charlottesville,

1982). In addition to the results for the different forecasting methods, the paper reports the results of using other measures of predictive accuracy, including the mean difference.

[10] Historical market returns were calculated using data from R.G. Ibbotson and R.A. Sinquefield, *Stocks, Bonds, Bills and Inflation* (Charlottesville, VA: Financial Analysts Research Foundation, 1980). Tests of the accuracy of beta in predicting returns are really a joint test of the accuracy of the beta forecast and forecasts for the market return and the risk-free rate; all could be forecast imperfectly.

[11] For example, to develop the January 31, 1974 one-year perfect foresight forecast for any stock, the beta forecast for that stock as of January 31, 1974, the actual return on 90-day Treasury bills and the S&P 500 for the period February 1, 1974 to January 31, 1975, were combined.

Questions

1. According to Merrill Lynch, American Airlines' beta (unadjusted) equaled 2.04 early in 1974. Interpret the meaning of this beta.

2. Describe the steps taken by Merrill Lynch to estimate the beta (unadjusted) of a common stock.

3. Describe the uses of beta in practice; that is, for what purposes do practitioners use betas?

4. The average beta of public utility companies is about 0.65; the average for industrial companies is about 1.1. What factors might cause this difference in average betas?

5. Why does the error in forecasting beta decline as the number of stocks increases in a portfolio? Stated differently, why is it easier to forecast accurately the beta of a diversified portfolio in comparison to the beta of one stock?

6. In general, are betas estimated with historical data very reliable indicators of future betas? Describe the evidence supporting your answer.

10
Corporate Financing: Too Much Debt?

Robert A. Taggart, Jr.

Are U.S. corporations overburdened with debt? Since 1970, internal funds have been taking wider swings as percentages of total funds sources, as compared with the 1950s and 1960s. Furthermore, use of debt financing has been consistently higher since the mid-1960s than during previous periods throughout the century. And short-term debt has accounted for most of this rise.

After adjustment for inflation, however, the figures indicate that, since 1974, corporations have relied heavily on internal funds and cut their cost of debt financing to levels that are not high by historical standards. Despite fluctuations in internal funds and increased use of short-term debt, corporations do not appear to have significantly riskier capital structures than they've had in the past.

An examination of determinants of the composition of capital structure reveals that corporate reliance on debt financing increases as capital expenditures rise relative to available internal funds. Use of debt financing is limited, however, by investors' perceptions of the riskiness of the business environment and by relative supplies of federal government securities. Over long periods, furthermore, the tax system seems to affect the level of debt financing; corporate borrowing increases as personal income tax rates rise above corporate levels.

In 1984, new debt accounted for 45 percent of total sources of funds for U.S. nonfinancial corporations. Less than one-quarter of this new debt came from long-term bonds and mortgages; the rest represented short-term debt from a variety of sources. Moreover, 15 percent of net funds sources went, not for investment in new plant and equipment, but for the repurchase of outstanding common stock.

Robert A. Taggart, Jr., "Corporate Financing: Too Much Debt?" *Financial Analysts Journal* (May/June 1986): 35–42. Reprinted with permission.

At the time of this writing, Robert Taggart, Jr. was Professor of Finance, Boston University, and Research Associate, National Bureau of Economic Research. The author thanks the National Bureau of Economic Research for partial financial support of this research.

Do such developments reflect increasing financial weakness of U.S. business? Many observers seem to think so. Their fears have been stimulated by such highly publicized trends as the levered buyout boom, the growth of "junk" bond financing, and the shrinkage of equity bases that often accompanies corporate restructuring. In addition, the current period is only the latest in a series of surges in corporate debt financing. Previous notable episodes occurred in 1968–69, 1973–74, and 1978–79.

Each of these surges gave rise to similar fears over corporations' financial condition. It has been argued that corporations' reliance on debt financing, particularly short-term debt, has made them increasingly vulnerable to economic shocks. This reliance on debt financing is in turn blamed on a combination of factors, including the tax system's favored treatment of debt over equity, reduced availability of internally generated funds during inflationary periods, and unrealistic assessments of business risk by executives, entrepreneurs and corporate raiders.

This article examines more closely these allegations of corporate financial weakness by comparing recent corporate financing patterns against long-term trends and by analyzing the link between these patterns and potential causal factors. The conclusion emerges that, in many respects, the degree of financial weakening has been exaggerated. It must be conceded, nonetheless, that increased use of short-term debt and volatile capital market conditions have made corporate treasurers' lives more hectic.

The Historical Perspective

Figures A and B illustrate the yearly composition of funds sources for U.S. nonfinancial corporations during the 1946–84 period. Figure A shows the yearly flows of gross internal funds (retained earnings plus depreciation), total debt and new equity issues, all expressed as fractions of total sources of funds. Figure B shows the breakdown of total debt into long-term and short-term components.[1] The data are taken from the Federal Reserve's Flow of Funds Account.

The figures give a sense of the typical pattern in corporate financing over the course of the business cycle. The predominant feature of this pattern is the opposite movement of debt financing and the availability of internal funds. Toward the end of an expansion, and even into the early stages of a recession, the use of debt financing tends to increase sharply as capital spending and inventory investment outrun firms' generation of internal funds. Moreover, as Figure B makes clear, short-term debt accounts for the bulk of the increased debt financing during such periods. As the recession deepens, investment declines, and in the early stages of an expansion, internally generated funds typically come back faster than

---

[1] Footnotes appear at end of article.

Figure A   Fractions of Total Sources of Funds of U.S. Nonfinancial Corporations

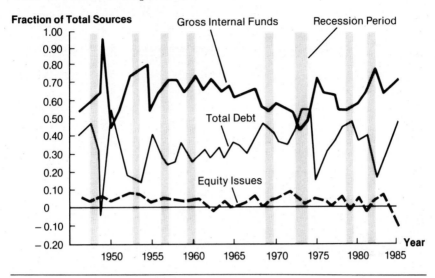

Source: Board of Governors of the Federal Reserve System.

Figure B   Short- and Long-Term Debt as Fractions of Total Sources of Funds of U.S. Nonfinancial Corporations

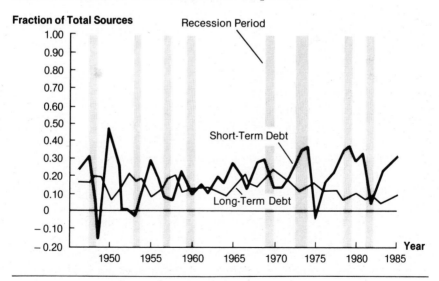

Source: Board of Governors of the Federal Reserve System.

Table I   **Composition of Funds Sources of U.S. Nonfinancial Corporations**

Period	(1) Total Debt	(2) Long-Term Debt*	(3) Total Short-Term Liabilities
1901–12	0.31	0.23	0.08
1913–22	0.29	0.12	0.17
1923–29	0.26	0.22	0.04
1930–39	−0.33	−0.05	−0.29
1940–45	0.15	−0.05	0.20
1946–49	0.30	0.18	0.12
1950–54	0.31	0.14	0.17
1955–59	0.31	0.14	0.17
1960–64	0.30	0.13	0.16
1965–69	0.40	0.15	0.25
1970–74	0.47	0.18	0.29
1975–79	0.38	0.12	0.27
1980–84	0.36	0.10	0.26

Sources: Board of Governors of the Federal Reserve System and R.W. Goldsmith, *Financial Intermediaries in the American Economy Since 1900.*

* Long-term debt consists of bonds and mortgages.

** Consists of bank loans, commercial paper, acceptances, finance company loans, and U.S. government loans.

investment spending. At such times, firms use these internal funds, as well as long-term debt, to reduce their reliance on short-term liabilities.

It should be noted that the year 1984 represents a departure, in some respects, from this typical cyclical pattern. It is unusual for both internal funds and total debt to move in the same direction as proportions of total funds sources. In fact, 1984 was the first year in the entire postwar period in which the fractions of total funds sources accounted for by internal funds, long-term debt and short-term debt all moved in the same direction. The reason, as Figure A shows, was the unprecedented extent of stock repurchasing during 1984.

Clearly, 1984 was an unusual year. But is there any indication of a definite trend toward financial weakness? It does appear that the composition of corporate funds flows has become more volatile since the early 1970s. After a period of relative stability from the late 1950s to the late 1960s, internal funds and short-term debt have been taking wider swings as percentages of total funds sources, much as they did in the decade immediately following World War II. Perhaps this is a sign that corporate treasurers have had to worry more about maintaining flexibility in recent years. However, Figures A and B give little indication of any steady trends. To make a better assessment of whether such trends exist, it is necessary to smooth out some of the short-run fluctuations.

(4) Short-Term Credit Market Debt**	(5) New Stock Issues	(6) Gross Internal Funds
	0.14	0.55
	0.11	0.60
	0.19	0.55
	0.19	1.14
	0.05	0.80
0.05	0.05	0.65
0.05	0.06	0.63
0.06	0.04	0.65
0.07	0.02	0.69
0.12	0.01	0.59
0.14	0.05	0.48
0.12	0.01	0.60
0.15	−0.02	0.66

Secular Patterns

Table I presents the composition of corporate funds flows over selected longer periods. To give a long-run perspective, the Flow of Funds data, which cover only the postwar period, have been supplemented by Raymond W. Goldsmith's estimates for the 1900–45 period.[2]

Table I suggests that corporations' use of debt financing has been consistently higher since the mid-1960s than during previous periods throughout the century. Although it has been substantially reduced during the most recent decade, debt usage still remains at levels that appear high by historical standards. Issuance of long-term debt, however, has not been unusually high. Rather, it is short-term debt that has accounted for much of the rise in total debt. This increase in short-term debt has come from both credit market instruments and spontaneous sources, such as trade debt and tax liabilities.

On the equity side of financing activity, the availability of internal funds has fluctuated considerably from period to period, but no obvious trend is discernible. What does seem clear is that new stock issues declined substantially as a source of funds beginning in the 1940s, and they have remained relatively small ever since.

In a broad sense, the trends indicated in Table I would seem to justify the concerns of those who feel that corporate financial strength has eroded. Greater reliance on debt, especially short-term debt, and the apparent reluctance to issue equity would appear to have exposed the corporate sector to increased financial risk.

Before this conclusion is accepted, however, it should be recognized that inflation can cause figures such as those displayed in Table I to give a distorted picture of corporate financing activity. In particular, traditional measures of corporate internal funds do not take into account the annual decline in the real value of outstanding liabilities caused by inflation.

Inflation Effects

Capital market participants may or may not anticipate the extent to which inflation will occur. If they do not, lenders suffer an uncompensated real loss. This loss can properly be considered a gain to shareholders and therefore a part of firms' profits. Moreover, even if this profit component does not manifest itself as an immediate cash inflow, it does allow firms to increase their debt in nominal terms without any increases in real burden.

If inflation is anticipated, however, lenders will protect themselves by demanding an inflation premium in the nominal interest rate. This premium does not represent additional real interest, but rather a repayment of real principal that compensates lenders for the decline in the real value of the debt that remains outstanding. As a debt repayment, this portion of interest payments should not be thought of as a current expense, or, it follows, a charge against profit. Similarly, an equal amount of new debt in a given period can be thought of as a rollover of that portion of the real principal that must be repaid, rather than as a net issuance of new debt.

Whether inflation is anticipated or not, then, one may make a case that conventional funds flow figures should be adjusted for inflation to give a more accurate picture of real financing activity. Accordingly, the figures reported in Table II have been adjusted by adding to each year's gross internal funds the decline during the year in the real value of debt outstanding at the beginning of that year.[3] This same amount has been subtracted from each year's net new debt issues. The unadjusted figures from Table I are also shown for comparison.

As one would expect, these adjustments make a substantial difference for the three most recent periods. Nevertheless, one would still infer that corporations made use of debt financing to an unprecedented extent during the 1965–74 period. Since that time, however, reliance on internal funds has been heavy, while debt issuance has declined to levels that are not high by historical standards.[4] In short, the adjusted figures are much less indicative of a steady, long-run trend toward greater reliance on debt financing. They suggest instead that, following the debt surge of 1965–74, corporations have reverted to more normal financing proportions.

Both the adjusted and unadjusted data give a strong impression that corporations have made substantial efforts since 1974 to assume a more conservative financial posture. Table III gives further indication of such efforts: Corporations have paid out smaller proportions of available internal funds as dividends during the most recent two periods than during any other period in the postwar era. This has helped to reduce their reliance on debt financing.

The preceding analysis suggests that the fear of a steady erosion in corporate financial strength is probably exaggerated, despite the evidence

Table II   Inflation-Adjusted Composition of Funds Sources

| | Fractions of Total Sources of Funds | | | |
| | Gross Internal Funds | | Total Debt | |
Period	(1) Unadjusted	(2) Adjusted*	(1) Unadjusted	(2) Adjusted*
1901–12	0.55	0.56	0.31	0.30
1913–22	0.60	0.67	0.29	0.22
1923–29	0.55	0.55	0.26	0.26
1930–39	1.14	1.23	−0.33	−0.39
1940–45	0.80	0.87	0.15	0.08
1946–49	0.65	0.72	0.30	0.24
1950–54	0.63	0.66	0.31	0.29
1955–59	0.65	0.68	0.31	0.28
1960–64	0.69	0.70	0.30	0.29
1965–69	0.59	0.63	0.40	0.36
1970–74	0.48	0.57	0.47	0.38
1975–79	0.60	0.70	0.38	0.28
1980–84	0.66	0.77	0.36	0.25

Sources: Unadjusted data, see Table I; beginning-of-period liabilities, Board of Governors of the Federal Reserve System and R.W. Goldsmith, R.E. Lipsey and M. Mendelson, *Studies in the National Balance Sheet of the United States,* 2 Vols. (Princeton: Princeton University Press, 1963); price level changes are measured by implicit GNP inflator for 1901–48, *Historical Statistics of the United States,* and by index of total cost and profit for nonfinancial corporations for 1949–84, *Economic Report of the President.*

* Any inflation-induced decline in the real value of beginning-of-period debt is added to gross internal funds (and subtracted from total debt) for each period. Total beginning-of-period debt outstanding is multiplied by the percentage change in the price level during each period to compute changes in real value.

of the postwar period. As Tables I and II indicate, the end of World War II is a potentially misleading reference point, because it followed a 15-year period of unusually low debt issuance.[5] When a longer-run view is taken, and especially when adjustments are made for the effects of inflation, any steady trend in debt financing is more difficult to detect.

Table III   Fraction of Available Internal Funds Paid Out as Dividends by U.S. Nonfinancial Corporations

| Period | Dividends as a Fraction of Dividends Plus Gross Internal Funds | |
	Unadjusted	Adjusted
1946–49	0.29	0.27
1950–54	0.28	0.27
1955–59	0.25	0.24
1960–64	0.24	0.24
1965–69	0.24	0.23
1970–74	0.24	0.21
1975–79	0.22	0.19
1980–84	0.22	0.19

Source: Board of Governors of the Federal Reserve System.

Furthermore, charges of financial weakness often ignore the substantial effort corporations have made over the past decade to rebuild their balance sheets. At the very least, this effort belies the notion that corporate treasurers have become too cavalier in their attitudes toward financial risk. Nevertheless, there can be little doubt about the increased use of short-term debt. This development, in conjunction with the recent volatility of internal funds, has necessitated more frequent trips to the capital market and has forced corporate treasurers to devote more attention to financial flexibility.

Determinants of Financing Patterns

While it is of some use to know whether corporations' current reliance on debt financing is heavy by historical standards, it must also be conceded that the world today is not the same as it used to be. We could more confidently assess recent corporate financing patterns if we knew something about the forces that have shaped them.

To understand these forces, we must consider the nature of corporate financing decisions. When a corporation finances its assets, it offers investors a set of financial services. That is, it packages the return stream from those assets in the form of different types of securities, each of which offers investors some combination of risk, return and liquidity.

In deciding what kind of financing package it wants to sell, the corporation must consider the competition. Financial institutions, government entities and foreign businesses all raise funds in the capital markets, hence compete with one another in offering financial services. Corporations must therefore compare the costs they would incur by offering a given financing package with the costs their capital market competitors would incur. In addition, they must consider the relative supplies of different types of securities that other capital market participants are offering.

The Corporate Choice

In theory, the comparative costs of different sources of financing will lead corporations to use internal funds first, before turning to debt and, finally, stock issues. This is because dealings with the capital markets incur transaction costs, both explicit and implicit. Among the implicit costs is the potential underevaluation of securities, particularly equity.

Management has inside information about a firm's prospects and, other things equal, it will try to sell securities when prices are favorable. But if investors interpret the announcement of a new equity issue as a sign that management feels the stock price is high, they may discount the stock.[6] The corporation may avoid this problem by using internal funds. Internal financing also allows the firm to avoid the double taxation inherent in paying out taxable dividends and then raising new money from investors' after-tax savings. The availability of internal funds relative to capital expenditure needs should thus be an important determinant of firms' financing proportions.

Once firms turn to external financing, the costs and benefits of debt become important. Corporate debt enjoys a net tax advantage, for example, when corporate tax rates exceed marginal personal tax rates. The relative structure of corporate and personal tax rates should therefore influence corporations' reliance on debt financing. To the extent that corporate rates do exceed marginal personal rates, the tax advantage to debt should also rise with inflation. Under those circumstances, the benefit corporations derive from the tax deductibility of the inflation premium in interest rates exceeds the extra taxes debtholders must pay on the inflation premium.

Debt issues will be limited, however, by the potential costs of financial distress and by the costs of resolving conflicts of interest between shareholders and debtholders. Both these costs increase when the firm faces a riskier environment. Business risk should therefore be another major determinant of corporations' reliance on debt financing.

Finally, corporations in the aggregate may find that heavy supplies of substitute debt securities limit their own ability to issue debt on advantageous terms. In particular, the federal government is a major issuer of low-risk, taxable bonds, and its financing activities may exert an important influence on corporate financing patterns.

Some Evidence

Table IV compares past patterns in corporate financing with some rough measures of the determinants discussed above. Column 2 shows the ratio of (unadjusted) gross internal funds to capital expenditures. For the most part, this ratio is inversely related to the fraction of total funds sources accounted for by debt. This is consistent with the idea that corporations place greatest reliance on debt financing in periods when internal funds are low relative to capital expenditure needs. This pattern is particularly evident in the 1965–69 and 1970–74 periods.

Column 3 gives average "debt incentive tax ratios" for different periods. This ratio, defined as the difference between corporate and personal tax rates, divided by one minus the personal tax rate, measures the net tax advantage to corporate debt.[7] When the ratio takes on higher values, corporate debt issuance yields greater tax advantages, and *vice versa*.

The figures suggest that the net tax advantage to corporate debt rose rapidly after World War II, but that it has been relatively constant since the early 1950s. To the extent corporate debt usage has risen in the postwar period, the increased tax advantage may have been a contributing factor. However, tax factors do not appear capable of explaining the fluctuations in financing proportions that have taken place over shorter periods.

Table IV   **Determinants of Corporate Debt Financing**

Period	(1)[a] Debt Financing Proportion	(2)[b] Gross Internal Funds as a Fraction of Capital Expenditures	(3)[c] Debt Incentive Tax Ratio
1901–12	0.31		0.00
1913–22	0.29		0.03
1923–29	0.26		0.11
1930–39	−0.33		−0.12
1940–45	0.15		0.23
1946–49	0.30	0.84	0.25
1950–54	0.31	0.82	0.37
1955–59	0.31	0.90	0.40
1960–64	0.30	0.96	0.40
1965–69	0.40	0.81	0.40
1970–74	0.47	0.70	0.40
1975–79	0.38	0.91	0.39
1980–84	0.36	0.94	0.37

[a] From Table I.

[b] From Board of Governors of the Federal Reserve System.

[c] Personal tax rate minus corporate tax rate all divided by one minus personal tax rate. Personal rate is measured as lowest statutory personal rate. Data taken from J.A. Pechman, *Federal Tax Policy,* 3d ed. (Washington, DC: Brookings Institution, 1977).

[d] Measured as average annual percentage change in implicit GNP deflator. Data taken from *Historical Statistics of the United States* and *Economic Report of the President.*

[e] Measured as average annual standard deviation of monthly changes in S&P 500 composite stock index. Data taken from Standard & Poor's *Trade and Securities Statistics.*

[f] From Board of Governors of the Federal Reserve System.

Column 4 shows average annual inflation rates for the different periods. High rates of inflation can increase the net tax advantage to corporate debt, and there is indeed some indication that rising inflation may be associated with increased debt financing. Note, however, that debt usage fell substantially during 1975–79—the same time average annual inflation rates reached their peak. The ability of inflation to explain short-term movements in total debt appears limited.

Inflation rates in recent years have been not only high on average, but also very uncertain. Inflation may have had a greater impact on the split between long and short-term debt than on fluctuations in total debt. The more uncertain the inflation rate, the more investors will demand an uncertainty premium as well as an inflation premium in long-term interest rates. This may lead corporations to reduce the issuance of long-term debt.[8]

Column 5 presents a rough proxy for the perceived risk of the economic environment, hence for the implicit costs debt financing imposes on corporations. Specifically, risk is measured by the averages of yearly standard deviations of the percentage changes in month-to-month stock prices for each of the different periods.[9]

(4)[d] Inflation Rate (% per year)	(5)[e] Perceived Risk (% per year)	(6)[f] Federal Borrowing as a Fraction of Total Borrowing
2.1	10.12	0.03
6.5	10.79	0.32
0.1	12.59	−0.11
−1.5	25.59	1.34
6.4	11.46	0.96
9.6	12.99	−1.12
2.7	8.15	0.10
2.7	9.14	0.04
1.5	8.95	0.09
3.9	8.96	0.07
6.5	12.44	0.10
8.4	10.35	0.20
7.3	15.91	0.30

Although the relation is not perfect for each period, there does seem to be a tendency, as theory would suggest, for perceived risk and debt financing proportions to move in opposite directions. This is particularly apparent during the Depression years, when perceived risk rose tremendously. The unusual stability of the 1950s and '60s may have laid the groundwork for the increase in debt that occurred toward the end of that period and somewhat beyond. Of special interest to the interpretation of current developments are the recent movements in perceived risk. Although debt financing increased during 1970–74, together with perceived risk levels, the continuing higher level of risk, especially in 1980–84, may have contributed to the subsequent decline in debt proportions.

The last column in Table IV shows federal government borrowing by domestic nonfinancial sectors during the various periods. These figures are intended to measure the supply of substitutes against which corporate debt securities must compete in the capital market. Although, again, the relation does not hold for each period, there does seem to be a tendency for corporations to scale back their debt financing when the federal government assumes a more dominant role in the market. During the past 10 years, for example, the increase in federal borrowing may have contributed to the decrease in corporate debt financing.

To summarize, the degree of corporate debt financing rises and falls with the extent of capital expenditures relative to available internal funds. When capital spending needs are heavy relative to internal funds, corporations increase their reliance on debt financing, but the extent to which they are willing to do so is tempered by perceptions of business risk and by relative supplies of federal government securities. Over long periods, the tax system, in conjunction with inflation, also seems to exert some effect on corporate debt financing, but its short-run influence is more difficult to detect. The effect of inflation may stem more from inflation uncertainty rather than taxes, and its influence may be felt, not so much on the total extent of debt financing, but on the split between long and short-term debt.

Are Capital Structures Riskier?

Corporations' use of debt financing reached 45 percent of total funds sources in 1984. Does this represent the continuation of an ominous trend? I believe the answer is no. Table I indicates that corporate debt financing has declined, on the whole, since 1974. When the data are adjusted for inflation, as in Table II, recent debt proportions do not appear unusually high by historical standards.

Certainly 1984 was unusual because of the large amount of stock repurchases. The rise of the levered buyout and other forms of corporate restructuring have evidently left their traces in the data. In view of the volatility of the composition of total funds sources over the past 15 years, however, it would be premature to conclude that these developments reflect any long-run trend toward riskier capital structures.

Have corporate executives shown an increased tendency to ignore business risk in their financing choices? In general, the evidence does not appear to support this claim. Recent increases in perceived risk have coincided with more conservative financing choices. Over the past 10 years, dividend payments have been restrained in order to conserve internal funds and reduce dependence on debt financing.

Is there nothing, then, to worry about? Before relaxing, you might take note of the sharp fluctuations in internal funds of late, as well as the increased use of short-term debt, which have placed a higher premium on corporate financial flexibility. As in the past, individual corporations will prove in the future to have made unfortunate financing choices today. But the corporate sector as a whole does not appear to be building a house of cards. To the extent that there is weakness in the U.S. financial system, the corporate sector is not the primary culprit.

Footnotes

[1] Long-term debt is defined to include bonds and mortgages. Short-term debt includes bank loans, commercial paper, acceptances, finance company loans, U.S. government loans, profit taxes payable and trade debt. Because some unknown fraction of loans is actually long-term debt, this categorization is imprecise. However, even long-term loans in recent years have often had floating rates, hence have some of the characteristics of short-term debt.

[2] See R.W. Goldsmith, *Financial Intermediaries in the American Economy since 1900* (Princeton: Princeton University Press, 1958). For a more complete discus-

sion of these long-term financing trends, see R.A. Taggart, Jr., *"Secular Patterns in the Financing of U.S. Corporations,"* in B.M. Friedman, ed. *Corporate Capital Structures in the United States* (Chicago: University of Chicago Press, 1985) and "Have U.S. Corporations Grown Financially Weak?" in B.M. Friedman, ed., *Financing Corporate Capital Formation* (Chicago: University of Chicago Press, 1986).

[3] This adjustment procedure is discussed in G.M. Von Furstenberg and B.G. Malkiel, "Financial Analysis in an Inflationary Environment," *Journal of Finance,* May 1977, pp. 575–88. Further discussion of the relation between inflation, profitability and the real value of corporate debt can be found in F. Modigliani and R.A. Cohn, "Inflation, Rational Valuation and the Market," *Financial Analysts Journal,* March/April 1979, pp. 24–44.

[4] Analysis of inflation-adjusted balance sheet debt ratios also yields the conclusion that current debt levels are not unusually high relative to historical experience. Estimates of the ratio of the market value of debt to both the market value of total capital and the replacement value of total assets are reported in Taggart, "Secular Patterns," *op. cit.*

[5] Analysis of liquidity ratios leads to a similar conclusion. Corporate liquidity has declined substantially in the postwar period, but it was at an unusually high level following heavy corporate purchases of federal government debt during the war. See Taggart, "Have U.S. Corporations Grown Financially Weak?" *op. cit.*

[6] For further discussion of this problem of asymmetric information, see S.C. Myers, "The Capital Structure Puzzle," *Journal of Finance,* July 1984, pp. 474–99.

[7] There is, of course, a whole spectrum of personal tax rates. The one used in these calculations is the lowest statutory personal rate. The figures in Table IV thus approximate true movements in the tax advantage to corporate debt as long as the personal rates in the entire tax structure tend to move together over time.

[8] Bradford Cornell elaborates on this argument in "The Future of Floating-Rate Bonds," in *Issues in Corporate Finance* (New York: Stern, Stewart, Putnam & Macklis, Ltd., 1983). For evidence that the uncertainty premium in long-term rates has been high in recent years, see Z. Bodie, A. Kane and R. McDonald, "Why Haven't Nominal Rates Declined?" *Financial Analysts Journal,* March/April 1984, pp. 16–27.

[9] Because the degree of debt financing itself exerts a positive influence on stock price volatility, the independent effect of risk is difficult to disentangle. A better measure of business risk *per se* would be a standard deviation of returns to total corporate assets. Unfortunately, the data required for that measure are not available for the entire period encompassed by Table IV.

Questions

1.   Gross internal funds generated by corporations for a given year equal retained earnings plus depreciation. Explain the reason for adding depreciation to retained earnings.

2.   Short-term debt has accounted for much of the rise in total debt since the mid-1960s. What effect does this phenomenon have on corporate risk? Explain.

3. In recent years have corporations increased or decreased their reliance on debt? What evidence supports your answer?

4. "In theory, the comparative costs of different sources of financing will lead corporations to use internal funds first, before turning to debt and, finally, stock issues." What are the cost advantages of internal funds over external funds?

5. Identify and explain the expected impact on corporate debt financing of the following changes:
    a. Internal funds increase as a fraction of capital expenditures.
    b. The difference increases between marginal corporate tax rates (T_c) and marginal personal tax rates (T_p).
    c. Environmental uncertainties increase the business risk faced by corporations.

6. In general, are corporate capital structures riskier in the 1980s than they were in the 1970s? Explain.

The Capital Structure Puzzle

Stewart C. Myers

This paper's title is intended to remind you of Fischer Black's well-known note on "The Dividend Puzzle," which he closed by saying, "What should the corporation do about dividend policy? We don't know." [6, p. 8] I will start by asking, "How do firms choose their capital structures?" Again, the answer is, "We don't know."

The capital structure puzzle is tougher than the dividend one. We know quite a bit about dividend policy. John Lintner's model of how firms set dividends [20] dates back to 1956, and it still seems to work. We know stock prices respond to unanticipated dividend changes, so it is clear that dividends have information content — this observation dates back at least to Miller and Modigliani (MM) in 1961 [28]. We do not know whether high dividend yield increases the expected rate of return demanded by investors, as adding taxes to the MM proof of dividend irrelevance suggests, but financial economists are at least hammering away at this issue.

By contrast, we know very little about capital structure. We do not know how firms choose the debt, equity or hybrid securities they issue. We have only recently discovered that capital structure changes convey information to investors. There has been little if any research testing whether the relationship between financial leverage and investors' required return is as the pure MM theory predicts. In general, we have inadequate understanding of corporate financing behavior, and of how that behavior affects security returns.

I do not want to sound too pessimistic or discouraged. We have accumulated many helpful insights into capital structure choice, starting with the most important one, MM's No Magic in Leverage Theorem (Proposition I) [31]. We have thought long and hard about what these insights imply for optimal capital structure. Many of us have translated

Stewart C. Myers, "The Capital Structure Puzzle," *Journal of Finance,* Vol. XXXIX, No. 3, (July 1984): 575-592. Copyright (c) 1984 the American Finance Association. Reprinted with permission.

At the time of this writing, Stewart C. Myers was affiliated with the Sloan School of Management, MIT, and the National Bureau of Economic Research.

these theories, or stories, of optimal capital structure into more or less definite advice to managers. But our theories don't seem to explain actual financing behavior, and it seems presumptuous to advise firms on optimal capital structure when we are so far from explaining actual decisions. I have done more than my share of writing on optimal capital structure, so I take this opportunity to make amends, and to try to push research in some new directions.

I will contrast two ways of thinking about capital structure:

1.   A *static tradeoff* framework, in which the firm is viewed as setting a target debt-to-value ratio and gradually moving towards it, in much the same way that a firm adjusts dividends to move towards a target payout ratio.

2.   An old-fashioned *pecking order* framework, in which the firm prefers internal to external financing, and debt to equity if it issues securities. In the pure pecking order theory, the firm has no well-defined target debt-to-value ratio.

Recent theoretical work has breathed new life into the pecking order framework. I will argue that this theory performs at least as well as the static tradeoff theory in explaining what we know about actual financing choices and their average impacts on stock prices.

Managerial and Neutral Mutation Hypotheses

I have arbitrarily, and probably unfairly, excluded "managerial" theories which might explain firms' capital structure choices.[1] I have chosen not to consider models which cut the umbilical cord that ties managers' acts to stockholders' interests.

I am also sidestepping Miller's idea of "neutral mutation."[2] He suggests that firms fall into some financing patterns or habits which have no material effect on firm value. The habits may make managers feel better, and since they do no harm, no one cares to stop or change them. Thus someone who identifies these habits and uses them to predict financing behavior would not be explaining anything important.

The neutral mutations idea is important as a warning. Given time and imagination, economists can usually invent some model that assigns

---

[1] The finance and economics literature has at least three "managerial" strands: (1) descriptions of managerial capitalism, in which the separation of ownership and control is taken as a central fact of life, for example Berle and Means [5]; (2) agency theory, pioneered for finance by Jensen and Meckling [18], and (3) the detailed analysis of the personal risks and rewards facing managers and how their responses affect firms' financing or investment choices. For examples of Strand (3), see Ross's articles on financial signalling [36, 37].

[2] Put forward in "Debt and Taxes," [27], esp. pp. 272–273. Note that Miller did not claim that all of firms' financing habits are neutral mutations, only that some of them may be. I doubt that Miller intended this idea as a strict null hypothesis (see below).

apparent economic rationality to any random event. But taking neutral mutation as a strict null hypothesis makes the game of research too tough to play. If an economist identifies costs of various financing strategies, obtains independent evidence that the costs are really there, and then builds a model based on these costs which explains firms' financing behavior, then some progress has been made, even if it proves difficult to demonstrate that, say, a type A financing strategy gives higher firm value than a type B. (In fact, we would never see type B if all firms follow value-maximizing strategies.)

There is another reason for not immediately embracing neutral mutations: we know investors are interested in the firm's financing choices, because stock prices change when the choices are announced. The change might be explained as an "information effect" having nothing to do with financing per se — but again, it is a bit too easy to wait until the results of an event study are in, and then to think of an information story to explain them. On the other hand, if one starts by assuming that managers have special information, builds a model of how that information changes financing choices, and predicts which choices will be interpreted by investors as good or bad news, then some progress has been made.

So this paper is designed as a one-on-one competition of the static tradeoff and pecking-order stories. If neither story explains actual behavior, the neutral mutations story will be there faithfully waiting.

The Static Tradeoff Hypothesis

A firm's optimal debt ratio is usually viewed as determined by a tradeoff of the costs and benefits of borrowing, holding the firm's assets and investment plans constant. The firm is portrayed as balancing the value of interest tax shields against various costs of bankruptcy or financial embarrassment. Of course, there is controversy about how valuable the tax shields are, and which, if any, of the costs of financial embarrassment are material, but these disagreements give only variations on a theme. The firm is supposed to substitute debt for equity, or equity for debt, until the value of the firm is maximized. Thus the debt-equity tradeoff is as illustrated in Fig. 1.

Costs of Adjustment

If there were no costs of adjustment, and the static tradeoff theory is correct, then each firm's observed debt-to-value ratio should be its optimal ratio. However, there must be costs, and therefore lags, in adjusting to the optimum. Firms cannot immediately offset the random events that bump them away from the optimum, so there should be some cross-sectional dispersion of actual debt ratios across a sample of firms having the same target ratio.

Figure 1   **The Static-Tradeoff Theory of Capital Structure**

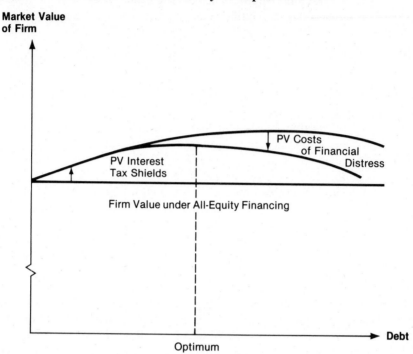

Large adjustment costs could possibly explain the observed wide variation in actual debt ratios, since firms would be forced into long excursions away from their optimal ratios. But there is nothing in the usual static tradeoff stories suggesting that adjustment costs are a first-order concern — in fact, they are rarely mentioned. Invoking them without modelling them is a cop-out.

Any cross-sectional test of financing behavior should specify whether firms' debt ratios differ because they have different optimal ratios or because their actual ratios diverge from optimal ones. It is easy to get the two cases mixed up. For example, think of the early cross-sectional studies which attempted to test MM's Proposition I. These studies tried to find out whether differences in leverage affected the market value of the firm (or the market capitalization rate for its operating income). With hindsight, we can quickly see the problem: if adjustment costs are small, and each firm in the sample is at, or close to its optimum, then the in-sample dispersion of debt ratios must reflect differences in risk or in other variables affecting optimal capital structure. But then MM's Proposition I cannot be tested unless the effects of risk and other variables on firm value can be adjusted for. By now we have learned from experience how hard it is to hold "other things constant" in cross-sectional regressions.

Of course, one way to make sense of these tests is to assume that adjustment costs are small, but managers don't know, or don't care, what the optimal debt ratio is, and thus do not stay close to it. The researcher then assumes some (usually unspecified) "managerial" theory of capital structure choice. This may be a convenient assumption for a cross-sectional test of MM's Proposition I, but it is not very helpful if the object is to understand financing behavior.[3]

But suppose we don't take this "managerial" fork. Then if adjustment costs are small, and firms stay near their target debt ratios, I find it hard to understand the observed diversity of capital structures across firms that seem similar in a static tradeoff framework. If adjustment costs are large, so that some firms take extended excursions away from their targets, then we ought to give less attention to refining our static tradeoff stories and relatively more to understanding what the adjustment costs are, why they are so important, and how rational managers would respond to them.

But I am getting ahead of my story. On to debt and taxes.

Debt and Taxes

Miller's famous "Debt and Taxes" paper [27] cut us loose from the extreme implications of the original MM theory, which made interest tax shields so valuable that we could not explain why all firms were not awash in debt. Miller described an equilibrium of *aggregate* supply and demand for corporate debt, in which personal income taxes paid by the marginal investor in corporate debt just offset the corporate tax saving. However, since the equilibrium only determines aggregates, debt policy should not matter for any single tax-paying firm. Thus Miller's model allows us to

---

[3] The only early cross-sectional study I know of which sidesteps these issues is MM's 1966 paper on the cost of capital for the electric utility industry [28]. Their "corrected" theory says that firm value is independent of capital structure except for the value added by the present value of interest tax shields. Thus tax-paying firms would be expected to substitute debt for equity, at least up to the point where the probability of financial distress starts to be important. However, the regulated firms MM examined had little tax incentive to use debt, because their interest tax shields were passed through to consumers. If a regulated firm pays an extra one dollar of interest, and thus saves T_c in corporate taxes, regulators are supposed to reduce the firm's pre-tax operating income by $T_c/(1-T_c)$, the grossed-up value of the tax saving. This roughly cancels out any tax advantage of borrowing. Thus regulated firms should have little incentive to borrow enough to flirt with financial distress, and their debt ratios could be dispersed across a conservative range.

Moreover, MM's test could pick up the present value of interest tax shields *provided* they adjusted for differences in operating income. Remember, interest tax shields are not eliminated by regulation, just offset by reductions in allowed operating income.

Thus regulated firms are relatively good subjects for cross-sectional tests of static tradeoff theories. MM's theory seemed to work fairly well for three years in the mid-1950s. Unfortunately, MM's equations didn't give sensible coefficients when fitted on later data (see for example, Robicheck, McDonald and Higgins [35]). There has been little further work attempting to extend or adapt MM's 1966 model. In the meantime, theory has moved on.

explain the dispersion of actual debt policies without having to introduce non-value-maximizing managers.[4]

Trouble is, this explanation works only if we assume that all firms face approximately the same marginal tax rate, and *that* is an assumption we can immediately reject. The extensive trading of depreciation tax shields and investment tax credits, through financial leases and other devices, proves that plenty of firms face low marginal rates.[5]

Given significant differences in effective marginal tax rates, and given that the static tradeoff theory works, we would expect to find a strong tax effect in any cross-sectional test, regardless of whose theory of debt and taxes you believe.

Figure 2 plots the net tax gain from corporate borrowing against the expected realizable tax shield from a future deduction of one dollar of interest paid. For some firms this number is 46 cents, or close to it. At the other extreme, there are firms with large unused loss carryforwards which pay no immediate taxes. An extra dollar of interest paid by these firms would create only a potential future deduction, usable when and if the firm earns enough to work off prior carryforwards. The expected realizable tax shield is positive but small. Also, there are firms paying taxes today which cannot be sure they will do so in the future. Such a firm values expected future interest tax shields at somewhere between zero and the full statutory rate.

In the "corrected" MM theory [28] any tax-paying corporation gains by borrowing; the greater the marginal tax rate, the greater the gain. This gives the top line in the figure. In Miller's theory, the personal income taxes on interest payments would exactly offset the corporate interest tax shield, provided that the firm pays the full statutory tax rate. However, any firm paying a lower rate would see a net loss to corporate borrowing and a net gain to lending. This gives the bottom line.

There are also compromise theories, advanced by D'Angelo and Masulis [12], Modigliani [30] and others, indicated by the middle line in the figure. The compromise theories are appealing because they seem less extreme than either the MM or Miller theories. But regardless of which theory holds, the *slope* of the line is always positive. The *difference* between (1) the tax advantage of borrowing to firms facing the full statutory rate, and (2) the tax advantage of lending (or at least *not* borrowing) to firms with large tax loss carryforwards, is exactly the same as in the "extreme" theories. Thus, although the theories tell different stories about aggregate supply and demand of corporate debt, they make essentially the same predictions about which firms borrow more or less than average.

---

[4] Although Miller's "Debt and Taxes" model [27] was a major conceptual step forward, I do not consider it an adequate description of how taxes affect optimum capital structure or expected rates of return on debt and equity securities. See Gordon and Malkiel [16] for a recent review of the evidence.

[5] Cordes and Sheffrin [8] present evidence on the cross-sectional dispersion of effective corporate tax rates.

Figure 2   **The Net Tax Gain to Corporate Borrowing**

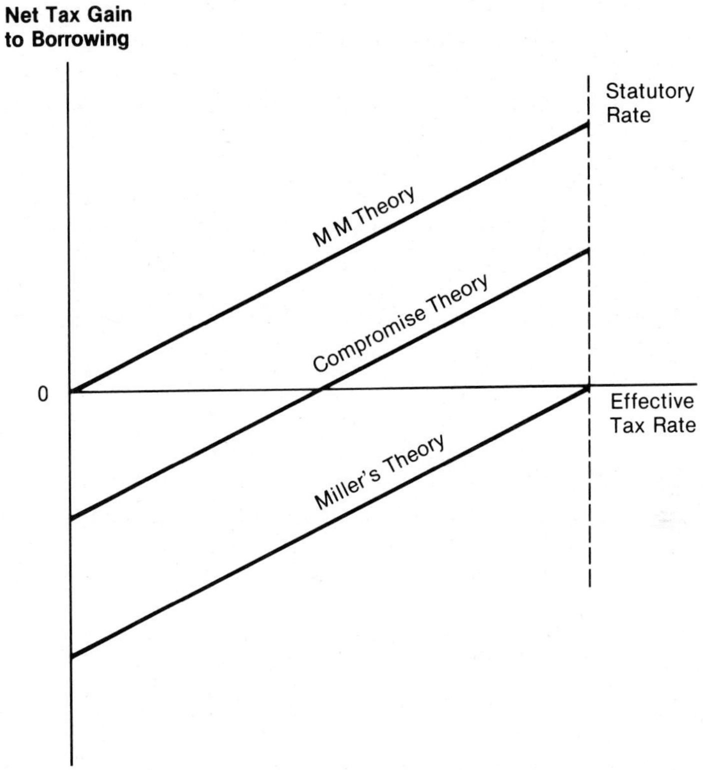

**Net Tax Gain
to Borrowing**

So the tax side of the static tradeoff theory predicts that IBM should borrow more than Bethlehem Steel, other things equal, and that General Motors' debt-to-value ratio should be more than Chrysler's.

Costs of Financial Distress

Costs of financial distress include the legal and administrative costs of bankruptcy, as well as the subtler agency, moral hazard, monitoring and contracting costs which can erode firm value even if formal default is avoided. We know these costs exist, although we may debate their magnitude. For example, there is no satisfactory explanation of debt covenants unless agency costs and moral hazard problems are recognized.

The literature on costs of financial distress supports two qualitative statements about financing behavior.[6]

---

[6] I have discussed these two points in more detail in [32] and [33].

1.   Risky firms ought to borrow less, other things equal. Here "risk" would be defined as the variance rate of the market value of the firm's assets. The higher the variance rate, the greater the probability of default on any given package of debt claims. Since costs of financial distress are caused by threatened or actual default, safe firms ought to be able to borrow more before expected costs of financial distress offset the tax advantages of borrowing.

2.   Firms holding tangible assets-in-place having active second-hand markets will borrow more than firms holding specialized, intangible assets or valuable growth opportunities. The expected cost of financial distress depends not just on the probability of trouble, but the value lost if trouble comes. Specialized, intangible assets or growth opportunities are more likely to lose value in financial distress.

The Pecking Order Theory

Contrast the static tradeoff theory with a competing popular story based on a financing pecking order:

1.   Firms prefer internal finance.

2.   They adapt their target dividend payout ratios to their investment opportunities, although dividends are sticky and target payout ratios are only gradually adjusted to shifts in the extent of valuable investment opportunities.

3.   Sticky dividend policies, plus unpredictable fluctuations in profitability and investment opportunities, mean that internally-generated cash flow may be more or less than investment outlays. If it is less, the firm first draws down its cash balance or marketable securities portfolio.[7]

4.   If external finance is required, firms issue the safest security first. That is, they start with debt, then possibly hybrid securities such as convertible bonds, then perhaps equity as a last resort. In this story, there is no well-defined target debt-equity mix, because there are two kinds of equity, internal and external, one at the top of the pecking order and one at the bottom. Each firm's observed debt ratio reflects its cumulative requirements for external finance.

The Pecking Order Literature

The pecking order hypothesis is hardly new.[8] For example, it comes through loud and clear in Donaldson's 1961 study of the financing practices of a sample of large corporations. He observed [13, p. 67] that

---

[7] If it is more, the firm first pays off debt or invests in cash or marketable securities. If the surplus persists, it may gradually increase its target payout ratio.

[8] Although I have not seen the term "pecking order" used before.

"Management strongly favored internal generation as a source of new funds even to the exclusion of external funds except for occasional unavoidable 'bulges' in the need for funds." These bulges were not generally met by cutting dividends: Reducing the "customary cash dividend payment . . . was unthinkable to most managements except as a defensive measure in a period of extreme financial distress" (p. 70). Given that external finance was needed, managers rarely thought of issuing stock:

Though few companies would go so far as to rule out a sale of common under any circumstances, the large majority had not had such a sale in the past 20 years and did not anticipate one in the foreseeable future. This was particularly remarkable in view of the very high Price-Earnings ratios of recent years. Several financial officers showed that they were well aware that this had been a good time to sell common, but the reluctance still persisted (pp. 57–58).

Of course, the pecking order hypothesis can be quickly rejected if we require it to explain everything. There are plenty of examples of firms issuing stock when they could issue investment-grade debt. But when one looks at aggregates, the heavy reliance on internal finance and debt is clear. For all non-financial corporations over the decade 1973–1982, internally generated cash covered, on average, 62 percent of capital expenditures, including investment in inventory and other current assets. The bulk of required external financing came from borrowing. Net new stock issues were never more than 6 percent of external financing.[9] Anyone innocent of modern finance who looked at these statistics would find the pecking order idea entirely plausible, at least as a description of typical behavior.

Writers on "managerial capitalism" have interpreted firms' reliance on internal finance as a byproduct of the separation of ownership and control: professional managers avoid relying on external finance because it would subject them to the discipline of the capital market.[10] Donaldson's 1969 book was not primarily about managerial capitalism, but he nevertheless observed that the financing decisions of the firms he studied were *not* directed towards maximizing shareholder wealth, and that scholars attempting to explain those decisions would have to start by recognizing the "managerial view" of corporate finance [14, Ch. 2].

This conclusion is natural given the state of finance theory in the 1960s. Today, it is not so obvious that financing by a pecking order goes against shareholders' interests.

External Financing with Asymmetric Information

I used to ignore the pecking order story because I could think of no theoretical foundation for it that would fit in with the theory of modern finance. An argument could be made for internal financing to avoid issue

---

[9] These figures were computed from Brealey and Myers [7], Table 14-3, p. 291.

[10] For example, see Berle [4], or Berle and Means [5].

costs, and if external finance is needed, for debt to avoid the still higher costs of equity. But issue costs in themselves do not seem large enough to override the costs and benefits of leverage emphasized in the static tradeoff story. However, recent work based on asymmetric information gives predictions roughly in line with the pecking order theory. The following brief exposition is based on a forthcoming joint paper by me and Nicholas Majluf [34], although I will here boil down that paper's argument to absolute essentials.

Suppose the firm has to raise N dollars in order to undertake some potentially valuable investment opportunity. Let y be this opportunity's net present value (NPV) and x be what the firm will be worth if the opportunity is passed by. The firm's manager knows what x and y are, but investors in capital markets do not: they see only a joint distribution of possible values $(\tilde{x}, \tilde{y})$. The information asymmetry is taken as given. Aside from the information asymmetry, capital markets are perfect and semi-strong form efficient. MM's Proposition I holds in the sense that the stock of debt relative to real assets is irrelevant if information available to investors is held constant.

The *benefit* to raising N dollars by a security issue is y, the NPV of the firm's investment opportunity. There is also a possible cost: the firm may have to sell the securities for less than they are really worth. Suppose the firm issues *stock* with an aggregate market value, when issued, of N. (I will consider debt issues in a moment.) However, the manager knows the shares are really worth N_1. That is, N_1 is what the new shares will be worth, other things equal, when investors acquire the manager's special knowledge.

Majluf and I discuss several possible objectives managers might pursue in this situation. The one we think makes the most sense is maximizing the "true," or "intrinsic" value of the firm's *existing* shares. That is, the manager worries about the value of the "old" shareholders' stake in the firm. Moreover, investors know the manager will do this. In particular, the "new" investors who purchase any stock issue will assume that the manager is *not* on their side, and will rationally adjust the price they are willing to pay.

Define ΔN as the amount by which the shares are over- or undervalued: $\Delta N \equiv N_1 - N$. Then the manager will issue and invest when

(1) $y \geq \Delta N$.

If the manager's inside information is unfavorable, ΔN is negative and the firm will always issue, even if the only good use for the funds raised is to put them in the bank—a zero-NPV investment.[11] If the inside information is favorable, however, the firm may pass up a positive-NPV investment opportunity rather than issue undervalued shares.

---

[11] If the firm always has a zero-NPV opportunity available to it, the distribution of $\tilde{y}$ is truncated at $\tilde{y}=0$. I also assume that $\tilde{x}$ is non-negative.

But if management acts this way, its decision to issue will signal bad news to both old and new shareholders. Let V be the market value of firm (price per share times number of shares) if it does *not* issue, and V' be market value if it does issue; V' includes the value of the newly-issued shares. Thus, if everyone knows that managers will act according to Inequality (1), the conditions for a rational expectations equilibrium are:[12]

(2a) $V = E(\tilde{x} \mid \text{no issue}) = E(\tilde{x} \mid y < \Delta N)$

(2b) $V' = E(\tilde{x} + \tilde{y} + N \mid \text{issue}) = E(\tilde{x} + \tilde{y} + N \mid y \geq \Delta N)$.

The total dollar amount raised is fixed by assumption, but the number of new shares needed to raise that amount is not. Thus ΔN is endogenous: it depends on V'. For example, if the firm issues, the fraction of all shares held by "new" stockholders is N/V'. The manager sees the true value of their claim as:

(3) $N_1 = \dfrac{N}{V^1} (x + y + N)$

Thus, given N, x and $y,$ and given that stock is issued, the greater the price *per share*, the less value is given up to new stockholders, and the less ΔN is.

Majluf and I have discussed the assumptions and implications of this model in considerable detail. But here are the two key points:

1. *The cost of relying on external financing.* We usually think of the cost of external finance as administrative and underwriting costs, and in some cases underpricing of the new securities. Asymmetric information creates the possibility of a different sort of cost: the possibility that the firm will choose *not* to issue, and will therefore pass up a positive-NPV investment. This cost is avoided if the firm can retain enough internally-generated cash to cover its positive-NPV opportunities.

2. *The advantages of debt over equity issues.* If the firm does seek external funds, it is better off issuing debt than equity securities. The general rule is, "Issue safe securities before risky ones."

---

[12] The simple model embodied in (1) and (2) is a direct descendant of Akerlof's work [1]. He investigated how markets can fail when buyers cannot verify the quality of what they are offered. Faced with the risk of buying a lemon, the buyer will demand a discount, which in turn discourages the potential sellers who do *not* have lemons. However, in Majluf's and my model, the seller is offering not a single good, but a partial claim on two, the investment project (worth y) and the firm without the project (worth x). The information asymmetry applies to both goods — for example, the manager may receive inside information that amounts to good news about x and bad news about y, or vice versa, or good or bad news about both.

Moreover, the firm may suffer by not selling stock, because the investment opportunity is lost. Management will sometimes issue even when the stock is undervalued by investors. Consequently, investors on the other side of the transaction do not automatically interpret every stock issue as an attempted ripoff — if they did, stock would never be issued in a rational expectations equilibrium.

This second point is worth explaining further. Remember that the firm issues and invests if y, the NPV of its investment opportunity, is greater than or equal to ΔN, the amount by which the new shares are undervalued (if $\Delta N > 0$) or overvalued (if $\Delta N < 0$). For example, suppose the investment requires $N = \$10$ million, but in order to raise that amount the firm must issue shares that are really worth $12 million. It will go ahead only if project NPV is at least $2 million. If it is worth only $1.5 million, the firm refuses to raise the money for it; the intrinsic overall value of the firm is reduced by $1.5 million, but the old shareholders are $0.5 million better off.

The manager could have avoided this problem by building up the firm's cash reserves — but that is hindsight. The only thing he can do now is to redesign the security issue to reduce ΔN. For example, if ΔN could be cut to $0.5 million, the investment project could be financed without diluting the true value of existing shares. The way to reduce ΔN is to issue the safest possible securities — strictly speaking, securities whose future value changes least when the manager's inside information is revealed to the market.

Of course, ΔN is endogenous, so it is loose talk to speak of the manager controlling it. However, there are reasonable cases in which the absolute value of ΔN is always less for debt than for equity. For example, if the firm can issue default-risk free debt, ΔN is zero, and the firm never passes up a valuable investment opportunity. Thus, the ability to issue default-risk free debt is as good as cash in the bank. Even if default risk is introduced, the absolute value of ΔN will be less for debt than for equity if we make the customary assumptions of option pricing models.[13] Thus, if the manager has favorable information ($\Delta N > 0$), it is better to issue debt than equity.

This example assumes that new shares or risky debt would be underpriced. What if the managers' inside information is *unfavorable,* so that any risky security issue would be *over*priced? In this case, wouldn't the firm want to make ΔN as *large* as possible, to take maximum advantage of new investors? If so, stock would seem better than debt (and warrants better still). The decision rule seems to be, "Issue debt when investors undervalue the firm, and equity, or some other risky security, when they overvalue it."

The trouble with this strategy is obvious once you put yourself in investors' shoes. If you know the firm will issue equity only when it is overpriced, and debt otherwise, you will refuse to buy equity unless the firm has already exhausted its "debt capacity" — that is, unless the firm has issued so much debt already that it would face substantial additional

---

[13] This amounts to assuming that changes in firm value are lognormally distributed, that managers and investors agree on the variance rate, and that managers know the current value of $\bar{x} + \bar{y}$ but investors do not. If there is asymmetric information about the variance rate, but not about firm value at the time of issue, the pecking order could be reversed. See Giammarino and Neave [15].

costs in issuing more. Thus investors would effectively force the firm to follow a pecking order.

Now this is clearly too extreme. The model just presented would need lots of fleshing out before it could fully capture actual behavior. I have presented it just to show how models based on asymmetric information can predict the two central ideas of the pecking order story: first, the preference for internal finance, and, second, the preference for debt over equity if external financing is sought.

What We Know About Corporate Financing Behavior

I will now list what we know about financing behavior and try to make sense of this knowledge in terms of the two hypotheses sketched above. I begin with five facts about financing behavior, and then offer a few generalizations from weaker statistical evidence or personal observation. Of course even "facts" based on apparently good statistics have been known to melt away under further examination, so read with caution.

Internal vs. External Equity

Aggregate investment outlays are predominantly financed by debt issues and internally-generated funds. New stock issues play a relatively small part. Moreover, as Donaldson has observed, this is what many managers say they are trying to do.

This fact is what suggested the pecking order hypothesis in the first place. However, it might also be explained in a static tradeoff theory by adding significant transaction costs of equity issues and noting the favorable tax treatment of capital gains relative to dividends. This would make external equity relatively expensive. It would explain why companies keep target dividend payouts low enough to avoid having to make regular stock issues.[14] It would also explain why a firm whose debt ratio soars above target does not immediately issue stock, buy back debt, and re-establish a more moderate debt-to-value ratio. Thus firms might take extended excursions *above* their debt targets. (Note, however, that the static tradeoff hypothesis as usually presented rarely mentions this kind of adjustment cost.)

But the out-of-pocket costs of *repurchasing* shares seems fairly small. It is thus hard to explain extended excursions *below* a firm's debt target by an augmented static tradeoff theory — the firm could quickly issue debt and buy back shares. Moreover, if personal income taxes are important in explaining firms' apparent preferences for internal equity,

---

[14] Regulated firms, particularly electric utilities, typically pay dividends generous enough to force regular trips to the equity market. They have a special reason for this policy: it improves their bargaining position vs. consumers and regulators. It turns the opportunity cost of capital into cash requirements.

then it's difficult to explain why *external* equity is not strongly *negative* — that is, why most firms haven't gradually moved to materially lower target payout ratios and used the released cash to repurchase shares.

Timing of Security Issues

Firms apparently try to "time" stock issues when security prices are "high." *Given that they seek external finance,* they are more likely to issue stock (rather than debt) after stock prices have risen than after they have fallen. For example, past stock price movements were one of the best-performing variables in Marsh's study [22] of British firms' choices between new debt and new equity issues. Taggart [39] and others[15] have found similar behavior in the United States.

This fact is embarrassing to static tradeoff advocates. If firm value rises, the debt-to-value ratio falls, and firms ought to issue *debt,* not equity, to rebalance their capital structures.

The fact is equally embarrassing to the pecking order hypothesis. There is no reason to believe that the manager's inside information is systematically more favorable when stock prices are "high." Even if there were such a tendency, investors would have learned it by now, and would interpret the firm's issue decision accordingly. There is no way firms can *systematically* take advantage of purchasers of new equity in a rational expectations equilibrium.

Borrowing against Intangibles and Growth Opportunities

Firms holding valuable intangible assets or growth opportunities tend to borrow less than firms holding mostly tangible assets. For example, Long and Malitz [21] found a significant negative relationship between rates of investment in advertising and research and development (R & D) and the level of borrowing. They also found a significant *positive* relationship between the rate of capital expenditure (in fixed plant and equipment) and the level of borrowing.

Williamson [41] reached the same conclusion by a different route. His proxy for a firm's intangibles and growth opportunities was the difference between the market value of its debt and equity securities and the replacement cost of its tangible assets. The higher this proxy, he found, the less the firm's debt-to-value ratio.

There is plenty of indirect evidence indicating that the level of borrowing is determined not just by the value and risk of the firm's assets, but also by the *type* of assets it holds. For example, without this distinction, the static tradeoff theory would specify all target debt ratios in terms of market, not book values. Since many firms have market values

---

[15] Jalilvand and Harris [17], for example.

far in excess of book values (even if those book values are restated in current dollars), we ought to see at least a few such firms operating comfortably at *very* high book debt ratios — and of course we do not. This fact begins to make sense, however, as soon as we realize that book values reflect assets-in-place (tangible assets and working capital). Market values reflect intangibles and growth opportunities as well as assets-in-place. Thus, firms do not set target book debt ratios because accountants certify the books. Book asset values are proxies for the values of assets in place.[16]

Exchange Offers

Masulis [23, 24] has shown that stock prices rise, on average, when a firm offers to exchange debt for equity, and fall when they offer to exchange equity for debt. This fact could be explained in various ways. For example, it might be a tax effect. If most firms' debt ratios are below their optimal ratios (i.e., to the left of the optimum in Figure 1), and if corporate interest tax shields have significant positive value, the debt-for-equity exchanges would tend to move firms closer to optimum capital structure. Equity-for-debt swaps would tend to move them farther away.

The evidence on exchanges hardly builds confidence in the static tradeoff theory as a description of financing behavior. If the theory were right, firms would be sometimes above, and sometimes below, their optimum ratios. Those above would offer to exchange equity for debt. Those below would offer debt for equity. In both cases, the firm would move closer to the optimum. Why should an exchange offer be good news if in one direction and bad news if in the other?

As Masulis points out, the firm's willingness to exchange debt for equity might signal that the firm's debt capacity had, in management's opinion, increased. That is, it would signal an increase in firm value or a reduction in firm risk. Thus, a debt-for-equity exchange would be good news, and the opposite exchange bad news.

This "information effect" explanation for exchange offers is surely right in one sense. Any time an announcement affects stock price, we can infer that the announcement conveyed information. That is not much help except to prove that managers have some information investors do not have.

The idea that an exchange offer reveals a change in the firm's target debt ratio, and thereby signals changes in firm value or risk, sounds plausible. But an equally plausible story can be told without saying anything about a target debt ratio. If the manager with superior information acts to maximize the intrinsic value of existing shares, then the announcement of a stock issue should be bad news, other things equal,

---

[16] The problem is not that intangibles and growth opportunities are risky. The *securities* of growth firms may be excellent collateral. But the firm which borrows against intangibles or growth opportunities may end up reducing their value.

because stock issues will be more likely when the *manager* receives bad news.[17] On the other hand, stock retirements should be good news. The news in both cases has no evident necessary connection with shifts in target debt ratios.

It may be possible to build a model combining asymmetric information with the costs and benefits of borrowing emphasized in static tradeoff stories. My guess, however, is that it will prove difficult to do this without also introducing some elements of the pecking order story.

Issue or Repurchase of Shares

The fifth fact is no surprise given the fourth. On average, stock price falls when firms announce a stock issue. Stock prices rise, on average, when a stock repurchase is announced. This fact has been confirmed in several studies, including those by Korwar [19], Asquith and Mullins [2], Dann and Mikkleson [10], and Vermaelen [40], and DeAngelo, DeAngelo and Rice [11].

This fact is again hard to explain by a static tradeoff model, except as an information effect in which stock issues or retirements signal changes in the firm's target debt ratio. I've already commented on that.

The simple asymmetric information model I used to motivate the pecking order hypothesis does predict that the announcement of a stock issue will cause stock price to fall. It also predicts that stock price should *not* fall, other things equal, if default-free debt is issued. Of course, no private company can issue debt that is absolutely protected from default, but it seems reasonable to predict that the average stock price impact of high-grade debt issues will be small relative to the average impact of stock issues. This is what Dann and Mikkleson [10] find.

These results may make one a bit more comfortable with asymmetric information models of the kind sketched above, and thus a bit more comfortable with the pecking order story.

That's the five facts. Here now are three items that do not qualify for that list—just call them "observations."

Existence of Target Ratios

Marsh [22] and Taggart [39] have found some evidence that firms adjust towards a target debt-to-value ratio. However, a model based solely on this partial adjustment process would have a very low R^2. Apparently the static tradeoff model captures only a small part of actual behavior.[18]

---

[17] This follows from the simple model presented above. See Myers and Majluf [34] for a formal proof.

[18] Of course, we could give each firm its own target, and leave that target free to wander over time. But then we would explain everything and know nothing. We want a theory which predicts how debt ratios vary across firms and time.

Risk

Risky firms tend to borrow less, other things equal. For example, both Long and Malitz [21] and Williamson [41] found significant negative relationships between unlevered betas and the level of borrowing. However, the evidence on risk and debt policy is not extensive enough to be totally convincing.

Taxes

I know of no study clearly demonstrating that a firm's tax status has predictable, material effects on its debt policy.[19] I think the wait for such a study will be protracted.

Admittedly it's hard to classify firms by tax status without implicitly classifying them on other dimensions as well. For example, firms with large tax loss carryforwards may also be firms in financial distress, which have high debt ratios almost by definition. Firms with high operating profitability, and therefore plenty of unshielded income, may also have valuable intangible assets and growth opportunities. Do they end up with a higher or lower than average debt-to-value ratio? Hard to say.

Conclusion

People feel comfortable with the static tradeoff story because it sounds plausible and yields an interior optimum debt ratio. It rationalizes "moderate" borrowing.

Well, the story may be moderate and plausible, but that does not make it right. We have to ask whether it explains firms' financing behavior. If it does, fine. If it does not, then we need a better theory before offering advice to managers.

The static tradeoff story works to some extent, but it seems to have an unacceptably low R^2. Actual debt ratios vary widely across apparently similar firms. Either firms take extended excursions from their targets, or the targets themselves depend on factors not yet recognized or understood.

At this point we face a tactical choice between two research strategies. First, we could try to expand the static tradeoff story by introducing adjustment costs, possibly including those stemming from asymmetric information and agency problems. Second, we could *start* with a story based on asymmetric information, and expand it by adding only those elements of the static tradeoff which have clear empirical support. I think we will progress farther faster by the latter route.

---

[19] For example, both Williamson [41] and Long and Malitz [21] introduced proxies for firms' tax status, but failed to find any significant, independent effect on debt ratios.

Here is what I really think is going on. I warn you that the following "modified pecking order" story is grossly oversimplified and underqualified. But I think it is generally consistent with the empirical evidence.

1.   Firms have good reasons to avoid having to finance real investment by issuing common stock or other risky securities. They do not want to run the risk of falling into the dilemma of either passing by positive-NPV projects or issuing stock at a price they think is too low.

2.   They set target dividend payout ratios so that normal rates of equity investment can be met by internally generated funds.

3.   The firm may also plan to cover part of normal investment outlays with new borrowing, but it tries to restrain itself enough to keep the debt safe — that is, reasonably close to default-risk free. It restrains itself for two reasons: first, to avoid any material costs of financial distress; and second, to maintain financial slack in the form of reserve borrowing power. "Reserve borrowing power" means that it can issue safe debt if it needs to.

4.   Since target dividend payout ratios are sticky, and investment opportunities fluctuate relative to internal cash flow, the firm will from time to time exhaust its ability to issue safe debt. When this happens, the firm turns to less risky securities first — for example, risky debt or convertibles before common stock.

The crucial difference between this and the static tradeoff story is that, in the modified pecking order story, observed debt ratios will reflect the cumulative requirement for external financing — a requirement cumulated over an extended period.[20] For example, think of an unusually profitable firm in an industry generating relatively slow growth. That firm will end up with an unusually low debt ratio compared to its industry's average, *and it won't do much of anything about it*. It won't go out of its way to issue debt and retire equity to achieve a more normal debt ratio.

An unprofitable firm in the same industry will end up with a relatively high debt ratio. If it is high enough to create significant costs of financial distress, the firm *may* rebalance its capital structure by issuing equity. On the other hand, it may not. The same asymmetric information problems which sometimes prevent a firm from issuing stock to finance real investment will sometimes also block issuing stock to retire debt.[21]

If this story is right, average debt ratios will vary from industry to industry, because asset risk, asset type, and requirements for external

---

[20] The length of that period reflects the time required to make a significant shift in a target dividend payout ratio.

[21] The factors that make financial distress costly also make it difficult to escape. The gain in firm value from rebalancing is highest when the firm has gotten into deep trouble and lenders have absorbed a significant capital loss. In that case, rebalancing gives lenders a windfall gain. This is why firms in financial distress often do not rebalance their capital structures.

funds also vary by industry. But a long-run industry average will not be a meaningful target for individual firms in that industry.

Let me wrap this up by noting the two clear gaps in my description of "what is really going on." First, the modified pecking order story depends on sticky dividends, but does not explain why they are sticky. Second, it leaves us with at best a fuzzy understanding of when and why firms issue common equity. Unfortunately I have nothing to say on the first weakness, and only the following brief comments on the second.

The modified pecking order story recognizes both asymmetric information and costs of financial distress. Thus the firm faces two increasing costs as it climbs up the pecking order: it faces higher odds of incurring costs of financial distress, and also higher odds that future positive-NPV projects will be passed by because the firm will be unwilling to finance them by issuing common stock or other risky securities. The firm may choose to reduce these costs by issuing stock now even if new equity is not needed immediately to finance real investment, just to move the firm *down* the pecking order. In other words, financial slack (liquid assets or reserve borrowing power) is valuable, and the firm may rationally issue stock to acquire it. (I say "may" because the firm which issues equity to buy financial slack faces the same asymmetric information problems as a firm issuing equity to finance real investment.) The optimal *dynamic* issue strategy for the firm under asymmetric information is, as far as I know, totally unexplored territory.[22]

References

1. Akerlof, G.A., "The Market for 'Lemons': Quality and the Market Mechanism," *Quarterly Journal of Economics,* 84 (August 1970), 488–500.

2. Asquith, P. and D.W. Mullins, "Equity Issues and Stock Price Dilution," Working Paper, Harvard Business School, May 1983.

3. Barges, A., *The Effect of Capital Structure on the Cost of Capital,* Prentice-Hall, Inc., Englewood Cliffs, N.J., 1963.

4. Berle, A., *The 20th Century Capitalist Revolution,* Harcourt, Brace and World, Inc., 1954.

5. Berle, A. and G. Means, *The Modern Corporation and Private Property,* MacMillan, New York, 1932.

6. Black, F., "The Dividend Puzzle," *Journal of Portfolio Management,* 2 (Winter 1976), 5–8.

7. Brealey, R.A. and S.C. Myers, *Principles of Corporate Finance,* 2nd Ed., McGraw-Hill Book Co., New York, 1984.

8. Cordes, J.J. and S.M. Sheffrin, "Estimating the Tax Advantage of Corporate Debt," *Journal of Finance,* 38 (March 1983), 95–105.

---

[22] If the information asymmetry disappears from time to time, then the firm clearly should stock up with equity before it reappears. This observation is probably not much practical help, however, because we lack an objective proxy for changes in the degree of asymmetry.

9. Dann, L.Y., "Common Stock Repurchases: An Analysis of Returns to Bondholders and Stockholders," *Journal of Financial Economics,* 9 (June 1981), 113–138.

10. Dann, L.Y. and W.H. Mikkleson, "Convertible Debt Issuance, Capital Structure Change and Financing-Related Information: Some New Evidence," Working Paper, Amos Tuck School of Business Administration, 1983.

11. DeAngelo, H., L. DeAngelo, and E.M. Rice, "Minority Freezeouts and Stockholder Wealth," Working Paper, Graduate School of Business Administration, University of Washington, 1982.

12. DeAngelo, H., and R. Masulis, "Optimal Capital Structure Under Corporate and Personal Taxation," *Journal of Financial Economics,* 8 (March 1980), 3–29.

13. Donaldson, G., *Corporate Debt Capacity: A Study of Corporate Debt Policy and the Determination of Corporate Debt Capacity,* Boston, Division of Research, Harvard Graduate School of Business Administration, 1961.

14. Donaldson, G., *Strategy for Financial Mobility,* Boston, Division of Research, Harvard Graduate School of Business Administration, 1969.

15. Giammarino, R.M. and E.H. Neave, "The Failure of Financial Contracts and the Relevance of Financial Policy," Working Paper, Queens University, 1982.

16. Gordon, R.H. and G.B. Malkiel, "Corporate Finance," in H. J. Aaron and J.A. Pechman, *How Taxes Affect Economic Behavior,* Brookings Institution, Washington, DC, 1981.

17. Jalilvand, A. and R.S. Harris, "Corporate Behavior in Adjusting Capital Structure and Dividend Policy: An Econometric Study," *Journal of Finance,* 39 (March 1984), 127–145.

18. Jensen, M.C. and W. Meckling, "Theory of the Firm: Managerial Behavior, Agency Costs and Capital Structure," *Journal of Financial Economics,* 3 (October 1976), 11–25.

19. Korwar, A.N., "The Effect of New Issues of Equity: An Empirical Examination," Working Paper, University of California, Los Angeles, 1981.

20. Lintner, J. "Distribution of Incomes of Corporations Among Dividends, Retained Earnings and Taxes," *American Economic Review,* 46 (May 1956), 97–113.

21. Long, M.S., and E.B. Malitz, "Investment Patterns and Financial Leverage," Working Paper, National Bureau of Economic Research, 1983.

22. Marsh, P.R., "The Choice Between Equity and Debt: An Empirical Study," *Journal of Finance,* 37 (March 1982), 121–144.

23. Masulis, R.W., "The Effects of Capital Structure Change on Security Prices: A Study of Exchange Offers," *Journal of Financial Economics,* 8 (June 1980), 139–177.

24. Masulis, R.W., "The Impact of Capital Structure Change on Firm Value," *Journal of Finance,* 38 (March 1983), 107–126.

25. Mikkelson, W.H., "Capital Structure Change and Decreases in Stockholders' Wealth: A Cross-Sectional Study of Convertible Security Calls," Forthcoming in B. Friedman, Ed., *Corporate Capital Structures in the*

United States, (National Bureau of Economic Research Conference Volume).

26. Mikkelson, W.H., "Convertible Calls and Security Returns," *Journal of Financial Economics,* 9 (June 1981), 113–138.

27. Miller, M., "Debt and Taxes," *Journal of Finance,* 32 (May 1977), 261–275.

28. Miller, M., and F. Modigliani, "Dividend Policy, Growth and the Valuation of Shares," *Journal of Business,* 34 (October 1961), 411–433. "Some Estimates of the Cost of Capital to the Electric Utility Industry, 1954–1957," *American Economic Review,* 56 (June 1966), 333–391.

29. Miller, M.H. and K. Rock, "Dividend Policy Under Information Asymmetry," Working Paper, Graduate School of Business, University of Chicago, November 1982.

30. Modigliani, F., "Debt, Dividend Policy, Taxes, Inflation and Market Valuation," *Journal of Finance,* 37 (May 1982), 255–273.

31. Modigliani, F. and M. Miller, "The Cost of Capital, Corporation Finance and the Theory of Investment," *American Economic Review,* 53 (June 1958), 261–297.

32. Myers, S., "Determinants of Corporate Borrowing," *Journal of Financial Economics,* 5 (November 1977), 147–176.

33. Myers, S., "The Search for Optimal Capital Structure," *Midland Corporate Finance Journal,* 1 (Spring 1984), 6–16.

34. Myers, S., and N. Majluf, "Corporate Financing and Investment Decisions When Firms Have Information Investors Do Not Have," *Journal of Financial Economics,* forthcoming.

35. Robicheck, A.A., J. McDonald and R. Higgins, "Some Estimates of the Cost of Capital to the Electric Utility Industry, 1954–1957: Comment," *American Economic Review,* 57 (December 1967), 1278–1288.

36. Ross, S.A., "Some Notes on Financial-Incentive Signalling Models, Activity Choice and Risk Preferences," *Journal of Finance,* 33 (June 1978), 777–792.

37. Ross, S.A., "The Determination of Financial Structure: The Incentive-Signalling Approach," *Bell Journal of Economics,* 8 (Spring 1977), 23–40.

38. Smith, C. and Warner, J., "On Financial Contracting: An Analysis of Bond Covenants," *Journal of Financial Economics,* 7 (June 1979), 117–161.

39. Taggart, R., "A Model of Corporate Financing Decisions," *Journal of Finance,* 32 (December 1977), 1467–1484.

40. Vermaelen, T., "Common Stock Repurchases and Market Signalling: An Empirical Study," *Journal of Financial Economics,* 9 (June 1981), 139–183.

41. Williamson, S., "The Moral Hazard Theory of Corporate Financial Structure: An Empirical Test," Unpublished Ph.D. Dissertation, MIT, 1981.

Questions

1.   Identify the different kinds of costs experienced by corporations in financial distress.

2. MBI Company's marginal tax rate is 34 percent. MBI pays $10 million of interest expense. How large is the tax shield created by MBI's interest payment? Explain what is meant by *present value of interest tax shields*.

3. Describe the static tradeoff hypothesis of corporate capital structure.

4. Asymmetric information exists when corporate managers have information not known by investors. Explain the role played by asymmetric information in understanding why corporate managers would prefer to issue low-risk bonds instead of common stock.

5. Explain why corporate managers might prefer internal financing over external financing.

6. Describe the pecking-order theory of corporate capital structure.

7. According to Myers, what are the five "facts" known about corporate financing behavior?

8. Sakan Cola Company's common stock trades at $15 per share, but Sakan's managers have reason to believe that it is worth $20 per share. They plan to introduce a profitable new drink called Sakan Orange, which will add $1 million to Sakan's equity value. Introduction of the new drink will require a $2 million investment. Sakan has 200,000 shares of common stock currently outstanding, making its aggregate equity value equal to $3 million.

    a. If Sakan issues common stock to finance the new project, how many shares will it need to issue? (Assume zero flotation costs.)

    b. According to management's beliefs, what is the true worth of the new issue of common stock?

    c. If issuing common stock is Sakan's only financing alternative, should it go forward with the investment plan? Explain.

PART III
CAPITAL BUDGETING

12
Capital Budgeting Practices of Twelve Large Manufacturers

Marc Ross

1. Introduction

Surveys of capital budgeting practices among large firms have indicated a widespread use of discounted cash flow (DCF) methods, especially internal rate of return.[1] At the same time, many firms state that they also continue to use simple payback or related methods [8]. The study reported here sheds light on the differences between theory and practice in the implementation of DCF analysis.

Surveys have shown that many firms use either a weighted average cost of capital or the cost of a specific source of funds in determining a hurdle rate. Most firms, however, employ some form of capital rationing—that is, they restrict capital expenditures even though it generally means neglecting profitable projects.[2] Under rationing, projects compete against each other, not against a profitability standard. The study reported here uses empirically determined hurdle rates and other data to examine these capital allocation practices.

A. The Alliance Study

The study, by the Alliance to Save Energy [1], was undertaken to evaluate tax incentives for industrial energy conservation. It was supported by the John D. and Catherine T. MacArthur Foundation. Data

Marc Ross, "Capital Budgeting Practices of Twelve Large Manufacturers," *Financial Management* (Winter 1986) Vol. 15, Iss. 4: 15–22. Reprinted with permission.

At the time of this writing, Marc Ross was a member of the faculty of the Physics Department at the University of Michigan, Ann Arbor.

The author would like to express his pleasure in working with the project group at the Alliance to Save Energy: Robin Miller, Bob Rauch, Mike Reid, and Jim Wolf, and Carliss Baldwin of the School of Business Administration, Harvard University for extensive comments on an early draft.

[1] Two recent surveys of the literature are those by Scott and Petty [9] and Gurnani [5].

[2] See the surveys by Gitman and Forrester [4] and Petty, Scott, and Bird [6]. A survey of capital budgeting practices is presented by Fremge [3].

were gathered, primarily in 1981–82, from 15 large firms, with three each from the steel, paper, aluminum, and petroleum refining industries. Since the author did not participate in the petroleum refining interviews, petroleum refining is omitted here. The firms studied account for about one-third of the combined sales of the four industries. Much of the information collected is proprietary and the firms cannot be identified.

Information was gathered from two sources at each firm: one to three days of interviews, and records of the analysis of energy-related investment projects. The interviews focused on examples of projects at the margin of acceptability and on the financial analysis of these projects.

Although the study was designed to address tax incentives, its field-study approach and its focus on energy conservation projects lent themselves to learning about the investment decision-making process in general. The field-study approach enabled examination of actual operating procedures; and, since energy conservation is not usually an area of proprietary concern, discussions were often open and information generously provided. Moreover, respondents stated that the capital budgeting process for energy conservation is essentially the same as for other discretionary projects of the same size.

B. The Sample Data

The firms typically categorize capital investments as either mandatory (regulations and contracts, capitalized maintenance, replacement of anti-quated equipment, product quality) or discretionary (expanded markets, new businesses, cost cutting). Decisionmaking is different for mandatory and discretionary projects. We culled the project data to omit (the few) projects that appeared to be mandatory. We also omitted many projects for which the financial information was inadequate for our analysis. The final sample contained some 400 projects: roughly 100 completed projects, almost all in 1980–81, and 300 projects either underway or prospective, primarily intended for the period 1982–85.

Interviews at the firms showed that most firms' decision-making processes are different for different project sizes. Typical levels of approval authority are shown in Exhibit 1. Using the size categories from Exhibit 1, we found the data to contain roughly 300 small and very small projects, 100 medium-sized projects, and 12 large projects. Unlike the samples of small and medium projects, that of large projects was probably not representative of those under consideration across these industries, because some firms did not provide data on large projects (due to proprietary concerns). In this study most of the information thus concerns discretionary projects of $10 million or less.

The data were complete (except for very small projects) for four of the twelve firms under consideration; *i.e.*, they spanned all energy-conservation projects under consideration regardless of project size. Complete records for projects based at one or more plants were obtained for five more firms. For the remaining firms only samples of the projects under consideration were obtained.

Exhibit 1   **Project Size and Decision-Making Authority**

Project Size	Typical Boundaries	Primary Site for Investment Decision
Very small	Up to $100,000	Plant
Small	$100,000 to $1 million	Division
Medium	$1 million to $10 million	Corporate investment committee
Large	Over $10 million	CEO & board

II. Example of a Project Proposal

Decisionmaking on smaller projects can be succinctly described by a hypothetical example. Typical features that we observed are incorporated; the specifics would, of course, vary.

Bill Johnson is part of an energy-conservation team (created in 1979) at a large plant of a basic-materials manufacturer. On the initiative of a vendor, he has identified an approach to cutting energy costs at a heater: advanced combustion controls, which could reduce excess air in the combustion zone.[3]

Bill looks into other approaches, such as total replacement of the heater or added heat exchangers (to capture heat from the stack gases to preheat the product). However, the projects overlap; he can advocate at most one.

Opinions on technical issues are sought out by Bill, especially from an operating engineer at the facility where the heater is located and from his supervisor. He obtains rough quotes from vendors and estimates annual benefits for several schemes. A critical test for the combustion-control option is passed in a discussion with the manager of the facility in question. These managers are typically like kings in their realms. Their tastes and the production problems they face may lead them to veto any modification out of hand. The facility manager is primarily concerned with technological risks, such as a long breaking-in period and possible operational problems. Use of automatic controls would involve operating the heater close to conditions that are analogous to being at the edge of a cliff; a small mistake could be very damaging. Bill selected a project for this particular heater in part because he knows that this facility manager is open to new technology. He is able to tell the manager that one of the control options has been applied in a similar situation and has operated without trouble.

Bill gets the go-ahead for detailed design work on the control option. One consideration is that, since the likely project cost is over $100,000 (but less than a million), the final investment decision would be made at

---

[3] His idea could also have come from an energy-conservation audit of the plant, corporate energy conservation staff, professional literature, or contacts with peers.

division headquarters. Bill knows that the plant manager has many things to ask for at the division and would prefer that the decision on this project be kept at the plant level. He cannot bring the cost below $100,000, however. He also knows that other alternatives would create a project in the $1 million to $10 million range, putting the final decision with the Corporate Investment Committee (CIC). Paradoxically, while he knows that the CIC is more generous in approving projects than the division, he wants to avoid going to the CIC because a very extensive case would have to be prepared, and enthusiastic support would be needed from the division, plant, and facility managers. That would be hard to get for a project that cuts costs but has no other production benefits. He has observed that higher-level managers give higher priority to new markets than to cost cutting and that lower-level managers give higher priority to maintaining and improving the manufacturing process (with respect to product quality, flexibility and reliability of production, production capacity, *etc.*) than to cost cutting.

The control system is designed by Bill with the help of a vendor and representatives of plant service organizations, and in collaboration with the operating engineer. He obtains good capital cost quotes and calculates initial-year operating costs and benefits. He calculates the ratio of capital cost to first year net benefits (without considering taxes) and calls this the payback.

Bill notes with concern that the cost is higher than his preliminary estimate, so that the payback is 1.7 years, near the cut-off on projects approved by the division in the past two years. Bill's plant is relatively modern and the businesses with which the heater is associated are sound; if the project were at a less-favored location, the division would certainly not approve it. A substantial risk that the plant or production line will be shut down creates an expectation of substantially reduced profitability, even where management does not expect the shutdown to occur soon.

Using a microcomputer, Bill calculates several after-tax DCF measures of investment worth. He has instructions for certain aspects of the evaluation: He must assign a ten-year life to all projects, although he suspects the life of this project will be shorter because the technology will probably become obsolete. He must use 6% per year escalation of all prices over the project life, in spite of the different expectations he has for natural gas and other factors.[4] He assumes that the heater is operated at design levels and that the energy saved per year is constant over the ten-year period. No risk assessment is included in the analysis. In any case, although the DCF evaluations are carried out, the project is discussed at the plant in terms of its 1.7 year payback.

The request for funds includes a two-page financial analysis prepared by a computer, a brief technical description of the project and very

---

[4] Although many interviewees in our study discussed the uncertainty of future energy prices, the recent steep drop in oil and gas prices was not expected or even hinted at by anyone in our interviews. In the following, no consideration of this price drop is made.

brief comments on its possible impacts on production and on pollution. The request is sent to the plant manager. He has an overview of the requests that will go from the plant to the division. Although he is not especially impressed by a cost-cutting project with this payback, he wants to get experience with advanced control systems and is satisfied the project will not interfere with production; so he approves the request. It is then forwarded to Corporate Engineering for technical evaluation. The plant manager or Corporate Engineering often returns a request at this stage, putting it on hold or asking for substantial changes. This time it goes through.

The request is sent to division headquarters as part of a group of requests. On the basis of an earlier planning process, the plant manager knows that the total requested is in line with the capital the division expects to allocate to his plant.

Decisionmakers at the division include a vice president who has responsibility for the products made at the facility in question. He has a good relationship with the facility manager and knows about the request from personal conversation. He notes the project's internal rate of return of 44%, but pays no attention to the NPV or profitability index, which are also shown in the financial analysis. He is accustomed to the fact that standard project life and escalation rates have been used in the evaluation, and believes this to be an effective procedure for preventing some plant managers from exaggerating the benefits of their projects. The vice president believes the engineering estimate of capital costs and initial benefits to be unbiased. He has his own ideas about rates of inflation, which lead him to feel that the calculated IRR may be a few points high. As an expert in the prospects of the business in question, he believes this facility will operate at a full schedule for the next few years and so he is satisfied with this aspect of the analysis.

The division has a fixed amount of capital to allocate, similar to that of the previous year.[5] At the critical meeting on the project in question, it is learned that the requests for mandatory projects are larger than usual.[6] Considering the funds remaining, if all discretionary projects were ranked by their IRR, this particular project would not make it. On the other hand, division management likes to approve requests from this plant manager because he is cautious in his proposals and is very effective in other respects. The project is approved but it is noted that implementation may be delayed.

---

[5] If division management wanted to, they could increase this capital allocation by making a good case for it. But this would require a major effort and would use up some of the division's "credit" with corporate headquarters. Division management feels it has more pressing problems to address.

[6] Requests for mandatory projects are not accompanied by financial analyses. They are generally approved after consideration of the project's nature and its cost, the priorities developed at the plant level, and the reputation of the plant and its management.

Exhibit 2   **Distribution of 12 Firms by Measure of Investment Worth Used for Smaller Projects**

Measures Calculated	Number of Firms	Measure Primarily Relied Upon	Number of Firms
IRR*	5	IRR, with both variable project life and price escalation	5
Simplified IRR and simple payback†	5	IRR, with fixed life and/or escalation	3
Simple payback only‡	2	Simple payback	4

* NPV and other DCF measures were also calculated but not referred to in discussion or in other documents.

† Of the five, one approximated the DCF calculation so it could be easily hand calculated, and all required use of a single economic life for all projects and/or a single uniform price escalation rate.

‡ Or a return on investment directly based on simple payback.

III. Financial Analysis of Projects

As the example suggests, many of the firms studied severely simplify the DCF evaluation of projects and, in any case, rely primarily on simple payback. (It should be kept in mind that projects of the kind under study have, as suggested in the hypothetical example, very simple benefit streams.) Exhibit 2 summarizes the observations at the twelve firms.

Not surprisingly, perhaps, sensitivity analysis for various potential risks is typically avoided. For example, reduced production because of weak sales or changes in the production process could affect the benefit stream from an energy-saving project. However, only a few of the firms studied have considered such contingencies. Two chemical firms retroactively studied the performance of energy-conservation projects associated with organic chemicals and found that, while engineering analyses proved fairly accurate in a narrow sense, benefits and economic lives tended to be less than predicted because of unanticipated changes in production rates and technology. These insights were not formally incorporated into the financial analyses.

The practice at most firms is thus to keep both the financial analysis of smaller projects, and the process of communicating this analysis to decisionmakers, extremely simple [7]. Decisions are then based on the primary quantitative measure from the analysis supplemented by informal adjustments made in the minds of decisionmakers. The analysis of large projects was more detailed in the few cases we saw. For example, detailed DCF analyses were carried out, often including sensitivity analyses with respect to parameters like rates of price escalation.

IV. Rates of Return for Project Approval

Many firms have internally published, or *de jure,* hurdle rates for project approval. These rates may or may not correspond to the apparent, or *de facto,* rates that empirically characterize projects actually approved. At some firms the *de jure* rates were described as being out of date or intended only for a first cut, to help decide if preparation of a project proposal merits more effort.

At some firms, however, the *de jure* and *de facto* rates are essentially the same. These firms have a decentralized capital budgeting process: Project decisions are made locally, with heavy reliance on a uniform rate of return criterion. Capital requirements are forwarded to higher management and, although there may be restraints at a given time or for a given business, the capital is typically provided. We call these flexible-budgeting firms.

A different approach to capital budgeting is followed at many firms. At these firms, project approval is not based on an announced or assumed hurdle rate. While people are typically aware, as suggested in the hypothetical example, of hurdle rates characterizing past decisions, the critical approval decision is based on competition among projects for an essentially fixed sum. We call firms employing this procedure capital-rationing firms.

The *de facto* rates reported here are all based on a uniform calculation of (nominal-dollar) internal rate of return (IRR).[7] For this purpose, we examined projects at flagship plants associated with relatively solid product lines with stable process technology and with well-established lives. For almost all the firms there were data on such projects. These projects roughly share the financial risks of the firm as a whole.

De facto hurdle rates for project approval were determined in part from the data on proposed and approved projects. Almost all projects in the sample were completed, approved, or expected to be approved. In other words, very few projects were being considered (and were included in the sample) which were not expected to be approved. The IRR distribution of these projects is very broad, but it has a few projects with IRRs that are close to the lowest IRR for an approved project. Hence, this lowest IRR is taken as the apparent hurdle rate. In addition, apparent hurdle rates were determined from information on projects specifically identified at the firm as barely acceptable. Hurdle rate results from these

---

[7] For comparative purposes it is important to choose project parameters that reflect the expectations at the firm, rather than mimicking the overly simple financial analyses sometimes made there. For example, in the cases of organic chemical products mentioned in the previous section, the adjustments suggested by the firms' studies were incorporated.

Exhibit 3   **Investment Hurdle Rates by Project Size:**
Flexible-Budgeting and Capital-Rationing Firms

	Hurdle Rate Range* (percent)		Number in Sample (firms, projects)	
	Flexible Budgeting Firms	Capital Rationing Firms	Flexible Budgeting Firms	Capital Rationing Firms
Size of Project †				
Small	14–17	35–60	(4,197)	(6,96)
Medium	14–17	25–40	(4,19)	(6,73)
Large	—	15–25‡	—	(3,12)

* Internal rate of return, discounting nominal dollar flows.
† See Exhibit 1 for definitions.
‡ Based on a very small project sample; return on least profitable project is shown.

two sources of information were consistent (within roughly ±5 percentage points in the rate of return).[8]

V. Hurdle Rate Results

Our information is consistent with the expectation that all twelve firms
had *de facto* hurdle rates for large projects close to the corporate average
cost of capital (about 15%).[9] Only four firms gave this treatment to the
smaller projects, however. For the other eight firms, hurdle rates for small
and/or medium projects were high. Among the eight, all six providing
information on small projects show very high hurdle rates (35% to 60%)
and all six providing information on medium projects show moderately
high hurdle rates (25% to 40%). These data are summarized in Exhibit 3.
    The firms studied thus fall into two classes:

(i)   firms with uniform *de facto* hurdle rates near the corporate average
      cost of capital for all discretionary projects, *i.e.*, flexible-budgeting
      firms, and

[8] Another issue in hurdle rate determination is possible time dependence. Were they rising
because of the 1982 recession? Were they falling because the best energy-conservation
projects had already been selected? Data from four firms that extended several years into the
past and/or were planned several years into the future showed no significant change in
hurdle rates. Interviews confirmed that there was no major change in project opportunities
and that the firms' financial practices were not changing rapidly, except for delays in capital
spending associated with the 1982 recession. These delays were not reflected in the
information we collected.

[9] Two of these firms showed us their methods of calculating cost of capital; they correspond
closely to textbook procedures. See, for example, Van Horne [10].

(ii)   firms with *de facto* hurdle rates that are high for small projects, moderately high for medium projects, and fairly near the cost of capital for large projects.

We found through interviews that most of the second group of firms explicitly employ capital rationing at lower levels of decisionmaking. That is, fixed sums are allocated to those groups, below the level of CEO and Board, that make decisions about capital projects, with the result that much less discretionary investment is undertaken in smaller projects than would be justified by conventional analysis. The rest of the firms in this group deny that they impose capital rationing, but at the plant/division level perceptions and behavior conform to capital rationing. The sample data suggest that the rationing of capital is most severe at plant and division levels, but, surprisingly, is often severe even at the level of the corporate investment committee (which typically makes the effective decision on medium-sized projects).

The results from our sample of firms are consistent with survey results that half or more of large firms impose capital rationing on all projects [4], [7]. Our new finding is that capital rationing, as practiced, has an especially severe impact on smaller projects.

Not surprisingly, financial analysis of smaller projects at flexible-budgeting firms tends to be more sophisticated than at capital-rationing firms. All of the former employ DCF analysis and essential attention is given to details in the calculation. At only one of the eight capital-rationing firms is a DCF analysis with essential details carried out.

Although the firms cannot be named, general observations can be made. The flexible-budgeting firms are all relatively strong financially. From comments made at a few capital-rationing firms, it seemed that interest coverage might be negatively correlated with the effective hurdle rate. It is, roughly. A linear regression (using data from nine firms) of hurdle rates, HR, for small projects (in percent) against interest coverage (four-year average), IC, yielded $HR = 60 - 5 \times IC$, with $r^2 \approx 0.5$. (The hurdle rates also correlate rather well with other financial characteristics of the firms.) The reason for such a correlation is probably related to inhibitions on capital spending resulting from the difficulties that firms with poorer ratings face in raising capital, as discussed subsequently.

VI. Possible Rationales for Severe Capital Rationing for Smaller Projects

The high hurdle rates for smaller projects do not primarily reflect greater uncertainty about return on investment for smaller projects at capital-rationing firms. Such concerns have, to a large degree, been taken into account:

(i)   Engineering data on the projects (*i.e.*, within their design context) is relatively accurate. This has been confirmed by retrospective studies of projects at several of the firms.

(ii)   The disadvantages of projects associated with less favored plants and product lines, with rapidly changing products and processes, and with short-lived types of equipment were compensated for in the hurdle-rate determinations. The sample of low-risk projects at flagship plants defines the hurdle rates for almost all the firms. Without doubt, incomplete financial analysis of smaller projects at most capital-rationing firms leads to some discounting by management of even the least risky projects. This does not appear, however, to be a major consideration.

There was no suggestion from our interviewees at capital-rationing firms that smaller projects at better plants and product lines suffer from a degree of uncertainty that would justify subjecting them to higher hurdle rates. Instead, as discussed at several interviews, *all* cost-cutting projects in the firm's major businesses suffer from the same downside uncertainty as the firm as a whole: the risk of low capacity utilization, especially during recessions. The evidence indicates, then, that limitations in capital budgeting procedures, rather than unusual risk levels, are the direct cause of high hurdle rates for smaller projects. What then is the cause of these capital budgeting procedures?

Two explanations were suggested at interviews at capital-rationing firms, both of which have merit:

(i)   The shadow cost of capital is much higher than the average cost of capital to the firm. Under this explanation, capital rationing is imposed on firms by outside suppliers of capital.

(ii)   Top corporate management is preoccupied with many other responsibilities and assigns low priority to cost cutting. Also top management feels unable to decentralize or delegate open-ended responsibility for investment in smaller projects, especially since information and decision costs for smaller projects are relatively high.

With respect to the first explanation, mature businesses typically provide for plant and equipment expenditures from their stream of earnings. For most of the capital-rationing firms the earnings would not be sufficient to allow expeditious implementation of all profitable cost-cutting projects. Our interviews showed that many perceived it would be potentially damaging for their firm to attempt to raise additional equity funds, and that lenders would resist the raising of debt money beyond some debt-equity or interest-coverage ratios (independent of the profitability of the investments). For example, rating services might draw negative conclusions about an attempt to raise additional capital, with the result that the firm could no longer borrow in certain markets and its bonds could not be purchased by certain institutional investors. The sense that an equity offering would, in particular, reduce stock prices is confirmed by a general analysis of public offerings of industrial stocks by Asquith and Mullins [2].

Interviewees perceived the effect to be strongly differentiated, however, depending on the general purpose of the investment: Debt *can* be raised by the capital-rationing firms without unacceptably weakening their financial rating for certain major acquisitions. In the recent past, many of the firms in the study have made major acquisitions. For added investment to modernize existing plants,. however, the cost of capital is perceived to be very high.

Let us turn to the second explanation. For firms in a poor financial position, a perception that characterized a majority of the capital-rationing firms, arrangements for any financing from outside sources would be extraordinarily time consuming for top management. Given their priorities, top management often copes with productivity improvement by allocating relatively small fixed sums to divisions and plants. That leaves them the time to carefully analyze the large projects and the modes of financing them.

A related perspective was offered at some interviews. Many energy-conservation projects' lack of impact on production capacity, product quality, and product flexibility is perceived as a reason for giving them a low priority. Cost-cutting projects can be postponed, it is thought, without losing much of the opportunity, whereas market opportunities associated with new or improved products or increased production may be altogether fleeting.

How important are the smaller projects being postponed, or neglected altogether, at capital-rationing firms? There was enough information from six of the firms to roughly answer this question. Smaller energy-conservation projects (*i.e.*, those decided below the CEO-Board level) accounted for 2% to 15% of total capital spending by these six firms. The highest fractions in this range were associated with flexible-budgeting firms or firms in very high energy-to-value-added businesses and the lowest fractions were associated with capital-rationing firms with somewhat lower energy costs. The average difference in these energy-conservation expenditures between flexible-budgeting and capital-rationing firms was roughly 10% of total plant and equipment expenditures.[10] In addition, the estimated returns for these smaller projects were substantially higher than for the average project.[11] One can infer that the profits being postponed by capital-rationing firms could be substantial.

---

[10] Of the six firms, four practice capital rationing, with two each in the high and lower energy to value-added categories. One flexible-budgeting firm is in each of the two energy to value-added categories.

[11] There are three principal reasons why there were so many highly profitable energy conservation projects: (i) rapidly increased prices for energy, (ii) dramatic improvements in available energy-related technology such as control systems, and (iii) qualitative changes in the management of energy projects (*e.g.*, assignment of responsibilities, improved engineering capabilities, metering, and new cost accounting procedures). Given fixed energy prices, this opportunity might be largely, but not completely, used up in five years at a flexible-budgeting firm. Other categories of small projects also offer high profitability for some of the same reasons, *e.g.*, automation based on new microprocessors.

The author concludes that capital rationing is not, as some might suspect, a rational scheme for focusing effort on the most profitable investment opportunities. The evidence on the high returns of smaller projects shows that the average large project is less profitable than the smaller projects being neglected by capital-rationing firms. Capital rationing is a bureaucratic process, which was not responsive at the time of our study to the substantial opportunities for profits offered by small and medium-sized energy-related projects.

VII. Suggestions for Improved Capital Budgeting

We will focus on suggestions for efficient involvement of top management in decisions on smaller projects.

(i)   Information on Individual Projects: Communication is difficult at large firms and people at all levels are busy, so the financial analysis of a smaller project and the reporting of it must be kept simple and intuitively clear. It should include easily digested information on the project's definition and input parameters, as well as internal evidence that the analysis has been done correctly and consistently with that of other projects.

(ii) Analysis of Groups of Projects: The second suggestion is less familiar. For those firms that feel unable to decentralize investment decisionmaking with uniform hurdle rates, we suggest that top management solicit from their staff, for selected plants and product lines, ambitious modernization proposals consisting of coherent combinations of smaller projects. The idea is to elicit a proposal for a program of smaller projects whose total cost is large enough to command the careful attention of top management on a par with large projects costing perhaps $100 million or more. Not only would such an approach make it possible for top management to evaluate the potential of smaller projects, but also it would free the people who define projects, like Bill Johnson of our hypothetical example, to consider competing projects of different size on their merits (without being biased by considering where the decision would be made) and to define a coherent program of projects rather than using a piecemeal approach.

It is essential that such modernization programs be solicited by top management and that the means of analyzing and presenting the programs be well developed.[12] Ad hoc efforts from below are not likely to succeed.

---

[12] Helpful software (ENVEST) has been developed by M.W. Reid at the Alliance to Save Energy.

VIII. Summary

Results have been presented from an in-depth study of capital budgeting for discretionary projects at twelve firms in the process industries. They indicate that, while discounted cash flow techniques are nominally used at most firms, it is important to ask whether the calculations are carried out incorporating essential details and whether it is a DCF criterion or simple payback that is actually relied on. For their smaller projects, most firms in the sample severely simplify their DCF analysis and/or rely primarily on simple payback.

Results (in eight of the twelve firms studied) also indicate that project approval at many firms follows different criteria depending on the locus of the decision. The effect of this is that smaller projects are subject to high *de facto* hurdle rates. At these firms only large projects are observed to face a hurdle rate near the cost of capital. Only four of the twelve firms studied impose uniform hurdle rates regardless of the locus of decisionmaking (or the size of project). Not surprisingly, firms with thorough financial analysis of smaller projects tend to be the same firms that do not discriminate against smaller projects.

These results suggest the importance of asking how capital budgeting practices differ at the plant, division, investment committee, and CEO and Board levels. A large firm's capital budgeting practices for smaller projects can be indicative of the firm's effectiveness in using information and skills from its lower levels.

References

1. Alliance to Save Energy, *Industrial Investment in Energy Efficiency: Opportunities, Management Practices, and Tax Incentives,* Washington, DC (July 1983).
2. P. Asquith and D.W. Mullins, Jr., "Equity Issues and Offering Dilution," *Journal of Financial Economics* (Jan./Feb. 1986), pp. 61–89.
3. J.M. Fremgen, "Capital Budgeting Practices: A Survey," *Management Accounting,* U.S. (May 1973), pp. 19–25.
4. L.J. Gitman and J.R. Forrester, Jr., "A Survey of Capital Budgeting Techniques Used by Major U.S. Firms," *Financial Management* (Fall 1977), pp. 66–71.
5. C. Gurnani, "Capital Budgeting: Theory and Practice," *Engineering Economist,* 30 (Fall 1984), pp. 19–46.
6. J.W. Petty, D.F. Scott, and M.M. Bird, "The Capital Expenditure Decision-Making Process of Large Corporations," *Engineering Economist,* 20 (Spring 1975), pp. 159–172.
7. E.M. Rudden, "The Misuse of a Sound Investment Tool," *The Wall Street Journal* (Nov. 1, 1982), p. 30.
8. L.D. Schall, G.L. Sundem, and W.R. Geijsbeek, Jr., "Survey and Analysis of Capital Budgeting Methods," *Journal of Finance* (March 1978), pp. 281–287.

9. D.F. Scott, Jr., and J.W. Petty, "Capital Budgeting Practices in Large American Firms: A Retrospective Analysis and Synthesis," *The Financial Review,* 19 (May 1984), pp. 111–123.

10. J.C. Van Horne, *Financial Management and Policy,* 5th ed., Englewood Cliffs, NJ, Prentice-Hall, 1980.

Questions

1. Describe the relationship between project size and level of decision-making authority in the typical manufacturing company.

2. Bill Johnson, as described in Section II, is part of an energy-conservation team. Bill is the sponsor of a capital project to cut energy costs at a heater.
    a. Identify the occupations of the people Bill interacts with as he pursues implementation of the project.
    b. Provide a critique of Bill's financial analysis of the project.

3. Which of the following capital-budgeting techniques do the 12 manufacturers use: payback period, internal rate of return, net present value, or profitability index? Explain.

4. The author divides the sample companies into two groups: *flexible-budgeting* firms and *capital-rationing* firms. What is the meaning of these terms?

5. What are the negative consequences of capital rationing? Why does capital rationing exist in some companies?

13

Capital Budgeting Practices in Large American Firms: A Retrospective Analysis and Synthesis

David F. Scott, Jr. and
J. William Petty II

For many years the procedures used by large corporations to evaluate capital-expenditure proposals have been identified and discussed in the financial management literature. This interest in the investment-analysis practices of firms is understandable, given the importance of such decisions to the financial health of the business unit. More detailed reasons that underlie why a firm should carefully select its capital projects are well-known and have been presented in several places [3]. There is no need to belabor them here.

The concern of academic researchers for the theory of capital investment decisions coupled with attentiveness to analysis procedures used by firms produced a stream of articles during the 1960s and 1970s that dealt with the integration of investment theory into investment practice. Such materials comprise a meaningful portion of this study. The objective of this paper is to present a synthesis of several important surveys into corporate capital budgeting practices. We summarize a series of earlier studies that document the practice of capital budgeting analysis by firms. Definite trends and disparities with normative prescriptions suggested by the current state of the financial management literature can be identified. Details concerning the target populations, sample sizes, and response rates for the major studies discussed in this review are summarized in the Appendix.

David F. Scott, Jr. and J. William Petty II, "Capital Budgeting Practices in Large American Firms: A Retrospective Analysis and Synthesis," *The Financial Review* (March 1984): 111–123. Reprinted with permission from the Eastern Finance Association.

At the time of this writing, David F. Scott, Jr. was affiliated with the University of Central Florida and J. William Petty II was affiliated with Abilene Christian University.

Goals, Organization, and Stages in the Investment Analysis Process

The discounting models generally purported by academics as being efficient in the selection of capital projects rely on the assumption that the firm should maximize the market value of its common shares. It is of direct interest, then, to examine the responses of corporate executives to questions concerning their perceptions of the objective(s) of financial management.

In personal interviews with eight medium to large firms conducted during 1969, Mao [12, p. 352] found that managers in general did *not* explicitly state that the objective of the firm was to maximize the market value of its common equity. This observation was substantiated by Petty, Scott, and Bird [17] in a survey of "Fortune 500" firms, where managements considered several *other* goals to be more important than the maximization of common stock price. The respondents in this 1975 study identified the following three goals as being most important to their firms [17, pp. 159–160]:

1. maximization of the percent return on total asset investment,

2. achievement of a desired growth rate in earnings per share,

3. maximization of aggregate dollar earnings.

Stock price maximization followed (lagged behind) the above objectives in order of importance. Operationally, the finance function in large enterprises seems to be multi-directed. Osteryoung's results [15] buttress this conclusion. Also focusing on the Fortune 500 population, Osteryoung reported in 1973 that 95 percent of his respondents used two or more goals in making capital investment decisions and 70.5 percent of the firms used three or more goals. In short, managements are operationally oriented, favoring goals that can be translated into measurable targets. Maximizing common stock price is an elusive goal compared to the more tangible nature of other objectives such as maximizing the percent return on investment. Additionally, during periods of depressed or steady stock prices, it might hold no appeal for either internal control or incentive purposes.

We next present the previously reported findings that relate to project origination and the remaining stages of the capital budgeting process. It is usual for firms to distinguish between replacement expenditures and major expenditures [7], or in a similar sense between proposals related to existing product lines as opposed to new product lines [17]. Istvan's study [7] of forty-eight large corporations, conducted during 1959, is the earliest empirical work analyzed in this review. Istvan noted that replacement proposals tend to be initiated by operating personnel. A full 79 percent of his participating firms stated that replacement proposals were originated either by operating personnel or division or plant managers. On the other hand, "major proposals" tend to flow from top

Table 1   **Difficulties Associated with the Stages of the Capital Budgeting Process**

Stage	Stages Considered to Be Most Difficult	
	Fremgen[a]	Gitman and Forrester[b]
Project definition and cash flow estimation	44%	64%
Financial analysis and project selection	12	15
Project implementation and review	44	20

[a] [5, p. 38].
[b] [6, p. 68].

management [7, p.10]. Likewise, in Petty, Scott, and Bird [17, p. 161], 30 percent of the participating firms indicated that more than 39 percent of project requests for existing product lines originate at the divisional office and plant levels. This response compared to 7 percent for a similar volume of proposals flowing from the central office level. For new product-line proposals, this latter figure rose to 13 percent with a corresponding reduction in those requests beginning at the divisional and plant levels.

There is evidence that academics spend a disproportionate (unjustified) amount of time on a particular stage of the capital budgeting process considered less difficult than others by managers. Table 1 is prepared from the works conducted by Fremgen [5] in 1971 and Gitman and Forrester in 1976 [6]. Fremgen's study involved 177 usable responses (a 71 percent response rate) to his questionnaire, while the Gitman and Forrester study received 110 responses (38.4 percent). Note that project definition and cash flow estimation is considered the "most difficult" aspect of the capital budgeting process. The financial analysis and project selection stage, which receives the most attention in the literature, is considered the *least* difficult of the three stages listed in Table 1. It is also noticeable that the more recent of these two studies (Gitman and Forrester [6]) found the initial stage of project definition and cash flow estimation to be notably more difficult. Sixty-four percent of the respondents ranked this initial phase as the most difficult stage in the Gitman and Forrester study, compared with 44 percent in Fremgen's effort. Concern on the part of executives over the increased uncertainty in the business environment may be having an impact. Specifically, such factors as inflation, energy shortages, or volatility on international currency markets might be impounded in these later responses.

Evaluation Methods

Five techniques are widely used in industrial practice to estimate the attractiveness of a capital project to the firm. Three of these are termed "theoretically correct" by academics; they include the net present value,

Table 2   Use of Discounted Cash Flow Techniques for
Evaluating at Least Some Prospective Expenditures

Year Published	Percent of Firms	Reference
1960	30	Miller [13]
1961	10[a]	Istvan [7]
1970	67[b]	Mao [12]
1970	61	Williams [21]
1972	57	Klammer [10]
1973	76	Fremgen [5]
1975	94	Brigham [1]
1975	66	Petry [16]
1975	58[c]	Petty, Scott, Bird [17]
1977	66[d]	Gitman and Forrester [6]
1978	86	Schall, Sundem, Geijsbeek [19]

[a] Only five of forty-eight firms

[b] Six of eight firms

[c] Based on *most* important technique used in the firm's investment decision process as it relates to new product lines. This probably understates the total percentage of respondents using *some* time-adjusted techniques.

[d] Based on *primary* evaluation technique used in the firm's investment decision process. This also probably understates the total percentage of respondents using *some* time-adjusted techniques.

internal rate of return, and profitability index discounting models. Alternatively, the average rate of return and payback period methods are labeled "theoretically incorrect." Of course variations on these themes abound, but by and large, these metrics are the ones commonly adopted by firms that attempt to compute expected benefits from proposed capital expenditures.

Table 2 is a chronological tabulation derived from several often-cited surveys of corporate capital budgeting practices. For the most part it identifies the percentage of survey respondents that stated their firm uses discounting (time-adjusted) methods to analyze *some* projects. Two exceptions are the studies by Gitman and Forrester [6] and Petty, Scott, and Bird [17]. In these studies the percentages reflect the extent that discounting methods comprise the *primary* evaluation technique used by the participating companies. In [6] and [17] the percentages are most likely biased downward.

The extensive use of discounting models by large American corporations is evident from an inspection of Table 2. The early investigations by Istvan [7, 8] and Miller [13] reported that 10 and 30 percent respectively of their responding firms employed the time-adjusted models to some extent. Studies published after 1969 have consistently noted that at least 57 percent of the participating companies use discounting techniques in their capital budgeting processes.

The movement towards the use of more sophisticated project evaluation procedures by major organizations in unequivocal. A nagging question, though, concerns the extent of such use.The recent study by Schall, Sundem, and Geijsbeek [19] is provocative in this regard. These authors surveyed 424 firms. A total of 189 responses was received, giving a response rate of 46.4 percent. It was found that while 86 percent of the firms used either the internal rate of return or net present value models in their procedures, only 16 percent used such discounting techniques without also using the payback period or average rate of return metrics [19, p. 282]. This same tendency to use theoretically incorrect models as supplementary or back-up tools has been reported elsewhere [17, p. 163]. It seems that we know little of the reasoning behind management's reluctance to abandon the cruder methods of estimating project worth.

In Table 3 the most-favored and least-favored evaluation methods as indicated by the various surveys are displayed. Two conclusions are offered. First, managements today emphatically prefer the internal rate of return technique over the alternatives. In seven of the ten studies that identified individual methods, the internal rate of return model was the most-favored. The Klammer study [10] lumped all discounting models together. Thus, no specific inference is possible from that paper. Of the studies noted in Table 3 that have been published after 1969, only one [19] reported a more popular technique than the internal rate of return. Second, recent evidence shows that the profitability index and net present value models are the least popular capital budgeting techniques. This fact indicates, again, that non-discounting models like the payback period and average rate of return are still prevalently used in combination with the

Table 3   The Most and Least Popular Evaluation Methods

Year Published	Most Popular	Least Popular	Reference
1960	PP[a]	DCF[b]	Miller [13]
1961	ARR	DCF and MAPI formula	Istvan [7]
1970	IRR	NPV and PI	Mao [12]
1970	IRR	PI	Williams [21]
1972	DCF	PP, PP reciprocal and urgency	Klammer [10]
1973	IRR	PI	Fremgen [5]
1975	IRR	PI	Brigham [1]
1975	IRR	NPV[c]	Petry [16]
1975	IRR	PI	Petty, Scott, Bird [17]
1977	IRR	PI	Gitman and Forrester [6]
1978	PP	NPV[c]	Schall, Sundem, Geijsbeek [19]

[a] The abbreviations used are as follows: PP is payback period, DCF is discounted cash flow techniques, ARR is average rate of return, IRR is internal rate of return, NPV is net present value, PI is profitability index.

[b] When DCF is used in this table, the survey did not distinguish among the various time-adjusted evaluation methods.

[c] The PI was not identified as a possible response in the questionnaire format.

Table 4 **Determination of the Discount Rate**

Method	Percent Using	Reference
Cost of a specific source of funds	26 17	Schall, Sundem, Geijsbeek [19] Petty, Scott, Bird [17]
Weighted average cost of capital	61 46 30	Brigham [1] [19] [17]
Historical rates of return (i.e., past experience)	20 13 10	[19] [17] [1]
Management determined target rate of return	40	[17]

time-adjusted methods — especially the internal rate of return. Despite the difficulties associated with the internal rate of return model, as viewed by academics, it is very popular with practitioners. Management seems unconcerned with (1) this model's violation of the value additivity principle, (2) the fact that its reinvestment rate assumption is something other than the market-determined cost of capital, and (3) the fact that under certain conditions it generates multiple rates of return for a single project.

Required Rates of Return

Use of a minimum return standard is as necessary to the operation of a capital budgeting system as is a method for calculating expected returns. Curiously, the bulk of the many surveys dealing with the capital budgeting process avoid questions aimed at understanding how the firm arrives at its required rate of return. Table 4 summarizes some of the available data.

The evidence is strong that large firms *do* employ required rates of return in their capital budgeting procedures [4]. Schall, Sundem, and Geijsbeek reported that 74 percent of their respondents used some type of discount rate [19, p. 283]. In the Petty, Scott, and Bird study 84 percent of the responding firms used at least one required rate of return [17, p. 169]. The evidence is also strong that across firms a variety of methods are employed to determine the discount rate.

In Table 4 it can be seen that from 30 to 61 percent of respondents in different surveys stated they compute a weighted average cost of capital. This technique dominates the other procedures reported as being in prevalent use. When a weighted cost of funds is used, most firms compute it on an after-tax basis [16, p. 62]. Little evidence is available to shed light on the specific weighting schemes used. Brigham [1, p. 20] mentioned that balance sheet figures (book weights) were used by a wide margin over other approaches. He could not discern, however, whether the weights represented *actual* book values at the time of the computation or some type of *target* capital structure weights.

Judgment still plays a major role in the assessment of capital costs. For example, historical rates of return and management-determined target rates continue to be popular "solutions" to this problem. One reason for this reluctance to accept a cost of capital computation might be concern over the wide range of values for the cost of capital that an analyst obtains when he or she uses different estimation models.

Recognition of Risk

The final aspect of the capital budgeting process that we consider in this review is that of risk assessment. Table 5 indicates the percent of firms which explicitly consider risk in their analysis of capital projects. Note that the data are not strictly comparable across the various studies. The 39 percent figure reported in the Klammer study [10] represents only those firms that use a *formal* method for considering risk. The percentages associated with the other studies in Table 5 are indicative of both formal and informal risk assessment. Three of the six studies generated a clustering of responses in the 67 to 71 percent range. It seems safe, then, to conclude that in excess of two-thirds of major U.S. firms are overtly concerned with project risk.

Table 6 identifies specific methods of risk adjustment in use. While the responses certainly vary, it is evident that the most common technique for considering risk is the risk-adjusted discount rate approach. This same conclusion was reached by Mao in his interview study [12, p. 356]. Other popular methods for considering risk include (1) changing the required payback period for a particular project and (2) application of probability factors to forecasted cash flows.

The surveys exhibit wide disparities concerning the payback period adjustment approach. Presumably, higher risk projects must "beat" a shorter payback period to be included in the firm's capital budget. Three of the surveys reported a rather low usage rate for this method (10 to 13

Table 5   **Explicit Consideration of Project Risk**

Year Published	Percent Considering Risk	Reference
1972	39[a]	Klammer [10]
1973	67	Fremgen [5]
1973	58	Brigham and Pettway [2]
1975	71	Petry [16]
1977	71	Gitman and Forrester [6]
1978	96[b]	Schall, Sundem, Geijsbeek [19]

[a] This percentage reflects only those firms that use a specific formal method for assessing risk.

[b] In this study, 36 percent of the respondents indicated use of a quantitative technique for assessing risk. The other 60 percent represents subjective adjustments.

Table 6 Risk Adjustment Methods

Method	Percent Using	Reference
Risk-adjusted discount rate	90	Schall, Sundem, Geijsbeek [19]
	58	Petry [16]
	54	Fremgen [5]
	43	Gitman and Forrester [6]
	37[a]	Petty, Scott, and Bird [17]
	21	Klammer [10]
	15[b]	Brigham and Pettway [2]
Changing the payback period	61[a]	[17]
	40	[2]
	27	[16]
	13	[6]
	10	[10]
	10	[19]
Adjusting cash flows by use of quantitative probability factors	32	[5]
	27	[6]
	25	[19]
	13	[10]
Sensitivity analysis	55[b]	[2]
	10	[19]
Simulation	27[a]	[17]

[a] Based on the sum of categories labeled "frequently" and "always" in this study.

[b] Based on the sum of categories labeled "primary" and "secondary" in this study.

Appendix A A Summary of Capital Budgeting Surveys

Author and Reference	Population Sampled
[1] Brigham	Selected financial executives and participants in executive development courses
[2] Brigham and Pettway	Electric utilities on Compustat public utility file
[5] Fremgen	*Dun and Bradstreet's Reference Book of Corporate Managements*
[6] Gitman and Forrester	Firms identified in *Forbes* which experienced significant stock price appreciation and capital expenditures
[8] Istvan	Selected large firms; all within the ten largest in their respective industries
[9] Kim	*Dun and Bradstreet Million Dollar Directory 1975;* all firms were in the machinery industry
[11] Klammer	Manufacturing firms on Compustat annual industrial file
[12] Mao	Selected large and medium firms
[13] Miller	*Fortune* 500 and American Institute of Management "Manual of Excellently Managed Companies"
[14] Neuhauser and Viscione	*Fortune* 500
[15] Osteryoung	*Fortune* 500
[16] Petry	*Fortune* 500, and each *Fortune* 50 list of Retailing, Transportation, and Utilities
[17] Petty, Scott, and Bird	*Fortune* 500
[18] Petty and Bowlin	Firms from membership in Financial Management Association
[19] Schall, Sundem, and Geijsbeek	Compustat annual industrial file with firms exceeding certain size and capital expenditure levels
[20] Viscione and Neuhauser	*Fortune* Second 500
[21] Williams	*Fortune* 500 plus selected small firms

[a] n.a. is not applicable

percent), so its actual adoption by large firms might either be waning or was overstated in some earlier studies [2, 17].

More agreement is found concerning the application of probability distributions to forecasted cash flows. About one-fourth of major companies seem to use this method. Moreover, it can be seen in Table 6 that simulation and sensitivity analysis are coming into their own as risk assessment techniques.

Summary

We have tried to provide a balanced synthesis of previous research relating to capital budgeting practices of large American firms. In studying this prior research from a chronological perspective, a definite trend becomes apparent. Corporate managements are gradually coming to use more sophisticated and theoretically sound approaches in their capital budgeting analyses. Several other conclusions can be drawn. First, the principal financial objective of large companies is the firm's return on total

Sample Size	Responses	Response Rate	Year Published
n.a.[a]	33	n.a.	1975
116	53	46	1973
250	177	71	1973
268	103	38	1977
n.a.	48	n.a.	1961
349	114	33	1979
369	184	50	1972, 1973
n.a.	8	n.a.	1970
200	127	64	1960
500	174	35	1973
137	94	69	1973
550	284	52	1975
500	109	22	1975
500	227	45	1976
424	189	45	1978
500	146	29	1974
147	100	68	1970

asset investment. Second, the initiation of new projects continues to be a bottom-up process. Third, the internal rate of return method has unequivocally moved into a preferred position *vis-a-vis* other evaluation techniques. The payback period, however, is still viewed as a strong supplementary tool. Fourth, management's concept of risk aligns reasonably well with theory; still, the application of this concept proves difficult from a practical basis. Finally, investment hurdle rates are regularly used in making accept-reject decisions, with the primary types being a *management-determined* target rate of return and a weighted cost of capital.

References

[1] Brigham, Eugene F. "Hurdle Rates for Screening Capital Expenditure Proposals." *Financial Management* (Autumn 1975): 17–26.

[2] ———, and Richard H. Pettway. "Capital Budgeting by Utilities." *Financial Management* (Autumn 1973): 11–22.

[3] Dean, Joel. "Measuring the Productivity of Capital." *Harvard Business Review* (January-February 1954): 120–9. Reprinted in Edward J. Mock. *Financial Decision-Making,* pp. 385–400. Scranton: International Textbook Co., 1967.

[4] Donaldson, Gordon. "Strategic Hurdle Rates for Investments." *Harvard Business Review* (March-April 1972): 50–58.

[5] Fremgen, James. "Capital Budgeting Practices: A Survey." *Management Accounting* (May 1973): 19–25. Reprinted in William J. Serraino et al. *Frontiers of Financial Management,* 2d ed., pp. 25–39. Cincinnati: South-Western Publishing Co., 1976.

[6] Gitman, Lawrence J., and John R. Forrester, Jr. "A Survey of Capital Budgeting Techniques Used by Major U.S. Firms." *Financial Management* (Fall 1977): 66–71.

[7] Istvan, Donald F. *Capital-Expenditure Decisions: How They Are Made in Large Corporations.* Bloomington, Indiana: Bureau of Business Research, Indiana University, 1961.

[8] ———. "The Economic Evaluation of Capital Expenditures." *Journal of Business* (January 1961): 45–51.

[9] Kim, Suk H. "Capital Budgeting Practices in Large Corporations and Their Impact on Overall Profitability." *Baylor Business Studies* (November-December 1978): 48–66.

[10] Klammer, Thomas. "Empirical Evidence of the Adoption of Sophisticated Capital Budgeting Techniques." *Journal of Business* (July 1972): 387–97.

[11] ———. "The Association of Capital Budgeting Techniques with Firm Performance." *Accounting Review* (April 1973): 353–64.

[12] Mao, James C.T. "Survey of Capital Budgeting: Theory and Practice." *Journal of Finance* (May 1970): 349–60.

[13] Miller, James H. "A Glimpse at Practice in Calculating and Using Return on Investment." *N. A. A. Bulletin* (now *Management Accounting*) (June 1960): 65–76.

[14] Neuhauser, John J., and Jerry A. Viscione. "How Managers Feel About Advanced Capital Budgeting Methods." *Management Review* (November 1973): 16–22. Reprinted in William J. Serraino et al. *Frontiers of Financial Management,* 2d ed., pp. 40–45. Cincinnati: South-Western Publishing Co., 1976.

[15] Osteryoung, Jerome S. "A Survey Into the Goals Used by Fortune's 500 Companies in Capital Budgeting Decisions." *Akron Business and Economic Review* (Fall 1973): 34–35.

[16] Petry, Glenn H. "Effective Use of Capital Budgeting Tools." *Business Horizons* (October 1975): 57–65.

[17] Petty, J. William; David F. Scott, Jr.; and Monroe M. Bird. "The Capital Expenditure Decision-Making Process of Large Corporations." *The Engineering Economist* (Spring 1975): 159–72.

[18] Petty, J. William, and Oswald D. Bowlin. "The Financial Manager and Quantitative Decision Models." *Financial Management* (Winter 1976): 32–41.

[19] Schall, Lawrence D.; Gary L. Sundem; and William R. Geijsbeek, Jr. "Survey and Analysis of Capital Budgeting Methods." *Journal of Finance* (March 1978): 281–7.

[20] Viscione, Jerry, and John Neuhauser. "Capital Expenditure Decisions in Moderately Sized Firms." *Financial Review* (1974): 16–23.

[21] Williams, Ronald B., Jr. "Industry Practice in Allocating Capital Resources." *Managerial Planning* (May-June 1970): 15–22.

Questions

1. According to corporate managers, project definition and cash flow estimation is the most difficult aspect of capital budgeting. Financial analysis and project selection is the least difficult aspect of capital budgeting. Paradoxically, many finance courses spend more time on analysis and selection than on definition and estimation. Explain this paradox.

2. Are corporate managers becoming more sophisticated in their analyses of capital projects? What evidence supports your answer?

3. In your opinion, why do corporate managers tend to prefer internal rate of return more than net present value?

4. Of the methods used in capital budgeting for determining the discount rate, which one is the most appealing theoretically?

5. Risk-adjusted discount rates and changing the payback period are two methods for recognizing risk in capital-budgeting analysis. Describe these two methods.

14

Corporate Strategy and the Capital Budgeting Decision

Alan C. Shapiro

The decade 1974 through 1983 was a dismal one for American business in general. It began with the deepest economic decline since the Depression and ended with national recoveries from back-to-back recessions in the early 1980s. Yet throughout these dark years, 13 companies on the Fortune 500 list of the largest U.S. industrial companies were money-making stars, earning consistently high returns. These firms averaged at least a 20 percent return on shareholders' equity (ROE) over this ten-year span. (To gain some perspective, a dollar invested in 1974 at a compound annual rate of 20 percent would have grown to $6.19 by the end of 1983, a healthy return even after allowing for the effects of inflation.) Moreover, none of these firms' ROE ever dipped below 15 percent during this difficult period.

The 13 were led by a profit superstar, American Home Products, whose ROE not only averaged 29.5 percent during the 1974–83 decade, but also has held above 20 percent for 30 straight years. To appreciate the significance of such a feat, one dollar invested at 20 percent compounded annually would be worth over $237 at the end of 30 years.

What type of firm can achieve such a remarkable record? Far from being the prototypical high-tech firm or a lucky oil company, American Home Products is the low-profile producer of Anacin, Chef Boy-Ar-Dee pasta products, Brach's candy, and Gulden's mustard, in addition to prescription drugs and nondrug products such as cardiovascular drugs, oral contraceptives, and infant formula.

In general, high technology firms were not well represented among the 13, which included just IBM and two pharmaceutical companies, SmithKline Beckman and Merck. IBM, moreover, with an average ROE of 20.5 percent, ranked only 11th out of the 13, far behind such low-tech

Alan C. Shapiro, "Corporate Strategy and the Capital Budgeting Decision," *Midland Corporate Finance Journal* (Spring 1985), 22–36. Reprinted with permission.

At the time of this writing, Alan C. Shapiro was Associate Professor of Finance at the Graduate School of Management of the University of California at Los Angeles.

firms as Dow Jones (26.3%), Kellogg (24.8%), Deluxe Check Printers (24.1%), and Maytag (23.1%). It was even less profitable than a steel company (Worthington Industries—23.9%) and a chemical firm (Nalco Chemical—21.5%).

The demonstrated ability for a firm such as Deluxe Check Printers—a firm on the trailing edge of technology, described as a "buggy whip company threatened with extinction by the 'checkless society'"—consistently to earn such extraordinary returns on invested capital must be due to something more than luck or proficiency at applying sophisticated techniques of investment analysis. That something is the knack for creating positive net present value (NPV) projects, projects with rates of return in excess of the required return. The scarcity of this skill is attested to by the fact that aggregate profits of $68.8 billion for the Fortune 500 in 1983 were, in real terms, 22 percent below the $43.6 billion earned in 1974, a recession year. Keep in mind also that the Fortune 500 have been disciplined savers, re-investing over $300 billion of retained earnings, in their businesses over the ten-year period. This massive reinvestment alone should have produced considerably higher real earnings than 1974's.

Exhibit 1   **13 Stars of the Decade 1974–1983**

Company	Average ROE 1974–1983	Total return to investors 1974–1983*
American Home Products	29.5%	6.6%
Dow Jones	26.3	29.8
Mitchell Energy	26.0	26.4
SmithKline Beckman	25.4	19.7
Kellogg	24.8	13.3
Deluxe Check Printers	24.1	13.4
Worthington Industries	23.9	41.7
Maytag	23.1	14.5
Merck	21.9	3.8
Nalco Chemical	21.5	11.4
IBM	20.5	11.3
Dover	20.3	26.6
Coca-Cola	20.3	2.9
Median total return to investors for the 13:	13.4%	
Median total return to investors for the Fortune 500:	13.6%	

* Total return to investors as calculated by *Fortune*, April 30, 1984. It includes both price appreciation and dividend yield to an investor and assumes that any proceeds from cash dividends, the sale of rights and warrant offerings, and stock received in spinoffs were reinvested at the end of the year in which they were received. The return reported is the average annual return compounded over the ten-year period.

Although the 13 have earned extraordinary returns on share-holders' equity capital, Exhibit 1 shows that returns to the shareholders themselves have been less than earthshaking. This is consistent with the efficient market hypothesis, the idea that prices of traded securities rapidly reflect all currently available information. Since the high return on equity capital earned by the 13 is not news to investors — these firms have consistently been outstanding performers — investors back in 1974 had already incorporated these expectations in their estimations of firm values. This means that a firm's expected high ROE is already "priced out" or capitalized by the market at a rate that reflects the anticipated riskiness of investing in the company's stock. As a result, investors will earn exceptional returns only if the firm turns out to do even better than expected, something that by definition is not possible to predict in advance. The fact that the 13's median annual total return to investors (stock price appreciation plus reinvested dividends) of 13.4 percent is almost identical to the Fortune 500's median return of 13.6 percent indicates that investor expectations about the relative performances of both groups of firms were subsequently borne out.

This illustrates the key distinction between operating in an efficient financial market and operating in product and factor markets that are less than perfectly competitive. One can expect to consistently earn excess returns only in the latter markets; competition will ensure that excess returns in an efficient market are short-lived. However, it is evident from the generally dismal performance of the Fortune 500 that it is no mean trick to take advantage of those product and factor market imperfections that do exist.

This evidence notwithstanding, it is usually taken for granted that positive NPV projects do exist and can be identified using fairly straight-forward techniques. Consequently, the emphasis in most capital budgeting analyses is on estimating and discounting future project cash flows. Projects with positive net present values are accepted; those that fail this test are rejected.

It is important to recognize, however, that selecting positive NPV projects in this way is equivalent to picking under-valued securities on the basis of fundamental analysis. The latter can be done with confidence only if there are financial market imperfections that do not allow asset prices to reflect their equilibrium values. Similarly, the existence of economic rents — excess returns that lead to positive net present values — is the result of monopolistic control over product or factor supplies (i.e., "real market imperfections").

It is the thesis of this article that generating projects likely to yield positive excess returns is at least as important as the conventional quantitative investment analysis. This is the essence of corporate strategy: creating and then taking advantage of imperfections in product and factor markets. Thus, an understanding of the strategies followed by successful firms in exploiting and defending those barriers to entry created by product and factor market imperfections is crucial to any systematic evaluation of investment opportunities. For one thing, it provides a qualitative means of identifying, or ranking, ex ante those projects most likely to have positive net present values. This ranking is useful because constraints of time and money limit the number and range of investment opportunities a given firm is likely to consider.

More important, a good understanding of corporate strategy should help uncover new and potentially profitable projects. Only in theory is a firm fortunate enough to be presented, at no effort or expense on its part, with every available investment opportunity. Perhaps the best way to gain this understanding is to study a medley of firms, spanning a number of industries and nations, that have managed to develop and implement a variety of value-creating investment strategies. This is the basic approach taken here.

The first section discusses what happens to economic rents over time, and thus to opportunities for positive NPV projects, in a competitive industry. The second section considers in more detail the nature of market imperfections that give rise to economic rents and how one can design investments to exploit those imperfections. The third section presents the available evidence on the relationship between various competitive advantages and rates of return on invested capital. The fourth introduces a normative approach to strategic planning and investment analysis. The fifth and final section deals with the rationale and means for domestic firms to evolve into multinational corporations.

Competitive Markets and Excess Returns

A perfectly competitive industry is one characterized by costless entry and exit, undifferentiated products, and increasing marginal costs of production. These undifferentiated products, also known as commodities, are sold exclusively on the basis of price. In such an industry, as every student of microeconomics knows, each firm produces at the point at which price equals marginal cost. Long-run equilibrium exists when price also equals average cost. At this point, total revenue equals total cost for each firm taken individually and for the industry as a whole. This cost includes the required return on the capital used by each firm. Thus, in the long run, the actual return on capital in a competitive industry must equal the required return.

Any excess return quickly attracts new entrants to the market. Their additional capacity and attempts to gain market share lead to a reduction in the industry price and a lowering of returns for all market participants. In the early 1980s, for example, the high returns available in the video-game market, combined with the ease of entry into the business, attracted a host of competitors. This led to a red-ink bath for the industry in 1983, followed by the exit of a number of firms from the industry. Conversely, should the actual return for the industry be below the required return, the opposite happens. The weakest competitors exit the industry, resulting in an increase in the industry price and a boost in the overall return on capital for the remaining firms. This process, which is now taking place in the oil refining business, continues until the actual return once again equals the required return.

The message from this analysis is clear: the run-of-the-mill firm operating in a highly competitive, commodity-type industry is doomed from the start in its search for positive net present value projects. Only firms that can bring to bear on new projects competitive advantages that are difficult to replicate have any assurance of earning excess returns in the long run. These advantages take the form of either being the low-cost producer in the industry or being able to add value to the product — value for which customers are willing to pay a high (relative to cost) price. The latter type of advantage involves the ability to convert a commodity business into one characterized by products differentiated on the basis of service and/or quality. By creating such advantages, a firm can impose barriers to entry by potential competitors, resulting in a less-than-perfectly competitive market and the possibility of positive NPV projects.

Barriers to Entry and Positive Net Present Value Projects

As we have just seen, the ability to discourage new entrants to the market by erecting barriers to entry is the key to earning rates of return that consistently exceed capital costs. If these barriers did not exist, new competitors would enter the market and drive down the rate of return to the required return. High barriers to entry and the threat of a strong reaction from entrenched competitors will reduce the risk of entry and so prolong the opportunity to earn excess returns.

This analysis suggests that successful investments (those with positive NPVs) share a common characteristic: they are investments that involve creating, preserving, and even enhancing competitive advantages that serve as barriers to entry. In line with this conclusion, the successful companies described by Thomas Peters and Robert Waterman in their bestseller, *In Search of Excellence,* were able to define their strengths — marketing, customer contact, new product innovation, low-cost manufacturing, etc. — and then build on them. They have resisted the temptation to move into new businesses that look attractive but require corporate skills they do not have.

A clearer understanding of the potential barriers to competitive entry can help to identify potential value-creating investment opportunities. This section now takes a closer look at the five major sources of barriers to entry — economies of scale, product differentiation, cost disadvantages, access to distribution channels, and government policy — and suggests some lessons for successful investing.[1]

Economies of Scale

Economies of scale exist whenever a given increase in the scale of production, marketing or distribution results in a less-than-proportional increase in cost. The existence of scale economies means that there are *inherent cost advantages in being large*. The more significant these scale economies, therefore, the greater the cost disadvantage faced by a new entrant to the market. Scale economies in marketing, service, research, and production are probably the principal barriers to entry in the mainframe computer industry, as GE, RCA, and Xerox discovered to their sorrow. It is estimated, for example, that IBM spent over $5 billion to develop its innovative System 360, which it brought out in 1963. In natural resource industries, firms such as Alcan, the Canadian aluminum company, and Exxon are able to fend off new market entrants by exploiting economies of scale in production and transportation.

High capital requirements go hand-in-hand with economies of scale. In order to take advantage of scale economies in production, marketing, or new product development, firms must often make enormous up-front investments in plant and equipment, research and development, and advertising. These capital requirements themselves serve as a barrier to entry; the more capital required, the higher the barrier to entry. This is particularly true in industries such as petroleum refining, mineral extraction, and mainframe computers.

A potential entrant to a market characterized by scale economies in production will be reluctant to enter unless the market has grown sufficiently to permit the construction and profitable utilization of an economically-sized plant. Otherwise, the new entrant will have to cut price to gain market share, destroying in the process the possibility of abnormal profits. By expanding in line with growth in the market, therefore, entrenched competitors can preempt profitable market entry by new competitors.

Consider, for example, the economics of the cement industry. The low value-to-weight ratio of cement makes the cement business a very regional one; beyond a radius of about 150 to 200 miles from the cement plant, the costs of transport become prohibitive unless cheap water or rail

---

[1] See, for example, Michael E. Porter, "How Competitive Forces Shape Strategy," *Harvard Business Review,* March-April 1979, pp. 137–145 for a good summary and discussion of these barriers to entry and their implications for corporate strategy.

transportation is available. At the same time, the significant economies of scale available in cement production limit the number of plants a given region can support. For instance, suppose that demand in a land-locked region is sufficient to support only one or two modern cement plants. By expanding production and adding substantial new capacity to that already available, a firm can significantly raise the price of market entry by new firms and make plant expansion or replacement by existing competitors look much less attractive. This type of move obviously requires a longer time frame and the willingness to incur potential losses until the market grows larger.

Scale economies are all-important in the grocery retailing business, on the level of the individual stores as well as the city-wide market. Whether a store has $100,000 or $10,000,000 in annual sales, it still needs a manager. In addition, the cost of constructing and outfitting a super-market doesn't increase in proportion to the number of square feet of selling space. Thus, the ratio of expenses to sales exhibits a significant decline as the volume of sales rises.

Similarly, whether it has 10 percent or 25 percent of a given market, a supermarket chain has to advertise and supply its stores from a warehouse. The higher the share of market, the lower the advertising cost per customer, the faster the warehouse will turn over its inventory, and the more likely its delivery trucks will be used to capacity. These cost efficiencies translate directly into a higher return on capital.

The relationship between the market dominance of a supermarket chain in a given market and its profitability is evident in the relative returns for firms following contrasting expansion strategies. Chains such as Kroger and Winn-Dixie, which have opted for deep market penetration in a limited geographic area (ranking number 1 or 2 in almost all their major markets), have realized returns on equity that far exceed their equity costs. On the other hand, chains such as A&P and National Tea, which expanded nationally by gaining toe-hold positions in numerous, though scattered markets, have consistently earned less than their required returns.

Computer store chains, to take another example, also enjoy signifi-cant economies of scale. These show up in the form of lower average costs for advertising, distribution, and training. Even more important, they receive larger discounts on their products from the manufacturers.

LESSON #1: Investments that are structured to fully exploit economies of scale are more likely to be successful than those that are not.

Product Differentiation

Some companies, such as Coca-Cola and Procter & Gamble, take advantage of *enormous advertising expenditures* and *highly developed marketing skills* to differentiate their products and keep out potential competitors wary of the high marketing costs and risks of new product introduction. Others sell expertise and high-quality products and service. For example, Nalco Chemical, a specialty chemical firm, is a problem-solver and counselor to its customers while Worthington Industries, which turns semifinished steel into finished steel, has a reputation for quality workmanship that allows it to charge premium prices. As indicated in the introduction to this article, both have been handsomely rewarded for their efforts, with average equity returns exceeding 20 percent annually from 1974 to 1983.

Pharmaceutical companies have traditionally earned high returns by developing unique products that are protected from competition by patents, trademarks, and brand names. Three outstanding examples are SmithKline Beckman's Tagamet, for treating stomach ulcers, and Hoffman-La Roche's tranquilizers, Librium and Valium. American Home Products also owes a great deal of its profitability to several patented drugs.

Similarly, the development of technologically innovative products has led to high profits for firms such as Xerox and Philips (Netherlands). A fat R&D budget, however, is only part of the activity leading to commercially successful innovations. To a great extent, the risks in R&D are commercial, not technical. Firms that make technology pay off are those that closely link their R&D activities with market realities. They always ask what the customer needs. Even if they have strong technology, they do their marketing homework. This requires close contact with customers, as well as careful monitoring of the competition. Studies also indicate that top management involvement is extremely important in those firms that rely heavily and effectively on technology as a competitive weapon. This requires close coordination and communication between technical and business managers.

Failure to heed that message has led to Xerox's inability to replicate its earlier success in the photocopy business. In addition to its revolutionary copier technology, Xerox developed some of the computer industry's most important breakthroughs, including the first personal computer and the first network connecting office machines. But, through a lack of market support, it has consistently failed to convert its research prowess into successful high-tech products.

Service is clearly the key to extraordinary profitability for many firms. The ability to differentiate its computers from others through exceptional service has enabled IBM to dominate the worldwide mainframe computer business with a market share of over 75 percent. Similarly, Caterpillar Tractor has combined dedication to quality with outstanding distribution and after-market support to differentiate its line of construction equipment and so gain a commanding 35 percent share of the world market for earth-moving machinery. American firms, such as the auto companies, that have been somewhat lax in the area of product quality have fallen prey to those Japanese firms for which quality has become a religion.

What may not be obvious from these examples is that it is possible to differentiate anything, even commodity businesses such as fast food, potato chips, theme parks, candy bars, and printing. The answer seems to be quality and service as companies like McDonald's, Disney, Frito-Lay, Mars, and Deluxe Check Printers have demonstrated. Cleanliness and consistency of service are the hallmarks of Disney and McDonald's, with both rating at the top of almost everyone's list as the best mass service providers in the world. Similarly, it is said that Mars' plants are kept so clean one can "eat off the factory floor."

High quality work and dependability have helped Deluxe Check Printers flourish in a world supposedly on the verge of doing without checks. It fills better than 95 percent of orders in two days, and ships 99 percent error free.

Frito-Lay's special edge is a highly motivated 10,000 person sales force dedicated to selling its chips. They guarantee urban supermarkets and rural mom and pop stores alike a 99.5 percent chance of a daily call. Although they get only a small weekly salary, the sales people receive a 10 percent commission on all the Lay's, Doritos, and Tostitos they sell. So they hustle, setting up displays, helping the manager in any way possible, all the while angling for that extra foot of shelf space or preferred position that can mean additional sales income. There are also tremendous side benefits to close contact with the market. Frito can get a market test rolling in ten days and respond to a new competitive intrusion in 48 hours.

A similar level of service is provided by Sysco, a $2 billion firm in the business of wholesaling food to restaurants and other institutional businesses. It is a very mundane, low-margin business — one where low cost is seemingly all that matters. Yet, behind its slogan, "Don't sell food, sell peace of mind," Sysco earns margins and a return on capital that is the envy of the industry. Even in that business, a large number of customers will pay a little more for personalized service. And in a low-margin business, a little more goes a long way.

Sysco's secret was to put together a force of over 2,000 "marketing associates" who assure customers that "98 percent of items will be delivered on time." They also provide much more, going to extraordinary lengths to produce a needed item for a restauranteur at a moment's notice. Chairman John Baugh summed it up as follows:

The typical food service company picks a case of frozen french fries out of the warehouse and drops it on the restaurant's back porch. Where is the skill in that? Where is the creativity? Service isn't a free lunch. The price tag (and cost) is higher; but even at the lower end of the market, most customers (not all, to be sure) will pay some additional freight for useful service.[2]

---

[2] Quoted in *Forbes*, October 11, 1982, p. 58.

Other firms have made their owners wealthy by understanding that they too are *selling solutions to their customers' problems,* not hardware or consumables. John Patterson, the founder of National Cash Register, used to tell salesmen: "Don't talk machines, talk the prospect's business." Thomas Watson, the founder of IBM, patterned his sales strategy on that admonition. Thus, while other companies were talking technical specifications, his salesmen were marketing solutions to understood problems, such as making sure the payroll checks came out on time.

These days, Rolm Corp., a leader in the crowded market for office communications systems, is taking a page out of IBM's book. It has built up a service force of over 3,400 employees whose main job is to reassure customers mystified by the complexities of modern technology, while selling them more equipment. The common strategic vision and approaches of the two firms may help explain why IBM, when it decided to enter the telecommunications business, did so by acquiring Rolm (in 1984) rather than another firm.

The contrast between the approaches followed by IBM and DEC is particularly revealing. DEC has developed excellent narrow-purpose minicomputers, trusting that application solutions can be developed by others to justify advanced technology. That simple strategy — selling machines on their merits to scientists and engineers — worked spectacularly for two decades, turning DEC into the world's second-largest computer company. One consequence of that strategy, however, is that DEC never needed to and never did develop the kind of marketing orientation IBM is noted for.

The advent of the personal computer, which can perform many of the functions of a minicomputer at a fraction of the cost, has underscored the shortcomings inherent in DEC's product-rather than market-oriented strategy. As its traditional business has stagnated, DEC has attempted to reposition itself to compete in the nimble new world of personal computers. But it has failed thus far to adapt marketing and sales strategies to the new, less technically sophisticated customers it has tried to attract.

The results are painfully obvious. On October 18, 1983, DEC's stock nose-dived 21 points after it announced that quarterly earnings would be 75 percent lower than the year before. Thus far at least, IBM, and its strategy of utilizing proven technology to market solutions to known problems, has prevailed in the marketplace.

LESSON #2: Investments designed to create a position at the high end of anything, including the high end of the low end, differentiated by a quality or service edge, will generally be profitable.

Cost Disadvantages

Entrenched companies often have cost advantages that are unavailable to potential entrants, independent of economies of scale. Sony and Texas Instruments, for example, take advantage of the *learning curve* to reduce costs and drive out actual and potential competitors. This concept is based on the old adage that you improve with practice. With greater production experience, costs can be expected to decrease because of more efficient use of labor and capital, improved plant layout and production methods, product redesign and standardization, and the substitution of less expensive materials and practices. This cost decline creates a barrier to entry because new competitors, lacking experience, face higher unit costs than established companies. By achieving market leadership, usually by price cutting, and thereby accumulating experience faster, this entry barrier can be most effectively exploited.

Proprietary technology, protected by legally enforceable patents, provides another cost advantage to established companies. This is the avenue taken by many of the premiere companies in the world, including 3M, West Germany's Siemens, Japan's Hitachi, and Sweden's L.M. Ericsson.

Monopoly control of low-cost raw materials is another cost advantage open to entrenched firms. This was the advantage held for so many years by Aramco (Arabian-American Oil Company), the consortium of oil companies that until the early 1980s had exclusive access to low-cost Saudi Arabian oil.

McDonald's has developed yet another advantage vis-a-vis potential competitors: it has already acquired, at a relatively low cost, many of the best fast-food restaurant locations. Favorable locations are also important to supermarkets and department stores.

A major cost advantage enjoyed by IBM's personal computer is the fact that software programs are produced first for it since it has a commanding share of the market. Only later—if at all—are these programs, which now number in the thousands, rewritten for other brands. Companies that don't develop IBM look-alikes must either write their own software, pay to have existing software modified for their machines, or wait until the software houses get around to rewriting their programs.

Sometimes, however, new entrants enjoy a cost advantage over existing competitors. This is especially true in industries undergoing deregulation, such as the airlines and trucking. In both of these industries, regulation long insulated firms from the rigors of competition and fare wars. Protected as they were, carriers had little incentive to clamp down on costs. And still they were quite profitable. The excess returns provided by the regulatory barrier to entry were divided in effect between the firms's stockholders and their unionized employees.

Deregulation has exposed these firms to new competitors not saddled with outmoded work rules and high-cost employees. For example, new low-cost competitors in the airline industry, such as People's Express and Southwest Airlines, have much lower wages (about half of what big airlines pay) and more flexible work rules (which, for example, permit pilots to load baggage and flight attendants to man reservations phones).

One firm that managed to stay ahead of the game is Northwest Airlines. For years, Northwest has been run as if competition were fierce, while still making the most of the protections of regulations. It gained a reputation for fighting labor-union demands and hammered away to increase productivity. As a result, Northwest's overhead costs are only about 2 percent of total costs, compared with about 5 percent for major competitors. Similarly, its labor costs are about two-thirds the industry average. Consequently, it is the most efficient of the major airlines, which has greatly enhanced its competitive position.

LESSON #3: Investments aimed at achieving the lowest delivered cost position in the industry, coupled with a pricing policy to expand market share, are likely to succeed, especially if the cost reductions are proprietary.

Access to Distribution Channels

Gaining distribution and shelf space for their products is a major hurdle that newcomers to an industry must overcome. Most retailers of personal computers, for example, limit their inventory to around five lines. Currently, over 200 manufacturers are competing for this very limited amount of shelf space. Moreover, the concentration of retail outlets among chains means that new computer makers have even fewer avenues to the consumer. This presents new manufacturers with a Catch-22: you don't get shelf space until you are a proven winner, but you can't sell until you get shelf space.

Conversely, well-developed, better yet unique, distribution channels are a major source of competitive advantage for firms such as Avon, Tupperware, Procter & Gamble, and IBM. Avon, for example, markets its products directly to the consumer on a house-to-house basis through an international network of 900,000 independent sales representatives. Using direct sales has enabled Avon to reduce both its advertising expenditures and the amount of money it has tied up in the business. Potential competitors face the daunting task of organizing, financing, and motivating an equivalent sales force. Thus, its independent representatives are the entry barrier that allows Avon consistently to earn exceptional profit margins in a highly competitive industry. Similarly, the sales forces of Frito-Lay, Sysco, and IBM help those firms distribute their products and raise the entry barrier in three very diverse businesses.

Conversely, the lack of a significant marketing presence in the U.S. is perhaps the greatest hindrance to Japanese drug makers attempting to expand their presence in the U.S. Marketing drugs in the U.S. requires considerable political skill in maneuvering through the U.S. regulatory process, as well as rapport with American researchers and doctors. This latter requirement means that pharmaceutical firms must develop extensive sales forces to maintain close contact with their customers. There are economies of scale here: the cost of developing such a sales force is the same, whether it sells one product or one hundred. Thus, only firms with extensive product lines can afford a large sales force, raising a major entry barrier to Japanese drug firms trying to go it alone in the U.S.

One way the Japanese drug firms have found to get around this entry barrier is to form joint ventures with American drug firms, in which the Japanese supply the patents and the American firms provide the distribution network. Such licensing arrangements are a common means of entering markets requiring strong distribution capabilities. Union Carbide, for example, follows a strategy of using high R&D expenditures to generate a diversified and innovative line of new products. Since each new product line requires a different marketing strategy and distribution network, firms like Union Carbide are more willing to trade their technology for royalty payments and equity in a joint venture with companies already in the industry.

LESSON #4: Investments devoted to gaining better product distribution often lead to higher profitability.

Government Policy

We have already seen in the case of the airline, trucking, and pharmaceutical industries that government regulations can limit, or even foreclose, entry to potential competitors. Other government policies that raise partial or absolute barriers to entry include import restrictions, environmental controls, and licensing requirements. For example, American quotas on Japanese cars have limited the ability of companies such as Mitsubishi and Mazda to expand their sales in the U.S., leading to a higher return on investment for American car companies. Similarly, environmental regulations that restrict the development of new quarries have greatly benefited those firms, such as Vulcan Materials, that already had operating quarries. The effects of licensing restrictions on the taxi business in New York City are reflected in the high price of a medallion (giving one the right to operate a cab there), which in turn reflects the higher fares that the absence of competition has resulted in.

A change in government regulations can greatly affect the value of current and prospective investments in an industry. For example, the Motor Carrier Act of 1935 set up a large barrier to entry into the business as it allowed the Interstate Commerce Commission to reject applicants to the industry. The Act also allowed the truckers themselves to determine their rates collectively, typically on the basis of average operating efficiency. Thus carriers with below-average operating costs were able to sustain above-average levels of profitability. It is scarcely surprising, then, that the major trucking companies pulled out all the stops in lobbying against deregulation. As expected, the onset of trucking deregulation, which greatly reduced the entry barrier, has led to lower profits for trucking companies and a significant drop in their stock prices.

LESSON #5: Investments in projects protected from competition by government regulation can lead to extraordinary profitability. However, what the government gives, the government can take away.

Investment Strategies and Financial Returns: Some Evidence

Ultimately, the viability of a value-creating strategy can only be assessed by examining the empirical evidence. Theory and intuition tell us that companies which follow strategies geared towards creating and preserving competitive advantages should earn higher returns on their investments than those which do not. And so they do.

William K. Hall studied eight major domestic U.S. industries and the diverse strategies followed by member firms.[3] The period selected for this study was 1975–1979, a time of slow economic growth and high inflation. These were especially hard times for the eight basic industries in Hall's study. They all faced significant cost increases that they were unable to offset fully through price increases. In addition, companies in each of these industries were forced by regulatory agencies to make major investments to comply with a variety of health, environmental, safety, and product performance standards. To compound their problems, competition from abroad grew stronger during this period. Foreign competitors achieved high market shares in three of the industries (steel, tire and rubber, and automotive); moderate shares in two others (heavy-duty trucks and construction and materials handling equipment); and entry positions in the other three (major home appliances, beer, and cigarettes).

The net result of these adverse trends is that profitability in the eight basic industries has generally fallen to or below the average for manufacturers in the United States. According to Table 1, the average return on equity for these eight industries was 12.9 percent, substantially below the 15.1 percent median return for the Fortune 1000. A number of firms in these industries have gone bankrupt, are in financial distress, or have exited their industry.

Yet this tells only part of the story. As Table 1 also shows, some companies survived, indeed prospered, in this same hostile environment. They did this by developing business strategies geared towards achieving one or both of the following competitive positions within their respective industries and then single-mindedly tailoring their investments to attain these positions:

---

[3] William K. Hall, "Survival Strategies in a Hostile Environment," *Harvard Business Review*, September-October 1980, pp. 75–85.

Table 1 **Return on Equity in Eight Basic Industries: 1975–1979***

Industry	Return on Equity	Leading Firm	Return on Equity
Steel	7.1%	Inland Steel	10.9%
Tire and rubber	7.4	Goodyear	9.2
Heavy-duty trucks	15.4	Paccar	22.8
Construction and materials handling eq.	15.4	Caterpillar	23.5
Automotive	15.4	General Motors	19.8
Major home appliances	10.1	Maytag	27.2
Beer	14.1	G. Heilman Brewing	25.8
Cigarettes	18.2	Philip Morris	22.7
Average — eight industries	**12.9**	**Average — leading companies**	**20.2**
Median — *Fortune* 1000	**15.1**		

1. Become the lowest total delivered cost producer in the industry, while maintaining an acceptable service/quality combination relative to competition.

2. Develop the highest product/service/quality differentiated position within the industry, while maintaining an acceptable delivered cost structure.

Table 2 provides a rough categorization of the strategies employed by the two top-performing companies in each of the eight industries studied. In most cases, the industry profit leaders chose to occupy only

Table 2 **Competitive Strategies Employed by Leaders in Eight Basic Industries***

Industry	Low Cost Leader	Meaningful Differentiation	Both Employed Simultaneously
Steel	Inland Steel	National	—
Tire and rubber	Goodyear	Michelin (French)	
Heavy-duty trucks	Ford, Daimler Benz (German)	—	—
Construction and materials handling equipment	—	John Deere	Caterpillar
Automotive	General Motors	Daimler Benz	—
Major home appliances	Whirlpool	Maytag	—
Beer	Miller	G. Heilman Brewing	—
Cigarettes	R.J. Reynolds	—	Philip Morris

* From William K. Hall, "Survival Strategies in a Hostile Environment."

one of the two competitive positions. Perhaps this is because the resources and skills necessary to achieve a low-cost position are incompatible with those needed to attain a strongly differentiated position.

At least three of the 16 leaders, however, combined elements of both strategies with spectacular success. Caterpillar has combined lowest-cost manufacturing with outstanding distribution and after-sales service to move well ahead of its domestic and foreign competitors in profitability. Similarly, the U.S. cigarette division of Philip Morris has become the industry profit leader by combining the lowest-cost manufacturing facilities in the world with high-visibility brands, supported by high-cost promotion. Finally, Daimler Benz employs elements of both strategies, but in different business segments. It has the lowest cost position in heavy-duty trucks in Western Europe, along with its exceptionally high-quality, feature-differentiated line of Mercedes Benz cars.

Other examples of the benefits of attaining the low-cost position in an industry or picking and exploiting specialized niches in the market abound. For example, the low-cost route to creating positive NPV investments has been successfully pursued in, of all places, the American steel industry. The strategy has involved building up-to-date mini-mills employing non-union workers who earn substantially less than members of the United Steelworkers Union. Mini-mills melt scrap, which is cheaper in the U.S. than anywhere else, and their modern plant and equipment and simplified work practices greatly reduce their need for labor. Chapparal Steel of Midlothian, Texas, a big—and profitable— mini-mill, has pared its labor costs to a mere $29 on a ton of structural steel. This compares with average labor costs of $75 a ton at big integrated U.S. plants.

The chief disadvantage is that their steelmaking capabilities are limited. They can't, for example, make the industry's bread-and-butter item: flat-rolled steel. But in the product areas where mini-mills do compete—rod, bar, and small beams and shapes—big producers have all but surrendered. So, too, have foreign mills. In just two years, Nucor Corp's mini-mill in Plymouth, Utah cut the Japanese share of California's rod and bar market from 50 to 10 percent.

Taking a different tack, Armstrong Rubber Co. has specialized in grabbing small market segments overlooked by its rivals. Today, Armstrong ranks second in industrial tires and second or third in both the replacement market for all-season radials and in tires for farm equipment and off-road recreational vehicles. Its niche-picking strategy relies heavily on the design and production innovations arising from its large investments in research and development.

A number of chemical firms, including Hercules, Monsanto, Dow, and Belgium's Solvay, have attempted to lessen their dependence on the production of commodity chemicals and plastics by investing heavily in highly profitable specialty products for such industries as electronics and defense. These specialty chemicals are typically sold in smaller quantities but at higher prices than traditional bulk commodity chemicals. Perhaps the most successful chemical "niche-picker" is Denmark's Novo Industri—one of the world's largest producers of enzymes and insulin, and a pioneer in genetic engineering techniques. Novo's continued success is largely due to its ability to find and exploit small but profitable market niches. For instance, industry analysts credit Novo's success at selling enzymes in Japan to the company's ability to outdo even Japanese purity standards and to concentrate on small specialty markets that Japan's chemical giants can't be bothered with. In fact, most of Novo's markets appear too small for giant chemical firms such as Germany's Hoechst or Du Pont to pursue.

James River Corp. has combined cost cutting with product differentiation to achieve spectacular growth and profits in the paper-goods industry, an industry where many companies are struggling to hold their own. Typically, James River buys other companies' cast-off paper mills and remakes them in its own image. It abandons all or most of the commodity-grade paper operations. It refurbishes old equipment, and supplements it with new machinery to produce specialty products (automobile and coffee filters, airline ticket paper, peel-off strips for Band-Aids, and cereal-box liners) that are aimed at specific markets and provide higher profits with less competition. At the same time, James River cuts costs by extracting wage concessions from workers and dismissing most executives. It also raises the productivity of those employees who stay by allowing many of them to join the company's lucrative *profit-sharing* programs. James River's success in following this two-pronged strategy is reflected in its 1983 net income of $55.1 million, 332 times larger than its 1970 earnings of $166,000.

Designing an Investment Strategy

Although a strong competitive edge in technology or marketing skills may enable a firm to earn excess returns, these barriers to entry will eventually erode, leaving the firm susceptible to increased competition. Existing firms are entering new industries and there are growing numbers of firms from a greater variety of countries, leading to new, well-financed competitors able to meet the high marketing costs and enormous capital outlays necessary for entry. Caterpillar Tractor, for example, faces a continuing threat from low-cost foreign competitors, especially Japan's Komatsu, which is second in worldwide sales. To stay on top, therefore, a firm's strategy must be constantly evolving, seeking out new opportunities and fending off new competitors.

Xerox clearly illustrates the problems associated with losing a competitive edge. For many years, Xerox was the king of the copier market, protected by its patents on xerography, with sales and earnings growing over 20 percent annually. The loss of its patent protection has brought forth numerous well-heeled competitors, including IBM, 3M, Kodak, and the Japanese, resulting in eroding profits and diminished growth prospects. Xerox has tried to transfer its original competitive advantage in technology to new products designed for the so-called office of the future. However, its difficulties in closely coordinating its R&D and marketing efforts have led to a series of serious, self-confessed blunders in acquisitions, market planning, and product development. For example, as mentioned earlier, the basic technology for the personal computer was developed by Xerox's Palo Alto Research Center in the early 1970s, but it remained for Apple Computer and IBM to capitalize on this revolutionary product.

More recently, Xerox's 1982 acquisition of Crum & Forster, a property and casualty insurance company, has called into question the company's strategy. It is unclear how Xerox, for whom high technology has been the chief competitive advantage, can earn excess returns in a business in which it has no experience. As we have already seen, firms that stick to their knitting are more likely to succeed than those that don't.

Common sense tells us that, in order to achieve excess returns over time, the distinctive competitive advantage held by the firm must be difficult or costly to replicate. If it is easily replicated, it will not take long for actual or potential competitors to apply the same concept, process, or organizational structure to their operations. The competitive advantage of experience, for example, will evaporate unless a firm can keep the tangible benefits of its experience proprietary and force its competitors to go through the same learning process. Once a firm loses its competitive advantage, its profits will erode to a point where it can no longer earn excess returns. For this reason, the firm's competitive advantage has to be constantly monitored and maintained so as to ensure the existence of an effective barrier to entry into the market. Should these barriers to entry break down, the firm must react quickly either to reconstruct them or build new ones.

Caterpillar has reacted to Komatsu's challenge by attempting to slash its costs, closing plants, shifting productions overseas, forcing union and nonunion workers alike to take pay cuts, eliminating many positions, and pressuring its suppliers to cut prices and speed deliveries. To get lower prices, the company is shopping around for hungrier suppliers, including foreign companies. This is reflected in its philosophy of worldwide sourcing, as described by its director of purchasing: "We're trying to become international in buying as well as selling. We expect our plants, regardless of where they're located, to look on a worldwide basis for sources of supply."[4] For example, German and Japanese companies now supply crankshafts once made exclusively in the U.S.

One important source of extra profit is the quickness of management to recognize and use information about new, lower-cost production opportunities. The excess profits, however, are temporary, lasting only until competitors discover these opportunities for themselves. For exam-

---

[4] As quoted in the *Wall Street Journal* (August 10, 1971), p. 1.

ple, purchasing the latest equipment will provide a temporary cost advantage, but this advantage will disappear as soon as competitors buy the equipment for their own plants. Only if the equipment is proprietary will the firm be able to maintain its cost advantage. Along the same line, many American electronics and textile firms shifted production facilities to Taiwan, Hong Kong, and other Asian locations to take advantage of lower labor costs there. However, as more firms took advantage of this cost reduction opportunity, competition in the consumer electronics and textiles markets in the U.S. intensified, causing domestic prices to drop and excess profits to dissipate. In fact, firms in competitive industries must continually seize new non-proprietary cost reduction opportunities, not to earn excess returns but simply to make normal profits, or just survive.

Similarly, marketing-oriented firms can earn excess returns by being among the first to recognize and exploit new marketing opportunities. For example, Crown Cork & Seal, the Philadelphia-based bottle-top maker and can maker, reacted to slowing growth in its U.S. business by expanding overseas. It set up subsidiaries in such countries as Thailand, Malaysia, Ethiopia, Zambia, Peru, Ecuador, Brazil, and Argentina. In so doing, as it turns out, they guessed correctly that in those developing, urbanizing societies, people would eventually switch from home-grown produce to food in cans and drinks in bottles.

Profitable markets, however, have a habit of eventually attracting competition. Thus, to be assured of having a continued supply of value-creating investments on hand, the firm must institutionalize its strategy of cost reduction and/or product differentiation. Successful companies seem to do this by creating a corporate culture—a set of shared values, norms, and beliefs—that has as one of its elements an obsession with some facet of their performance in the marketplace. McDonald's has an obsessive concern for quality control, IBM for customer service, and 3M for innovation. Forrest Mars set the tone for his company by going into a rage if he found an improperly wrapped candy bar leaving the plant. In order to maintain its low-cost position in the structural steel market, Chapparal Steel has teams of workers and foremen scour the world in search of the latest production machinery and methods.

Conversely, AT&T's manufacturing orientation, which focused on producing durable products with few options, was well-suited to the regulated environment in which it operated throughout most of its existence. But such an inward-looking orientation is likely to be a significant barrier to the company's ability to compete against the likes of IBM and other market-oriented, high-tech companies that react quickly to consumer demand. Prior to the breakup of AT&T, the manufacturers at Western Electric, AT&T's manufacturing arm, freely decided which products to make and when. They controlled the factories, supplying telephones to a captive market of Bell companies. AT&T was essentially an order taker, no more needing a sales force than any other utility does.

There were no competitors forcing quicker market reaction nor any marketers challenging manufacturers' decisions.

Although AT&T claims that it is now "market-driven," evidence abounds that the company's older, entrenched manufacturing mentality is still dominant. Unless AT&T can change its corporate culture—a difficult and demanding task for any company, much less for a giant set in its ways—and marry manufacturing and marketing, it will have a difficult time competing with firms such as IBM in the office automation and computer businesses it has set its sights on.

The basic insight here is that sustained success in investing is not so much a matter of building new plants as of seeking out lower-cost production processes embodied in these plants, coming up with the right products for these plants to produce, and adding the service and quality features that differentiate these products in the marketplace. In other words, it comes down to people and how they are organized and motivated. The cost and difficulty of creating a corporate culture that adds value to capital investments is the ultimate barrier to entry; unlike the latest equipment, money alone can't buy it.

In the words of Maurice R. (Hank) Greenberg, president of American Insurance Group (A.I.G.), a worldwide network of insurance companies that has enjoyed spectacular success by pioneering in territory relatively unpopulated by competitors, "You can't imitate our global operation. It's just incapable of being reproduced. Domestically, we have some imitators for pieces of our business, but not the entire business. And in any event, you can only imitate what we've done. You can't imitate what we're thinking. You can't copy what we're going to do tomorrow."[5]

Corporate Strategy and Foreign Investment

Most of the firms we have discussed are multinational corporations (MNCs) with worldwide operations. For many of these MNCs, becoming multinational was the end result of an apparently haphazard process of overseas expansion. But, as international operations become a more important source of profit and as domestic and foreign competitors become more aggressive, it is apparent that domestic survival for many firms is increasingly dependent on their success overseas. To ensure this success, multinationals must develop global strategies that will enable them to maintain their competitive edge both at home and abroad.

Overseas Expansion and Survival

It is evident that if one's competitors gain access to lower-cost sources of production abroad, following them overseas may be a prerequisite for domestic survival. One strategy often followed by firms for whom cost is

[5] Wyndham Robertson, "Nobody Tops A.I.G. in Intricacy—or Daring," *Fortune*, May 22, 1978, p. 99.

the key consideration, such as Chapparal Steel, is to develop a global scanning capability to seek out lower-cost production sites or production technologies worldwide.

Economies of Scale

A somewhat less obvious factor motivating foreign investment is the effect of economies of scale. We have already seen that in a competitive market, prices will be forced close to marginal costs of production. Hence, firms in industries characterized by high fixed costs relative to variable costs must engage in volume selling just to break even.

A new term has arisen to describe the size necessary in certain industries to compete effectively in the global marketplace: *world scale*. These large volumes may be forthcoming only if firms expand overseas. For example, companies manufacturing products such as mainframe computers that require huge R&D expenditures often need a larger customer base than that provided by even a market as large as the United States in order to recapture their investment in knowledge. Similarly, firms in capital-intensive industries with significant economies of scale in production may also be forced to sell overseas in order to spread their overhead over a higher volume of sales.

To take an extreme case, L.M. Ericsson, the highly successful Swedish manufacturer of telecommunications equipment, is forced to think internationally when designing new products since its domestic market is too small to absorb the enormous R&D expenditures involved and to reap the full benefit of production scale economies. Thus, when Ericsson developed its revolutionary AXE digital switching system, it geared its design to achieve global market penetration.

Many firms have found that a local market presence is necessary in order to continue selling overseas. For example, a local presence has helped Data General adapt the design of its U.S. computers and software to the Japanese market, giving the company a competitive edge over other U.S. companies selling computers in Japan. Data General has also adopted some Japanese manufacturing techniques and quality-control procedures that will improve its competitive position worldwide.

More firms are preparing for global competition. For example, although Black & Decker has a 50 percent market share worldwide in power tools, new competitors like the Japanese are forcing the company to change its manufacturing and marketing operations. Black & Decker's new strategy is based on a marketing concept known as "globalization," which holds that the world is becoming more homogenized and that distinctions between markets are disappearing. By selling standardized products worldwide, a firm can take advantage of economies of scale, thereby lowering costs and taking business from MNCs that customize products for individual markets. Until recently, the latter strategy of customization was the one that Black & Decker followed: the Italian subsidiary made tools for Italians, the British subsidiary tools for Britons.

By contrast, Japanese power-tool makers such as Makita Electric Works don't care that Germans prefer high-powered, heavy-duty drills and that Americans want everything lighter. Instead, Makita's strategy, which has been quite successful, is based on the notion that if you make a good drill at a low price, it will sell from Brooklyn to Baden-Baden. In response, Black & Decker recently unveiled 50 new power tools, each standardized for world production. It plans to standardize future products as well, making only minimal concessions, which require only minor modifications, to cultural differences.

Knowledge Seeking

Some firms enter foreign markets for the purpose of gaining information and experience that is expected to prove useful elsewhere. For instance, Beecham, an English firm, deliberately set out to learn from its U.S. operations how to be more competitive, first in the area of consumer products and later in pharmaceuticals. This knowledge proved highly valuable in competing with American and other firms in its European markets. Unilever, the Anglo-Dutch corporation, learned to adapt to world markets, with impressive results, the marketing skills it acquired in the U.S. through its American affiliate Lever Bros.

In industries characterized by rapid product innovation and technical breakthroughs by foreign competitors, it pays constantly to track overseas developments. The Japanese excel in this. Japanese firms systematically and effectively collect information on foreign innovation and disseminate it within their own research and development, marketing, and production groups. The analysis of new foreign products as soon as they reach the market is an especially long-lived Japanese technique. One of the jobs of Japanese researchers is to tear down a new foreign computer and analyze how it works as a base on which to develop a product of their own that will outperform the original. In a bit of a switch, as pointed out above, Data General's Japanese operation is giving the company a close look at Japanese technology, enabling it quickly to pick up and transfer back to the United States new information on Japanese innovations in the areas of computer design and manufacturing. Similarly, Ford Motor Co. has used its European operations as an important source of design and engineering ideas and management talent.

Designing a Global Expansion Strategy

The ability to pursue systematically policies and investments congruent with worldwide survival and growth depends on four interrelated elements.

1.   The first, and the key to the development of a successful global strategy, is to understand and then capitalize on those factors that have led to success in the past. In order for domestic firms to become global competitors, therefore, the sources of their domestic advantage must be transferable abroad. A competitive advantage predicated on government regulation, such as import restrictions, clearly doesn't fit in this category.

2. Second, this global approach to investment planning necessitates a systematic evaluation of individual entry strategies in foreign markets, a comparison of the alternatives, and selection of the optimal mode of entry.

3. The third important element is a continual audit of the effectiveness of current entry modes. As knowledge about a foreign market increases, for example, or sales potential grows, the optimal market penetration strategy will likely change.

4. Fourth, top management must be committed to becoming and/or staying a multinational corporation. Westinghouse demonstrated its commitment to international business by creating a new position of President-international and endowing its occupant with a seat on the company's powerful management committee. A truly globally oriented firm — one that asks, "Where in the *world* should we develop, produce, and sell our products and services?" — also requires an intelligence system capable of systematically scanning the world and understanding it, along with people who are experienced in international business and know how to use the information generated by the system.

Summary and Conclusions

We have seen that rates of return in competitive industries are driven down to their required returns. Excess profits quickly attract new entrants to the market, lowering returns until actual and required returns are again equal. Thus, the run-of-the-mill firm operating in a highly competitive market will be unable consistently to find positive net present value investments — ones which earn excess returns relative to their required returns. The key to generating a continual flow of positive NPV projects, therefore, is to erect and maintain barriers to entry against competitors. This involves either building defenses against potential competitors or finding positions in the industry where competition is the weakest.

The firm basically has two strategic options in its quest for competitive advantage: it can seek lower costs than its competitors or it can differentiate its product in a number of ways, including high advertising expenditures, product innovation, high product quality, and first-rate service.

Each of these options involves a number of specific investment decisions: construction of efficient-scale facilities and vigorous pursuit of cost reduction through accumulated experience, in the case of cost leadership; if product differentiation is the main goal, the focus is on advertising, R&D, quality control, customer-service facilities, distribution networks and the like. The more an investment widens a firm's competitive advantage and reduces the chances of successful replication by competitors, the greater the likelihood that investment will be successful.

Despite our understanding of the subject matter, it is difficult to give a set of rules to follow in developing profitable investment strategies. If it were possible to do so, competitors would follow them and dissipate any excess returns. One must be creative and quick to recognize new opportunities. Nevertheless, without dictating what should be done in every specific circumstance, there are some basic lessons we have learned from economic theory and the experiences of successful firms. The basic lessons are these:

1. Invest in projects that take advantage of your competitive edge. The corollary is, stick to doing one or two things and doing them well; don't get involved in businesses you are unfamiliar with.

2. Invest in developing, maintaining, and enhancing your competitive advantages.

3. Develop a global scanning capability. Don't be blindsided by new competitors or lower-cost production techniques or locations.

4. Pick market niches where there is little competition. Be prepared to abandon markets where competitors are catching up and apply your competitive advantages to new products or markets.

Assuming that a firm does have the necessary resources to be successful internationally, it must carefully plan for the transfer of these resources overseas. For example, it must consider how it can best utilize its marketing expertise, innovative technology, or production skills to penetrate a specific foreign market. Where a particular strategy calls for resources the firm lacks, such as an overseas distribution network, corporate management must first decide how and at what costs these resources can be acquired. It must then decide whether (and how) to acquire the resources or change its strategy.

Questions

1. The Coca-Cola Company earned an average annual return on shareholder equity of 20.3 percent during 1974–1983. During this same period, shareholders averaged only 2.9 percent annually on their investment in Coca-Cola's common stock. Explain why the shareholders earned only 2.9 percent annually while the company earned 20.3 percent annually.

2.   Describe the characteristics of a perfectly competitive market. Why is it useful to understand these characteristics, even though perfectly competitive markets do not exist?

3.   ". . . a firm can impose barriers to entry by potential competitors, resulting in a less-than-perfectly competitive market and the possibility of positive NPV projects." Interpret the preceding statement. What kind of barriers to entry can a firm impose?

4.   IBM is more profitable in the mainframe computer business than GE, RCA, and Xerox. Kroger and Winn-Dixie are more profitable supermarkets than A&P and National Tea. What factors account, in part, for these differences in profitability?

5.   Briefly describe the strategic advantages of the following companies: (a) Coca-Cola, (b) Nalco Chemical, (c) Frito-Lay, (d) McDonald's, (e) Southwest Airlines, (f) Avon, (g) Vulcan Materials, and (h) Daimler Benz.

6.   What basic strategies in capital budgeting does the author recommend?

15

Finance Theory and Financial Strategy

Stewart C. Myers

Despite its major advances, finance theory has had scant impact on strategic planning. Strategic planning needs finance and should learn to apply finance theory correctly. However, finance theory must be extended in order to reconcile financial and strategic analysis.

Strategic planning is many things, but it surely includes the process of deciding how to commit the firm's resources across lines of business. The financial side of strategic planning allocates a particular resource, capital.

Finance theory has made major advances in understanding how capital markets work and how risky real and financial assets are valued. Tools derived from finance theory, particularly discounted cash-flow analysis, are widely used. Yet finance theory has had scant impact on strategic planning.

I attempt here to explain the gap between finance theory and strategic planning. Three explanations are offered:

1. Finance theory and traditional approaches to strategic planning may be kept apart by differences in language and "culture."

2. Discounted cash flow analysis may have been misused, and consequently not accepted, in strategic applications.

3. Discounted cash flow analysis may fail in strategic applications even if it is properly applied.

Each of these explanations is partly true. I do not claim that the three, taken together, add up to the whole truth. Nevertheless, I will describe both the problems encountered in applying finance theory to strategic planning, and the potential payoffs if the theory can be extended and properly applied.

Reprinted by permission of Stewart C. Myers, "Finance Theory and Financial Strategy," *Interfaces* (January-February 1984): 126–137. Copyright 1984 The Institute of Management Sciences, 290 Westminster Street, Providence, Rhode Island 02903, USA. At the time of this writing, Stewart C. Myers was affiliated with the Sloan School of Management at the Massachusetts Institute of Technology.

The first task is to explain what is meant by "finance theory" and the gap between it and strategic planning.

The Relevant Theory

The financial concepts most relevant to strategic planning are those dealing with firms' capital investment decisions, and they are sketched here at the minimum level of detail necessary to define "finance theory."

Think of each investment project as a mini-firm, all-equity financed. Suppose its stock could be actively traded. If we know what the mini-firm's stock would sell for, we know its present value, and therefore the project's present value. We calculate the net present value (NPV) by subtracting the required investment.

In other words, we calculate each project's present value to investors who have free access to capital markets. We should therefore use the valuation model which best explains the prices of similar securities. However, the theory is usually boiled down to a single model, discounted cash flow (DCF):

$$PV = \sum_{t=1}^{T} \frac{C_t}{(1 + r)^t},$$

where

PV = present (market) value;

C_t = forecasted incremental cash flow after corporate taxes — strictly speaking the mean of the distribution of possible $\tilde{C}_t$'s;

T = project life (C_T includes any salvage value);

r = the opportunity cost of capital, defined as the equilibrium expected rate of return on securities equivalent in risk to the project being valued.

NPV equals PV less the cash outlay required at $t=0$.

Since present values add, the value of the firm should equal the sum of the values of all its mini-firms. If the DCF formula works for each project separately, it should work for any collection of projects, a line of business, or the firm as a whole. A firm or line of business consists of intangible as well as tangible assets, and growth opportunities as well as assets-in-place. Intangible assets and growth opportunities are clearly reflected in stock prices, and in principle can also be valued in capital budgeting. Projects bringing intangible assets or growth opportunities to the firm have correspondingly higher NPVs. I will discuss whether DCF formulas can capture this extra value later.

The opportunity cost of capital varies from project to project, depending on risk. In principle, each project has its own cost of capital. In practice, firms simplify by grouping similar projects in risk classes, and use the same cost of capital for all projects in a class.

The opportunity cost of capital for a line of business, or for the firm, is a value-weighted average of the opportunity costs of capital for the projects it comprises.

The opportunity cost of capital depends on the use of funds, not on the source. In most cases, financing has a second-order impact on value: You can make much more money through smart investment decisions than smart financing decisions. The advantage, if any, of departing from all-equity financing is typically adjusted for through a somewhat lowered discount rate.

Finance theory stresses cash flow and the expected return on competing assets. The firm's investment opportunities compete with securities stockholders can buy. Investors willingly invest, or reinvest, cash in the firm only if it can do better, risk considered, than the investors can do on their own.

Finance theory thus stresses fundamentals. It should not be deflected by accounting allocations, except as they affect cash taxes. For example, suppose a positive-NPV project sharply reduces book earnings in its early stages. Finance theory would recommend forging ahead, trusting investors to see through the accounting bias to the project's true value. Empirical evidence indicates that investors do see through accounting biases; they do not just look naively at last quarter's or last year's EPS. (If they did, all stocks would sell at the same price-earnings ratio.)

All these concepts are generally accepted by financial economists. The concepts are broadly consistent with an up-to-date understanding of how capital markets work. Moreover, they seem to be accepted by firms, at least in part: any time a firm sets a hurdle rate based on capital market evidence, and uses a DCF formula, it must implicitly rely on the logic I have sketched. So the issue here is not whether managers accept finance theory for capital budgeting (and for other financial purposes). It is why they do not use the theory in strategic planning.

The Gap between Finance Theory and Strategic Planning

I have resisted referring to strategic planning as "capital budgeting on a grand scale," because capital budgeting in practice is a bottom-up process. The aim is to find and undertake specific assets or projects that are worth more than they cost.

Picking valuable pieces does not insure maximum value for the whole. Piecemeal, bottom-up capital budgeting is not strategic planning.

Capital budgeting techniques, however, ought to work for the whole as well as the parts. A strategic commitment of capital to a line of business is an investment project. If management does invest, they must believe the value of the firm increases by more than the amount of capital committed — otherwise they are throwing money away. In other words, there is an implicit estimate of net present value.

This would seem to invite the application of finance theory, which explains how real and financial assets are valued. The theory should have direct application not only to capital budgeting, but also to the financial side of strategic planning.

Of course it has been applied to some extent. Moreover, strategic planning seems to be becoming more financially sophisticated. Financial concepts are stressed in several recent books on corporate strategy [Fruhan 1979; Salter and Weinhold 1979; and Bierman 1980]. Consulting firms have developed the concepts' strategic implications [Alberts 1983].

Nevertheless, I believe it is fair to say that most strategic planners are not guided by the tools of modern finance. Strategic and financial analyses are not reconciled, even when the analyses are of the same major project. When low net present value projects are nurtured "for strategic reasons," the strategic analysis overrides measures of financial value. Conversely, projects with apparently high net present values are passed by if they don't fit in with the firm's strategic objectives. When financial and strategic analyses give conflicting answers, the conflict is treated as a fact of life, not as an anomaly demanding reconciliation.

In many firms, strategic analysis is partly or largely directed to variables finance theory says are irrelevant. This is another symptom of the gap, for example:

1. Many managers worry about a strategic decision's impact on book rate of return or earnings per share. If they are convinced the plan adds to the firm's value, its impact on accounting figures should be irrelevant.

2. Some managers pursue diversification to reduce risk — risk as they see it. Investors see a firm's risk differently. In capital markets, diversification is cheap and easy. Investors who want to diversify do so on their own. Corporate diversification is redundant; the market will not pay extra for it.

If the market were willing to pay extra for diversification, closed-end funds would sell at premiums over net asset value, and conglomerate firms would be worth more to investors than their components separately traded. Closed-end funds actually sell at discounts, not premiums. Conglomerates appear to sell at discounts too, although it is hard to prove it, since the firm's components are not traded separately.

Much of the literature of strategic planning seems extremely naive from a financial point of view. Sometimes capital markets are ignored. Sometimes firms are essentially viewed as having a fixed stock of capital, so that "cash cows" are needed to finance investment in rapidly growing lines of business. (The firms that pioneered in strategic planning actually had easy access to capital markets, as do almost all public companies.) Firms may not like the price they pay for capital, but that price is the opportunity cost of capital, the proper standard for new investment by the firm.

The practical conflicts between finance and strategy are part of what lies behind the recent criticism of U.S. firms for allegedly concentrating on quick payoffs at the expense of value. U.S. executives, especially M.B.A.s, are said to rely too much on purely financial analysis, and too little on building technology, products, markets, and production efficiency. The financial world is not the real world, the argument goes; managers succumb to the glamour of high finance. They give time and talent to mergers, spinoffs, unusual securities, and complex financing packages when they should be out on the factory floor. They pump up current earnings per share at the expense of long-run values.

Much of this criticism is not directed against finance theory, but at habits of financial analysis that financial economists are attempting to reform. Finance theory of course concentrates on the financial world — that is, capital markets. However, it fundamentally disagrees with the implicit assumption of the critics, who say that the financial world is not the real world, and that financial analysis diverts attention from, and sometimes actively undermines, real long-run values. The professors and textbooks actually say that financial values rest on real values and that most value is created on the left-hand side of the balance sheet, not on the right.

Finance theory, however, is under attack too. Some feel that any quantitative approach is inevitably short-sighted. Hayes and Garvin, for example, have blamed discounted cash flow for a significant part of this country's industrial difficulties. Much of their criticism seems directed to misapplications of discounted cash flow, some of which I discuss later. But they also believe the underlying theory is wanting; they say that "beyond all else, capital investment represents an act of faith" [Hayes and Garvin 1982, p. 79]. This statement offends most card-carrying financial economists.

I do not know whether "gap" fully describes all of the problems noted, or hinted at, in the discussion so far. In some quarters, finance theory is effectively ignored in strategic planning. In others, it is seen as being in conflict, or working at cross-purposes, with other forms of strategic analysis. The problem is to explain why.

Two Cultures and One Problem

Finance theory and strategic planning could be viewed as two cultures looking at the same problem. Perhaps only differences in language and approach make the two appear incompatible. If so, the gap between them might be bridged by better communication and a determined effort to reconcile them.

Think of what can go wrong with standard discounted cash flow analyses of a series of major projects:

1. Even careful analyses are subject to random error. There is a 50 percent probability of a positive *NPV* for a truly border-line project.

2. Firms have to guard against these errors dominating project choice.

3.   Smart managers apply the following check. They know that all projects have zero *NPV* in long-run competitive equilibrium. Therefore, a positive *NPV* must be explained by a short-run deviation from equilibrium or by some permanent competitive advantage. If neither explanation applies, the positive *NPV* is suspect. Conversely, a negative *NPV* is suspect if a competitive advantage or short-run deviation from equilibrium favors the project.

In other words, smart managers do not accept positive (or negative) *NPV*s unless they can explain them.

Strategic planning may serve to implement this check. Strategic analyses look for market opportunities — deviations from equilibrium — and try to identify the firm's competitive advantages.

Turn the logic of the example around. We can regard strategic analysis which does not explicitly compute *NPV*s as showing absolute faith in Adam Smith's invisible hand. If a firm, looking at a line of business, finds a favorable deviation from long-run equilibrium, or if it identifies a competitive advantage, then (efficient) investment in that line must offer profits exceeding the opportunity cost of capital. No need to calculate the investment's *NPV:* the manager knows in advance that *NPV* is positive.

The trouble is that strategic analyses are also subject to random error. Mistakes are also made in identifying areas of competitive advantage or out-of-equilibrium markets. We would expect strategic analysts to calculate *NPV*s explicitly, at least as a check; strategic analysis and financial analysis ought to be explicitly reconciled. Few firms attempt this. This suggests the gap between strategic planning and finance theory is more than just "two cultures and one problem."

The next step is to ask why reconciliation is so difficult.

Misuse of Finance Theory

The gap between strategic and financial analysis may reflect misapplication of finance theory. Some firms do not try to use theory to analyze strategic investments. Some firms try but make mistakes.

I have already noted that in many firms capital investment analysis is partly or largely directed to variables finance theory says are irrelevant. Managers worry about projects' book rates of return or impacts on book earnings per share. They worry about payback, even for projects that clearly have positive *NPV*s. They try to reduce risk through diversification.

Departing from theoretically correct valuation procedures often sacrifices the long-run health of the firm for the short, and makes capital investment choices arbitrary or unpredictable. Over time, these sacrifices appear as disappointing growth, eroding market share, loss of technological leadership, and so forth.

The non-financial approach taken in many strategic analyses may be an attempt to overcome the short horizons and arbitrariness of financial analysis as it is often misapplied. It may be an attempt to get back to fundamentals. Remember, however: finance theory never left the fundamentals. Discounted cash flow should not in principle bias the firm against long-lived projects, or be swayed by arbitrary allocations.

However, the typical mistakes made in applying DCF do create a bias against long-lived projects. I will note a few common mistakes.

Ranking on Internal Rate of Return

Competing projects are often ranked on internal rate of return rather than *NPV*. It is easier to earn a high rate of return if project life is short and investment is small. Long-lived, capital-intensive projects tend to be put down the list even if their net present value is substantial.

The internal rate of return does measure bang per buck on a DCF basis. Firms may favor it because they think they have only a limited number of bucks. However, most firms big enough to do formal strategic planning have free access to capital markets. They may not like the price, but they can get the money. The limits on capital expenditures are more often set inside the firm, in order to control an organization too eager to spend money. Even when a firm does have a strictly limited pool of capital, it should not use the internal rate of return to rank projects. It should use *NPV* per dollar invested, or linear programming techniques when capital is rationed in more than one period [Brealey and Myers 1981, pp. 101–107].

Inconsistent Treatment of Inflation

A surprising number of firms treat inflation inconsistently in DCF calculations. High nominal discount rates are used but cash flows are not fully adjusted for future inflation. Thus accelerating inflation makes projects — especially long-lived ones — look less attractive even if their real value is unaffected.

Unrealistically High Rates

Some firms use unrealistically high discount rates, even after proper adjustment for inflation. This may reflect ignorance of what normal returns in capital markets really are. In addition:

1.   Premiums are tacked on for risks that can easily be diversified away in stockholders' portfolios.

2.   Rates are raised to offset the optimistic biases of managers spon-
soring projects. This adjustment works only if the bias increases
geometrically with the forecast period. If it does not, long-lived
projects are penalized.

3.   Some projects are unusually risky at inception, but only of normal-
risk once the start-up is successfully passed. It is easy to classify this
type of project as "high-risk," and to add a start-up risk premium to
the discount rate for all future cash flows. The risk premium should
be applied to the startup period only. If it is applied after the startup
period, safe, short-lived projects are artificially favored.

Discounted cash flow analysis is also subject to a difficult organizational problem. Capital budgeting is usually a bottom-up process. Proposals originate in the organization's midriff, and have to survive the trip
to the top, getting approval at every stage. In the process political
alliances form, and cash flow forecasts are bent to meet known standards.
Answers — not necessarily the right ones — are worked out for anticipated challenges. Most projects that get to the top seem to meet
profitability standards set by management.

According to Brealey and Myers's Second Law, "The proportion of
proposed projects having positive NPV is independent of top management's estimate of the opportunity cost of capital" [Brealey and Myers
1981, p. 238].

Suppose the errors and biases of the capital budgeting process make
it extremely difficult for top management to verify the true cash flows,
risks and present value of capital investment proposals. That would
explain why firms do not try to reconcile the results of capital budgeting
and strategic analyses. However, it does not explain why strategic
planners do not calculate their own *NPV*s.

We must ask whether those in top management — the managers who
make strategic decisions — understand finance theory well enough to use
DCF analysis effectively. Although they certainly understand the arithmetic of the calculation, they may not understand the logic of the method
deeply enough to trust it or to use it without mistakes.

They may also not be familiar enough with how capital markets
work to use capital market data effectively. The widespread use of
unrealistically high discount rates is probably a symptom of this.

Finally, many managers distrust the stock market. Its volatility
makes them nervous, despite the fact that the volatility is the natural
result of a rational market. It may be easier to underestimate the
sophistication of the stock market than to accept its verdict on how well
the firm is doing.

Finance Theory May Have Missed the Boat

Now consider a firm that understands finance theory, applies DCF analysis correctly, and has overcome the human and organizational problems
that bias cash flows and discount rates. Carefully estimated net present

values for strategic investments should help significantly. However, would they fully grasp and describe the firm's strategic choices? Perhaps not.

There are gaps in finance theory as it is usually applied. These gaps are not necessarily intrinsic to finance theory generally. They may be filled by new approaches to valuation. However, if they are, the firm will have to use something more than a straightforward discounted cash flow method.

An intelligent application of discounted cash flow will encounter four chief problems:

1.   Estimating the discount rate,

2.   Estimating the project's future cash flows,

3.   Estimating the project's impact on the firm's other assets' cash flows, that is through the cross-sectional links between projects, and

4.   Estimating the project's impact on the firm's future investment opportunities. These are the time series links between projects.

The first three problems, difficult as they are, are not as serious for financial strategy as the fourth. However, I will review all four.

Estimating the Opportunity Cost of Capital

The opportunity cost of capital will always be difficult to measure, since it is an expected rate of return. We cannot commission the Gallup Poll to extract probability distributions from the minds of investors. However, we have extensive evidence on past average rates of return in capital markets [Ibbotson and Sinquefield 1982] and the corporate sector [Holland and Myers 1979]. No long-run trends in "normal" rates of return are evident. Reasonable, ballpark cost of capital estimates can be obtained if obvious traps (for example, improper adjustments for risk or inflation) are avoided. In my opinion, estimating cash flows properly is more important than fine-tuning the discount rate.

Forecasting Cash Flow

It's impossible to forecast most projects' actual cash flows accurately. DCF calculations do not call for accurate forecasts, however, but for accurate assessments of the mean of possible outcomes.

Operating managers can often make reasonable subjective forecasts of the operating variables they are responsible for—operating costs, market growth, market share, and so forth—at least for the future that they are actually worrying about. It is difficult for them to translate this knowledge into a cash flow forecast for, say, year seven. There are several reasons for this difficulty. First, the operating manager is asked to look into a far future he is not used to thinking about. Second, he is asked to express his forecast in accounting rather than operating variables. Third, incorporating forecasts of macroeconomic variables is difficult. As a result, long-run forecasts often end up as mechanical extrapolations of short-run trends. It is easy to overlook the long-run pressures of competition, inflation, and technical change.

It should be possible to provide a better framework for forecasting operating variables and translating them into cash flows and present value—a framework that makes it easier for the operating manager to apply his practical knowledge, and that explicitly incorporates information about macroeconomic trends. There is, however, no way around it: forecasting is intrinsically difficult, especially when your boss is watching you do it.

Estimating Cross-Sectional Relationships between Cash Flows

Tracing "cross-sectional" relationships between project cash flows is also intrinsically difficult. The problem may be made more difficult by inappropriate project definitions or boundaries for lines of businesses. Defining business units properly is one of the tricks of successful strategic planning.

However, these inescapable problems in estimating profitability standards, future cash returns, and cross-sectional interactions are faced by strategic planners even if they use no financial theory. They do not reveal a flaw in existing theory. Any theory or approach encounters them. Therefore, they do not explain the gap between finance theory and strategic planning.

The Links between Today's Investments and Tomorrow's Opportunities

The fourth problem—the link between today's investments and tomorrow's opportunities—is much more difficult.

Suppose a firm invests in a negative-*NPV* project in order to establish a foothold in an attractive market. Thus a valuable second-stage investment is used to justify the immediate project. The second-stage must depend on the first: if the firm could take the second project without having taken the first, then the future opportunity should have no impact on the immediate decision. However, if tomorrow's opportunities depend on today's decisions, there is a time-series link between projects.

At first glance, this may appear to be just another forecasting problem. Why not estimate cash flows for both stages, and use discounted cash flow to calculate the *NPV* for the two stages taken together?

You would not get the right answer. The second stage is an option, and conventional discounted cash flow does not value options properly. The second stage is an option because the firm is not committed to undertake it. It will go ahead if the first stage works and the market is still attractive. If the first stage fails, or if the market sours, the firm can stop after Stage 1 and cut its losses. Investing in Stage 1 purchases an intangible asset: a call option on Stage 2. If the option's present value offsets the first stage's negative *NPV,* the first stage is justified.

The Limits of Discounted Cash Flow

The limits of DCF need further explanation. Think first of its application to four types of securities:

1. DCF is standard for valuing bonds, preferred stocks and other fixed-income securities.

2. DCF is sensible, and widely used, for valuing relatively safe stocks paying regular dividends.

3. DCF is not as helpful in valuing companies with significant growth opportunities. The DCF model can be stretched to say that Apple Computer's stock price equals the present value of the dividends the firm may eventually pay. It is more helpful to think of Apple's price, P_0, as:

$$P_0 = \frac{EPS}{r} + PVGO,$$

where

EPS = normalized current earnings
r = the opportunity cost of capital
$PVGO$ = the net present value of future growth opportunities.

Note that *PVGO* is the present value of a portfolio of options — the firm's options to invest in second-stage, third-stage, or even later projects.

4. DCF is never used for traded calls or puts. Finance theory supplies option valuation formulas that work, but the option formulas look nothing like DCF.

Think of the corporate analogs to these securities:

1. There are few problems in using DCF to value safe flows, for example, flows from financial leases.

2. DCF is readily applied to "cash cows" — relatively safe businesses held for the cash they generate, rather than for strategic value. It also works for "engineering investments," such as machine replacements, where the main benefit is reduced cost in a clearly defined activity.

3. DCF is less helpful in valuing businesses with substantial growth opportunities or intangible assets. In other words, it is not the whole answer when options account for a large fraction of a business' value.

4.   DCF is no help at all for pure research and development. The value of R&D is almost all option value. Intangible assets' value is usually option value.

The theory of option valuation has been worked out in detail for securities — not only puts and calls, but warrants, convertibles, bond call options, and so forth. The solution techniques should be applicable to the real options held by firms. Several preliminary applications have already been worked out, for example:

1.   Calculations of the value of a federal lease for offshore exploration for oil or gas. Here the option value comes from the lessee's right to delay the decisions to drill and develop, and to make these decisions after observing the extent of reserves and the future level of oil prices [Paddock, Siegel, and Smith 1983].

2.   Calculating an asset's abandonment or salvage value: an active second-hand market increases an asset's value, other things equal. The second-hand market gives the asset owner a put option which increases the value of the option to bail out of a poorly performing project [Myers and Majd 1983].

The option "contract" in each of these cases is fairly clear: a series of calls in the first case and a put in the second. However, these real options last longer and are more complex than traded calls and puts. The terms of real options have to be extracted from the economics of the problem at hand. Realistic descriptions usually lead to a complex implied "contract," requiring numerical methods for valuation.

Nevertheless, option pricing methods hold great promise for strategic analysis. The time-series links between projects are the most important part of financial strategy. A mixture of DCF and option valuation models can, in principle, describe these links and give a better understanding of how they work. It may also be possible to estimate the value of particular strategic options, thus eliminating one reason for the gap between finance theory and strategic planning.

Lessons for Corporate Strategy

The task of strategic analysis is more than laying out a plan or plans. When time-series links between projects are important, it's better to think of strategy as managing the firm's portfolio of real options [Kestler 1982]. The process of financial planning may be thought of as:

1.   Acquiring options, either by investing directly in R&D, product design, cost or quality improvements, and so forth, or as a by-product of direct capital investment (for example, investing in a Stage 1 project with negative *NPV* in order to open the door for Stage 2).

2.   Abandoning options that are too far "out of the money" to pay to keep.

3.   Exercising valuable options at the right time—that is, buying the cash producing assets that ultimately produce positive net present value.

There is also a lesson for current applications of finance theory to strategic issues. Several new approaches to financial strategy use a simple, traditional DCF model of the firm [For example, Fruhan 1979, Ch. 2]. These approaches are likely to be more useful for cash cows than for growth businesses with substantial risk and intangible assets.

The option value of growth and intangibles is not ignored by good managers even when conventional financial techniques miss them. These values may be brought in as "strategic factors," dressed in non-financial clothes. Dealing with the time-series links between capital investments, and with the option value these links create, is often left to strategic planners. But new developments in finance theory promise to help.

Bridging the Gap

We can summarize by asking how the present gap between finance theory and strategic planning might be bridged.

Strategic planning needs finance. Present value calculations are needed as a check on strategic analysis and vice versa. However, the standard discounted cash flow techniques will tend to understate the option value attached to growing, profitable lines of business. Corporate finance theory requires extension to deal with real options. Therefore, to bridge the gap we on the financial side need to:

1.   Apply existing finance theory correctly.

2.   Extend the theory. I believe the most promising line of research is to try to use option pricing theory to model the time-series interactions between investments.

Both sides could make a conscious effort to reconcile financial and strategic analysis. Although complete reconciliation will rarely be possible, the attempt should uncover hidden assumptions and bring a generally deeper understanding of strategic choices. The gap may remain, but with better analysis on either side of it.

References

Alberts, W.A. and McTaggart, James M. 1984, "Value based strategic investment planning," *Interfaces,* Vol. 14, No. 1 (January-February), pp. 138–151.

Bierman, H. 1980, *Strategic Financial Planning,* The Free Press, New York.

Brealey, R.A. and Myers, S.C. 1981, *Principles of Corporate Finance,* McGraw-Hill Book Company, New York.

Foster, G. 1978, *Financial Statement Analysis,* Prentice-Hall, Inc., Englewood Cliffs, New Jersey.

Fruhan, W.E., Jr., 1979, *Financial Strategy: Studies in the Creation, Transfer and Destruction of Shareholder Value,* Richard D. Irwin, Inc., Homewood, Illinois.

Hayes, R.H. and Garvin, D.A. 1982, "Managing as if tomorrow mattered," *Harvard Business Review,* Vol. 60, No. 3 (May-June), pp. 70–79.

Holland, D. M. and Myers, S. C. 1979, "Trends in corporate profitability and capital costs," in R. Lindsay, ed., *The Nation's Capital Needs: Three Studies,* Committee on Economic Development, Washington, DC.

Ibbotson, R.G. and Sinquefield, R.A. 1982, *Stocks, Bonds, Bills and Inflation: The Past and the Future,* Financial Analysts Research Foundation, Charlottesville, Virginia.

Myers, S.C. and Majd, S. 1983, "Applying option pricing theory to the abandonment value problem," Sloan School of Management, MIT, Working Paper.

Paddock, J.L.; Siegel, D.; and Smith, J.L. 1983, "Option valuation of claims on physical assets: the case of offshore petroleum leases," Working Paper, MIT Energy Laboratory, Cambridge, Massachusetts.

Salter, M.S. and Weinhold, W.A. 1979, *Diversification Through Acquisition,* The Free Press, New York.

Questions

1. "The opportunity cost of capital depends on the use of funds, not on the source." Explain the meaning of this statement.

2. The objective of capital budgeting is to invest in projects that are worth more than they cost. Explain how net present value relates to this objective.

3. Why do capital projects have net present values of zero in long-run competitive equilibrium? Do capital projects necessarily have net present values of zero in short-run competitive equilibrium? Explain.

4. Explain why net present value, properly used, will not bias a company against long-lived capital projects.

5. According to the author, what are some possible misuses of finance theory in capital budgeting?

6. Define a call option and a put option.

7. Financial analysts who properly apply discounted cash flow in capital budgeting may still encounter problems in estimating: (a) the discount rate, (b) future cash flows from the project, (c) the impact of the project on cash flows of other company projects, and (d) the impact of the project on the company's future investment opportunities. Describe why an analyst might experience difficulty in estimating each of these four variables.

How American Can Allocates Capital

Richard J. Marshuetz

We're entering another age of conglomerates. Having pruned unprofitable divisions in the late 1970s, many large American companies once again are merging with or acquiring diverse businesses. Whether it's Nestlé's bid for Carnation, American Standard's acquisition of Trane, or Champion International's purchase of St. Regis, the corporate rush is on to buy assets that will complement and expand strategic capabilities.

Having restructured, however, these companies face the same problems as their counterparts of the late 1960s and early 1970s did— how to meet the variety of strategic demands made on them by these different businesses and, more exactly, how to determine which projects to fund. A major problem is that most of these companies have trimmed their headquarters and staff operations down to the corporate bone in a push toward decentralization. A skeletal corporate staff or one wedded to past definitions of success may not be ready to meet conflicting demands effectively.

Theorists have come up with suggestions for coping with this problem, but translating their theories into practice has not proved simple. Some companies have given up before they have started or have stuck to their old ways. In this article, Richard Marshuetz explains how a group of managers at American Can developed a modern system to tailor the corporation's capital allocation process to the needs of its various businesses. He outlines the system's rationale, shows how it functions, and recounts how his group won over the company's skeptics.

Weighed down by sagging profits from overcapacity in the late 1970s, American Can faced a growing demand for funds in various forms from myriad businesses. What had been a normal management responsibility—deciding which strategy deserved how much capital—became

Reprinted by permission of the *Harvard Business Review*. "How American Can Allocates Capital" by Richard J. Marshuetz (January-February 1985), 82–91. Copyright © 1985 by The President and Fellows of Harvard College; all rights reserved. At the time of this writing, Richard J. Marshuetz was vice president and chief financial officer of American Can's Specialty Retailing Sector.

the overriding challenge of the early 1980s under a cacophony of competing demands:

- The metal can business continually demanded capital to buy equipment to eliminate lead-soldered seams and improve manufacturing productivity.

- Dixie disposable cups needed to match its competitors' advance into plastics.

- The plastic toothpaste tube business required new equipment for expansion.

- The Musicland retail record store chain needed more locations and planned a wider selection of entertainment products.

- The mail-order business, Fingerhut, wanted to bring out new products and to spend to expand the impact of its mailing lists.

- Packaging alternatives lower in cost than metal cans and glass bottles required heavy outlays for R&D and new production capabilities.

William S. Woodside, American Can's chairman and chief executive officer, first responded to the challenge by divesting several capital-intensive businesses and acquiring a group of financial services companies. Second, he called on the company's managers to create a structure that would help the company make better strategic choices as well as give the managers of each operating unit as much independence as possible so that they could be more responsive to their markets.

While business unit managers were given new freedom to run their businesses, the important corporate trade-offs could not be left to the undeniably acute intuition of middle managers or to the rules of thumb of the industry. Instead, American Can needed a synthesis of prevailing theories of strategic planning, capital allocation, and management decentralization in order to decide on major strategies and to allocate the funds necessary to support them.

A corporate effort resulted from Woodside's call. Headquarters staffs were pared down. The vice president of strategic planning, Robert M. Abramson, set out to forge a better link between the strategic planning process and an existing semiautonomous function called capital coordination, which had for years evaluated large requests for plants and equipment. An eight-member corporate operating committee was disbanded, and with it went cumbersome monthly corporate reviews of each business.

The new structure (see the *Exhibit*) inextricably links investment and strategic planning decisions from the beginning; deliberations start at the business unit level and end with review and approval by corporate management. It looks complex but is actually quite simple. The Office of the Chairman, which includes the chairman, the vice chairman, the

Exhibit **American Can Company's Management Structure**

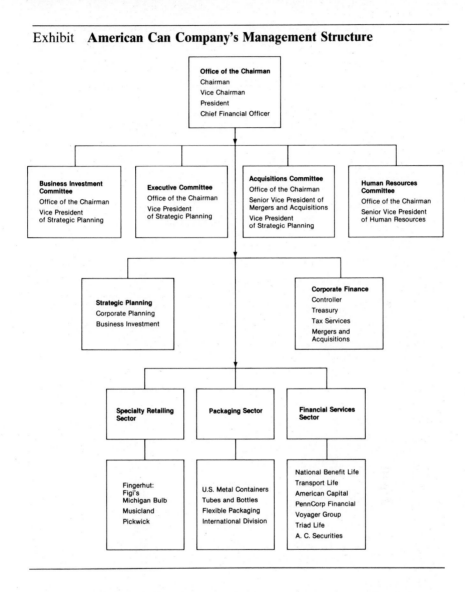

president, and the chief financial officer, is a four-person team that heads up the Business Investment, Executive, Acquisitions, and Human Resources committees. The vice president of strategic planning joins the four-person team on the first three committees; he is responsible for two major departments, corporate planning and business investment — descendants of the old capital coordination department.

The key to success is the distinction between decisions that support daily operations and those that determine the future of each business. Daily operations are in the hands of business unit managers; plans for the future — investment decisions — are reviewed by corporate staff.

Drawing such a distinction may seem simple in theory, but putting it into practice required a major commitment of management time and resources in order to:

- Distinguish between operating and investment decisions.

- Link investments with business plans.

- Develop uniform criteria to select the best investments.

- Delegate approval authority for smaller investments.

- Keep the entire management process simple and efficient.

- Win over a large number of management skeptics, who had watched a variety of fashionable techniques come and go over the last decade.

The commitment paid off. The losses of 1982 turned to profits in 1983, and earnings per share were up by two-thirds in the first six months of 1984. For the most part, management is decentralized, for unit managers run their companies with a dramatically increased autonomy. At the same time, the corporate staff channels the major decisions that should be controlled by senior management and gets a better understanding of how to link strategy with investment.

Defining an Investment

Throughout its history, American Can's investment decisions had revolved around plants and equipment—fixed capital. The variety of investments possible, however, in such nonpackaging businesses as the Musicland record store chain, the Fingerhut mail-order company, and the new financial services businesses made this definition obsolete. Decisions about new product development, advertising, credit terms, and inventory can set the future direction and determine future returns of several of these businesses just as productive capacity dictates major strategies in packaging.

We could not base a broader definition on balance sheet or income statement accounting treatment or on the sheer size of an expenditure. Buyers of aluminum in the metal can businesses routinely, and we feel correctly, tie up amounts in the double-digit millions, as do buyers of records and tapes and Fingerhut's wide assortment of goods. We also excluded the impact of financing decisions from our definition. Some argued that a leased item was not an investment, especially if it contained a 30- or a 60-day escape clause. We concluded that a leased item could be an investment if the intent was to continue leasing on a long-term basis.

Having ruled out most conventional distinctions, we concluded that the key to differentiating between an operating and an investment decision is the extent to which the proposed expenditure determines the future course of a business. Expenditures that fit within the investment definition come under one of five categories:

- New product development programs.

- Business expansion into new geographic areas.

- Major spending to increase and hold market share, such as more intense sales coverage, a large sustained advertising campaign, and a structural change in prices.

- Discretionary spending to increase a business's or a product's life expectancy.

- Productivity and quality improvement expenditures.

We can usually differentiate between investments and operations decisions with these categories. When a dispute arises, the key questions are, Does the expenditure have long-run consequences? Is the decision outside the ordinary course of business? If the unit proposing the investment puts special emphasis on it or involves a higher level of management in deliberations, we consider the project an investment decision and therefore, if it is large, subject to the corporate allocation procedure.

Fingerhut Companies, Inc., for example, wanted to market video-cassette recorders, which it had never sold before and which required a big inventory buildup. Fingerhut's management had also wanted to market a line of handmade items for sale under the label "Artisans of China." The unit wished to sell both product lines by mail and argued that both were routine operating decisions.

The corporate strategic planning staff disagreed. The Artisans of China program represented an investment decision, while expansion into VCR marketing did not. Even though the commitment of resources was large in both cases, introducing VCRs only extended an existing product line. It did not create a new one. The VCRs would be market tested, purchased, promoted, and sold routinely. While management could not guarantee successful VCR sales, the risks were much less formidable than the risks involved in starting a new business like the Artisans of China.

Fingerhut proposed the "Artisans" concept as a distinct new business aimed at an upscale market. Because the business was discretionary and relatively risky, within Fingerhut it was reviewed outside the normal business process. By our definition, Artisans represented an investment decision and was therefore subject to corporate approval. Fingerhut's managers did not welcome this "intrusion" into their business; they still don't. But they do recognize a responsibility at the corporate level to allocate resources in the most promising way possible.

In the rare instances when such disputes arise, the business unit and the corporate strategic planning staff have generally resolved it and have only infrequently referred the decision to a sector executive or the Business Investment Committee.

Linking Investments to Plans

Business unit managers usually come up with the ideas for investments and express them formally during the strategic planning process; from then on, investments are linked to strategic plans. As a result, the criteria for evaluating the investment are the same as for evaluating the plan — the impact of an investment on the competitive position of a business, as measured by the amount, timing, and risk of the investment's cash flows. Even if an investment opportunity surfaces outside the planning cycle, the managers reviewing and approving it will be familiar enough with business unit strategies to evaluate the opportunity according to the same criteria.

We have taken great care to put the results of discounted cash flow analysis in the context of a project's impact on competitive position as well as its exposure — how much money will be at risk for how long. The focus is on general management issues — price, volume, quality, customer selection, service level and cost, competitive reaction, suppliers' reliability, and the business's ability to implement the project on schedule and on budget.

In developing these criteria, it's been difficult to argue with the axiom that managers should never invest money for a lower rate of return than the stockholders could earn elsewhere at a comparable level of risk. But the axiom has glaring shortcomings for a manager who must choose between conflicting investments. A hurdle rate oversimplifies the decision a business unit general manager faces in evaluating investments. The business may need a marginal investment just to prevent deterioration of its competitive position. Indeed, managers must balance these marginal investments with superior ones to earn more than the cost of capital on their total portfolios.

But thinking in terms of *only* pursuing investments that return more than their cost of capital is about as useful as encouraging managers to perform *only* to earn a bonus. Roofs need repairing; a sales organization needs a marginal product to support the sale of a more profitable one. Sometimes an exit barrier may make running an entire business for a return below its cost of capital an attractive alternative in the short run.

A good example is the high cost of closing an old plant, which can trigger large payments of severance and accelerated pension benefits. For a limited time, it might make sense to run the plant at a marginal rate of return while normal retirements and attrition reduced the work force and the closing costs.

While the use of DCF techniques helps determine the specific contribution of a single investment, we do not use hurdle rates to select the interrelated set of investments that yield the best overall return.

It is also difficult to quantify the total value of an investment. Determining the capital required to launch a new product and project the resulting sales, profits, and cash flow may be easy; quantifying the product's impact on a business's competitive position is not. The manager must consider the product's halo effect on employees—its internal motivational value—and the degree to which the product deters competitors and affects other businesses. Less obvious perhaps is the tendency to underestimate competitors. When it plans to add new equipment or expand its sales force, a business will automatically project a subsequent sales increase. But what about the reaction of a competitor who loses business? Will it cut prices and reduce the industry's overall pricing structure? If the manager excludes this possibility, he or she may overstate investment return projections.

Finally, narrowly focused quantitative analysis only shows what happens if an investment *is* implemented and does not examine the consequences if the investment is *not* implemented. If the business doesn't introduce a new product, will it leave a hole a competitor will try to fill? Will our costs be too high and allow a lower-cost competitor to gain market share at our expense?

We also test a project's sensitivity to potential pitfalls. In the case of a new product, for example, what if volume falls short or a competitor forces prices down or a weak economy results in disappointing prices and volumes?

Delegating Approval Authority

Four levels of executives have the authority to approve investments — the board of directors, the Business Investment Committee, the sector executives, and the business units' general managers.

In deciding how to delegate authority, corporate management wanted to limit its involvement in all but the most important investment decisions. To measure importance, we wanted to incorporate the size of the project, its level of risk, and the amount of managerial discretion over its outcome.

Size alone seemed an inadequate criterion. Sometimes large dollar investments contain little risk and pay back rapidly (for example, increases in capacity to produce patented products). Small dollar investments like air emission compliance projects are based on new technology that is sometimes highly risky but offers management little discretion. Others are large and risky, but management has flexibility in the amount and timing of expenditure (for example, an expansion overseas).

Despite the variety of these components, we simply could not find a straightforward way to incorporate them. In this conflict between practical simplicity and theoretical perfection, simplicity won. Size would serve to isolate the projects that would have to be submitted for approval. We decided to add up all the dollars of the expenses involved in a project, which include:

- Research, development, and initial marketing and sales expenses.

- Capital and start-up costs of plants and equipment.

■   The maximum working capital exposed prior to the point when an investment begins to return cash.

■   The maximum income-producing assets required by statute to support insurance liabilities before new products begin to pay back.

■   The net present value of leases.

Once the proposal's value is calculated, the approval process begins. The business units' general managers' approval extends to projects amounting to $250,000; sector executives may approve projects of up to $1 million; the Business Investment Committee approves projects of between $1 million and $3 million; and the board of directors has responsibility for anything larger than $3 million. These levels may be raised as we gain experience.

Setting levels for investment approval determines only one thing, however—who has the authority to approve the investment. The intensity of analysis is another issue. Sometimes a small investment will receive close scrutiny, either because it represents the seed money for a larger program—like a prototype machine—or because it offers corporate management an opportunity to review the progress and outlook of major strategic programs.

The opposite is also true. Sometimes the rationale behind very large investments is so clear-cut as not to require much analysis or discussion—for example, when technological advances allow new equipment to be made smaller, operate faster, and sell for less money. Fingerhut recently requested capital to expand printing capacity, either by getting a new generation of equipment or constructing a new building; limited analysis was required.

To streamline the decision-making process, we had to put it into the hands of as few executives as possible and make certain that the minimum amount of analysis was required to reach a decision. Although many sources provide expert support, only the project sponsor and a corporate reviewer from Strategic Planning's business investment department actually draft and review the request at the corporate level.

Designated by the business unit's general manager, the project sponsor steers the investment request from inception through approval. The sponsor usually represents the department that will implement the project and not the financial staff. The chief task is to draft the request by incorporating summaries from marketing, operations, manufacturing, finance, legal, tax, human resources, and other functions.

A Bias toward Approval?

Once the business unit's general manager approves the project, the corporate business investment department assigns a staff member as reviewer. The reviewer moves the request through the normal corporate process, resolves sticking points, and drafts a review letter to the sector executive or the Business Investment Committee. A bias toward approval among the staff members discourages an unfocused search for more information. Only questions that are essential for a decision are answered.

This bias does not mean that every request is approved. But by the time investment proposals are presented, most issues have been dealt with in a rigorous planning and plan review cycle and such matters of fact as engineering feasibility, costs, and strategic fit have been resolved. Many proposals have been scaled down or dropped because the right resources are not available, the proposal is inconsistent with strategic objectives, or the investment will not generate the requisite returns.

The approval process concentrates on the judgment calls and ensures the use of current information. If the company adds capacity, will targeted customers convert to the new products? Will the capacity preempt competitive expansion? Will prices and volumes hold so that the return is worthwhile? Will we achieve cost reduction targets? In these key issues, the staff takes an "innocent until proven guilty" attitude but it is unbending in ensuring that the issues on which a decision depends receive appropriate attention.

Relating the analysis directly to the issues on which approval depends usually starts before a request is written. The project sponsor from the business unit and a member of the corporate business investment department get together to pinpoint risks, outline key issues, and agree on the level of analysis necessary for a recommendation of approval. When funds are requested to develop and market a new product in any business, the business investment staff works with the business unit to identify reasonable upper and lower sales volume limits as well as the assumptions about profit margins. When the business unit provides sufficient evidence that sales and margins will fall within these limits, the business investment staff recommends approval. Although such recommendation does not guarantee success, the overall record of the staff is quite good.

Converting the Skeptics

As a result of the buildup of the corporate staff in the 1970s and the layering of analytic procedures, business units viewed any new change skeptically. Our decision to revamp capital allocation was no different. The fact that corporate management had withdrawn from operating decisions was overlooked by unit managers who were suspicious of the broadened scope of the investment definition. Some claimed they had no investment decision to make. Others complained that the definition would take corporate headquarters into areas where it had nothing to offer.

Overcoming this initial, understandable resistance took time. First, top management had to support the concept, even when easy answers were not forthcoming. Second, we involved as few people as possible in implementing the planning and appropriations process. Third, we made certain that members of the business investment department had had operations experience. Expecting to return to those responsibilities after a short staff tenure, they viewed the assignment as an opportunity to participate in top-level decision making and to broaden their skills. Finally, we put a lot of energy into an informal selling effort. The chairman publicly reiterated his support, and the staff worked face-to-face with operating managers as often as possible.

In addition, we have seized every opportunity to win over the remaining skeptics, a process best exemplified by the experience with the financial services businesses. The company acquired eight businesses between 1982 and 1984 and in a short time had to develop a way to evaluate major investments. We took a two-pronged approach. Corporate planning worked with the newly acquired financial services businesses to develop plans and understand the relationship between new investment and future cash flows. Meanwhile, the business investment department analyzed and submitted requests for the cash infusions needed to support insurance already in the works.

While cash infusions were really not discretionary because they were required by statute, these early projects provided an opportunity for the managements of financial services to work with the staff of American Can. Organizational and communication barriers began to fall, allowing a shift in focus from the allocation of funds needed to support existing policies to real discretionary decisions — whether to come out with new insurance products or to expand major businesses.

Gradually, the business investment staff has gained credibility. Although some staff members have demonstrated technical strategic planning and financial analytic skills, other have brought only work experience and common sense to the job. We have avoided bringing in analysts from outside American Can Company or its subsidiaries. When a job on the staff opens up, general managers and sector executives suggest candidates. The vice president of strategic planning, in consultation with members of the Office of the Chairman, selects the head of the business investment department. The managing director of the business investment department, in consultation with general managers of the business units, selects the persons for the remaining two jobs.

Plant and sales managers, financial executives from the corporate controller's department, and the head of finance and planning from one of American Can's consumer businesses have all been successful on the business investment staff. Most have gone on to greater responsibilities.

Marketing the Idea

In introducing the new structure for capital allocation to managers, simplicity was an overriding goal. We distributed a business investment policy manual, which presents the highlights of the new process and describes how it fits into the overall management of American Can. Next, a member of the business investment staff visited most of the business units to make a short presentation covering highlights of the resource allocation process and respond to a variety of questions and objections. Concerns like these, for example, came up:

"We don't have any investment decisions in our business, except to determine whether to purchase a computer." Such a contention could only be true if all future direction-setting decisions had been made in the past.

"We're not asking the corporation for money; we are using only our own money for this investment." All funds belong to the stockholders, and stockholders do not care where cash flow comes from nearly as much as where it goes. Allocating these funds to obtain the best overall return is one of corporate management's most important responsibilities.

"Even our general manager delegates these decisions; why do they have to be approved at sector or corporate levels?" We often heard this complaint from newly acquired businesses but found, on close examination, that in the past the general manager had either given the final go-ahead for large investments or had such a thorough awareness of the business unit's operations that approval had taken place subtly and informally over time. The distance between businesses and the diversity among managers require a more formal process at American Can.

"Corporate management doesn't understand what we're up against." This common complaint has a parallel in the normal loan approval process at a bank. Banks cannot understand all the intricacies of corporate customers, but they must be satisfied that they understand where their depositors' money goes and what the risks and expected results are. Corporate management is in a similar position: it may say yes or no to an investment; it will sometimes offer advice or specify conditions under which funds can be spent; but generally it will not change a request.

"General managers and sector executives should be free to spend within the limits agreed to in the planning process." While the most frequent objection, this lacks credibility for two reasons. First, no plan is written or reviewed in the kind of detail necessary for a commitment to be guaranteed on all proposed investment decisions for the next year. Second, conditions change, both for the business unit and for the corporation.

"It's a nuisance! Every time I want a piece of equipment, I have to go through the appropriation process." The time and effort the appropriation process requires are warranted for major decisions. In fact, most of the alternatives would be more of a nuisance. Routine — and sometimes unnecessary — meetings gobble up large chunks of executives' time. Our appropriation process is triggered only by a request to spend money, and it always results in a decision.

This kind of give-and-take has been essential to our success in implementing the new policy. We have carefully avoided discussion of risk premiums, beta factors, and hurdle rates and have instead stuck to the subjects business managers deal with in the conduct of business —

customers, products, service, costs, suppliers, competitors, employees, and the economy.

A Normal Cycle

The two phases of the planning and appropriation process start at the business unit level and finish with top management's review and approval. (For a look at the kinds of decisions that need to be made, please see the insert.)

The Gamma Success

American Can has long monitored packaging trends and funded a large R&D budget that has produced several successes, including the laminated toothpaste tube and the two-piece metal food can that eliminates lead solder seams. Despite the packaging industry's declining profitability and the company's redirection of resources into other businesses, the company still carefully looks for growth opportunities in packaging.

Since the mid-1970s, for example, American Can has been developing an oxygen barrier plastic bottle to replace glass. Preferred to glass bottles because they are lighter, shatter resistant, and squeezable, plastic bottles are usually oxygen-permeable and not suitable for oxygen-sensitive products. In addition, plastics that provide an oxygen barrier are very expensive.

By the early 1980s, the long R&D process had culminated in a breakthrough called barrier coextrusion blow molding, a process in which various plastics are sandwiched together and blown into bottle molds. We chose Gamma as the bottle's brand name. American Can's market research showed substantial consumer preference for it rather than the usual glass bottle.

Despite the bottle's consumer appeal, the company's course was anything but clear. Cash was tight; management did not view packaging as its primary growth vehicle; we were a small contender against the giants of the bottle business; we did not know the size of the potential market. Nor did we know whether food processing customers would convert their filling lines to handle our new bottle.

We had to select customers and products carefully to capitalize on our technological lead time, synchronize our capacity buildup with our customers, achieve a rapid payback,

The strategic planning cycle begins in early winter when the Executive Committee agrees to a planning calendar. Next, top-level managers of each business unit identify or reaffirm appropriate strategies. The metal container business, for example, may reaffirm its marketing concentration in profitable segments while it cuts costs to exploit a strong position in the mature metal container industry. Fingerhut may continue to seek rapid sales growth in the expanding mail-order industry.

Operating managements then summarize their list of recommended investments. They incorporate the cash flows of each investment in the

---

and still live within our cash constraints. Though the prototype bottles were promising, we had to quickly prove we could produce commercial quantities at acceptable cost.

In 1981, a developmental program targeted potential end-use products and customers, confirmed product compatibility, outlined timing, costs, and revenues for Gamma's commercialization, and at the same time gained approval for the purchase of an expensive prototype machine. By 1982, the company had produced commercial quantities of the Gamma bottle and H.J. Heinz had developed introductory plans for ketchup — a natural application for a squeezable container. Test markets showed that consumers liked the new package, so we adjusted strategic plans upward.

New investment was now required, and a second blow-molding machine was approved in the last quarter of 1982. Still, we had much uncertainty about longer-run demand because Heinz had not yet started the commercial rollout of its ketchup bottles and was unsure about which sizes would be most popular in plastic. Management justified the second machine on the basis of sales estimates from Heinz and analysis of other uses for the machine should Heinz change its mind.

On the strength of Heinz's initial test results, our company approved two more blow-molding machines in 1983. The business unit reestimated the project's future and reaffirmed the decision to concentrate on major-brand products.

Today, we still have technological lead time on competitors and the Gamma bottle is a success. Its development and commercialization have gone smoothly because management has continually updated plans as results have come in. We scrutinized each decision to commit large increments of capital and compared them with overall plans. Throughout the process, we have been able to balance our larger concerns with the requirements of the Gamma project.

financial projections of each business; then the corporate planning department consolidates those financial projections in late spring and, with the corporate treasury, provides an assessment of the corporation's available cash flow.

At the same time, the other half of the strategic planning staff—business investment—consolidates and ranks the major investment decisions and provides the forum in which the range of the corporation's investment choices can be viewed outside the context of individual business units. After reviewing data supplied by business units, business investment normally recommends which investments to speed up, which to stretch out, and possibly which to drop.

Review and approval of plans take place in early summer. As corporate management seeks the best mix of risks and rewards within corporate constraints, it may revise plans. The end product is acceptance of each business unit's plan and its list of investment projects based on three assumptions: first, a unit's performance will come close to the projections in the plans; second, the performance of other units will come close to their cash generation or use projections; and third, the details of the major investments will be similar to the abbreviated overview shown in each business's plan.

Beginning the Appropriations Process

The appropriations process begins when it is time to spend money on a specific investment. Then managers need to verify the three basic assumptions; agreement in principle from the planning process must be turned into a contract to spend money in the appropriations process.

Business units write an investment request, which describes the investment, discusses its impact on competitive position, highlights the key issues on which the decision depends, and estimates its risk and sensitivities. The request also sets forth the alternatives, including the consequences of doing nothing, and provides a cash flow projection and a calculation of the internal rate of return, the net present value, and the payback, if appropriate. The business unit's general manager then approves all projects and sends those over $250,000 to the business investment department for review.

The business investment department examines each major request—about 150 annually—and crystallizes issues from a corporate point of view. Will the request from one business unit affect the customers or the suppliers of another? Do the appropriate functional experts, including corporate engineering, human resources, taxes, information systems and services, accounting and treasury, agree? The business investment department also checks details and adjusts for the current environment and ensures that the analytical work is comparable to that of other projects and businesses.

After the review, a letter summarizes the proposal, emphasizes critical issues and risks, and provides a recommendation of approval (or specifies conditions under which an investment should be approved). It goes first to the sector executive who has final approval authority for projects under $1 million. Projects of more than $1 million do not reach the Business Investment Committee unless the sector executive approves the project. Rarely does either the sector executive or the Business Investment Committee turn down a proposal. The business unit usually withdraws a doomed project first.

Business Investment Committee members and the sector executive may raise questions about the project or about progress in an associated strategy. In the process, they discuss the risks and offer advice on implementation. Their approval of a proposed investment gives a clear decision to implement new strategic expenditures.

Balancing Strategy and Operations

In this company's turbulent environment, we've been challenged to maintain continuity in business operations. The strategic planning and business investment processes have been invaluable in helping corporate management put short- and long-term objectives in perspective and balance sources and uses of funds. For example, because the mission of the metal packaging business is to generate cash, it must be very selective in its investments. Although we have rationalized and cut costs since 1972, we continue to lead the metal container industry in converting to lead-free food cans and to two-piece beer and beverage cans with stay-on openers. These improvements require huge investments for automated equipment, for welders, for two-piece can machines, and for entirely new plants.

In our tube business, we invest in laminated tube equipment to accommodate growth in dentifrice and to convert pharmaceutical products from metal to laminated tubes. During 1983, we approved projects to produce more laminated tubes at lower cost. The key questions are: How fast will the market become saturated? How can we most efficiently maintain our low-cost position?

In coextruded films, we have added capacity and developed a tubular water-quench process to produce lower-cost, higher-quality film for cheese wraps, hot dogs, and other meat products. The key issue: how to convert the customer to the new process. Although we produce a low-cost, high-quality product, we are its only supplier and important customers have been reluctant to substitute it as long as it is available from only one source. We have had to balance the cost of large-capacity additions against the risk of competition, low prices, and the possibility of low returns.

In specialty retailing, Fingerhut has dramatically increased its mailing list and computer capacity, approved new facilities, added new printing equipment, and acquired the Figi's and Michigan Bulb companies. Musicland has opened new stores and installed one of the most modern inventory management systems in specialty retailing. This company has also made substantial investments in marketing computer software, movies, and other new products.

In the financial services sector, new facilities, new computer systems, improved telecommunications, major expansion of existing lines of business, and new products have all been approved.

Resistance and Breakthrough

The system allows us to make difficult choices and trade-offs on the basis of acts, not personalities, history, or rules of thumb. The measures are consistent for all business units, and each incremental allocation is tailored to an overall plan for the corporation that supports its direction.

Turfmanship is alive and well at American Can; business units take a healthy interest in maintaining their independence. Although management has communicated the new policy well, misunderstandings do occur. Rules have been bent by business units, but clear violations have been few. Most conflicts between the managing director of the business investment department and the business units' general managers have been settled. Resolution at this level is encouraged by the consistent support given to the business investment policy by corporate management. Unresolved differences between the business investment staff and the business units' general managers are brought to the attention of the sector executive. While questions of interpretation have been referred to the Business Investment Committee, no clear violation of policy has risen above the sector level.

The most frequent resistance to the new policy comes in the form of a delayed submission of an investment request — until events in the marketplace or elsewhere call for approval under crisis conditions (e.g., "build the plant, or watch our competitors walk away with the business"). This kind of manipulative behavior is disruptive. But it is also self-limiting because no general manager wants the reputation of consistently surprising and pressuring corporate management.

The capital allocation process at American Can is a major step forward in the practical application of management science. It has improved our ability to deploy resources in a way that generates promising returns while giving business units enough independence to respond to their marketplaces. We have reduced the number of people involved in decisions, concentrated staff support in the hands of fewer individuals, and cut the cost of the whole allocation process. Most important, we believe these changes have contributed greatly to our current success and have provided a strong management framework on which to build for the future.

Questions

1.   In many companies, capital budgeting and strategic planning are separate functions involving different sets of people. Explain how

American Can linked these two functions. What advantages flow from this linkage?

2. How does American Can distinguish between expenditures for operations and investments? Identify examples of each type of expenditure.

3. Describe American Can's procedure for approval of capital projects.

4. What steps does American Can take to understand and limit risks of capital investments?

5. What role does a business unit of American Can play in capital budgeting?

Applying Behavioral Finance to Capital Budgeting: Project Terminations

Meir Statman and David Caldwell

Standard financial theory offers managers decision rules that are designed to maximize the value of the firm. A central rule of capital budgeting prescribes that investment projects be selected, continued, or terminated based on their net present values. In particular, the choice between continuation and termination should be made by comparing the project's net present value under the two alternatives.

The net present value approach to project termination has been investigated by Bonini [1], Dyl and Long [3], Gaumnitz and Emery [5], Howe and McCabe [7], and Robichek and Van Horne [17, 18]. While these investigations vary in many aspects, they share the conclusion that sunk costs should be ignored and that projects should be terminated when the expected present value of cash flows, given that the project is terminated today, is greater than the expected present value of cash flows given that the project is continued for at least one additional period. Do managers follow this advice? We suggest that managers tend to become entrapped into losing projects and throw good money after bad as they attempt to rescue them.

Termination decisions are difficult even when they are wise. Consider, for example, the report by Russell [19] on the development of an eight-inch floppy disk drive (half-height, double-sided, double density, one megabyte capacity) by the Shugart Corporation.

Meir Statman and David Caldwell, "Applying Behavioral Finance to Capital Budgeting: Project Terminations," *Financial Management* (Winter 1987) Vol. 16, Iss. 4: 7–15. Reprinted with permission.

At the time of this writing, both authors were members of the faculty of the Leavey School of Business and Administration, Santa Clara University. Meir Statman was with the Department of Finance and David Caldwell was with the Department of Management.

The authors wish to thank Melanie Austin, Keith Brown, George Pinches, Robert Taggart, James Van Horne and two anonymous reviewers for comments on an earlier draft. Meir Statman acknowledges support from a Batterymarch Fellowship.

The disk-drive project was initially seen as a profitable project by Shugart Corporation, a company that has already established itself as a leader in disk drives. Shugart started the project in 1980, and supported it generously. The project was abandoned in 1983, after severe time and cost overruns and long after disk drives by competitors had been designed into computers that Shugart considered as part of its market. Below are comments by people who were involved in the project.

V.P. Finance: "I was Controller then. The V.P. of Finance and I presented an economic justification for eliminating this product in August 1982. We felt very strongly about it. We presented the analysis at the executive staff meeting. The V.P. of the Disk-Drive Division immediately championed the product and signed up for lower costs. He also argued the asset recovery issue. I find that if any champion is willing to stick up for a project, then the financial analysis is rejected. Personalities are very important around here."

V.P. Marketing: "In November 1982 the executive staff discussed ending this project. The Disk-Drive Division championed the product quite strongly. I feel it was an emotional decision to continue, because in this same time frame the Disk-Drive Division had begun to protest that a lot of their talent was being drained to go work on a new venture group within the company. Keeping the project going was a way to placate the people by giving them more time to make it come out right and not have to admit defeat. By April 1983 I was aware that our competition, who had gotten the product to market, was also suffering because total demand was not as great as expected. This project had horrendous milestone and target misses. I talked with the division V.P. and the president about it."

Resistance to project termination can be very expensive. For example, the Lockheed L-1011 airplane would have bankrupted the company if not for a federal government bailout. (See Reinhardt [16].) The program was terminated in 1981. The amount of good money thrown after bad can be gleaned from the fact that Lockheed's stock price increased by 18% on the day following the termination announcement. Lockheed's case is not unique. A study by Statman and Sepe [25] showed that announcements of termination of losing projects are generally associated with positive abnormal returns on the stock of the terminating companies.

This paper has two parts. The first presents behavioral finance, a framework that is consistent with a tendency to become entrapped and resist project terminations. The second part of the paper describes structures, such as organizational hierarchies and hostile takeovers, that are designed to overcome the resistance to project terminations.

I. Behavioral Finance

Behavioral finance is a descriptive theory of choice under uncertainty. It contains four elements: (1) framing mental accounts according to prospect theory, (2) evaluating mental accounts according to prospect theory, (3) regret aversion, and (4) self-control.

Past and expected cash flows associated with a project are framed into mental accounts and evaluated according to the rules of prospect theory. Regret aversion serves to deter managers from terminating projects. Self-control is employed to explain how managers force themselves to terminate projects.

Behavioral finance has been applied earlier to the issues of dividends (Shefrin and Statman [21]), the realization of gains or losses on securities (Shefrin and Statman [22]), and the use of options (Shefrin and Statman [23]).

A. *Prospect Theory: Framing Mental Accounts and Evaluating Them*

Managers who make decisions on the initiation, continuation, and termination of projects make a series of choices, or gambles, based on uncertain cash flows. Managers who follow the net present value rule, as prescribed by standard financial theory, frame these cash flows in a way that we call economic accounting. However, we believe that managers use mental accounting to frame cash flows. The crucial point that distinguishes the two in our context is that sunk costs are ignored in economic accounting, but not in mental accounting.

Kahneman and Tversky's [9] prospect theory divides the choice process into two phases. The first phase involves framing by which mental accounts are created. The second phase involves evaluation of these mental accounts and choice. The following example illustrates the construction of accounts and their evaluation.[1]

A person is involved in a business venture in which he has already lost $2,000. Now he faces a choice between a sure gain of $1,000 and an even chance to win $2,000 or nothing. What will he choose?

An account, economic or mental, is similar to a checking account. A person who uses the rules of economic accounting forms two accounts. The first account contains a loss of $2,000, and it is now closed. The second account is an account that will contain $1,000 when closed if the sure gain is chosen. It will contain $2,000 or zero when closed if the gamble is chosen. The $2,000 lost earlier is sunk cost, reflected in the closed account, and it has no bearing on the choice between the sure amount and the gamble. The rules of economic accounting lead a person to choose the $1,000 sure gain over the gamble if risk aversion is assumed.

Kahneman and Tversky noted that people do not adapt easily to losses. A person who uses mental accounting and who has not adapted to his $2,000 loss sees only one account that is open and registers a $2,000 loss. In other words, sunk costs are not ignored. This person frames

---

[1] Our discussion is not intended to capture all the aspects of prospect theory. The theory is presented fully in Kahneman and Tversky [9].

his choice between the sure gain and the gamble as a choice between (a) closing the account with a loss of $1,000 (i.e., the $2,000 original loss less the $1,000 gain), and (b) closing the account with a loss of $2,000 or a loss of zero, depending on the outcome of the gamble. Kahneman and Tversky argue that people display risk-seeking behavior when faced with a choice between a sure loss and a gamble, and they are likely to choose the $2,000 or zero gamble over the sure $1,000.

The implications of this analysis for project continuation and abandonment are important. Economic accounting dictates that the $2,000 sunk cost be ignored and that the project be abandoned, if risk aversion is assumed. However, it is likely that the problem is framed according to mental accounting where sunk costs are not ignored. In that case, the even chance to lose $2,000 or nothing that comes with continuing the project for another period will be chosen over the sure loss of $1,000 that comes with project abandonment; thus, projects that should be abandoned according to the prescription of standard financial theory might be continued according to the perspective of behavioral financial theory.

B. Aversion to Regret

An individual who has not adapted his asset position to losses is likely to be entrapped into continuing the project. He makes a distinction between unrealized "paper" losses and "realized" losses, and he adapts his asset position only when the losses are realized. Kahneman and Tversky [10] and Thaler [29] suggested that people are reluctant to realize loss because realization induces regret. Kahneman and Tversky wrote:

Regret is a special form of frustration in which the event one would change is an action one has either taken or failed to take . . . regret is felt if one can readily imagine having taken an action that would have led to a more desirable outcome. This interpretation explains the close link between the experience of regret and the availability of choice: actions taken under duress generate little regret. The reluctance to violate standard procedures and to act innovatively can also be an effective defense against subsequent regret because it is easy to imagine doing the conventional thing and more difficult to imagine doing the unconventional one. (p. 173)

In his discussion of regret, Thaler [29] pointed out that regret will be acute where an individual must take responsibility for the final outcome. Thaler explained the reluctance of soldiers to trade patrol assignments even when such trades would make assignments more convenient for all individuals.

If two men trade assignments and one is killed, the other must live with the knowledge that it could (should?) have been he. By avoiding such trades these costs are reduced. Since the opportunity to exchange assignments must surely be a valued convenience, the observed resistance to trading suggests that the potential responsibility costs are non-trivial. (p. 52)

The effects of responsibility on entrapment are illustrated in an experiment by Staw [26]. Staw asked his subjects to play the role of corporate executives making decisions about the allocation of research and development funds to various projects.[2]

The decision material described the Adams and Smith Company, a large technologically oriented firm that is suffering declining profitability. Each subject was provided with descriptions of the company's two divisions (Industrial Products and Consumer Products) and ten years of sales and earnings data. Staw manipulated the degree of responsibility of the subjects for the decision. In the "high personal responsibility" case, the subjects themselves chose one of the two divisions and invested $10 million in it. In the "low personal responsibility" case, subjects were told that a financial officer who preceded them had already chosen the division for investment.

Later, subjects received a second part of the case which included sales and profit results based on the five-year period following the initial $10 million investment. One-half of the subjects received data indicating that their chosen division was improving. The other half received data indicating that their chosen division was deteriorating further. All subjects were told that they had an additional budget of $20 million to distribute between the two divisions.

Staw found that the interaction between personal responsibility and decision consequences was very strong. In the second part of the experiment, subjects allocated the highest amounts to the division they had chosen in the first part, where the initial decision had negative consequences, and where subjects had high personal responsibility for that decision.[3]

---

[2] Economists tend to treat evidence from experiments with caution and are reluctant to conclude that similar results would be obtained in real life settings. Two specific challenges to experiments are usually raised. First, students are most often used as subjects for experiments. Are they representative of the larger population? Second, compensation paid subjects is not always related to their performance. Are experiment results sensitive to incentives?

Psychologists have recognized these challenges. Experiments with professionals (*e.g.,* executives, psychologists, physicians) as subjects yield results similar to those with students as subjects. And experiments where substantial monetary incentives are offered yield results similar to those with experiments where no such incentives are provided. Moreover, it is unlikely that robust results would be obtained if subjects selected answers randomly. Rather, the robust results obtained in experiments suggest that subjects take their roles seriously.

[3] The Staw case did not provide subjects with information about expected future cash flows from the two divisions. Therefore, the results cannot preclude the possibility that the decision to invest in the deteriorating division is consistent with the net present value prescription of standard financial theory. Specifically, it is possible that subjects properly ignored the sunk costs in the deteriorating division and chose to invest in it because they thought that further investment in it had a higher net present value that was higher than the net present value of further investment in the other division. However, in a recent experiment Hoskin [6] provided subjects with information about expected future cash flows and other information needed for the calculation required by standard financial theory. He found that the resistance to project termination is dominant even when standard financial theory prescribes termination.

The Staw experiment indicates that high personal responsibility increases the resistance to project termination. That relationship is consistent with the link between regret and the availability of choice. A manager who chooses to accept a project has a choice between acceptance and rejection. The regret that this manager feels when he terminates the project is greater than the regret felt by a manager who terminates a project that has been accepted earlier by another manager.

The strong effect of personal responsibility is extended in experiments which show that insecurity on the part of the manager and resistance on the part of his or her superiors is associated with increased entrapment. Consider the following experiment by Fox and Staw [4].

The experiment is based on the "Adams and Smith" case presented earlier. Responsibility for the funding decision was manipulated in two aspects, job insecurity and resistance. In the "high insecurity" condition, subjects were told that they now assume the position of vice president of finance at Adams and Smith, a significant promotion from their earlier position. However, the title of the position is acting vice president. Subjects were told further that the position might become permanent, or they might be demoted, based on their performance. In the interim, subjects have to deal with other executives who are well qualified and envious of the subject's position and who are not likely to provide much assistance. In the "low insecurity" condition, subjects were told that the position of vice president of finance is permanent and that other executives are happy with the choice and likely to provide support.

As in Staw [26] each subject was asked to choose one of two divisions for an initial investment of $10 million. In the "high resistance" condition, subjects received a negative evaluation from the board of directors on their funding decision. The board members were very dissatisfied and firmly convinced that the choice was wrong, but reluctantly deferred to the subject's judgment. In the "low resistance" condition, subjects received a positive evaluation from the board of directors on their funding decision.

In the second stage of the experiment, all subjects were told that the results of the initial investment decision met with little success and that more funds were needed for research and development. Subjects were asked to allocate an amount ranging from $0 to $20 million to their previously chosen division.

Analysis of the results showed that both insecurity and resistance increase the commitment of subjects to their previously chosen division. Subjects in the "high insecurity" condition allocated significantly more funds than did subjects in the "low insecurity" condition. Similarly, subjects in the "high resistance" condition allocated more funds than subjects in the "low resistance" condition.

The degree to which personal responsibility contributes to the reluctance to terminate projects is modified by conditions of resistance and insecurity. However, reluctance to terminate projects exists even in the absence of personal responsibility. It is probably a manifestation of a societal norm. This suggestion is supported by the results of an experiment by Staw and Ross [28] in which subjects received a description of an administrator responsible for alleviating poor housing conditions.

Subjects were informed about the administrator's actions in response to the housing problem, actions taken over a period of several years. Half the subjects were told that the administrator was consistent in his actions (consistency condition). The other half were told that the administrator continuously changed his policies in response to negative feedback concerning previous decisions (experimental condition). Housing conditions remained bleak regardless of the administrator's decisions. The administrator in the "consistency condition" was entrapped, ignoring negative feedback and persisting with his original policy. However, the experimenting administrator was not entrapped and changed his policies in response to feedback. Subjects judged the consistent manager much more favorably than the experimenting one. This suggests that consistent, rather than experimental, behavior is considered socially desirable.[4]

C. Self-Control

The pain of regret is felt most acutely when a project is terminated and a loss is realized. People tend to procrastinate when confronted with losses as a way to postpone that pain.

Procrastination is a manifestation of a self-control problem. It is similar in nature to the difficulty people have in completing their tax forms early, even when a refund is waiting. The manager who chooses to continue the project rather than realize the $2,000 loss in the earlier example may be aware of the economic accounting argument that favors project abandonment. Yet the manager may find it difficult to take action consistent with economic accounting. This self-control problem can be analyzed within the Thaler and Shefrin [30] framework where it is treated as an intrapersonal agency conflict between a rational, forward-looking principal and an emotional, myopic agent. The rational principal understands the benefits associated with following the prescriptions of standard financial theory. However, action can be taken only by the emotional agent and that agent is the one who will suffer the pain of regret that comes with loss realization. Procrastination helps the agent postpone the pain. The proposition that a self-control problem may lead to the reluctance to realize losses is supported by the link between the personal responsibility for the initial decision and the reluctance to realize losses in the subsequent stage.

---

[4] Staw and Ross noted that the tendency to rate favorably the consistent manager was most pronounced where managers were used as subjects. The tendency was less pronounced where undergraduate business students were used as subjects, and it disappeared where psychology students were used as subjects.

II. Structures for Project Termination Decisions

A. The Two Faces of Commitment

Behavioral finance provides a framework, supported by experiments, that is consistent with the tendency to resist project terminations. In the following sections we suggest that people are generally aware of this tendency and that important aspects of organizations and financial markets reflect attempts to cope with it.

The tendency to become committed and the difficulty of disengaging from commitment are pervasive. People who undertake projects or who join existing projects tend to become committed to them. Moreover, commitment is generally regarded by society as positive. We admire people who are not deterred by failure and who persist in the pursuit of their goals. Commitment to losing projects imposes great costs, and it is tempting to devise solutions that will reduce these costs. However, commitment is useful as a motivator, compelling people to work harder and accomplish more than they would otherwise. Examples abound about committed project "champions," who were able to complete projects successfully by intense effort. (See, for example, Kidder [11].) Perhaps becoming "fanatically committed" is necessary for success in the face of perceived failure (Quinn [15]). Commitment, then, has two faces. Commitment helps people generate the force needed to complete difficult projects. However, commitment also entraps people into losing projects.

One possible remedy for the tendency to become entrapped is to teach people to distinguish projects where commitment plays a positive role from those where it plays a negative role. Specifically, people can be taught to ignore sunk costs and frame projects according to the prescriptions of economic accounting. They might learn to be committed to projects with positive net present value, but disengage from those with negative net present value. (See, for example, Northcraft and Wolf [13].) Indeed, such teaching may be one of the greatest contributions of business school teachers to their students. However, as Thaler [29] noted, anyone who has tried to teach his or her students to ignore sunk costs knows that the advice is not intuitively obvious. As the experiments demonstrate, the tendency to become committed is ingrained. We lack mechanisms to turn it off or regulate it well.

B. Regret and Self-Control

The difficulty of learning to distinguish projects where commitment plays a positive role from projects where it plays a negative role is not an intellectual difficulty; the net present value prescription of standard financial theory is fairly simple. Rather, the difficulty is largely a manifestation of a self-control problem. Termination means that a mental account is now closed at a loss; the loss is now admitted as fact. The rational internal "principal" may understand the benefits of terminating losing projects but finds it difficult to force the emotional internal "agent" to take the required action.

Rules are useful in self-control. For example, traders often use internally enforced iron-clad rules to force themselves to realize losses. Consider the following statement by a professional trader:

I have a hard and fast rule that I never let my losses on a trade exceed ten percent. Say I buy a ten-dollar stock. As soon as it goes to nine dollars, I must sell it and take a loss. Some guys have a five percent rule. Some may have fifteen. I'm a ten man. The thing is, when you're right you're making eighths and quarters. So you can't take a loss of a point. The traders who get wiped out hope against hope. I've seen a good hundred come and go since I've been here in 1964. They're stubborn. They refuse to take losses. (Quoted in Kleinfield [12], pp. 17–18.)

Two rules are useful in the context of project terminations: first, a rule that mandates an explicit formulation of projects according to the principles of economic accounting and specifies that only projects with positive expected net present value be accepted, and second, a rule that mandates periodic reviews of the net present value of each project. Continuation of a project beyond each review is contingent on a finding of an expected net present value that is higher than the termination value. These rules can be enforced internally by the project manager, but internal enforcement in the presence of severe self-control problems is difficult. As noted by the professional trader quoted earlier, many fail to abide by internally enforced rules.

C. Rules Enforced within the Company

Externally enforced rules can be useful where internally enforced rules fail. Specifically, companies can devise formal structures whereby people other than project managers and their teams evaluate each project periodically and decide on continuation or termination according to the prescriptions of economic accounting. Indeed, periodic structured reviews of projects are common in companies. Project "milestones" are an integral part of many projects' plans and progress is compared to these milestones.

Comparison to milestones can be an effective way to identify projects that deserve termination, but it is effective only if the rules are followed strictly. Effective reviews require precommitment of decisions to milestones. Precommitment means that a project's plan identifies milestones such that termination is automatic if they are not reached.

Iron-clad precommitment will be suboptimal in some instances. Information arrives continuously and some of it might justify modifications or postponement of milestones. However, decisions based on precommitment may still be superior to decisions based on biased information. Specifically, we know that entrapped project managers tend to promote their failing projects, and distort or filter negative information as they do so. (See Caldwell and O'Reilly [2].) Accurate information can provide a way out of the costly choice between reliance on outdated information and reliance on updated but possibly biased information.

Finance people often serve as a source of accurate project information, but it is not better knowledge that makes their analysis more accurate. Indeed, project managers probably possess the best information about their projects. However, project managers are also project champions, likely to be entrapped in the commitment to their projects and likely to conceal negative information.

The important aspect of the finance function is an absence of commitment to the project. Finance people are valuable when they are "objective" and they can remain objective only as long as they are not entrapped in the project. They play their role effectively when they serve as "anti-champions," exposing rosy projections provided by project champions. Of course, playing the role of anti-champion is not easy. Project managers often complain that finance people are not "team players"; they are antagonistic nay-sayers. Antagonism is unpleasant, and finance people are always tempted to join the team. However, structured and civilized antagonism serves a useful purpose in the facilitation of project terminations.

Finance people can play their anti-champion role effectively when chief executives provide them with power equal to that of the project champions. As the Shugart case illustrates, not all chief executives provide that power. Finance people are frequently left with only the role of the "bean counter."

Commitment to losing projects can be eliminated in other ways. For example, "workout" units for nonperforming loans have been established by some banks (Staw [27]). Loan officers are likely to be committed to their original loan decisions. They are likely to accept disadvantageous arrangements rather than close a mental account at a loss and admit that a loan is bad. However, officers in the workout unit have little commitment to the decision to grant the loan. They are more likely to be aggressive in pursuit of payment even when aggressive pursuit might disclose that earlier loan decisions were faulty. (The loan officers' problem also illustrates the fact that outsiders, such as bankers, can be "sucked in" and become committed to projects that they oversee.)

Outside consultants sometimes serve a function similar to that of the workout unit. Consultants are often accused of charging money for "borrowing your watch to tell you the time." However, while consultants lack complete knowledge, they possess the objectivity of a person who is not entrapped.[5]

---

[5] Sah and Stiglitz [20] suggest that hierarchies are useful because they reduce the likelihood that bad projects will be chosen. For example, in a hierarchy with two levels, only projects that pass two independent examinations are undertaken. We suggest that hierarchies are useful partly because they provide a mechanism to terminate projects even when some levels of the organization are entrapped. It would be useful to develop tests that will distinguish between the organizational consequences of two approaches.

D. Rewards and Penalties

The pain of regret comes even where no one but the individual who is involved knows that a termination occurred. A stockholder who realizes a "paper" loss feels the pain of regret even when he or she alone knows about the purchase and the subsequent sale of the stock. However, the pain of regret is intensified where the termination is known to others, and it is intensified further where company penalties such as demotion or pay cut are involved. Substantial company penalties may lead project champions to "double up," increase commitment and continue to invest in losing projects rather than admit failure.

The two faces of commitment are evident here. High rewards for success and high penalties for failure increase the level of commitment to projects. These rewards and penalties add power to the intrinsic rewards and penalties and to those provided by society. High commitment to projects enhances the likelihood that they will be completed successfully, but it also increases the likelihood of entrapment. The beneficial effects of rewards and penalties on commitment are often emphasized while the link between commitment and entrapment is often ignored. Perhaps we need a better balance.

A good reward system also encourages project managers to provide accurate information. That is important because project managers know more about their projects than anyone else, and accurate information is crucial for correct continuation or termination decisions. A reward system that favors those who disclose bad news early is likely to counter the tendency to increase commitment to losing projects.

The pain of regret is particularly intense where project managers are placed in situations of "high insecurity" and "high resistance" (Fox and Staw [4]). Managers who feel that their positions are not secure or that their decisions are resisted by superiors are more likely to be entrapped than managers who are secure in their position and who have the trust of their superiors. Trust on the part of superiors does not mean that they suspend criticism. It only means that superiors acknowledge that the task is difficult and that failure might not necessarily be due to fault on the part of a project manager.[6]

---

[6] A letter sent to Charles F. Kettering by the Executive Committee of General Motors provides an excellent example of the needed balance between trust and criticism:
November 30, 1921

Dear Kettering:
It is most important in our opinion that your mind be kept free from worries foreign to the development of the air cooled car and other laboratory work.
In the development and introduction of anything so radically different from standard practice as the air cooled car is from the regular water cooled job, it is quite natural that there should be a lot of "wiseacres" and "know-it-alls" standing around knocking the development.
In order that your mind may be completely relieved as to the position of the undersigned with respect to the air cooled development, we beg to advise as follows:

E. Enforcement by Outsiders

Even top-level managers do not always confront the problem of entrapment. Indeed, sometimes the project that needs termination is the overall strategy of top management. Intervention from the outside is needed in such cases. As Jensen [8] noted, takeovers offer a way to terminate losing strategies and projects. He wrote:

> Managers often have trouble abandoning strategies they have spent years devising and implementing, even when those strategies no longer contribute to the organization's survival. Such changes often require abandonment of major projects, relocation of facilities, changes in managerial assignments, and closure or sale of facilities or divisions. It is easier for new top-level managers with no ties with current employees or communities to make such changes. (p. 9)

New top-level managers are similar to consultants and "workout" units. They are likely to be successful, not because they know more than the deposed managers; rather, they are likely to be successful because they have no ties or commitments to existing strategies and projects.

F. After Termination

The pain of regret comes when losses are realized, but losses are losses only when they are framed as such. Even failing projects have redeeming features. For example, they provide greater understanding of technologies or consumers. Focusing on the gains and deemphasizing the losses might be derided as useless "sour grapes" rationalization, but such derision misses the usefulness of framing losses as gains. It is easier to terminate projects with gains than it is to terminate projects with losses.

The knowledge that terminations bring pain is not new to companies. Many companies offer "outplacement" services to dismissed employees. Outplacement services are structured on the premise that dismissed (terminated) employees have to be helped through their pain,

---

1st: We are absolutely confident in your ability to whip all problems in connection with the development of our proposed air cooled cars.

2nd: We will continue to have this degree of confidence and faith in you and your ability to accomplish this task until such time as we come to you and frankly state that we have doubt as to the possibility or feasibility of turning the trick and you will be the first one to whom we will come.

We are endeavoring in this letter to use language such as will result in the complete elimination of worry on your part with respect to our faith in you and this work and if this language fails to create this result, then won't you kindly write us quite frankly advising in what respect we have failed?

Due to the fact that criticisms are bound to continue until the air cooled cars are in active production and use, would it not be well for you to agree with us that at any time you have occasion to pause and wonder about our faith and confidence in you and this development, that you will pull this letter out of your desk and read it again, after which you will write to us in consideration of our frankly stating that we will write to you first in case of any doubt? (From Sloan [24])

well beyond the problems that accompany loss of income. It is ironic that companies acknowledge the pain of dismissed employees yet ignore the pain of employees, such as project managers, who are retained while their projects are terminated. Project managers whose projects are terminated often become isolated and alienated within their companies even when they should not carry blame for the failures of their projects. Perhaps companies can use some of the techniques of outplacement services to help managers of terminated projects.

III. Conclusion

Commitment has two faces. The first is a motivating face that helps us generate the force needed to surmount obstacles that seem insurmountable and accomplish goals that seem impossibly remote. The second face of commitment is wasteful. Commitment can easily turn into entrapment where good money is thrown after bad in the pursuit of impossible goals.

Behavioral finance offers a useful framework for the analysis of the pervasive tendency to cross the line from commitment as motivation to commitment as entrapment. In particular, projects are framed as mental accounts where sunk costs are not ignored, and entrapment is likely where termination results in a loss relative to sunk costs. Termination induces the pain of regret and projects are continued so as to postpone that pain.

Individuals and companies have recognized the problem of entrapment and have developed some structures for project termination decisions. For example, periodic reviews where accomplishments are compared to project milestones are used by top management to control the commitment of project managers. Project audits by finance people and outside consultants serve to control the tendency of project managers to hide and distort negative information. Finally, takeovers are used as a tool for project terminations where companies have not been able to muster sufficient resources to do so.

References

1. C.P. Bonini, "Capital Investment Under Uncertainty with Abandonment Options," *Journal of Financial and Quantitative Analysis* (March 1977), pp. 39–54.

2. D.F. Caldwell and C.A. O'Reilly, "Response to Failure: The Effects of Choice and Responsibility on Impression Management," *Academy of Management Journal* (March 1982), pp. 121–136.

3. E.A. Dyl and H.W. Long, "Abandonment Value and Capital Budgeting," *Journal of Finance* (March 1969), pp. 88–95.

4. F.V. Fox and B.M. Staw, "The Trapped Administrator: Effects of Job Insecurity and Policy Resistance Upon Commitment to a Course of Action," *Administrative Science Quarterly* (March 1979), pp. 449–471.

5. J.E. Gaumnitz and D.R. Emery, "Asset Growth, Abandonment Value and the Replacement Decision of Like-for-Like Capital Assets," *Journal of Finance and Quantitative Analysis* (June 1980), pp. 407–419.

6. B. Hoskin, "Accounting Methods and the Framing of Sunk Costs," Working paper, Duke University (February 1986).

7. K.M. Howe and G.M. McCabe, "On Optimal Asset Abandonment and Replacement," *Journal of Financial and Quantitative Analysis* (September 1983), pp. 295–305.

8. M.C. Jensen, "The Takeover Controversy: Analysis and Evidence," Forthcoming in *Knights, Raiders and Targets: The Impact of the Hostile Takeover,* J.C. Coffee, L. Lowenstein, and S. Rose-Ackerman (Editors), Oxford University Press, 1987.

9. D. Kahneman and A. Tversky, "Prospect Theory: An Analysis of Decision Under Risk," *Econometrica* (March 1979), pp. 263–291.

10. ――― "The Psychology of Preferences," *Scientific American* 246: (January 1982), pp. 167–173.

11. T. Kidder, *The Soul of a New Machine*. New York, Little Brown and Co., 1981.

12. S. Kleinfield, *The Traders*. New York, Holt, Rinehart and Winston, 1983.

13. G.B. Northcraft and G. Wolf, "Dollars, Sense, and Sunk Costs: A Life Cycle Model of Resource Allocation Decisions," *Academy of Management Review* (January 1984), pp. 225–234.

14. G.E. Pinches, "Myopia, Capital Budgeting and Decision Making," *Financial Management* (Autumn 1982), pp. 6–19.

15. J.B. Quinn, "Technical Innovation, Entrepreneurship and Strategy," *Sloan Management Review* (Spring 1979), pp. 19–30.

16. U.E. Reinhardt, "Break-even Analysis for Lockheed's TriStar: An Application of Financial Theory," *Journal of Finance* (September 1973), pp. 821–838.

17. A.A. Robichek and J.C. Van Horne, "Abandonment Value and Capital Budgeting," *Journal of Finance* (December 1967), pp. 577–598.

18. ――― "Abandonment Value and Capital Budgeting: Reply," *Journal of Finance* (March 1969), pp. 96–97.

19. C.A. Russell, "Problems in Ending a Project: Theory and Case Study," Term paper, Santa Clara University (November 1983).

20. R.K. Sah and J.E. Stiglitz, "The Architecture of Economic Systems: Hierarchies and Polyarchies," *American Economic Review* (September 1986), pp. 716–727.

21. H.M. Shefrin and M. Statman, "Explaining Investor Preference for Cash Dividends," *Journal of Financial Economics* (June 1984), pp. 253–282.

22. ――― "The Disposition to Sell Winners Too Early and Ride Losers Too Long: Theory and Evidence," *Journal of Finance* (July 1985), pp. 777–790.

23. ――― "Applying Behavioral Finance to the Use of Options," Working Paper, Santa Clara University (May 1987).

24. A.P. Sloan, Jr., Edited by J. McDonald with C. Stevens, *My Years with General Motors*. Garden City, NY, Doubleday (1972).

25. M. Statman and J.F. Sepe, "Project Termination Decisions and the Market Value of the Firm," Working Paper, Santa Clara University (June 1986).

26. B.M. Staw, "Knee-deep in the Big Muddy: A Study of Escalating Commitment to a Chosen Course of Action," *Organizational Behavior and Human Performance* (June 1976), pp. 27–44.

27. ———— "Escalating at the Credit Window: Bank Decisions on Non-performing Loans," Unpublished manuscript, University of California (1984).

28. B.M. Staw and J. Ross, "Commitment in an Experimenting Society: An Experiment on the Attrition of Leadership from Administrative Scenarios," *Journal of Applied Psychology* (June 1980), pp. 249–260.

29. R. Thaler, "Toward a Positive Theory of Consumer Choice," *Journal of Economic Behavior and Organization* (March 1980), pp. 39–60.

30. R. Thaler and H. Shefrin, "An Economic Theory of Self-control," *Journal of Political Economy* (April 1981), pp. 392–410.

Questions

1. Provide an example of a sunk cost in capital budgeting. Explain why sunk cost is irrelevant to capital-budgeting analysis.

2. If you are risk averse, then which of the following probability distributions would you prefer?

Distribution A		Distribution B	
P_i	O_i	P_i	O_i
1.0	$100,000	0.5	$200,000
		0.5	0

where P_i is the probability of the outcome O_i. Explain your preference in terms of risk aversion.

3. Why might the original sponsor of a capital project support continuation of the project after recommendations by external consultants to abandon the project?

4. Describe the "two faces" of commitment.

5. What was the Executive Committee of General Motors trying to accomplish in its letter (see footnote 6) to Charles F. Kettering?

6. How can companies avoid the problem of becoming entrapped in a losing project?

PART IV
MANAGING WORKING CAPITAL

18
Management of Excess Cash: Practices and Developments

Ravindra R. Kamath, Shahriar Khaksari,
Heidi Hylton Meier, and
John Winklepleck

I. Introduction

Cash management, a long neglected aspect of financial management, has received increasing attention from both practitioners and academicians in recent years. High and volatile interest rates have increased the opportunity cost of holding idle cash and have intensified cash managers' efforts in expediting the collection process and optimizing the disbursement system. In addition, a more centralized cash management system, complemented by an electronic communication and transfer system, has enhanced cash managers' ability to make more productive uses of excess cash balances. The Federal Reserve System's attempts to reduce float through quicker check clearing and various changes in the regulatory environment have led to severe competition among financial institutions as well as innovation of new instruments. This in turn has provided further ammunition to money managers in their efforts to achieve greater efficiency.

It is felt that by relying on three distinctly different surveys of Fortune's second 500 firms over the 1979–84 period, the present study can add significantly to the insights provided by the earlier studies [3, 4, 5, 9]. Furthermore, these surveys provided an opportunity to capture the dynamic nature of cash management practices, trends, and the environment in which they operate. More specifically, the objective of this study is to obtain the following information:

Ravindra R. Kamath, Shahriar Khaksari, Heidi Hylton Meier, and John Winklepleck, "Management of Excess Cash: Practices and Developments," *Financial Management* (Autumn 1985) Vol. 14, Iss. 3: 70–77. Reprinted with permission.
At the time of this writing, Ravindra R. Kamath was Professor of Finance, Cleveland State University; Shahriar Khaksari was Assistant Professor of Finance, Cleveland State University; Heidi Hylton Meier was a D.B.A. student, Kent State University; and John Winklepleck was Assistant Vice President, Commercial Banking Division, Central National Bank, Cleveland, Ohio.

Exhibit 1   Characteristics of Surveys

	1979	1982	1984
Sample Size	250*	500	480†
Number of Responses	129	211	199
Unusable Responses	4	2	2
Response Rate	50%	42%	41.5%
Percentage of Companies that Invested Their Excess Cash in Money Market Instruments	87.2%	89.5%	95.94%

* In 1979, 250 questionnaires were sent to all odd-numbered companies in the second FORTUNE 500.

† FORTUNE magazine halted publication of its second 500 industrials after 1982. Thus, unlike the 1979 and 1982 surveys for which we used the prior year's listing, the 1984 survey relied on the 1982 listings. Consequently twenty of the listed companies, which had ceased to exist due to mergers, takeovers, or even outright failures, were excluded from our sample.

(i)   The number of industrial firms that invest cash in money market instruments.

(ii)   The instruments that have been used by these firms and those that were held in the year concurrent with each survey.

(iii)   The ranking of factors managers used when choosing an investment.

(iv)   The typical dollar amounts invested in each instrument.

(v)   The extent of premature liquidation in the secondary market.

(vi)   The cash forecasting techniques employed.

(vii)   The ability of those firms to borrow at below-prime interest rates.

Exhibit 2   Respondent Characteristics*

Total Assets in Millions of $ at the End of	Under $100	$100–$199	$200–$299
1978	21.10	52.29	17.43
1981	17.10	42.49	24.87
1983	12.57	39.43	23.43

Sales in Millions of $ for the Year	Under $100	$100–$199	$200–$299
1978	0.92	47.71	25.68
1981	1.04	30.73	30.73
1983	6.58	25.66	31.58

Average Size of Money Market Portfolio in Millions of $ in	Under $1	$1–$4.99	$5–9.99
1978	13.46	31.73	15.38
1981	1.67	30.17	25.70
1983	5.59	22.91	18.99

* The tables contain the percentage of respondents in each group and the means and standard deviations of assets, sales and portfolio size, respectively.

II. Methodology

Fortune's second 500 industrial companies [6, 7, 8] were the target
population in all three surveys. The questionnaires were sent to the
highest ranking financial officer of each firm in the first quarter of 1979,
1982, and 1984.[1]

In Exhibit 1, the sample sizes for each survey are shown along with
the usable response rates. As shown, the percentage of responding firms
committing their excess cash to money market instruments (MMI's)
shows a gradual increase between the 1979 survey and the 1984 survey
with only 4% of the respondents in the latest survey not investing in
MMI's.

III. Respondents' Profiles

Exhibit 2 presents general information on the responding firms. The mean
of the average money market portfolio as a percentage of the mean
year-end total assets of the respondents, MS/TA, can be found to equal

[1] Since many of the questions dealt with respondents' practices or experience in the years
preceding the survey years, the years 1978, 1981, and 1983 are shown wherever appropriate
in the text or the exhibits.

$300–$399	$400–$499	$500 and over	Mean (Std. Dev.)
3.67	3.67	1.84	172.96(105)
8.29	2.59	4.66	214.86(199.01)
10.29	5.71	8.57	243.89(182.55)

$300–$399	$400–$499	$500 and over	Mean (Std. Dev.)
22.02	3.67	—	226.92(92)
19.79	16.15	1.56	271.75(108.53)
19.08	9.21	7.89	276.48(163.57)

$10–19.99	$20–49.99	$50 and over	Mean (Std. Dev.)
19.23	16.34	3.86	11.48(12.82)
24.02	13.85	5.59	12.75(16.45)
18.99	23.14	8.38	18.34(23.15)

Exhibit 3   **Number of Different Money Market Instruments Used in a Year***

	Number of Different Types of Instruments Used									
Year	1	2	3	4	5	6	7	8	9 or >9	Mean
1978	10.10	16.51	21.10	22.02	13.76	11.01	1.83	2.75	0.92	3.72
1981	8.74	16.94	21.31	20.22	12.02	13.66	7.10	—	—	3.79
1983	9.29	12.57	17.49	15.30	19.67	14.21	8.74	2.73	—	4.18

* Table contains percentages of respondents using a given number of different types of instruments except for the mean values.

6.64%, 5.93%, and 7.52% in 1978, 1981, and 1983, respectively. This decrease in the MS/TA ratio from the 1978 level to the 1981 level followed by a large increase could reflect the general downturn in economic and business conditions in 1981 and subsequent upturn in 1983.

IV. Employment of Money Market Investments

The sample firms were asked to indicate the average number of different security types in their money market portfolios. Exhibit 3 shows a rather wide distribution of responses. To explore the relationship between the size of money market portfolios and the number of instruments held, sample portfolios were grouped into large and small portfolios, where the large portfolio group consisted of companies with an average MMI investment of $10 million or more. The average number of instruments for this group increased from 4.65 in 1978 to 5.13 in 1983, compared to an increase from 3.17 to 3.90 over the same period for the small portfolio group.

V. Money Market Instruments

Respondents' usage of each MMI, both in the survey years and in the five-year period just prior to each survey, are shown in Exhibit 4. Repurchase agreements (repos) were the most frequently used investment outlets over the period of the study. In the five-year period ending in 1983, almost 93% of the responding firms had relied on them at one time or another as a vehicle of short-term investment. Negotiable certificates of deposit (NCD's) and commercial paper ranked second and third. In 1983, for example, these two instruments were relied upon about equally (68.7% and 68.3%). In comparison, Mathur and Loy's study [5] found commercial paper, domestic CD's, repos, and Eurodollar time deposits to be the four most popular MMI's. In yet another study, by Gitman, Moses, and White [4], the top four rankings of the respondents' preferences were captured by commercial paper, repos, treasury bills, and NCD's. In none

---

Exhibit 4   Usage of Various Money Market Instruments (tabular values are % of respondents using each instrument)

Instrument	During 1979	1/74– 12/78	During 1981	1/77– 12/81	During 1983	1/79– 12/83
Bankers' Acceptances	31.2	42.2	36.6	65.5	34.4	58.4
Negotiable CD's	78.0	90.9	71.3	87.1	68.7	90.6
Commercial Paper	70.6	79.8	77.0	89.0	68.3	85.4
Eurodollar CD's	22.0	28.5	37.4	52.3	39.9	57.5
Eurodollar Deposits	22.0	26.7	52.6	59.9	52.5	65.6
Repurchase Agreements	87.2	88.1	87.8	94.2	76.5	92.9
Tax Exempt Notes	8.3	20.2	12.2	23.3	18.7	33.6
Treasury Bills	41.3	60.6	44.1	68.9	42.9	68.4
Other instruments*	11.9	14.7	27.7	51.4	35.2	61.9

* Includes money market funds, Merrill Lynch Ready Asset account, Canadian CD's and variable preferred, among others.

---

of the studies did bankers' acceptances rank high on the preference list. A more detailed comparison of the current results with those of other previous studies is shown in Exhibit 5.

According to Exhibit 4, Eurodeposits have become the fastest growing group of securities in the money market portfolios of the second tier of the Fortune 1000 companies. Until 1978, only 26.7% of the respondents had used this instrument; however, by 1983, over 65% of all respondents had used it at one time or another. In 1983 alone, for example, 52.5% of the respondents relied on Eurodeposits compared to 42.9% who relied on Treasury bills. Exhibit 6 is useful in understanding the growing use of Eurodeposits and Eurodollar CD's. This exhibit summarizes the main reason(s) identified by the respondents for their reluctance to use an MMI. In the 1979 survey, the respondents cited "lack of familiarity" as the predominant reason for shying away from Eurodeposits as well as Eurodollar CD's. While that reason was still present in the responses of the 1982 and 1984 survey, it did not seem to be the major objection it once was. Instead, the creditors' restrictions and company policy dominated the list of reasons for cash managers' reluctance to use the Eurodollar securities. Based on the phenomenal growth in the use of Eurodollar securities, which is evident from Exhibit 4, it appears that even the second tier of Fortune companies have become more aware of the opportunities provided by Euromarkets and are slowly catching up with the multinational corporations and financial institutions which have been active participants in those markets for many years.[2]

---

[2] In their explanation of interest rate differentials between domestic and offshore banks, Feiger and Jacquillat [2] have noted that most borrowers are still rather unsophisticated in international banking and, thus, view a CD from a foreign branch as a different item than a CD from a parent in the U.S. However, according to them, this sophistication is growing.

Exhibit 5   **A Comparison of the Usage of MMI as Reported by Different Studies§**

Money Market Instrument	Present Study 1984 Survey Only	
	Rank	%
Repurchase Agreements	1	76.5
Negotiable Certificates of Deposit	2	68.7
Commercial Paper	3	68.3
Foreign Short-Term Securities	4	‡58.7
Treasury Securities	5	42.9
Bankers' Acceptances	6	34.4
Federal Agency Issues	*—	—
Federal Funds	*—	—
Tax Exempt Securities	8	18.7
Other	7	35.2
None		†4.06

* These categories of MMI did not appear in these respective studies of securities.

† Percentage of respondents that did not invest their excess cash in MM Instruments.

‡ Includes Eurodollar deposits as well as Eurodollar CD's.

§ The Mathur/Loy study [5] is not included specifically here because no such data were available. They noted that the four most popular MMI's were commercial paper, domestic CD's, repurchase agreements, and Eurodollar time deposits.

VI. Money Market Instrument Preferences with Respect to Maturity

To add another dimension to the information summarized in Exhibit 4, respondents were also asked which three MMI's they preferred when they wanted to invest for less than 30 days and for 30 days or more. The responses are summarized in Exhibit 7. Repos were preferred for terms of less than 30 days in all three surveys, while for longer-term investments, negotiable CD's were the preferred MMI's. Commercial paper was the second most preferred instrument in all three surveys for both holding periods. Once again, it is worth noting that Eurodeposits were found to be the third most popular MMI's irrespective of the desired holding period, in both the 1982 and 1984 surveys. In contrast, Treasury bills lost ground in successive surveys for both holding periods.

VII. Investment Criteria

To evaluate the relative importance of MMI investment criteria, survey participants were asked to rank six specific criteria, ranging from preservation of capital to convenience. The responses, separated into two investment size categories, are summarized in Exhibit 8. The findings

Smith and Sell Study (1978)		Gitman/Moses/White Study (1976)		Gitman/Goodwin Study (1977)	
Rank	%	Rank	%	Rank	Mean Rank
*—	—	2	74.5	3	2.90
2	63	4	69.4	2	2.73
1	64	1	77.6	1	2.33
*—	—	7	17.3	8	4.08
3	57	3	72.4	4	3.09
5	36.0	5	58.2	6	3.63
4	38	6	45.9	7	3.79
*—	—	9	8.2	5	3.33
*—	—	*—	—	*—	—
5	18	8	12.2	9	4.33
	—		†9.2		—

indicate that concern for preservation of capital was the dominant factor for choosing MMI's, followed by rate of return. In the two most recent surveys, company policy was found to capture the third rank, just over the concern for liquidity. It is not clear, however, just what combination of factors is subsumed under company policy. To better understand the importance of each criterion relative to the most dominant criterion,

Exhibit 6   A Summary of Reasons behind Respondents' Reluctance to Use a MMI

Name of MMI	Reasons*
Bankers' Acceptance	(1) Low yield (2) Not familiar
Certificates of Deposit	(1) Low yield (2) Others: Creditor's restrictions, Company policy, Liquidity
Commercial Paper	(1) Risk (2) Creditor's restrictions (3) Others: Low yield, Company policy, Poor liquidity
Eurodollar CD's	(1) Creditor's restrictions (2) Company policy (3) Risk (4) Others: Not familiar, Admin. cost, Maturity
Eurodollar Deposits	(1) Creditor's restrictions (2) Risk (3) Company policy (4) Others: Not familiar, Inconvenient, Admin. cost
Repurchase Agreements	(1) Low yield (2) Others: Risk
Short-Term Tax Exempt Notes	(1) Not useful taxwise (2) Low yield (3) Others: Not familiar, Low liquidity
Treasury Bills	(1) Low yield

* Very common reasons are numbered and those reasons that were mentioned less frequently are listed in "others" category.

Exhibit 7   **Money Market Instrument Preferences for Different Holding Periods (1 = most preferred and 9 = least preferred)**

	Rankings					
	Funds Invested for Less than 30 days			Funds Invested for More than 30 days		
	1978	1981	1983	1978	1981	1983
Bankers' Acceptances	6	7	7	5	5	6
Negotiable CD's	3	4	4	1	1	1
Commercial Paper	2	2	2	2	2	2
Eurodollar CD's	7	6	5	6(tie)	6	4
Eurodollar Deposits	4(tie)	3	3	6(tie)	3	3
Repurchase Agreements	1	1	1	4	7	7(tie)
Tax-Exempt Notes	9	9	9	9	9	9
Treasury Bills	4(tie)	5	6	3	4	5
Other Instruments	8	8	8	8	8	7(tie)

preservation of capital, relative importance indices are shown in parentheses in Exhibit 8. For example, the relative importance of the rate of return criterion is between 82% and 86% that of preservation of capital. Accordingly, it could be concluded that concern for the rate of return is not far behind concern for capital preservation. Because of differences in the list of criteria presented to survey respondents, it is difficult to compare these results with those of previous studies [3, 4, 9]. It is clear from those studies, however, that factors related to safety of principal and yield rank highest in importance. This result could be explained by the manner in which the cash manager's performance is evaluated. It is also consistent with Exhibit 6, which lists the reasons behind respondents' reluctance to use bankers' acceptances, CD's, repurchase agreements, and Treasury bills as the low yield of these instruments for the level of risk involved as perceived by them.

VIII. Typical Dollar Denomination of Investments in Various MMI's

Exhibit 9 reveals that the most common denomination for each of the various investments was in the $1,000,000 to $4,999,999 range. Furthermore, the concentration of MMI's in this category has been increasing. The typical dollar denomination of $1–5 million is, of course, in accordance with the average market denomination,[3] but it might also reflect the efforts to lower transaction costs.

---

[3] For example, Cook and Summers [1] indicate the following typical denominations: commercial paper, $2 million; CD's, $1 million; most repos, $1 million or more; and Euro CD's, $250,000 to $5 million.

Exhibit 8   **Rankings and Relative Importance* of Factors Considered in Making Money Market Investments (1 = most important and 6 = least important)**

	Rankings (Relative Importance) Investment Between					
	$100,000–$999,999			$1,000,000–$4,999,999		
	1978	1981	1983	1978	1981	1983
Company Policy	4(71.6)	3(70.2)	3(75.1)	3(70.0)	3(72.3)	3(75.6)
Convenience	5(54.2)	5(50.8)	5(53.2)	5(50.1)	5(46.7)	5(48.1)
Liquidity	3(74.7)	4(69.9)	4(73.5)	4(71.2)	4(68.0)	4(72.8)
Preservation of Capital	1(100.0)	1(100.0)	1(100.0)	1(100.0)	1(100.0)	1(100.0)
Rate of Return	2(84.7)	2(85.6)	2(83.6)	2(82.3)	2(82.4)	2(83.6)
Other Restrictions such as Creditor	6(3.3)	6(1.7)	6(1.8)	6(3.2)	6(2.3)	6(1.9)

* Since there are six criteria, each criterion, or factor, would have a certain frequency for it under the classification of "most important" "second most important," and so on, as assigned by the respondents in each survey. The frequency of responses under the "most important" were assigned a weight of six, the responses of "second most important" a weight of five, all the way down to a weight of one to responses of the "least important" classification. By multiplying the response frequencies by the appropriate weights and adding, a total score was obtained for each criterion, which in turn was utilized to rank them. The total score of each criterion was then divided by the highest total score (that of "preservation of capital" in each case here) and multiplied by 100 to arrive at the relative importance scores. For example, in 1981, for investments of $1 million to $5 million, the "rate of return" criterion shows a relative importance of 82.4. This score could be interpreted as meaning that the respondents of that survey were saying that the concern over "rate of return" was about 17.6% less important than their concern for the "preservation of capital" in choosing money market instruments for investing over $1 million.

IX. Cash Forecasting Techniques

A section of the questionnaire dealt with cash forecasting techniques. As seen in Exhibit 10, the cash budget was the most popular forecasting tool with the method of historical trends coming in a distant second. Some of the "other" reported tools were the zero balance account, daily cash balance techniques, and regression analysis. Some respondents in the latest survey reported that their banks determined the amount of excess cash that could be invested in money market instruments.

X. MMI Holding Plans and the Actual Experience

In each survey the participants were asked if they intended to hold their MMI's until maturity (or until the originally agreed-upon liquidation date). As shown in Exhibit 11, about 92.5% of the respondents, on average, claimed that they did intend to hold the MMI's until their maturity. This finding is in agreement with Smith and Sell's [9] findings that the buy and hold until maturity strategy was preferred by an

Exhibit 9   **Typical Dollar Denominations of Investments in Various Money Market Instruments (tabular values are percentages of respondents using each instrument)**

Instrument		Denomination Amount			
		$100,000– $499,999	$500,000– $999,999	$1M– $4,999,999	$5M and over
Bankers' Acceptances	1978	16.67	33.33	50.00	—
	1981	17.98	21.35	58.43	2.25
	1983	20.00	15.56	61.11	3.33
Negotiable CD's	1978	19.39	26.53	52.04	2.04
	1981	11.27	19.72	61.27	7.74
	1983	14.29	15.71	62.86	7.14
Commercial Paper	1978	18.39	25.29	55.17	1.15
	1981	9.93	22.52	60.93	6.62
	1983	6.80	17.01	63.95	12.24
Eurodollar CD's	1978	18.75	18.75	62.50	—
	1981	—	12.16	74.32	13.52
	1983	4.71	14.12	68.24	12.93
Eurodollar Deposits	1978	20.00	16.67	63.33	—
	1981	7.06	12.94	67.06	12.94
	1983	6.86	17.65	65.69	9.80
Repurchase Agreements	1978	21.88	20.83	54.17	3.12
	1981	16.68	21.88	53.75	7.69
	1983	13.70	22.60	54.79	8.91
Tax-Exempt Notes	1978	35.00	25.00	40.00	—
	1981	18.75	15.63	59.38	6.24
	1983	8.70	21.74	58.70	10.86
Treasury Bills	1978	21.21	18.18	59.09	1.52
	1981	16.67	18.89	53.33	11.11
	1983	14.58	11.46	63.54	10.42
Other Instruments	1978	25.00	16.67	50.00	8.33
	1981	14.29	14.29	64.27	7.15
	1983	2.38	9.52	83.34	4.76

overwhelming majority of the respondents as compared to strategies like *ad hoc* decisions, play-the-yield curve, portfolio perspective, or others.

To compare respondents' intentions with their actual experience in that same year, they were also asked to report the dollar percentage of MMI's they liquidated prior to their originally intended dates. The findings, reported in Exhibit 12, show that the respondents' experience is remarkably consistent with their intentions. This suggests that the second tier of the Fortune 1000 firms have been rather effective in forecasting the amounts and durations of excess cash to be invested in money market instruments.

XI. Management of Short-Term Borrowings

Short-term borrowing and investment of excess cash are closely related, since the need for both arises from variances between actual and forecasted levels of cash. To get an indication of how effectively firms

Exhibit 10   **Methods Used to Determine the Amounts and Duration of Cash Available for Investing in Marketable Securities (tabulated numbers are percentages of respondents)**

	1978	1981	1983
Cash Budget			
yes	87.16	84.70	83.61
no	2.75	2.73	1.64
no response	10.09	12.57	14.75
Historical Trends			
yes	40.37	40.98	40.98
no	19.26	17.49	16.94
no response	40.37	41.53	42.08
Other Methods*			
yes	0.92	10.38	10.38
no	—	—	0.55
no response	99.08	89.62	89.07
Cash Budget & Historical Trends			
yes	36.70	38.80	39.34

* "Other" includes responses such as "our bank determines the amount of excess cash that can be invested and the duration for which it can be invested," regression analysis, zero balance account, *etc.*

Exhibit 11   **Respondent Intentions to Hold MMI's until Maturity or until Their Original Agreed-upon Liquidation Date**

Percentage Responding	1978	1981	1983
Yes, they intended to hold the marketable securities until their maturity	89.91	96.13	91.38
No, they did not intend to hold the marketable securities until maturity	10.09	3.87	8.62

Exhibit 12   **Premature Liquidation of Money Market Investments**

% of MMI's (in $) Liquidated Prematurely	Percentage of Respondents in		
	1978	1981	1983
0	82.57	82.87	74.14
>0 but < =5	10.09	9.14	16.66
>5 but < =10	5.50	5.14	4.02
>10 but < =20	0.92	0.57	2.30
>20 but < =35	—	1.14	0.58
>35 but < =60	—	0.57	0.58
>60	0.92	0.57	1.72

Exhibit 13   **Borrowing at Sub-Prime Rates**

		% Responding	
Question	**Response**	**In 1981**	**In 1983**
Were you able to borrow at sub-prime rates?	yes	63.02	53.45
	no	16.15	10.92
	funds not needed	20.83	35.63
		In 1982	**In 1984**
Do you expect to be able to borrow at sub-prime rates?	yes	78.95	63.59
	no	11.05	13.87
	will not need	10.00	22.54

manage their short-term borrowing, respondents were asked to indicate (i) if they were able to borrow at a sub-prime rate and, (ii) if they expected to raise funds at sub-prime rates. The responses, summarized in Exhibit 13, are somewhat surprising. In the 1982 survey, 63% of the respondents indicated that they had succeeded in borrowing at below-prime rates in 1981 and about 79% expected to do so in 1982. The figures in the 1984 survey were 53.5% and 63.5%, respectively. Given the turbulent economic environment of the 1980s, the achievements of the respondents can be interpreted as either excellent planning and cash forecasting on their part or the deficiency of the prime rate as a bench mark. Note that the prime rate in the past had been defined as the rate at which banks lend money to their most creditworthy customers. Yet, even the firms that claimed to have had only a few opportunities to invest in MMI's, or that referred to themselves as "net borrowers" for the most part in 1981, were generally able to borrow at sub-prime rates that year and were confident of doing so again in 1982.[4]

XII. Summary and Conclusions

The economic and regulatory environment of recent years has compounded the task of cash management. To gain information on current practice, this study examined survey evidence on the management of excess cash for the second Fortune 500 firms. The primary results emerging from three surveys of these firms conducted in 1979, 1982, and 1984 are summarized in the following paragraphs.

Repurchase agreements were the most preferred marketable securities followed by negotiable certificates of deposit, commercial paper, and Eurodollar securities. Over the six-year study period, Eurodollar securities experienced the largest rise in usage. Treasury bills, on the other

[4] It is possible that some of the respondents had to maintain large compensating balances in order to be able to borrow at sub-prime rates.

hand, seemed to have lost their appeal to cash managers, despite the overall growth in financial markets.

For maturities of less than 30 days, repos were the highest ranked securities while NCD's captured that highest rank for longer maturities in all three surveys. Commercial paper was the second most preferred instrument in all three surveys for both of the maturity categories.

"Preservation of capital" was found to be the most important MMI selection criterion, irrespective of the size of the investment, followed by yield, company policy, liquidity, and convenience. An analysis of relative importance indicated that the respondents' concern for rate of return is only about 16% less important than preservation of their invested capital.

Cash budgeting was reported to be the most widely used cash forecasting technique. About 85% of the respondents relied on this method, while about 40% relied on historical trend analysis to forecast their cash positions. The fact that firms did not seem to prematurely liquidate their MMI investments very frequently, and their apparent ability to borrow at sub-prime rates suggests that cash budgeting and forecasting have been carried out rather effectively by the second tier of the Fortune 1000 firms.

In closing, it is believed that by relying on three surveys of the same target population and the general consistency of the results obtained, this study has succeeded in providing further insights into the corporate practices of investment in marketable securities.

References

1. T. Cook and B.J. Summers, *Instruments of Money Market,* Federal Reserve Bank of Richmond, 1981.

2. G. Feiger and B. Jacquillat, *International Finance: Text and Cases,* Boston, MA, Allyn & Bacon, 1982, pp. 237–239.

3. L.J. Gitman and M.D. Goodwin, "An Assessment of Marketable Securities Management Practices," *The Journal of Financial Research,* Vol. II, No. 2 (Fall 1979), pp. 161–169.

4. L.G. Gitman, E.A. Moses, and I.T. White, "An Assessment of Corporate Cash Practices," *Financial Management* (Spring 1979), pp. 32–41.

5. I. Mathur and D. Loy, "Corporate-Banking Cash Management Relationships: Survey Results," *Journal of Cash Management* (October/November 1982), pp. 35–46.

6. "The 2nd 500: The Fortune Directory of the Largest U.S. Industrial Corporations," *Fortune* (June 18, 1978), pp. 156–184.

7. "The 2nd 500: The Fortune Directory of the Largest U.S. Industrial Corporations," *Fortune* (June 16, 1981), pp. 174–195.

8. "The 2nd 500: The Fortune Directory of the Largest U.S. Industrial Corporations," *Fortune* (June 15, 1982), pp. 196–224.

9. K.V. Smith and S.B. Sell, "Working Capital Management in Practice," in K.V. Smith (ed.), *Readings on the Management of Working Capital* 2nd ed., New York, West Publishing Company, 1980, pp. 51–84.

Questions

1. What is cash management? What major activities are included in cash management?

2. In which money market instrument (MMI) do industrial companies most frequently invest? Which MMIs rank second and third?

3. Describe the criteria used by industrial companies to select MMIs for investment. Note the relative importance of each criterion.

4. What is the purpose of cash budgeting? Approximately what percentage of industrial companies engage in cash budgeting?

19

What You Should Know about Repos

Daniel L. Kovlak

A repurchase (repo) agreement is an agreement in which an investor (buyer-lender) transfers cash to a broker-dealer or a financial institution (seller-borrower). The broker-dealer or financial institution transfers securities to the entity and promises to later repay the cash plus interest in exchange for the same securities. (This description is from the viewpoint of a savings and loan association or a state or local government; banks and broker-dealers call this agreement a "reverse repurchase agreement.")

There are several types of repo agreements. If the same securities are returned, the agreements are sometimes referred to as "vanilla" or "plain vanilla" agreements because there is nothing complicated about these transactions. In "dollar repurchase agreements," different securities are returned. There are two types of dollar repo agreements: fixed coupon repo agreements in which different securities are returned but with the same stated interest rate and with maturities similar to the securities transferred, and yield maintenance agreements in which different securities are returned that provide the seller-borrower with a yield as specified in the agreement.

This article focuses on those agreements in which the same securities are returned. An example of such a repo transaction on the trade date is shown in Figure 1. The transaction at maturity is shown in Figure 2.

The terms of repo agreements also vary. "Overnight repo agreements" mature in one day. "Term repo agreements" are those that mature in more than one day. "Open repo agreements" have no specific maturity; both parties have the right to close the transaction at any time. "Repo agreements to maturity" are those that mature on the same day as the underlying securities.

Daniel L. Kovlak, "What You Should Know about Repos," *Management Accounting,* May 1986: 52–56. Reprinted with permission from *Management Accounting,* U.S.A. Copyright 1986 by National Association of Accountants, Montvale, N.J. 07645. All rights reserved. At the time of this writing, Daniel L. Kovlak was a practice fellow from Peat, Marwick, Mitchell & Co. at the Governmental Accounting Standards Board (GASB) in Stamford, Connecticut.

Figure 1   **Repurchase-Reverse Repurchase Agreement Using Full Coupon Treasury Securities as Collateral**

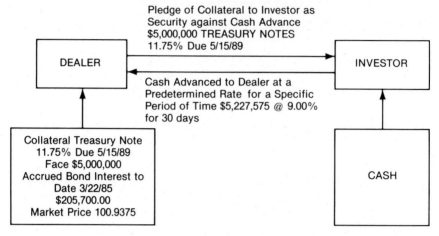

$$\begin{array}{c}\text{Face}\\\text{value}\end{array} \times \left(\begin{array}{c}\text{Market}\\\text{price}\end{array} - \begin{array}{c}\text{Initial}\\\text{margin}\end{array}\right) + \begin{array}{c}\text{Accrued}\\\text{bond}\\\text{interest}\end{array} = \begin{array}{c}\text{Agreed upon}\\\text{value of collateral}\end{array}$$

$5,000,000 \times (100.9375 - .500 \text{ price points}) + 205,700.00 = \$5,227,575$

(1) Trade date/settlement date dealer delivers collateral to investor on a delivery versus payment basis with payment equal to the agreed value of the collateral for repurchase.

(2) During the life of the Repurchase-Reverse Repurchase agreement there may be fluctuations in collateral value due to market price movements and interest payments on the underlying security. These variations and interest paydowns must be monitored on a daily basis by both sides to insure proper collateralization levels and maintenance of initial margin levels.

Investors invest in repos because they want to obtain a better yield on their temporarily idle cash. In a repurchase agreement, when the investor transfers money to the seller-borrower, the investor receives as collateral government securities or government agency securities (such as GNMA, FNMA, and so forth). In most cases, the market value of those securities is in excess of the amount of cash transferred. This excess is called a "haircut" and protects the buyer-lender against fluctuations in the market value of the underlying securities. At the end of the repo agreement term, the buyer-lender returns the securities in exchange for the original amount of the agreement plus interest.

Figure 2   **At Maturity***

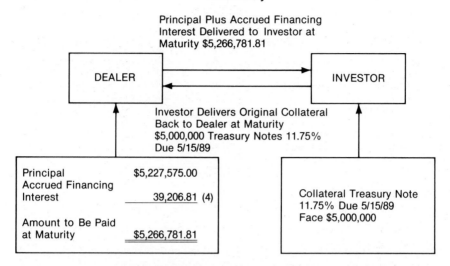

At Maturity*

Principal Plus Accrued Financing
Interest Delivered to Investor at
Maturity $5,266,781.81

| DEALER | | INVESTOR |

Investor Delivers Original Collateral
Back to Dealer at Maturity
$5,000,000 Treasury Notes 11.75%
Due 5/15/89

Principal	$5,227,575.00
Accrued Financing	
Interest	39,206.81 (4)
Amount to Be Paid	
at Maturity	$5,266,781.81

Collateral Treasury Note
11.75% Due 5/15/89
Face $5,000,000

(3)   At maturity the investor delivers the collateral back to the dealer on a delivery versus payment basis. At maturity the repurchase price includes the initial principal advanced, plus the sum of the daily financing accrual at the predetermined rate.

(4)   Principal   × Rate   × Number of days   = Accrued interest
          $5,227,575 × 9.0%   ×   30   = $39,206.81

* These examples do not contemplate the repurchase-reverse repurchase agreement crossing a coupon payment date, which would require use of various collateralization procedures.

Repo Environment: $300 Billion Market

In the book *The Money Market* published in 1983, Marcia Stigum estimates that between $150 and $160 billion of overnight repo agreement transactions occur each day. In addition, there are approximately $200 to $300 billion of term repo agreements outstanding. These numbers are probably significantly higher now because the U.S. government's debt has increased significantly since 1983, and U.S. government debt is financed through treasury bills, bonds, and notes. Government securities usually are the underlying securities, or collateral, for repo agreements, which is why investors think repo agreements are so safe.

There are 36 primary government securities dealers and approximately 200 secondary dealers. Primary dealers are permitted to make direct bids on new Treasury offerings. They submit daily reports of market activity and positions and monthly financial statements to the Federal Reserve Bank of New York and are subject to its informal

Table 1   **Past Disasters Involving Repos**

Dealers	Date	Total Losses in Millions	Major Industries
Bevill, Bresler & Schulman	April 1985	$240	Savings & Loan Associations
ESM	March 1985	$300	State & Local Governments Savings & Loan Associations*
Lion Capital	May 1984	$ 89	69 Municipalities (60 N.Y. State School Districts)
RTD Securities	May 1984	$ 5	8 Municipalities (7 N.Y. State School Districts)
Lombard-Wall	August 1982	$ 55	N.Y. State Dormitory Authority
Drysdale	May 1982	$160	Banking (Chase)
		$849	

* Led to the closing of the 71 S&Ls in Ohio for several days in March 1985.

oversight. Secondary dealers cannot bid on new offerings and are largely unregulated. Certain secondary dealers, including banks and Securities & Exchange Commission broker-dealers, may be regulated by federal bank regulators or the SEC. Most secondary dealers, however, are unregulated. Because of this fact and because of a lack of investor awareness of the risks, there have been a number of losses in recent years (Table 1).

The most recent loss occurred in April 1985 when Bevill, Bresler and Schulman, a small government securities dealer in New Jersey, failed. Losses in that case have been estimated to be as high as $240 million. Those losses were incurred mostly by savings and loan associations and banks.

In March 1985, ESM Government Securities also went bankrupt, leaving its investors with losses of up to $300 million. In this case, local governments, in addition to savings and loan associations, were the losers. Home State Savings and Loan in Cincinnati, Ohio, had over $150 million invested with ESM, which led to a run on the savings and loan associations in Ohio. As a result, 71 savings and loan associations in Ohio were closed until they could prove they qualified for federal insurance. Municipalities that had repos with ESM included Toledo, Ohio ($19 million); Beaumont, Texas ($20 million); and Pompano Beach, Florida ($12 million).

How do these losses occur? In both situations, these losses resulted from the fact that the buyer-lender in the repo agreement did not take delivery of the securities underlying the agreement. If the investors had taken delivery of the securities, either physically or through an independent third party, they could have sold those securities and recovered the amount of their investments. However, if broker-dealers are requested to deliver securities in a repo agreement, most lower the interest rate for the repo agreement. Many investors, therefore, do not take possession of the securities because they naturally want to realize the highest rate.

Because delivery was not required, some government securities dealers were entering into several repurchase agreement transactions and were using the same securities as collateral for each of the transactions. In that case, some of the repo agreement transactions were not collateralized.

What Are the Risks?

The two major risks associated with repo agreements are credit risk and market risk. Credit risk is the risk that the other party to the transaction will not fulfill its obligation. This risk can be associated with the dealer of the repo agreement or with a third party holding the underlying securities (collateral). Credit risk exposure can be affected by a large concentration of investments with any one dealer.

Market risk is the risk that the market value of the underlying securities will decline. Market risk is affected by the length to maturity of the repo agreement, the extent that the underlying securities exceed the amounts invested, and the frequency at which the amount of collateral is adjusted for changing market values.

There are several ways an investor can minimize risks. An investor should always know the dealer. An investor can obtain information about the dealer by reviewing its credit rating and the latest financial statements. Regardless of the personal relationships that exist between the investor and a dealer, a financial review should be performed periodically. Lavish offices, impressive yachts, or expensive entertainment flaunted by dealers often can mislead investors.

Dealers offering excessively high interest rates also should be avoided. There is usually a good reason why a dealer is offering higher rates than other dealers. In many cases, it is because he really needs the business. As with other investments, the rate of return is related to the risks involved.

The best way investors in repo agreements can avoid significant losses and minimize credit risk is to take physical possession of the securities or have them delivered to an independent third party (custodian). The investor should never permit the dealer or the dealer's agent to hold the underlying securities. Those securities need to be accessible to the investor in the event of a dealer failure.

Another precaution the investor should take to minimize market risk is to "mark-to-market." This phrase means that the market value of the underlying securities should be checked periodically to determine that it is in excess of the amount of the repo agreement. If the market value of the underlying securities falls below the value of the investment, the investor should insist on receiving more securities or a return of cash.

Written agreements also limit risk when entering into repo agreements. A written agreement can be drafted for each repo transaction or a master agreement can be written that covers all repo transactions with that dealer. These agreements should clearly establish the rights of each of the parties to the transactions. Moreover, investors should also enter into agreements with the custodian holding the underlying securities. Custodial agreements should specify the custodian's responsibilities, which include: disbursing cash for repo agreements only when the underlying securities are delivered; obtaining additional securities or a return of cash if the required margin on a repo agreement is not maintained because of market fluctuations; holding the securities separately from all other securities of the custodian; and reporting periodically to the investor on the market value of underlying securities.

What Is Being Done to Protect Investors?

A number of organizations have taken steps to protect investors and prevent losses in repo transactions. The American Institute of CPAs issued its "Report of The Special Task Force on Audits of Repurchase Securities Transactions" in June 1985. This report describes the risks associated with repo agreements and the audit implications of these transactions. The AICPA also has drafted a Statement of Position (SOP) that will soon be issued by its Savings and Loan Association Committee to supplement the Savings and Loan Association Audit Guide. The draft SOP requires certain disclosures of repo agreement and reverse repurchase agreement transactions.

The Governmental Accounting Standards Board (GASB) issued an exposure draft of a statement of "Accounting and Financial Reporting for Deposits with Financial Institutions, Investments (including Repurchase Agreements), and Reverse Repurchase Agreements" in June 1985. The GASB believes the risks associated with repo agreements also exist for deposits with financial institutions when the deposits are in excess of insured amounts and collateral has not been received for those amounts. The proposed statement would require disclosure of legal or contractual provisions for deposits and investments, including repurchase agreements, and reverse repurchase agreements. In addition, certain disclosures would be required as of the balance sheet date. The purpose of these disclosures is to help financial statement users to assess the risks the governmental entity is taking with its investments.

In January 1986, the Securities & Exchange Commission issued "Disclosure Amendment to Regulation S-X regarding Repurchase and Reverse Repurchase Agreements." The Federal Reserve Bank is in the process of holding a number of educational programs to educate the public about repurchase agreements, their risks, and safeguards against those risks. They have issued a brochure, "It's 8:00 a.m. . . . Do You Know Where Your Collateral Is?"

In September 1985, the Government Securities Act of 1985 was passed by the U.S. House of Representatives. The bill would create a nine-member Government Securities Rule-making Board, a self-regulatory organization composed of industry and investor representatives under the supervision of the Federal Reserve Board. The new board would set minimum capital standards requirements and adopt bookkeeping, reporting, and other rules for all government securities dealers, including the approximately 200 currently unregulated dealers. In addition to this bill, the Senate has two other proposals that deal with this matter.

In January 1986, the U.S. Treasury and the Federal Reserve Board agreed to allow state and local governments to establish accounts with the Federal Reserve Banks for safekeeping of government securities. This agreement will allow governments to provide for better safekeeping and third-party verification of the securities underlying their repo agreements.

Many people believe that there has been an overreaction to recent failures of government securities dealers. They believe that because these failures have been well publicized, most investors are aware of the risks involved in repo agreements and will protect themselves against future failures. This argument is challenged by critics who point out that even though the failures of 1982 and 1984 were well publicized, the 1985 losses still occurred! In light of this experience it is hard to believe that without some action, other failures will not occur.

To help protect against these types of losses, corporate treasurers, investment officers of savings and loan associations, state and local governments, and other organizations need to be fully aware of the risks involved in repo agreements. Users of financial statements cannot assess the risks of these types of organizations without reviewing and understanding financial statement disclosures about those risks. Finally, it would seem that more regulation of the government securities industry is needed to guard against inadequately capitalized or unscrupulous dealers.

Questions

1. Describe a typical repurchase agreement.

2. Repurchase (repo) agreements are classified in the following ways: (a) reverse agreements, (b) plain vanilla agreements, (c) dollar agreements, (d) overnight agreements, (e) term agreements, (f) open agreements, and (g) agreements to maturity. Briefly describe each of these agreements.

3. What risks are faced by an investor in repos?

4. What can an investor in repos do to reduce the risk?

Commercial Paper: New Tunes on an Old Instrument

Patricia Segall

The commercial paper market, like the Stephen Leacock character, has leaped on its horse and galloped off in all directions at once. The market has become bigger, domestic credit ratings are now widespread, collateralized issues are prominent, and small companies are tapping the market. Banks are taking on additional roles, insurance companies are guaranteeing the paper, groups of modest-size businesses are issuing their own paper, and money market mutual funds are investing funds in commercial paper. The horse has even galloped abroad, where the European commercial paper market is beginning to take off.

The Domestic Market

Originally, we all understood commercial paper to be a short-term corporate I.O.U., with a maturity of no more than 270 days. By keeping the maturity to 270 days or less, and by using the proceeds to finance current transactions, commercial paper is exempt from SEC registration requirements. This minimizes the time and cost of preparing a commercial paper issue.

The issuer of the paper typically has been a blue-chip corporation such as Coca Cola and IBM. In the past, the issuer pledged no assets, only its liquidity, estimated potential earnings, and reputation. However, much of that is changing.

Patricia Segall, "Commercial Paper: New Tunes on an Old Instrument," *The Journal of Commercial Bank Lending* (April 1987): 16–23. Copyright 1987 by Robert Morris Associates. Reprinted with permission from *The Journal of Commercial Bank Lending*, April 1987.

At the time of this writing, Patricia Segall was a research assistant in the Economics Group of The Chase Manhattan Bank, N.A., New York City. The author is grateful to Gregory Hoelscher for his patience and support in preparing this article.

Figure 1   **Commercial Paper Outstanding**

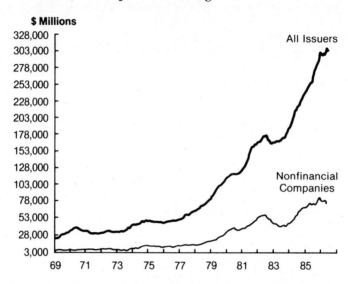

Rating of Commercial Paper

The current volume of commercial paper in the U.S. is about $300 billion, an increase of approximately 39% since 1984 (see Figure 1). Commercial paper was issued by only very strong firms, whose liquidity seemed beyond question. The buyers of commercial paper saw little risk in their purchase. The few defaults that did take place were mainly smaller companies, so the effect was to limit the market to bigger, better known firms.

But in 1970, when Penn Central went bankrupt with $82 million in commercial paper outstanding, fear entered the picture. The credit rating of a company became very important. In 1977 the SEC ruled that commercial paper bought by institutional investors would have to be backed by additional capital held by dealers if the paper was not rated by at least two rating firms. Since the dealers did not want to bear the cost of raising additional capital, virtually all commercial paper is now rated.

Bank Backup Lines of Credit

One of the early innovations was the emergence of bank lines of credit to back new issues of nonfinancial commercial paper. In 1966 interest rates in the open market rose above legal ceilings on bank CDs. This made it difficult for banks to raise funds for corporate loans. Consequently, banks encouraged their strongest customers to issue commercial paper and provided backup lines of credit to be used in the event of liquidity problems or inability in rolling over expiring paper.

Banks earn a fee for supplying lines of credit to the commercial paper issuers and can thus offset some of their competitive losses to the commercial paper market. The issuer pays the bank a fee or keeps a compensating balance, the former becoming the more commonly used method, in exchange for the right to come in and borrow money from the bank should liquidity problems arise.

While bank fees for these lines are less profitable than providing a direct bank loan, these arrangements do not tie up capital. Instead, the issuers and banks create an agreement, a contingent liability, that ensures payment if the issuer cannot repay. This commitment provides safety for the investors, and since issuers rarely use their bank lines, it has virtually no effect on the bank's capital.

At this point, however, it may be important to note that the issuance of lines or letters of credit, that is, off-balance-sheet activity, has recently grabbed the attention of those in the banking industry. According to some, global market integration and innovation are acting in tandem to lessen the importance of the role banks play as creditor for prime borrowers.

In addition are the impositions of reserve requirements and capital adequacy controls. Those banks which are especially sensitive to these regulations have reacted in a variety of ways, some of which have included shifting to off-balance-sheet activities; that is, a shift from a traditional source of income, lending, to fee income. This shift has not gone unnoticed, and many concerned regulators are proposing to extend these regulations to all off-balance-sheet activities, thus requiring that capital be maintained for certain off-balance-sheet activities. To date, there has been no official ruling, but it will be interesting to see the outcome and subsequent effect on the industry.

Entrance of Small Companies

Seeing that the commercial paper market was an efficient way to obtain cheap, short-term funds, cheaper than bank loans, small companies wanted in. By using bank lines of credit, insurance company guarantees, and the like, smaller companies entered the market. These guarantees and bank lines of credit increase the company's credit rating, which greatly reduces their borrowing costs. In essence, these devices enhance the credit standing of the issuer by borrowing the name of a large financial institution. The increase in paper placed by dealers is a good way to observe the increase in small companies' use of the market since these companies do not find it cost effective to maintain their own sales force.

Collateralized Issues

Another new technique is the use of collateralized issues. In 1983, a group of rent-a-car licensees formed a company and issued commercial paper backed by a bank letter of credit, for which they pledged titles to their cars. Large firms and savings and loan institutions now pledge receivables and other assets as collateral for their commercial paper.

One of the quickest credit enhancements to take hold benefits the thrift industry: A savings and loan sets up an independent subsidiary to which it sells its highly rated government-backed paper. The subsidiary, in turn, uses the paper as collateral and issues the commercial paper in the name of the savings and loan. This paper can guarantee to the investor that the debt will be repaid, even if the S & L fails.

Government-backed securities, credit card receivables, mortgage obligations, and the like all serve as collateral. This allows companies that otherwise would have been denied access to the market, or which would have received very low ratings, to become well-rated participants in the market. At the same time, collateral raises the credit rating and thus lowers financing costs for those already in the market. These collateralized issues have secured top credit ratings.

Effect of MMMFs

The rapid growth of money market mutual funds (MMMFs) has also deepened the commercial paper market by providing a demand for the growing supply of paper. More than 40% of the growth in MMMFs from 1979 to 1985 was invested in the commercial paper market. MMMFs now hold approximately $98 billion of commercial paper or over 30% of the total commercial paper outstanding (see Figure 2).

The European Market

The European counterpart of the U.S. commercial paper market developed from the Euronote market. Euronotes are defined as short-term promissory notes arranged with a form of medium-term bank backup, that is, a source that the issuer can draw on if his note cannot be placed at an attractive rate.

Attractive Foreign Regulations

From the Euronote market, today's European commercial paper (ECP) has evolved. ECP is defined as a Euronote without a committed backup facility. In the 1970s, the European commercial paper market's main participants were big American multinationals. They used the market to obtain funds for the operations of their foreign subsidiaries, due to the Interest Equalization Tax Act (IET) and the Office of Foreign Direct Investment (OFDI) regulations.

The IET was a tax on foreign securities in the domestic market. The controls set by the OFDI were restrictions on the outflow of capital from parent companies to their foreign affiliates. The IET raised the cost for foreign subsidiaries of U.S. companies to issue securities in the U.S.

Figure 2   **Money Market Mutual Funds**

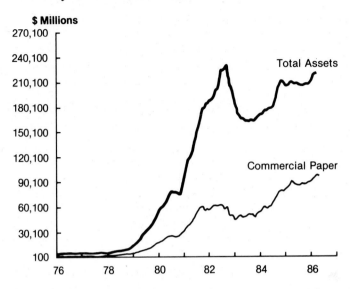

market, while the OFDI made it disadvantageous for parent companies to export funds abroad. Both sets of regulations drove multinational companies to the European market for their financing needs. Once these restrictions were dropped, the European market, which was not offering great cost advantages, disappeared.

But that has all changed. The ECP market is back and beginning to boom. The volume (as of June 1986) of ECP outstanding was approximately $1.7 billion. Considering the fact ECP did not make its comeback until late 1984, this growth is impressive. Broader definitions of ECP, which include Euronotes, produce volume estimates of between $15 and $20 billion.

Factors Contributing to ECP's Growth

Several factors have contributed to ECP's recent growth. One is the decreased attractiveness of syndicated loans to borrowers. Other forms of debt financing appeared that offered more appealing rates. Many issuers became dissatisfied with the Euronote market; setting up a note facility, arranging the backup, and so forth became costly and time consuming. Another reason for growth was that many investors felt uneasy about parking all their money in banks. They wanted to diversify out of bank risk and wanted attractive alternatives to bank deposits. ECP provided one.

Recent developments in the ECP market suggest that it is developing along the lines of the U.S. market. Average maturity in the U.S.

is 22 days. A three- or six-month maturity for ECP is the norm, although the market is experiencing more and more odd-dated maturities, akin to the domestic market. This feature allows borrowers to tailor the paper to fit specific short-term financing requirements.

LIBOR (defined as the London Interbank Offered Rate on Euro-dollar deposits traded between banks) is still used as a "proxy" for the rate on ECP, since most ECP is tied to LIBOR. This too is changing as the market shifts away from bank investors. Although approximately two-thirds of the participants in the market are still banks, a growing proportion of them are nonbank investors. The market has recently witnessed several issues where the pricing was done on an absolute rate basis.

Until recently, ECP could be issued only in Eurodollars and European Currency Units (ECUs). Absence of denomination in other currencies was perhaps due mainly to regulatory prohibitions by the home country of the issuer regarding short-term securities. Recently there have been programs denominated in Euro Dutch guilders and sterling, due to lifting of these regulations. Two things should be noted though. First, most of the big Euro Commercial Paper houses are institutions that have had good experience with U.S. dollar investors, and as such, the U.S. money center and investment banks lead the market. Second, the demand for ECP may only be for that which is denominated in "strong" currencies.

Increased Competition between European and U.S. Markets

The issuance costs of the European and U.S. markets have become increasingly competitive. Previously, the "classic arbitrage" was to issue commercial paper in the U.S. and then reinvest the funds in either Euro CDs or LIBOR deposits. Increased arbitrage helped narrow the spread between U.S. and European rates which in turn increased participation in the European market. The most important decline is that of the LIBOR/U.S. commercial paper rate spread: In 1982, the spread was 89 basis points; in 1984, 42 basis points; and as of July 1986, 29 basis points. As spreads between the two markets narrow, borrowers may find it hard to resist another source of short-term funds.

Currently, ratings are not required in the ECP market. European investors are much more name conscious than their U.S. counterparts, placing more emphasis on name recognition than on a company's credit ratings. Standard & Poor's and Moody's have set up offices in London to begin rating European companies, but many issuers feel the time and effort required to receive the rating are not worth it. They would prefer to avoid the credit ratings and thus shave a few extra points off their costs. In addition to not paying the rating fee, issuers avoid the possible outcome of obtaining a less than desirable rating, and they keep their financial information confidential. However, some investors, financial institutions and perhaps even issuers believe that a rating system would provide order, uniformity, decrease some price distortion, and perhaps even add a degree of safety to the market.

Challenges for U.S. Banks

The implications of a thriving commercial paper market for the commercial banking system are, one can say with great confidence, less than exhilarating. It is impossible, of course, to pinpoint the reduction in bank loans that is a direct consequence of growth in the commercial paper market. However, it does seem clear that many firms that would ordinarily turn to banks are meeting at least part of their short-term financial needs through the sale of commercial paper.

From January 1985 through June 1986, commercial paper (including nonfinancial) grew from $245 billion to $303 billion. Commercial and industrial loans at commercial banks grew from $474 billion to only $508 billion over the same period. The growth in commercial paper was almost twice the growth in bank loans. Even if the growth in commercial paper has not come exclusively at the expense of bank loans, it remains true that bank lending rates have tended to exceed commercial paper rates by a considerable margin.

Decline in Bank Loan Profitability

The margin of profitability on bank loans has declined sharply. Banks' largest and best customers can obtain funds more cheaply in the commercial paper market. Therefore, banks are losing traditional customers and income. At this point, the future of bank borrowing and commercial paper as primary financing sources is not clear. Three forces that have had and will continue to have a major role in shaping the future of the short-term lending market in the U.S. are discussed below.

Higher Cost of Funds

The average cost of funds for banks rose in the 1980s, leading to higher loan rates in relation to commercial paper rates. The phase-out of regulation Q, which placed a ceiling on the interest rates banks could pay to depositors, means that banks must now pay a higher rate of interest on most deposits.

Another contributing factor to the increasing cost of funds for banks has been the higher market interest rates on bank-purchased deposits in relation to commercial paper rates during the past few years. These higher rates may have been due to a risk premium that banks pay for funds during periods of high interest rates, such as the early 1980s, when their borrowers are more likely to default. The well-publicized LDC (lesser developed country) debt problems were also most likely an important cause of that higher relative cost.

Effect of Regulatory Practices

A second reason for the stagnation in C & I (commercial & industrial) loans is that regulatory practices have limited the returns on bank loan portfolios. Reserve requirements raise the effective cost of bank funding. Banks must keep a percentage of deposits on reserve. These reserves earn no interest, and in periods of rising interest rates, the opportunity cost of holding these reserves increases. Stricter capital requirements have forced banks to substitute more expensive funding (equity and long-term debt) for short-term deposits to raise their capital bases. This then may start a cycle of unintended consequences: Higher funding costs put the best credits out of reach for some banks, these banks are left with making much riskier transactions and meeting stricter capital requirements, which leads to higher cost of funds for banks, and the cycle begins again.

Evolution of the Commercial Paper Market

A third contributing factor to the substitution of commercial paper for bank loans is no doubt the evolution of the commercial paper market itself. A larger pool of commercial paper investors makes the market more liquid, which in turn draws more investors to it. A larger supply of paper is then more easily absorbed. The catalysts for growth in the investor base were MMMFs and the inflows of capital from abroad. These two sectors have added about $48 billion to their commercial paper holdings in the past three years.

The commercial paper market has developed into such an efficient market for borrowing money that banks have turned elsewhere for income: asset sales, bond trading, and other nonlending activities. But looking on the bright side, recent declines in interest rates mean that spreads between commercial paper rates and bank lending rates should narrow, perhaps leading to renewed growth in bank loans at the expense of commercial paper. The real question is where will the market go next?

Questions

1. Commercial paper has been defined traditionally as short-term, unsecured promissory notes issued by large corporations. In what way(s) has some recently issued paper broken with tradition?

2. Describe the role played by commercial banks in some issues of commercial paper.

3. What financial institution is the major purchaser of commercial paper? Provide evidence supporting your answer.

4. What factors have contributed to the growth in dollar volume of European commercial paper? Has the European market overtaken the U.S. market?

5. Describe the challenge presented by commercial paper to U.S. commercial banks.

21
How and Why to Hedge a Short-Term Portfolio
Ira G. Kawaller

Managers of short-term fixed income securities structure their portfolios in order to benefit from their implicit or explicit forecasts of the direction of interest rates and changes in the shape of the yield curve. Such structuring of a portfolio is a dynamic process, however, as changing economic conditions frequently affect investors' forecasts and thus foster recurring—if not continual—reevaluations of optimal portfolio design.

When a portfolio adjustment becomes appropriate, the portfolio manager has two choices: to liquidate portions of the portfolio and reallocate the capital to other issues or to effect a synthetic restructuring through the use of interest rate futures. This paper focuses on the second alternative. It describes: how to construct an appropriate hedge for a portfolio of short-term, fixed income securities; why a manager might want to hedge; and the risks inherent in hedging with futures contracts.

Constructing the Hedge

In implementing a hedging program, the manager hopes to use short-term interest rate futures—Treasury bill futures, Certificate of Deposit futures, or Eurodollar futures—to create an offset from the profit generated by the futures position to the change in the capital value of the portfolio due to a rise in interest rates. Each of these futures contracts is traded at the Chicago Mercantile Exchange. They are bought and sold on the floor of the exchange using an open outcry auction process. Prices quoted for these instruments are *index values,* constructed by subtracting the interest rate on the futures contract from 100.00. For example, a futures

Ira G. Kawaller, "How and Why to Hedge a Short-Term Portfolio," *Journal of Cash Management* (January/February 1985): 26–30. Reprinted with permission of the *Journal of Cash Management*.

At the time of this writing, Ira G. Kawaller was affiliated with the Chicago Mercantile Exchange.

rate of 9.07% would translate to a futures *price* of 90.93; and for each increase (decrease) of the futures *rate,* the futures price would decrease (increase) an equal number of basis points. (A basis point is one hundredth of a percent or .0001.) Thus, to hedge against a rising interest rate, which would adversely affect any fixed income asset holdings, one would be a seller of futures contracts.

The hedge allows the manager to continue to hold the cash market securities and to accrue interest, while at the same time it prevents net worth from deteriorating. As a practical matter, the hedge also precludes any appreciation of the net worth due to a decline in interest rates, for if such a change were to occur, a perfect hedge would effectively forego this benefit through losses in the futures market.

The first step in constructing a hedge for a short-term fixed income portfolio is to segment the portfolio by *instrument* (e.g. Treasury bills, CDs, Commercial Paper, etc.) and *maturity.* Individual hedge positions would be calculated for each category of security represented in the portfolio, with the overall hedge simply being a consolidation of all of the individual hedges.

For short-term instruments, the best futures contract to use as a hedge vehicle would be chosen from Treasury bill futures, Certificate of Deposit futures, and Eurodollar futures, using the contract whose underlying interest rate offers the highest correlation to the cash market interest rate to be hedged. For those security categories that happen to be the underlying instruments of existing futures contracts (e.g., three-month Treasury bills, three-month Certificates of Deposit, or three-month Eurodollar deposits) the choice of contract is obvious. In each case the appropriate hedge would involve shorting (or selling) one associated contract for each million dollars of the portfolio.

For other categories of securities, more discretion comes into play. Consider the case of the portfolio manager who owns $100 million in six-month Treasury bills and decides to hedge against the risk that interest rates are about to rise, causing the capital value of this investment to decline. Determining the proper hedge requires three steps:

- Identifying which rate between the three-month Treasury bill rate, the three-month Certificate of Deposit rate, and the three-month Eurodollar rate offers the highest correlation with the six-month Treasury bill rate in order to determine which futures contract would serve as the best hedge.

- Calculating the price effect on the portfolio that results from a one basis point change in the six-month Treasury bill rate.

- Making a judgment as to the expected relationship between changes in rates of the six-month bill and changes in rates on futures contracts that are to be used as a hedge.

Assume the correlation study indicates that Treasury bill futures offer the best hedge protection for the six-month cash Treasury bills. The next step is calculating the hedge ratio: For short-term fixed-income securities, the value of a basis point is calculated simply by multiplying the principal value times one basis point (.0001) times the maturity of the instrument (days divided by 360). Thus, the value of a basis point in this example is $100,000,000 × (.0001) × (180/360) or $5,000. As the value of a basis point on a Treasury bill futures contract is $25 (as is the case for the other two short-term interest rate futures, as well), the hedge ratio would be $5,000/$25 or 200 contracts—*provided the rates on the futures were expected to move exactly the same number of basis points as the rate on the six-month instruments.* If one held the view that these two rates would move somewhat differently, however, the hedge ratio would be affected.

Suppose, for instance, one expected the interest rate future to move, say, 125 basis points each time the six-month Treasury bill rate moved 100 basis points. In this case, the simplistic hedge of 200 contracts would have to be adjusted by multiplying 200 times the ratio 100/125 or 0.8. In other words, the appropriate hedge would be 200 × 0.8 or 160 contracts. The general formula for determining the appropriate number of contracts for the hedge of any particular money market instrument is shown in Exhibit 1.

Determination of the factor must take into account two components. The first involves the relationship between the underlying instrument upon which the future is based and the instrument for which hedging is desired; the second component involves the relationship between the future and its underlying instrument—the *basis*. One can be exactly correct about the relationship between the two cash instruments, yet the factor may be off because of an unanticipated development of the basis. The appropriate factor must reflect both of these considerations accurately for the hedge to be perfect.

Unfortunately, no simple, objective methodology for calculating this factor is available. The uninitiated may be tempted to compare time series data on the change in the futures rate versus changes in the rate on the portfolio instrument (e.g., using regression analysis). However, results of such an analysis will be highly dependent upon the specific time period from which the data are collected. Grossly different results may be obtained depending on whether the data used in the regression reflect an upward or downward sloping yield curve or whether rates are generally rising or declining.

Exhibit 1

$$\text{Number of Contracts} = \left(\frac{\text{Value of .01 Cash Portfolio}}{\text{Value .01 on Future}}\right) \times \text{Factor}$$

$$\text{where Value of .01} = \text{Principal} \times (.0001) \times \frac{\text{days}}{360} \text{ and}$$

$$\text{Factor} = \frac{\text{Expected rate move on cash}}{\text{Expected rate move on future}}$$

The problem is illustrated by the following example: suppose the hedge were desired at a time when futures rates were 50 basis points above the spot market Treasury bill rate; suppose further that the futures contracts were expected to be held until they expired, when the spot/future differential would converge to zero basis points. If the spot market rate were to *rise* 100 points in that period, the futures rate would only increase by 50 basis points; but if the spot market rate were to *fall* by 100 basis points, the futures rate would decline by 150 points. A regression carried out under the first scenario would suggest a larger factor, while a regression under the second scenario would yield a smaller factor. Unless one happened to choose data from past periods that turned out to be similar to the forthcoming hedge period, the regression results would be inappropriate.

Perhaps a preferred approach would be to compare the changes of the rates on the instrument to be hedged with the changes of the rates on the instrument that underlies the future. In the above example, for instance, a comparison would be made with the change in six-month Treasury bill rates and the change in three-month Treasury bill rates. Under this approach, the manager may be able to predict whether the hedge will overperform or underperform. Hedging when the futures rate is below that of the underlying security (the rate on the *cash* three-month Treasury bill, in this case) is generally attractive — provided the hedge is liquidated *only* after this difference (the basis) has narrowed. In this case the hedger will "earn" the convergence between the rate on the futures contract and the rate on the underlying instrument, while insulating the portfolio from the spot market rate move. At some times, it may even be attractive to hedge simply to capture this basis adjustment, even if the forecasted rate environment is not particularly adverse.

Assuming these issues can be resolved and the manager ultimately determines a factor that he is willing to accept, it is important to recognize that the hedge must be adjusted as time passes. With a declining maturity of the cash instrument (as days pass), the value of the basis point on the cash position declines. After two weeks, for example, the value of the basis point will decline from $5,000 to $4,611.11——$100,000,000 × (.0001) × (166/360) or $4,611.11. Provided the 166-day bill (previously 180-day bill) will still move with a factor equal to 0.8, the correct hedge at this point would be ($4,611.11/$25) × .8 or about 148 contracts.

Over the elapsed two weeks (10 trading days), 12 contracts should have been liquidated in some phased-out method. Some might choose to liquidate one contract a day for four days and two contracts on the fifth day, and so on. Others might feel more comfortable liquidating two contracts every other day.

Beyond the choice of the specific contract, the question remains as to which contract *month(s)* should be chosen. This decision essentially involves a comparison of relative value of alternative futures months as well as a consideration of liquidity. Typically, the most actively traded contracts, and thus the most liquid, are the contracts with the nearest expiration dates. Using contracts with the greatest liquidity provides the hedger with the most flexibility to manage the hedge and to liquidate positions. Often, however, a manager might be willing to trade liquidity for relative value. For example, assuming the correct hedge involved selling 100 contracts, and the third contract out were judged to be "over valued," the hedger might be induced to use this contract as a hedge vehicle. It is beyond the scope of this paper to get into pricing or relative value issues.

Still another possibility is spreading the contracts out among a number of different months. For example, hedging six-month instruments one would sell two successive contract months, three contract months for nine month instruments, four contract months for one-year instruments, etc. *Stripping* contracts in this manner tends to mitigate some portion of the yield curve risk inherent in the determination of the factor. Put another way, when stripping contracts, the factor used for the calculation of the correct number of contracts in the hedge should measure only the relative rate due to quality difference between the cash market instruments to be hedged and the instruments underlying the futures, as the strips of futures generally behave more like the six-month, nine-month, and one-year rates, respectively, rather than behaving like the three-month rate underlying the contract. If one wanted to *stack* contracts in one contract month, on the other hand, the factor should reflect anticipated yield curve changes, as well as quality effects.

Why Hedge?

Now that the idea of hedging and the methodology of constructing a hedge have been explained, one might reasonably wonder why such an activity should be undertaken. After all, if the manager is simply concerned that interest rates will rise and the capital value of his portfolio will decline, why wouldn't he simply liquidate the portfolio?

In fact, liquidating the portfolio — or portions thereof — might be the most appropriate decision; but hedging may be more appropriate in certain cases. The manager's most prudent course is to evaluate both liquidating the portfolio and hedging the portfolio and then to choose the alternative that provides the greater advantage.

As mentioned above, one possible reason for hedging a portfolio may be to capture the income from a converging basis. Two other conditions might also make hedging particularly attractive: (1) hedging may be the preferred way of dealing with an anticipated rise in interest rates when portions of the portfolio are not actively traded or because the size of the position is so large that a liquidation could only be accomplished at a seriously depressed price; and (2) the results generated from the reinvestment of the liquidated capital would be less than the forthcoming accrual of interest associated with the existing portfolio instrument.

Of these two reasons for hedging, the first is fairly obvious and needs no further explanation. The second reason becomes relevant when the yield curve is sufficiently upward sloping. The perfect hedge on a portfolio, or a segment of a portfolio, would protect the capital value of the asset while allowing interest to accrue. Consider imposing a hedge on the above $100 million in six-month Treasury bills. If the hedge were to work perfectly, the changes in the portfolio value associated with an interest rate change would be entirely offset, but the changes in the value of the portfolio associated with time passing would still be realized. This income would be the discount that would be earned over time. At the time the hedge is being considered, the manager would want to evaluate the effective rate of return that is associated with earning this remaining discount and compare this return to that anticipated from reinvesting the capital in a shorter term security. In an upward sloping yield curve environment the reinvestment rate may be quite inferior to the returns available from the hedged portfolio.

The Risks — probably not perfect hedge

Does designing and implementing hedges as described above promise a perfect performance? Probably not. This hedge construction *assumes* that the relationship between the interest rate move on the future and the interest rate move on the cash instrument (the factor) is a specific value. If this assumption proves to be incorrect, the hedge will not offset the change in the value of the cash position exactly. The mismatch may work to the benefit of the investment manager or to his detriment, but one cannot anticipate the outcome. There are four different cases:

- Interest rates rise and the actual adjustment factor exceeds the expected adjustment factor (that is, cash rates move more than anticipated relative to futures rates): results in a loss on the portfolio with a less than fully offsetting gain on the hedge.

- Interest rates rise and the actual adjustment factor falls short of the expected adjustment factor: results in losses on the cash position and even greater profits on the hedge.

- Interest rates decline and the adjustment factor exceeds the expected adjustment factor: results in gains on the cash portfolio and less than fully offsetting losses on the hedge.

- Interest rates decline and the adjustment factor falls short of the expected adjustment factor: results in gains on the portfolio and even greater losses on the hedge.

These four cases reflect the primary risk, that the assumed factor in the hedge ratio calculation may turn out to be inappropriate. They also demonstrate, however, that coincident with risk is additional opportunity (i.e., better than anticipated performance).

A secondary risk deals with the very nature of a futures contract and the cash flow obligation that is inherent in its use. Once the hedge is in place, as the futures price changes each day, the change in the value of the futures contract is passed between the two parties of the trade, making use of the exchange's Clearing House as an intermediary. For example, assume the hedge works as anticipated. That is, interest rates rise on both the cash instrument to be hedged and the futures contracts, thus the futures price declines and profits accrue to the short hedger. In this case, the hedger would receive the change in the value of the contract due to the price change. This *variation margin* could be reinvested, and hedge results would be enhanced. Unfortunately, just the opposite can occur with detrimental effects. That is, rather than interest rates rising, interest rates could decline, resulting in hedge losses. The overall assessment of the hedge performance should reflect the opportunity costs associated with financing these losses. Moreover, even though losses on futures will ultimately balance gains on the cash position, the benefit accruing on the cash side often is not realized until long after variation losses have been paid. Due to the high-leverage nature of the futures contract, the cash flow requirements of the losing futures position may be quite onerous in certain times, possibly straining borrowing constraints.

Summary

Fully hedging a portfolio involves maintaining an appropriate number of futures contracts such that if interest rates rise and the value of the portfolio declines, the futures hedge should generate profits equal to the loss on the portfolio. Alternatively, if interest rates decline and the value of the portfolio increases, an equal loss will arise from the futures hedge.

Importantly, whether a futures hedge generates profits or losses is *not* an indication of the hedge's effectiveness. Instead, it is a measure of the manager's skill in anticipating an adverse interest rate movement. Hedging is simply one possible defensive tactic. It should be viewed as an alternative to restructuring the portfolio.

Restructuring a portfolio will protect or enhance returns if the interest rate view proves correct, but can be detrimental if the view proves incorrect. In the same way, futures positions will generate profits in the first case and losses in the second. The appropriate measure of the hedge's effectiveness, therefore, is the comparison of the overall portfolio performance that would result under restructuring versus the overall performance that would result from incorporating a hedge.

Assuming a defensive measure is desired, hedging will be the preferred approach when (1) a "cash/futures" adjustment appears to be favorable, (2) the liquidation of the portfolio would involve selling at a seriously depressed price, or (3) the reinvestment rates for shorter termed instruments are unattractive. One who chooses to hedge at these times will outperform the manager with the same goals who ignores the futures markets and instead deals exclusively with cash instruments.

Defining Selling Terms

Calvin M. Boardman and Kathy J. Ricci

Credit management is a major part of a company's working capital management. The extension of credit is a valuable sales tool, but it may also create a considerable drain on a firm's financial resources including the cash flow you monitor. As you extend credit, the time it takes to acquire the cash from a sale increases. This may cause a firm to increase its borrowings and thus its costs of financing. It also increases the costs of following through on overdue invoices. The ultimate costs, those of nonpayment, may be very high.

To encourage prompt payment when credit is extended, many firms offer cash discounts for early payment or charge a financing fee for late payment. Many credit executives use these practices in combination. The extent to which they have been applied in practice varies, however. If more buyers and sellers understood how these practices save both of them money, their use would probably be more widespread. Since the seller controls the selling terms, as a credit exec you should reevaluate the selling terms of your credit policy and be prepared to convince your customers why they should want to follow those terms.

The Seller's Perspective

There are various factors to consider when a firm decides whether or not to offer a cash discount for early payment of invoices, and, if a discount is offered, how much it should be. Discounts may vary from product to product and market to market. The payment due date must be considered along with the firm's added cost on a credit sale, including the value of the

Calvin M. Boardman and Kathy J. Ricci, "Defining Selling Terms," *Credit & Financial Management* (April 1985): 31–33. Reprinted with permission from *Credit & Financial Management,* copyright April 1985, published by the National Association of Credit Management, 8815 Centre Park Drive, Columbia, MD 21045.

At the time of this writing, Calvin M. Boardman was Associate Professor of Finance, University of Utah, and Kathy J. Ricci was Internal Auditor, American Savings and Loan. The views expressed are the opinions of the authors and are not intended to represent the official views of the University of Utah or American Savings and Loan.

firm's investment in the sale (the cost of the goods sold on credit) during the period before the cash payment is received.

The process of determining discount policy involves many issues, such as estimates of payment arrivals, expected changes in sales volume, the percentage of discounted credit sales and any changes in the bad debt loss rate resulting from discount policy changes. In "Determining the Cash Discount in the Firm's Credit Policy," Ned Hill and Kenneth Reiner present a formula combining the above variables that compares the present value of cash flow patterns under existing credit policy to those expected under the suggested credit policy. A new cash discount should be offered only when the present value of the cash flow under the proposed policy is greater than that under current policy.

Hill and Reiner examine the variables in the formula and come to the following five conclusions which all argue in favor of frequent reviews of a firm's cash discount policy.

1. Products with different variable costs should have different credit terms. In general, the lower the variable costs, the higher the feasible discount.

2. Since the cash discount offered depends on the firm's own cost of funds, managers should consider changing credit policy as the firm's opportunity costs change.

3. The timing of cash flow is critical to the discount decision model. The manager must consider not only how the discounts shift some payments forward but also how the timing of cash flows from the nondiscount-taking customers are affected.

4. Since the cash discount depends on how sensitive demand is to price changes, knowledge of price elasticity is important.

5. Bad debt losses affect the maximum justifiable discount. Firms with higher bad debt loss rates can afford to offer higher cash discounts, provided the discount helps reduce the loss.

Certainly the firm offering the cash discount faces a loss of full payment if the discount is taken. These losses could be large if the discount percentage is high and many customers take the discount option. However, these losses are offset by at least four advantages of the lower early payment. Cash is received sooner, reducing the firm's need to borrow or allowing more cash for investment. Returns on these investments begin earlier. Bad debt losses and costs of obtaining payment are reduced if customers pay early. Since a cash discount may be considered, in effect, a price reduction, sales volume may increase. Whether or not these benefits offset the cash discounts should be the focus of study for any company contemplating a cash discount.

Another practicality is that once a company sets what it considers its "correct" cash discount, the marketplace may dictate some other rate. If it is determined that 1/10, net 20 is optimal, and the company's competitors offer 2/10, net 30, the firm is faced with a decision to conform or lose sales. This reevaluation does not mean that the process of determining the optimal rate is a meaningless exercise. It would certainly point out the costs of conformity and the need to recoup those costs in other ways.

In addition to offering a cash discount, a service or finance charge may be levied on late payments to encourage timely payment. It can also be viewed as a way to pass financing costs on to the customer. Thus, one would expect a service charge to bear a close relationship to the charging firm's cost of capital. Additionally, the amount will be affected by the competition's practice with respect to service charges. Often, the rate is also regulated by the state in which the company does business.

The Buyer's Perspective

Certainly, there are two sides to these cash discount and service charge transactions. Thus far, we have examined the issue from the seller's viewpoint. What about the buyer?

The buyer's most straightforward cost is the service charge. It is included on the monthly statement as an additional cost of buying from a particular firm and not paying on time. The annualized percent is easily estimated by multiplying the monthly percent by 12.

The cost of not taking a discount is more difficult to determine. If a 2 percent discount offer is not taken, a very real cost is incurred. If the credit terms are 2/10, net 30, and the 2 percent discount is passed and the net amount paid at 30 days, an annualized cost of 37.2 percent is incurred. This percentage is calculated using the equation: discount percent divided by 100−discount percent multiplied by 365 divided by the number of days the credit is outstanding−discount period.

$$\frac{2}{98} \times \frac{365}{30 - 10} = 37.2\%$$

The latter half of the equation annualizes the passed discount so that comparative analysis can be performed. It also points out that if the discount is passed, adding time to the actual payment date decreases the effective cost of passing the discount. For example, if the customer passes the 2 percent discount on a 2/10, net 30 discount, but waits until the 60th day to pay, the annualized cost decreases to 14.9 percent.

While waiting longer to pay does reduce this type of cost, others may be incurred. The company can lose credit standing, be placed on C.O.D. or even refused shipment. Service charges are likely to be levied as well.

An examination of costs of passing a discount and incurring a service charge from the buyer's viewpoint illustrates the consequences of delaying payment. Using the 2/10, net 30 terms and an annualized service charge of 21 percent, the following three observations can be made:

1.   The annualized total costs of delaying payment when both condi-
      tions occur is higher than many may realize.

2.   The annualized total costs decrease as time passes until, on the
      365th day, the total would be 23 percent.

3.   Other costs begin to be incurred at 120 days and, if quantifiable,
      would certainly make the total costs even higher. If these costs were
      truly understood, most borrowers would borrow if they had to,
      probably at a lower rate, to pay off the outstanding account.

Credit Practices of Sellers

In order to determine company credit practices in setting cash discounts
and service charges, we mailed a questionnaire to 666 credit execs in
retail, wholesale, manufacturing and service industries who were members of NACM-Intermountain. We received 391 responses (almost 59%).
The largest percentage of the companies were located in Utah (64.2%), in
the sales range of $1 million to $9.9 million, and were in the wholesale
industry.

      We asked the participants what credit terms they offered. C.O.D.
was the only payment term for 5.6 percent of the respondents. About 40
percent of these were in the retail industry, and the others were spread
almost evenly over the other industries.

      About 67 percent of the 391 firms offered credit but no cash
discounts. Of these, 21 percent offered terms of net 10 and a little over
half of those offered terms of net 30. The companies offering credit but no
discounts were spread over the retail, wholesale, manufacturing and
service industries fairly evenly. Approximately 69 percent of the retailers,
58.6 percent of the wholesalers, 66 percent of the manufacturers and 72
percent of the service companies offered credit but no cash discounts.

      About 27 percent of the 391 firms offered credit with accompanying
cash discounts available for early payment. Of those firms, 25 percent
offered terms of 1/10, net 30 while 68 percent of those firms offered 2/10
net 30. The other 7 percent offered a wide range of cash discount terms.

      Cash discount offers appeared to be industry-related. The wholesale
industry offered 78.7 percent of its customers cash discounts, more than
double the percentage of all the other industries combined. The retail,
manufacturing and service industries offered cash discounts to 56 percent, 64.2 percent and 36 percent of their customers, respectively.

      Although cash discounts are offered to encourage timely payment,
they are only an advantage to the sellers if their customers take them. In
our survey, 24.8 percent of the respondents found that 0 to 20 percent of
their customers took offered discounts, while 26.4 percent found that 81
to 100 percent of their customers took the discounts. At the top end, there
was little differentiation by industry. For example, 29.1 percent of the
retail firms had a high success rate and 32 percent of the manufacturing

firms had a high success rate. At the low end, industry influence was more apparent. Wholesale firms had few customers that did *not* take a discount, while 57 percent of the service firms took no or very few discounts.

The other major method of encouraging timely payment, the service charge, was widely used by responding firms. About 79 percent of all responding firms levied a service charge for late payment. Half of these were wholesale companies, 23 percent were retail, 14 percent were manufacturing and 6.5 percent were service companies. The percentages seem lopsided only because 41 percent of the firms answering the survey were wholesale firms.

It appears that the wholesale industry was the most aggressive in managing its accounts receivable. The most popular range for service charges was 15 to 20 percent, and 82.6 percent of the wholesaling companies said they charged a rate in this area, with 13.7 percent charging more than 20 percent as a service charge.

Of the companies that levy service charges, 51 percent do so as of the net date. This trend is so in each of the industry categories: 47.1 percent of the wholesalers, 54 percent of the retailers, 48 percent of the manufacturers and 58 percent of the service companies gave this answer. A significant percentage use the invoice date as the relevant date.

We also found that 11.2 percent of firms levying service charges do not attempt to call the customer regarding payment. A total of 22.4 percent of all industries do acquire 61 to 80 percent of the service charges. Once again, the breakdown between industries produces a wide range of success: 31.7 percent of the wholesalers achieve 61 to 80 percent of their service charges, whereas only 9.6 percent of the retailers collect within this range from their customers.

Both cash discounts and service charges are used to encourage prompt payment. During times of tight money, the timely receipt of monies owed becomes critical. It would be expected that firms would be aggressive in using the tools available to them; however, this was not usually the case. Only 30.4 percent of all firms utilized both tactics.

Again the wholesale firms were in the lead with 49 percent utilizing both methods of accounts receivable management. A total of 22.2 percent of all manufacturing firms, 19.4 percent of all retail firms and only 5.6 percent of all service firms employed both cash discounts and service charges. Possible reasons for not using both techniques are competitive pressures, a reluctance to be aggressive and ignorance of their effectiveness in motivating timely customer payments.

The Merits of Timely Payment

Delaying payment can be a costly move for both sellers and buyers. Sellers lose the use of the money, incur additional collection costs and run the risk that payment may never occur. Buyers lose access to cash discounts, may incur a service charge and may have their credit rating tarnished in the process. Any buyer contemplating a delay in payment must consider all the costs involved. This understood, firms may be more likely to pay on time.

The evidence shows that many firms do not take advantage of the myriad tools of credit management at their disposal. When used properly, these tools can yield impressive results. Of the industries studied, the wholesale industry appears most aggressive in its handling of accounts receivable. Certainly the evidence shows that understanding the economics of delayed payment and using this knowledge with your customers can be effective in encouraging early payment and should be done more regularly.

Questions

1. Identify the financial advantages and disadvantages of granting credit and of *not* granting credit to customers.

2. What factors should a credit manager consider when establishing policy on granting cash discounts for early payment?

3. Suppliers to Rinco, Inc., grant credit terms of 1/10, net 20, but Rinco pays 15 days after the net date. What is Rinco's opportunity cost of forgoing the 1 percent cash discount? What other costs might Rinco incur?

4. Answer the following true-false questions based on the survey results reported by the authors:

    T   F   Most companies sell goods on a C.O.D. basis.

    T   F   Most companies offer a cash discount for early payment.

    T   F   Among companies offering a cash discount for early payment, the terms 2/10, net 30 are frequently offered.

    T   F   Many companies levy a service charge for late payment, which is defined as any payment after the net date.

23
Survey of Current Practices in Establishing Trade-Credit Limits
Scott Besley and Jerome S. Osteryoung

Introduction

While some viable efforts to derive a rational credit-limit model for trade credit have appeared over the years, this area still is only beginning to construct a solid theoretical base. Until now, academicians have offered few alternatives to the dilemma facing practitioners: how to set credit limits for receivables. Two very important questions naturally arise. Is it a normal practice of firms to establish credit limits for their trade-credit customers? And, if so, what are the reasons for and the methods used in setting these limits?

Two surveys conducted in the early 1970s give some indication of the methodologies employed to establish credit limits. First, Davey's [4] study of 119 firms in twenty-three industries (sales ranged from $4 million to $6 billion) revealed that most firms (69 percent) relied on credit ratings supplied by mercantile agencies, such as Dun and Bradstreet, when determining credit limits. Later, Kirkman [5] surveyed British corporations and discovered a similar result. In addition, he found that 90 percent of the firms in the study assigned credit limits to at least a portion of their customers. Yet, only one-half of the firms imposed limits for all of their credit customers.

Scott Besley and Jerome S. Osteryoung, "Survey of Current Practices in Establishing Trade-Credit Limits," *The Financial Review* (February 1985): 70–82. Reprinted with permission from the Eastern Finance Association.

At the time of this writing, Scott Besley was affiliated with the University of South Florida and Jerome S. Osteryoung was affiliated with Florida State University.

Neither survey was designed explicitly to investigate the practices of establishing credit limits for trade customers.[1] Rather, the object of each was a general investigation of accounts receivable practices to determine whether firms offer cash discounts, the normal length of credit terms, how receivables are monitored and controlled, and so on. Unlike the surveys of Davey and Kirkman, the study presented in this paper is designed specifically to update current knowledge concerning the techniques applied by businesses to establish purchasing limits for credit customers. Succinctly stated, the goal is to answer the questions posed above by examining extant credit-limit practices employed by trade creditors.

Methodology and Sample Characteristics

A survey was administered in Fall of 1982 with the assistance of the Credit Research Foundation, Incorporated (hereafter CRF).[2] The membership of the Foundation, which numbered approximately 510 firms at the time of the survey, served as the population for the study. Each member firm was sent a survey package containing both a pre-tested questionnaire and a cover letter signed by Dr. George N. Christie, the executive vice president of the CRF, with instructions to return the completed questionnaire to the CRF.[3,4]

Questionnaire Characteristics

The questionnaire contained a total of seventeen questions and relevant instructions. Other than some questions used to elicit firm characteristics such as industry classification and total size, all of the questions were "close-ended" with respect to the possible answers. The close-ended

---

[1] The term trade customers is used throughout this paper to designate customers other than those who purchase final goods and services. That is, firms such as manufacturers or suppliers who issue credit to other firms are extending trade credit (see Brealey and Myers [1], p. 547). Since those who receive trade credit can be labeled trade credit customers, trade customers is a general term for all purchasers of goods and services from firms that grant trade credit.

[2] This study was accomplished with the assistance of and the partial funding by the Credit Research Foundation, Incorporated. Much gratitude is extended to that organization and its members for the cooperation received. Of course, any errors in this paper are the sole responsibility of the authors, and not the Foundation.

[3] Prior to surveying the entire membership, a pilot study was conducted to fine tune the questionnaire. The purpose of the pre-test was to determine whether the respondents' interpretation of each question included in the survey was as intended. About twenty-five randomly selected firms participated in the pilot study. After the pre-test of the questionnaire, some questions were re-designed to help eliminate any ambiguities that existed.

[4] The survey packages were distributed and collected by the CRF to insure the anonymity of the respondents in the data processing stage of the study. Problems concerning specific questionnaires could be answered by CRF because each respondent was assigned a number code. This code allowed the CRF to identify the company by name and industry if the firm had to be contacted.

questions included a list of alternatives from which the respondent could choose.[5] For these questions, the respondent was able to specify an option not included in the list by marking the selection "other" and then stating the appropriate reply. In addition, for three of the close-ended questions the respondents were allowed multiple selections. These particular questions were designed expressly to elicit whether more than one method or reason was responsible for a firm's credit-limit position. If two or more responses were chosen, a follow-up question required the respondent to specify which was the principal factor.

Sample Characteristics

The sample used in this study is comprised of data collected from 234 completed surveys.[6] Tables 1 and 2 indicate that the characteristics of the responding companies are varied with respect to firm size and industry classification. On the other hand, the data did reveal that more than 83 percent of the respondents to some extent are involved in manufacturing.

Survey Results[7]

On the whole, the results of the survey support the previous findings of Kirkman [5] that most firms impose credit limits for at least some of their trade customers. In addition, the results yield a general implication similar to the one given by Davey [4] that the nature of the procedures commonly utilized to establish the trade-credit limits is rather subjective.

---

[5] In an effort to avoid an ordering bias, two survey forms were created. (For an explanation of ordering biases, see Webster [6].) The only difference in the forms was the order of the alternatives for the "close-ended" questions. In addition, to determine if an ordering bias existed, the data were statistically tested with respect to the frequency of response for each alternative and the survey form. The tests' findings suggest that the ordering of the alternatives for the "close-ended" questions was not an important problem for this study. At a 0.10 significance level none of the hypotheses of independence were rejected. And the level of rejection could be raised to .35 if the "multivariate statistics" selection was eliminated from the question that elicited the combination of methods employed to set limits. The reason for this was because all of those who responded to this option had the same form of the questionnaire.

[6] Five of the respondents indicated that they were either commercial factors or financial institutions. The data from these cases were omitted for two reasons. First, much of the information on these questionnaires was incomplete and inconsistent. But, more important, financial concerns do not sell manufactured products and, therefore, accounts receivable are not created per se. Instead, factors and banks are third parties in the trade-credit process since essentially their role is to lend funds based on an aggregation of outstanding credit accounts, not to generate, or solicit, the original account.

[7] Not every survey was complete, because some of the respondents had not answered all of the questions. The missing responses generally applied only to the open-ended questions. And, as it turned out, in every instance, the remainder of the questionnaire was completed sufficiently to retain the firm as a member of the sample. In any event, the number of missing cases for each question was not significant to the findings of this study. Therefore, while the tabulations of the data report missing responses for particular sections, the discussion is generalized for all of the observations in the sample.

Table 1   Industry Classifications[a]

Industry	Absolute Freq	Relative Freq (pct)	Cumul. Freq (pct)
Mining	18	7.7	7.7
Food	31	13.2	20.9
Textiles	11	4.7	25.6
Chemical	49	20.9	46.6
Forest	16	6.8	53.4
Building	19	8.1	61.5
Metals	23	9.8	71.4
Machine	22	9.4	80.8
Electrical	22	9.4	90.2
Other	23	9.8	100.0
Total	234	100.0	

234 Valid Cases   0 Missing Cases

[a] Each firm was classified according to the industrial coding scheme of *Compustat* [2], which is a four-digit number identifying a specific Standard and Poor's industry classification. A list of the industry codes can be found in any *Compustat* manual. For the purposes of this study, only the first two digits of the industry code were utilized.

Table 2   Total Assets (millions of dollars)

Interval	Absolute Freq	Relative Freq (pct)	Adjusted Freq[a] (pct)	Cumul. Freq (pct)
$0–50	24	10.3	12.2	12.2
>$50–100	13	5.6	6.6	18.8
>$100–250	31	13.2	15.7	34.5
>$250–500	22	9.4	11.2	45.7
>$500–1000	28	12.0	14.2	59.9
>$1000–2500	29	12.4	14.7	74.6
>$2500–5000	25	10.7	12.7	87.3
>$5000–10000	20	8.5	10.2	97.5
>$10000	5	2.1	2.5	100.0
No Response	37	15.8	Missing	100.0
Total	234	100.0	100.0	

Mean	1990.209	Std Dev	3035.264
Minimum	1.000	Maximum	20429.000

197 Valid Cases   37 Missing Cases

[a] The relative frequency computation is based on the entire sample of 234 firms, while the adjusted relative frequency is calculated by excluding the 37 respondents who chose not to reply to this particular question. Thus, the adjusted relative frequency computation is based on a sample of 234 − 37 = 197 firms.

General Credit-Granting Characteristics

None of the respondents indicated that it is normal to conduct business entirely on a cash-only basis. Instead, more than 87 percent of the firms reported that from 91 percent to 100 percent of their goods and services are sold on credit. Further, the data disclose that credit sales constitute more than 80 percent of the aggregate annual sales amount for almost 96 percent of the sample members. Thus, for nearly all of the firms contained in the sample, credit sales represent a very significant portion of total revenues. In fact, only four respondents (less than 2 percent of the sample) indicated cash sales comprise a majority of total annual revenues. But this is not surprising, considering members of a credit organization were sampled.

When asked about the use of credit limits, only five respondents indicated that they do not normally impose limits on the amount of outstanding credit for at least some customers. Of those 229 firms which restrict credit purchases (nearly 98 percent of the sample), more than 43 percent stated they assign limits to all of their credit customers, while 80 percent use limits for 90 percent or more. Moreover, about 80 percent of the sample indicated limits are employed for a majority of their customers. Therefore, the findings suggest that a very large portion of the firms extending trade credit to some degree limit the credit purchases for most of their customers.

Why Limits Are Applied on an Individual Account Basis

Those respondents who revealed they restrict customers' accounts were asked to specify *all* of the reasons for administering credit limits. If two or more responses were chosen as reasons for applying limits, the respondent was requested to specify which reply represented the principal reason. Table 3 presents the results of this inquiry.

Notice that more than one-half of the respondents (53.1 percent) regard risk exposure as the primary ground for establishing limits, while 28 percent indicate the reason is due to the financial condition of the credit customer. Actually, there may not be a clear distinction between these two explanations, since a customer with a poor financial position exposes the lending company to a higher degree of default risk, in relative terms, than a financially sound customer would. Consequently, in aggregate, the results show that, for 81 percent of the companies sampled, the basis for concern when limiting trade-credit purchases is exposure to risk. None of the respondents indicated that either the economy or the financial position of the firm is a *primary* reason for assigning credit limits.

Methods of Establishing Credit Limits

A logical complement to the question of why credit limits are assigned is to ask how the limits are determined. The techniques employed by firms

Table 3   Reason(s) for Imposing Credit Limits

	Primary Reason	
Reason	Count	Pct of Cases
Credit Reputation	7	3.1
Experience with Customer	13	5.8
Customer Financial Position	63	27.9
Lender Financial Position	0	0.0
Limited Funds for Receivables	0	0.0
Control Exposure to Risk	120	53.1
New Credit Customer .	1	0.4
Tradition of Lending Firm	8	3.5
Industry Practice	2	0.9
Weak Economy	0	0.0
Legal Reasons	1	0.4
Other Reasons	11	4.9
Total Responses	226	100.0

Number of firms responding   226

to establish limits are listed in Table 4. Again, multiple responses were permitted.

No evidence has been presented to suggest firms rely on credit-limit models or algorithms other than those based heavily on subjective

Table 4   Method(s) of Establishing Credit Limits

	Primary Method	
Method	Count	Pct of Cases
Industry Guidelines	0	0.0
New Customer — Low Limit	2	0.9
Customer's Needs — Time	13	5.8
Permit Amount Desired	11	4.9
% of Balance Sheet Acct	8	3.5
Average Order Size	0	0.0
Based on # of Suppliers	0	0.0
Agency Ratings	17	7.5
Point Scoring Systems	2	0.9
Mathematical Programming	4	1.8
Expected Profit Analysis	1	0.4
Multivariate Statistics	1	0.4
Ratio Analysis	47	20.8
Judgment	119	52.7
Other Methods	1	0.4
Total Responses	226	100.0

Number of firms responding   226

Secondary Reason(s)			
Count	**Pct of Cases**	**Total Count**	**Pct of Cases**
128	56.6	135	59.7
135	59.7	148	65.5
80	35.4	143	63.3
1	0.4	1	0.4
7	3.1	7	3.1
60	26.5	180	79.6
82	36.3	83	36.7
46	20.4	54	23.9
19	8.4	21	9.3
31	13.7	31	13.7
7	3.1	8	3.5
16	7.1	27	11.9
612		838	

decision-making practices. The data in Table 4 indicate this is true. Surprisingly, however, the results suggest that pure judgment is the principal instrument used by a majority of firms to decide the maximum levels of credit purchases to permit trade customers. Nearly 53 percent of

Secondary Method(s)			
Count	**Pct of Cases**	**Total Count**	**Pct of Cases**
4	1.8	4	1.8
41	18.1	43	19.0
88	38.9	101	44.7
48	21.2	59	26.1
60	26.5	68	30.1
50	22.1	50	22.1
15	6.6	15	6.6
112	49.6	129	57.1
16	7.1	18	8.0
7	3.1	11	4.9
35	15.5	36	15.9
10	4.4	11	4.9
142	62.8	189	83.6
63	27.9	182	80.5
21	9.3	22	9.7
712		938	

Table 5   **Reason(s) Receivables in Aggregate Restricted**

Reasons	Primary Reason	
	Count	Pct of Cases
Limited Funds to Invest	1	11.1
Weak Economy	0	0.0
Avoid Large Bad Debts	4	44.4
Poor Financial Position	0	0.0
Limited Production Capabilities	0	0.0
More Profitable Alternatives	3	33.3
Other Reasons	1	11.1
Total Responses	9	100.0

Number of firms responding   9

the financial executives sampled disclosed that judgment is the *primary* method of establishing lines of credit.

Closer examination of the data reveals some supplemental information regarding the combination of credit-limit techniques employed by the sample firms. Specifically, of the respondents who indicated judgment is the *primary* method employed to establish credit limits, 84 percent stated financial statement analysis (ratio analysis) also is used in the decision. The reverse does not hold, since only 68 percent of those who principally rely on ratio analysis also include judgment of the trade customer's creditworthiness in the decision-making process. Further, in either case, about 60 percent of the respondents reported their firms examine the ratings supplied by mercantile agencies to supplement the decision.

Restricting Accounts Receivable in Aggregate

At least in theory, firms granting trade credit may have to turn down acceptable credit sales because funds required to support (finance) the additional accounts are not available, or can be utilized more efficiently elsewhere in the asset structure.[8] Therefore, each respondent was asked: "Does your firm restrict the *total amount* of accounts receivable it has outstanding at any time?" The question specified four replies from which to choose: (1) always, (2) most of the time, (3) sometimes, and (4) never.

Only nine of the 234 respondents (3.8 percent) revealed they ever restrict receivables in aggregate. None of the firms enforce this strategy all of the time. Two of the nine respondents indicate total receivables are

---

[8] Capital budgeting theory suggests that a firm may not be able to invest in all of its acceptable capital projects because of limited long-term funds. (See Brealey and Myers [1], Copeland and Weston [3], and Weingartner [7], among others, for an explanation of capital rationing.) Logically, short-term funds also are not unlimited resources, and firms, therefore, are subject to a total funds constraint. If true, efficient funds rationing is an important consideration for the financing of *all* assets, not just those termed capital assets.

Secondary Reason(s)		Total Count	Pct of Cases
Count	Pct of Cases		
0	0.0	1	11.1
3	33.3	3	33.3
3	33.3	7	77.8
0	0.0	0	0.0
0	0.0	0	0.0
0	0.0	3	33.3
0	0.0	1	11.1
6		15	

restricted most of the time, while the remaining seven consider such a limitation an infrequent necessity.

Table 5 summarizes the reasons the nine respondents restrict the total dollars outstanding in receivables at any time. Though the findings are tenuous because of the small sample size, it appears the restriction of receivables in aggregate is a consequence either of funds rationing resulting from limited resources or of an attempt to avoid large bad debts.

Measure of Financial Variables in Credit Decisions

The last section of the questionnaire was devoted to the investigation of the accuracy of measure for financial variables generally considered important to the decision-making process involved in credit management. Five factors (variables) were presented to the respondents, who were asked to indicate whether measurement is attempted, and, if so, the level of accuracy attainable. The variables which were included are those mentioned most often in the literature, especially in articles that propose credit-management algorithms for practical applications. Table 6 contains the results of this question.

Notice that in every case more than 84 percent of the respondents whose firm's policy it is to measure these credit factors indicated they can obtain at least an adequate estimate for the variables. A rather small number stated that either they have to rely upon a poor estimate or the value cannot be estimated. At the same time, except for the firm's cost of capital, not many of the firms (less than 10 percent) indicated it is possible to attain an exact value for the measure in question. This is not surprising considering both the theoretical and practical refinement of the models employed to measure the cost of capital compared to the methods available for measuring the more credit-related variables.

Table 6   Measurement Accuracy of Credit Variables

Variable	Measure		
	Do Not Est.	Cannot Est.	Poor Est.
Default Probability	17[c] 7.9[d]	6[c] 2.8[d] (3.0)[e]	19 8.8 (9.6)
Delinquency Probability	9 4.2	2 0.9 (9.7)	5 2.3 (2.4)
Credit Limit[f]	38 17.7	5 2.3 (2.8)	15 7.0 (8.5)
Receivables Opportunity Cost	81 37.7	5 2.3 (3.7)	16 7.4 (11.9)
Cost of Capital	49[c] 22.8[d]	3[c] 1.4[d] (1.8)[e]	7 3.3 (4.2)

[a] Nineteen of the questionnaires contained *no* response at all for this section.

[b] The row subtotal excludes those respondents who reported they do *not* measure the variable in question. It includes only those firms that indicated the particular variable is measured. Therefore, the subtotal row count equals the row total count less the cell count for "Do Not Est." in that respective row. The subtotal percentage computation follows directly.

[c] Count.

[d] Percent of total.

[e] Percent of subtotal.

[f] At first glance, there appears to be an inconsistency between the number of respondents who reported they do not *measure* credit limits (i.e., thirty-eight) and the number who state they do not *impose* credit limits (i.e., five). However, closer inspection reveals that thirty-one of the thirty-eight "Do Not Estimate" responses (81.6 percent) corresponded to methods of setting credit limits that actually do not require measurement per se (i.e., judgement, permit amount desired, start new customers at an arbitrarily low amount, and so on).

Tests for Dependencies

Where applicable, chi-square tests were employed to determine whether there was an association between the responses to the questions and the firm's size or its industry classification. Generally speaking, the results demonstrate no discernable relation between the size of a firm nor the industry classification and the responses given for the reasons credit limits are imposed, the methods employed to set limits, or the reasons total accounts receivable are restricted. In fact, most of the independence tests are rejected only at a significance level greater than .30. Though not as strong, the conclusions are identical when the responses of how accurately credit variables can be measured are evaluated. Therefore, the general conclusion is that the credit-limit practices of the firms in this study are neither size dependent nor industry dependent.

	Measure			
	Adeq Est.	Good Est.	Exact Value	Row Total[a] (Subtotal)[b]
	96	75	2[c]	215
	44.7	34.9	0.9[c]	(198)
	(48.5)	(37.9)	(1.0)[c]	
	57	139	3	215
	26.5	64.7	1.4	(206)
	(27.7)	(67.5)	(1.5)	
	96	56	5	215
	44.7	26.0	2.3	(177)
	(54.2)	(31.6)	(2.8)	
	46	54	13	215
	21.4	25.1	6.0	(134)
	(34.3)	(40.3)	(9.7)	
	32	72	52[c]	215
	14.9	33.5	24.2[d]	(166)
	(19.3)	(43.4)	(31.3)[e]	

Implications

The results of this study should be generalized only for the membership of the CRF. But, since the members are provided information specifically pertinent to trade-credit-granting procedures, perhaps they are more aware than nonmembers of existing practices. Consequently, it might be expected that credit-limit policies established by the general population of firms are no better than those of the general membership of the CRF. In this light, the implications reported here, to some extent, reflect the characteristics of the more general population.

Clearly, firms use credit limits as a means of controlling exposure to the risk associated with granting trade credit. The findings of this investigation indicate that the concern for risk concentrates on the individual account. Very few of the lending firms intentionally restrict accounts receivable in aggregate; rather, the total of receivables is constrained only by the combination of the customers' credit limits. Essentially, then, firms do not consider funds limitations a major obstacle to financing receivables. Conceivably the sentiment is that customers refused credit will tend to purchase elsewhere. And, therefore, perhaps credit managers believe the opportunity cost of declining credit to potentially profitable customers is greater than the cost of additional funds necessary to support the credit extended to those customers. It seems the possibility of lost sales in the future dominates the current credit-granting decision. (One respondent commented that the firm would "most likely lose the sale" if credit is not granted for the total amount requested.)

As a risk management mechanism, the basis of credit-limit method-ologies is unsophisticated. More than 80 percent of the firms surveyed employ quite subjective techniques as the primary means of establishing limits for their credit customers. This finding could be a signal that the more complex and sophisticated algorithms constructed by theoreticians are not practicable because the input variables required to operationalize such models either cannot be measured adequately or are not measured by practitioners. Interestingly, though, the data from this study suggest that this is not true. Rather, the respondents are convinced that they receive adequate estimates of financial variables such as default probabil-ity, delinquency cost, credit limits, accounts receivable opportunity cost, and cost of capital. *If* the measures *actually* are as accurate as the results suggest, the implication is that the inputs necessary for the theoretical algorithms can be sufficiently estimated.[9] Therefore, there must be another explanation why the theoretical models are not popular with practitioners. Unfortunately, this study has not addressed this subject. Even so, it is proposed that there are three possible explanations: (1) the more technical models are not understood by practitioners; (2) current credit-limit theory is not practicable; and/or, (3) credit managers have little confidence that such techniques are superior to judgment. In any event, academicians should endeavor to discover the needs of prac-titioners and develop a theory to satisfy these needs.

References

[1] Brealey, Richard, and Stewart Myers. *Principles of Corporate Finance.* Second Ed. New York: McGraw-Hill, 1984.

[2] *Compustat.* Standard & Poor's Compustat Services, Inc. Denver, Colorado: Investors Management Science, Inc., 1982.

[3] Copeland, Thomas E., and J. Fred Weston. *Financial Theory and Corporate Policy.* Reading, Massachusetts: Addison-Wesley Publishing Company, 1983.

[4] Davey, P.J. *Managing Trade Receivables.* New York: The Conference Board, 1972.

[5] Kirkman, P.R.A. *Modern Credit Management: A Study of the Management of Trade Credit Under Inflationary Conditions.* London: George Allen and Unwin, 1977.

[6] Webster, Jr., Frederick E. *Marketing Communication: Modern Promotional Strategy.* New York: The Ronald Press Company, 1971.

---

[9] Care must be taken in generalizing these results to the operationality of all credit-limit models and to all companies. Besides the fact that only a portion of the total population was included in the survey, the manner in which the question was presented leaves two additional questions unanswered. First, how accurate are the financial managers' impres-sions of the adequacy of the measures of the financial variables? Perhaps the measures are not as accurate as (or even more accurate than) the financial manager is convinced. And, second, what is the expense involved in attaining an accurate measure? If the cost of measurement outweighs the overall benefits realized by greater accuracy, then refining the metric to attain the accuracy is an unsound decision.

[7] Weingartner, H. Martin. "Capital Rationing: Authors in Search of a Plot." *Journal of Finance* XXXII (December 1977): 1403–31.

Questions

1. Describe the evidence indicating that companies normally impose credit limits on their customers.

2. What are the principal reasons given for imposing credit limits on customers?

3. What are the principal methods used to establish credit limits on customers?

4. Suppose that you overhear the following exchange in the credit department of a manufacturer:

    Salesperson: *"If we don't give Alley Company the $100,000 credit line it wants, we will lose them as a customer!"*

    Credit Manager: *"But Alley has only a $25,000 line with us."*

    Salesperson: *"I know. I know. We should increase the line."*

    Credit Manager: *"I don't know. It worries me."*

    What factors should be considered in the decision to increase Alley Company's credit limit?

Factoring Accounts Receivable

Edward J. Farragher

In many firms, managers who are marketing or production oriented often give insufficient attention to accounts receivable. This can cause a slowdown in cash receipts and/or abnormal credit losses. Fortunately, such firms can eliminate delayed collections and credit loss by factoring their accounts receivable. This article provides survey evidence of the characteristics of factoring and proposes a methodology for separate evaluation of its credit management and financing services. It is intended to help treasury managers broaden their perspective as suggested by Hill and Ferguson [3].

Credit Administration Services

Factoring is a credit management service whereby a client firm sells its accounts receivable to a factor who guarantees the amount and timing of the cash due. Factors generally do not deal with clients on an emergency basis but rather establish ongoing relationships with minimum annual factoring requirements. The survey data indicate that the respondents favor a minimum annual accounts receivable factoring volume of $750,000 to $1,000,000 per year. At present, factoring activity mainly includes textile-related products with some expansion into the furniture, sporting goods and toy industries (Exhibit 1).

As owner of the accounts receivable, a factor typically assumes all credit management responsibilities — analysis, accounting, collection and bad-debt loss exposure. Additionally, a factor may provide cash advances to clients. The respondent's perceptions of the relative importance to clients of each these services is indicated in Exhibit 2.

A factor usually assumes a client's credit exposure by purchasing approved accounts receivable without recourse. The factor expects to provide faster, better and lower cost credit analyses because it has

Edward J. Farragher, "Factoring Accounts Receivable," *Journal of Cash Management* (March/April 1986): 38–42. Reprinted with permission of the *Journal of Cash Management*.

At the time of this writing, Edward J. Farragher was affiliated with DePaul University.

Exhibit 1   **Involvement in Various Industries**

Industry	Average Level of Involvement*	Growing Involvement Yes	No
Manufacturing:			
Finished Apparel	6.38	18	3
Textile Mill Products	5.71	14	7
Furniture/Fixtures	3.00	11	10
Plastic	2.05	3	18
Food	1.81	4	17
Electrical	1.67	4	17
Toys	1.62	4	17
Shoes	1.57	3	18
Lumber/Wood	1.57	3	18
Scientific Instruments	1.52	4	17
Wholesaling:			
Sporting/Toys	2.71	11	10
Furniture/Furnishings	2.67	8	13
Apparel	2.33	4	17
Electrical	1.62	3	18
Hardware/Plumbing	1.57	2	19
Lumber/Construction Materials	1.43	4	17
Auto Parts	1.43	3	18
Paper/Paper Products	1.29	3	18

* On a scale of one (Rarely Involved) to seven (Heavily Involved).

Note: Questionnaires were sent to all 33 members of the National Commercial Finance Association, the trade association of the accounts receivable factoring industry; 21 usable responses were received. The data show that the respondents were high level and, hopefully, well-informed managers.

in-depth, up-to-date credit files; full-time, experienced credit managers; and, through computerization, significant economies of scale. The factor only assumes losses due to nonpayment for financial reasons. The client bears any losses due to product disputes. Because a factor is larger and more diversified than its clients, it is able to assume more credit exposure.

Exhibit 2   **Relative Importance of Services Provided to Their Customers**

Service	Relative Importance*
Credit Analysis	6.48
Bad-Debt Loss Exposure	6.33
Cash Advance	5.52
Collection	5.29
Accounting	4.81

* On a scale of one (Not Important) to seven (Very Important).

This allows clients to handle a greater volume of business and to sell to borderline credit risk customers. A client also benefits from the improved consistency/quality of receivables cash flow. Late payments are eliminated because the factor guarantees the amount and timing of payment, and planning is improved because uncertainty in accounts receivable collection is no longer a problem.

Most factoring is on a notification basis whereby a client's customers are notified that a factor has purchased the receivables and are instructed to pay the factor. Factors prefer this method because it provides direct interaction with a client's customers, thus easing their ability to obtain the up-to-date information essential for accurate credit analysis. Additionally, it provides a factor with direct control over collection of accounts receivable. Another client benefit is that the factor becomes the collection agency and assumes the risk of being viewed negatively when a customer is paying late. There is less animosity between a client and its customers because the client can disavow late payment collection practices by blaming a third party—the factor. In turn, the factor can be more determined in its collection activities since it is not overly concerned about a client's customer complaints.

In return for its credit management services, a factor receives a percentage of the face value of the receivable. The survey indicated that the fee ranges from .35% to 4.0%, with an average of 1.03%. It is a negotiated rate dependent upon the:

- Stability of the client's product line
- Financial quality of client's customers
- Client's annual credit sales volume
- Average dollar amount per invoice
- Number of separate customers of client
- Length of client's credit terms.

The more stable a client's product line and the higher financial quality of its customers, the lower the fee because a factor assumes less risk. The higher a client's credit sales volume and the larger the average dollar amount per invoice, the greater are a factor's economies of scale and, thus, the lower the fee. The fewer customers a client has, the lower the fee because the factor is required to gather credit information and prepare analysis for fewer firms. The longer a client's payment period, the greater is the factor's credit exposure, resulting in a higher fee. Exhibit 3 indicates the relative importance factors assign to each of these items.

When deciding whether to factor, a firm should compare, on a present value basis, its in-house credit costs with the cost of factoring. This involves an extensive accounting effort to identify all costs that can be eliminated by factoring. An illustration of the in-house credit management versus the factoring decision process is provided in Appendix A.

Exhibit 3   **Relative Importance in Fee Determination**

Factor Fee Determinants	Relative Importance*
Financial Stability of Client's Customers	6.14
Client's Annual Factoring Volume	6.05
Average Dollar Amount per Invoice	5.71
Number of Repeat Customers per Invoice	4.90
Client's Credit Period	4.57
Financial Stability of Client	4.48

* On a scale of one (Not Important) to seven (Very Important).

Financing Services

A factor typically does not pay a client immediately upon purchase of accounts receivable. The payment date depends on the type of factoring: maturity or discount. *Maturity factoring* (illustrated in Appendix A) involves cash payment on either the actual or average due date of the accounts receivable. Maturity factoring provides only credit management and bad-debt loss protection, not cash advances. *Discount factor* provides credit management, bad-debt loss protection and the option of taking cash advances. The survey indicates that approximately 55% of factoring volume is on a discount basis, 36% on a maturity basis and 9% is customized to a client's wishes. Whether a firm using discount factoring should take cash advances depends on the effective annual rate of interest for factor-provided financing vis-a-vis the effective cost of alternative financing sources. Appendix B provides an illustration of the amount and time of cash flows with discount factoring.

Summary

For many firms, factoring provides a means for obtaining credit management and short-term financing. A firm must perform a cash flow analysis of in-house versus factoring credit management costs when deciding whether to use maturity factoring and must compare the effective annual cost of cash advances with the cost of alternative sources of financing when deciding whether to take cash advances. The successful cash manager must be aware of the distinct credit management and cash advance services a factor can provide and must work together with the credit manager in jointly determining whether to use the services of a factor. A thorough awareness of nontraditional cash management functions, such as factoring, should provide significant potential for broadening the scope of cash management to include the entire cash flow timeline.

References

1. Boldin, Robert J. and Patti D. Feeney, "The Increased Importance of Factoring," *Financial Executive,* April 1981, pp. 19–21.

2. Boldin, Robert J. and Susan J. Mulholland, "A Banker's Primer on Factoring," *The Bankers Magazine,* January-February 1981, pp. 73–77.

3. Hill, Ned C. and Daniel M. Ferguson, "Cash Flow Timeline Management: The Next Frontier of Cash Management," *Journal of Cash Management,* May/June 1985, pp. 12–22.

4. Moore, Carroll G., "Factoring—A Unique and Important Form of Financing and Service," *The Business Lawyer,* Vol. XIV, No. 3.

5. National Commercial Finance Conference, *Special Bulletin No. 62: Impact of Factoring Costs on Procedures and Rates,* New York (1974).

6. _____ , *Special Bulletin No. 84: Seminar on Atypical Factoring Arrangements,* New York (1979).

7. _____ , *Special Bulletin No. 93: Factoring: Past, Present and Future,* New York (1980).

Questions

1. Define *factoring* and identify the services typically provided by factors. Distinguish between maturity factoring and discount factoring.

2. Which manufacturers commonly use factoring?

3. In a factoring arrangement, who bears the risk of customers not paying because of bankruptcy? Because of product disputes?

4. Factors charge a fee for credit management services usually within the range of 0.35 percent to 4.0 percent. What would cause the factor's fee to be in the high end of this range?

5. Tres Faux Wholesalers' monthly credit sales are $2 million. Credit terms are 2/10, net 60, and 20 percent of receivables are paid on the 10th. Because of financial difficulties experienced by its customers, Tres Faux's bad-debt expense averages 0.5 percent of monthly credit sales. Credit department costs are 2 percent of monthly credit sales and are paid on the 30th. Tres Faux has never experienced customer disputes over the quality of its products. Fechere Factoring offers to buy Tres Faux's accounts receivable on a maturity basis for a 2 percent fee. Tres Faux uses a 10 percent discount rate for the analysis of its receivables. Based on present value analysis, should Tres Faux factor its receivables? Show calculations supporting your answer. (See Appendices.)

Appendix A

A manufacturing firm sells $1,000,000 per month on credit with terms of 2/10; Net 60. Historically, 20% of the accounts receivable are discounted and paid on the 10th, the bad-debt loss rate is 1%, and credit department costs, 2% of the face amount of accounts receivable, are paid on the 30th. It is expected that 5% of the accounts will be disputed and not paid until the 120th day after sale. A factor offers to buy all of the manufacturer's accounts receivable on a maturity basis charging a 1½% fee. The factor will make a cash settlement on the net date (60th) less a 5% holdback for non-payment due to product quality disputes. It is expected that all such disputes will be settled and the factor will release the holdback on the 120th day. The manufacturer has a 10% opportunity rate of return. The following present value analysis of the incremental cash flows indicates that the manufacturing firm should factor its accounts receivable.

Day

10th	Discounted Payments	
	Collect $1,000,000 × 20% =	$200,000
	Discounts $200,000 × 2% =	($4,000)
30th	Credit Department Costs	
60th	Collection of Balance less Disputed Payments	
	$800,000 − (5%)($1,000,000)	
	Payment from Factor $1,000,000 less:	
	$15,000 Factor fee	
	$4,000 Discount	
	$50,000 Holdback	
120th	Collection of Disputed Accounts less Bad Debt Loss	
	$50,000 − (1%)($1,000,000)	
	Factor Releases Holdback	

Cash without Factoring	Cash with Factor	Incremental Cash due to Factoring	10% Discount Rate	Present Values
196,000		(196,000)	.9973	(195,470)
(20,000)		20,000	.9918	19,835
750,000				
		181,000	.9837	178,050
	931,000			
40,000		10,000	.9675	9,675
	50,000			
Present Value Advantage to Factoring				$ 12,090

Appendix B

It was decided (Appendix A) that the manufacturer should factor its accounts receivable. Now the question becomes should it take cash advances from the factor. The factor will charge 17% simple interest with a 90% client availability allowance. The client availability allowance indicates the maximum amount of client equity which the factor will advance. It depends upon the client's financial character, the likelihood of excessive product quality disputes and the liquidation value of the factored accounts receivable. The client equity is equal to the face value of the factored accounts receivable less potential early payment discounts, the factor fee and the product quality holdback. Assuming the manufacturer takes the maximum cash advance, the amount and timing of the cash flows are as follows:

Factored Accounts Receivable	$1,000,000
Less: Potential Early Payment Discounts	(4,000)
Factor Fee	(15,000)
Product Quality Dispute Holdback	(50,000)
Client Equity	$931,000
Availability Allowance	× 90%
Maximum Cash Advance	$837,900

Cash Advance Outstanding	Interest Rate	Days	Interest Expense
$837,900	17%	10	$ 3,900
$641,900*	17%	50	$14,950
		Total Interest	$18,850

(* $837,900 Cash Advance less $196,000 early payments)

Whether or not the manufacturer should take the factor's cash advance would depend on its annual percentage cost of 17% as compared to the availability and cost of alternative sources of short-term financing.

	Amount	Cash Received	Date Cash Received
Factored Accounts Receivable	$1,000,000		
Less: Factor Fee	(15,000)		
Early Payment Discounts	(4,000)		
Interest Expense	(18,850)		
Gross to Manufacturer	$ 962,150		
Less: Cash Advance	(837,900)	$837,900	1st
Net to Manufacturer	$124,250		
Less: Product Quality Holdback	(50,000)		
Cash to Manufacturer	$74,250	$74,250	60th
Release of Product Quality Holdback		$50,000	120th
Total Cash Received		$962,150	

How Economic Order Quantity Controls Inventory Expense

Frank M. Tiernan and Dennis A. Tanner

Inventory control and the proper recognition of inventory costs are critical factors for the efficient management and operations of a firm. A recent survey of financial management textbooks reveals standard discussions of such inventory control tools as economic order quantity (EOQ), order point formula (OP), and optimum safety stock levels.

Of particular importance to this article is the discussion about the optimum lot-size or EOQ, whereby the optimum size of an order is determined on the basis of the demand for inventory, holding or carrying costs, and procurement or ordering costs. The standard treatment of the deterministic EOQ model ultimately reduces to a single number, which is identified as the optimum order size for a given set of costs. Recognition of uncertainty is introduced through the use of safety stocks and stochastic models for demand estimation. Yet, even with the proper adjustments for uncertainty, the optimum order size is still expressed in terms of a single value.

In practice, it is alleged that the EOQ formula is rigidly adhered to with the fear that substantial penalties will be incurred for even slight deviations from the optimum order size. However, Arthur Snyder suggests that the EOQ can be interpreted as a range which would provide flexibility to the firm's inventory control process. (See Arthur Snyder, "Principles of Inventory Management," *Financial Executive*, April 1964, p. 13–21.)

For example, a firm might be in a situation where the EOQ is 18 units, and a standard lot size is 20 units. Faced with this problem, the firm must decide whether to break the standard lot size or order the additional

Frank M. Tiernan and Dennis A. Tanner, "How Economic Order Quantity Controls Inventory Expense," *Financial Executive* (July 1983): 46–47, 49–52. Used by permission from *Financial Executive*, Copyright 1983 by Financial Executives Institute.

At the time of this writing, Frank M. Tiernan was Associate Professor of Finance at Drake University and Dennis A. Tanner was Dean of the College of Business Administration at Winona State University.

units. Snyder indicates that there appears to be a rather wide range of order quantities that could be used by the firm without significantly affecting the total inventory cost. Yet, some questions about the range EOQ model still remain. It is the purpose of this article to investigate the range EOQ concept as a means of efficient inventory control and to list the conditions under which such a model would be appropriate.

Total inventory cost is a compilation of a number of different cost factors which are accumulated into a cost minimizing objective function. (The development of the standard EOQ model has been adapted from the previous work of William Beranek — see *Working Capital Management,* Wadsworth Publishing Co., Inc., 1966, and "Financial Implications of Lot-size Inventory Models," *Management Science,* April 1967.) If one assumes a total demand of D units is to be used at a constant rate over some planning horizon, then the ordering cost R can be expressed as a function of demand with both fixed and variable cost factors. If:

k = the fixed reorder cost incurred with each order
b = the incremental cost of ordering one additional unit of inventory
Q = the size (in units) of the order

then the ordering cost for one order can be expressed by the following:

(1) $R = k + bQ$

The total ordering cost over the planning horizon would therefore depend on the number of orders placed or D/Q. Thus,

(2) $R (D/Q) = (k + bQ) D/Q$, or

(3) $R (D/Q) = kD/Q + bD$

which represents the total ordering cost for the entire planning period.

The holding or carrying cost is generally expressed as a function of the average inventory on hand over the time interval between orders. By assuming a roughly constant usage rate for each time interval, the average inventory is estimated by dividing the order quantity in half. If h denotes the holding cost per unit of inventory for the entire planning horizon, then

(4) $H = hQ/2$

represents the total holding cost for the entire period. Total inventory cost C is then the sum of Equations 3 and 4 or

(5) $C = kD/Q + bD + hQ/2.$

The order quantity Q represents the controllable variable, which can be varied in order to minimize the total cost C. By differentiating Equation 5 with respect to Q, setting the right side of the resulting equation equal to zero and solving for Q, the standard EOQ equation would be obtained:

(6) $Q^* = \sqrt{2kD/h}$

(Q^* represents the optimum quantity of inventory.)

It is at this point that Snyder argues that two misconceptions exist concerning the use of the EOQ equation. These misconceptions are as follows:

- The EOQ is a specific quantity.
- A small deviation from this specific quantity substantially increases the total cost per unit.

Through examples and graphs, Snyder develops the concept of an EOQ range as opposed to the use of a specific quantity. As shown in Figure 1, the total cost curve has relatively steep slopes on either side of the EOQ point, which seems to suggest that slight deviations from the EOQ could be costly. However, if the same cost curve is plotted, as in Figure 2, with a different scale for the quantity ordered, the cost curve appears to be relatively flat about the EOQ point, suggesting that even substantial errors in order size may not significantly affect the total inventory cost. Thus, a broad range of order sizes could be used to replenish depleted inventory stocks.

It was on the basis of this graphic analysis and some hypothetical inventory problems that Snyder concluded that the range EOQ concept would be a useful tool in formulating an inventory control program and that wide deviations from the EOQ point (25 percent to 50 percent) would not prove to be excessively expensive. Reacting to these findings, further investigation of the range EOQ concept seemed to be warranted, with particular emphasis on the cost parameters of the EOQ model.

Testing the EOQ Concept

It is hypothesized that different combinations of ordering costs and holding costs will give rise to different-shaped total inventory cost curves; substantial differences will be observed in the minimum total cost level at

Figure 1   **Total Cost Curve with Narrow EOQ Range**

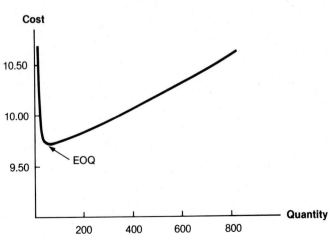

Figure 2   **Total Cost Curve with Wide EOQ Range**

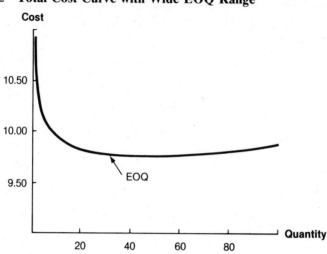

the various EOQ points. There are a priori reasons to believe that as either of the relevant costs are increased, the total inventory cost curve will change shape, thereby reflecting a change in cost. This belief is based on Equations 5 and 6, which define the cost relationships so that as the ordering and/or holding costs change, the EOQ point and the total cost curve will shift. In addition, low ordering and holding costs will, in all likelihood, lead to a highly insensitive total cost curve with respect to the quantity ordered, whereas high ordering and holding costs will result in a highly sensitive inventory cost curve. Thus, the sensitivity of the total inventory cost curves can be evaluated by analyzing the percentage change in cost for a given percentage change in the order size.

The specific hypotheses which will be examined are that different cost combinations will produce different-shaped total cost curves and that the sensitivity of the total inventory cost will be directly related to the magnitudes of the ordering and holding costs.

It is convenient to look at several examples to demonstrate the changing shape of the total cost curve for differing values of the ordering

Table 1   **Values of the Parameters for Tests of the EOQ Model**

Case	Fixed Ordering Cost (k)	Incremental Ordering Cost (b)	Holding Cost (h)
A	$ .10	$.02	$ .01
B	50.00	.02	.01
C	.10	.02	20.00
D	50.00	.02	20.00

(k) and holding (h) cost parameters. Four cases have been selected to illustrate the effect upon total inventory cost of high and low values for each of the parameters. Because the incremental ordering cost (b) does not affect the slope of the curve (Equation 6), it will have an arbitrarily assigned value in all cases. Furthermore, the value of demand (D) will also be held constant as it affects the slope of the curve in precisely the same way as the value of k. (The level of demand may in fact be viewed as a variable, and the effect of relatively high and low demand upon the total cost curve is discussed later.)

The parameter values for the four different cases are presented in Table 1. Case A represents one extreme where order costs (k) and holding costs (h) are both very low: $.10 fixed cost per order and $.01 per unit per period carrying cost. Case D represents the other extreme, where both ordering and holding costs are extremely high: $50 and $20, respectively. The two mixed cases are Case B with high ordering and low holding costs and Case C with low ordering and high holding costs. Demand is 1000 units for the planning period, and the values of Q and C are calculated from Equations 5 and 6.

Case A represents a situation where both costs are extremely low. The graph in Figure 3 confirms that there is a broad range of values about the EOQ point where the total cost curve does not increase rapidly. This suggests that total inventory cost is highly insensitive to errors in the specification of order size, and it appears to be the special case alluded to by Snyder. When considering Case D, by comparison, where the ordering and holding costs are very high, a broad range of total cost values does not exist. Errors in specifying Q cause much more rapidly increasing costs on either side of the optimum order point, as illustrated in Figure 4. Thus, both the shape and the absolute level of the total cost curve in Case D are substantially different from the results in Case A.

Although Cases A and D demonstrate the extremes in ordering and holding costs, both cases yield rather moderate values for the economic order quantity. Not surprisingly, when ordering costs are high and holding costs are low, as in Case B, a single large order provides more than enough inventory to meet present demand. As indicated in Figure 5, Case B is similar to Case A in total cost pattern because large errors in the order size do not significantly increase the overall inventory cost. This negligible change in cost is due in part to the large optimum order quantity

Level of Demand (D)	Economic Order Quantity (Q)	Total Inventory Cost (C)
1000	141	$ 21.41
1000	3162	51.62
1000	3	83.33
1000	71	1434.23

Figure 3   **Total Cost Curve for Case A**

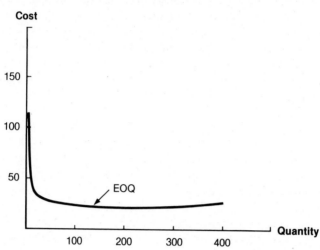

for Case B (3162 units). Case C (Figure 6) is characterized by low order costs and high holding costs, indicating that extremely small and frequent orders are appropriate. When comparing Case C and Case D, errors in the order size (Q) will typically result in relatively large errors in total cost (C), because holding costs are high. However, Case C differs from Case D in that total inventory costs are uniformly lower and slightly less sensitive to errors in Q.

Figure 4   **Total Cost Curve for Case D**

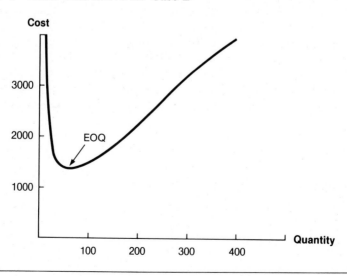

Figure 5   **Total Cost Curve for Case B**

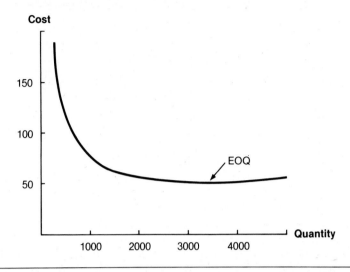

A sensitivity analysis of the various cases confirms the previous findings with regard to the degree of variability of the total inventory cost for a given specified error in the order quantity. The results of the sensitivity analysis, as presented in Table 2, indicate that total cost in Case A is highly insensitive to large errors in order size, whereas total cost in Case D is highly sensitive to such errors. For example, doubling the order size (+100 percent) results in a 1.65-percent increase in total

Figure 6   **Total Cost Curve for Case C**

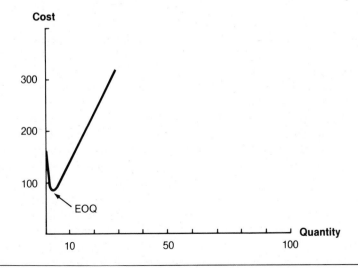

Table 2   **Percentage Change in Total Inventory Cost for a Given Percentage Change in Order Size away from the Optimum Order Quantity**

Case	−50%	−10%	−1%	+1%	+10%	+100%
A	1.65	0.03	0.000003	0.000003	0.03	1.65
B	15.31	0.28	0.000003	0.000003	0.28	15.31
C	18.99	0.35	0.000004	0.000004	0.35	18.99
D	24.65	0.45	0.000005	0.000005	0.45	24.65

inventory cost for Case A; the same error in order size for Case D results in an increase of 24.65 percent in total costs. Because of the high ordering and holding costs, Case D is most sensitive to errors in order size. Case C, with low ordering and high holding costs, is the closest to Case D in overall cost sensitivity. This suggests that holding costs, high in both Cases C and D, have a greater impact on total inventory cost than does the cost of ordering. While it was found that the results for Case B more closely approximate the results from Case A, there are some important differences. Although Case B graphically appears to be similar to Case A, the results in Table 2 indicate that equal percentage errors in A and B result in significantly different cost effects, so that total inventory costs are much more sensitive to changes in order size for Case B than Case A. (Even though Case B has a higher percentage change in total cost for a given percentage change in order size than in Case A, this result is not true when viewed in an absolute sense.)

The effect of the level of demand upon the shape of the total cost curve is similar to that of the effect of the fixed order cost. As can be seen from Equations 5 and 6, any change in demand level will affect the shape of the cost curve in the same way as a change in the level of fixed order costs. Introducing the level of demand as a variable, rather than as a constant as assumed in Equations 5 and 6, will further accentuate the shape of the cost curve. Higher levels of demand will increase the total cost curve and make the shape of the total cost curve less flat and more sensitive to deviations in order quantities from the optimum EOQ. This suggests that as demand is rising for a product or a firm, the importance of inventory control increases.

Four cases with different combinations of high and low ordering and holding costs have been considered in order to evaluate the appropriateness of the range EOQ concept. Total inventory cost for each case was analyzed through the use of graphs and sensitivity analysis. The results of this analysis confirmed the hypothesis that different cost parameters cause different shapes in the total inventory cost curves. Extreme cases were tested and found to be significantly different in terms of the shape of the total inventory cost curves and in terms of the sensitivity of those cost curves to errors in the specification of order size (Q). Only in the low ordering cost/low holding cost case were percentage changes in C found to be insensitive to changes in Q. The other three cases exhibited increasing degrees of sensitivity with respect to Q, as the ordering and/or holding costs were increased.

The total inventory cost curves were substantially different from each other: Two cases exhibited relatively flat curves while the other two cases exhibited relatively pointed curves. This result appears to have been caused primarily by the changes in the holding cost per unit of inventory. The flatness of the total inventory cost curves over a wide range near the optimum order size can be attributed to the extremely low holding cost. It was only after this cost was increased that the total cost curves substantially changed shape. It is of particular importance to the firm's inventory control process that the holding cost appears to be the most critical parameter of the EOQ model. Errors in the estimation of holding costs could significantly change the shape and the sensitivity of the total cost curve. As pointed out in the work of William Beranek, errors in estimating holding cost may be quite common if a firm fails to properly recognize the financial arrangements needed to support the inventory. Thus, careful attention should be given to the estimation procedures for the parameters of the EOQ model, with specific emphasis on the holding costs.

To answer the question that was initially raised concerning the appropriate use of the range EOQ concept, the findings suggest that when the cost parameters are relatively low, a broad range of order sizes would be available to the firm to restock its inventory. More specifically, when the holding costs are low, the firm could expect a flat segment in the total cost curve about the EOQ point. However, when holding costs are high, the firm should exercise caution in reordering inventory and should attempt to determine the sensitivity of the total inventory cost to different order sizes.

Questions

1.   What is the purpose of the EOQ model?

2.   Explain why total order cost and total holding cost are inversely related.

3.   Total inventory cost C can be shown as follows:
     $$C = kD/Q + bD + hQ/2$$
     where k is fixed cost per order, D is demand for units over the planning period, Q is number of units per order, b is incremental cost of ordering one additional unit of inventory, and h is holding cost per unit of inventory for the planning period. Show the steps for deriving the EOQ model from the above equation.

4.   Using graph paper, plot total inventory cost C as a function of order quantity Q for the following two cases:

ABCs of Figuring Interest

Anne Marie LaPorte

Interest represents the price borrowers pay to lenders for credit over specified periods of time. The amount of interest paid depends on a number of factors: the dollar amount lent or borrowed, the length of time involved in the transaction, the stated (or nominal) annual rate of interest, the repayment schedule, and the method used to calculate interest.

If, for example, an individual deposits $1,000 for one year in a bank paying 5 percent interest on savings, then at the end of the year the depositor may receive interest of $50, or he may receive some other amount, depending on the way interest is calculated. Alternatively, an individual who borrows $1,000 for one year at 5 percent and repays the loan in one payment at the end of a year, may pay $50 in interest, or he may pay some other amount, again depending on the calculation method used.

Simple Interest

The various methods used to calculate interest are basically variations of the simple interest calculation method.

The basic concept underlying simple interest is that interest is paid only on the original amount borrowed for the length of time the borrower has use of the credit. The amount borrowed is referred to as the principal. In the simple interest calculation, interest is computed only on that portion of the original principal still owed.

Example 1: Suppose $1,000 is borrowed at 5 percent and repaid in one payment at the end of one year. Using the simple interest calculation, the interest amount would be 5 percent of $1,000 for one year or $50 since the borrower had use of $1,000 for the entire year.

When more than one payment is made on a simple interest loan, the method of computing interest is referred to as "interest on the declining balance." Since the borrower only pays interest on that amount of

Anne Marie LaPorte, "ABCs of Figuring Interest," *Business Conditions* (Federal Reserve Bank of Chicago, September 1973): 3–11.

original principal which has not yet been repaid, interest paid will be smaller the more frequent the payments. At the same time, of course, the amount of credit the borrower has at his disposal is also smaller.

Example 2: Using simple interest on the declining balance to compute interest charges, a loan repaid in two payments — one at the end of the first half-year and another at the end of the second half-year — would accumulate total interest charges of $37.50. The first payment would be $500 plus $25 (5 percent of $1,000 for one-half year), or $525; the second payment would be $500 plus $12.50 (5 percent of $500 for one-half year), or $512.50. The total amount paid would be $525 plus $512.50, or $1,037.50. Interest equals the difference between the amount repaid and the amount borrowed, or $37.50. If four quarterly payments of $250 plus interest were made, the interest amount would be $31.25; if 12 monthly payments of $83.33 plus interest were made, the interest amount would be $27.08.

Example 3: When interest on the declining balance method is applied to a loan that is to be repaid in two equal payments, payments of $518.83 would be made at the end of the first half-year and at the end of the second half-year. Interest due at the end of the first half-year remains $25; therefore, with the first payment the balance is reduced by $493.83 ($518.83 less $25), leaving the borrower $506.17 to use during the second half-year. The interest for the second half-year is 5 percent of $506.17 for one-half year, or $12.66. The final $518.83 payment, then, covers interest of $12.66 plus the outstanding balance of $506.17. Total interest paid is $25 plus $12.66, or $37.66, slightly more than in Example 2.

This equal payment variation is commonly used with mortgage payment schedules. Each payment over the duration of the loan is split into two parts. Part one is the interest due at the time the payment is made, and part two — the remainder — is applied to the balance or amount still owed. In addition to mortgage lenders, credit unions typically use the simple interest/declining balance calculation method for computing interest on loans. Consumer instalment loans are normally set up on this method and a number of banks have also begun offering personal loans using this method.

Other Calculation Methods

Add-on interest, bank discount, and compound interest calculation methods differ from the simple interest method as to when, how, and on what balance interest is paid. The "effective annual rate," or the annual percentage rate, for these methods is that annual rate of interest which when used in the simple interest rate formula equals the amount of interest payable in these other calculation methods. For the declining balance method, the effective annual rate of interest is the stated or nominal annual rate of interest. For the methods to be described below, the effective annual rate of interest differs from the nominal rate.

Add-on Interest: The More Frequent the Payments, the Higher the Effective Rate

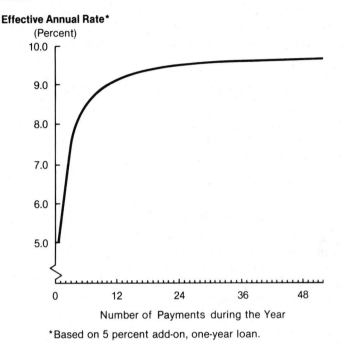

Effective Annual Rate*
(Percent)

*Based on 5 percent add-on, one-year loan.

Add-on Interest

When the add-on interest method is used, interest is calculated on the full amount of the original principal. The interest amount is immediately added to the original principal and payments are determined by dividing principal plus interest by the number of payments to be made. When only one payment is involved, this method produces the same effective interest rate as the simple interest method. When two or more payments are to be made, however, use of the add-on interest method results in an effective rate of interest that is greater than the nominal rate. True, the interest amount is calculated by applying the nominal rate to the total amount borrowed, but the borrower does not have use of the total amount for the entire time period if two or more payments are made.

Example 4: Consider, again, the two-payment loan in Example 3. Using the add-on interest method, interest of $50 (5 percent of $1,000 for one year) is added to the $1,000 borrowed, giving $1,050 to be repaid; half (or $525) at the end of the first half-year and the other half at the end of the second half-year.

Recall that in Example 3, where the declining balance method was used, an effective rate of 5 percent meant two equal payments of $518.83

were to be made. Now with the add-on interest method each payment is $525. The effective rate of this 5 percent add-on rate loan, then, is greater than 5 percent. In fact, the corresponding effective rate is 6.631 percent. This rate takes into account the fact that the borrower does not have use of $1,000 for the entire year, but rather use of $1,000 for the first half-year, and, excluding the interest payment, use of $508.15 for the second half-year.

To see that a one-year, two equal payment, 5 percent add-on rate loan is equivalent to a one-year, two equal payment, 6.631 percent declining balance loan, consider the following. When the first $525 payment is made, $33.15 in interest is due (6.631 percent of $1,000 for one-half year). Deducting the $33.15 from $525 leaves $491.85 to be applied to the outstanding balance of $1,000. The second $525 payment covers $16.85 in interest (6.631 percent of $508.15 for one-half year) and the $508.15 balance due.

In this particular example, using the add-on interest method means that no matter how many payments are to be made, the interest will always be $50. As the number of payments increases, the borrower has use of less and less credit over the year. For example, if four quarterly payments of $262.50 are made, the borrower has the use of $1,000 during the first quarter, around $750 during the second quarter, around $500 during the third quarter, and around $250 during the fourth and final quarter. Therefore, as the number of payments increases, the effective rate of interest also increases. For instance, in the current example, if four quarterly payments are made, the effective rate of interest would be 7.922 percent; if 12 monthly payments are made, the effective interest rate would be 9.105 percent. The add-on interest method is commonly used by finance companies and some banks in determining interest on consumer loans.

Bank Discount

When the bank discount rate calculation method is used, interest is calculated on the amount to be paid back and the borrower receives the difference between the amount to be paid back and the interest amount. In Example 1, a 5 percent $1,000 loan is to be paid back at the end of one year. Using the bank discount rate method two approaches are possible.
Example 5: The first approach would be to deduct the interest amount of $50 from the $1,000, leaving the borrower with $950 to use over the year. At the end of the year he pays $1,000. The interest amount of $50 is the same as in Example 1. The borrower in Example 1, however, had the use of $1,000 over the year. Thus, the effective rate of interest using the bank discount rate method is greater than that for the simple interest rate calculation. The effective rate of interest here would be 5.263 percent — i.e., $50 ÷ $950 — compared to 5 percent in Example 1.
Example 6: The second approach would be to determine the amount that would have to be paid back so that once the interest amount was

Compound Interest: Over Time, Compounding Increases the Amount of Interest Paid

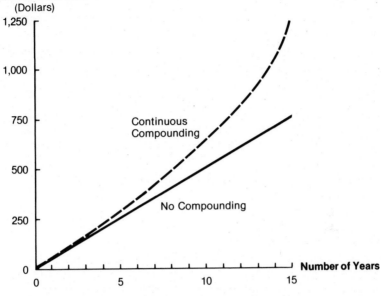

*Amount paid on $1,000 at 5 percent annual interest rate.

deducted, the borrower would have the use of $1,000 over the year. This amount is $1,052.63, and this becomes the face value of the note on which interest is calculated. The interest amount (5 percent of $1,052.63 for one year) is $52.63, and this is deducted leaving the borrower with $1,000 to use over the year. The effective rate of interest, again, is 5.263 percent. The bank discount method is commonly used with short-term business loans. Generally there are no intermediate payments and the duration of the loan is one year or less.

Compound Interest

When the compound interest calculation is used, interest is calculated on the original principal plus all interest accrued to that point in time. Since interest is paid on interest as well as on the amount borrowed, the effective interest rate is greater than the nominal interest rate. The compound interest rate method is often used by banks and savings institutions in determining interest they pay on savings deposits "loaned" to the institutions by the depositors.

Example 7: Suppose $1,000 is deposited in a bank that pays a 5 percent nominal annual rate of interest, compounded semi-annually (i.e., twice a year). At the end of the first half-year, $25 in interest (5 percent of $1,000 for one-half year) is payable. At the end of the year, the interest amount is calculated on the $1,000 plus the $25 in interest already paid, so that the second interest payment is $25.63 (5 percent of $1,025 for one-half year). The interest amount payable for the year, then, is $25 plus $25.63, or $50.63. The effective rate of interest is 5.063 percent which is greater than the nominal 5 percent rate.

The more often interest is compounded within a particular time period, the greater will be the effective rate of interest. In a year, a 5 percent nominal annual rate of interest compounded four times (quarterly) results in an effective annual rate of 5.0945 percent; compounded 12 times (monthly), 5.1162 percent; and compounded 365 times (daily), 5.1267 percent. When the interval of time between compoundings approaches zero (even shorter than a second), then the method is known as continuous compounding. Five percent continuously compounded for one year will result in an effective annual rate of 5.1271.

How Long Is a Year?

In the above examples, a year is assumed to be 365 days long. Historically, in order to simplify interest calculations, financial institutions have often used 12 30-day months, yielding a 360-day year. If a 360-day year is assumed in the calculation and the amount borrowed is actually used by the borrower for one full year (365 or 366 days), then interest is paid for an additional 5/360 or 6/360 of a "year." For any given nominal rate of interest, the effective rate of interest will be greater when a 360-day year is used in the interest rate calculation than when a 365-day year is used. This has come to be known as the 365-360 method.

Example 8: Suppose $1,000 is deposited in a bank paying a 5 percent nominal annual rate of interest, compounded daily. As pointed out earlier, the effective annual rate of interest for one year, based on a 365-day year, is 5.1267 percent. The interest payable on the 365th day would be $51.27. Daily compounding means that each day the daily rate of 0.0137 percent (5 percent divided by 365 days) was paid on the $1,000 deposit plus all interest payable up to that day. Now suppose a 360-day year is used in the calculation. The daily rate paid becomes 0.0139 percent (5 percent divided by 360 days) so that on the 365th day the interest amount payable would be $52. The effective annual rate of interest, based on a 360-day year, would be 5.1997 percent.

Example 9: Suppose that a $1,000 note is discounted at 5 percent and payable in 365 days. This is the situation discussed in Example 5 where, based on a 365-day year, the effective rate of interest was seen to be 5.263 percent. If the bank discount rate calculation assumes a 360-day year, then the length of time is computed to be 365/360 or 1 1/72 years instead of one year, the interest deducted (the discount) equals $50.69 instead of $50, and the effective annual rate of interest is 5.267 percent.

When Repayment Is Early

In the above examples, it was assumed that periodic loan payments were always made exactly when due. Often, however, a loan may be completely repaid before it is due. When the declining balance method for calculating interest is used, the borrower is not penalized for prepayment since interest is paid only on the balance outstanding for the length of time that amount is owed. When the add-on interest calculation is used, however, prepayment implies that the lender obtains some interest which is unearned. The borrower then is actually paying an even higher effective rate since he does not use the funds for the length of time of the original loan contract.

Some loan contracts make provisions for an interest rebate if the loan is prepaid. One of the common methods used in determining the amount of the interest rebate is referred to as the "Rule of 78." Application of the Rule of 78 yields the percentage of the total interest amount that is to be returned to the borrower in the event of prepayment. The percentage figure is arrived at by dividing the sum of the integer numbers (digits) from one to the number of payments remaining by the sum of the digits from one to the total number of payments specified in the original loan contract. For example, if a five-month loan is paid off by the end of the second month (i.e., there are three payments remaining), the percentage of the interest that the lender would rebate is $1 + 2 + 3 = 6 \div 1 + 2 + 3 + 4 + 5 = 15$, or 40 percent. The name derives from the fact that 78 is the sum of the digits from one to 12 and, therefore, is the denominator in calculating interest rebate percentages for all 12-period loans.

Application of the Rule of 78 results in the borrower paying somewhat more interest than he would have paid with a comparable declining balance loan. How much more depends on the effective rate of interest charged and the total number of payments specified in the original loan contract. The higher the effective rate of interest charged and the greater the specified total number of payments, the greater the amount of interest figured under the Rule of 78 exceeds that under the declining balance method. (See chart.)

The difference between the Rule of 78 interest and the declining balance interest also varies depending upon when the prepayment occurs. This difference over the term of the loan tends to increase up to about the one-third point of the term and then decrease after this point. For example, with a 12-month term, the difference with prepayment occurring in the second month would be greater than the difference that would occur with prepayment in the first month; the third-month difference would be greater than the second-month difference; the fourth month (being the one-third point) would be greater than both the third-month difference and the fifth-month difference. After the fifth month, each succeeding month's difference would be less than the previous month's difference.

Interest Paid under the Rule of 78 Is Always More than under the Declining Balance — but How Much More Depends on:

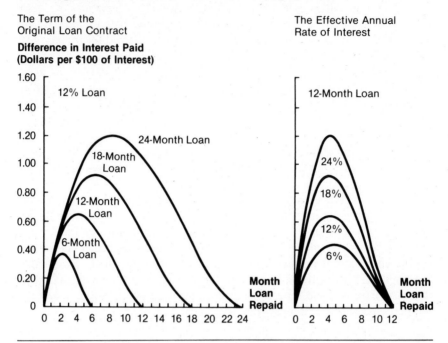

The Term of the
Original Loan Contract

The Effective Annual
Rate of Interest

Example 10: Suppose that there are two $1,000 loans that are to be repaid over 12 months. Interest on the first loan is calculated using a 5 percent add-on method which results in equal payments of $87.50 due at the end of each month ($1,000 plus $50 interest divided by 12 months). The effective annual rate of interest for this loan is 9.105 percent. Any interest rebate due because of prepayment is to be determined by the Rule of 78.

Interest on the second loan is calculated using a declining balance method where the annual rate of interest is the effective annual rate of interest from the first loan, or 9.105 percent. Equal payments of $87.50 are also due at the end of each month for the second loan.

Suppose that repayment on both loans occurs after one-sixth of the term of the loan has passed, i.e., at the end of the second month, with the regular first month's payment being made for both loans. The interest paid on the first loan will be $14.74, while the interest paid on the second loan will be $14.57, a difference of 17 cents. If the prepayment occurs at the one-third point, i.e., at the end of the fourth month (regular payments having been made at the end of the first, second, and third months), interest of $26.92 is paid on the first loan and interest of $26.69 on the second loan, a difference of 23 cents. If the prepayment occurs later, say at the three-fourths point, i.e., at the end of the ninth month (regular payments having been made at the end of the first through eighth months), $46.16 in interest is paid on the first loan and $46.07 in interest is paid on the second loan, a difference of but 9 cents.

Bonus Interest

Savings institutions are permitted to pay interest from the first calendar day of the month on deposits received by the tenth calendar day of the month, and also on deposits withdrawn during the last three business days of a month ending a regular quarterly or semi-annual interest period. If a savings institution chooses to do this, then it is paying for the use of the depositor's money for some period of time during which the savings institution does not have the use of the money. The effective rate of interest is, therefore, greater than it would be otherwise.

Example 11: Suppose that on January 10, $1,000 is deposited in a bank paying 5 percent interest compounded daily based on a 365-day year and that funds deposited by the 10th of any month earn interest from the 1st of that month. On the following December 31, 355 days after the deposit is made, interest for 365 days is payable on the deposit, or $51.27. The bank, however, had the use of the funds for only 355 days. The effective rate of interest, or that rate which when compounded daily for 355 days would yield the interest amount $51.27, is 5.1408 percent.

Although savings institutions choosing to pay interest for these grace periods are prohibited from advertising an effective yield which takes this into account, depositors should be aware of the effect such practice has on the price paid for the use of their money.

Charges Other than Interest

In addition to the interest which must be paid, loan agreements often will include other provisions which must be satisfied. Two of these provisions are mortgage points and required (compensating) deposit balances.

Mortgage Points

Mortgage lenders will sometimes require the borrower to pay a charge in addition to the interest. This extra charge is calculated as a certain percentage of the mortgage amount and is referred to as mortgage points. For example, if 2 points are charged on a $10,000 mortgage, then 2 percent of $10,000, or $200, must be paid in addition to the stated interest. The borrower, therefore, is paying a higher price than if points were not charged—i.e., the effective rate of interest is increased. In order to determine what the effective rate of interest is when points are charged, it is necessary to deduct the dollar amount resulting from the point calculation from the mortgage amount and add it to the interest amount to be paid. The borrower is viewed as having the mortgage amount less the point charge amount rather than the entire mortgage amount.

Example 12: Suppose that 2 points are charged on a 20-year, $10,000 mortgage where the rate of interest (declining balance calculation) is 7 percent. The payments are to be $77.53 per month. Once the borrower pays the $200 point charge, he starts out with $9,800 to use. With payments of $77.53 a month over 20 years, the result of the 2 point charge is an effective rate of 7.262 percent.

The longer the time period of the mortgage, the lower will be the effective rate of interest when points are charged because the point charge is spread out over more payments. In the above example, if the mortgage had been for 30 years instead of 20 years, the effective rate of interest would have been 7.201 percent.

Required (Compensating) Deposit Balances

A bank may require that a borrower maintain a certain percentage of the loan amount on deposit as a condition for obtaining the loan. The borrower, then, does not have the use of the entire loan amount but rather the use of the loan amount less the amount that must be kept on deposit. The effective rate of interest is greater than it would be if no compensating deposit balance were required.

Example 13: Suppose that $1,000 is borrowed at 5 percent from a bank to be paid back at the end of one year. Suppose, further, that the lending bank requires that 10 percent of the loan amount be kept on deposit. The borrower, therefore, has the use of only $900 ($1,000 less 10 percent) on which he pays an interest amount of $50 (5 percent of $1,000 for one year). The effective rate of interest is, therefore, 5.556 percent as opposed to 5 percent when no compensating balance is required.

Summary

Although not an exhaustive list, the methods of calculating interest described here are some of the more common methods in use. They serve to indicate that the method of interest calculation can substantially affect the amount of interest paid, and that savers and borrowers should be aware not only of nominal interest rates but also of how nominal rates are used in calculating total interest charges.

Questions

1.   Suppose that you borrow $10,000 for one year at a 10 percent annual interest rate.
      a.   Using the simple interest calculation, you pay $ _____ interest at the end of the year.

      b.   Using simple interest on the declining balance, you repay the loan with semiannual payments of $5,500 and $5,250. In this case, your total interest charge for the year is $ _____ .

      c.   Using simple interest on the declining balance, you repay the loan with two equal semiannual payments of $5,378.05 each. In this case, your total interest charge for the year is $ _____ .

      d.   Explain why the total interest charge in Part b is smaller than that in Part c.

2.   Suppose that you borrow $10,000 for one year at a nominal interest rate of 10 percent per year. The lender calculates interest using the add-on method.

      a.   What is the dollar size of your payments if you pay semiannually? Quarterly?

      b.   Calculate the effective rate (percent per year, compounded annually) for semiannual payments and for quarterly payments.

3.   Bosch Company plans to borrow $10,000 for one year. The nominal interest rate is 10 percent annually, and the lender will discount the loan. What effective rate does Bosch have to pay?

4.   How much money would Bosch Company (in Question 3) have to borrow in order to have $10,000 to use during the year? What is Bosch's effective rate?

5.   Why might a lender define a year as being 360 days?

6.   Explain the "Rule of 78." What is it used for? What is the origin of the number 78?

7.   WMB Inc. plans to borrow $10,000 for one year. The nominal interest rate is 10 percent annually, and the lender will discount the loan. The lender also requires that 20 percent of the loan be kept in a non-interest-bearing account. What is WMB's effective rate?

Business Loans at Large Commercial Banks: Policies and Practices

Randall C. Merris

Commercial bank lending was once a fairly simple business. Business loans were nearly all short term and carried fixed interest rates. Any other details, except possibly collateral requirements, were left to informal agreements between a bank and its customers.

Business lending began getting more complex in the 1930s as many banks started making term loans—loans with maturities of more than a year. Relations between banks and business borrowers have been growing more complex—and more formal—ever since, the formality of term loans are now being applied to many short-term loans as well.

Part of the push for more complicated loan arrangements—and, therefore, a greater variety in the kinds of agreements—has been the need for banks and borrowers to protect themselves from movements in interest rates over the credit cycle. Increases in market rates boost bank costs of funding outstanding loans. They also increase the opportunities for more lucrative new credits elsewhere. Reductions in market rates lower the interest costs of other debt financing available to bank loan customers.

Floating rates have probably been the most important innovation in bank lending since the advent of the term loan. Provisions for adjusting loan rates periodically give banks and borrowers some protection against market rate fluctuations. By combining some of the advantages of term and short-term loans, floating rates have allowed banks to compete effectively for their share of the business credit market—even in the face of increased competition from the commercial paper market and other nonbank credit suppliers. At the same time, use of floating rates has encouraged changes in the other terms and conditions of business lending.

Randall C. Merris, "Business Loans at Large Commercial Banks: Policies and Practices," *Economic Perspectives* (Federal Reserve Bank of Chicago, November/December 1979): 15–23.

This article examines business lending practices at large banks, especially toward commercial and industrial loans. These loans to businesses other than financial institutions most clearly reflect the recent directions in bank lending policy. Pricing, maturities, and other lending terms depend on the particular bank and borrower negotiating the credit, as well as the use of the loan proceeds—such as, to provide working capital, cover accounts receivable, or finance expenditures on plant and equipment.

Term Loans

Term loans range in maturity from just over a year to more than ten years. Banks once held loans with maximum maturities of five to seven years. For customers that needed longer terms, banks participated with other lenders. A bank might, for example, take the first five years of credit, with an insurance company taking the rest to maturity, often under different terms and conditions. Banks are more inclined now to take all the term credits themselves or to participate with other banks, each taking part of the loan for the whole maturity.

With the future always uncertain, lengthening the maturity structure of bank loan portfolios might seem to mean banks were taking more risks. But at least half the term lending at large banks calls for periodic adjustment of loan rates.

Costs are nearly always higher for initiating term loans than short-term loans. Considerable negotiation is required, usually at top levels of management and often with legal staffs representing the bank and the borrower. And voluminous documentation is needed to cover both the terms and conditions of the loan. Administrative costs are also high, especially in the frequent situations where the bank and borrower need to keep in touch throughout the life of the loan.

Agreement has to be reached not only on the amount of the loan and its price but also any number of other points:

Loan commitment — an arrangement for the borrower to draw down loans and sometimes even a schedule for disbursing the funds. As the funds are made available to the borrower whether he uses them or not, a fee is sometimes charged on the amount of the commitment not used.

Instalment schedule — a timetable for paying down the principal and interest. Payments are most often due monthly, quarterly, or semiannually.

Supporting balance requirement — the borrower's obligation to maintain demand deposits that help offset the cost of funding the loan. A bank may require that even a loan commitment be backed by demand deposits.

Collateral — property put up against a loan. Banker and borrower must agree on the physical nature of the collateral, its value, and the care to be taken in its handling and protection.

Fall of the Real Bills Doctrine . . .

Though term loans were sometimes made for special purposes, most banks offered only short-term credit until well into this century. This was because bank policies were based on the commercial loan theory of credit, an American adaptation of the Real Bills Doctrine in England.

According to this doctrine, the only appropriate bank loans were short-term, self-liquidating notes. By self-liquidating, bankers meant loans that led to enough increase in sales and near-term profits to cover repayment. Loans for plant and equipment did not usually qualify, the reasoning being that several years might be needed before returns on fixed capital were enough to retire the debt.

Some business loans were renewed routinely, even as early as the 1830s, with the result that nominally short-term credit arrangements were actually long term. Not until the 1920s, however, was the commercial loan theory seriously challenged. The idea that loans needed to be self-liquidating began losing credibility for several reasons:

- The realization that the commercial loan theory did not provide the monetary policy advantages its proponents claimed.

- The practice of financing long-term projects by borrowing from one bank to pay off another—sequential bank financing.

- The emergence of the view that banks could gain liquidity better from their non-loan assets and their liabilities.

Proponents of the Real Bills Doctrine had long argued that the requirement that bank loans be self-liquidating made the money supply expand and contract with the needs of business. However, bankers became increasingly aware, especially in looking back on the Panic of 1907, that the policy did not prevent severe contractions, bank deposit runs, or bank failures.

Many banks, meanwhile, had imposed the rule that customers had to have all their loans at the bank paid up sometime during the year. This clean-up rule, meant to strengthen the commercial loan theory, actually had the opposite effect. Annual clean-ups tended to encourage short-term borrowing first at one bank, then another, and then back at the first bank—all to extend effective credit periods for fixed-capital purposes.

Renewals, sequential financing across banks, and the clean-up rule together debased the short-term loan doctrine. It took a new theory of bank management, however, to utterly discredit the commercial loan theory.

The new theory took the view that as most business loans were not actually liquid, they did not serve as a funding cushion against unexpected deposit withdrawals. In place of short-term loans, the theory turned for liquidity to other assets—such as government and corporate securities, bankers' acceptances, and commercial paper—that could be sold with little loss of their capital value. A forerunner to modern liability management, the new theory also noted that banks could acquire liquidity through Federal Reserve borrowings and interbank sale of bonds under repurchase agreements.

Together, these changes both in attitude and in the structure of banks' short-term investment portfolios helped foster some growth of term lending in the 1920s.

Protective covenants—a requirement that the borrower do certain things, as for example, keep working capital above some minimum level during the credit term or furnish the bank periodic financial reports. Covenants can also require that the borrower not do certain things without the bank's approval—for example, expand its fixed assets, undertake further external financing, enter a merger, or acquire an affiliate.

Some of the costs of initiating and administering term loans are charged directly to borrowers as fees. But there is, of course, an interest rate at which banks are willing to absorb the remaining costs of term lending.

Revolving Credits

Revolving credits were once treated as short-term loans, which followed the banking convention that all loans had to be paid up sometime during the year—the annual clean-up rule. They now fall somewhere between term loans and short-term loans. Customers with revolving credits can borrow and repay repeatedly over the life of the agreement (usually two or three years) as long as the debt outstanding does not exceed the amount originally agreed on.

As many banks have relaxed the clean-up rule, however, allowing continuous indebtedness, revolving credits often qualify now as an intermediate form of term lending. Some contracts, in fact, include conversion clauses that allow credits to continue as term loans when the revolving credit agreement expires. Under such contracts, the period of revolving credit is often viewed as the first years of a term loan.

. . . and Rise of Term Lending

Although Real Bills persisted into the 1930s, events gave impetus to term lending.

- The slack demand for short-term loans during the Depression—even at a prime rate of 1½ percent from 1933 on—gave banks incentives and opportunities to shift into some higher yielding term loans.

- The Banking Acts of 1933 and 1935 limited bank activities in corporate security markets, leading banks to substitute term lending.

- The establishment of deposit insurance in 1933 reduced the likelihood of financial panics and deposit runs, encouraging some lengthening of the maturity of bank loan portfolios.

- A change in Federal Reserve rules in 1933 allowing loans of all maturities to be used as assets for discounts and advances at Federal Reserve banks increased the liquidity of term loans.

- Under the revision of bank examination standards in 1934, term loans were no longer routinely classified as "slow."

- With modern amortization gaining general acceptance, term loans, which had usually called for payment of principal and interest at maturity, were made payable in annual, semiannual, quarterly, or monthly instalments. Instalment payments smoothed the flow of interest and principal back to the bank and, by demonstrating a borrower's ability to repay, helped banks monitor term loans and identify problem credits.

- Banks were encouraged to help finance the recovery, and followed the examples set by the Federal Reserve and Reconstruction Finance Corporation in making direct term loans to business.

The change was marked. A Federal Reserve survey in 1939 showed term loans accounted for a fourth of the dollar volume of business loans at the banks sampled—39 percent at the banks sampled in New York. More than a third of the banks, however, showed no more than five term loans on their books. A 1946 survey of member banks showed term lending accounting for more than a third of the dollar volume of business loans.

Short-Term and Term Loans as Substitutes

Distinctions between term and short-term loans have sometimes been misleading. The most detailed survey of continuous indebtedness through renewal of short-term loans was conducted nearly 25 years ago in the Cleveland Federal Reserve District. The survey showed that half of the dollar holdings of short-term business loans outstanding at member banks in the district were obligations of borrowers continuously in debt to the same bank for at least two years. A fourth of the short-term credit was owed by businesses in debt to the same bank continuously for at least five years. Only 8 percent of this credit was to customers in debt to the same bank no longer than three months.

As long as loans are renewable, some borrowers with long-term financing needs might actually prefer short-term loans. Initiation costs are lower. And as the contracts are less detailed, they are less likely to put operating constraints on the borrower.

Continuous indebtedness of this kind may not be to the bank's advantage, however, especially if it has to renew credit to prevent a loan default or bolster future demand for loans or other bank services. The prospects of renewal requests increase uncertainties for the bank. A borrower may feel that the loan can be renewed. But the bank cannot be sure renewal will be requested. Even if a bank has done very well in predicting renewal requests and sorting out the loans it feels obligated to renew, this ability is a poor second for certain knowledge of the length of indebtedness agreed on when the credit was first made.

Short-term loan renewals can, of course, be appropriate at times, as for example, when the need for longer-term credit was not anticipated. But the flexibility of term loans nowadays reduces the need for renewals. The term loan itself can be written to capture one of the main advantages of short-term loan renewal—periodic adjustment in the interest rate. Floating rates substitute directly for the privilege of banks to change the interest rate when a short-term loan is renegotiated at maturity.

Both bank and borrower find advantages in negotiating the *effective* maturity at the outset instead of a *nominal* maturity that can be renewed. Sure of the maturity of a loan, a bank can absorb some of the other risks elsewhere in a loan agreement or lower the average loan rate. Assured of credit for the full term, a borrower is spared the real (albeit sometimes small) risk that a renewal request might be denied.

Loan Commitments

Loan commitments, once informal credit lines available to customers that kept adequate balances at a bank, are now more apt to be firm agreements laying out a bank's obligation to provide credit in the future (including the amount of the credit and the rate to be charged) and often the customer's obligation to pay fees on the credit availability. The change has come with

Floating Loan Rates . . .

Banks have been devising alternatives to fixed-rate pricing of business loans for decades. Graduated rates on some term loans appeared in the late 1930s. This scheme, applying progressively higher rates to later years of maturity, did not provide floating rates, of course. Term premiums to be added to the loan rate for later years were set when the loan was originated. The loan rate did not move with market rates, and the bank had no influence on it over the life of the loan.

Floating rates came into use in the late 1940s, with the introduction of formulas involving the addition of a quarter of a percentage point or more to the Federal Reserve discount rate. Floating rates were not widely used, however, as long as the discount rate and other rates remained fairly stable.

When the discount rate began changing more often in the early 1950s — and lagging hikes in the prime rate — banks switched the floating-rate base to the prime, a rate more closely reflecting market forces. Floating rate provisions, limited almost entirely to term loans, were not nearly as common as today.

The big change came in the mid-1960s, with the advent of modern bank liability management, growth of money-market funds, and more changes in short-term rates. Floating rates gave banks a way of making sure returns on outstanding loans — both long and short-term — moved with the costs of funds.

. . . and the Formulas for Computing Them

Essentially two types of prime-based formulas are used in calculating floating rates:

- Prime-plus. The more conventional of the two, this method calls for an add-on factor to adjust for default risk and provide a term premium for long-term credit. An example is the prime rate plus 2 percentage points — "prime *plus* 2."

- Times-prime. Becoming more common, this method calls for multiplication of the prime by a factor to adjust for credit risk and a term premium. An example is the prime multiplied by 1.2 — "1.2 *times* prime."

With either example, a prime rate set initially at 10 percent results in a floating loan rate of 12 percent.

Differences follow, however, if the prime rate is any rate other than 10 percent. With reductions in the prime rate, floating rates based on times-prime pricing decline faster than plus-prime rates. And increments in the prime result in faster increases in times-prime rates than in plus-prime rates.

Suppose, for instance, that an initial 10 percent prime is hiked to 12 percent. The prime-plus-2 loan rate moves from 12 percent to 14. The 1.2-times-prime rate moves from 12 percent to 14.4. If the prime is lowered from 10 percent to 8, the plus-prime rate falls from 12 percent to 10, but the times-prime rate drops to 9.6 percent.

Banks sometimes combine the two methods. An example is 1.09 times the *sum* of prime plus 1 percentage point—a floating rate equal to 1.09 *times* the prime plus 1.09 percentage points. Again, if the prime rate is set initially at 10 percent, the combination method leads to about the same floating rate as the basic methods—for example, 1.09 times 10 percent plus 1.09 percentage points, or roughly 12 percent. Effects for the combination method at any other prime, however, are the same as times-prime pricing, given the same multiplicative factors in the formulas.

As times-prime rates vary more than plus-prime rates over the interest-rate cycle, they have greater implications for changing bank loan revenue and, therefore, total profits.

One of the main reasons for times-prime pricing is that when the prime rate is raised, bank costs of funding outstanding loans in interest-sensitive markets may go up faster than the prime. The greater-than-proportional increase in the loan rate from times-prime pricing helps compensate banks for lagged upward responses of the prime rate.

The drift away from compensating balances also helps explain the growing use of times-prime pricing. The trend toward higher loan rates and lower required demand-deposit balances has, in fact, been a major factor in the use of more complicated floating-rate formulas.

The idea is to raise the loan rate enough to offset the loss of loanable funds when compensating balance requirements are eased. But the cost to a bank of foregoing these balances varies over interest-rate and credit cycles. When credit demand rises and banks scramble for ever more costly money-market funds, earlier reductions in compensating balances become increasingly costly. If rates are adjusted by the times-prime formula, explicit reimbursement to the bank increases as the prime rate rises. That is, an escalating rate premium replaces the supporting deposit balances.

Against these advantages of floating rates must be set the main disadvantage — the greater variation in loan revenue over the credit cycle. The disadvantage of floating rates becomes most apparent when market rates are falling. If formula loan rates are geared to fall as fast as money market rates, or even faster, bank profit margins on outstanding loans can be squeezed. Banks can immunize part of their business-loan portfolios from movements in money-market rates and the prime by continuing to make fixed-rate loans to customers interested primarily in loan-rate certainty.

the growth of both term loans and revolving credits and the greater use made of formal commitments for short-term lending.

The Federal Reserve Survey of Loan Commitments at Selected Large Banks for April 1979 showed $68 billion outstanding in unused formal agreements. Of these unused formal commitments, 16 percent was for term loans, 71 percent was for revolving credits, and the remaining 13 percent was mostly for short-term credits. Loans that had been made under formal commitments totaled $76 billion.

Despite the trend toward formalization of loan commitments, informal but confirmed lines of credit still accounted for much of the unused commitments. A total of $95 billion in unused credit was available to business borrowers under informal but confirmed lines, compared with the $68 billion in formal commitments. Use of informal lines was much less, however. Loans outstanding under confirmed lines amounted to $29 billion, compared with the $76 billion in loans that had been made under formal commitments.

Compensating Balances

Although many banks still require compensating (or supporting) balances, with the trend toward explicit pricing of bank services, less emphasis is put on these balances than in the past. As a result, required balances are being replaced in many cases by explicit fees and increases in lending rates.

Where demand-deposit balances are still used, the requirement is usually stated as an average deposit balance equal to a percentage of the loan or commitment. A typical requirement is an average balance of 15 percent of the loan. Another is 10 percent of the loan, plus 10 percent of the unused commitment — 10 percent of the total commitment.

Negotiations sometimes result in higher requirements on the loan commitments than on the loans themselves. In other cases, balance requirements are set higher on loans than on commitments.

Pressure from a credit customer to shift the balance requirement one way or the other gives a bank some indication of how the commitment is to be used. If the borrower wants the balance requirement on the commitment reduced enough to have the loan requirement raised an equal amount, he clearly expects to make little use of the loan commitment — less than half of it on average. If he expected to use most of the commitment, he would want the opposite, with more of the balance requirement on the unused commitment.

Loan Prepayments

Prepayment provisions in loan contracts spell out the penalty costs (premiums) charged for paying a loan before it matures. Until the 1960s, banks usually did not charge premiums when loans were paid off (or paid down) before maturity, provided the funds came from operating earnings or other internal sources. Although substantial premiums were often imposed on prepayments financed from other borrowing, especially from other banks, many banks in the 1950s actually encouraged prepayments from a firm's retained earnings.

Banks today often impose substantial penalties on the prepayment of fixed-rate loans, the intentions being to hold borrowers to the full terms of their contracts in return for the banks' having to risk a rise in interest rates.

If term borrowers could prepay their loans at will, with no direct or implied costs, they would in effect control maturities. As banks could not be sure of the repayment dates, prime-setting decisions would have to be based on probable prepayments, with banks undoubtedly charging more to compensate for the uncertainty.

Prepayment of floating-rate loans is seldom a problem. Borrowers have little incentive to prepay loans when the rates move with the costs of credit generally. Even if other interest rates fall a little faster than the floating rate, or rise a little slower, the substantial costs of originating other credit are apt to lock a customer into the existing loan.

Whether the rates are fixed or floating, then, most term loans run to maturity. And as a result, outstanding term loans are essentially immune to changes in the prime rate.

There are limits, of course, to the changes that can be made in prime rates. If floating rates went up too much or did not respond to drastic reductions in market rates, borrowers would stand the prepayment penalties and term loans outstanding would fall.

Secured Loans

Although large corporations with top credit ratings routinely receive unsecured bank loans, many business borrowers have to post collateral.

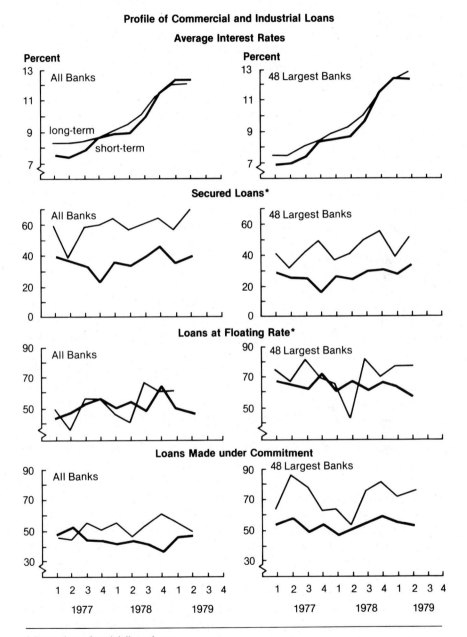

Profile of Commercial and Industrial Loans

Average Interest Rates

* Proportions of total dollar volumes
Source: Federal Reserve Survey of Terms of Bank Lending. The survey data are taken from about 340
banks selected to represent all sizes of banks. The data are collected from one business week in the
middle month of each calendar quarter. Short-term loans have original maturities of less than one year,
and term loans have maturities of one year or more.

The amount of collateral and the type depend on the customer's credit rating, the size and maturity of the loan, and the purpose of the credit. Because of risk factors involved in some types of term credit, term loans are more apt to be secured than are short-term loans.

The most recent trend in secured bank lending is the kind of asset-based lending long handled by commercial finance companies. Large banks and their holding companies have become active in this specialized form of secured lending by acquiring existing finance companies, establishing new commercial-finance affiliates, and restructuring their own lending policies for closer management and monitoring of the collateral behind secured loans. The inroads large banks have made into asset-based lending represent a competitive response — especially to attract small business borrowers — and awareness of the need for adequate collateralization as an adjunct to the risk-bearing business of modern bank lending.

Recent Pricing Tactics

When loan demand eases and money-market rates fall, large money-center banks come under pressure to lower their prime-rate quotations in an effort to attract more new business loan customers. This was the situation in 1976 and 1977. Because of floating-rate provisions in outstanding business loans, however, reductions in the prime rate aimed at bolstering new loans call for forfeitures of revenue on floating-rate loans already on the books. Bank concern over loss of this revenue can slow the lowering of the prime.

When two large banks in a money-center have significantly different proportions of their loan portfolios in floating-rate loans — especially if the loans are priced by different formulas (see box) — the one with the larger proportion may well be at a disadvantage in lowering its prime. These interbank differences in floating-rate loans help to explain split-rate primes — different prime rates at various money-center banks.

Large banks have tried several loan pricing policies aimed at bolstering loan demand and at the same time protecting profit margins on outstanding loans. One policy, dating from the 1950s, specifies ranges in which floating rates can be revised, as for example, an initial loan rate of 6 percent with the rate floating from 4 percent to 8 percent.

Some banks redesigned the cap-rate feature a few years ago by offering floating rates that would not average more than an agreed-on rate over the life of the loan. Because these cap rates combined the borrowing advantages of both fixed rates and floating rates, they gained some customer acceptance in 1971 and 1972.

When open-market rates rose, in 1973 and 1974, however, pushing up funding costs, profit margins on outstanding cap-rate loans dwindled. The upper limit on average interest costs became a ceiling that made further rate increases impossible. Banks have paid little attention to this type of loan since. They have also shown few inclinations to adopt minimum-rate features that would limit the decline in loan rates when the prime was lowered.

Another technique for bolstering loan demand while protecting bank loan income has been floating rates tied to base rates other than the prime. This pricing feature is often tailored to the needs (and competitive environment) of large multinational corporations with access to credit markets abroad.

One of the rates that moves somewhat independently of the regular prime rate quotations governing other floating rates is the London Interbank Offering Rate (LIBOR), a short-term European money-market rate. Although this is the most common formula rate for these loans, such U.S. money-market rates as the commercial paper rate and secondary certificate of deposit rate are also used. In some cases, large banks have revised their overseas lending policies to provide credit in the European market at rates tied either to their U.S. prime rate or to LIBOR, depending on the expected changes in the prime-LIBOR rate spread.

Business lending strategies refined at large banks during a time of rising interest rates will be tested when demand for loans eases and interest rates fall. As pressures build for banks to lower their prime rates from the above-15 percent levels of recent months, a large part of their current loan portfolios will still be on the books.

Banks have been preparing for an eventual downturn by diversifying their business loans, interspersing fixed-rate loans with loans written to various formula rates based on prime and other rates. Their success in pursuing this diversification strategy will be reflected in how well their prime rates follow declines in market rates.

Since revisions in prime rates usually lag behind changes in market rates, the tendency is for the spread to widen when rates fall rapidly. If, after adjustment for the lag, the prime rate still responds sluggishly to easing market conditions, banks may have to rethink some of their explicit pricing methods for business lending.

Questions

1. Why do origination costs of a five-year bank loan usually exceed those of a one-year bank loan?

2. Describe the following three types of bank loans: (a) term loan, (b) revolving credits, and (c) short-term loan.

3. Assume that you plan to borrow $1 million for five years from a commercial bank. Under what circumstances would you prefer a floating-rate loan instead of a fixed-rate loan?

4. Assume that you plan to borrow $1 million for five years from a commercial bank. The bank will make you a floating-rate loan. You may choose either of the following formulas for setting the bor-

rowing rate, which will be adjusted quarterly: (a) prime + 2, (b) 1.2 × prime, or (c) 1.09 × (prime + 1.09). The prime rate at the time of borrowing is 10 percent. Which formula would you choose? Explain. To help with your decision, graph the borrowing rate as a function of the prime rate—i.e., put the borrowing rate on the vertical axis and the prime rate on the horizontal axis.

5.   Al Priest and Company can borrow $100,000 from either the Riverdale Bank or the Elm Hall Bank. All loan terms, except one, are identical at both banks. Riverdale requires a compensating balance equal to 15 percent of the loan commitment. Elm Hall requires a compensating balance of 10 percent of the loan commitment plus 10 percent of any borrowings against the commitment. From which bank should Al Priest and Company borrow the $100,000? Explain.

Asset-Based Revolvers
Financing Growth with a Loan that Minimizes the Balance
Barry Herskowitz and David A. Kaplowitz

Profits and growth represent a double-edged sword to the problem of cash flow. Profits give rise to tax payments, and growth requires increasing investments in accounts receivable and inventory. Executives who attempt to solve this problem by stretching the company's credit are risking the loss of discounts and jeopardizing the supplier-customer relationship, which takes years to establish.

Financing growth with a term loan usually requires that the company borrow a lump sum and make subsequent periodic repayments of principal and interest. Because it is difficult to forecast external financing needs, organizations tend to (1) borrow more than they need and invest excess loan proceeds in money market instruments that yield returns that are less than the cost of borrowed funds or (2) borrow less than they require and leave themselves without sufficient funds to finance growth. Principal repayments of term loans have especially adverse effects on cash flow because they do not give rise to tax deductions.

Raising additional equity is another way to finance growth. It is, however, an expensive source of funds, especially for a privately owned company, because of the related issuance costs and the dilution of the ownership interest of existing shareholders.

A better way to obtain financing for growth may be the asset-based revolving credit loan. In this type of loan agreement, a lender allows a company to borrow at any time before the expiration of the agreement an

Barry Herskowitz and David A. Kaplowitz, "Asset-Based Revolvers," *Journal of Accountancy* (July 1986): 97–104. Reprinted with permission from the *Journal of Accountancy*. Copyright (c) 1986 by American Institute of Certified Public Accountants, Inc. Opinions of the authors are their own and do not necessarily reflect policies of the AICPA.

At the time of this writing, Barry Herskowitz was Assistant Professor of Accounting at Marymount Manhattan College, New York City. David A. Kaplowitz was a vice president for new business development at Manufacturers Hanover Commercial Corporation, New York City.

amount equal to predetermined percentages of the defined values of accounts receivable and inventories. This article describes these loans from the borrower's and lender's perspectives.

A Word about Factoring

Asset-based lending is sometimes confused with factoring. The major difference is that a factor purchases the accounts receivable of its client and assumes the related credit and collection risk. The factor has no recourse to its client if a receivable is uncollectible.

Under an asset-based lending arrangement, the lender takes a security interest in the receivables (and other assets if applicable) and the borrower retains the credit and collection risk. Factoring has historically been associated with the textile and apparel industries.

Profile of a Borrower

A typical borrower in an asset-based lending arrangement is a leveraged manufacturer or wholesaler that has a sizable investment in quality inventory and receivables. The borrower would have a need for permanent working capital financing that it couldn't presently amortize or "clean up." Such a need would disqualify the borrower for traditional bank financing. Retailers and companies engaged in high-tech activities aren't good candidates for this type of financing because of the risks associated with consumer receivables and high-tech inventories.

We believe that many CPAs in industry and in practice will find this financing technique suitable for a business that requires financing for growth and expansion. An asset-based revolver can also serve as an integral component of the financing of an acquisition. It is especially attractive to companies with annual revenues of $5 million to $100 million and with limited access to the credit and capital markets.

How Asset-Based Revolvers Work

With an asset-based revolving loan agreement, the lender obligates itself to loan to the borrower an amount that equals an agreed-upon percentage ("advance rate") of the outstanding eligible accounts receivable plus an agreed-upon percentage of eligible merchandise inventory. The lender takes a security interest in these assets.

After the initial loan is disbursed, the subsequent cash collections received by the borrower from its customers are remitted to the lender to reduce the revolving loan. The borrower borrows money periodically by instructing the lender to wire transfer funds into its bank account on the day that it requires funds. All of the borrower's cash receipts and disbursements, therefore, are funneled through the asset-based loan.

"Eligible accounts receivable" usually is defined as gross accounts receivable minus reserves for returns, discounts and other credits, slow-paying accounts (usually over 60 days past the due date on the invoice), foreign receivables, deferred shipment transactions and receivables due from affiliates and suppliers. The accounts receivable advance rate is determined by the lender after analysis of the borrower's creditworthiness, products sold and the credit profile of its customers. A typical accounts receivable advance rate is between 75 percent and 85 percent of eligible accounts receivable.

Eligible inventory includes finished goods and raw materials owned by and in the possession of the borrower valued for advance purposes on a FIFO basis net of reserves for obsolescence and for declines in market value. Work in process and supplies usually aren't considered eligible inventory. The advance rate varies from 20 percent to 60 percent of eligible inventory and is influenced by the borrower's gross profit percentage and creditworthiness and the inventory's turnover rate, marketability, perishability and obsolescence risk.

The balance sheet of the XYZ Distribution Corporation (Exhibit 1) indicates that a term loan of $1 million is payable on November 1, 1985. XYZ refinances the loan by entering into an asset-based revolving loan agreement. Exhibit 2 illustrates how much XYZ can borrow if the lender advances 80 percent on eligible accounts receivable and 50 percent on inventory.

The Borrower's Responsibilities

A distinguishing feature of asset-based financing is the close monitoring by the lender. Because the loan balance changes on a daily basis, reflecting advances and collections, the lender is interested in the

Exhibit 1   XYZ Distribution Corporation Balance Sheet (October 31, 1985)

Assets		Liabilities and Shareholders' Equity	
Cash	$ 40,000	Accounts payable	$ 500,000
Accounts receivable minus allowance for doubtful accounts of $40,000	960,000	Accrued expenses	200,000
Inventory—finished goods	1,200,000	Term loan payable 11/1/85	1,000,000
Total current assets	2,200,000	Total current liabilities	1,700,000
Leasehold improvements and equipment, net	500,000	Shareholders' equity	1,000,000
Total assets	$2,700,000	Total liabilities and shareholders' equity	$2,700,000

Exhibit 2   Calculation of XYZ's Loan Availability (October 31, 1985)

The amount of the eligible accounts receivable, inventory and their respective advance rates determines the maximum amount that can be borrowed. XYZ Distribution Corporation will borrow $1 million to repay its maturing term loan. XYZ will also have the ability to borrow additional funds up to $321,280 because of the level of its eligible accounts receivable and inventory.

Gross accounts receivable	$1,000,000
Minus allowances for	
Slow-paying accounts (60 days past due)	50,000*
Receivables from foreign customers	30,000*
Eligible accounts receivable	920,000
Advance rate	× 78.4**
Maximum amount that can be borrowed against accounts receivable	$ 721,280
Inventory—finished goods	$1,200,000
Advance rate	× 50%*
Maximum amount that can be borrowed against inventory	$ 600,000
Maximum amount that can be borrowed against accounts receivable and inventory	$1,321,280
Amount borrowed to refinance maturing term loan	1,000,000
Loan availability on October 31, 1985	$ 321,280

* Determined by representatives of the lender.

** Assume an 80 percent advance rate on accounts receivable minus 2 percent reserve for future discounts and returns.

relationship between the outstanding loan balance and the related assets in which it holds a security interest. Consequently, the lender requires periodic collateral reports from the borrower.

Once or twice a week (or more or less frequently if warranted), the borrower reports and pledges its recently created receivables to the lender. The report summarizes the sales total since the previous assignment and is accompanied by a copy of the borrower's sales or invoice register. The borrower remits its receivable collections by depositing customer checks in the lender's bank account or by setting up a lockbox in the lender's bank and sending the checks there directly. These cash remittances are summarized by the borrower on periodic collection reports.

Having these frequent reports on sales and collections enables the lender to calculate, on an ongoing basis, the borrower's gross accounts receivable. The gross accounts receivable total is then reconciled to the borrower's monthly aging to ensure that reporting is accurate. Inventory totals are "confirmed" monthly by the borrower based on its perpetual records, physical counts or estimated value (using the gross profit method of calculation).

The lender is concerned with asset quality as well as with asset quantity and, therefore, audits the borrower's collateral records. Before making a new loan, and on a periodic basis afterward, the lender's auditor will examine the borrower's general ledger, accounts receivable and payable subsidiary ledgers, cashbooks and inventory records, as well as the related sales and purchase invoices, shipping and receiving documents, bank statements and physical inventory counts. The auditor is especially interested in verifying that receivables are not assigned to the lender before the related merchandise is shipped. In addition, the auditor examines the receivables for any unusual changes in turnover and bad debts. Large or frequent credit memos and a deterioration of the overall accounts receivable aging are also subject to investigation.

The lender also analyzes the borrower's financial condition by requiring periodic interim and annual financial statements. The borrower is also asked to prepare cash flow projections on an annual basis.

The assumptions used in preparing the projections are of critical importance. The assumptions regarding future sales growth, gross profit margins, asset turnover, operating-expense ratios, interest rates and capital expenditures should be conservative and should bear a reasonable relationship to the borrower's historic operating performance. Asset-based lenders place more emphasis on cash flow projections than on financial ratio analyses to assess the borrower's ability to service its debt.

The lender's evaluation of the quality of the borrower's management team is another variable that greatly affects the decision on whether to provide credit. The lender's evaluation includes an analysis of the borrower's past operating performance, operating and financial controls, and the depth of management's business and industry experience. The lender is especially interested in management's commitment to the organization, as evidenced by its equity investment, ownership percentage and contractual performance incentives. If certain managers are considered indispensable, the lender will require "key person" life insurance.

Pricing

Financial institutions tend to charge borrowers a floating rate of one to three percentage points above prime. The increment over prime is determined by the lender's perceived level of risk, competitive pressures from other lenders, collateral protection and the size of the lender's commitment. Because the lender's cost of servicing the revolver is high, reflecting the constant collateral monitoring and the periodic audits, higher rates are charged for smaller commitments. Lenders may charge a monthly management fee of $500 to $1,000 for small loans (under $1 million commitments) to compensate themselves for the cost of monitoring and auditing the collateral. An annual commitment fee of one-quarter to one-half of one percent may be charged on the unused available portion of the revolving line for a larger loan.

Exhibit 3   **XYZ's Loan Statement (November 1985)**

Date	Gross accounts receivable— beginning of day	Gross sales for the day	Returns and credits	Cash collections	Gross accounts receivable— end of day
1	$1,000,000	$ 38,000		$ 90,000	$ 948,000
2	948,000	35,000		23,000	960,000
3	960,000	42,000		25,000	977,000
29	1,029,000	45,000		65,000	1,009,000
30	1,009,000	43,000		37,000	1,015,000
Total	—	$844,000	$9,000	$820,000	—

The loan agreement usually allows the financial institution to charge a minimum rate of interest but rarely specifies a maximum rate. The rate is increased if a "360-day year" is used in calculating the interest. The lender is contractually allowed to increase the loan balance (to calculate interest) by a collection-day factor of two or three days because the loan balance is reduced by the day's cash receipts, which aren't immediately usable by the lender. Thus, if a borrower's average daily cash receipts are $20,000, its loan balance will be increased by $40,000 or $60,000 for the purpose of calculating interest. Compensating balances are not required.

Advantages to the Borrower

A borrower that negotiates an asset-based revolving loan agreement is benefited in several ways.

Minimized Loan Balance

The borrower automatically reduces its loan balance by the incoming receipts on a daily basis. An advance is requested on the day that funds

Exhibit 4   **Calculation of XYZ's Loan Availability (November 1985)**

Date	Gross accounts receivable	Reserves for foreign and slow-paying accounts*	Eligible accounts receivable	Maximum amount that can be borrowed on accounts receivable**
1	$ 948,000	$80,000	$868,000	$680,512
2	960,000	80,000	880,000	689,920
3	977,000	80,000	897,000	703,248
29	1,009,000	80,000	929,000	728,336
30	1,015,000	80,000	935,000	733,040

* Adjusted once a month.
** Eligible accounts receivable plus $600,000 applicable to inventory.
*** Eligible accounts receivable times 78.4 percent.

Loan balance— beginning of day	Advances by lender	Cash collections	Loan balance— end of day
$1,000,000		$ 90,000	$ 910,000
910,000		23,000	887,000
887,000	$300,000	25,000	1,162,000
1,032,000		65,000	967,000
967,000		37,000	930,000
—	$750,000	$820,000	—

are required. These factors minimize the loan balance, which, in turn, reduces the aggregate interest expense. The borrower operates with a perpetual cashbook balance of zero, and the task of cash management is simplified.

Flexible Borrowing Capability

The borrower in effect has a credit line equal to its loan availability. The loan availability, which can be calculated on a daily basis by the lender's account officer, represents the maximum amount that can be borrowed on the date of the calculation.

This flexible borrowing capacity allows the borrower to take advantage of favorable discounts and purchasing opportunities offered by suppliers if the loan availability is sufficient. XYZ Distribution's loan statement for November 1985 (see Exhibit 3) has been used in calculating the company's loan availability for that month (see Exhibit 4).

Maximum allowable loan balance***	Loan balance — end of day	Loan availability
$1,280,512	$ 910,000	$370,512
1,289,920	887,000	402,920
1,303,248	1,162,000	141,248
1,328,336	967,000	361,336
1,333,040	930,000	403,040

Delayed Principal Repayment

The revolver usually doesn't require repayment of the principal until the loan agreement expires. This delay gives the borrower the opportunity to conserve cash and plan ahead for the refinancing of the principal balance outstanding at the expiration date. Interest usually is calculated on a monthly basis and added to the loan balance on the first day of the following month.

Increased Borrowing Capacity

Many borrowers have accounts receivable and inventory increases that are proportional to their revenue increases. Thus a 20 percent increase in revenue generally will result in a 20 percent increase in collateral value and borrowing capacity. (Usually the financial institution will limit both its overall loan commitment and the amount it will lend against inventory.)

Advantages to the Lender

Asset-based lending is highly profitable for most financial institutions because the interest rates are higher than in traditional bank lending. Most money-center and large regional banks have asset-based lending subsidiaries or divisions. Independent finance companies are also involved in this type of lending; however, many independent finance companies have been acquired by the money-center and large regional banks in recent years.

Role of the CPA

CPAs, in industry or in practice, can play a vital role in obtaining asset-based financing for managements or clients — especially for medium-sized companies. The probability of obtaining financing is increased if the company has financial statements that have been independently audited. If the loan commitment is large, the lender will require audited annual financial statements from the borrower while the agreement is in effect. The CPA is, moreover, frequently involved in structuring and negotiating the terms of the loan agreement and also can provide guidance in the preparation of financial projections.

Questions

1. Describe an asset-based revolving loan agreement.

2. Explain why work-in-process inventory and supplies are usually ineligible to serve as collateral for bank loans.

3.   Indicate which of the following statements are true and which are false:

T   F   Factoring receivables is the pledging of receivables for a loan.

T   F   The advance rate for typical accounts receivable is greater than the advance rate for typical inventories.

T   F   Providers of asset-based financing need to monitor the borrower's collateral.

T   F   Banks usually charge borrowers the prime rate for asset-based revolving loan agreements.

4.   What are the advantages to the borrower of an asset-based revolving loan agreement?

Interest Rate Swaps: A New Tool for Managing Risk

Jan G. Loeys

Introduction

Sharp movements of interest rates in recent years have created serious problems for firms in which the maturity of their assets does not match the maturity of their liabilities. For example, some financial institutions and other corporations have long-term, fixed-rate assets financed with short-term liabilities. Such firms experience an earnings squeeze whenever market interest rates rise unexpectedly, because their cost of borrowing rises faster than the yield on their assets. As a result, many firms look for ways to reduce the sensitivity—or exposure—of their earnings to interest rate fluctuations. A recent technique that allows firms to hedge (reduce) this exposure is the "interest rate swap." Used first in the Eurobond market during 1981, interest rate swaps have taken the market by storm; and now the volume of interest rate swaps in the United States alone is close to $80 billion.

Why are interest rate swaps so popular? What are the advantages of this instrument over other hedging techniques, such as refinancing the firm's debt or purchasing interest rate futures? The answers to these questions require first an explanation of what interest rate swaps are and how they can be used to reduce interest rate risk.

Jan G. Loeys, "Interest Rate Swaps: A New Tool for Managing Risk," *Business Review* (Federal Reserve Bank of Philadelphia, May/June 1985), 17–25.

At the time of this writing, Jan Loeys was a Senior Economist in the Macroeconomics Section of the Research Department of the Federal Reserve Bank of Philadelphia. The author is indebted to Charles Gibson for helpful comments.

What Are Interest Rate Swaps?

An interest rate swap typically involves two firms that want to change their exposure to interest rate fluctuations in opposite directions. For example, one firm has long-term assets that yield a fixed rate of return; but it also has liabilities with interest payments that fluctuate with market rates of interest (that is, floating rate liabilities).[1] This firm loses when interest rates rise unexpectedly, because the interest cost of its liabilities rises but the revenue from its (fixed-rate) assets remains the same. Conversely, this firm gains from an unexpected drop in interest rates. This sensitivity of a firm's net earnings to interest rate fluctuations is the firm's *exposure to interest rate risk*. The other firm involved in the swap faces the opposite situation: its assets yield a return that fluctuates with market rates, but the interest payments on its liabilities are fixed for a longer period of time. A rise in interest rates benefits this firm, because its revenues rise faster than its cost of borrowing; but a drop in market rates reduces its net earnings.

When two firms such as these have opposite interest risk exposures, one has the makings of a swap. In a typical swap the two firms get together — sometimes through an intermediary — and, in effect, exchange some of their interest payments. A firm with floating-rate liabilities essentially takes over some of the interest payments of a firm with fixed-rate liabilities, and in return the firm with the fixed-rate liabilities takes over some of the interest payments of the firm with floating-rate liabilities. For example, a firm that has liabilities on which the interest rate fluctuates with the 3-month Treasury bill (T-bill) rate could agree to pay another firm a fixed rate of 12 percent on an agreed upon dollar amount (principal) in exchange for a floating-rate payment of 50 basis points over the 3-month T-bill rate on the same principal. *In effect,* one firm converts the interest payments on its liabilities from a floating-rate to a fixed-rate basis, and the other converts its liabilities from fixed to floating rate. (For a more detailed discussion of the mechanics of swap arrangements, see HOW A SWAP WORKS.) Parties to a swap agree to make *interest payments* to each other — they do not actually swap liabilities, nor do they lend money to each other. Each firm remains responsible for paying the interest and principal on its own liabilities. Therefore, swaps do not appear on a firm's balance sheet; instead they are used to alter the exposure to interest rate risk implied by the balance sheet.

In just a few years, interest rate swaps have become very popular as a hedging instrument (see FROM ZERO TO $80 BILLION IN THREE YEARS). But why are firms using swaps rather than other more established hedging techniques, such as purchasing interest rate futures?

---

[1] There are two types of floating-rate debt: one is a short-term liability that has to be refinanced frequently; the other is a long-term liability on which the interest rate fluctuates with the interest rate of a specific market instrument.

Swaps: Longer than Futures, but More Expensive

Futures are contracts that generate cash flows that can be used to reduce a firm's interest risk exposure. An interest rate futures contract is an agreement to buy or sell a certain financial asset, such as a T-bill, for a specific price at a specific date in the future. During the life of the futures contract, each time the market value of the asset falls (interest rates rise), the seller in the contract makes a profit, and receives cash, and the buyer takes a loss, and pays cash, and vice versa if the asset's market value rises.[2]

Consider again the case of a thrift institution that has long-term fixed-rate assets, like mortgages, that it funds with short-term liabilities, like certificates of deposit (CDs). If interest rates rise unexpectedly, this thrift will lose — it suffers reduced net earnings. But the thrift could hedge

---

How a Swap Works

The following example is based on an actual transaction that was arranged by an investment bank between a large thrift institution and a large international bank; it is representative of many swaps that have been arranged since 1982. "Thrift" has a large portfolio of fixed-rate mortgages. "Bank" has most of its dollar-denominated assets yielding a floating-rate return based on LIBOR (the London Interbank Offered Rate).

On May 10, 1983, the "Intermediary," a large investment bank, arranged a $100 million, 7-year interest rate swap between Thrift and Bank. In the swap, Thrift agreed to pay Bank a fixed rate of 11 percent per year on $100 million, every 6 months. This payment covered exactly the interest Bank had to pay on a $100 million bond it issued in the Eurodollar market. Thrift also agreed to pay Bank the 2 percent underwriting spread that Bank itself paid to issue this bond. In exchange, Bank agreed to make floating-rate payments to Thrift at 35 basis points (.35 percent) below LIBOR. Intermediary received a broker's fee of $500,000.

---

[2] Cash flows are generated because the exchange where the contract is traded requires that both the buyer and seller in a futures contract post a certain margin. If the price of the underlying asset falls, the buyer has to deposit additional funds with the exchange to maintain the margin requirement, and the seller has his account credited by the same funds. Margins may consist of Treasury securities. For more details, see Howard Keen, Jr., "Interest Rate Futures: A Challenge for Bankers," *Business Review* (November/December, 1980), pp. 13–25; Mark Drabenstott and Anne O'Mara McDonley, "Futures Markets: A Primer for Financial Institutions," Federal Reserve Bank of Kansas City *Economic Review* (November 1984), pp. 17–23; and Nancy Rothstein (ed.), *The Handbook on Financial Futures* (New York: McGraw-Hill, 1984).

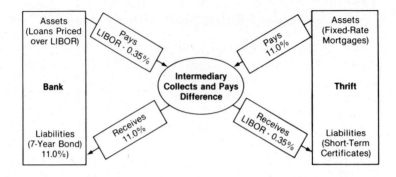

Twice a year, intermediary (for a fee) calculates Bank's floating-rate payment by taking the average level of LIBOR for that month (Col. 2), deducting 35 basis points, dividing by 2 (because it is for *half* a year), and multiplying by $100 million (Col. 3). If this amount is larger than Thrift's fixed-rate payment (Col. 4), Bank pays Thrift the difference (Col. 5). Otherwise, Thrift pays Bank the difference (Col. 6).

1	2	3	4	5	6
		Floating-Rate Payment 1/2 (LIBOR-	Fixed-Rate Payment	Net Payment from Bank to	Net Payment from Thrift to
Date	LIBOR	0.35%)	1/2 (11%)	Thrift	Bank
May 1983	8.98%	—	—	—	—
Nov 1983	8.43%	$4,040,000	$5,500,000	0	$1,460,000
May 1984	11.54%	$5,595,000	$5,500,000	$95,000	0
Nov 1984	9.92%	$4,785,000	$5,500,000	0	$ 715,000
May 1985	8.44%	$4,045,000	$5,500,000	0	$1,455,000

The swap allows both Bank and Thrift to reduce their exposure to interest rate risk. Bank can now match its floating-rate assets priced off LIBOR with an interest payment based on LIBOR, while the fixed-rate interest payments on its bond issue are covered by Thrift. At the same time, Thrift can hedge part of its mortgage portfolio, from which it receives fixed interest earnings, with the fixed-rate payment it makes to Bank. However, the floating-rate payment that Thrift receives is linked to LIBOR while its cost of borrowing is more closely linked to the T-bill rate. Since LIBOR and the T-bill rate do not always move in tandem, Thrift is still exposed to fluctuations in the relation between LIBOR and the T-bill rate.

its interest rate risk with a futures contract to deliver (sell) a CD. Then, if interest rates rise, the market value of the CD falls, and the thrift receives a cash flow. This cash inflow offsets the reduced net earnings from the higher interest cost of the thrift's short-term liabilities. When interest rates *drop,* the futures contract produces a cash outflow, but this loss is offset by a lower interest cost on the thrift's short-term liabilities. By buying enough of these futures contracts, the thrift can, in principle, fully hedge its exposure to interest rate fluctuations.

One disadvantage of futures is that they are standardized contracts that exist only with certain specific delivery dates and deliverable types of financial instruments.[3] In particular, futures are available only for delivery dates at 3-month intervals out to about 2-1/2 years. This makes it impossible to hedge interest rate risk beyond 2-1/2 years.[4] Interest rate swaps, in contrast, are private contracts with virtually every aspect of the agreement open to negotiation. Consequently, a swap can be tailor-made to fulfill one firm's particular needs, assuming another firm can be found to fit the other end of the contract. This flexibility allows firms to set up long-term arrangements — most swaps have a final maturity of three to ten years — thereby filling the gap left by futures.

The ability to customize interest rate swaps does not come without its disadvantages. The lack of product standardization makes it more difficult to find another party and to negotiate a mutually agreeable contract. It also costs more to close out a swap contract if the need arises, than a futures contract position, which can be closed out readily. Apart from certain fixed costs of setting up an account with a trader and meeting regulatory requirements, the brokerage costs of initiating and eventually closing out a futures contract are 2 to 5 basis points. This is much lower than the arrangement fee of about 25 basis points that most swap brokers charge (not including additional fees for settling and guaranteeing the agreement).

Because swaps are agreements between private parties, they also have the disadvantage that one of the parties may default and thus be unable to continue the agreement. Although the other party has no

---

[3] The four delivery dates are March, June, September, and December. The deliverable assets are Treasury bills, notes, and bonds; Bank and Eurodollar CDs; Sterling CDs and Gilts; and Ginny Maes. However, there are no interest rate futures on the prime rate or on the London Interbank Offered Rate (LIBOR), although many firms have their cost of borrowing tied to either of these two rates. Firms that use, say, a T-bill futures to hedge their LIBOR-based borrowing are still exposed to fluctuations in the relation between the T-bill rate and LIBOR. Swaps, though, frequently have the same problem as it is difficult to find two firms with opposite exposure to the same market rate of interest (see the example in HOW A SWAP WORKS).

[4] As a practical matter, a firm that wants to hedge as closely as possible, say, a 5-year fixed-rate asset when only 2-1/2 year futures contracts are available, has to buy the contract with the longest available delivery date and then replace it every three months with the new 2-1/2 year contract. In this way, the firm can keep the delivery date of its futures contract as close to 2-1/2 years as possible. The firm will keep doing this until the remaining maturity of the asset reaches 2-1/2 years.

principal at risk, it would again be stuck with an interest risk exposure. It could negotiate a new swap arrangement with another firm, but the terms of that agreement would depend on current market interest rates, which may be more or less advantageous to the firm. Default risk can be reduced by requiring collateral, standby letters of credit, or a third-party guarantee—all of which are costly.[5] Futures, on the other hand, are guaranteed by the exchange in which the contracts are traded and by the funds that both parties to a futures contract must hold on margin with the exchange.

From Zero to $80 Billion in Three Years

Interest rate swaps first emerged in the Eurobond market in late 1981.[a] Large international banks, which do most of their lending on a floating-rate basis, were involved in the first swaps so that they could use their fixed-rate borrowing capacity to obtain lower-cost floating-rate funds. Initially, the swapping partners consisted mainly of utilities and lower-rated industrial corporations that preferred fixed-rate financing. During 1982, the first domestic interest rate swap occurred between the Student Loan Marketing Association (Sallie Mae) and the ITT Financial Corp., with Sallie Mae making floating-rate payments to ITT. Since then, the market has grown tremendously; in 1984 about $80 billion in swap agreements were concluded.[b] Any large corporation can now use interest rate swaps as an instrument for asset-liability management.

Both investment banks and commercial banks have been active in arranging interest rate swaps. These intermediaries earn fees by bringing the different parties together, by acting as settlement agent (that is, collecting and paying the net difference in the interest payments), and by serving as guarantor of the agreement. Most intermediaries have recently gone beyond their initial role of merely bringing different parties together and function also as dealers. As a dealer, the intermediary is also the counterparty to each swap it "sells." That is, each party has an agreement only with the intermediary and is totally unaware of who might be on the other side of the swap. This arrangement allows the intermediary to sell one leg of the swap before selling the other and to work with an inventory of as yet unmatched swap agreements. The existence of dealers also facilitates an informal secondary market in swaps, where

---

[5] Often the third-party guarantee is provided by the intermediary who would be required to step in and take over the obligation of the defaulting party. So far, there have been no reports of defaults on a swap agreement.

parties to a swap can sell their position to the intermediary or to another party, thereby increasing the liquidity of this instrument.

A typical swap involves a bond issue for $25 to $75 million with a 3 to 10 year maturity on one side, and a floating-rate loan on the other side. Initially, this floating-rate loan was priced at a fraction over LIBOR, the London Interbank Offered Rate. Recently floating-rate loans have also been using the prime rate, the T-bill rate, or other indices of the cost of short-term borrowing.

The most common type of swap is the one described above: a dollar fixed-rate loan swapped for a dollar floating-rate loan, otherwise called the "plain-vanilla" swap. However, several variations on this basic swap have emerged in the market. One such variation is a floating-to-floating swap where parties agree to swap floating rates based on different indices. For example, a bank with assets tied to the prime rate and liabilities based on LIBOR may want to swap the interest payments on its liabilities with payments on a prime-tied, floating-rate loan. Another type of arrangement involves currency swaps such as a swap of a sterling floating-rate loan for a dollar fixed-rate loan. For firms whose assets are denominated in a different currency than are its liabilities, this type of swap may be more appropriate. Finally, rather than exchanging interest payments on liabilities, swaps can also be used to exchange yields on *assets* of different maturities or currencies.

The interest rate swap market has proven to be very flexible in adjusting its product to new customer needs. This innovativeness all but guarantees that swaps will remain a permanent feature of international capital markets.

[a] For more technical and institutional details on interest rate swaps, see Carl R. Beidleman, *Financial Swaps: New Strategies in Currency and Coupon Risk Management* (Homewood, Illinois: Dow Jones-Irwin, 1985); and Boris Antl (ed.), *Swap Financing Techniques* (London: Euromoney Publications Limited, 1983).

[b] Since there are no official reporting requirements on swaps, estimates of the size of this market vary tremendously. The amount of $80 billion, as estimated by Salomon Brothers (see *The Economist,* March 16, 1985, p. 30, Table 16), appears to be somewhere in the middle.

To reduce the costs stemming from the customized nature of swaps, many intermediaries have started to standardize the contract terms of swap agreements, such as the type of floating interest rate, repricing dates, and margin or collateral requirements.[6] As a result, interest rate swaps may become similar to futures contracts, but with longer periods available for hedging.

Given a choice, firms that want to reduce their exposure to interest rate fluctuations for up to 2-1/2 years may be better off with interest rate futures than with swaps because futures are less costly to use than swaps.[7] For longer-term hedges, interest rate swaps are a more appropriate, though relatively more expensive, hedging instrument.

Swaps: More Flexible and Cheaper than Refinancing

Rather than using complicated instruments such as swaps and futures, it may seem a lot less trouble for a firm to adjust its exposure directly by issuing liabilities (debt) with the pricing characteristics it desires. For example, a firm that has only floating-rate liabilities but now desires more fixed-rate liabilities, could buy back some of its floating-rate liabilities and issue fixed-rate liabilities instead; that is, it could refinance some of its liabilities. However, "sellers" of interest rate swaps claim that swaps may be less costly than refinancing for several reasons. One is that firms with lower credit ratings may have to pay relatively higher interest rates—that is higher quality spreads—in the fixed-rate market than in the floating-rate market. Thus, they claim, such firms should borrow in the floating-rate market and then swap, if they desire fixed-rate liabilities. Another reason is that swaps circumvent transactions costs associated with refinancing—such as legal fees, advertising, and regulatory restrictions—because swaps do not involve new borrowing; they only involve the exchange of interest payments on existing liabilities. To understand the advantages swaps can have over refinancing requires a closer look at these quality spread differentials and transactions costs.

Quality Spread Differentials

A quality spread is the premium that a borrower with a low credit rating has to pay over a borrower with a high credit rating. For example, during 1982 when interest rate swaps first became popular in the U.S., the quality spread between Aaa and Baa rated firms in the fixed-rate

---

[6] For more details, see "Swaps: Managing the Future," *Euromoney* (October 1984), pp. 201–221; and "Making a Market in Slightly Used Swaps," *Institutional Investor* (November 1984), pp. 77–84.

[7] Firms could also use options in this case. An option is the right (rather than the commitment) to buy or sell an asset before a certain date in the future. Options are not discussed in this paper because a comparison of options with swaps is very similar to a comparison of futures with swaps. Options, like futures, are mostly standardized products, traded mostly on organized exchanges, and available only up to 2 years. However, certain over-the-counter options are increasingly available for longer periods.

Table 1   **Quality Spread Differentials**

Issued By	Interest Rate on Liabilities	
	Floating Rate	Fixed rate
Company (Baa)*	T-bill + 1.0%	16.0%
Bank (Aaa)*	T-bill + 0.5%	14.0%
Quality spread:	0.5%	2.0%

* Credit ratings are in parentheses. Baa is the lower rating.

corporate bond market was over 2 percentage points, a post-war high.[8] At the same time, these quality spreads were less than 1 percentage point in the floating-rate market.

To see how interest rate swaps could exploit this apparent difference in quality spreads, consider an example typical of many of the early swaps. "Company" is a manufacturer whose assets yield a fixed rate of return. Company finances a major part of its assets by borrowing at a floating rate of 1 percentage point above the 3-month T-bill rate. Company prefers to finance its assets with a fixed-rate bond issue, but because of its low Baa credit rating it would have to pay, say, 16 percent.

On the other side is "Bank," a large international bank, with a portfolio of commercial loans on which it charges a rate based on the 3-month T-bill rate. Bank currently finances its portfolio by issuing CDs at 1/2 percentage point above the 3-month T-bill rate. Given its high Aaa credit rating it has the option of borrowing in the bond market at a fixed rate of 14 percent. Table 1 shows the different alternatives for the two firms. Note that the quality spread is 1/2 percentage point in the floating-rate market, and 2 percentage points in the fixed-rate market.

If each simply wanted to match maturities, Bank would borrow in the floating-rate market at 1/2 percentage point above the T-bill rate and Company would borrow in the bond market at 16 percent. But both borrowers could reduce their cost of borrowing if Bank borrows at a fixed rate and Company borrows at a floating rate and they swap interest payments, with Company agreeing to pay Bank, say, an additional 1 percentage point. In effect, this means that Bank borrows at a 14 percent interest rate, pays Company the T-bill rate plus 1 percentage point (Company's borrowing cost), and receives payments from Company at a 15 percent interest rate. On net, Bank makes interest payments at the T-bill rate [14% + (T-bill rate + 1%) − 15%]. On the other side of the transaction, Company in effect borrows at the T-bill rate plus one percentage point, pays Bank a 15 percent interest rate, and receives

[8] Aaa and Baa are credit ratings assessed by Moody's Investors Services, Inc., a major credit-rating agency. This rating system consists of 10 grades, ranging from Aaa (highest quality) to Baa (medium quality) to Caa (poor quality) to D (default).

payments from Bank at the T-bill rate plus one percentage point. On net, then, Company makes interest payments at a 15 percent interest rate [(T-bill rate + 1%) + 15% − (T-bill rate + 1%)].[9] As a result, Bank effectively borrows at the T-bill rate, better than it could do by itself, and Company borrows at a fixed 15 percent, less than the 16 percent it would have to pay if it had entered the bond market on its own. The source of this reduction in borrowing costs is the difference in quality spreads between the fixed-rate and the floating-rate market. By being able to borrow at a fixed rate through Bank, Company saves more than enough over its own fixed-rate cost of borrowing to compensate Bank for Company's higher (than Bank's) cost of borrowing in the floating-rate market (1/2 percentage point).

The reduction in borrowing costs made possible by these quality spread differentials has been a major selling point for swaps. These cost reductions may be more apparent than real, however. There is a lot of evidence that financial markets are efficient, and that pure arbitrage profits are not readily available.[10] Market efficiency suggests that the difference in quality spreads between fixed-rate and floating-rate markets — 200 vs. 50 basis points in the example — reflects differences in risk to lenders in these respective markets. Indeed, the quality spread that is typically quoted does not refer to debt of the same maturity. The floating-rate debt that firms use as a basis for swaps is mostly short- to medium-term, while the fixed-rate debt consists of long-term bonds.[11] Debt-holders consider *short-term* debt less risky than long-term debt because they have the option not to renew the debt if the firm looks shakier than anticipated. Therefore, debt-holders require smaller quality spreads on short-term debt than on long-term debt. The possibility that debt will not be renewed, however, makes issuing short-term debt rather than long-term debt more risky to *equity-holders*. Issuing short-term rather than long-term debt therefore merely shifts risk from debt-holders to equity-holders.[12] A firm that considers swapping the floating-rate

[9] As explained in HOW A SWAP WORKS, only the *difference* between these two flows of payment actually changes hands. Unless the T-bill rate is above 14 percent, company pays the difference between 14 percent and the T-bill rate.

[10] For a survey of the evidence, see Thomas E. Copeland and J. Fred Weston, *Financial Theory and Corporate Policy,* Second Edition (Reading: Addison-Wesley, 1983).

[11] The floating-rate debt that firms use as a basis for a floating-to-fixed interest rate swap consists mostly of bank credit, commercial paper, certificates of deposits (CDs), and floating-rate notes (FRNs). More than 90% of commercial and industrial loans by U.S. banks are short term. Commercial paper usually has a maturity of 3 to 6 months, while most large negotiable CDs of financial institutions are for 6 months or less. Although FRNs have stated maturities of 7 to 15 years, almost all FRNs issued in the U.S. have covenants that give the holder the right to redeem the note at 3-year intervals, thereby reducing the effective maturity of these FRNs to 3 years. Some of the FRNs that do show large quality spreads usually give the issuer the option to exchange the issue for fixed-rate debt before a certain date. Thus, these last FRNs are more like fixed-rate bonds.

[12] For a formal treatment of this issue, see Thomas Ho and Ronald Singer, "Bond Indenture Provisions and the Risk of Corporate Debt," *Journal of Financial Economics* (1982), pp. 375–406.

interest on its short-term debt for a fixed-rate interest payment as an alternative to borrowing directly long term must take into account that the lower cost of borrowing produced by the swap comes at the cost of increased risk to the firm's equity-holders.

Quality spread differentials may seem to offer profit opportunities, and they may look like a good reason to use swaps instead of refinancing. But market efficiency suggests that true profit opportunities are likely to be short-lived at best, and that most of the time they are illusory. But there are more solid reasons why refinancing is more costly than interest rate swaps, and they are transactions costs and other non-interest costs (as opposed to interest costs in the form of high quality spreads).

Transactions Costs

Refinancing can take a lot of time, while a swap can be arranged within a few days. To refinance, a firm has to buy back its outstanding liabilities, which can be expensive, or wait until these liabilities mature. Then the firm must try to convince its regular lenders to provide a different type of funds. A thrift, for example, may have to expend much time, effort, and expense to convince its depositors of short-term funds to invest instead in long-term time deposits.

If a firm's regular customers are unwilling to provide, say, fixed-rate funds, the firm can look to alternative markets, such as the domestic or the Eurodollar bond market. Bond markets, however, are costly to use. Domestic bond markets, for one, are highly regulated. To issue a new domestic bond, a firm has to register with the Securities and Exchange Commission (SEC) and meet its disclosure requirements.[13] In addition, a prospective bond issuer is well-advised to obtain a credit rating from the major rating agencies, such as Moody's, or Standard and Poor's, which requires additional expense. The actual selling of a bond issue involves other costs such as advertising, legal fees, and an underwriting spread — that is, the difference between what the firm issuing the debt receives and the (higher) price that ultimate investors pay for the debt. This spread, which runs anywhere from 25 to 500 basis points and which averages about 80 basis points for investment grade debt, serves as payment to the underwriter (or underwriter's syndicate) for distributing the issue to the ultimate investors, and for committing himself to buy that part of the issue that is not bought by the public at a given price.

As an alternative to the domestic bond market, a firm also can try the Eurodollar bond market. Eurodollar bonds are dollar-denominated bonds issued by international syndicates anywhere outside the United States. The Eurobond market has the advantage that it is almost totally

---

[13] Under SEC rule 415 firms can shortcut the normally lengthy registration procedure by filing a single registration statement covering securities they expect to sell from time to time within two years. These firms can then sell securities "off the shelf" whenever they choose. However, this procedure is only available to the largest and most creditworthy corporations.

unregulated (that is, there are almost no registration or disclosure requirements), so that issuing a bond does not take a lot of time. On the negative side, however, underwriting spreads on Eurodollar bonds are three to four times those on domestic bond issues. Also, because there are no disclosure requirements in Eurobond markets, investors are reluctant to lend to firms that do not have an excellent credit rating. Therefore, for relatively unknown firms the Eurodollar bond market is even less accessible than the domestic bond market.

The existence of interest rate swaps makes it possible for firms to borrow in the markets in which they have a comparative advantage rather than refinancing in markets in which they don't. These firms can then swap interest payments with firms that have a comparative advantage in another market to achieve the interest payments characteristics they desire. Comparative advantage can take the form of lower interest costs and lower transactions costs. Such lower costs can be the result of name recognition, an established retail network for issuing liabilities, government subsidies and regulations, or other attributes associated with borrowing or lending in certain markets. For example, international banks have the name recognition that allows them to borrow in the Eurodollar market. Domestic banks and thrifts, on the other hand, have the retail network and deposit insurance that give them a comparative advantage in attracting retail savings-type deposits. Interest rate swaps allow banks and thrifts to protect themselves against interest rate risk without having to give up the retail (short-term) savings market in which most of them specialize.

Summary

The high interest rate volatility of recent years has induced many firms to look for ways to protect their profit margins — to hedge — against interest rate fluctuations. A recent and popular technique is the interest rate swap, in which different parties *in effect* swap the interest rate payments on each other's liabilities. An interest rate swap typically allows a firm with floating-rate liabilities to exchange its floating-rate interest payments with another party for fixed-rate payments, thereby effectively acquiring a fixed-rate cost of borrowing.

In only a few years, interest rate swaps have become very popular hedging instruments because frequently they are better suited or less expensive than other hedging techniques, such as purchasing interest rate futures or refinancing the firm's debt. Because interest rate futures are standardized products traded on an organized market, they are inexpensive to use. But because of their standardization, they do not always meet a firm's specific requirements to hedge its interest rate risk exposure. In particular, futures have delivery dates only out to 2-1/2 years, while there is no such limit for swaps. Swaps are freely negotiated agreements between private parties, and, therefore, they can be tailor-made. But this customization makes swaps more expensive to use than futures.

Interest rate swaps can also be very useful when the high costs of entering a market as a new borrower make it too expensive for a firm to obtain directly the type of financing it needs to achieve its desired interest risk exposure. A firm may find that attracting fixed-rate financing in the bond market, for example, is very costly because of high underwriting fees, disclosure costs, or the high risk premium that relatively unknown borrowers may have to pay. An interest rate swap allows a firm to exchange interest flows in order to achieve the desired characteristics of its interest payments without changing the structure of its balance sheet. Interest rate swaps are thus an indirect way of entering financial markets in situations where firms find it very costly to obtain financing directly.

Questions

1.   Company A and Company B have assets and liabilities described as follows:

Company	Assets	Liabilities
A	Fixed rate	Floating rate
B	Floating rate	Fixed rate

Which company gains when interest rates rise unexpectedly? Explain.

2.   Explain how Company A and Company B in the preceding question could benefit from an interest rate swap with each other.

3.   Company A (in Question 1) could hedge its position by selling interest rate futures — say, a contract to deliver sometime in the future a Treasury bill. Then, if interest rates rise, the market value of the T-bill falls, and Company A makes a profit. This profit offsets the increased cost of Company A's liabilities. Explain how Company B can use interest rate futures to hedge its position.

4.   What are the advantages and disadvantages of interest rate swaps in comparison to interest rate futures, for hedging purposes?

5.   Company C pays 2 percentage points above the 3-month T-bill rate on its liabilities. It would prefer to finance its assets with a fixed-rate bond, but it would have to pay 18 percent. Company D pays 1 percentage point above the 3-month T-bill rate on its liabilities. Company D can issue fixed-rate bonds at 14 percent, if it so chooses. Describe an interest rate swap between Companies C and D wherein they both appear to benefit.

PART V
ANALYZING AND PLANNING
FINANCIAL PERFORMANCE

Financial Analysis among the Fortune 500 Firms

Alan K. Reichert and James S. Moore

Introduction

Financial analysis has the potential for providing a rigorous foundation for financial decision-making at all levels of business organization. The fundamental goal frequently associated with management in the United States is to direct the operations of their firm in a manner consistent with shareholder wealth maximization. This goal has important financial implications regarding the securing of funds at the lowest possible cost and the allocation of funds across a wide range of investment opportunities in an attempt to optimize the fundamental risk/return trade-off.

The use of financial analysis techniques should not be viewed as a goal in itself, but as a vehicle for making sound financial decisions which contribute to general corporate objectives. The academic community has assisted in the development of a wide range of analytical tools for financial analysis. The ascent of university-trained corporate managers into positions with significant decision-making authority has created the opportunity to fuse "classroom theory" and "boardroom reality." The intent of this study is to investigate the extent and manner in which modern financial management techniques are being employed by the nation's largest corporations. More specifically, the research was designed to answer the following key questions:

- Do specific industries more actively employ certain analytical tools?

- Are larger firms with potential economies-of-scale more likely to adopt sophisticated financial management techniques?

- To what extent do firms employ capital budgeting techniques which incorporate the time value of money?

Alan K. Reichert and James S. Moore, "Financial Analysis among the Fortune 500 Firms," *Journal of Cash Management* (November/December 1984): 26–31. Reprinted with permission of the *Journal of Cash Management*.

At the time of this writing, Alan K. Reichert was affiliated with Illinois State University and James S. Moore was affiliated with Indiana University–Purdue University at Fort Wayne.

Exhibit 1   Utilization Rates for Selected Financial Techniques

	Total Number Responding
A. Which of the following financial techniques are commonly used to evaluate *division performance*?	
1) Profit margin on sales	266
2) Return on assets or ROI	281
3) Financial ratio analysis	232

	Total Number Responding
B. *Working Capital Techniques*	
1) Projected cash budget	298
2) Breakeven analysis	298
3) Analysis of financial and operating leverage	298
4) Sales forecasting models	298
5) Sources and uses of funds	298
6) Cash management models	298
7) Inventory management models	298
8) Statistical credit scoring models	298
C. *Capital Budgeting Techniques*	
1) Average rate of return	298
2) Payback period	298
3) Net present value	298
4) Internal rate of return	298
5) At least one of AROR* or Payback	298
6) At least one of NPV or IRR	298
D. *Forecasting/Operations Research Techniques*	
1) Macro-economic modeling and simulation	298
2) Project/product financial analysis and modeling	298
3) Optimal transportation modeling	298
4) Linear programming**	261
5) Goal programming**	261
6) Program evaluation and review techniques (PERT)**	261

* Average rate of return.

** These techniques were included in the later surveys only.

- To what extent do major corporations employ a wide variety of analytical techniques in the financial decision making process?

Sampling Procedure

In order to determine what important techniques are currently employed by corporate managers, several surveys of major U.S. corporations were made during 1980 and 1981. A questionnaire addressed to the chief financial officer was sent to the corporate headquarters of each firm on the May 1980 Fortune 500 list. The survey sought to establish a basic profile

Use of Technique	
Yes (percent)	No (percent)
94.0	6.0
94.3	5.7
75.4	24.6

Extent of Use		
Frequently (percent)	Seldom (percent)	Never (percent)
91.9	5.4	2.7
37.9	50.0	12.1
59.7	30.5	9.7
71.5	21.8	6.7
91.0	7.7	1.3
61.7	25.5	12.8
56.0	30.2	13.8
10.1	28.5	61.4
59.1	17.4	23.5
79.9	14.4	5.7
68.1	22.1	9.7
66.4	17.8	15.8
87.2	12.8	
86.2	13.8	
34.9	28.9	36.2
59.7	23.2	17.1
21.5	35.9	42.6
24.5	41.8	33.7
21.8	33.3	44.8
38.3	31.8	29.9

of the respondents' organizational structure and to identify the primary analytical tools used in risk assessment, working capital management, capital budgeting, and forecasting/operations research modeling. A total of 298 firms responded to the questionnaire for a 60 percent response rate. A breakdown of respondents by industry type and asset size indicates that the survey sample is representative of the population of Fortune 500 firms.

Survey Results

Survey data presented in Exhibit 1, Part A indicate that the vast majority of all respondents (95 percent) are organized along divisional lines. The number of distinct subsidiaries ranged anywhere from zero to over a thousand, with 19 being the median number. Divisional performance is evaluated by standard profit margin and return on investment techniques by virtually all respondents. A smaller proportion (75 percent) employ a more comprehensive program of financial ratio analysis. Other miscellaneous evaluation techniques were reported by 36 percent of the respondents. Cash flow analysis was the most common of these miscellaneous techniques. Furthermore, for those firms organized along divisional lines, virtually all operate each division as a distinct profit center and monitor division profitability on a monthly basis.

An examination of the utilization rates for specific working capital techniques in Part B of Exhibit 1 indicates the most frequent use of cash budgeting techniques and sources and uses of funds analysis. Frequent utilization of the remaining working capital techniques was reported by approximately 60 percent of the firms with the notable exception of breakeven analysis and statistical credit scoring models.

Examining the various financial techniques employed in long-term investment decisions (Part C of Exhibit 1), the most frequently used capital budgeting technique is the payback period. Almost 80 percent of the respondents indicated frequent use of this technique. On the other hand, given the large dollar amounts and long lives associated with major capital investment projects, some form of time-adjusted cash flow technique such as net present value (NPV) or internal rate of return (IRR) is useful in the measurement of relative project risk and return. Eighty-six percent of those responding acknowledged regular employment of at least one of these time-sensitive evaluation techniques. In the area of forecasting and operations research techniques, approximately 60 percent of the firms frequently conduct comprehensive project/product financial simulations (Part D of Exhibit 1). The remaining analytical techniques are regularly employed by only 20 to 40 percent of the respondents.

Industry Breakdown

The utilization of specific financial techniques was analyzed by industry groups to determine if certain categories were more likely to either under-utilize or to over-utilize formal quantitative methods. A cross tabulation of responses by industry identified ten financial techniques where the pattern of responses differed significantly. For each of these techniques, Exhibit 2 on pages 394–395 indicates the percentage of firms within a given industry that reported *frequent* use of that particular technique. For example, among firms in the food, beverage, and tobacco group, 33 percent indicated frequent use of breakeven analysis, 58 percent reported frequent use of sales forecasting models, etc. These industry specific utilization rates can be compared to the percentages at the bottom of each column which indicate the percent of all 298 respondents who regularly employ the specific financial technique in question.

The results appear to identify several industry groups which are unique. Industries which *under*-utilize modern financial techniques include textiles, apparel, and vinyl flooring; metal products fabrication; shipbuilding, railroads, and transportation equipment; and publishing. For example, the metal products fabrication industry is unique in its infrequent use of working capital techniques. The textile, apparel and vinyl flooring group plus the shipbuilding, railroads, and transportation equipment industry both reported a marked lack of interest in operations research procedures such as PERT, linear programming, and transportation modeling. These industry groups also reported infrequent use of time-adjusted capital budgeting techniques.

In contrast to the industry groups mentioned above, the respondents in the computer and office equipment industry appear to be leaders in the utilization of modern financial techniques. This group reported a utilization rate for all of the techniques of at least one standard deviation above the composite utilization rate. To illustrate, 100 percent of the sample reported using sales forecasting and inventory models, plus some form of time-adjusted capital budgeting technique (e.g., IRR, NPV) on a frequent basis. Furthermore, firms in the aerospace and motor vehicle industries, and the pharmaceutical, soap, and cosmetic groups reported above average utilization rates for a number of important financial techniques.

Firm Size

The sample was analyzed by firm size to test the hypothesis that firms with potential economies-of-scale are more likely to adopt sophisticated financial management tools. Exhibit 3 on pages 396–397 presents the statistical results for three asset size groups. The results indicate that out of the twenty-three techniques, eleven utilization rates appear to be *directly* related to firm size. Size related financial techniques include sales forecasting models, cash and inventory management models, statistical credit scoring models, internal rate of return, and all but one of the forecasting/operations research techniques (goal programming). Consider, for example, the use of IRR which is employed on a frequent basis by close to 66 percent of all respondents. The size analysis reveals that the percentage of firms which employ IRR on a frequent basis increases from 55% for the small size category to 71% for the medium size group, and 91% for the largest asset category. Only two techniques, profit margin analysis and payback period, appear to be inversely related to firm size and in both cases the decline in utilization rates is limited to the largest firms with assets in excess of $5 billion.

Bundling Analytical Techniques

In an effort to determine the extent to which firms employ a variety of formal procedures in their overall decision-making process, a large number of statistical cross tabulations were made between techniques

Exhibit 2   Percentage of Firms Indicating Frequent Use of Various Financial Techniques

Industry	Sample Size	Breakeven Analysis	Sales Forecast Models	Cash Management Models
Mining, Crude Oil	7	43	43*	43*
Food, Beverage, & Tobacco	40	33	58	53
Textile, Apparel, Vinyl Flooring	10	40	60	20*
Paper	13	23	62	69
Publishing	10	20*	70	60
Chemical	25	16*	84	56
Petrol. Refining	22	50	64	59
Rubber & Plastic	5	60*	100*	60
Glass, Concrete, Etc.	12	8*	83	100
Metal Manufacturing	24	33	71	67
Metal Products Fabrication	15	33	60	40*
Electronics and Appliances	21	29	88*	67
Shipping, Rail, Road, Etc.	6	50	33*	67
Scientific & Photo Equipment	11	46	82	73
Motor Vehicles	16	56*	88*	81*
Aerospace	7	43	71	57
Pharm., Soap & Cosmetics	14	57*	79	71
Office & Computer Equipment	8	63*	100*	100*
Industrial & Farm Equipment	23	57*	78	52
Music, Toys, Sporting Goods	2	50	100*	100*
Not Identified	7	43	43	57
Composite Rate	298	38%	72%	62%
Standard Deviation		14.7	14.7	16.0
Level of Significance (X^2)		0.4	.11	.10

* An asterisk indicates that the utilization rate for a specific industry is at least one standard deviation from the all industry composite utilization rate given at the end of the table. Contingency table tests using the Chi-square variable (X^2) are frequently used to determine whether or not a systematic relationship exists between two or more variables. This is accomplished by comparing observed cell frequencies with those that would be expected in the absence of a statistically significant relationship between the variables.

In Exhibit 2, a X^2 level of significance of 0.10 or less for a given column (i.e., a specific financial technique) indicates that significant differences between industries exist in terms of their utilization of that specific technique. A X^2 value greater than 0.10 suggests that little or no difference exists between industries.

within each of the major working capital, capital budgeting, and forecasting/operations research categories. In almost 80 percent of the cases the various techniques were interrelated in a statistically significant manner. While one cannot infer from these results that firms frequently employ several complementary financial techniques on the *same* project, the results do indicate that these firms frequently employ a variety of analytical tools in the financial decision-making process. In effect these firms have assembled what might be considered a "tool kit" of analytical techniques that are frequently used to analyze a number of key financial issues. Similar results were obtained for the various capital budgeting, forecasting, and operations research techniques.

Investment Management Models	Internal ROR	NPV or IRR	Macro Models	Transportation Models	Linear Programming	P.E.R.T.
43	86*	100*	29	43*	29	43
43	63	95	28	13	34	37
50	30*	50*	0*	0*	0*	11*
54	77	77	54	37	23	46
20*	90	90	30	0*	11	11*
48	80	92	52*	32	46*	38
64	73	91	36	41*	50*	45
80*	60	80	0*	20	0*	0*
42	58	83	50	25	18	45
42	54	8*	33	17	15	30
13*	33*	67*	20*	7*	8*	31
76*	71	86	43	10	6*	50
67	33*	67*	17*	17	0*	17*
82*	55	91	27	27	0*	33
75	75	94	69*	13	14	29
71	100*	100*	29	29	20	80*
79*	64	86	21	43*	42*	58*
88*	100*	100*	50	50*	60*	80*
78*	57	78	26	17	14	52
0*	100*	100*	50	0*	50*	0*
57	100	100	43	29	43	14
56%	66%	86%	35%	22%	25%	38%
20.0	17.3	11.0	15.2	13.1	17.1	16.1
.00	.09	.13	.00	.02	.11	.15

Analysis of utilization rates for techniques between major categories also provided consistent and statistically significant results. For example, the frequent use of operations research tools is strongly tied to that of the more sophisticated time-adjusted capital budgeting techniques. Furthermore, employment of selected working capital management procedures, namely sales forecasting and cash inventory management models, are also shown to be statistically linked to the use of at least one of the discounted cash flows techniques (NPV or IRR) and *all* of the operations research procedures. Thus, the results suggest that firms not only employ a variety of techniques within a given analytical category but frequently utilize analytical techniques from among several different categories.

Summary

The survey results are consistent with the hypothesis that strong emphasis is being placed upon rigorous financial analysis in today's high risk, increasingly competitive corporate environment. Furthermore, there

Exhibit 3   Survey Results by Firm Size

	$0-1 Billion (143 Firms)		$1-5 Billion (115 Firms)	

A. Which of the following techniques are commonly used to evaluate division performance?

	Yes	No	Yes	No
1) Profit margin	97.7%	2.3%	95.0%	5.0%
2) Return on Assets or ROI	93.3	6.7	94.4	5.6
3) Financial Ratio Analysis	72.2	27.8	79.6	20.4

B. Working Capital Techniques

Percent of Respondents Indicating "Frequent" Use of Various Financial Techniques

1) Projected cash budget	90.2	93.9
2) Breakeven analysis	32.2	40.9
3) Financial and operating leverage analysis	58.0	60.9
4) Sales forecasting models	66.4	76.5
5) Sources and uses of funds	88.1	92.2
6) Cash management models	52.4	68.7
7) Inventory management models	46.9	61.7
8) Statistical credit scoring models	3.5	14.8

C. Capital Budgeting Techniques

1) Average rate of return	58.0	60.9
2) Payback period	81.1	81.7
3) Net present value	67.8	64.3
4) Internal rate of return	55.2	71.3
5) At least one of ARR or payback	88.1	87.8
6) At least one of NPV or IRR	81.8	87.8

D. Forecasting and Operations Research Techniques

1) Macro-economic modeling and simulation	23.8	40.9
2) Project/product financial analysis and modeling	53.1	61.7
3) Optimal transportation modeling	9.1	28.7
4) Linear programming	14.8	29.5
5) Goal programming	18.5	28.4
6) Program evaluation and review techniques	29.6	48.4

* In Exhibit 3, a X^2 level of significance of 0.10 or less for a given row (i.e., specific financial technique) indicates that significant differences exist between the three categories of firm size in terms of their utilization of that specific technique. A X^2 value greater than 0.10 suggests that little or no size relationship exists.

appears to be a high degree of compatibility between the financial techniques employed by practitioners and those advocated by academics. Major U.S. corporations are making financial decisions with the aid of a relatively wide range of modern management techniques. On the other hand, the movement to implement new financial techniques has developed somewhat unevenly with certain industries more actively involved than others. For example, industries producing office equipment and computers, soap, cosmetics, pharmaceuticals, motor vehicles, and

Over $5 Billion (32 Firms)		Composite Results (290 Firms)		Summary Statistics*		
				X^2	Degree of Freedom	Significance

A. Which of the following techniques are commonly used to evaluate division performance?

Yes	No	Yes	No			
78.6%	21.4%	94.6%	5.4%	16.43	2	.0003
96.7	3.3	94.1	5.9	.52	2	.7693
73.9	26.1	75.4	24.6	1.49	2	.4750

B. Working Capital Techniques

Percent of Respondents Indicating "Frequent" Use of Various Financial Techniques

93.8		92.1		5.61	4	.2303
53.1		37.9		6.18	4	.1859
59.4		59.3		1.33	4	.8562
81.3		72.1		9.11	4	.0585
100		91.0		4.83	4	.3048
78.1		61.7		12.75	4	.0125
75.0		55.9		11.20	4	.0244
21.9		10.0		15.04	4	.0046
56.3		59.0		.40	4	.9825
71.9		80.3		3.08	4	.5447
78.1		67.6		4.73	4	.3160
90.6		65.5		18.35	4	.0011
81.3		87.2		1.16	2	.5586
96.9		85.9		5.49	2	.0643
59.4		34.5		22.73	4	.0001
81.3		59.7		11.65	4	.0201
50.0		21.4		42.29	4	.0000
56.5		24.1		27.18	4	.0000
21.7		22.5		6.23	4	.1824
52.2		38.7		13.08	4	.0109

aerospace products appear to be leaders in the adoption of comprehensive financial techniques. The metal products fabrication, textile, apparel and vinyl flooring industries appear substantially less committed to such techniques.

Furthermore, many firms employ a variety of analytical tools. As firms begin to introduce formal techniques in one area there is a strong likelihood that they will begin to employ sophisticated analytical tools in other areas as well.

In summary, this study has concentrated on the major U.S. corporations that comprise the Fortune 500 list and found them to be active, yet selective users of formal analytical procedures as aids in their financial and operational decision-making.

Questions

1. Which working-capital techniques are used most frequently by U.S. companies? Which technique is used least frequently?

2. Describe the frequency of corporate use of the following techniques: (a) payback period, (b) net present value, (c) internal rate of return, (d) linear programming, and (e) PERT.

3. Industrial leaders in the use of modern financial techniques appear to be office equipment manufacturers, aerospace and motor vehicle companies, and pharmaceutical companies. Industries showing less interest in these techniques include textiles, metal products fabrication, shipbuilding, and publishing. In your opinion, what accounts for the difference between these two groups in the use of modern financial techniques?

4. The use rate of forecasting and operations research techniques increases with the size of corporations. Explain what might account for this relationship.

Cash Flows, Ratio Analysis and the W. T. Grant Company Bankruptcy

James A. Largay III and
Clyde P. Stickney

Although they surfaced as a gusher rather than a trickle, the problems that brought the W. T. Grant Company into bankruptcy and, ultimately, liquidation, did not develop overnight. Whereas traditional ratio analysis of Grant's financial statements would not have revealed the existence of many of the company's problems until 1970 or 1971, careful analysis of the company's cash flows would have revealed impending doom as much as a decade before the collapse.

Grant's profitability, turnover and liquidity ratios had trended downward over the 10 years preceding bankruptcy. But the most striking characteristic of the company during that decade was that it generated no cash internally. Although working capital provided by operations remained fairly stable through 1973, this figure (which constitutes net income plus depreciation and is frequently referred to in the financial press as "cash flow") can be a very poor indicator of a company's ability to generate cash. Through 1973, the W. T. Grant Company's operations were a net user, rather than provider, of cash.

Grant's continuing inability to generate cash from operations should have provided investors with an early signal of problems. Yet, as recently as 1973, Grant stock was selling at nearly 20 times earnings.

James A. Largay III and Clyde P. Stickney, "Cash Flows, Ratio Analysis and the W. T. Grant Company Bankruptcy," *Financial Analysts Journal* (July/August 1980): 51–54. Reprinted with permission.

James Largay is Professor of Accounting at the College of Business and Economics, Lehigh University. This article was written while he was Coopers & Lybrand Visiting Associate Professor of Accounting at The Amos Tuck School of Business Administration, Dartmouth College. Clyde Stickney is Associate Professor of Accounting at The Amos Tuck School of Business Administration, Dartmouth College. The authors thank the Tuck Associates Program for its financial support.

Investors placed a much higher value on Grant's prospects than an analysis of the company's cash flow from operations would have warranted.

The W. T. Grant Company was the nation's largest retailer when it filed for protection of the Court under Chapter XI of the National Bankruptcy Act on October 2, 1975. Only four months later, the creditors' committee voted for liquidation, and Grant ceased to exist. The collapse of Grant is a business policy professor's dream—ambiguous marketing strategy, personnel compensation based on questionable incentive schemes, financially and administratively unsound credit operations, centralization versus decentralization issues and poorly conceived and poorly executed long-range plans. Problems of this magnitude do not develop overnight, although they often surface as a gusher rather than a trickle.

As we will show, a traditional ratio analysis of Grant's financial statements would not have suggested the existence of many of these problems until approximately 1970 or 1971. As recently as 1973, Grant stock was selling at nearly 20 times earnings. Perhaps investors believed that Grant would continue to prosper despite many years of consistent but lackluster performance; after all, the company had been in existence since the turn of the century, paying dividends regularly from 1906 until August 27, 1974. But Grant's demise should not have come as a surprise to anyone following its fortunes closely; a careful analysis of the company's cash flows would have revealed the impending problems as much as a decade before the collapse.

Stock Prices and Ratio Analysis

Prior to 1971, Grant's stock had tended to perform like other variety store chain stocks. Beginning in June or July of 1971, however, the stock price performance of Grant and the other variety chains parted ways.

Exhibit I presents data on monthly closing prices and various ratios from Grant's financial statements for the 10 years preceding bankruptcy in 1975. The top panel shows the December 31 closing price for Grant's stock for each year expressed as a ratio of the closing price on December 31, 1964 (i.e., the December 31, 1964 closing price equals 100). It also shows the values of the Standard & Poor's Variety Chain Stock Price Index and the Standard & Poor's 500 Composite Stock Price Index at the end of each year, each expressed as a ratio of its value on December 31, 1964.

The bottom four panels in Exhibit I show the trends in Grant's profitability, turnover, liquidity and solvency ratios over the fiscal periods between 1966 and 1975 (ending January 31 of each year). The profitability, turnover and liquidity ratios trended downward over this 10-year period. The solvency ratios reflect increasing proportions of liabilities in the capital structure. The most significant deterioration in these ratios,

Exhibit I W. T. Grant Company Stock Prices and Selected Ratios for the Fiscal Years Ending January 31, 1966 to 1975

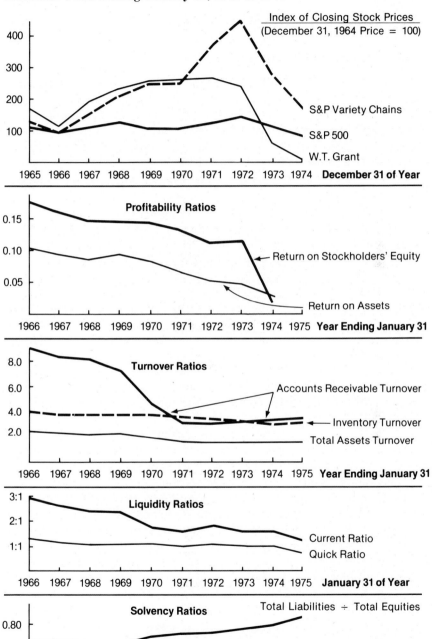

however, occurred during the 1970 and 1971 fiscal periods, leading the stock market's recognition of Grant's problems by approximately one year.

Net Income and Cash Flows

The most striking characteristic of the Grant Company during the decade before its bankruptcy was that it generated virtually no cash internally. The company simply lost its ability to derive cash from operations. After exhausting the possibilities of its liquid resources, it had to tap external markets for funds. As the failure to generate cash internally continued, the need for external financing snowballed.

Most textbooks in corporate finance, investments and financial statement analysis devote little attention to computing or using cash flow from operations. Yet the calculations are straightforward enough. One starts with working capital provided by operations from the statement of changes in financial position, adds changes in current asset accounts (other than cash) that decreased and current liability accounts that increased and subtracts changes in current asset accounts (other than cash) that increased and current liability accounts that decreased. In accounting terms, the calculation is equivalent to adding credit changes in working capital accounts and subtracting debit changes. Exhibit II summarizes the process of converting working capital provided by operations to cash flow provided by operations.

Exhibit III graphs Grant's net income, working capital provided by operations and cash flow provided by operations for the 1966 to 1975 fiscal periods. Note how poorly working capital provided by operations correlates with cash flow from operations. The financial press frequently refers to "cash flow," defined as net income plus depreciation. This measure of cash flow approximates working capital provided by operations, which (as Exhibit III shows) may prove a very poor surrogate for the cash flow actually generated by operations.

While Grant's net income was relatively steady through the 1973 period, operations were a net user, rather than provider, of cash in all but two years (1968 and 1969). Even in these two years, operations provided only insignificant amounts of cash. Grant's continuing inability to generate cash from operations should have provided investors with an early signal of problems.

Was the Market for Grant Stock Efficient?

In an efficient market, stock prices continually reflect all publicly available information about a company's past performance and future prospects. The evidence presented here, however, seems to suggest that the W.T. Grant Company was a counterexample to market efficiency.

Exhibit II   Computing Cash Flow Provided by Operations from Published Financial Statements

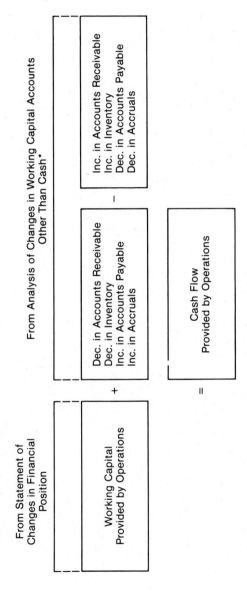

* Accounts such as "Bank Loans" and "Current Portion of Long-Term Debt" must be excluded from the analysis. Even though treated as current liabilities, they represent neither cash provided nor cash used by operations.

Exhibit III   **W. T. Grant Company Net Income, Working Capital and Cash Flow from Operations for Fiscal Years Ending January 31, 1966 to 1975**

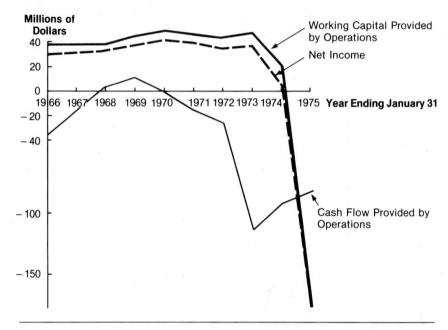

Operations were a net user of cash in eight of Grant's last 10 years. Between January 31, 1966 and January 31, 1973, Grant's sales nearly doubled, but its earnings and earnings per share remained virtually unchanged. Despite its failure to translate vastly increased sales into additional profits, Grant's price-earnings ratio on January 31, 1973 was about twice what it had been on January 31, 1966.

We compared Grant's price-earnings ratios with those of similar variety chains (Kresge, McCrory, Murphy and Woolworth) over the 1965–75 period. Until 1973, Grant's price-earnings multiple tended to exceed the multiples of the other variety chains, with the exception of Kresge. Traders in Grant stock during the company's last decade placed a much higher value on Grant's prospects than an analysis of the company's cash flow from operations would have warranted.

Questions

1.   W. T. Grant filed for bankruptcy in 1975 and was liquidated in 1976. In what year did investors recognize the severity of W. T. Grant's problems? What evidence supports your answer?

2.   In what year did traditional financial ratios indicate the severity of W. T. Grant's problems? What evidence supports your answer?

3.   Based on your answers to Questions 1 and 2, do you think that investors were too slow in recognizing W. T. Grant's problems? Explain.

4.   Define the term *cash flow provided by operations*.

5.   Describe the pattern before bankruptcy of W. T. Grant's cash flow provided by operations.

6.   Was the market for W. T. Grant's common stock efficient? Explain.

Financial Statement Analysis — A Two-Minute Drill

William L. Stone

Commercial loan officers often face the situation where they would like to make a quick appraisal of a financial statement. Some loan requests, for example, can be declined in short order because the financial statements reflect a weak condition. However, loan officers must have the skill to focus on those factors that would reveal that further discussion is fruitless. More important, they should be able to develop several pertinent questions regarding the problem areas of a company's operation as revealed by a brief analysis of the financial statements.

It is not uncommon for a loan applicant to present a loan officer with two or three years of financial statements in support of an application being presented orally. The loan officer does not have the luxury of analyzing the statements thoroughly while the applicant patiently sits in silence. The applicant, of course, is anxious and apprehensive about laying out the company's financial history to the banker. Most applicants can tolerate a minute or two of idleness while the loan officer reviews the statements. The limit, however, is about two minutes.

Within that two-minute period, the loan officer should be able to make an analysis that is thorough enough to reveal the company's problem areas on which the subsequent questioning should focus. This article will explain how those two minutes can be spent most efficiently so that the loan officer will have a clear picture of the company's financial strengths and weaknesses.

William L. Stone, "Financial Statement Analysis — A Two-Minute Drill," *The Journal of Commercial Bank Lending* (November 1983): 11–19. Copyright 1983 by Robert Morris Associates. Reprinted with permission from *The Journal of Commercial Bank Lending*, November 1983.

At the time of this writing, William L. Stone was a vice president at Bank of the West, San Jose, California.

Cautions

Several cautions, while obvious, require emphasis before proceeding. First, the two-minute drill that is presented here should not be taken as a substitute for a thorough analysis of the credit once the applicant has left the bank. Loan officers should not permit themselves to fall into the trap of thinking that they have completely analyzed the financial statements once they have completed the two-minute drill.

Second, the analysis suggested here does not concern itself with nonfinancial factors such as management quality, market, products, prospects, the economy, and a myriad of other factors that are crucial to the success of every business. This system of analysis relates only to relationships of figures on the financial statements.

Third, since speed is of the essence in this analysis, rough rounding off is recommended. For example, $93,439 may be appropriately rounded off to $90,000 or even $100,000. Further, it is not important that the classification of assets and liabilities as current or noncurrent be carefully scrutinized. If, for instance, the statement shows prepaid assets of $18,713 as a current asset and it is your bank's practice to treat prepaid assets as noncurrent, it is not important, unless the amount is unusually large, that the current assets as shown on the statement be adjusted for the purposes of this analysis. One could argue that accuracy will suffer at the expense of speed, but as will be seen, we will work with estimates as indications of problem areas.

Fourth, there appears to be, in the writer's experience, some differences throughout the country about standards of liquidity, leverage, and profitability. Readers should establish their own standards if those suggested here are significantly different from their own. Keep in mind, however, that the standards presented here lend themselves to the computations.

Six Standards for Comparison

Three ratios—current, debt-to-worth, and net profit margin—and three turnovers—receivables, inventory, and payables—form the basis of the two minute drill. These six relationships (turnovers are often referred to as ratios, but in the strictest sense, they are not ratios) were selected for several reasons. First, they are important indicators of a specific aspect of a company's financial condition. Second, taken together, they are indicative of the three important areas for credit purposes: liquidity, leverage, and profitability. Third, we can establish a standard that is easy to compute and understand against which a company's performance can be measured.

It is the third factor that is essential to this system of analysis. Loan officers often hedge on the subject of an acceptable or unsatisfactory figure for a given ratio with the comment that "every business is different.'' While it is true that every business is different, it is also true that the performance of a wide range of companies can be compared to a series of standards in an effort to establish a line of inquiry for the loan officer. The point, of course, is that management may have an entirely reasonable explanation for the company's performance being substantially different from the standard. If, though, the loan officer did not have the standard as a means of comparison, the difference in the company's operation might not have been revealed.

It is, then, the thesis of this article that by comparing the company's three ratios and three turnovers to the standards explained here, we will determine quickly what areas of the company's operation require further inquiry. The advantage of the system of analysis suggested here is that after studying the statements for less than two minutes, loan officers will be able to ask some pertinent questions about the business in the initial interview, even if they have never seen the applicant or the statements before.

Refer to Table 1 for a summary balance sheet and profit and loss statement for Wobbly Widgets, Inc., which will be used as the statement to be analyzed. Each of the ratios and turnovers will be discussed. First,

Table 1   **Wobbly Widgets, Inc.**

Balance Sheet
December 31, 1982

Assets		Liabilities and Net Worth	
Cash	$ 18.3	Accounts Payable	$ 87.8
Accounts Receivable	248.6	Notes Payable	32.0
Inventory	77.4	Current Portion Term Debt	22.6
Prepaid Assets	10.0	Accrued Liabilities	13.7
Current Assets	354.3	Current Liabilities	156.1
Fixed Assets (net)	210.0	Term Debt	110.0
Total Assets	$564.3	Total Liabilities	266.1
		Net Worth	298.2
		Total Liabilities & Net Worth	$564.3

Profit and Loss Statement
for the Twelve-Month Period Ended December 31, 1982

Sales	$1,314.6
Cost of Goods Sold	739.2
Gross Profit	575.4
Operating Expenses	448.1
Operating Profit	127.3
Income Taxes	53.6
Net Income	$ 73.7

the standard for each will be established. Second, the fastest method for mentally computing the ratio or turnover will be explained. Since the use of even a small, hand calculator might intimidate the applicant, it is recommended that the loan officer develop the skill to make the computations mentally. After some practice, the calculations suggested here can be made faster mentally than by using a calculator.

Current Ratio

The generally accepted standard for the current ratio—current assets divided by current liabilities—is 2.0. In practice, a current ratio of 2.0 appears to be more of a goal, or comfort figure, than a minimally accepted standard, but it does serve as a good figure to use as a standard.

To compute the current ratio mentally, it is best to look first at current liabilities, round it off, and double that figure. For Wobbly Widgets, current liabilities rounded off is 160. Twice 160 is 320. If current assets were 320, the current ratio would be 2.0. Current assets, though, total 354.3. An estimate of the current ratio is 2.1. If current assets were between 160.0 and 320.0, the current ratio would be between 1.0 and 2.0. The lending officer must estimate the current ratio, but it is important to recognize that the precise calculation is simply irrelevant. Rather, we wish to estimate the current ratio (and all of the other ratios presented here) as an indication of whether or not there is a problem in the company's financial health. Once you have estimated the current ratio, jot it down (see Table 2) and go on to the next ratio, keeping in mind that a current ratio of 2.1 indicates a satisfactory position.

Notice that we looked at current liabilities before current assets. The rationale for this approach is that it is easier to double a number than it is to divide it by two. If we looked at current assets first, we would have to divide it by two, mentally, to establish a point of reference. Certainly, we could use that approach, but since our overriding objective is to make the analysis quickly, we should pick the easiest type of computation. In this case, multiplying is easier than dividing.

Debt-to-Worth Ratio

As with the current ratio, the standard for the debt-to-worth ratio is 2.0. However, of the six relationships we will study, this one will cause the greatest disagreement about the standard. Some banks will probably not entertain the application of a company whose ratio is as high as 2.0, whereas other banks consider 4.0 an acceptable figure.

First, look at total liabilities. On most CPA-prepared statements, a total liabilities figure is not shown, so the first step is to add up current liabilities and noncurrent liabilities. Second, is total liabilities more than or less than net worth (compute and use tangible net worth if there is a significant amount of intangible assets)? If total liabilities and net worth are approximately the same, determine whether the ratio should be .9 or

1.1, jot it down, and go on to the next ratio. If total liabilities are significantly more than net worth, round off the net worth figure and double it. What, then, is the relationship between total liabilities and two times net worth? The process is one of narrowing down total liabilities to an approximate multiple of net worth.

In the case of Wobbly Widgets, net worth is slightly more than total liabilities, so the approximate ratio is .9. If total liabilities were 512.0, for example, we would estimate debt to worth at 1.7 (500 ÷ 300), indicating that total liabilities were somewhat less than twice net worth. Again, jot down the estimated debt-to-worth figure and go on to the next ratio.

Net Profit Margin

The generally accepted average for net profit margin—net profit divided by net sales—is 5%, which will serve as a good standard for our purposes. The computation of the net profit margin is the most difficult relationship to compute mentally. The first step is to round off net sales. In the case of Wobbly Widgets, we should use 1,300 as the sales figure. The next step is to move the decimal point two places to the left, or 13 in this case. If net profit were 13, then the net profit margin would be 1%. In our case, net profit is significantly more than 13. Two approaches are possible at this point. The first one is to move the decimal point on the sales figure one place to the left, or 130, which represents 10% net profit, and compare it to the actual figure. A second approach is to divide 13 into 70. In Wobbly's case, 13 cannot be easily divided into 70 mentally, so we should return to the first approach. We observe that the actual figure 70 is well below the 10% figure of 130. Half of 130, or 10% of sales, is 65, which would represent 5% of sales. Since our net profit figure is 70, net profit is approximately 6% of sales. The actual net profit margin (73.7 divided by 1314.6) is 5.61%, which makes our 6% estimate correct for our purposes.

Again, the mental computation of the net profit margin is the most difficult of the six relationships discussed here. It is the writer's experience that the computation is often intimidating to many people, particularly those who do not feel proficient at math. In this case, however, the concept is not difficult; it is the mechanics that cause the difficulty. Once the concept is understood, practice is all it takes to make a reasonably accurate and quick estimate of the net profit margin.

Accounts Receivable Turnover

The accounts receivable turnover compares accounts receivable to sales. Generally it is assumed that all sales are on a credit basis. If loan officers have information to the contrary, they should adjust the sales figure accordingly to reflect only credit sales. There are several ways to compute the accounts receivable turnover. The computation used here will be accounts receivable divided by sales times the number of days in the period covered by the profit and loss statement. For annual statements, 360 days is used as the number of days in a year. The other turnovers are computed in the same manner. The resulting answer is expressed in days and is intended to represent the average amount of time that each dollar of receivables (and inventory and payables) stays on the books.

From time to time, significant variances occur in these accounts in a given company and within industries. Furthermore, it must be remembered that the figure shown on the balance sheet may or may not be representative of the average level of receivables (or inventory or payables) during the year. These possible distortions notwithstanding, we can establish our standard for all three turnovers as 36 days. As a practical matter, 36 days would generally indicate a very favorable turnover, which should be considered when comparing the actual figures to our standard.

Since the computation of the turnovers is a two-step process, mental computation would be very difficult. We can, however, simplify the process. First, round off the sales figure and move the decimal one place to the left. The resulting number, 130 in Wobbly's case, represents 10% of sales. Since annual sales, 1,300 for Wobbly, represents 360 days of sales, receivables of 130 would represent 36 days of sales. Second, compare the 10% of sales figure (130) to accounts receivable. Wobbly's accounts receivable are 248.6, or almost twice as much as the 10% figure. Therefore, accounts receivable are remaining on the books for an average of slightly less than the 72 days. The writer recommends rounding off turnovers to multiples of five days. In this case, if Wobbly's accounts receivable were 125.0, 35 days would be a reasonable estimate. If they were 300.0, 80 days—slightly more than twice 36 days—would be a reasonable estimate.

Inventory Turnover

As noted above, the computation of the inventory turnover is similar to the accounts receivable turnover. The only difference is that inventory is compared to cost of goods sold. The computation is otherwise the same. First, round off cost of sales and move the decimal one place to the left. The resulting number, 74 in Wobbly's case, represents 10% of the cost of sales. Disregarding seasonal factors, the first 74 of cost of sales expense should be incurred in the first 10%, or 36 days, of the year. If, then, Wobbly's inventory were 74, we could conclude that the company had inventory on hand 36 days.

Such a conclusion presumes one additional factor. The inventory (and accounts payable) turnover should compare inventory (and accounts payable) to purchases. In a number of cases, however, the purchases figure is not available. In other cases, it can only be found in a supplemental schedule or in the footnotes. Further, over the period of a year, the difference between purchases and cost of sales does not generally vary significantly. As a result, most analysts use the cost of sales when computing inventory and accounts payable turnovers. For our purpose, the accuracy achieved in using the purchases figure will usually not justify the time required to find that figure.

In the case of Wobbly, inventory is slightly more than 10% of cost of sales, so we can estimate Wobbly's inventory turnover to be 40 days. If inventory were 150, we would estimate the turnover to be 50 days. The key element of the computation is to compare 10% of the annual cost of sales to the actual inventory figure, remembering that 10% of the annual cost of sales represents 36 days.

Accounts Payable Turnover

To estimate the accounts payable turnover, compare the same 10% of the annual cost of sales figure to actual accounts payable and estimate the turnover. If, for example, the accounts payable figure were 74, we would conclude that on the average, accounts payable are paid when they are 36 days old. In Wobbly's case, accounts payable total 88, so we would estimate the turnover to be 45 days.

Analysis

The writer suggests that loan officers have a simple worksheet available that looks like Table 2.

A quick glance at Table 2 reveals that the company's financial condition for 1982 is pretty much in line except for the accounts receivable. The trap into which many loan officers fall is to stop once a chart such as Table 2, or a spread sheet, is completed. On the contrary, no analysis has been accomplished yet. The numbers do not have any meaning until the loan officer understands what the numbers mean. What, for instance, do the numbers in Table 2 indicate about the company's liquidity, leverage, and profitability? What problems—and therefore what areas of further inquiry—are indicated by the figures in Tables 1 and 2?

It should occur to readers that unless they go through an exercise such as the two-minute drill, they will have difficulty knowing what line

Table 2   **Sample Worksheet**

	1980	1981	1982
CR			2.1
D/W			0.9
NPM			5%
AR T/O			70
INV T/O			40
AP T/O			45

of inquiry to pursue. The two-minute drill gives the loan officer the opportunity to focus on those areas of apparent weakness. An important side benefit is that the applicant realizes right away that the loan officer "understands" the applicant's business because he can ask direct, pertinent questions after only a brief review of the statements, for example, "What is your difficulty in collecting the money owed to you?" "Do you have a lot of obsolete inventory?" "Are you being pressured by your trade creditors to bring your payables current?"

Conclusion

It is worth emphasizing again the cautions that appear near the beginning of this article. Briefly, the two-minute drill is not intended to be a substitute for a thorough analysis of a credit. Rather, it provides quick estimates of several important financial relationships that can serve as a basis for inquiries in the early stages of the application process.

Initially, the shortcuts presented here might appear to be too complex to be of any value. They are not. *Every* loan officer should be able to develop the skill to complete the two-minute drill for a single statement in less than two minutes. Once loan officers have developed that skill, they will conduct more effective and productive initial interviews and will increase their own level of self-confidence in dealing with applicants. Try it. It will work.

Questions

1.   Use the financial data for Wobbly Widgets, Inc. to calculate the following ratios: (a) current ratio, (b) debt-equity ratio, (c) after-tax profit margin, (d) average collection period, (e) days' sales in inventory, and (f) average payables period. (Note: These financial ratios are the same as those suggested by the author; the names used here reflect common usage among analysts.)

2.   According to the author, what values for the financial ratios in Question 1 should be used in the "Two-Minute Drill?"

3.   BFM Company's balance sheet for the year ending December 31, 19X9, is as follows:

Cash	$ 14,000	Accounts payable	$ 70,000
Receivables	130,000	Other current	35,000
Inventory	150,000		
		Current liabilities	$105,000
Current assets	$294,000	Long-term debt	160,000
Fixed assets (net)	300,000		
		Total debt	$265,000
Total assets	$594,000	Common equity	329,000
		Total claims	$594,000

BFM's sales for the year were $1,100,000; cost of goods sold equaled $800,000; and earnings after taxes were $50,000. Use the "Two-Minute Drill" to assess BFM's financial strengths and weaknesses. Note: (a) Do not use a calculator or formal calculations; make mental calculations only. (b) Time yourself; try to do the exercise in two minutes!

Business Credit Skills

Anthony Alan Kelley

In the last 20 years, commercial credit evaluation has evolved from an intuitive art shrouded in mystique to a developing quantitative science. Commercial credit executives have gained new insights into financial analysis and have had to come to grips with both quantitative and weighted quantitative analysis. They no longer rely on vague generalities that once characterized the art of credit decision-making and are beginning to design sophisticated computer models based on quantitative research using techniques like multiple discriminant analysis (MDA).

Traditionally, credit execs have concentrated on the four C's of credit: character, capacity, capital and condition, or have been financial statement arithmetic buffs. All one had to do was assess the quality of the C's and one had an unquestionably fine account. The other alternative was to figure all types of mathematical ratios until somehow a clear picture of the firm would emerge. However, although volumes were written describing the details of where to get the information and how to calculate each ratio, no one adequately described how one put all of this information together to make a decision.

Credit lines were traditionally set by one of four methods. As described by Frank Wey in "Establishing Credit Lines By Formula" (C&FM, May 1983), some were set at whatever the need was, some at 10 percent of net worth, some at a percentage of the highest credit reported by credit references and some by pure gut feeling. None of the four had any scientific basis.

These methods were used primarily to prevent bad debt losses. However, as management recognized that bad debt losses have not been a significant factor in American business in the past 30 years (median of 0.0767 percent of sales) and as interest rates have climbed, the emphasis has turned toward controlling the cost of carrying accounts receivable.

Anthony Alan Kelley, "Business Credit Skills," *Credit & Financial Management* (December 1985): 11, 12, 15, 16. Reprinted with permission from *Credit & Financial Management,* Copyright December 1985, published by the National Association of Credit Management, 8815 Centre Park Drive, Columbia, MD 21045.

At the time of this writing, Anthony Alan Kelley, ABCE, was assistant manager, wholesale operations, AT&T Consumer Products, St. Louis, Missouri.

This has accelerated the need for a scientific approach toward setting credit lines during the last 15 years with the development of computerized statistical packages and the basic research of scholars such as Beaver and Altman. Development of scientific techniques has also received support from marketing executives as many viewed traditional judgment systems of credit as allowing too much room for bias and inaccuracy.

The current financial analysis models are viewed as an integral part of modern financial theories. Even company-designed systems consider each account as part of a portfolio that the credit executive administers. These models have also been integrated into the investment theories of predicting corporate earnings and the theory of efficient capital markets.

The traditional approach to credit evaluation required that each customer be evaluated individually and proclaimed that no two credit execs would come to the same decision given the same situation. This viewpoint is that credit evaluation is an art and that all attempts to quantify the credit decision will end in frustration.

The C's of Credit

In his book, "Commercial Credit and Collection Practice," published in 1957, Watrous Irons held that credit's job is to evaluate the client's "credit power" to obtain the optimum volume of sales against expenses for extending credit. Each client must be classified in terms of the degree of credit risk involved based on the four C's of credit. Somehow the credit executive is to assess the client's character based on his knowledge of the management of the firm. By examining the financial statements, the credit exec is to assess the firm's capacity and capital. These are to be judged on the basis of efficiency of use and not on size. The financial status can be judged by comparison with similar firms in the same industry and by looking for trends in the key financial ratios.

This picture of the firm must then be viewed in light of the prevailing conditions. The state of the business cycle combined with the hazards of the client's business will affect its future. Labor conditions, local economic conditions and government regulations and policies will affect the firm. Most of all, changes in consumer demands affecting the vitality of the industry will affect the firm.

These factors must somehow be evaluated to determine a reasonable credit line. After determining the debt-paying ability and the merchandise requirements, Irons said, the credit line is set at a certain percentage of the client's net worth or working capital.

Individual Evaluation

Writing in "Credit and Collection Management," William Schultz and Hedwig Reinhardt add that the credit decision must be modified by the selling firm's position in the market and its own profit margin. Because each client is an individual, they maintain that the relative weight assigned to each of the C's of credit must be individually determined. They further add to the confusion by pointing out that financial statement analysis suffers from two problems: many customer financial statements are inadequate and there is a lack of standardization due to varying accounting conventions. This makes comparing firms to an industry very difficult.

They also add two other methods of establishing a credit line. The credit line can be set high enough to cover the order or on a follow-the-leader basis where it is established at the highest credit level granted by other firms.

Standard Comparisons

Robert Bartels, in "Credit Management," further enlarges the C's of credit to add collateral and country. He considers the extent of collateral of the client to be important enough to be added as another factor. He also recognizes that different cultural influences exist in other countries that must affect international credit decisions.

Bartels also expands on the traditional C's of credit. He defines character to include not only the background of the firm's officers, but the payment and discount policy of the firm that affect the routines for paying bills. He includes the size of the firm in capacity as well as the management expertise, debt capacity and the profit margin of the client. He identifies capital in terms of its liquidation value as well as its equity interest on the books.

Statement analysis is an important part of customer evaluation. He believes that one should set up a standard model of an ideal firm's financial ratios and measure the client against this standard. Bartels does realize that statement analysis is not always possible with small businesses. In this case, he suggests conducting a break-even analysis on the individual firm. He maintains that whatever the circumstances, credit scoring is used only by less experienced credit personnel. Credit appraisal involves four steps. One searches for evidence of creditworthiness, sorts and evaluates the evidence, interprets the meaning of the evidence and judges the creditworthiness of the client. Unfortunately, he neglects to explain how each step is done.

Credit Information

In his book "Consumer and Commercial Credit Management," Robert Cole emphasizes the quality and quantity of credit information gathered on a client. He maintains that there is a direct correlation between this information and the frequency of loss. Each customer must be considered as an individual analytical and interpretational problem. Commercial credit decisions are unique because of the distance between the client and the creditor, the range of clients from very small to very large and the varying conditions that each client faces. Therefore, there can be no fixed standards.

The creditor must answer certain questions about a client. The identity and legal responsibility of the client must be established. The history and business background of the firm must be researched. The character and responsibility of management must be ascertained. The client must have financial ability as well as current financial strength and an outlook for the future. Past and present payment history will reveal much about the firm.

In order to answer the questions properly, the creditor must choose sources of information carefully. They must be selected for their accuracy, depth of information, speed, cost, trade coverage and variety and frequency of reports.

Cole views statement analysis as valuable in determining whether a firm is an efficient business machine. Therefore, one must consider ratios against given industry standards. One must also consider the trend and direction of the business since statements are an indication of past history. Because of this, he prefers future cash flow projections when evaluating financial statements.

All of these authors describe in detail what factors must be considered when evaluating a client. The traditional method of client evaluation relies heavily on financial statement analysis. Unfortunately, there is no clear system of integrating all financial factors into a credit decision. However, the basic assumption of the traditional credit approach is that, as Roy Foulke says, "Every managerial policy, or absence of managerial policy, is reflected somewhere in the figures; in the balance sheet, in the income statement or in the reconciliation of surplus."

Traditional Financial Statement Analysis

Financial statement analysis began with an article by Alexander Wall published in the "Federal Reserve Bulletin" in 1919. In his book "How to Evaluate Financial Statements," he expanded his explanation and laid the foundation for traditional statement analysis. Wall's analysis concentrated on property statements, the modern balance sheet. He introduced concepts of working capital, defined as the difference between current assets and current liabilities, the use of common size statements, the beginnings of ratio analysis and trend analysis.

The basis of his analytical system was to reduce the numbers on the balance sheet to percentages of the total, producing what he called common size statements. He felt that by comparing these common size statements for different companies, deficiencies in one company could be spotted. By comparing two years' statements for the same firm, trends in the changes of assets could be spotted.

He introduced 10 financial ratios to be used in statement analysis. The current ratio indicates a firm's relative liquid strength to pay current debts. The merchandise receivables ratio checks the change in the current ratios from year to year to see if they are due to purely mathematical influences. The net worth to fixed assets ratio indicates the degree to which equity has financed long term investments, and net worth to debt indicates the source of operating funds.

Wall also relates sales to receivables, inventory, fixed assets, net worth and profits. The relationship with receivables and inventory indicates the currency of these assets. The comparison with fixed assets and net worth implies the effectiveness of the capital investment. The relationship to profits indicates the extent to which sales exceed cost. By comparing profits to net worth, he indicates the size of the return to the investor.

Wall recognizes that these ratios have varying value to the financial analyst. Therefore, he goes on to develop a weighted index, giving greater emphasis to the current and worth-debt ratios. Emphasis on sales ratios is greatly reduced. Finally, he suggests that these ratios should be compared to industry standards. He uses the industry indexes, developed by the Robert Morris Associates (RMA) under his direction and supervision, to create four risk classes, based on the current ratio index.

Wall's classic work established many of the basic concepts of financial statement analysis. Later authors built on this foundation, extending the potential of ratio analysis.

Income Statement and Break-Even Analysis

John Myer expanded Wall's work to include the income statement and a discussion of break-even analysis. In his book, "Financial Statement Analysis," he wrote that the income statement summarizes the operations of the firm and clearly shows the net result of operations. His technique centers around vertical (Wall's common-size percentage) and horizontal (Wall's year-to-year comparison) analysis and forms the basis of modern financial statement analysis technique.

Before he discussed financial statement analysis, he explained the problems associated with the statements themselves. He points out that it is difficult to compare firms and develop industry averages because of these problems. Many firms have different though legitimate accounting assumptions that have a major effect on their financial statement. For example, it is almost impossible to compare a last in, first out (LIFO) inventory with a first in, first out (FIFO) inventory. Many firms also have different year ending dates. This means that it is impossible to compare financial statements because they cover different expanses of time. Therefore, he felt that, until uniform accounting methods and closing dates are instituted, no acceptable standard ratios can exist. He recommends the self-contained method of analysis that relies strictly on the statements of the individual firm without comparison to industry averages.

When examining the balance sheet, Myer concentrates on changes and percentage changes in individual items from year to year, instead of looking only at the relation of each item to the total. He maintains that these changes reflect the effects of the conduct of business by management. These effects are of great value in forming an opinion regarding the progress of the firm.

Myer examined what causes a variation in income reported on the income statement. One primary technique he introduced was break-even analysis. He figured the minimum level of sales needed to sustain fixed costs plus variable costs associated with that level of sales. When this point is identified, subsequent changes in the sales level can be used to predict future profits or losses. He also recognized the effect of rising price levels due to inflation on trend analysis. He recommended adjusting all yearly figures to compensate for the rise in the general level of prices.

In contrast to Wall, Mayer held that it is not productive to try to summarize financial ratios by assigning arbitrary weights to the ratios and combining them to determine an index number. He felt that this implied a precise relationship between ratios existed. For him, this showed "how seductive statistical methods may become to one who does not properly understand them." He recognized that the results displayed in the financial statement reflect not only the abilities of the firm's management, but also factors beyond management's control. Therefore, he said, even though statement analysis is the center of any credit evaluation, the explanations for the results and the implications for future results often are beyond the firm's scope.

Expansion of Financial Analysis

Roy Foulke expanded on these early works in 1961. In "Practical Financial Statement Analysis," he went into greater detail on each of the ratios and their use in internal statement analysis. While the ratios he used are somewhat different from other authors', they attempt to measure the same factors: profitability, leverage, solvency, efficiency and liquidity. Foulke relies heavily on the technique of comparing these ratios against industry standards. Through this comparison, he classifies customers according to their standing in the industry to determine their risk.

He also explores a technique for examining small businesses that do not fit the standard ratio technique. Here he falls back on the percentage of the total method. However, he figures this on a percentage of total sales. Costs are figured as a percentage of total sales and compared against previous years and overall industry indexes. While he admits this is not precise, it is due to a lack of detailed financial information.

Foulke also introduces the possibility of profit manipulation in great detail. He maintains that it is important to obtain management antecedent information in order to judge whether this may have occurred. His solution lies in a detailed examination of the capital surplus. Since accounting rules allow great flexibility in this area, a detailed verification of the contents of retained earnings is essential.

Integration with Credit Decisions

In "Financial Statement Analysis Theory, Application and Interpretation," Leopold Bernstein relates the detailed technical tools of financial statement analysis to the credit decision-making process. His major approach involves the use of "building blocks" to arrive at a decision. He points out that the way in which these building blocks are used depends on the purpose of the analyst. Financial statement analysis must be flexible to allow for the great diversity of decisions that depend on this process for data. Bernstein defines the process of financial statement analysis as "the application of analytical tools and techniques to financial statements and data in order to derive from them measurements and relationships which are significant and useful for decision making." It must convert data into input that can be used in making credit and financial decisions.

He also examines the statement of changes in financial position of the firm. He maintains that it sheds light on how liquidity is changing over time. It also shows what assets are being acquired and how they are financed. It is definitely useful in projecting operating results because it highlights the distinction between net income and funds provided by operations. It provides a summary of the firm's investment policies and evidence concerning the intentions of management.

The building block approach involves two steps: defining the objective of the analysis, and identifying the degree of emphasis and priority of the six areas of evaluation. These areas include short-term liquidity, funds flow, capital structure and long-term solvency, return on investment, asset utilization and operating performance. The credit decision-maker cannot ignore any of these areas, but is mainly interested in short-term liquidity and long-term solvency. However, Bernstein points out that many of these areas directly affect others. For example, operational problems may result in a serious drain of funds that will lead to short-term liquidity problems.

Bernstein hails the modern computer as a tool that can facilitate calculations useful in analyzing financial information. However, he is skeptical that it can ever be used to make financial judgments. He maintains that "the computer lacks the ability to make intuitive judgments or to gain insights, capabilities which are essential to a competent and imaginative financial analysis." He also points out that the lack of consistent accounting data prevents a straightforward computer analysis. The major use of computers will be the availability of information through sources like Compustat.

Cash and Funds Flows

The Credit Research Foundation has suggested an additional technique for the credit analyst. This is to project future cash and funds flow based on past financial statements and expected events. This technique can be most effective when future plans of the firm are known.

Because credit evaluation involves forecasting future payments, this technique is both very promising and very inaccurate when the future environment changes. The best source of information for this technique is found in past statements of changes in financial position of the firm. As described in "The Credit Management Handbook," the technique involves projecting how future financial statements will look based on all available sources of information. While based on past data, the final result of this process must be highly subjective by nature.

Financial statement analysis has become a useful tool for evaluating the management of a firm. Various techniques have developed and been refined. Common size statements express each item as a percentage of the total statement and allow comparisons between different size firms. Standard ratios of various items show operating relationships. Both these techniques allow comparisons against a standard industrial index.

Trends can be discerned by comparing statements over periods of time. Forecasts of future funds and cash flows can be projected from past information. Even small firms can be judged on a percentage of sales analysis. Break-even analysis can also be useful in projecting the future course of the firm.

All of these techniques are only as good as the information they provide. Differences in accounting conventions prevent precise comparisons. Traditional analysts insist that problems like these prevent any use of the computer in credit decision-making.

Questions

1. What are the traditional four C's of credit? What two C's did Robert Bartels add? Define each of these six C's of credit.

2. Alexander Wall began writing about financial statement analysis in 1919. He introduced the concepts of working capital, common-size statements, and trend analysis. Describe each of these concepts.

3. In the analysis of financial statements, what information does industry comparative analysis add to trend analysis?

4. Critics and analysts alike point out difficulties in financial statement analysis, because "there is a lack of standardization due to varying accounting conventions." John Myer points out that "it is almost impossible to compare a last in, first out (LIFO) inventory with a first in, first out (FIFO) inventory. Many firms also have different year ending dates." In view of these accounting problems, why do so many analysts continue to analyze financial statements?

The Current Ratio Revisited

Mary M. K. Fleming

The current ratio is frequently used to determine if a firm can meet its short-term obligations. But this simple calculation can be manipulated to make a wobbly balance sheet look good. In assessing a firm's health, the wise investor or creditor will look beyond the current ratio to a number of other critical factors.

The current ratio has long been used by investors and creditors as a gauge to determine if a firm can meet its short-term obligations. Because their cash management depends on timely cash receipts, short-term creditors are understandably concerned that debtors make cash payments on time. If a firm is to survive and prosper, funds must be readily available for current operations. Recessions and unfavorable economic conditions increase the need for a comfortable margin to meet maturing obligations, as losses may come from liquidating securities, receivables, and inventories.

The current ratio is a simple calculation: current assets divided by current liabilities. Current assets consist primarily of cash, marketable securities, receivables, inventories, and perhaps some nominal assets as prepayments. The adequacy of the ratio is assessed by rules of thumb that take into consideration such factors as the type of industry and credit practices. A two-to-one ratio frequently is mentioned as one that is satisfactory for many companies.

Because inventories can drag down the current ratio, the *quick ratio* (also called the acid test) is sometimes advanced as a better gauge of a firm's ability to meet obligations. The quick ratio is the current assets minus inventories divided by the current liabilities. Again, rules of thumb are used to assess if the quick ratio is acceptable; a popular quick ratio is one-to-one. Note that if a firm has a two-to-one current ratio, inventories must be 100 percent of the short-term debt before it can have a one-to-one quick ratio.

Mary M. K. Fleming, "The Current Ratio Revisited," reprinted from *Business Horizons* (May/June 1986): 74–77. Copyright 1986 by the Foundation for the School of Business of Indiana University. Used with permission.

At the time of this writing, Mary M. K. Fleming was a professor of accounting at California State University, Fullerton.

Weaknesses of the Current Ratio

A low current ratio is frequently thought to indicate liquidity problems, whereas a firm with a high ratio is considered financially sound. This is too simple, however. Observation of trends is important in ratio analysis, but evaluation of the trend of the current ratio is difficult. Other than a ratio of one-to-one, an equal numeric increase in current assets and debt, such as results from the purchase of inventory on account, will cause a decline in the ratio. An equal decrease will result in an increased current ratio. Thus, the current ratio can change rapidly during a short time.

This phenomenon also makes the current ratio subject to manipulation when management wishes to window-dress financial statements to make them appear more favorable than they really are. As Figure 1 illustrates, a firm can improve its current ratio simply by paying a portion of its debt immediately before the balance sheet date.

A related problem is that not all current assets and liabilities are equally current. Most current liabilities are payable within a relatively short period of time, often 30 days or less, whereas it can take months to convert a large percentage of the current assets into cash. This situation is especially true for manufacturers of products with long lead times. Industry norms or credit practices may also cause collection of the receivables to be slow.

Excessive emphasis on the traditionally favorable current ratio is questionable because a high current ratio is the arithmetic result of either large short-term assets or small short-term debt, or a combination of the two. Yet, when the individual assets composing the numerator of the

---

Figure 1   **Window-Dressing with the Current Ratio**

In the following example, a year-end payment of $50,000 results in an immediate "improvement" in the current ratio from 1.25 to 1.36.

	Before	**After**
Current Assets	$\dfrac{\$200,000}{\$160,000} = 1.25$	$\dfrac{\$200,000 - \$50,000}{\$160,000 - \$50,000} = 1.36$
Current Liabilities		

If management wants a ratio in excess of two, additional payments of $35,000 financed through long-term debt would accomplish this objective.

$$\frac{\$150,000 + \$35,000 - \$35,000}{\$110,000 - \$35,000} = 2.00$$

The higher the ratio before the manipulation tactic, the larger the improvement in the ratio. In the first example, payment of a $50,000 liability results in a .11 increase (1.36 − 1.25 = .11). However, if the ratio were originally 1.67, the change would be .47 (2.14 − 1.67 = .47).

Before	**After**
$\dfrac{\$200,000}{\$120,000} = 1.67$	$\dfrac{\$200,000 - \$50,000}{\$120,000 - \$50,000} = 2.14$

current ratio formula are analyzed, profits are enhanced when most of these assets are kept at a minimum.

Critical Factors

Wise investors and creditors look beyond the surface of the current ratio. They ask crucial questions, such as:

- Is a line of credit readily accessible should the firm run into financial difficulties?

- Can noncurrent assets be liquidated to meet an unexpected cash need?

- Has the firm been profitable over the long term?

- What are future profit expectations?

- How sound are other indicators of financial stability?

Knowing the length of time that the firm has been experiencing unsatisfactory current ratios helps pinpoint whether present operations are typical. A high current ratio can accompany unsatisfactory business conditions or poor management. During recessions, management may be reluctant to replace inventories; thus, inventories and accounts payable are kept at a minimum. Or accounts receivable may be unduly large because of poor credit and collection policies and practices. On the other hand, profitable operations may accompany a falling ratio — for example, when a large income tax payment is owed as a result of high year-end sales.

Mix of Assets

Because each asset does not have the same measurement base or cash conversion cycle, consideration must be given to the mix of the current assets. A large cash balance is undesirable because cash doesn't earn interest, or, if so, at nominal rates. Payments to creditors may be delayed by restrictions on cash accounts.

Marketable securities, to be classified as such, must be readily marketable, and management must intend to liquidate them in the current period. Hence, marketable securities are shown on the balance sheet at the lower of cost or market. Still, not all securities possess the same degree of marketability, and the market price can fluctuate substantially during a short time. It may be preferable to consider other means of short-term financing in lieu of suffering losses from forced liquidation of marketable securities.

The measurement base for receivables is *net realizable value*; that is, the amount that the firm expects to be able to collect in cash.

Generally, net realizable value consists of historical credit sales, less an allowance for uncollectible accounts. Judgment is an important factor in determining the amount of uncollectibles. Composition of the receivables must be examined: open accounts receivable do not carry interest, notes usually do, and credit card receivables generate favorable carrying charges — favorable to the recipient, that is.

Accounts receivable turnover and the average collection period (number of days of receivables) provide some indication of the quality and collectibility of receivables. The faster the turnover, the greater the credence that can be given to current and quick ratios. If discounts are provided, collection periods should be short. To what extent would customers be lost if the collection period were reduced? The answer may depend on industry practices. Poor collection practices result in increased record-keeping cost and bad debts. Encouraging cash sales is one way to minimize receivable balances.

Inventories

Inventories should be viewed with caution. They tie up company funds, become obsolete or unsalable, and increase storage costs. The amount of unrealized profit in the inventory is critical. The higher the unrealized profit, the more favorable the situation. From an accounting point of view, unrealized profit is the result of the inventory cost flow method; hence, during inflation LIFO (last in, first out) is preferable. However, LIFO also results in a lower asset base and, therefore, in a less favorable current ratio. The current ratio is also affected by the peaks and valleys in accounts payable as inventory is not replenished evenly throughout the month.

As with receivables, a turnover ratio and the number of days on hand can be computed to ascertain the presence of obsolete inventory or pricing problems. These measures are often too crude to determine the quality, condition, and salability of the inventory. An important factor is the lead time necessary to manufacture the goods, sell them, and collect the receivables. Profits are enhanced by short operating cycles and rapid turnover of receivables and inventories. Rapid turnover minimizes current asset values and is therefore compatible with a low current ratio and favorable cash flow. An elementary example, which easily proves this point, is described in Figure 2.

The impact of a more rapid turnover of inventory is more difficult to compute. Much depends upon the elasticity of demand. If sales can be increased accordingly, the more rapid the turnover of inventory, the higher the profit. Considering $75,000 of inventory for both firms and only the change in inventory turnover, in the example in Figure 2, Firm B's gross profit per month is $25,000 ($100,000 minus $75,000) more than Firm A. If additional sales cannot be made, higher profits result from the savings in inventory holding costs from less inventory and from the

Figure 2 How Turnover on Receivables and Inventory Affects Liquidity

Suppose Firm A has the following condensed balance sheet.

Current Assets of Firm A		Current Liabilities	
Cash	$ 6,000	Due in 10 days	$ 80,000
Marketable securities		Due in 30 days	30,000
(cost=market)	20,000	Due beyond 30 days	5,000
Accounts receivable	150,000		$115,000
Inventory	75,000		
	$251,000		

Current ratio = $251,000/$115,000 = 2.18
Quick ratio   = $176,000/$115,000 = 1.53

If liquidity is measured by the current (2.18) and quick (1.53) ratios, this firm appears to be in a favorable financial situation.

Now, let us compare the balance sheet of Firm A with Firm B's. They are identical *except* that Firm B collects its receivables twice as fast and maintains 25 percent less inventory. Firm B's balance sheet is as follows:

Current Assets of Firm B		Current Liabilities	
Cash	$ 6,000	Due in 10 days	$ 80,000
Marketable securities (cost=market)	20,000	Due in 30 days	30,000
Accounts receivable	75,000	Due beyond 30 days	5,000
Inventory	56,250		$115,000
	$157,250		

Current ratio = $157,250/$115,000 = 1.37
Quick ratio   = $101,000/$115,000 = .88

Many would argue that Firm B's current (1.37) and quick (.88) ratios indicate unsatisfactory liquidity.

Which firm is in a better position to pay its obligations? Assume that each firm's monthly credit sales are $150,000. The markup on cost is 100 percent, sales are incurred evenly throughout the month, and there are 360 days in a year. Other assumed data are:

	A	B
Receivables		
Turnover per year	12	24
Number of days	30	15
Inventory		
Turnover per year	12	16
Number of days	30	22.5

How well will each firm be able to meet its maturing liabilities?

Firm A	10 Days	30 Days
Cash on hand	$ 6,000	$ 6,000
Receivables	50,000	150,000
	56,000	156,000
Liabilities due	(80,000)	(110,000)
Cash balance	($24,000)	$46,000

Firm B	10 Days	30 Days
Cash on hand	$ 6,000	$ 6,000
Receivables	75,000	175,000
	81,000	181,000
Liabilities due	(80,000)	(110,000)
Cash balance	$ 1,000	$ 71,000

Firm A is unable to pay its liabilities that come due in 10 days even if it liquidates all of its securities, whereas Firm B will not have to sell its securities. Both firms can pay their 30-day obligations, but Firm B will have $25,000 ($71,000 − $46,000) more cash on hand at the end of the month than Firm A, exclusive of the $20,000 received for the securities. Thus, Firm B has superior liquidity despite its inferior ratios.

Figure 3   The Defensive-Interval Ratio

The formula for the defensive-interval ratio is:

$$\frac{\text{Cash + marketable securities + receivables}}{\begin{array}{c}\text{Projected daily operational expenditures minus noncash charges}\\ \text{(Cost of goods sold + cash expenses other than inventory purchases)}\end{array}}$$

Like the current ratio, the defensive-interval ratio is deceiving when collection of receivables is slow. For Firms A and B, the ratios are:

$$\text{Firm A } \frac{\$6,000 + \$20,000 + \$150,000}{(\$75,000 + \$20,000)/30} = 56 \text{ days}$$

$$\text{Firm B } \frac{\$6,000 + \$20,000 + \$75,000}{(\$75,000 + \$20,000)/30} = 32 \text{ days}$$

Although it would appear that 56 days provide a relatively higher degree of protection than do 32 days, Firm B's position is superior in cash flow and profits.

---

opportunity cost of whatever return could be earned on the $18,750 ($75,000 minus $56,250) less capital invested in inventory.

Defensive-Interval Ratio

To combat the problems of the current ratio, the defensive-interval ratio is computed. This ratio measures how long a firm can operate on present liquid resources without having to resort to the next period's revenue. It indicates the firm's ability to meet its basic operational costs, and therefore it provides a margin of safety to creditors. The higher the number of days, the sounder the firm. Figure 3, which is based on data in Figure 2 and assumes monthly cash expenses other than inventory purchases of $20,000, illustrates the defensive-interval ratio.

Investors and creditors should be skeptical of high current ratios. One ratio—or even one period's ratio—is seldom a meaningful measure of a company's profit, liquidity, or future success. It is necessary to examine many critical factors before extensive credit is offered to a firm or before capital is invested in it. Nor does a high current ratio necessarily denote good cash management. As a key element in determining liquidity, expected cash flow must be thoroughly studied.

Questions

1.   One rule of thumb states that a company's current ratio should be 2.0, and another states that a company's quick ratio should be 1.0. "Note that if a firm has a two-to-one current ratio, inventories must be 100 percent of the short-term debt before it can have a one-to-one quick ratio." Taken together, do the two rules of thumb provide bad advice? Explain.

2.   Three companies — Loliq, Medliq, and Hiliq — are similar in most respects, but they have differing current ratios:

Loliq	Medliq	Hiliq
$CR = \dfrac{\$50}{\$100} = 0.5$	$CR = \dfrac{\$100}{\$100} = 1.0$	$CR = \dfrac{\$200}{\$100} = 2.0$

What happens to their current ratios when each company uses $25 to pay accounts payable? What mathematical principles do these cases illustrate?

3.   Are the companies in Question 2 more or less liquid after they make the $25 payment? What are your assumptions in answering this question?

4.   Trumpet Company's balance sheet for the year ending July 31, 19X4, is as follows:

Cash	$ 10,000	Current liabilities	$ 50,000
Marketable securities	50,000	Long-term debt	100,000
Accounts receivable	100,000	Total liabilities	$150,000
Inventory	140,000	Owner equity	350,000
Fixed assets	200,000		
Total assets	$500,000	Total claims	$500,000

a. Calculate Trumpet Company's current ratio.

b. Assess Trumpet Company's liquidity.

c. Is it possible that Trumpet Company has excess liquidity? What are the negative consequences of excess liquidity? Assuming that it has excess liquidity, what steps should Trumpet Company take?

Break-even Analysis and Operating Leverage

Dev Strischek

The recessions we have suffered over the past ten years have forced us to focus our attention on how much our commercial borrowers depend on sales stability, real sales growth, and adequate profit margins to repay their debts. Volatile sales may not always cover overhead, and price increases that lag behind rising expenses mean that cost-push inflation will negate the additional profits. The successful firm sets prices that simultaneously attract enough demand and yield enough margin to cover all costs and generate the desired income.

The purpose of this article is to examine two closely linked techniques that can provide commercial bankers with answers to two basic questions:

1. What level of sales is necessary to break even?
2. How sensitive are profits to changes in sales?

A banker should know how much his borrower must sell to cover all his costs and how much profits will change when sales rise or fall. Both questions are crucial to estimating the time and profitability of repayment.

Break-even Analysis

Break-even analysis is undertaken to determine what sales level will allow a firm to cover all its costs. The banker's principal use of this technique is to compare actual cumulative sales to the break-even point to determine if and when his borrower will be earning a profit and generating funds for loan repayment.

Dev Strischek, "Break-even Analysis and Operating Leverage," *The Journal of Commercial Bank Lending* (October 1983): 32–41. Copyright 1983 by Robert Morris Associates. Reprinted with permission from *The Journal of Commercial Bank Lending*, October 1983.

© 1983 by Robert Morris Associates. The author is senior vice president, Barnett Bank of Palm Beach County and an Associate in RMA's Florida Chapter. He also heads RMA's national Credit Division Council and is former president of RMA's Florida Chapter.

Variable and Fixed Costs

Break-even sales occur at that point where revenues cover all costs. Costs are classified into two groups, variable costs and fixed costs. By definition, sales cause variable costs, so variable costs change as sales change. If there were no sales, there would be no variable costs. Examples of variable costs include sales commissions, direct labor, raw materials, and freight and shipping.

Important to later discussion in this article, cost of goods sold tends to behave as a variable cost because most of its components are usually classified as variable costs. Expenses for such components as direct labor and materials would not be incurred if there were no sales.

In contrast, fixed costs do not vary with sales. Even if there were no sales, these costs would still be incurred. Examples of fixed costs include officers' salaries, rent and lease expense, general and administrative expenses, utilities expenses, and property taxes and licenses.

Many of the so-called operating expenses are essentially fixed costs because they would have to be paid regardless of the sales level.

Differentiating between fixed and variable costs is usually the hardest step in break-even analysis. However, a short-cut method that lumps together all the "hard-to-classify" expenses as fixed costs will be shown later to result in a good but conservative banker's approximation of the break-even point.

Calculation of the Break-even Point

The break-even point can be calculated graphically or algebraically. We will discuss the graphic approach first because it illustrates some basic points about break-even analysis. The data for both our proofs will be derived from income and expense data for the Breakfast Corporation portrayed in Figure 1.

The concept underlying the graphic approach is that break even occurs where sales equal costs. So the two axes of the graph in Figure 2 have equivalent scales. We assign sales to the horizontal axis and costs to the vertical axis because dependent variables are customarily assigned to the vertical axis. We are assuming that some of our costs' existence depends on the making of sales.

Our first step is to graph the fixed costs. Figure 1 indicates that they total some $350,000. The horizontal line extending from the 350 mark on the vertical "cost" axis of Figure 2 implies that regardless of the sales level, Breakfast Corporation must spend annually $350,000 in fixed costs.

Our second step is to graph the variable costs. By definition, these costs vary in direct proportion to sales, and Figure 1's data indicate that variable costs totaled $2.8 million on sales of $3.6 million. Thus, variable costs amounted to $78 of every $100 of sales. We overlay the variable cost wedge on top of the fixed costs' horizontal line to arrive at a total cost line which when intersected by a break-even sales-costs line will give us the break-even point.

Figure 1   **Income and Expense Data of the Breakfast Corporation for the Year Ended 12/31/81**

Income Statement	$M	% of Sales
Sales	3,600	100.0
Cost of Goods Sold	2,700	75.0
Gross Profit	900	25.0
Operating Expenses	435	12.1
Earnings before Interest and Taxes	465	12.9
Interest Expense	15	.4
Profit before Taxes	450	12.5

Expenses	Costs ($M)		
	Fixed	Variable	Total
Materials		1,800	1,800
Labor		900	900
Commissions		100	100
General and Administrative	145		145
Depreciation	40		40
Interest	15		15
Rent	150		150
Total	350	2,800	3,150

At zero sales, we have no variable costs, but at $100,000, we would have $78,000, which is shown in Figure 2 as point A. Likewise, the $200,000 sales level would require $156,000 of variable costs and is identified as point B. Another way of describing points A and B is that at the $100,000 level, total costs equal $428,000 ($350,000 of fixed costs plus $78,000 of variable costs) and that at the $200,000 level, total costs equal $506,000 ($350,000 of fixed costs plus $156,000 of variable costs). By connecting points A and B, we can construct a total costs line.

Our final step is to draw in the break-even sales line. This break-even line will always be equidistant from both the vertical and horizontal axes because along the break-even line, costs must equal sales. Where this line intersects our total cost line, we will have our break-even sales point. By dropping a line down to the horizontal axis, we can determine break-even sales. Casual observation of Figure 2 suggests that the break-even sales point is about $1.6 million. At that level, $1.25 million of variable costs are incurred, leaving $350,000 of margin to be contributed toward covering the $350,000 of fixed costs.

The graphic approach is visually rewarding as an illustration of the break-even concept, but it is too imprecise and too time-consuming to be useful in timely, accurate problem-solving. A formula would serve us better, and if we retrace the steps we took in the graphic solution, we can derive an equation for estimating the break-even sales point.

Figure 2 **Break-even Graph**

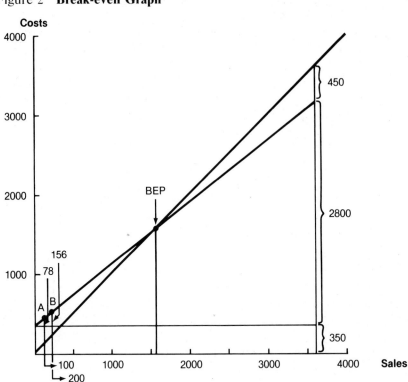

First, let us consider the role played by profit margins. We incur variable costs any time we make sales, so we assume that we must first pay our variable costs. The remainder is then available to cover fixed costs. We call this difference the "contribution" because it represents the revenues remaining after paying variable costs that can be contributed to covering the fixed costs.

We can express the contribution as a percent of sales because it is usually a stable relationship. This contribution margin can then be applied to a sales figure to yield the amount available to cover fixed costs. The following proof outlines the derivation of the break-even formula:

Break-even sales (BES) = variable costs (VC) + fixed costs (FC)

$$BES = VC + FC$$

$$S - VC = FC$$

$$S - VC = \text{contribution to covering fixed costs}$$

$$\frac{S - VC}{S} = CM, \text{ contribution margin as a \% of sales}$$

$$\frac{S - VC}{S} = \frac{FC}{S}$$

$$CM = \frac{FC}{S}$$

$$BES = \frac{FC}{CM}$$

Thus, break-even sales can be calculated by dividing the contribution margin into fixed costs.

Breakfast Corporation's $1.6 million graphic solution is substantiated by the formula's solution of $1,576,576.

$$BES = \frac{FC}{CM}$$

$$= \frac{350,000}{(800,000/3,600,000)} = \frac{350,000}{22.2\%}$$

$$= \frac{350,000}{.222} = \underline{\underline{1,576,576}}$$

Simplifications

The contribution margin bears a canny resemblance to gross profit margin (GPM), and for just a small trade-off in precision, there is much to be gained by a short-cut method substituting gross profit margin for contribution margin.

The first advantage is simplification of the break-even concept. Calculating the break-even point of any business becomes a simple matter of dividing the firm's fixed costs by its GPM.

The second advantage of this short-cut approach is that the break-even point calculated is a little higher than under the more precise method of carefully isolating variable costs from fixed costs. Figure 1 indicates that Breakfast Corporation's gross profit was $900,000 versus a contribution of $800,000. The $100,000 difference is the sales commission expense which is classified as a fixed cost under the short-cut method so that the gross profit margin can be used as the contribution margin. The result is that the short-cut method yields a higher and more conservative break-even point of $1,800,000 than the precise method's $1,576,000:

Calculation of Break-even Sales ($M)	Method	
	Precise	Short-Cut
Sales	3,600	3,600
VC	2,800	2,700
Contribution	800	900
Contribution/Sales = CM	$\frac{800}{3,600} = 22.2\%$	$\frac{900}{3,600} = 25.0\%$
FC	350	450
FC/CM = BES	1,576	1,800

What we have accomplished so far is how to graphically or algebraically calculate the break-even sales point. We can approximate the BES point by dividing the gross profit margin into the rest of a company's expenses, which are assumed to be fixed. The short-cut method gives us bankers a margin for error to protect us from our borrowers' optimistic sales projections as well as a simple formula for calculating the break-even point.

Goals and the Break-even Point

The lower the break-even point, the lower the sales level needed to generate a profit. Lowering the break-even point is a function of three alternatives:

1. Increasing the selling price per unit
2. Reducing the variable cost per unit
3. Reducing fixed costs

However, these simple alternatives are not so simple to apply, and where the contribution margin is very narrow, much more revenue is required to cover fixed costs. For example, if Breakfast Corporation's gross profit margin slipped from 25% to 10%, it would have to increase sales by a 2.5 multiple from $1.8 million to $4.5 million to cover its $450,000 of fixed costs. In effect, the contribution margin exerts a sort of inverse leverage on sales, so the lower the contribution margin is, the higher the break-even sales required. Moreover, if fixed costs rise, each incremental increase in these costs requires additional sales at some multiple of the fixed costs. One way of calculating this multiple is to measure what impact a change in sales has on profits. This multiple is sometimes called the operating leverage.

Operating Leverage

Operating leverage compares the gross profit earned on sales to the fixed costs, and we define operating leverage as the contribution available to cover fixed costs in relation to operating income. In "short-cut" terms, we can approximate operating leverage by dividing before-tax profits into the gross profit:

$$\text{Operating leverage} = \frac{\text{contribution to fixed costs}}{\text{operating income}}$$

$$= \frac{\text{sales} - \text{variable costs}}{\text{sales} - \text{variable costs} - \text{fixed costs}}$$

$$= \frac{\text{gross profit}}{\text{profit before taxes}} = \frac{\text{GP}}{\text{PBT}}$$

The operating leverage (OL) ratio will tell us how much each 1% change in sales will change operating income. If the ratio is 2.0, then a

10% increase in sales will result in a 20% increase in before-tax profits. A 10% drop in sales will cut before-tax profits by 20%.

Operating Leverage Ratio

Indeed, Breakfast Corporation's operating leverage is 2.0, and 10% changes in sales do result in 20% changes in profits:

Breakfast Corporation Income Statement ($M)	1981	Change in Sales	
		+10%	−10%
Sales	3,600	3,960	3,240
COGS	2,700	2,970	2,430
GP	900	990	810
−FC	450	450	450
PBT	450	540	360
% INCR (DECR) PBT	—	20%	(20%)
OL = GP/PBT	2.0X	—	—

Used in this context, the operating leverage ratio gives us some measure of the sensitivity of the bottom-line to changes in sales. It follows that risk-averse bankers should be wary of borrowers and industries with high operating leverage and volatile sales.

Industry Data

Industry statistics suggest that operating leverage tends to increase as products move through the distribution channel from manufacturers through wholesalers to retailers. For example, the 1981–82 women's clothing operating leverage ratios rise from a manufacturer's 6.0 through the wholesaler's 9.0 to the retailer's 16.2, according to Figure 3. Thus, a 10% drop in sales would mean a 60% drop in before-tax profits at the women's clothing manufacturing level, a 90% decline at the wholesale level, and a 162% fall at the retail level.

The higher operating leverages at the retail level suggest that retailers have higher fixed costs and inherent riskier situations that justify their generally fatter gross profit margins. Retailers are also at the end of the distribution channel and more directly exposed to shifts in ultimate consumer demand.

The three years of data in Figure 3 also reflect the volatility of the operating leverage ratios. The ratios change from year to year in response to changing conditions in the economy and the industry. Although operating leverage still tends to increase as goods flow from the manufacturing to the retail level, bankers must also be cognizant of the business cycle stage and the industry's condition.

Figure 3   **Operating Leverage by Level of Distribution**

		As % of Sales					
Industry		1979–80		1980–81		1981–82	
SIC	Name	GP	PBT	GP	PBT	GP	PBT
2335	mfr, women's clothing	28.3	4.1	26.8	2.9	28.3	4.7
5137	whl, women's clothing	28.5	3.1	25.5	2.5	25.2	2.8
5621	ret, women's clothing	40.8	2.7	40.9	2.6	40.5	2.5
2512	mfr, furniture	23.1	3.4	23.6	3.8	23.1	2.8
5021	whl, furniture	28.0	3.7	29.4	3.1	29.2	2.2
5712	ret, furniture	39.9	4.0	40.2	2.7	39.2	1.6
2084-5	mfr, wine & liquor	21.6	4.5	23.9	4.3	21.6	3.0
5182	whl, wine & liquor	21.1	3.0	21.2	2.7	21.8	2.7
5921	ret, wine & liquor	20.6	2.5	20.5	1.6	21.4	3.4
3143	mfr, shoes	22.5	3.2	24.4	5.5	25.6	5.6
5139	whl, shoes	23.7	2.8	24.4	1.1	26.8	4.2
5661	ret, shoes	41.8	4.4	42.4	3.6	41.3	2.9

Source: *1982 Annual Statement Studies* (Philadelphia: Robert Morris Associates, 1982). Statistics are drawn from comparative historical data columns.

Break-even Sales and Operating Leverage

The formula below shows the relationship between a firm's annual sales and its break-even sales point. Breakfast Corporation's operating leverage of 2.0 means it breaks even at 50% of its annual sales:

$$\text{Break-even Sales} = \frac{(\text{OL} - 1)}{\text{OL}} \ (\text{Annual Sales})$$

$$= \frac{(2 - 1)}{2} \ (\text{Annual Sales})$$

$$= 50\% \times \text{Annual Sales} = .50 \times 3{,}600{,}000$$

$$= 1{,}800{,}000$$

If its operating leverage ratio had been 4, 75% of Breakfast's annual sales would be required just to break even. At a ratio of 10, 90% of sales would be required to break even. If Breakfast Corporation's year-end is December 31, and 6-month sales are $1.8 million, the banker can probably feel reasonably comfortable that Breakfast will have a profitable year with a 2.0 operating leverage. That comfort level would be considerably less at the end of June if Breakfast had a 10.0 operating leverage and needed 90% of annual sales to break even. Obviously, the higher the operating leverage, the higher the sales level required to break even.

Operating Leverage (GP/PBT)		
1979–80	**1980–81**	**1981–82**
6.9	9.2	6.0
9.2	10.2	9.0
15.1	15.7	16.2
6.8	6.2	8.2
7.6	9.5	13.3
10.0	14.9	24.5
4.8	5.6	7.2
7.0	7.8	8.1
8.2	12.8	6.3
7.0	4.4	4.6
8.5	22.2	6.4
9.5	11.8	14.2

Summary

Break-even analysis can tell the banker what sales level his borrower must achieve to cover all his costs. A short-cut approach to finding the break-even sales point is to divide the gross profit margin into all the operating expenses. The result usually has a safety margin on the high side to protect the banker against the borrower's optimistically low break-even sales points.

Operating leverage provides a clue to sales-profit sensitivity. Dividing the gross profit by the before-tax profit yields a ratio that tells by how much a given change in sales will be magnified and carried to the bottom line. Higher operating leverage means bigger swings in profits as sales vary. Operating leverage appears to increase as goods flow from manufacturers through wholesalers to retailers. Thus, the risk of profit downswings in recessions seems to increase as goods move to the ultimate consumer.

As operating leverage declines, so will the break-even point. Lower operating leverage occurs when the gross profit margin increases as a result of higher unit selling prices, lower unit costs, or lower fixed costs. Rising operating leverage means potentially greater profit volatility and higher break-even sales levels, so appraising the borrower's credit risk may be improved if its break-even point and operating leverage are monitored periodically.

Questions

1. Define the terms *variable cost* and *fixed cost*. Provide examples of each type of cost.

2. The author calculates break-even sales for Breakfast Corporation as follows:

$$\text{BES} = \frac{\text{FC}}{\text{CM}}$$

$$= \frac{\$350,000}{(\$800,000/\$3,600,000)}$$

$$= \frac{\$350,000}{0.222} = \$1,576,576$$

Because he includes interest expense in fixed costs, we might call $1,576,576 the *total cost* break-even level. Calculate the *operating* break-even level by excluding interest expense from fixed costs.

3. Describe the short-cut method for calculating break-even sales. Why does this method produce only an approximation?

4. Use the short-cut method to calculate break-even sales for Hollywood Corporation:

Hollywood Corporation
Income Statement for the Year Ending
12-31-X5

Net sales	$6,000
Cost of goods sold	4,000
Gross profit	$2,000
Operating expense	1,000
EBIT	$1,000
Interest expense	400
Earnings before taxes	$ 600

5. Calculate Hollywood Corporation's (Question 4) degree of operating leverage using the short-cut method. Interpret your answer.

6. Check your answer to Question 4 using the following equation:

$$\text{Break-even sales} = \frac{\text{OL} - 1}{\text{OL}} \text{ (Annual sales)}$$

OL is the degree of operating leverage that you calculated in Question 5.

7. Retailers of women's clothing tend to have higher operating leverage than do manufacturers of women's clothing. This fact *suggests* that the retailers face higher risks than do the manufacturers. Explain why this suggestion is not necessarily true.

PART VI
INSTITUTIONAL FEATURES OF LONG-TERM FINANCING

Low-Grade Bonds: A Growing Source of Corporate Funding

Jan Loeys

In recent years, a growing part of corporate borrowing has taken the form of "low-grade bonds." Called "junk bonds" by some, and "high-yield bonds" by others, these bonds are rated as speculative by the major rating agencies, and they are therefore considered more risky than high- or investment-grade bonds. Lately, low-grade bonds have received a lot of public attention because of their use in corporate takeovers. But in fact, most low-grade bond issues are not used for this purpose.

Corporations that now issue low-grade bonds are firms that, because of their lack of size, track record, and name recognition, used to borrow mostly via bank loans or privately placed bonds. Recently, investors have become more willing to lend directly to smaller and less creditworthy corporations by buying these low-grade bonds. There are several reasons for the new popularity of these bonds. But before discussing those reasons, it is useful to examine in more depth exactly what low-grade bonds are and how their market first developed.

What Are Low-Grade Bonds?

Low-grade bonds represent corporate bonds that are rated below investment grade by the major rating agencies, Standard & Poor's and Moody's. These ratings, which firms usually request before issuing bonds to the public, reflect each agency's estimate of the firm's capacity to honor its debt (that is, to pay interest and repay principal when due). The highest rating is AAA (for firms with an "extremely strong" capacity to pay interest and repay principal), and then AA ("very strong"), A ("strong"), and BBB ("adequate"). Bonds rated BB, B, CCC, or CC are

Jan Loeys, "Low-Grade Bonds: A Growing Source of Corporate Funding," *Business Review* (Federal Reserve Bank of Philadelphia, November/December 1986): 3–12.

At the time of this writing, Jan Loeys was a Senior Economist in the Macroeconomics Section of the Research Department at the Federal Reserve Bank of Philadelphia.

regarded as "speculative" with respect to the issuer's capacity to meet the terms of the obligation.[1] Firms generally strive to maintain at least a BBB rating because many institutions or investment funds cannot, because of regulation, or will not, because of firm policy, invest in lower-grade bonds. This explains why bonds rated below BBB are also known as "below-investment" grade bonds.

There is no set formula for determining a bond rating—the rating agencies say they look at the entire spectrum of financial and product market conditions. But a certain issue may be considered too risky to be rated investment grade for several reasons. For one, certain financial ratios—such as a high debt-equity ratio or a high ratio of interest expenses to total income—may indicate that even moderate fluctuations in cash flow could endanger the issuer's capacity to pay the bondholders. Or the firm's assets may not be well diversified (too dependent upon a single product), which also makes the firm's revenues highly variable. Alternatively, if the firm is relatively new and thus lacks a proven track record, the firm's cash flow might be hard to predict. Finally, the firm or its industry may be considered in decline, which increases the likelihood of a default.

The Market for Low-Grade Bonds

Low-grade bonds have received widespread attention from the press in recent years, largely because of their association with certain corporate takeover techniques.[2] But low-grade bonds have been around for a long time. In fact, during the 1920s and 1930s, about 17 percent of domestic corporate bond offerings (that is, new issues) were low grade.[3] Furthermore, as the Depression of the 1930s wore on, many bonds that were originally issued with a high-grade rating were downgraded to below-investment grade. These so-called "fallen angels" were bonds of companies that had fallen on hard times. By 1940, as a result of both these downgradings and the earlier heavy volume of new low-grade offerings, low-grade bonds made up more than 40 percent of all bonds outstanding.

After 1940, the market for new public offerings of low-grade bonds shrank significantly. Many investors avoided low-grade bonds due to their

---

[1] These are the ratings for Standard & Poor's. The corresponding ratings for Moody's are Aaa, Aa, A, Baa, Ba, B, Caa, and Ca, with ratings below Baa considered below investment grade. For both agencies, the rating C is reserved for bonds on which no interest is being paid, while bonds rated D are in default.

[2] For a discussion of these issues, see Kevin F. Winch and Carol Kay Brancato, "The Role of High-Yield Bonds (Junk Bonds) in Capital Markets and Corporate Takeovers: Public Policy Implications," in *The Financing of Mergers and Acquisitions,* Hearing before the Subcommittee on Domestic Monetary Policy of the Committee on Banking, Finance and Urban Affairs, House of Representatives, 99th Congress, 1st session (May 3, 1985), pp. 246–297.

[3] See W. Braddock Hickman, *Corporate Bond Quality and Investor Experience* (Princeton University Press, 1958), p. 153.

Figure 1   **New Domestic Corporate Bond Issues: 1978–1985**

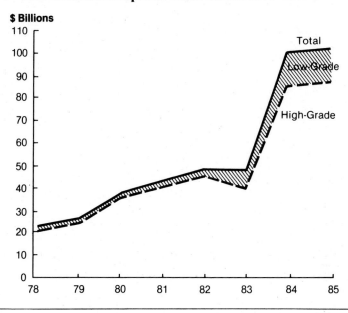

Source: Edward I. Altman and Scott A. Nammacher, "The Anatomy of the High Yield Debt Market:
1985 Update," Morgan Stanley (June 1986) Table 2. Data do not include exchange offers, secondary
offerings, tax exempts, convertible bonds, or government bonds.

high default rate during the 1930s—an average of almost 10 percent of
outstanding low-grade bonds (valued at par) defaulted each year.[4] Most
additional low-grade bonds represented only new fallen angels. By the
mid-1970s, only about 4 percent of all public corporate bonds outstanding
in the U.S. consisted of low-grade bonds.[5]

In 1977, Drexel Burnham Lambert, an investment bank that was
already making a secondary market in fallen angels, started an effort to
revitalize the market for original-issue low-grade bonds by underwriting
new issues and subsequently making a secondary market in them. By
1982, low-grade bond issuance had grown gradually to about $2.8 billion
per year (or 6 percent of total corporate bonds issued publicly that year).
In 1983, the market started growing much faster, reaching an annual issue
volume of about $15 billion in 1985 (or 15 percent of total corporate issues
that year; see Figure 1). Most low-grade bonds were issued by industrial

[4] See W. Braddock Hickman, *Corporate Bond Quality and Investor Experience*, p. 189.

[5] Edward I. Altman and Scott A. Nammacher, "The Anatomy of the High Yield Debt
Market," Morgan Stanley (September 1985), Table 2. These and the following data refer
only to publicly issued, nonconvertible debt that is rated below BBB (or Baa). Including
unrated debt, which would probably be low grade if it were rated, and debt that is
convertible into stock, would raise the outstanding amount of low-grade bonds by up to
30 percent.

Figure 2   **Historical Default Rates on Low-Grade Bonds: 1970–1985**

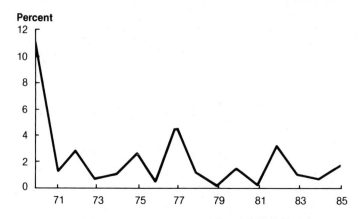

Source: Edward I. Altman and Scott A. Nammacher, "The Anatomy of the High Yield Debt Market: 1985 Update," Morgan Stanley (June 1986) Table 10.

companies and utilities, accounting for more than a third of the bonds raised by these firms in 1985. By the end of 1985, the total stock of low-grade bonds outstanding reached about $75 billion (or 14 percent of the total), less than a third of which consisted of fallen angels.

Historically, default rates on low-grade bonds have been much higher than those on high-grade bonds, lending credibility to the speculative rating of low-grade bonds. A recent study finds that between 1970 and 1984, this average annual default rate for low-grade bonds was only 2.1 percent, while the default rate for investment-grade debt was close to zero percent.[6] This average for low-grade bonds, however, hides a lot of year-to-year variability: it varied from a high of 11.4 percent in 1970, when Penn Central went under, to a mere 0.15 percent in 1981, when only two firms defaulted on their bonds (see Figure 2).

To compensate investors for the risk they bear by holding low-grade debt — or indeed any debt of private firms — rather than (presumably) default-free Treasury securities, firms promise to pay higher yields on their debt than the Treasury does.[7] This difference between yields is called a "risk premium." In general, the lower a firm's rating, the higher

---

[6] Edward I. Altman and Scott A. Nammacher, "The Anatomy of the High Yield Debt Market: 1985 Update," Morgan Stanley (June 1986), Table 10. One must be careful in interpreting these data. A default does not necessarily mean that bondholders lose all of their investment. If the firm in default has some assets left, bondholders may still retrieve part of their investment, although it may be some time before these funds are returned.

[7] Sometimes this compensation takes the form of a "warrant," which gives the bondholder the right to buy equity in the firm at an attractive price, or an option to convert the bond to the common stock of the firm. These so-called "equity kickers" allow bondholders to benefit from any improvements in the value of the firm.

Figure 3 Promised Yields on Treasury and Corporate Bonds

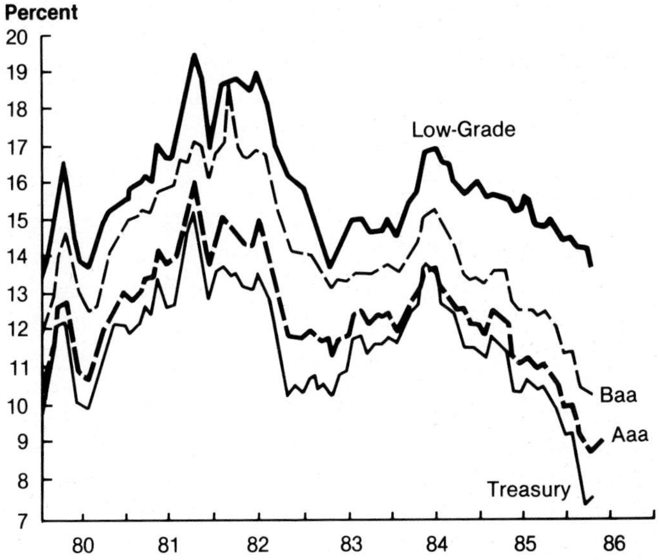

Source: Salomon Brothers and Moody's.

the risk premium will be. As Figure 3 shows, high-grade (AAA) bonds usually yield only 50 to 100 basis points more than Treasury bonds, while medium-rated (BBB) bonds may yield from 150 to 300 basis points above Treasury yields. The risk premium of lower-grade bonds over Treasuries, however, has run from 300 to 600 basis points over the last five years. But default risk is probably not the only reason for these yield differentials. Low-grade bonds may require a higher return to compensate investors for the fact that the secondary market for low-grade securities is much less liquid than that for Treasury securities.[8]

Actual realized returns frequently differ from promised returns, however. Aside from the promised return, the actual return includes capital gains and losses due to defaults, upgradings and downgradings, and changes in market interest rates. For example, from 1978 to 1985, low-grade bonds realized an average annual return of 12.9 percent, compared with 10.8 percent on Treasury bonds.[9]

---

[8] In addition, unlike most Treasury securities, most corporate bonds are callable; that is, the issuer has the option to pay off part (or all) of the issue at a predetermined price during a predetermined period prior to maturity. The issuer pays for this option in the form of a higher yield.

[9] Edward I. Altman and Scott A. Nammacher, "The Anatomy of the High Yield Debt Market: 1985 Update," Table 1. See also Marshall E. Blume and Donald B. Keim, "Risk and Return Characteristics of Lower-Grade Bonds," Rodney L. White Center for Financial Research, University of Pennsylvania (August 1986).

This average return hides a lot of variability, however. In 1983, low-grade bonds outperformed Treasury securities by almost 20 percentage points (see Figure 4). But in 1982, and again in 1985, as yields on new Treasury issues dropped much more than the yield on new low-grade issues, the larger capital gains on Treasury securities allowed them to beat low-grade bond returns by almost 10 percentage points. Therefore, although low-grade bonds have yielded a higher return than Treasury or investment-grade bonds on average, there is no guarantee that they will do so in any given year.

The recent revival of the low-grade bond market raises the question of why this product has become successful again. One popular misconception is that these bonds are used solely to finance corporate takeovers. But while the sudden rise in corporate mergers and acquisitions in the last few years did contribute to the growth in low-grade bond offerings, the market had taken off well before the first major use of low-grade bonds in corporate takeover attempts in 1983. And even in 1985—a year of unprecedented merger activity—low-grade bonds issued for takeover purposes made up only about 38 percent of total low-grade bond issuance (see LOW-GRADE BONDS AND TAKEOVERS). Rather than reflecting a rise in one particular use for low-grade bonds, the reemergence of the market paralleled more fundamental changes in financial markets that made low-grade bonds relatively more attractive compared with other forms of financing.

Figure 4   **Realized Yields on Treasury and Low-Grade Bonds**

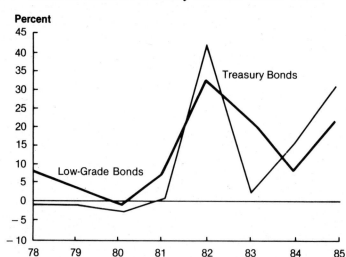

Source: Edward I. Altman and Scott A. Nammacher, "The Anatomy of the High Yield Debt Market: 1985 Update," Morgan Stanley (June 1986) Table 1.

Low-Grade Bonds and Takeovers

Low-grade bonds became the center of public attention because of their association with corporate takeover attempts. In a takeover, one firm or a set of investors acquires the stock (and thus ownership) of another firm. When the stock purchase is not financed with cash or newly issued stock of the acquiring firm, the acquisition is financed by borrowing funds. As a result, equity in the combined firm is replaced with debt and its debt-equity ratio rises. Many of these cases involve so-called "leveraged buyouts" (LBOs), in which a group of investors, usually including the management of the firm being acquired, buy out stockholders in order to take the firm private.[a]

In the past, there was little LBO borrowing and what there was took the form of bank loans. However, because an increased debt-equity ratio raises the default risk of a firm's debt, bank loans usually come with a lot of restrictions and collateral requirements. In response to an increased demand for LBO financing, Drexel Burnham Lambert, in late 1983, started using its extensive network of private and institutional buyers of low-grade debt to float LBO bonds. These bonds are frequently rated below investment grade, especially when they are junior to already existing debt, and when cash flow projections barely exceed the higher required interest payments. The flexibility of this new source of LBO financing allows some investors to attempt acquisitions of firms several times their own size.[b]

In contrast to the amount of public discussion about this topic, low-grade bond issues actually involved in takeovers make up only a small part of the market. During 1984, LBOs amounted to only $10.8 billion, compared with $122.2 billion in

[a] For details, see Carolyn K. Brancato and Kevin F. Winch, "Merger Activity and Leveraged Buyouts: Sound Corporate Restructuring or Wall Street Alchemy?" U.S. Congress, House Committee on Energy and Commerce, Subcommittee on Telecommunications, Consumer Protection, and Finance, 98th Congress, 2nd Session (November 1984).

[b] Early in 1986, the Board of Governors of the Federal Reserve System ruled that bonds that are issued by a corporation with no business operations and no assets other than the stock of the target company are functionally equivalent to borrowing to buy stock (that is, buying stock on margin). Therefore, these bonds are subject to a 50 percent margin as required by Regulation G. That is, only 50 percent of the stock purchase can be financed with borrowed funds. However, the Board specifically excluded bonds that are issued simultaneously with the consummation of the merger or LBO — a standard practice in LBOs — because the assets of the firm, and not its stock, would be the source of repayment of the bond issue. For details, see Federal Reserve System 12 C.F.R. Part 207 (Regulation G; Docket No. R-0562).

total merger and acquisition activity.[c] Drexel estimates that of about $14 billion in publicly issued low-grade bonds in 1984, only "approximately 12% was issued in acquisition or leveraged buyout transactions, of which a de minimis amount was connected with the financing of unsolicited acquisitions."[d] By 1985, however, other analysts had estimated that the proportion of new low-grade issues used to finance acquisitions and LBO transactions had risen to 38 percent.[e]

[c] W.T. Grimm & Co., "1984 Merger/Acquisitions Set Ten-Year Record: Total Dollar Value Rose 67% to a Record-Breaking $122.2 Billion," (Chicago: W.T. Grimm & Co., 1985). Press release, undated, duplicated.

[d] Drexel Burnham Lambert, Inc., "Acquisitions and High Yield Bond Financing," submitted to the Subcommittee on Telecommunications, Consumer Protection, and Finance (March 20, 1985), p. 14.

[e] Martin Fridson and Fritz Wahl, "Plain Talk About Takeovers," *High Performance* (February 1986), p. 2. Fridson and Wahl use a more restrictive definition of the size of the low-grade market than Drexel does.

Why Did the Market Grow?

The main alternative to issuing public debt securities directly in the open market is to obtain a loan from a specialized financial intermediary that issues securities (or deposits) of its own in the market. These alternative instruments usually are commercial bank loans — for short- and medium-term credit — or privately placed bonds — for longer-term credit. Unlike publicly issued bonds, privately placed bonds can be sold directly to only a limited number of sophisticated investors, usually life insurance companies and pension funds.[10] Moreover, privately placed bonds are held for investment purposes rather than for resale, and they have complex, customized loan agreements (covenants). The restrictions in the covenants range from limits on dividend payments to prohibitions on asset sales and new debt issues. They provide a series of checkpoints that permit the lender to review actions by the borrower that have the potential to impair the lender's position.[11] Thus, these agreements have to be regularly renegotiated prior to maturity. As a result, these privately placed bonds in effect are much more like loans than public securities.

[10] The Securities Act of 1933 exempts privately placed bonds from the normal registration process that the Securities and Exchange Commission enforces on public securities offerings. For more details on this market, see John D. Rea and Peggy Brockschmidt "The Relationship Between Publicly Offered and Privately Placed Corporate Bonds," Federal Reserve Bank of Kansas City *Economic Review*, (November 1973), pp. 11–20, and Patrick J. Davey, "Private Placements: Practices and Prospects," *The Conference Board Information Bulletin* (January 1979).

[11] See Edward Zinbarg, "The Private Placement Loan Agreement," *Financial Analysts Journal* (July/August 1975) pp. 33–35 and 52.

Before the reemergence of original-issue low-grade bonds, only large, well-known firms with established track records found it economical to raise money by issuing their own debt securities in the public capital markets. For smaller, relatively new or unknown firms, the expense was usually prohibitive. Because of the risk of underwriting low-grade bonds, investment bankers would demand hefty underwriting fees. Also, less creditworthy issuers would have had to pay a very high premium on their debt because investors perceived them as particularly risky investments.

Such borrowers thus found it more economical simply to obtain a loan from a bank or to place a private bond issue with a life insurance company. These alternatives proved cheaper because banks and life insurance companies specialize in credit analysis and assume a large amount (if not all) of a borrower's debt. Consequently, they could realize important cost savings in several functions, such as gathering information about the condition of debtor firms, monitoring their actions, and renegotiating loan agreements.

The reemergence of a market for public original-issue low-grade bonds suggests that this situation is changing. Certain lower-rated corporations now apparently find it economical to issue their own bonds directly in the public capital markets (see THE GROWTH OF SECURITIES MARKETS). As with many financial innovations, it is impossible to identify all the factors responsible for this development. But it is possible to suggest several important ones that may have made a contribution to the reemergence of original-issue low-grade bonds, and three seem particularly noteworthy—a greater demand by investors for marketable assets; lower information costs; and changes in investors' risk perceptions.

Marketability vs. Covenant Restrictions

One reason for the growth in the public issuance of low-grade bonds is that buyers of privately placed bonds have become more willing to trade some of the safety they found in the contractual restrictions they placed on borrowers in return for the marketability and higher yields of publicly issued low-grade bonds. Private placements are bilateral, customized loan agreements with complex contractual restrictions on borrowers' actions. However, the lack of standardization of these covenants and the frequent need for renegotiation when borrowers want to transgress the covenant restrictions make it very costly to have a lot of lenders per issue, or to change the identity of the lenders. As a result, there is not much of a secondary market for private placements. That is, they are not marketable.

Low-grade bonds, in contrast, are public securities and are issued with relatively simple, standardized contracts without cumbersome restrictions on borrowers' actions, in order to facilitate their trading in a secondary market. And in exchange for the added freedom from covenant restrictions, borrowers pay a higher yield on low-grade bonds than on

The Growth of Securities Markets

The growth of low-grade bond offerings is not an isolated phenomenon. In several other financial markets there is also a growing tendency for corporate borrowing to take the form of negotiable securities issued in the public capital markets rather than in the form of nonmarketable loans negotiated with financial intermediaries. For example, in the short-term credit market, commercial paper has become increasingly competitive with bank loans. By the end of 1985, bank loans constituted only 24 percent of short-term debt at large manufacturing firms, compared with 59 percent in early 1974.[a] And even in the Eurodollar market, large corporations are more frequently bypassing syndicated loans in favor of financing arrangements that allow them to issue debt under their own names. In fact, by 1985, financing in the form of securities made up 80 percent of total funds raised in international financial markets, compared to only 33 percent in 1980.[b]

This move towards borrowing in the form of securities reduces the role of the traditional intermediary that just makes loans and issues deposits. These financial intermediaries will still help link ultimate savers and borrowers, although the way in which they do business may change substantially. The traditional intermediary provides all forms of financial intermediation under one roof: it pools the funds of many small savers, issues insured deposits, provides a payments mechanism, and lends out the funds in a different form to a diverse set of borrowers. The new growth of securities markets implies an "unbundling" of this process with many of these services being provided by different intermediaries: a commercial bank or thrift may originate the loan; an investment bank may package it into a security and distribute it; an insurance company may insure it; and a mutual or pension fund may end up financing it by attracting funds from a large number of small savers.

[a] Large manufacturing firms with more than $1 billion in assets. Source: *Quarterly Financial Report*, U.S. Department of Commerce (1st Quarter 1975), p. 69, and (4th Quarter 1985), p. 134.

[b] *Financial Market Trends*, OECD (March 1986), p. 7, and earlier issues. See also *Recent Innovations in International Banking*, Bank for International Settlements (April 1986), Chapter 5.

private placements. The marketability and liquidity of low-grade bonds still are not comparable to those of Treasury or high-grade bonds. But the recent development of a secondary market for low-grade bonds and the increasing number of dealers in this market do make these securities much more liquid and marketable than privately placed bonds.

Historically, life insurance companies, to which most private placements were sold, had no great need for marketability or liquidity. They held long-term liabilities and received highly predictable cash flows. They had no particular preference for marketable securities because they expected to hold their investments to maturity.

But recent economic developments have forced life insurance companies to abandon their traditional buy-and-hold-to-maturity policy and to become more active in money management.[12] On the asset side, life insurance companies, as well as other financial intermediaries, have been faced with increased interest rate volatility and higher credit risk.[13] On the liability side, increases in loan requests by holders of whole life insurance policies and the growth of "separate accounts" — accounts managed temporarily for pension funds or other types of mutual funds — convinced life insurance companies that their liabilities have become much more volatile. In order to gain more flexibility in responding to unexpected cash outflows or to changing perceptions about firms, industries, or interest rates, life insurance companies shifted their investment focus away from nonmarketable, illiquid assets, such as private placements, toward publicly traded securities, including low-grade bonds.[14]

Information Costs

A second factor contributing to the growth of the low-grade bond market is that, in recent years, it has become much easier for individual and institutional investors to obtain and maintain information about the condition of corporate borrowers. Thus lenders are now more likely to find it cost-effective to lend directly to smaller and less well-known corporations, rather than indirectly through financial intermediaries such as commercial banks.

[12] See James J. O'Leary, "How Life Insurance Companies Have Shifted Investment Focus," *Bankers Monthly Magazine* (June 15, 1982), pp. 2–28, and Timothy Curry and Mark Warshawsky, "Life Insurance Companies in a Changing Environment," *Federal Reserve Bulletin* (June 1986), pp. 449–459.

[13] The early 1980s saw severe sectoral problems — for example in the farm and the energy sectors — and a third-world debt crisis. From 1980 to 1983, the business failure rate — that is, the annual number of failures per 10,000 listed enterprises — averaged 76, more than twice its level during the 1970s. See *The Economic Report of the President* (Washington, DC: GPO, February 1986), Table B-92. For evidence on interest volatility, see Harvey Rosenblum and Steven Strongin, "Interest Rate Volatility in Historical Perspective," Federal Reserve Bank of Chicago *Economic Perspectives* (January/February 1983), pp. 10–19.

[14] Timothy Curry and Mark Warshawsky, "Life Insurance Companies in a Changing Environment," p. 456, report that: "In recent years, however, life insurance companies have been committing to private placements smaller percentages of their investable cash flow: 25 to 30 percent in 1984, down from a historical level of 40 to 50 percent."

Indeed, recent technological improvements in such areas as data manipulation and telecommunications have reduced greatly the costs of obtaining and processing information about the conditions—whether international or domestic, industry-wide or firm-specific—that affect the value of a borrowing firm. Any analyst now has computerized access to a wealth of economic and financial information at a relatively low cost. New information reaches investors across the world in a matter of minutes. Given the reduction in information costs, the cheapest method of lending to certain smaller and less creditworthy borrowers may no longer require a specialized intermediary as the sole lender to these borrowers, especially after recognizing the other expenses of using the intermediary.[15] For many institutional investors—such as mutual funds, pension funds, and insurance companies—the costs of being informed about certain borrowers have dropped enough that it has become profitable to acquire relatively small amounts of debt directly from those firms. As a result, firms that now issue their own low-grade bonds in the open market face a growing acceptance of their securities.

Risk Perceptions

A third explanation of the growth in low-grade bond offerings is more on the psychological side. Investors are not only better informed about the risks they take on, but they may have also become more willing to invest in risky securities. After the 1930s, the market for newly issued low-grade bonds shrank as most investors—with the losses incurred during the Depression still vividly in mind—turned to high-grade securities and left it to financial intermediaries to manage the risk of lending to less creditworthy borrowers. But as time passed and the memory of the 1930s faded, portfolio managers probably started to discount the probability that the economy would again become subject to a major system-wide shock.[16] It is thus possible that, as new generations of portfolio managers with no direct experience of the Depression took over, financial markets as a whole became more receptive to riskier securities, such as low-grade bonds.

Summary

Low-grade bonds are bonds that are rated "speculative" by the major rating agencies and that are therefore considered very risky investments.

---

[15] These added costs of using a financial intermediary instead of lending directly to a firm by buying its debt securities involve, for example, taxes, administration costs, and the costs of monitoring the condition and behavior of the intermediary.

[16] For a discussion of this type of behavior, see Jack Guttentag and Richard Herring, "Credit Rationing and Financial Disorder," *The Journal of Finance* (December 1984), pp. 1359–1382. As an example, the authors describe the behavior of a driver who has just witnessed a car accident. His immediate reaction is to drive much more cautiously. But gradually, as time passes and the image of the accident recedes from memory, the driver reverts to less cautious behavior.

These bonds are either corporate bonds that have been downgraded, or, more recently, bonds that are issued originally with a rating below investment grade. Original-issue low-grade bonds are issued mostly by corporations that previously borrowered in the form of commercial loans or privately placed bonds.

Several factors seem to have contributed to the growth in low-grade bond offerings. For one, increased volatility in their sources of funds and a worsening of interest rate and credit risk have forced life insurance companies, which are the major buyers of private placements, to shift their investment focus towards assets that are somewhat more marketable and liquid, such as low-grade bonds. Also, improvements in computer technology have lowered the information and monitoring costs of investing in securities and have thus allowed smaller and less known corporations to borrow directly from private and institutional investors. Third, it may be that the favorable post-World War II default experience on low-grade bonds has made investors more receptive towards investing directly in riskier securities, including low-grade bonds.

The growth in low-grade bond offerings thus represents mostly a rechanneling of corporate borrowing, away from individually negotiated loans, towards public securities. As such, it exemplifies a continuing effort by financial market participants to search out the most cost-effective way to channel funds from lenders to borrowers.

Questions

1. What are junk bonds?

2. Describe the historical record of default rates of low-grade bonds.

3. Describe the historical record of rates of return on low-grade bonds.

4. Low-grade bonds are often associated with corporate takeovers; that is, a company issues low-grade bonds to finance the purchase of another company. Does the empirical evidence support the belief that low-grade bonds are issued primarily to finance takeovers?

5. "The risk premium of lower-grade bonds over Treasuries, however, has run from 300 to 600 basis points over the last five years." In your opinion, does the risk premium of low-grade bonds justify their purchase by investors, who become exposed to their default risk?

6. What reasons does the author give for the growth in the issuance of low-grade bonds?

Nonconvertible Preferred Stock Financing and Financial Distress: A Note

R. Charles Moyer, M. Wayne Marr, and Robert E. Chatfield

Nonconvertible preferred stock does not play a major role in the financing of most corporations, with the exception of public utilities. Donaldson (1962) hypothesized that nonconvertible preferred stock will be issued primarily by industrial (non-utility) firms facing financial difficulties. This article investigates this hypothesis. Our results support the financial-distress hypothesis and indicate that industrial issuers of nonconvertible preferred stock have a lower relative market value, a lower interest coverage ratio, a lower level of retained earnings, and a lower equity ratio than do non-issuers.

I. Introduction

Because preferred stock has played a minor role in the long-term financing plans of United States corporations, little research attention has focused on this financial instrument. Donaldson (1962) discussed the rationale for a corporation's issue of preferred stock. In particular, Donaldson hypothesized that when cash inadequacy threatens corporate survival, the relative risk between preferred stock and long-term debt

R. Charles Moyer, M. Wayne Marr, and Robert E. Chatfield, "Nonconvertible Preferred Stock Financing and Financial Distress: A Note," *Journal of Economics and Business* (February 1987): 81–89. Reprinted with permission.

R. Charles Moyer is from Wake Forest University. M. Wayne Marr is from Virginia Polytechnic Institute and State University. Robert E. Chatfield is from University of Nevada, Las Vegas. Address correspondence to Professor R. Charles Moyer, Babcock School, Wake Forest University, P.O. Box 7659, Winston-Salem, NC 27109.

The authors wish to acknowledge the assistance of Phil Sisneros, who did much of the statistical analysis in this article and the thoughtful comments of the participants in the University of Oklahoma and Texas Tech University Finance workshops.

changes. With possible bankruptcy on the horizon, corporations may be inclined to issue higher-cost preferred stock instead of lower-cost long-term debt. With imperfect market information about the potential future financial condition of a firm, the firm may be able to achieve some cost-of-capital benefits by issuing preferred stock rather than debt and common equity. Fisher and Wilt (1968) conclude that as long as preferred stock dividends are not a tax-deductible expense for the issuing firm, the use of preferred stock by large industrial (non-utility) firms is likely to be minimal. For a firm facing financial difficulty and the potential of negative future earnings (and 0% effective tax rates), the tax deductibility of interest payments is no longer important. For these firms, preferred stock becomes an attractive financing alternative because of the reduced risk of forced bankruptcy if preferred stock dividends cannot be paid (as compared to the failure to pay bond interest). The value of this benefit depends, of course, on asymmetries in information relative to the future condition of the firm. If investors fully perceive this increased risk of financial distress, the preferred stock will be priced accordingly. In addition, we would expect to find other firms with low effective marginal tax rates to have some preference for the issuance of preferred stock because of the before-tax cost advantages to an investing corporation arising from the 85% corporate preferred stock dividend exclusion.

This article empirically examines the hypothesis that nonconvertible preferred stock is issued primarily by non-utility firms facing financial difficulties. The article does not address the broader issues of the determinants of aggregate preferred stock financing, although the incidence of impending financial distress may have implications for macro-level studies of preferred stock financing activity.

This article is organized as follows. Section II examines the extent of use and the characteristics of preferred stock issued by industrial firms from 1974 to 1980. Section III develops reasons why financially distressed firms may find preferred stock to be a relatively attractive financing instrument. Section IV reports the results of empirical tests of the hypotheses. Section V summarizes the major conclusions from the study.

II. Preferred Stock Use and Characteristics

Before the 1970s, preferred stock issues constituted about 3% of the total dollar amount of new corporate securities issued. Table 1 shows that during the 1970s, convertible and nonconvertible preferred stock issues made up over 6.6% of the total dollar amount of new corporate securities issued. Sorenson and Hawkins (1981) suggested that the relative increase in preferred stock issues resulted from increases in demand for preferred stock by insurance companies and other institutional investors.

Table 2 indicates that utilities have issued well over half of the preferred stock sold between 1970 and 1980 (by total dollar amount), although a definite downward trend in the utility share of this market has

Table 1   **New Security Offerings for Selected Years**

Year	Total Issues ($ Bil)	Percentage		
		Common Stock	**Bonds**	**Preferred Stock**
1970	$38.9	18.6%	77.8%	3.6%
1971	45.0	20.6	71.3	8.1
1972	39.7	27.0	64.6	8.4
1973	31.7	24.1	65.4	10.5
1974	37.7	10.5	83.5	6.0
1975	53.6	13.8	79.7	6.5
1976	53.4	15.5	79.2	5.3
1977	54.2	15.0	78.0	7.0
1978	47.2	16.0	78.0	6.0
1979	51.5	15.0	78.0	7.0
1980	72.9	23.0	72.0	5.0

Source: *Monthly Statistics*, various issues 1970 through 1981, Securities and Exchange Commission.

occurred. Industrial corporations that include manufacturing companies and extractive companies increased their use of preferred stock during the 1970s. Table 2 shows that industrial firms issued about 4% of the convertible and nonconvertible preferred stock by total dollar amount in 1970. By 1980, industrial firms issued about 30% of preferred stock by total dollar amount. During the same period, financial and real estate firms also increased their use of preferred stock.

Table 2   **Convertible and Nonconvertible Preferred Stock Offerings by Industry**

Year	Total Issues ($ Bil)	Percentage		
		Utility	**Industrial**	**Other**
1970	$1.39	90.5%	3.7%	5.8%
1971	3.68	92.5	5.5	2.0
1972	3.37	92.2	6.2	1.6
1973	3.34	94.0	3.8	2.2
1974	2.25	93.9	5.1	1.0
1975	3.46	76.1	17.7	6.2
1976	2.80	77.4	17.1	5.5
1977	3.92	61.1	14.5	24.4
1978	2.83	68.8	17.3	13.9
1979	3.53	64.4	23.9	11.7
1980	3.63	53.8	30.5	15.7

Source: *Monthly Statistics*, various issues 1970 through 1981, Securities and Exchange Commission.

Definitions: Utility includes electric, gas, water, and telephone companies. Industrial includes manufacturing and extractive companies. Other includes transportation, sales, consumer finance, financial, and real estate companies.

Table 3   **Industrial Nonconvertible Preferred Stock Issues**[a]

Company	Placement	($ Million)	Year
Ashland Oil	Private	$50.0	1974
Hooker Chemical	Private	30.0	1975
International Harvester	Private	50.0	1975
Occidental Petroleum	Private	75.0	1975
Quaker Oats	Private	50.0	1975
Ashland Oil	Private	50.0	1976
AMAX	Private	150.0	1977
Certain-Teed	Private	40.0	1977
Ethyl	Private	40.0	1977
General Cable	Private	25.0	1977
Itel	Public	52.5	1977
Kaneb Services	Private	25.0	1977
NL Industries	Private	50.0	1977
Norin	Public	15.0	1977
Northwest Industries	Private	50.0	1977
Occidental Petroleum	Public	100.0	1977
Reichhold Chemicals	Private	35.0	1977
Allis Chalmers	Private	30.0	1978
Chrysler	Public	250.0	1978
Combustion Equipment	Private	29.0	1978
IC Industries	Private	100.0	1978
Kerr-Glass Manufacturing	Private	15.0	1978
McQuay-Perfex	Private	10.0	1978
Occidental Petroleum	Public	75.0	1978
Wickes	Private	25.0	1978
Allied Chemical (2 issues)	Private	260.0	1979
Ameron	Private	15.0	1979
Grumman	Public	50.0	1979
Kerr-Glass Manufacturing	Private	14.0	1979
International Paper	Private	300.0	1979
Flexi-Van Corporation	Public	37.5	1979
Petro-Lewis	Public	26.5	1979
Lone Star Industries	Private	41.0	1980
Mesa Petroleum (2 issues)	Private	210.0	1980
Sta-Rite Industries	Private	10.4	1980
Toro	Private	15.0	1980

Source: *Registration and Offering Statistics File*, Securities and Exchange Commission, 1982.

[a] 10 million dollars or greater.

Between 1974 and 1980, 38 industrial nonconvertible preferred stock issues of $10 million or more were sold. These issues are identified in Table 3. Only 32 distinct companies are listed (among the 38 issues) because several companies issued preferred stock more than once during this period. In addition to the issues listed in Table 3, a number of smaller private-placement offerings were tendered. An examination of the 38 issues reveals several common features. The common features are the sinking fund, the call provision, and the voting-rights provision.

Thirty-seven issues have a sinking fund requiring the cumulative redemption of a specific number of shares of stock per year after a deferment period. Sinking fund requirements range from 3% to 34% of the face value of the issue, with a mean of 11% per year. In 90% of the issues, the sinking fund begins in the sixth year or later. After that time, the firm normally has a noncumulative option to retire an additional 100% of the minimum mandatory requirement. Most stocks are redeemable at par or at the initial offering price.

All of the issues have a call provision. Call prices range from 5% to 10% above the offering price and gradually decline over time to the issue price. Call deferment periods vary from immediately callable to a 10-year deferment period, with the majority callable at five years.

One-third of the issues give preferred stockholders full voting rights; that is, the preferred stockholder receives one vote for each share held. The other two-thirds carry only contingent voting rights: giving stockholders the right to elect at least two directors if four or more quarterly dividends have been passed. (The Securities and Exchange Commission opposes the issuance of preferred stock without, at least, contingent voting rights. The New York Stock Exchange will not list a preferred stock unless it offers holders contingent voting rights.) In addition, preferred stockholders must approve by at least a two-thirds majority: 1) any charter or bylaw change that may materially affect the position of preferred stockholders; 2) amendments to the certificate of incorporation that change the priorities of the preferred stock with respect to a claim on earnings and assets; 3) mergers or consolidations; and 4) voluntary liquidations.

III. The Financial Distress Hypothesis

Preferred stock dates back to the 1830s, when Maryland road and canal companies found obtaining capital from investors on reasonable terms impossible. The companies appealed to the state to provide funds to complete their construction projects. The legislature provided the funds, but only after the companies agreed to pay a fixed dividend on the stock purchased by the state. Later, in the 1840s and 1850s, railroads began using this same method to finance construction projects. At this time many of the railroads were financially distressed. They sought state aid, but it was only provided under the condition that investors purchase additional stock from the company. In order to attract investors, stock with a fixed dividend was offered. Evans (1929) reports that these were the first true preferred stocks in the United States. Thus, from its earliest days, preferred stock came into existence because of the inability of financially distressed firms to sell common stock or to borrow additional funds on reasonable terms.

How can the behavior of the industrial firms that issue nonconvertible preferred stock be reconciled with the normally high after-tax cost of preferred financing? Donaldson (1962) has argued that for a financially healthy firm, the legal fact that preferred dividends do not have to be paid on a regular basis is of little value, because they will be forced to behave *as if* these preferred dividends were mandatory. The reason is that when a firm fails to pay preferred dividends, it is precluded from paying common dividends. The cessation of common dividends would do serious damage to the market price of the firm's common stock.

In contrast, a firm facing possible cash inadequacy severe enough to threaten its ability to survive may find the flexibility offered by preferred stock worth the cost. Furthermore, many firms that face financial difficulty have an expectation of a 0% effective tax rate. Given this possibility, the relative cost disadvantage of preferred stock may not exist. If the firm regains its financial health, it can always call the preferred stock and eliminate this "high-cost" source of funds. Thus, we can expect many preferred stock-issuing firms to be experiencing current or imminent financial difficulties. Empirical evidence in support of this hypothesis is offered in the next section.

IV. Discussion of Results

The sample of firms used to test the financial-distress hypothesis consists of the 25 industrial firms issuing preferred stock for which complete data were available (on both the firm and a group of non-issuing firms in the same industry SIC code) during the 1974–1980 period. Data were also collected for industry control groups that did not issue preferred stock during the 1974–1980 period. The control groups include all non-issuing firms on the primary, supplementary, and tertiary files of *Compustat* with the same four-digit SIC code as the issuing firm, except for firms with missing or incomplete data and firms with total assets of less than $1 million. Data for both the issuing firm and the non-issuing control group were based on financial statements for the first full year preceding the date of the preferred stock offering. Table 4 lists the issuing firms and the number of firms in the control group of non-issuing firms. In the case of firms that made multiple offerings during the 1974–1980 period, data were collected only for the most recent offering.

A total of nine financial ratios are computed for the issuing firm and for the non-issuing control group. The industry average for the control group is computed as a weighted (by total asset) average of the companies in the industry. The first four ratios were chosen based on their relationship with financial distress and their use in past studies of financial distress, such as Beaver (1967). The ratios calculated are:

1. *Common equity to total assets:* Issuing firms are hypothesized to have lower equity ratios than are non-issuers, indicating the need for an equity infusion.

2. *Market price of common equity to book value per share:* The market to book ratio provides an indication of the future earnings capacity and risk of a firm relative to the historical cost of the equity-financed

Table 4 Issuing and Non-Issuing Firms in Sample

Issuing Company	SIC	Firms in Non-Issuing Control Group
Quaker Oats	2000	16
International Harvester	3711	8
Ashland Oil	2911	39
AMAX Inc.	1000	10
Certain-Teed	3290	4
Ethyl Corporation	2810	4
Kaneb Services	1381	15
NL Industries	3533	10
Northwest Industries	3310	38
Reichhold Chemicals, Inc.	2820	1
Allis Chalmers Corp.	3530	4
Combustion Equipment Corp.	3558	6
IC Industries	4011	11
Chrysler Corporation	3711	8
Occidental Petroleum	1311	47
Ameron, Inc.	3270	7
Flexi-Van Corporation	7394	4
Grumman Corporation	3721	7
International Paper	2600	26
Kerr-Glass Manufacturing	3221	5
Petro-Lewis	1311	48
Wickes	5211	5
Lone Star Industries	3241	8
Mesa Petroleum	1311	51
Toro	3520	7

assets of the firm. As such, the market to book ratio for issuing firms is expected to be less than that for non-issuers.

3. *Earnings before interest and taxes to total interest:* This interest-coverage variable indicates the ability of a firm to meet its fixed interest obligations. Issuing firms are expected to be less able to meet their fixed obligations than are non-issuing firms.

4. *Cash flow to total debt:* This ratio, the best bankruptcy predictor used by Beaver (1967), is expected to be lower for issuing firms than for non-issuing firms.

In addition to these four ratios, we have also analyzed the five ratios used by Altman (1968) in his well-known bankruptcy forecasting model. These ratios are:

5. *Working capital to total assets:* Issuing firms, if financially distressed, should have a lower working capital ratio than will non-issuing firms.

6. *Retained earnings to total assets:* This ratio is expected to be lower for issuing firms, indicating that they have generated insufficient profits or experienced losses in the past.

7.   *Earnings before interest and taxes to total assets:* This measure of profitability would be expected to be lower for issuing firms if the financial-distress hypothesis is true.

8.   *Market value of equity to book value of total debt:* Financially distressed firms are expected to have a significantly lower market value–based equity to debt ratio reflective of their relatively poor earnings, poor expected earnings, higher risk, and/or higher relative levels of debt.

9.   *Sales to total assets:* Altman hypothesized that financially distressed firms would have lower total asset turnover ratios than would financially healthy firms.

Table 5 summarizes the results of this ratio analysis for issuing and non-issuing firms. Six of the nine ratios have the hypothesized relationship and four are statistically significant.

Issuing firms have a significantly lower ratio of market price of common stock to book value of common stock than do non-issuing firms. A market to book ratio below 1 (e.g., 0.90 for the issuing group) is indicative of a firm earning and expected to continue earning a lower return on book equity than its market cost of equity. In contrast, a market to book ratio in excess of 1 (e.g., 1.28 for non-issuing firms) is indicative

Table 5   Ratio Analysis for Issuing and Non-Issuing Firms

Ratio	Issuing Group Mean	Non-Issuing Group Mean	*t* Value
1. Common equity / Total assets	41.20%	44.61%	−1.47
2. Market price common stock / Book value common stock	0.90	1.28	−2.39[a]
3. Earnings before interest and taxes / Total interest	5.22	10.97	−3.44[a]
4. Cash flow / Total debt	0.21	0.25	−1.57
5. Working capital / Total assets	20.78%	19.55%	0.36
6. Retained earnings / Total assets	26.78%	32.57%	−2.52[a]
7. Earnings before interest and taxes / Total assets	14.02%	13.65%	0.22
8. Market value of equity / Book value of total debt	83.74%	131.65%	−2.66[a]
9. Sales / Total assets	1.30	1.11	1.18

[a] Significant at the 0.05 level.

of a firm earning and expected to continue earning a higher return on book equity than its market cost of equity capital.

Issuing firms have a dramatically lower total-interest coverage ratio (5.22 times) than do non-issuing firms (10.97 times). Because earnings before interest and taxes to total assets are not relatively low for issuing firms, these firms must have relatively high interest charges. This may be caused by the issuing firms' greater use of financial leverage and a higher cost of debt. This is verified by the lower common equity to total assets ratio for issuing firms.

Consistent with the issuing firms' greater use of financial leverage are the results from the retained earnings to total assets ratio and the market value of equity to book value of total debt ratio. Both are significantly lower for issuing firms, indicating a deficiency in the amount of equity in their capital structures. Although not significant at the 5% level, the lower common equity to total assets ratio and the lower cash flow to total debt ratio for issuing firms are both consistent with the greater use of financial leverage.

Three ratios indicated the opposite of the hypothesized relationships, but in no case were the results from these ratios statistically significant. The sales to total assets ratio from Altman's bankruptcy study came the closest to refuting our hypothesis. This is not unexpected. A later study by Moyer (1977) indicated that this ratio adds nothing to the explanatory power of the bankruptcy model and could even detract from its explanatory power.

The results displayed in Table 5 are consistent with the financial-distress hypothesis. Each ratio either indicates issuing firms to be financially distressed relative to non-issuing firms or indicates no statistically significant difference. A look at Table 4 and a bit of casual empiricism also strengthens the argument. Several of the issuing firms have experienced near or total financial failure since they issued preferred stock. These firms include International Harvester, Chrysler Corporation, and Wickes (a subsidiary of Wickes — Gamble-Skogmo — had also issued income bonds a few years prior to Wickes's 1982 bankruptcy filing). Table 4 identifies a number of oil and gas firms — Occidental Petroleum, Ashland Oil, Petro-Lewis, and Mesa Petroleum. These firms faced low or zero effective tax rates because of the special tax preferences available to firms in that industry during the 1970s. Among the non-industrial, non-utility firms that have made use of preferred stock over the past decade are several airlines. Issuers include American, Eastern, and the now-bankrupt Braniff. Notably absent from the group of issuers are the financially stronger lines like Delta and United.

V. Conclusions and Implications

Preferred stock continues to play only a minor role in the long-term financing plans of U.S. industrial firms, with the exception of the utility industries. For those firms that have made use of preferred stock financing during the past decade, evidence was presented that supports the financial-distress hypothesis. Thus, the use of preferred stock may be viewed as a signal to the financial markets that the firm expects low effective future tax rates and/or anticipates a deterioration in the firm's future financial condition.

Given the relative insignificance of preferred stock financing by industrial firms, one can also consider the appropriateness of its use in utility capital structures. The typical electric utility capital structure contains 12% preferred stock financing. If utilities can justify the use of a security with the characteristics of preferred stock to raise funds, a superior alternative exists. Income bonds and preferred stock do not dilute ownership or entail bankruptcy costs. But income bonds' interest is a tax-deductible cost, unlike that of preferred dividends. Although infrequently used, evidence from McConnell and Schlarbaum (1981) supports the use of income bonds as a viable capital market instrument.

References

Altman, Edward I. Sept. 1968. "Financial ratios, discriminant analysis and the prediction of corporate bankruptcy." *Journal of Finance,* 23(4):589–609.

Beaver, William H. 1967. "Financial ratios as predictors of failure." *Empirical Research in Accounting: Selected Studies,* Supplement to Vol. 5, *Journal of Accounting Research.*

Donaldson, Gordon. July/Aug. 1962. "In defense of preferred stock." *Harvard Business Review.*

Evans, George H., Jr. March 1929. "The early history of preferred stock in the United States." *American Economic Review.*

Fisher, Donald E., and Wilt, Glenna A. Sept. 1968. "Nonconvertible preferred stock as a financing instrument." *Journal of Finance,* 23(4):611–624.

McConnell, John J., and Schlarbaum, Gary G. Jan. 1981. "Returns, risks, and pricing of income bonds, 1956–76 (does money have an odor?)." *Journal of Business.*

Moyer, R. Charles. Spring 1977. "Forecasting financial failure: A re-examination." *Financial Management.* 6(1):11–17.

Sorenson, Eric H., and Hawkins, Clark A. Nov. 1981. "On the pricing of preferred stock." *Journal of Financial and Quantitative Analysis.*

1981. U.S. Department of Energy. *Statistics of Privately Owned Electric Utilities in the United States, 1980 Annual.* Washington, D.C.: U.S.G.P.O.

Questions

1.   Describe the historical record of new security offerings — common stock, bonds, and preferred stock — by corporations.

2.   Define the following characteristics of preferred stock: sinking fund, call provision, and voting rights.

3. Why do financially weak industrial companies tend to issue preferred stock whereas financially strong industrial companies do not?

4. Selected financial characteristics of industrial companies that issue preferred stock tend to differ from those of industrial companies that do not. What differences between issuers and non-issuers would you expect in the following financial ratios: (a) market price of common stock divided by book value of common stock, (b) interest coverage ratio, (c) retained earnings divided by total assets, and (d) market value of equity divided by book value of debt? Explain.

Of Financial Innovations and Excesses

James C. Van Horne

One of the bedrocks of our financial system is financial innovation, the life blood of efficient and responsive capital markets. Even a casual review of the changes that recently have occurred in the financial services industry leaves one in awe. The last six years have witnessed the greatest number of financial innovations in our nation's history, reflecting vitality and the forces of competition. In this address, I wish to consider financial innovation in the good and in the bad. There is much good, as I think we will come to agree. However, some things labelled financial innovations have little or no substance when we peel away the veneer, other than to their promoters.

I. Foundations for Innovation

Briefly reviewing, a financial innovation may be either a new product, such as zero coupon bonds, or a new process, such as a new delivery system for electronic funds transfer. With financial innovations, very seldom do we observe the introduction of something entirely new. Rather, innovation typically involves modification of an existing idea, either a product or a process. The dramatic technological breakthroughs that occur in the product markets usually are not found in the financial markets.

For an idea to be viable as a financial innovation, it must make the markets more efficient in an operational sense and/or more complete. The purpose of financial markets, of course, is to channel the savings of

James C. Van Horne, "Of Financial Innovations and Excesses," *The Journal of Finance* Vol. XL, No. 3 (July 1985): 621–631. Copyright (c) 1985 the American Finance Association. Reprinted with permission.

At the time of this writing, James C. Van Horne was the A. P. Giannini Professor of Finance at Stanford University.

society to the most profitable investment opportunities on a risk-adjusted return basis. These opportunities may originate in the private sector, and involve a rate of return on investment, or in the public sector, where a social return is involved. In all cases, there is a cost to the financial intermediation process by which savings flows are allocated; the process is not frictionless. This cost is represented by the difference, or spread, between what the ultimate saver receives for funds and what the ultimate borrower pays (holding risk constant), as well as by the inconvenience to one or both parties.[1] A financial innovation may make the market more efficient by reducing the cost of financial intermediation to consumers of financial services. Either the spread, as defined above, is lowered or inconvenience costs are reduced.

A second foundation for financial innovation is the movement toward market completeness. A complete market exists when every contingency in the world corresponds to a distinct marketable security.[2] In contrast, incomplete markets exist when the number and types of securities available do not span these contingencies. In other words, there is an unfilled desire for a particular type of security on the part of an investor clientele. An example would be the desire for zero coupon bonds by pension funds prior to 1981. If the market is incomplete, it pays a financial intermediary or a direct borrower to exploit the opportunity by tailoring security offerings to the unfilled desires of investors, whether those desires have to do with maturity, coupon rate, protection, call feature, cash-flow characteristics, or whatever. As with most things, it is a matter of degree. The sheer number of different types of securities necessary to make the market truly complete is bound to result in an incomplete market in the real world. The issue is whether a sufficient number of time-state claims exist to make the market reasonably complete, not entirely so.

Thus, financial innovations occur in response to profit opportunities which, in turn, arise from inefficiencies in financial intermediation and/or incompleteness in financial markets. If markets are truly competitive, the profitability of a financial innovation to its original promoter will decline over time. A profitable innovation, of course, invites others to enter the marketplace with a like product or process. As this occurs, promoter profit margins erode and financial service consumers increasingly benefit vis-à-vis the promoter. In other words, as a financial innovation becomes seasoned, promoter profit margins decline, and the benefits of the innovation increasingly are realized by the consumer. At least that is how it should work, and usually does.

---

[1] As these notions are well known and further explanation is found in Van Horne [18], Chapter 1, I do not dwell on them.

[2] See Hirshleifer [7], Chapter 9, for additional explanation and mathematical expression.

II. Stimuli for Change

In steady-state market equilibrium, it would not be possible to make the market more efficient and/or more complete. Within the boundaries of search costs, all opportunities for profitable exploitation through financial innovation would be exhausted. Indeed, an unchanging world would be marked by a lack of new financial products and processes. The environment must change for there to be exploitable opportunities and for us to witness widespread financial innovation. During the last six years, a confluence of events has created a receptive atmosphere for financial innovation. With each important change in atmosphere, a flurry of activity occurs, the sum of which can only be described as dazzling. Changes which prompt financial innovation include: (1) volatile inflation rates and interest rates; (2) regulatory changes and circumvention of regulations; (3) tax changes; (4) technological advances; (5) the level of economic activity; and (6) academic work on market efficiency and inefficiencies. While there may be disagreement as to their relative importance, most people agree that these factors are highly influential.[3] Let us consider them in turn.

With volatile inflation and fluctuating nominal and real rates of interest, new products are designed to reduce such risk. Put another way, a changing inflation and interest-rate environment creates demand for different types of financial instruments. New deposit and investment accounts as well as floating rate loans are examples of responses to these stimuli. In part, the trend toward increased negotiability of financial instruments is the result of interest-rate volatility. The considerable variability of inflation and interest rates over the last ten years has caused reevaluation of existing financial instruments with new and, oftentimes, better instruments being proposed.

The second factor, regulatory change and circumvention of regulations, also has prompted many a financial innovation. Beginning in the early 1970s, a number of innovations occurred simply to get around existing regulations. In the late 1970s and accelerating rapidly in the 1980s, we have had deregulation of the financial services industry. Boundaries that functionally separated financial institutions were lowered and, in a number of cases, removed altogether. When constraints are reduced, of course, market participants enter new lines of business possessing previously unattainable profit and/or risk reduction possibilities.[4] On the other hand, when constraints are first imposed, or existing restrictions increased, portfolio adjustments also occur. Here financial

---

[3] See Silber [14], who categorizes a number of financial innovations as to exogenous cause.

[4] Silber [15], pp. 64–66, portrays financial institutions as maximizing a utility function subject to constraints. As the constraints are changed, the shadow prices change. Financial innovation is said to be an adaptive response to these shadow price changes.

innovation tends to be defensive in nature, aimed at restoring profitability and/or at risk reduction.

In recent years, most regulatory changes have reduced or removed restrictions. With financial deregulation, the distinction between commercial banks, savings and loan associations, investment banks, insurance companies, mortgage bankers, large retailers, and financial conglomerates, e.g., American Express, has blurred. Alas, it no longer is possible for a financial institution to remain in a nice, safe niche. With each step down the deregulatory road, financial innovation becomes increasingly necessary for survival.[5] This powerful force has been one of the most important stimuli for change. Only recently has it been blunted by the aftershocks of the Continental Illinois debacle. In addition to domestic deregulation, many capital and currency constraints to international borrowing and lending have been reduced.

The third factor, alteration in tax laws, also motivates financial innovation. When after-tax returns on financial instruments are impacted by tax legislation, new financial products often emerge as do revisions in existing products. In particular, changes in the differential taxation of interest and dividend income versus capital-gains income affects the market equilibrium process, often in dramatic ways. In turn, this opens things up for financial innovation. The closing of tax loopholes, as occurred in the Deficit Reduction Act of 1984, also alters market equilibrium in restricting the use of certain financial products. As a result, new degrees of market incompleteness are introduced. The final form and effect of the 1985 Tax Act remain to be seen.

Technological advances provoke process change more than they do product change. The computer age has brought with it a continual broadening of applications to the financial services industry and a lowering of costs per transaction. Electronic funds transfers, automatic teller machines, point-of-sale terminals, credit-card data processing, personal computers which permit in-home financial transactions, and telecommunications all have changed dramatically the way financial products are provided and the way they are priced. Speed and accuracy per transaction are increased, and structural costs have been lowered through automation. In most areas of financial service, efficiency in delivery is crucial.[6] Less efficient producers are left behind in the competitive arena. While there is a place for financial boutiques in special niches, the overall financial services industry is dominated by cost effectiveness. The shakeout continues, and most agree that there will be fewer financial service providers in the future than there are now.

Changes in the level of economic activity may stimulate financial innovation. In a period of economic prosperity, many financial institutions are eager to try new ideas in their relentless pursuit of growth.

---

[5] For an excellent analysis of the effects of deregulation, see Gart [6].

[6] For an overall evaluation of the effect of computers and telecommunications technology on the financial services industry, see Shrivastava [13].

However, in a steep recession, such as occurred in 1981 to 1982, the emphasis shifts to risk reduction and liquidity. To take international banking as an example, the financial innovations which occurred in the 1970s were mainly directed at business expansion. Currency option loans, parallel loans, special swap arrangements, and many other innovations were undertaken in the quest of higher loan volume. New business, generally at low spreads, was the result. With the surfacing of problem loans to developing countries in the 1980s, the posture of international banks changed to "battening down the hatches" through risk reduction moves. What innovation that occurs is largely in this vein.[7] This tendency is accentuated by domestic loan problems. In summary, variation in the level of economic activity affects not only the magnitude and type of funds needed, but also the risk attitudes of financial institutions and other market participants. In turn, these affect financial innovations in our society.

Last, but certainly not least, is all of the academic work on asset pricing, options, interest rates, futures markets, and derivative securities. The financial community has become increasingly receptive to these ideas, as it is clear that it can profit from them. Also, as more MBA and other students trained in modern finance become a part of the financial community, they prompt changes along such lines.

III. Some Financial Innovations

Thus, the stimuli to financial innovation are many. In response, a vast number of innovations have occurred during the past six years. Some of the better known are shown in Table I, according to whether the innovation was a product or a process. Similar to Silber [14], I have endeavored to categorize these more recent innovations as to primary cause(s). The numbers to the right represent the six factors described before. The more basic foundation, of course, is the opportunity to make the market more efficient and/or more complete and, by so doing, realize a profit and/or reduce risk. The profit/risk reduction motive is the fundamental reason behind the financial innovations observed. The first five external factors change the environment in which profit and risk reduction opportunities arise. The sixth, academic work, is more fundamental in its influence.

In Table I, we see that innovations often were prompted by changes in more than one factor. For products, a dominant theme is volatile inflation and interest rates. For processes, the major cause is technological advances. As one reflects on this list of well-known financial innovations or, for that matter, on any similar listing, most of us would agree that our financial system is well served by their occurrence. In the face of so

---

[7] See Prussia [12] for a discussion of this point.

Table I   A Partial Listing of Recent Financial Innovations
(1978–1984)

	Primary Cause[a]
Products	
Money market investment accounts	1, 2
Super NOW accounts	1, 2
Interest rate and stock index futures markets	1, 2, 6
Options on futures contracts	1, 2, 6
Municipal bond mutual funds	1, 3
Zero coupon bonds and coupon stripping	1, 6
Adjustable rate preferred stock	1, 3
New variations of adjustable rate mortgages	1, 2, 6
Securitization of pass-through and other mortgages	1, 2, 5
IRA accounts	3
Universal life insurance policies	1
Currency option loans	1
Interest rate swaps and currency swaps	1
Forward interest rate loan contracts, with ceilings and floors	1
Bonds with put options	1, 3
Issuance of and investment in high-yield (junk) bonds	1, 6
Processes	
Automatic teller machines	2, 4
Point-of-sale terminals	4
Financial transactions by personal computer	4
Shelf registrations	2
Electronic security trading	2, 4
Electronic funds transfer	4
New variations in credit card processing	4

[a] Cause notation: 1, volatile inflation and interest rates; 2, regulatory; 3, tax law change; 4, technological advance; 5, level of economic activity; and 6, academic work.

much change, financial innovation is absolutely essential if markets are to serve their vital role in the overall financial services industry. But all is not rose-colored.

IV. Alleged Innovations and Excesses

There has been a recent wave of enthusiasm for financial innovation. This enthusiasm is not surprising in view of the changing financial environment in which we live and all the innovations that have gone before. Nowdays, almost any proposal gets a receptive ear, unlike the past when proposed changes were viewed with innate skepticism. Never has the time been riper for new ideas. Certainly, this reduction in hostility benefits the financial markets to some extent.

However, it also allows certain deals to be masqueraded as financial innovations. When the mask is removed, we find little or no substance.

Still other ideas have substance, but the promoters have eaten not only the icing of the cake but also the cake itself. Yet promoters continue to be invited to the financial innovation ball, although perhaps only with new masks. The eagerness of financial-service consumers for almost anything new has allowed investment banks and other financial institutions to propose things lacking in the foundation of making the financial markets more efficient operationally and/or more complete. Indeed, there appears to be little reluctance to try out a new product or process, no matter how far out it might seem or how rich it is priced.[8]

Understandably the promoter wishes to make a profit regardless of whether an idea has substance. As long as people believe the proposal is a panacea for certain ills, promoters will exploit the opportunity. However, I find disturbing the case being made for such things as: defeasance; certain interest-rate swaps; schemes to dedicate bond portfolios in such a way as to take money out of a defined benefit pension plan; financial institutions issuing put options against new and existing bonds in order to alter accounting income; equity-for-debt swaps; the sale of high-yield (junk) bonds to savings and loan associations; and leveraged buyouts, whether financed with loans or with junk bonds. Many are designed to produce accounting profits with little or no economic gains.

And yet, alleged innovations continue to be sold with handsome fees to the promoters and, in mirror image, costs to the other parties involved. With the large number of bright people at investment banks and other financial institutions, it is not surprising that new ideas are continually spawned. The surprising part, at least to me, is that some of them can be sold as financial innovations when, upon close inspection, we find that they are not. In light of the rapid changes in the external environment, there are bound to be bad as well as good ideas in the on-going quest for true financial innovation. However, we would expect ideas without underlying substance to languish. How then do we explain their flourishing along with ideas that we all would agree are true financial innovations? How do we explain the very high and relatively long-lasting promoter profits associated with certain true financial innovations? Are not the financial markets rational and competitive?

I am not sure I have so much answers to these question as I do an observation. The enthusiasm for new ideas seems to me to have resulted in excesses. To a degree, a "herd" instinct appears. In the case of the corporation, a manager does not want to miss out on a perceived good thing if everyone else is doing it. Savings-and-loan association, commercial-bank, and insurance-company executives are attracted to a new repackaging of mortgaged-backed securities, even though they could manufacture essentially the same thing themselves at a lower cost. Like ants attracted to the honey pot, this is a bonanza for financial promoters.

---

[8] Kaufman [9] likens such introductions to new clothes designs where there is great demand to wear a first-of-a-kind outfit. While many do not go into mass production, there is still high initial interest.

Each time a defeasance plan, leveraged buyout, or new type of mortgage-backed security is sold, substantial promoter fees are realized. But do they make money the old fashioned way by earning it? I think not in many cases.

V. Bubbles and Balloons

Is there a bubble effect that allows an idea to be paraded in the guise of a financial innovation? We all are reminded of some of the famous bubbles of the past: the South Sea Company in England in the early 18th century, originated supposedly as a monopoly on trade to the south seas; tulip-mania in Holland in the 1630s, where a single tulip bulb once sold for many years' salary; and the electric utility boom in this country in the 1920s, which permitted excessive pyramiding of stock values.[9] It is difficult to make the case that a speculative bubble of this type is prevalent in ideas paraded as financial innovations. Perhaps some euphoric excesses, or as Adam Smith would say, "over trading," but not bubbles as usually defined.

A bubble, of course, implies an eventual bursting. If the time and magnitude of the burst were known in advance, all participants would be so guided. With completely rational expectations, bubbles simply would not occur.[10] A bubble depends on irrational behavior at least part of the time, with prices rising in anticipation of a further positive expected rate of price change. Such price movements eventually occur independent of any fundamental valuation principles, and further speculative price increases become a self-fulfilling prophecy.[11] The psychology of the crowd simply takes over and prices rise. Market values deviate from fundamental values, based on the information set available at the time. In a given period, the bubble will either remain, and usually by so doing grow bigger, with probability x or burst, with probability $1 - x$.

The longevity of a bubble typically depends on how long it has lasted to date as well as on any special news. Eventually, those with inside information and/or with an eye to the fundamentals begin to withdraw. Others come to the realization that the price will not go higher and there develops a race to get out. The ensuing panic brings with it a sharp price drop and by definition, the bubble is burst.[12] In effect, no more suckers

---

[9] For detailed descriptions of the first two bubbles, see Mackay [11], Chapters 2 and 3 of a book originally published in 1841. For the electric utility situation, see Williams [19], Chapter 25. See also Kindleberger [10] for a lively description of historical bubbles and financial panics.

[10] For proof of this proposition within rational expectations equilibrium, see Tirole [16].

[11] Flood and Garber [4] develop a linear model for analyzing bubbles in the market for foreign exchange and gold monetization.

[12] For a modeling of this phenomenon, as well as an attempt to identify bubbles through analysis of variance bounds being broken, see Blanchard and Watson [3].

can be found. Therefore, a bubble implies irrational behavior. While initially people may behave in a rational manner, a speculative fever eventually grips them. The euphoric atmosphere results in price rises in excess of what the fundamentals would dictate. Eventually the bubble bursts and the price debacle which follows brings misery to those left holding the bag.

The various devices recently conceived and sold as financial innovations are not bubbles, although some of the same excesses are present. Despite the excessive zeal with which I believe "hot" ideas are bought, there is not nearly the devastation that is wrought by the bursting of a speculative bubble. A balloon might be a better metaphor for certain financial promotions. It is blown up to be sure, but not to the extent it pops. The eventual deflation is less abrupt.

For example, the Federal Home Loan Mortgage Corporation (FHLMC; Freddie Mac) introduced collateralized mortgage obligations (CMOs) in 1983, a product that essentially divides mortgage-backed securities into up to four maturity groups. In addition, the FHLMC guarantees a minimum cash flow against excessive prepayment and certain default risk, so there are benefits to the investor other than just cash-flow repackaging. While the initial offerings yielded about 100 basis points less than comparable pass-through mortgage investments, that spread declined to 40 basis points by 1984. Competition and increasingly wiser investors simply let some of the air out of the balloon. Clearly, CMOs offer benefits to the parties involved, so there is a foundation for their existence. However, the initial pricing and reception by the market mainly rewarded the promoter. Whether this large initial profit was the result of asymmetry in sophistication between worldly wise promoters and less sophisticated thrift-institution executives, as suggested by Kaufman [9], is conjecture. These managers appear no more eager than others to swill the heady brew of a dazzling new financial instrument.

Another example of a balloon was the 1982 to 1984 explosion of instruments tailored so the corporate investor could take advantage of the 85 percent tax exemption of dividend income. Adjustable rate preferred stocks (ARPS), ARPS mutual funds, stock funds which hedge risk through options and pass the dividend income along to the corporate investor, convertible adjustable preferred stock (CAPS), and convertible exchangeable subordinated debentures were manifestations of this phenomenon. Never have financial promoters shown greater imagination; they lifted the tax avoidance industry to a new level of illusion. As might be expected, promoter fees were high, but initial demand proved extraordinary. For adjustable rate preferred stocks, investor excesses were particularly evident. At the peak in February of 1983, an ARPS security was priced with an adjustable return nearly 500 basis points below the yield on the appropriate benchmark, Treasury security. At that point, the balloon quickly deflated, and the negative differential declined. The 1984 Tax Act further deflated this balloon, but opportunities have not been extinguished.

Other examples of balloons could be illustrated, but they would tell much the same story. To be sure, many of the things proposed are financial innovations in that they have the potential to make the financial markets more efficient and/or more complete. Because of excessive zeal on the demand and/or supply side, however, the benefits to financial-service consumers are either wiped out by promotion fees or reduced substantially by them. Still other promotions are lacking in economic foundation and appeal to different instincts, often accounting related.

VI. Cost of Excesses

What are the costs of balloons and various alleged but unfounded financial innovations? They are the out-of-pocket expenses paid to promoters and investment managers together with certain dislocations in resource allocation. To the extent that promoter and other fees are excessive, this lessens or, in the extreme, eliminates the benefit of an innovation to consumers of financial services. With respect to dislocations, when decisions are geared to accounting as opposed to economic profits, as I believe is the case with defeasance, certain security swaps and putable bond arrangements, resources may be dissipated. The focus on short-run accounting profitability may be at the expense of longer run economic profits. Capital resources may be misallocated in less than optimal plant and equipment decisions. Much human talent—investment bankers, commercial bankers, other financial institution personnel, lawyers, and accountants—could be used in more fruitful endeavors. In fact, the dislocation costs of physical and human capital are likely to exceed the out-of-pocket costs.

Should we be apprehensive about what probably at worst is an excess? I believe that we should be concerned, and that the cost to society, although not large, is still significant. If true financial innovation is to play its creative role in the development of our financial markets, the promotion of certain schemes is disfunctional. One might ask why if markets are rational will not such plans be exposed for what they are and wither or, in the case of a true financial innovation, high initial promoter fees diminish more rapidly? In an idealized and completely rational expectations world, excesses of the sort described would not occur. However, I believe that irrationality prevails at times and this is the ground in which less than fully productive and/or barren seeds are planted. At the time of the planting, many believe the seeds will bear bountiful fruit and consequently, are willing to pay handsomely for them. After all, they are planted in a field where many a true financial innovation thrives.

Clearly, it is difficult to distinguish the good seed from one that ultimately proves to be less than fully productive or, in the extreme, barren. Still the simple question of whether a proposal will make the markets more efficient or complete usually will reveal whether the seed is barren. While ultimately the market will decide, I believe that excesses sometimes develop and that they extend too long before being corrected by market forces. It is wishful thinking to expect promoters to be self-policing in the things proposed and in the fees extracted. After all, it is the profit motive that gives rise to financial innovation. Also, I would disdain the Securities and Exchange Commission policing such activities, as many worthwhile financial innovations would be choked off in regulatory bureaucracy. FASB surveillance of the corporate accounting implications of a new financial idea is similarly ineffective. No, the ultimate discipline must come from the market, but hopefully an increasingly better informed and suspicious market — a market able to respond rationally and effectively to the cascade of financial ideas thrust upon it.

VII. Observations on the Future of Financial Innovation

What about the future? I believe financial innovation will continue to flourish, as financial markets and the financial services industry become even more competitive. The essential ingredient — change — is all about us. Changes in regulations, tax laws, and technology continue to unfold at almost a frightening clip. Inflation is more stable now than it has been in recent years, but we know this can change rather quickly. Interest rates, both nominal and real, behave in ways difficult to explain by past experience. International events continue to create uncertainty. In this atmosphere, financial innovation should thrive. However, the thrust of financial institutions will shift, as more marketable, depersonalized, rate-sensitive instruments are offered. Further shakeouts and consolidations of financial institutions are inevitable. The failing business doctrine has allowed large financial institutions to acquire organizations nationwide, thereby circumventing laws designed to preclude national deposit institutions. Recent regulatory changes have opened up the insurance industry to competition from other financial institutions. However, concern with the financial stability of banks, thrifts, insurance companies, and security firms has led to recent cries for reregulation.

The increasing sophistication of financial service delivery systems is making efficiency and breadth of services important. These characteristics sometimes can be achieved by merger or by linking together with other financial institutions to provide nationwide or even international service. Such joint ventures are particularly evident in the electronic funds transfer, credit card, and mutual fund areas. The differences between depository institutions, investment banks, insurance companies, telecommunication companies, mutual funds, and retailers are diminishing; the areas of business overlap are expanding. Geographic and product differentiation, once the hallmarks of the financial services industry, are becoming increasingly difficult to sustain.[13] Whether reregulation occurs and reduces this trend remains to be seen.

On balance, there is every reason to believe that the rapid and far reaching financial innovations of the last six years will continue. The times are ripe for such occurrences. Different innovations to be sure. For one thing, deregulation already is well along the road to completion. The initial, rather sweeping, changes will be followed by refinements, or perhaps even by reversals if reregulation occurs. In the unfolding process of financial innovation, I imagine that we will continue to observe excesses of the sort described. However, these may not be as large as in the past. The marketplace for new ideas should become wiser, what with increased experience with financial innovation. Hopefully, it will become sharper in its ability to discriminate. Hefty and sustained promotion fees, misallocation of resources, and the bad image finance conveys to some in our society as a result of promotion abuses are things we could better do without. Still the ultimate discipline and correction must come from the market.

While the times are ripe for financial innovation, they also are receptive for financial research. Formal tools of analysis can be brought to bear to give us more insight, both theoretically and empirically, into the rapidly changing financial environment in which we live. It is exciting, at the same time sobering, to realize that macro finance considerations are unavoidable in a field largely dominated heretofore with micro considerations.

References

1. George Benston, ed. *Financial Services: The Changing Institutions and Government Policy.* Englewood Cliffs, NJ: Prentice-Hall, 1983.

2. Fischer Black and Myron Scholes. "From Theory to a New Financial Product." *Journal of Finance* 29 (May 1974), 399–412.

3. Olivier J. Blanchard and Mark W. Watson. "Bubbles, Rational Expectations, and Financial Markets." In Paul Wachtel (ed.), *Crises in the Economic and Financial Structure.* Lexington, MA: Lexington Books, 1982, pp. 295–315.

4. Robert P. Flood and Peter M. Garber. "Bubbles, Runs and Gold Monetization." In Paul Wachtel (ed.), *Crises in the Economic and Financial Structure.* Lexington, MA: Lexington Books, 1982, 275–93.

5. Benjamin M. Friedman. "Postwar Changes in the American Financial Markets." In Martin Feldstein (ed.), *The American Economy in Transition.* Chicago: University of Chicago Press, 1980, pp. 9–78.

6. Alan Gart. *The Insider's Guide to the Financial Services Revolution.* New York: McGraw-Hill, 1984.

7. J. Hirshleifer. *Investment, Interest, and Capital.* Englewood Cliffs, NJ: Prentice-Hall, 1970.

---

[13] For a further discussion of the future as it pertains to the financial services industry, see Gart [6].

8. Edward J. Kane. "Technological and Regulatory Forces in the Developing Fusion of Financial-Services Competition." *Journal of Finance* 39 (July 1984), 759–72.

9. George G. Kaufman. "The Role of Traditional Mortgage Lenders in Future Mortgage Lending: Problems and Prospects." Paper presented at the Conference on Housing Finance, HUD, March 30, 1984.

10. Charles P. Kindleberger. *Manias, Panics, and Crashes.* New York: Basic Books, 1978.

11. Charles Mackay. *Extraordinary Popular Delusions and the Madness of Crowds.* New York: Harmony Books, 1980. (Originally published in 1841 by Richard Bentley Publishers, London.)

12. Leland S. Prussia. "Structural Change and Innovation in International Banking." Paper presented at the American Finance Association Meetings, December 29, 1983.

13. Paul Shrivastava. "Strategies for Coping with Telecommunications Technology in the Financial Services Industry." *Columbia Journal of World Business* 18 (Spring 1983), 19–25.

14. William L. Silber. "The Process of Financial Innovation." *American Economic Review* 73 (May 1983), 89–95.

15. ——— . "Towards a Theory of Financial Innovation." In William L. Silber (ed.), *Financial Innovation.* Lexington, MA: Lexington Books, 1975, pp. 53–85.

16. Jean Tirole. "On the Possibility of Speculation under Rational Expectations." *Econometrica* 50 (September 1982), 1163–81.

17. Robert M. Townsend. "Financial Structure and Economic Activity." *American Economic Review* 73 (December 1983), 895–912.

18. James C. Van Horne. *Financial Market Rates and Flows,* 2nd ed. Englewood Cliffs, NJ: Prentice-Hall, 1984.

19. John Burr Williams, *The Theory of Investment Value.* Amsterdam: North-Holland Publishing. 1964.

Questions

1.   "For an idea to be viable as a financial innovation, it must make the markets more efficient in an operational sense and/or more complete." Explain these two conditions for viable innovations.

2.   Changes in the environment lead to changes in operational efficiency and completeness of financial markets, which in turn lead to opportunities for financial innovation. What financial innovations have been spawned by changes in each of the following variables: (a) inflation rates and interest rates, (b) government regulation, (c) tax laws, (d) technology, (e) level of economic activity, and (f) academic research?

3.   "On balance, there is every reason to believe that the rapid and far reaching financial innovations of the last six years will continue. The times are ripe for such occurrences." Describe (invent) a financial innovation that differs from those of the past. What advantage does your suggested innovation produce; that is, what makes your suggested innovation viable?

39
Does Dividend Policy Matter?
Richard A. Brealey

Six years ago, Fischer Black, professor of finance at M.I.T., wrote an article entitled "The Dividend Puzzle." The puzzle referred to was that despite considerable debate and research, there is little agreement among economists, managers and investors about the stock price consequences of, and thus the corporate motives for, paying cash dividends. Does a high payout increase the stock price, reduce it, or make no difference at all?

Defining Dividend Policy

Part of the reason for this continuing controversy is that different people mean different things by dividend policy. So let me start by explaining what I mean by the term.

A company's dividend decisions are often mixed up with other financing and investment decisions. Some companies finance capital expenditures largely by borrowing, thus releasing cash for dividends. In this case, the higher dividend is merely a by-product of the borrowing decision. Other companies pay low dividends because management is optimistic about the company's future and wishes to retain earnings for expansion. In this case, the dividend is a by-product of management's capital budgeting decision.

It is therefore important to begin by isolating the effects of dividend policy from those of other financial management decisions. The precise question we should ask, then, is: "What is the effect of a change in cash dividends, given the firm's capital-budgeting and borrowing decisions?"

Richard A. Brealey, "Does Dividend Policy Matter?" *Midland Corporate Finance Journal* (Spring 1983): 17–25. Reprinted with permission.

At the time of this writing, Richard A. Brealey was Midland Bank Professor of Corporate Finance and Director of the Institute of Finance and Accounting at the London Business School.

Note: Several paragraphs in this article have been loosely adapted from *Principles of Corporate Finance* by Richard Brealey and Stewart Myers, Copyright McGraw-Hill Book Co., 1981.

If we fix the firm's investment outlays, borrowing, and operating cash flow, there is only one source of additional dividend payments: a stock issue. For this reason, I define dividend policy as the trade-off between retaining earnings on the one hand, and paying out cash and issuing new shares on the other.[1]

We know that the value of the firm depends on a number of factors. It may be affected by the plant and equipment that it owns, how much debt it issues, how hard the managers work and so on. If we want to know whether dividend policy as such is important, we should hold these other factors constant and ask whether, given the firm's investments, capital structure and management incentives, the level of payout makes any difference.

No financial manager can avoid taking a view on this question. If you are involved in the company's dividend decision, you have an obvious interest in how that decision will affect your shareholders. If you are concerned with capital investment appraisal, you need to know whether the firm's cost of capital depends on its payout policy. (For example, if investors prefer companies with high payouts, management should be more reluctant to take on investments financed by retained earnings.) And, if you have responsibility for the pension fund, you will want to know whether it is better to invest more in high- or low-payout stocks.

Why Dividend Policy May *Not* Matter

There is now substantial agreement among academic economists that, as defined above, dividend policy is largely irrelevant apart from possible tax effects.[2] The reason for this, stated most simply, is that the money for new investments must come from somewhere. Once you have fixed on a sensible debt policy, any increase in dividends must be matched by a corresponding issue of equity. So management's choice, as we have observed, is between retaining earnings or simultaneously paying them out as dividends and issuing stock to replace the lost cash. To suggest that you can make shareholders better off by paying them money with one hand and taking it back with the other is rather like suggesting that you can cool the kitchen by leaving the refrigerator door open. In each case, you are simply recycling.

Of course, a higher payout could affect the share price if it was the only way that the shareholder could get his hands on the cash. But, as

---

[1] This trade-off may seem artificial at first, for we do not see companies scheduling a stock issue with every dividend payment. But there are many firms that pay dividends and also issue stock from time to time. They could avoid the stock issues by paying lower dividends. Other companies restrict dividends so that they *do not* have to issue shares.

[2] The irrelevance of dividend policy in perfect markets was demonstrated by Merton Miller and Franco Modigliani in "Dividend Policy, Growth and the Valuation of Shares," *Journal of Business* 34 (October 1961), 411–432.

long as there are efficient capital markets, a shareholder can always raise cash by selling shares. Thus, the old shareholders can "cash in" on their investment either by persuading management to pay a higher dividend or by selling some of their shares. In either case there will be a transfer of value from old to new shareholders. Because investors do not need dividends to get their hands on cash, they will not pay higher prices for the shares of firms with a high payout. Therefore, firms ought not to worry about dividend policy.

Just as a high payout policy does not in itself raise firm value, so a low payout policy also cannot affect value. The argument is essentially the same. If you hold capital expenditure constant and pay lower dividends, then you will have more cash than you need. In the United States you can hand this cash back to the shareholders by repurchasing the shares of your own company. In countries where this is not permitted, you can hand the cash back by purchasing the shares of other companies.

Of course, all this ignores the costs involved in paying dividends and buying or selling shares. For example, if the company needs the cash, it is likely to be somewhat cheaper to retain it than to pay it out and make a stock issue. But these are matters of fine tuning and should not absorb large amounts of management time.

Some Common Misunderstandings

Some people find it difficult to accept the notion that, apart from tax considerations, dividend policy should not affect the value of the firm. For example, in the UK in 1975 the Diamond Commission received submissions from both the investment community and the trade unions about the effect of dividend control. The representatives of the investment community pointed out that the value of a share is equal to the discounted value of the expected stream of dividends. Therefore, they claimed, legislation that holds down dividends must also hold down share prices and increase companies' cost of capital.

The trade union representatives also thought that dividend policy is important. They argued that dividends are the shareholders' wages and so it was only equitable that the government's incomes policy should include control of dividends. Both sides ignored the secondary effects of dividend control. If a company raises its dividend, it must replace the cash by making a share issue. So the old shareholder receives a higher current dividend, but a proportion of the future dividends must be diverted to the new shareholders. The present value of these foregone future payments is equal to the increase in the current dividend.

Another common misunderstanding is the so-called "bird-in-the-hand" fallacy. Dividends, it is suggested, are more predictable than capital gains because managers can stabilize dividends, but cannot control stock price. Therefore, dividend payments are safe cash in hand while the alternative capital gains are at best in the bush.

But, the important point to remember, once again, is that as long as management's dividend policy does not influence its investment and capital structure decisions, a company's *overall* cash flows are the same regardless of its payout policy. The risks borne by its stockholders are likewise determined only by its investment and borrowing policies. Thus, it seems odd to suggest that while dividend policy has no effect on the firm's total cash flow, it nevertheless can still affect its risk.

The actual effect of a dividend increase is not to decrease the fundamental riskiness of the stock, but to transfer ownership and, hence, risk from "old" to "new" stockholders. The old stockholders — those who receive the extra dividend and do not buy their part of the stock issue undertaken to finance the dividend — are in effect disinvesting: that is, their stake in the firm is reduced. They have indeed traded a safe receipt for an uncertain capital gain. But the reason their money is safe is not because it is special "dividend money," but because it is in the bank. If the dividend had not been increased, the stockholders could have achieved an equally safe position just by selling shares and putting the money in the bank.

The old shareholder who receives and banks his dividend check has a safer asset than formerly, whereas the new shareholder who buys the newly issued shares has a riskier asset. Risk does not disappear; it is simply transferred from one investor to another, just as it is when one investor sells his stock to the other.

A third common objection to the dividend irrelevance argument is that many investors for reasons good or bad like high dividends. This may well be the case just as many people like to own motor cars, television sets and so on. But it does not mean that you can get rich by going into the dividend-manufacturing business any more than you can do so by going into the car or television business. A high-payout policy will only increase the stock price if there are not enough high-payout companies to satisfy the clientele for such stocks.

Why Dividend Policy *Seems* to Matter

If there is such widespread agreement that dividend policy does not matter aside from the tax consequences, why do so many managers believe it to be important? The obvious explanation is that the economists have got it wrong again. But I suspect that the real reason is that the economists and managers are talking about different issues.

For example, although I have suggested that low-payout stocks sell for as high a price as high-payout stocks, I also believe that the stock price is likely to rise if the dividend is unexpectedly increased. In other words, *unexpected changes* in a company's dividend matter even though the expected *level* of dividends does not. The reason for this has mostly to do with how managements typically set dividend policy.

Studies of corporate dividend policy suggest that most companies have a conscious or, at least, some subconscious long-term target payout rate.[3] If management attempted to adhere to a target every year, then the level of the dividend would fluctuate as erratically as earnings. Therefore, they try to smooth dividends by moving only partway toward the target payout in each year. They also take into account expected future earnings, as well as current earnings, in setting a long-run target. From long experience, investors are aware of this, and thus often interpret a large dividend increase as a sign of management's optimism about the company's prospects.

Thus, because unanticipated dividend changes convey information to the market about the outlook for profits, it makes sense to establish a reasonable set of investor expectations and to take these expectations into account when you decide on the annual payment.

A second reason that managers believe that the dividend decision is important is because they assume that it will affect the investment decision. In other words, they will say things like "If we pay this high dividend, then we won't have enough money to go ahead with our capital expenditure program." They are, therefore, implicitly rejecting the alternative of an equity issue. For example, many companies are reasonably tolerant of appropriation requests that can be financed out of retained earnings, but seem to impose much more stringent criteria on expenditure proposals that would involve a new issue of stock. In these cases the dividend decision feeds back on the investment decision and, therefore, it makes sense to take account of investment opportunities when setting the dividend level.

In both of these examples dividend policy appeared to matter. But in fact it was not the dividend policy as such that was important, but the company's investment policy and investors' expectations of future earnings.

Dividends and Taxes

The only serious challenge to those who believe that dividend policy does not matter comes from those who stress the tax consequences of a particular dividend policy.

[3] In the mid-1950s John Lintner conducted a series of interviews with corporate managers about their dividend policies. The results are presented in an article entitled "Distribution of Incomes of Corporations among Dividends, Retained Earnings, and Taxes," *American Economic Review*, 46:97–113 (May 1956). Lintner came to the conclusion that the dividend payout depends largely on two variables: the firm's current earnings and the dividend for the previous year (which in turn depends on that year's earnings and the prior year's dividend). The current dividend is thus generally a weighted average of past earnings, placing the heaviest weights on more recent years.

A more recent study by Eugene Fama and Harvey Babiak confirmed these results, demonstrating that the probability of a dividend increase depends largely on how consistently earnings have risen over the two or three years prior to the dividend change. See E. F. Fama and H. Babiak, "Dividend Policy: An Empirical Analysis," *Journal of the American Statistical Association*, 63:1132–1161 (December 1968).

If there were no taxes, investors would have no incentive to prefer one particular group of stocks. So they would hold well-diversified portfolios that moved closely with the market. But the fact that investors pay taxes at different rates on investment income provides an incentive for them to hold different portfolios. For example, the millionaire who is highly taxed on his dividend income has an incentive to slant his portfolio towards the low-payout stocks, even though this results in a less well-diversified portfolio. This extra demand by highly taxed investors for low-yield stocks will cause their prices to rise. As a result, tax-exempt investors such as pension funds will be induced to slant their portfolios towards the high-yielding stocks even though this causes their portfolios also to be less well-diversified. In between these two extremes is the investor with an "average" rate of tax. He has no incentive to slant his portfolio towards one particular group of stocks and will, therefore, invest in a well-diversified portfolio of high- and low-yielders.

The investor who pays tax at the average rate will be prepared to hold a well-diversified portfolio of both high- and low-yielders only if they offer him equal returns after tax.[4] But, if the returns are to be equal *after* tax, the high yielders must offer a higher return *before* tax. Thus, given two stocks which promise equal total returns (dividends plus capital gains) to investors, the stock that provides more of its return in the form of dividends will have a higher pre-tax expected return, and thus a lower stock price, than the one whose return is expected mostly in the form of capital gain.

The tax argument against high payouts is persuasive, but its advocates have so far failed to answer an important question: If generous dividends lead to generous taxes, why do companies continue to pay such dividends? Would they not do better to retain the earnings and avoid stock issues or, if they have excess cash, would it not be preferable to use it to repurchase stock? It is difficult to believe that companies are really foregoing such a simple opportunity to make their shareholders better off. Maybe there are offsetting advantages to dividends that we have not considered, or perhaps investors have ways to get around those extra taxes.

Merton Miller and Myron Scholes are among those who believe that the tax laws allow investors to avoid paying extra taxes on dividends.[5] For example, they point out that you can offset interest on personal loans against investment income. Such a strategy increases the risk of one's portfolio. But this increase in risk can be avoided or neutralized by channeling the borrowed funds through tax-exempt institutions like

---

[4] Michael Brennan showed that two stocks with equal risk should offer the same expected returns net of the average rate of tax. This average tax rate is a complicated average whose weight depends on each investor's wealth and aversion to risk.

[5] See M.H. Miller and M. Scholes. "Dividends and Taxes," *Journal of Financial Economics*, 6 (December 1978) 333–364.

insurance companies or pension funds. As an example, one could eliminate taxes on investment income without any increase in risk by using the personal loan to pay the premiums on a life insurance policy.

It is hard to know how literally to take Miller and Scholes's argument. There is no doubt that wealthy people are aware of the tax advantages of saving through insurance policies and pension plans. But the "average" tax rate on dividends is clearly not zero. So the puzzle has not entirely gone away: If taxes on dividend income do reduce the value of high-payout stocks, why do firms pay such high dividends?

The Empirical Evidence

The obvious way out of such a dilemma is to look at the evidence and test whether high-yielding stocks offer higher returns. Unfortunately, there are difficulties in measuring these effects.

One problem is to disentangle the effect of dividend yield from the effect of other influences. For example, most economists believe that risky stocks offer higher expected returns, and many believe that small company stocks also do so. Researchers have developed techniques for removing the effect on return of differences in risk, but there has been little attempt to disentangle the possible influences of yield and company size.

With the benefit of hindsight, we know some stocks have high yields because the dividend turned out to be higher than expected; others provided low yields because the dividend was lower than expected. Clearly what we want to measure is whether stocks that offer a higher *expected* yield also have a higher expected total return. To do that, however, it is necessary to estimate the dividend yield investors expected.

A third problem is that nobody is quite sure what is meant by a high dividend yield. For example, utility stocks are generally regarded as offering high yields. But are their yields high throughout the year, or only in the dividend month, or on the dividend day? Except at the time of the dividend payment, utility stocks effectively have zero yield and are thus perfect holdings for the highly taxed millionaire. The millionaire could avoid all taxes by selling the stock to a securities dealer just before the dividend date, and buying it back after. Since the securities dealer is taxed equally on dividends and capital gains, he should be quite content to hold the stock over the ex-dividend date. Thus, as long as investors can pass stocks freely between one another at the time of the dividend payment, we should not expect to observe any tax effect by dividends on stock prices. But if there are costs to avoiding taxes in this way, then any yield effect should become stronger as the ex-dividend day approaches.

A fourth problem is that most empirical studies have looked for a straight-line relationship between yield and return. But if there are any asymmetries in the tax system, that may not be the case. For example, if

Table 1   **Some Tests of the Effect of Yield on Returns**

Test	Test Period	Interval	Implied Tax Rate Percent	Standard Error of Tax Rate
Brennan (1970)	1946–65	Monthly	34	12
Black & Scholes (1974)	1936–66	Monthly	22	24
Litzenberger & Ramaswamy (1979)	1936–77	Monthly	24	3
Litzenberger & Ramaswamy (1982)	1940–80	Monthly	14–23	2–3
Rosenberg & Marathe (1979)	1931–66	Monthly	40	21
Bradford & Gordon (1980)	1926–78	Monthly	18	2
Blume (1980)	1936–76	Quarterly	52	25
Miller & Scholes (1981)	1940–78	Monthly	4	3
Stone & Bartter (1979)	1947–70	Monthly	56	28
Morgan (1982)	1946–77	Monthly	21	2

investors do not receive a tax refund on stocks that are sold short, there could be stocks traded only among millionaires and other stocks traded only by pension funds. In this case, there would be no single tax rate that clears the market and the relationship between yield and return would no longer be a straight-line one.[6] Stocks with above-average yields might be owned by pension funds, and priced to give the same expected pre-tax returns. By contrast, stocks offering below-average yields must all be owned by taxpayers, and priced to offer the same expected after-tax return.

Given these difficulties in measuring the relationship between yield and return, it is not surprising that different researchers have come up with somewhat different results. Table 1 summarizes the results of some of these empirical tests. Notice that in each of these tests the estimated tax rate was positive. In other words, over long periods of time, high-yielding stocks appeared to have offered higher returns, thus implying lower prices, than low-yielding stocks.

But if, at this point, the dividends-are-bad school can claim that the weight of evidence is on its side, the contest is by no means over. Not only are many of the empirical problems unsolved, but the standard errors in Table 1 show that the estimated tax rate is not always significantly different from zero.

Summary and Conclusion

It is difficult to summarize the dividend puzzle, and harder still to draw firm conclusions.

---

[6] Michael Brennan, for example, in an unpublished working paper entitled ''Dividends and Valuation in Imperfect Markets: Some Empirical Tests,'' argues that the relationship is not linear.

Almost no academic economist believes that paying out higher percentages of corporate earnings leads to higher stock prices. There is an important school which argues that taxes reduce the value of high-payout stocks. And, although there are unresolved problems of method, empirical tests of the issue to date provide tentative confirmation of an adverse tax effect on stock prices from higher dividends.

In setting the target payout, therefore, one should not dismiss entirely the tax argument against generous dividends. At the very least, management should adopt a target payout that, on the basis of its future capital requirements, is sufficiently low to minimize its reliance on external equity. In addition, the target payout should probably recognize that surplus funds can better be used to repurchase stock than to pay dividends.

There is little doubt, however, that sudden *changes* in dividend policy can cause dramatic changes in stock price. The most plausible reason for this reaction is the information investors read into dividend announcements. It is therefore important to define the firm's target payout as clearly as possible and to avoid unexpected changes in dividends. If it becomes necessary to make a sharp change in the level of the dividend, or in the target payout ratio, management should provide as much forewarning as possible, and take considerable care to ensure that the action is not misinterpreted.

References

Black, F., "The Dividend Puzzle," *Journal of Portfolio Management* 2 (Winter 1976).

Black, F. and M. Scholes, "The Effects of Dividend Yield and Dividend Policy on Common Stock Prices and Returns," *Journal of Financial Economics* 1 (May 1974), 1–22.

Blume, M.E., "Stock Returns and Dividend Yields: Some More Evidence," *Review of Economics and Statistics* (November 1980), 567–577.

Bradford, D.F. and R.H. Gordon, "Taxation and the Stock Market Valuation of Capital Gains and Dividends," *Journal of Public Economics* 14 (1980), 109–136.

Brennan, M.J., "Taxes, Market Valuation and Corporate Financial Policy," *National Tax Journal* 23 (December 1970), 417–427.

Hess, P., "The Empirical Relationship between Dividend Yield and Stock Returns: Tax Effect or Non-stationarity in Expected Returns," Unpublished Ph.D. dissertation.

Litzenberger, R.H. and K. Ramaswamy, "The Effects of Dividends on Common Stock Prices: Tax Effects or Information Effects?" *Journal of Finance* (May 1982), 429–443.

Litzenberger, R.H. and K. Ramaswamy, "Dividends, Short Selling Restrictions, Tax-Induced Investor Clienteles and Market Equilibrium," *Journal of Finance* 35 (May 1980), 469–482.

Miller, M.H. and F. Modigliani, "Dividend Policy, Growth and the Valuation of Shares," *Journal of Business* 34 (October 1961), 411–432.

Miller, M.H. and M. Scholes, "Dividends and Taxes," *Journal of Financial Economics* 6 (December 1978), 333–364.

Miller, M.H. and M. Scholes, "Dividends and Taxes: Some Empirical Evidence," *Journal of Political Economy* 90 (1982).

Morgan, I.G., "Dividends and Capital Asset Prices," *Journal of Finance* 37 (September 1982), 1071–1086.

Rosenberg, B. and V. Marathe, "Tests of Capital Asset Pricing Model Hypotheses," in H. Levy (ed.) *Research in Finance I*, Greenwhich, Conn: JAI Press (1979).

Sharpe, W.F. and H.B. Sosin, "Risk, Return and Yield: New York Stock Exchange Common Stocks 1928–1969." *Financial Analysts Journal* (March/April 1976), 33–42.

Stone, B.K. and B.J. Bartter, "The Effect of Dividend Yield on Stock Returns: Empirical Evidence on the Relevance of Dividends," W.P.E.-76-78, Georgia Institute of Technology, Atlanta, Georgia.

Questions

1. How does the author define *dividend policy*?

2. In what way is the argument that dividend policy can increase shareholder wealth like trying to cool the kitchen by leaving open the refrigerator door?

3. Evaluate the following arguments for the importance and relevance of dividends:
    a. The value of a share of common stock equals the present value of future dividends. Therefore, if you reduce dividends, you also reduce share value.
    b. Dividend payments reduce the risk perceived by investors and thus increase share value.
    c. Many investors like dividends because they need the income to cover expenses. These investors bid up the stock price of companies that pay dividends.

4. Unexpected changes in dividends per share often cause a change in a company's stock price. Does this statement imply that dividend policy matters? Explain.

5. Why are the personal tax rates of a company's shareholders relevant to the company's dividend policy?

6. Transaction costs include: (a) the costs of investors buying and selling shares, and (b) the costs of companies paying dividends and issuing shares. In what way are these costs relevant to a company's dividend policy?

A Survey of Management Views on Dividend Policy

H. Kent Baker, Gail E. Farrelly, and Richard B. Edelman

I. Introduction

The effect of dividend policy on a corporation's market value is a subject of long-standing controversy. Black [2, p. 5] epitomizes the lack of consensus by stating, "The harder we look at the dividend picture, the more it seems like a puzzle, with pieces that just don't fit together."

Because the academic community has been unable to provide clear guidance about dividend policy, a shift in emphasis is proposed. In the spirit of Lintner's seminal work [11], we asked a sample of corporate financial managers what factors they considered most important in determining their firm's dividend policy. Our objectives were as follows:

  (i) to compare the determinants of dividend policy today with Lintner's behavioral model of corporate dividend policy and to assess management's agreement with Lintner's findings;

 (ii) to examine management's perception of signaling and clientele effects; and

(iii) to determine whether managers in different industries share similar views about the determinants of dividend policy.[1]

H. Kent Baker, Gail E. Farrelly, and Richard B. Edelman, "A Survey of Management Views on Dividend Policy," *Financial Management* Vol. 14, Iss. 3 (Autumn 1985): 78–84. Permission granted by the Financial Management Association and authors.

At the time of this writing, H. Kent Baker and Richard B. Edelman were affiliated with the Kogod College of Business Administration, The American University, Washington, D.C. and Gail E. Farrelly was affiliated with Rutgers University, Newark, New Jersey.

The authors wish to express their appreciation to Robert A. Taggart and the two anonymous referees for their helpful suggestions.

[1] Whether industry regulation influences dividend policy is a potentially rich issue, since it is quite conceivable that regulation creates incentives for management to adopt a different payout policy than nonregulated firms. Although briefly addressed in this article, this issue has been examined elsewhere by Edelman, Farrelly, and Baker [6].

The remaining portion of this paper consists of three sections. Section II sets forth the survey design. Section III presents the research findings and compares them with theory and other empirical evidence. Section IV discusses conclusions and limitations of the study. Because research on dividend policy is already well documented [3], a separate section on the dividend literature is not provided. Instead, relevant aspects of the literature are incorporated into Section III.

II. Survey Design

The firms surveyed were listed on the New York Stock Exchange (NYSE) and classified by four-digit Standard Industrial Classification (SIC) codes. A total of 562 NYSE firms were selected from three industry groups: utility (150), manufacturing (309), and wholesale/retail (103).

A mail questionnaire was used to obtain information about corporate dividend policy. The questionnaire consisted of three parts: (i) 15 closed-end statements about the importance of various factors that each firm used in determining its dividend policy; (ii) 18 closed-end statements about theoretical issues involving corporate dividend policy, and (iii) a respondent's profile including such items as the firm's dividends and earnings per share.

A pilot test of the preliminary questionnaire was conducted among 20 firms selected from the three industry groups but not included in the final sample of 562 firms. The final survey instrument was then sent to the chief financial officers (CFOs) of the 562 firms, followed by a second complete mailing to improve the response rate and reduce potential nonresponse bias. The survey, which was conducted during the period between February and April 1983, did not require firms to identify themselves.

The survey yielded 318 usable responses (a 56.6% response rate), which were divided among the three industry groups as follows: 114 utilities (76.0%), 147 manufacturing firms (47.6%), and 57 wholesale/retail (55.3%). Based on dividend and earnings per share data provided by the respondents, the 1981 average dividend payout ratios were computed. The payout ratio of the responding utilities (70.3%) was considerably higher than for manufacturing (36.6%) and wholesale/retail (36.1%).[2]

---

[2] In the electric utility segment, the dividend payout ratio can be distorted by non-cash items such as allowance for funds used during construction (AFUDC). *Moody's Public Utility Manual* reports that in 1981 (the year surveyed), AFUDC made a substantial contribution to electric utility net income. In that year, average earnings per share for the industry was $10.16 from which $7.16 was paid in dividends. This represents an average utility payout of 70.5% in contrast with 34% in the other segments. If AFUDC is excluded from net income, earnings are $4.79 per share. Earnings at this level would represent a utility payout ratio of nearly 150%.

III. Results and Discussion

A. Determinants of Dividend Policy

Lintner's classic 1956 study [11] found that major changes in earnings "out of line" with existing dividend rates were the most important determinant of the company's dividend decisions. However, because these managers believed that shareholders preferred a steady stream of dividends, firms tended to make periodic partial adjustments toward a target payout ratio rather than dramatic changes in payout. Thus, in the short run, dividends were smoothed in an effort to avoid frequent changes.

Fama and Babiak's [8] examination of several alternative models for explaining dividend behavior supports Lintner's position that managers increase dividends only after they are reasonably sure that they can permanently maintain them at the new level.

To examine how well Lintner's model describes current practice, the respondents were asked to indicate the importance of each of 15 factors in determining their firm's actual dividend policy. A five-point equal interval scale was used for this purpose: 0 = no importance, 1 = slight importance, 2 = moderate importance, 3 = great importance, and 4 = maximum importance. It should be noted that the questionnaire does not follow Lintner's model exactly.

Exhibit 1 provides summary statistics on the major determinants of corporate dividend policy as reported by the three industry groups.[3] The results show that the same four determinants (identified later by "D") are considered most important by the three industry groups when ranked by the mean response. The determinant numbers represent the order in which each factor was presented in the questionnaire.

The most highly ranked determinants are the anticipated level of a firm's future earnings (D1) and the pattern of past dividends (D9). The high ranking of these two factors is consistent with Lintner's findings.

A third factor cited as important in determining dividend policy is the availability of cash (D8). Although Lintner does not directly address this determinant, Van Horne [19, p. 23] and Weston and Brigham [20, p. 675] note that liquidity is an important managerial consideration.

A fourth major determinant is concern about maintaining or increasing stock price (D7). This concern is particularly strong among utilities, who ranked this factor second in importance.

Firms in the other industry segments surveyed also have non-cash items charged or added to their income figure. However, Compustat shows no equivalent items in those segments which are consistently used by all firms and have such a profound effect on reported income. It is our belief that with or without an adjustment in the utility payout ratio for AFUDC, utilities can be viewed as high payout firms relative to manufacturing and wholesale/retail firms.

[3] Summary statistics on all 15 determinants of corporate dividend policy are available from the authors.

Exhibit 1 Major Determinants of Corporate Dividend Policy

Determinant	Level of Importance				
	None 0	Slight 1	Moderate 2	Great 3	Maximum 4
1 Anticipated level of firm's future earnings		3.40%	6.80%		89.80%
		1.75	14.04		84.21
		1.75	7.89		90.35
9 Pattern of past dividends		6.12	29.25		64.63
		1.75	29.82		68.42
		2.63	25.44		71.93
8 Availability of cash		14.29	22.45		63.27
		22.81	21.05		56.14
		21.24	34.51		44.25
7 Concern about maintaining or increasing stock price		13.61	44.22		42.18
		15.79	28.07		56.14
		3.51	22.81		73.68

* An asterisk indicates inadequate cell size and the chi-square test may not be valid.

† Underlining indicates a significant relationship at the .05 level of significance. Mfg = manufacturing; W/R = wholesale/retail; Util = utility.

B. Issues Involving Dividend Policy

The study's second objective was to investigate CFO's perceptions of certain specific issues. The respondents were asked to indicate their general opinion about each of 18 closed-end statements based on a seven-point interval scale: -3 = strongly disagree, -2 = moderately disagree, -1 = slightly disagree, 0 = no opinion, $+1$ = slightly agree, $+2$ = moderately agree, and $+3$ = strongly agree. Exhibit 2 provides summary statistics on the responses to each of the 18 statements (identified later by "S") for the three industry groups. The statement numbers refer to the order in which the statements appeared in the questionnaire.

Attitudes on Lintner's Findings. One issue was the level of agreement with statements supporting Lintner's research findings, namely, S2, S3, S9, S10, and S17. The results show that several such statements command the highest level of agreement. For example, two of the highest ranked statements were that a firm should avoid making changes in its dividend rates that might soon have to be reversed (S10) and should strive to maintain an uninterrupted record of dividend payments (S17). Respondents also generally agreed that a firm should have a target payout ratio and should periodically adjust the payout toward the target (S3).

Lintner's field work also suggests that managers focus on the change in the existing rate of dividend payout, not on the dollar amount of

Mean	Rank	Standard Deviation	X^2 Probability	Industry
3.20	1	.74		Mfg
3.12	1	.71	.4572*	W/R
3.21	1	.66		Util
2.73	2	.89		Mfg
2.86	2	.74	.4390*	W/R
2.94	3	.78		Util
2.70	3	1.04		Mfg
2.42	4	1.15	.0273†	W/R
2.35	4	1.02		Util
2.30	4	.87		Mfg
2.47	3	.85	.0001†	W/R
2.96	2	.79		Util

dividends (S9) so that investment requirements generally have little effect on modifying the pattern of dividend behavior (S2). On average, managers expressed no strong opinion on either of these statements.

Although management's perceptions could differ significantly from actual decisions, the results in Exhibit 1 do not suggest this. That is, managers' views about continuity of dividend policy seem to be translated into factors (D1 and D9) that are in fact consistent with dividend continuity.

Attitudes on Theoretical Issues.   A major controversy in the literature involves the relationship between dividends and value. Miller and Modigliani (MM) [15] suggest that dividend policy has no effect on the value of the corporation in a world without taxes, transaction costs, or other market imperfections. However, dividends may be relevant to the extent that market imperfections exist. Some of the explanations for dividend relevance include signaling and clientele effects.

Exhibit 2 shows that respondents from all three industry groups agreed relatively strongly that dividend payout affects common stock prices (S1). The utilities showed the highest level of agreement with this statement. These results seem consistent with the finding reported in Exhibit 1 that concern about maintaining or increasing stock price (D7) is a major determinant of corporate dividend policy, especially for utilities.

Management attitudes were also sought on several other theoretical issues. The first issue involves signaling effects. Managers have access to information about the firm's expected cash flows not possessed by outsiders and thus, changes in dividend payout may provide signals about

Exhibit 2   Issues Involving Corporate Dividend Policy

Statement	Disagreement −3 −2 −1	0	Agreement +1 +2 +3
10 A firm should avoid making changes in its dividend rates that might have to be reversed in a year or so.	1.37% 7.02 .00	11.64% 5.26 8.77	86.99% 87.72 91.23
4 Reasons for dividend policy changes should be adequately disclosed to investors.	2.05 .00 .88	20.55 19.30 28.95	77.40 80.70 70.18
17 A firm should strive to maintain an uninterrupted record of dividend payments.	1.36 3.51 .00	25.85 10.53 6.14	72.79 85.96 93.86
3 A firm should have a target payout ratio and periodically adjust the payout toward the target.	7.53 3.51 10.53	29.45 17.54 24.56	63.01 78.95 64.91
1 Dividend payout affects the price of the common stock.	6.80 7.02 3.51	39.46 42.11 21.93	53.74 50.88 74.56
7 Investors have different perceptions of the relative riskiness of dividends and retained earnings.	.69 3.57 1.76	45.83 42.86 35.96	53.47 53.57 62.28
14 Dividend payments provide a "signaling device" of future prospects.	6.80 7.02 7.02	38.10 49.12 42.11	55.10 43.86 50.88
5 The market uses dividend announcements as information for assessing security value.	5.52 8.77 5.26	55.86 52.63 42.98	38.62 38.60 51.75
9 A change in the existing dividend payout is more important than the actual amount of dividends.	10.27 21.05 34.21	49.32 50.88 44.74	40.41 28.07 21.05
16 A stockholder is attracted to firms which have dividend policies appropriate to the stockholder's particular tax environment.	6.85 10.53 6.14	58.22 45.61 39.47	34.93 43.86 54.39
15 Capital gains expected to result from earnings retention are riskier than are dividend expectations.	6.29 15.79 9.65	58.04 52.63 51.75	35.66 31.58 38.60
6 Management should be responsive to its shareholders' preferences regarding dividends.	12.33 8.77 7.02	54.11 56.14 40.35	33.56 35.09 52.63
12 Investors in low tax brackets are attracted to high-dividend stocks.	10.96 15.79 9.65	63.01 56.14 50.00	26.03 28.07 40.35
2 New capital investment requirements of the firm generally have little effect on modifying the pattern of dividend behavior.	21.92 31.58 24.78	38.36 31.58 23.89	39.73 36.84 51.33
11 Stockholders in high tax brackets are attracted to low-dividend stocks.	19.31 17.86 14.91	57.93 55.36 41.23	22.76 26.79 43.86
8 Dividend distributions should be viewed as a residual after financing desired investments from available earnings.	28.08 38.60 61.95	36.30 26.32 27.43	35.62 35.09 10.62
13 Financing decisions should be independent of a firm's dividend decisions.	43.54 49.12 38.60	27.21 22.81 28.07	29.25 28.07 33.33
18 Investors are basically indifferent between returns from dividends versus those from capital gains.	55.48 60.71 76.32	38.36 33.93 18.42	6.16 5.36 5.26

* An asterisk indicates inadequate cell size and the chi-square test may not be valid.

† Underlining indicates a significant relationship at the .05 level of significance. Mfg = manufacturing; W/R = wholesale/retail; Util = utility.

Mean	Rank	Standard Deviation	χ^2 Probability	Industry
2.47	1	.91		Mfg
2.16	2	1.46	.0155*†	W/R
2.61	2	.77		Util
2.09	2	1.28		Mfg
2.14	3	1.04	.3189*	W/R
2.02	3	1.09		Util
1.97	3	1.05		Mfg
2.28	1	1.25	.0001*†	W/R
2.63	1	.72		Util
1.47	4	1.50		Mfg
2.09	4	1.20	.1715	W/R
1.42	6	1.65		Util
1.41	5	1.02		Mfg
1.46	5	1.23	.0059†	W/R
1.99	4	1.22		Util
1.38	6	1.04		Mfg
1.34	6	1.28	.3286*	W/R
1.62	5	1.16		Util
1.37	7	1.35		Mfg
1.18	7	1.26	.6904	W/R
1.19	10	1.38		Util
1.02	8	1.29		Mfg
1.07	8	1.47	.2040	W/R
1.33	8	1.39		Util
.86	9	1.60		Mfg
.40	12	1.67	.0001†	W/R
−.21	16	1.85		Util
.80	10	1.32		Mfg
.88	10	1.48	.0225†	W/R
1.37	7	1.29		Util
.76	11	1.37		Mfg
.51	11	1.47	.2816	W/R
.85	12	1.44		Util
.68	12	1.52		Mfg
.91	9	1.52	.0240†	W/R
1.22	9	1.47		Util
.50	13	1.41		Mfg
.39	13	1.57	.1057	W/R
.86	11	1.47		Util
.38	14	1.88		Mfg
.09	15	1.97	.0786	W/R
.72	14	2.05		Util
.24	15	1.56		Mfg
.29	14	1.59	.0075†	W/R
.83	13	1.61		Util
.13	16	1.97		Mfg
−.07	16	2.12	.0001†	W/R
−1.35	17	1.78		Util
−.36	17	2.12		Mfg
−.58	17	2.04	.7495	W/R
−.10	15	2.04		Util
−1.33	18	1.50		Mfg
−1.46	18	1.54	.0103†	W/R
−1.77	18	1.30		Util

the firm's future cash flows that cannot be communicated credibly by other means. With some exceptions, empirical studies indicate that dividend changes convey some unanticipated information to the market [1, 5, 9, 10, 16, 21].

Three statements involved signaling effects (S4, S5, and S14). The respondents from all three industry groups agreed, on average, that dividend payments provide a "signaling device" of future company prospects (S14) and that the market uses dividend announcements as information for assessing security value (S5). The respondents also demonstrated a high level of agreement that the reasons for dividend policy changes should be adequately disclosed to investors (S4).

Another theoretical issue concerns the extent to which investors with different dividend preferences form clienteles. Two possible reasons for the formation of clienteles are different perceptions of the relative riskiness of dividends and retained earnings and different investor tax brackets. Although the research evidence is mixed, it does lean toward the existence of clientele effects [7, 12, 17].

Seven statements involved clientele effects (S6, S7, S11, S12, S15, S16, and S18) and these commanded mixed agreement. Respondents from all three industry groups thought that investors have different perceptions of the relative riskiness of dividends and retained earnings (S7) and hence are not indifferent between dividend and capital gain returns (S18). Yet, there was only slight agreement that a stockholder is attracted to firms with dividend policies appropriate to that stockholder's tax environment (S16) and that management should be responsive to its shareholders' dividend preferences (S6). However, the utilities differed from the other two groups, expressing significantly higher levels of agreement on S16 and S6.

C. Industry Influence on Dividend Policy

The study's final objective was to investigate differences in managers' attitudes across three broad industry groups. Studies by Dhrymes and Kurz [4], McCabe [13], and Michel [14] have previously detected some effect of industry classification on corporate dividend policy. However, Rozeff [18] concluded that a company's industry does not help to explain its dividend payout ratio. Rozeff's conclusion is not applicable to utilities since he intentionally excluded regulated companies because their policies may be affected by their regulatory status.

Chi-square analysis was used to test for differences in the responses among the three industry groups. In order to perform these tests and to avoid inadequate cell sizes, both the five-interval importance scale and the seven-interval disagreement-agreement scale were collapsed into three classes as shown in Exhibits 1 and 2, respectively. Nevertheless, some warnings about low cell counts resulted because of the highly skewed nature of the responses. These tests showed that the responses of the three groups differed significantly at the .05 level among eight of the 15 determinants of dividend policy (partly shown in Exhibit 1) and nine of the 18 issues (Exhibit 2).

Further Chi-square tests were performed using pair-wise comparisons between the industry groups on all 15 determinants and 18 issues. The results revealed that the manufacturing and wholesale/retail firms had no significant differences in responses at the .05 level for those questions with adequate cell sizes. Hence, the differences occurred primarily as a result of the utilities' responses relative to either manufacturing or wholesale/retail.

The reported differences between the utilities and the other firms may be due to regulation. For example, since regulation gives utilities monopoly power over a product enjoying steady demand, their earnings are comparatively stable. Their risk of having to reduce dividends because of an unexpected decline in earnings is thus less than that for many other companies.

It is also plausible that regulation creates incentives for management to adopt a different payout policy than nonregulated firms. This incentive may stem from the fact that funds retained inside the firm are implicitly subject to expropriation by the regulators in future rate cases. Hence, managers of regulated firms may view the world differently than managers operating in a competitive environment.

On the other hand, the differences may have nothing to do with regulation *per se* but with other characteristics. For example, Rozeff [18] notes that the apparently significant industry effect found in past studies results from the fact that other variables are often similar within a given industry. These similarities are the fundamental reason why companies in the same industry have similar dividend payouts.

Utilities are high payout firms relative to the two other groups and this characteristic makes them different. To control for dividend payout, the responses by managers in the highest payout quartile for 1981 of nonregulated firms (51 firms) were compared with the utilities (114 firms).[4]

With a few exceptions, the results were strikingly similar to those in Exhibit 2. Although the mean rankings changed little, the responses of the higher payout nonregulated firms more closely resembled the utilities on two statements—namely, dividend payout affects the price of the common stock (S1) and management should be responsive to its shareholders' dividend preferences (S6).

Overall, the findings suggest that the attitudes of even high-payout nonregulated firm managers are different from those of utility managers. Hence, regulation may be responsible for some of the relations observed.

---

[4] Summary statistics of high payout regulated and nonregulated firms are available from the authors.

IV. Conclusions

Before drawing any conclusions, several limiting aspects of this research should be noted. Survey research typically involves some non-response bias and although steps were taken to ensure a high response rate, this study is no exception. The problem of nonresponse bias is potentially greatest among manufacturing firms which had the lowest response rate. Another limiting factor is that views about dividend policy were obtained only from chief financial officers. Although CFOs' views should reflect the attitudes of top management more generally, CFOs are not the only individuals involved in dividend policy decisions. Finally, coverage is restricted to three broad industry groups representing only New York Stock Exchange firms.

With these caveats in mind, several conclusions emerge from this survey. First, the results show that the major determinants of dividend payments today appear strikingly similar to Lintner's behavioral model developed during the mid-1950s. In particular, respondents were highly concerned with dividend continuity.

Second, the respondents seem to believe that dividend policy affects share value, as evidenced by the importance attached to dividend policy in maintaining or increasing stock price. Although the survey does not uncover the exact reasons for their belief in dividend relevance, it does provide evidence that the respondents are generally aware of signaling and clientele effects.

Finally, the opinions of the respondents from the utilities differ markedly from those of the other two industries. The results suggest that managers of regulated firms have a somewhat different view of the world than managers operating in a competitive environment. Thus, it may be worthwhile to segregate regulated from nonregulated firms when examining dividend policy.

References

1. P. Asquith and D. Mullins, Jr., "The Impact of Initiating Dividend Payments on Shareholders' Wealth," *Journal of Business* (January 1983), pp. 77–96.

2. F. Black, "The Dividend Puzzle," *Journal of Portfolio Management* (Winter 1976), pp. 5–8.

3. T.E. Copeland and J.F. Weston, *Financial Theory and Corporate Policy,* Reading, MA, Addison-Wesley, 1983.

4. P.J. Dhrymes and M. Kurz, "Investment, Dividend, and External Finance Behavior of Firms," in R. Ferber (ed.), *Determinants of Investment Behavior,* New York, Columbia University Press, 1967, pp. 427–467.

5. K.M. Eades, "Empirical Evidence on Dividends as a Signal of Firm Value," *Journal of Financial and Quantitative Analysis* (November 1982), pp. 471–500.

6. R.B. Edelman, G.E. Farrelly, and H.K. Baker, "Public Utility Dividend Policy: Time for a Change?" *Public Utilities Fortnightly* (February 21, 1985), pp. 26–31.

7. E.J. Elton and M.J. Gruber, "Marginal Stockholder Tax Rates and the Clientele Effect," *Review of Economics and Statistics* (February 1970), pp. 68–74.

8. E.F. Fama and H. Babiak, "Dividend Policy: An Empirical Analysis," *Journal of the American Statistical Association* (December 1968), pp. 1132–1161.

9. C. Kwan, "Efficient Market Tests of the Informational Content of Dividend Announcements: Critique and Extension," *Journal of Financial and Quantitative Analysis* (June 1981), pp. 193–206.

10. P.M. Laub, "On the Informational Content of Dividends," *Journal of Business* (January 1976), pp. 73–80.

11. J. Lintner, "Distribution of Incomes of Corporations Among Dividends, Retained Earnings and Taxes," *American Economic Review* (May 1956), pp. 97–113.

12. R.H. Litzenberger and K. Ramaswamy, "The Effect of Personal Taxes and Dividends on Capital Asset Prices: Theory and Empirical Evidence," *Journal of Financial Economics* (June 1979), pp. 163–196.

13. G.M. McCabe, "The Empirical Relationship Between Investment and Financing: A New Look," *Journal of Financial and Quantitative Analysis* (March 1979), pp. 119–135.

14. A. Michel, "Industry Influence on Dividend Policy," *Financial Management* (Autumn 1979), pp. 22–26.

15. M.H. Miller and F. Modigliani, "Dividend Policy, Growth, and the Valuation of Shares," *Journal of Business* (October 1961), pp. 411–433.

16. S.H. Penman, "The Predictive Content of Earnings Forecasts and Dividends," *Journal of Finance* (September 1983), pp. 1181–1199.

17. R.R. Pettit, "Taxes, Transactions Costs and Clientele Effects of Dividends," *Journal of Financial Economics* (December 1977), pp. 419–436.

18. M.S. Rozeff, "Growth, Beta and Agency Costs as Determinants of Dividend Payout Ratios," *Journal of Financial Research* (Fall 1982), pp. 249–259.

19. J.C. Van Horne, *Financial Management and Policy,* 6th ed., Englewood Cliffs, NJ, Prentice-Hall, 1983.

20. J.F. Weston and E.F. Brigham, *Managerial Finance,* 7th ed., Hinsdale, IL, Dryden Press, 1981.

21. J.R. Woolridge, "The Information Content of Dividend Changes," *Journal of Financial Research* (Fall 1982), pp. 237–247.

Questions

1.   Define the term *dividend payout ratio*. What is the average payout ratio for utility companies? Manufacturers? Wholesalers and retailers?

2. Describe the corporate dividend policy envisioned by John Lintner.

3. What are the major determinants of corporate dividend policy according to the survey respondents? Explain how these determinants affect dividend policy.

4. "Dividend payments provide a *signaling device* of future prospects." What does this statement mean?

5. Do the survey respondents agree that a dividend clientele exists? Explain.

Management's View of Stock Repurchase Programs

H. Kent Baker, Patricia L. Gallagher, and Karen E. Morgan

Since the mid-1960s companies have been reacquiring their own shares in great numbers. In fact, during the past several years firms seem to have become increasingly aware of the impact that buying back stock can have on meeting corporate objectives and satisfying shareholders. But why do some corporations repurchase their own stock while others do not and what are the causes of the recent increase in stock repurchases?

This study attempts to document the reasons underlying the current proliferation of common stock repurchases and to compare the rationale of financial managers with theory. The value of this investigation lies not only in providing an empirical explanation of an important trend but also in investigating the relationship between the theory and practice of stock buybacks. As Levy and Sarnat [9, p. 273] note, "the ultimate test of the theory of corporate finance is not its formal elegance but lies in our ability to apply the theoretical concepts to actual business problems." Hence, the "reality test" of the theory underlying stock repurchases rests with whether the theory is borne out by actual practice.

I. Stock Repurchases in Perspective

A. Trends in Stock Repurchases

Although companies have bought back their stock for many years, three periods with high growth activity are the mid-1960s, 1973–74, and 1977–79. Table 1 shows the total number of shares repurchased by New

H. Kent Baker, Patricia L. Gallagher, and Karen E. Morgan, "Management's View of Stock Repurchase Programs," *The Journal of Financial Research*, Vol. IV, No. 3 (Fall 1981): 233–247. Reprinted with permission.

At the time of this writing, H. Kent Baker was Professor of Finance at American University, Patricia L. Gallagher was a financial analyst in international communications with Communications Satellite Corporation, and Karen E. Morgan was a financial analyst with American Satellite Company.

TABLE 1　Stock Repurchase Activity by NYSE Listed Firms 1962–79

Year	Common Shares Repurchased (in millions)*	Midpoint S&P 500 Index**
1962	—	61.73
1963	31.40	68.86
1964	<u>54.38</u>	80.86
1965	<u>40.41</u>	87.12
1966	<u>45.84</u>	83.63
1967	26.05	88.99
1968	41.18	98.66
1969	55.22	97.70
1970	55.93	81.38
1971	28.51	97.48
1972	47.55	110.40
1973	<u>128.85</u>	106.18
1974	<u>95.63</u>	81.04
1975	43.94	82.83
1976	37.15	98.85
1977	<u>56.51</u>	98.86
1978	<u>94.87</u>	96.95
1979	<u>119.29</u>	103.72

* New York Stock Exchange, "The Monthly Report of Changes in Treasury Stock," various issues [20].

** Standard and Poor's Statistical Service [13, p. 4].

NOTE: Periods of relatively high repurchase activity are underlined.

York Stock Exchange listed firms from 1963–79. When the amount of repurchased shares is compared to the mid-point of the high and low values of the *Standard & Poor's 500 Index* from 1963–79 [14], only a low correlation, *i.e.*, $r = .35$, exists between repurchase activity and the level of stock prices. Lagging repurchase activity one year behind the movement of this index increases the correlation coefficient to .69. Thus, repurchase activity seems to be moderately related to the movement of stock prices when repurchases are viewed as a lagged variable.

While recent repurchases are below the 1973 peak, the current period is distinguished by the relative size of the buybacks. In 1973, companies typically repurchased between 50 to 200 thousand shares, yet beginning with the most recent stock repurchase trend in 1977, announced repurchase plans in the millions of shares are not uncommon [12]. For example, firms which have reacquired at least a million shares included Sears, Roebuck and Co., Ashland Oil, Dow Chemical, IBM, Syntex, and U.S. Industries [10,16].

Another emerging trend is the small but growing number of firms using tender offers for corporate buybacks. For example, Communications Satellite Corporation was able to repurchase 2 million of its shares through a tender offer. Ennis Business Machines and Ethyl Corp. also used this method to reacquire shares [10].

Certain market conditions tend to make reacquisitions of stock favorable. One condition contributing to the increase in stock repurchases is the amount of idle cash held by many corporations. Thus, repurchasing stock appears a profitable means of disposing of excess liquidity, especially if the firm's stock price is depressed or below book value. Hilton Hotels, for example, repurchased 1.87 million shares because it believed that its stock was undervalued relative to the estimated fair market value per share [10].

Even firms without idle cash are buying back their stock. Despite high interest rates such firms as Transamerica, Monogram Industries, and GEICO have increased their long-term debt in order to shrink the amount of equity. The decision to repurchase stock is viewed as a means of enhancing the value of the remaining stock, cutting the cost of capital, and yielding cash savings because dividends are not paid on treasury stock, retired or cancelled shares [3,4].

The low value of stock prices is another factor contributing to the trend toward increased stock repurchases. If a company's current market price is less than its book value, a company's own stock becomes an attractive investment outlet. Inflation may also reduce the market value of a stock. Modigliani and Cohn, [11, p. 24] allege that " . . . because of inflation-induced errors, investors have systematically undervalued the stock market by 50 percent."

All of these conditions tend to provide a favorable climate for stock repurchases. Consequently, it is not surprising to note that earlier periods of high repurchase growth were characterized by similar conditions. During 1973–74, for example, rapid inflation, highly liquid corporations, and depressed stock prices also existed [22].

B. Possible Motivations for Stock Repurchases

Although many theoretical reasons exist for corporations repurchasing their own stock, the relative importance of these reasons may change over time. That is, the rationale underlying the current repurchase trend may differ from the mid-1960s or the 1973–74 period. Consequently, changing market conditions may cause managers to rank certain theoretically correct arguments as unimportant to their repurchase decision. Past empirical studies regarding reacquisitions confirm that several of the frequently mentioned theoretical reasons for repurchase are infrequently cited by managers [1].

One often mentioned reason for stock repurchases is that management may feel that buying its own stock is an effective means of utilizing idle cash. That is, if excess liquidity remains after making all profitable investments, a firm can either repurchase its own shares or distribute a cash dividend to dispose of excess cash. Thus, a repurchase may be an appealing investment for a non-growth firm [3] or a firm whose stock is selling at a low price and/or below book value. Although some firms have recently opted for paying higher cash dividends, Ellis [5] notes that a dividend distribution may not be the most advantageous alternative because of the relative inflexibility in distributing dividends and the fluctuating nature of corporate liquidity. A higher dividend payout may also have negative tax effects on owners.

Companies also repurchase shares for merger and acquisition purposes. Under the present tax structure, a company can be acquired less expensively using an exchange of stock offer rather than cash. A cash purchase is subject to capital gains taxes, if the basis is less than the acquisition price. In an exchange-of-stock merger, the capital gains liability is deferred [4]. As a consequence of a 1977 change in *SEC* requirements, the advantage of repurchased shares for use in mergers and acquisitions has been diminished. Now, a firm generally cannot apply the pooling-of-interest accounting treatment to mergers involving treasury stock if the merger takes place within two years of the stock repurchase [20]. Repurchased shares may still possess the advantage for mergers and acquisitions, stock options, conversions, and similar transactions because they reduce the dilution of earnings per share *(EPS)* and avoid the large costs associated with the issuance of new stock. A study of Rosenburg and Young [13] supports the belief that a firm can prevent dilution of *EPS* by repurchasing stock.

Companies may also consider repurchasing to adjust their leverage position [17]. That is, firms with redundant liquid assets and unused debt capacity could repurchase their own stock to reach a more nearly optimal capital structure. While empirical research indicates that most companies choosing to repurchase have low debt ratios and excessive liquidity [7], managers themselves have not frequently cited beneficial leverage as a reason for buybacks [1,8].

Reacquiring shares may also create additional demand in the marketplace and thus provide either price support or yield a higher price. Although the financial press often cites this potential advantage [10,16], Young's empirical study [19] refutes this reasoning. Young found that the repurchase firm's stock market performance approximately equaled the performance of the market and concluded that the price movement following a repurchase is not favorable. In a later study, Stewart [15] noted several deficiencies in Young's work, and after making appropriate corrections suggested that repurchase firms outperformed non-repurchase firms several years following the repurchase and that companies doing a moderate level of repurchasing have the best price performance.

Numerous other reasons cited in the literature for share repurchase include eliminating a large block of stock overhanging the market [5], thwarting an attempted takeover [18], reducing the number of small investors to lessen servicing costs and obtaining greater control of the company [8], serving as a substitute for paying dividends [17], fulfilling stock option and employee stock purchase programs, and using the reacquired stock for the conversion of convertible preferreds or debentures [10]. While all of these items are plausible reasons for repurchasing stock, few have attempted to document the relative importance of these various reasons over different periods of repurchase growth [1, 22].

Theoretically, repurchase decisions should help maximize the wealth of owners by raising earnings per share and bolstering the market price of the stock. Shareholders may also gain a potential tax advantage due to the lower tax rate on capital gains of repurchased shares compared with cash dividends [2]. Elton and Gruber [6] point out that the tax advantage associated with repurchases applies only to investors preferring future gains to current income. The importance of income tax considerations as a repurchase motive was noted by Guthart [8] but was not found in Austin's empirical study [1] during the same 1960s time period.

II. Methodology and Overall Responses

To determine the underlying reasons for the current trend in stock repurchases, a survey of the chief financial officers of two groups of firms — repurchasers and non-repurchasers — was performed. The repurchase group consisted of a random sample of 150 New York Stock Exchange listed firms selected from the *NYSE* monthly report of changes in treasury stock for the period December 23, 1977, to May 25, 1979 [21]. Preferred stock repurchases were not represented because the primary reason for reacquiring preferred was for retirement which was generally less costly than calling the stock [1]. The non-repurchasers consisted of a random sample of those *NYSE* firms not on the repurchase list.

A survey instrument consisting of 25 closed-end questions and six multiple choice or open-end questions was mailed to the chief financial officer of each of the 300 firms. Respondents were asked to indicate their level of agreement-disagreement based on a seven-point semantic differential scale to each of the 25 closed-end questions which relate to published statements about repurchases. When responding to these questions, financial managers were asked to think only of their own firms.

The responses to the 25 closed-end questions were ranked by their mean scores on the level of agreement-disagreement and a Spearman's rank correlation was computed. The null hypothesis to be tested was that no association existed between the ranking of the two groups regarding these questions. A one-tail test was used since a positive association was predicted. Chi-square tests were also performed on each closed-end statement to determine whether the repurchasers and non-repurchasers answered in a similar fashion. To avoid problems of small cell size, the seven-point scale was collapsed to three categories: agree, disagree, and no opinion; and the chi-square test was then computed.

Although the response rate was quite high, 48.7 percent (73 of 150) for the repurchase group and 42.0 percent (63 of 150) for the non-repurchase group, the potential of non-response bias does exist which can affect the validity of the findings. Because the respondents were not required to identify themselves, a technique designed to increase both the response rate and candor of responses, specific non-respondents could not be identified. Therefore, as a proxy measure of non-response bias the responses from a complete second mailing to the same group were compared to those of the first based on the premise that later respondents tend to have more similar characteristics of non-respondents than early respondents. No significant differences were found between the responses of the early and late respondents, which tends to lessen, but not eliminate, the concern over potential non-response bias.

Although it would have been interesting to know something about the relative size, profitability, and growth histories of the respondent firms, such information was not requested in the questionnaire. Although the repurchase and non-repurchase groups could differ in either financial condition or growth prospects, such potential differences apparently do not significantly affect the results given the overall consistency of the two groups' responses. Systematic differences could also exist within each group but again data do not exist to allow for statistical testing.

Admittedly, the research methodology and questionnaire design involve a risk-return tradeoff. Increasing the length of the questionnaire and requiring disclosure of respondents potentially decrease the response rate and increase non-response bias. The decision was made in favor of receiving more responses at the cost of obtaining slightly less information about the two sample groups.

A. Managers' Opinions on Repurchases

The mean responses of the two groups, stock repurchasers and non-repurchasers, based on the level of agreement-disagreement, are shown in Table 2. The rankings of the statements receiving the highest and lowest level of agreement are reasonably consistent for both repurchasers and non-repurchasers. For example, the financial executives responding apparently believe stock repurchasers make a good investment when their firm's stock price is depressed (#1) but not necessarily when below book value per share (#21). By reducing the number of shares outstanding (#3), managers perceive the reacquisition of shares as positively affecting per share earnings and stock price (#5). Both repurchasers and non-repurchasers also agree that stock repurchases, by increasing the debt ratio, may have a harmful effect on the firm's capital structure (#4).

Another reason for reacquiring shares is to use repurchased shares for stock option privileges and employee bonus plans (#2). This motive appears to take precedence over such reasons as mergers and acquisitions (# 8), conversions of preferred or debentures (#12), tax benefits to shareholders (#15), and gaining greater internal control (#24).

B. Type of Decision

To determine how the financial managers regard their repurchase decisions, they were asked to select among four choices — dividend, investment, financing and other. Only managers engaging in stock repurchases were asked to respond because they were actually involved in the repurchase decision making process. As shown in Table 3, most managers

TABLE 2 Opinions about Stock Repurchases

Strongly Disagree −3	Moderately Disagree −2	Slightly Disagree −1	No Opinion 0	Slightly Agree +1	Moderately Agree +2	Strongly Agree +3

Statement	Repurchases (n = 73) Mean Rank*		Non-Repurchases (n = 63) Mean Rank*	
1. Stock repurchases are a good investment when management feels the firm's stock price is depressed.	1.63	1	.48	4
2. An important reason for repurchasing shares is to provide for stock option privileges or bonuses for employees.	1.01	2	.30	7.5
3. Stock repurchases can remove a large block of stock overhanging the market.	.97	3	.98	2
4. Stock repurchases, by increasing the debt ratio, may have a harmful effect on the firm's capital structure.	.95	4	1.06	1
5. By increasing earnings per share, stock repurchases have a favorable effect on a firm's stock price.	.92	5	.84	3
6. Stock repurchases enable management to express confidence in the firm.	.38	6	−.32	19.5
7. Stock repurchases are likely to bolster a firm's stock price because the floating supply of stock is reduced.	.18	7	−.02	13
8. Repurchased shares are a less expensive means of obtaining shares for acquisition purposes than a new issue.	.16	8	−.08	14
9. By enabling a firm to pay a higher dividend per share, stock repurchases make a firm's stock more attractive to investors.	.10	9.5	.29	9
10. Once a firm has established its optimal capital structure, stock repurchases are an effective means of maintaining that structure.	.10	9.5	−.10	15
11. Stock repurchases provide a relatively riskless means for investment when a firm needs to employ excess cash.	.06	11	−.64	22
12. An important reason for stock repurchase is to provide common shares for conversion purposes.	−.08	12	−.22	16
13. Stock repurchases can be especially valuable to make a significant shift in the capital structure within a short time period.	−.11	13	.30	7.5
14. If excess cash cannot be profitably employed for reinvestment in the firm, stock dividends rather than cash dividends are preferred.	−.14	14	−.32	19.5
15. Investors prefer the long-term gains of stock repurchases versus dividends because of favorable tax treatment.	−.15	15	.11	11
16. Stock repurchases provide a means of putting a floor under a firm's stock price.	−.21	16	−.30	17
17. Stock repurchases can have an adverse impact on the firm's image.	−.25	17	.44	5

continued

TABLE 2 **continued**

Strongly Disagree −3	Moderately Disagree −2	Slightly Disagree −1	No Opinion 0	Slightly Agree +1	Moderately Agree +2	Strongly Agree +3

Statement	Repurchases (n = 73) Mean Rank*		Non-Repurchases (n = 63) Mean Rank*	
18. Firms which engage in stock repurchases have fewer good investment opportunities than ones that do not.	−.33	18	.43	6
19. Firms which repurchase substantial amounts of stock generally have poorer growth rates than ones which do not.	−.41	19	.16	10
**20. The small investor is more likely to take advantage of a stock repurchase than an institutional investor. Thus, it is an effective means of reducing marginal costs.	−.59	20	.05	12
21. Stock repurchases are attractive only when the firm's stock price is below book value per share.	−.66	21	−.33	21
22. Stock repurchases are an effective means of obtaining shares in order to issue stock splits or stock dividends.	−.77	22	−1.08	24
**23. Stock repurchases on a regular and systematic basis are not feasible because of such uncertainties as the tax treatment of such a program and the effect on market price.	−.90	23.5	−.32	18
24. By gaining greater internal control, stock repurchases are an effective means of staving off an attempted takeover.	−.90	23.5	−.65	23
25. Stock repurchases may be viewed as a substitute for paying cash dividends.	−1.43	25	−1.19	25

*The ranking of the responses is on the basis of mean scores.
**Chi-square test is significant at the .01 level.

(50.7 percent) view stock repurchases as an investment decision. The second highest category, *i.e.*, as a means of obtaining shares for employee stock options and bonuses, represents a write-in opinion under the "other" category. Only 15.1 percent viewed repurchases as a financing decision and none saw repurchases as a dividend decision.

C. *Repurchase Techniques*

Another area of concern involves the method by which companies actually obtain reacquired shares. Table 4 indicated that 64.4 percent of the repurchase firm respondents purchase shares in the open market. While tender offers are reportedly being used more frequently for odd-lot buyback (10), their use is still relatively minor.

Table 3   **Repurchasing Group's Response on the Nature of the Repurchase Decision**

Type	Frequency	Percent
Investment Decision	37	50.7
*Necessity for Stock Options/Bonuses	15	20.5
Financing Decision	11	15.1
**Other	9	12.3
Dividend Decision	0	0
No Answer	1	1.4
Total	73	100.0

* This response represented a write-in as part of the "other" category.

** Other reasons cited were to remove an overhanging block of stock, to prevent dilution, to obtain shares for acquisition purposes and to remove small or fractional shares.

D. Motivation for Repurchase

The repurchase firm executives were also asked to indicate the major reason underlying their repurchase of stock. Table 5 indicates that two reasons predominate—a good investment of excess cash and use in employee bonus or stock option plans. Repurchasing shares for the purpose of acquiring other firms, avoiding dilution of shares, or removing an overhanging issue was cited infrequently.

E. Ongoing Repurchase Programs

The financial executives of repurchase firms were also asked whether they have an ongoing repurchase program and the reason for it. Table 6 shows that 30 of the 73 responding firms have such plans. The managers

Table 4   **Methods Used to Repurchase Stock**

Method	Frequency	Percent
Open Market Purchase	47	64.4
Tender Offer	6	8.2
Open Market and Other (Exchange, Unsolicited Block, Private Placement)	6	8.2
Unsolicited Block Purchase	5	6.8
Individual Share Purchase	4	5.5
Other*	5	6.8
Total	73	99.9**

* Other includes private placement and combinations of methods such as tender offer and open market purchase.

** Does not add to 100.00 due to rounding.

Table 5   **Reasons for Repurchasing Stock**

Reason	Frequency	Percent
Good Investment of Excess Cash	25	34.2
Employee Bonus or Stock Option Plans	25	34.2
Possible Acquisitions	6	8.2
Avoid or Reduce Dilution of Shares	4	5.5
Put a Floor on the Stock Price or Remove Overhanging Blocks	4	5.5
Conversion Purposes	3	4.1
Other*	4	5.5
No Answer	2	2.7
Total	73	100.0

* Other reasons cited are to obtain an optimal capital structure, to reduce small holdings or fractional shares, to increase earnings per share, and to stave off a takeover.

have reasons for ongoing plans similar to those reported for repurchases in general. The only difference lies in the greater use of repurchases to satisfy various employee-related plans.

F. Reasons for Not Repurchasing Stock

Table 7 reports the reasons that companies do not engage in stock repurchases. Almost half (47.6 percent) indicated that no excess cash is available for repurchases. Other minor reasons for not repurchasing stock include the lack of attractiveness of the stock as an investment and the lack of need of the stock for employee benefit plans, acquisitions and other purposes.

G. Disadvantages of Stock Repurchases

Table 8 provides the primary disadvantages of repurchasing stock from the perspective of both repurchasers and non-repurchasers. The belief that stock reacquisition reduces equity capital which could prove detrimental to the firm's capital structure or impair its debt capacity is

Table 6   **Reasons for Ongoing Repurchase Program**

Reason	Frequency	Percent
Employee Bonus or Stock Option Plans	14	46.7
Good Investment of Excess Cash	6	20.0
Possible Acquisitions	3	10.0
Stock Dividends	1	3.3
No Answer	6	20.0
Total	30	100.0

Table 7   Reasons for Not Repurchasing Stock

Reason	Frequency	Percent
No Excess Cash	30	47.6
Stock Not Needed for Employee Benefit Plans, Acquisitions or Other Purposes	6	9.5
Forbidden by a Constraint	6	9.5
Not An Attractive Investment	6	9.5
Current Debt Level Too High	5	8.0
Optimal Capital Structure Required More, Not Fewer, Shares Outstanding	5	8.0
Other*	2	3.2
No Answer	3	4.8
Total	63	100.1**

* Other includes the fear of being viewed as manipulation by stockholders and the stock price being too high.

** Does not add to 100.0 due to rounding.

Table 8   Disadvantage of Stock Repurchases

Disadvantage	Repurchasers	Non-Repurchasers	Frequency	Percent
Reduces Equity Capital Which May Be Detrimental to the Capital Structure or Impair Debt Capacity	25	20	45	33.1
Reduces Funds for Future Growth, Dividends, or Other Investments	8	12	20	14.7
Implies Lack of Internal Growth or Better Investment Opportunities	9	11	20	14.7
Provides No Disadvantages under the Right Circumstances	13	6	19	14.0
Appears as Manipulation	1	5	6	4.4
Results in Accounting Problems (*e.g.*, pooling of interests)	3	2	5	3.7
Affects Stock Price Adversely	3	2	5	3.7
More Costly than Issuing New Shares	1	0	1	.7
No Answer	10	5	15	11.0
Total	73	63	136	100.0

foremost in the minds of financial managers. Another concern is that if cash is used to repurchase stock then funds are reduced for future growth, dividends or other investments.

It is also worth noting that some managers believe that stock repurchases may suggest potentially negative connotations about the firm such as a lack of internal growth or better investment opportunities. Some concern is also expressed that repurchases may be viewed as manipulation or adversely affect the stock price. Although these opinions are voiced by relatively few managers, they suggest that reacquisitions are perceived as having a potentially negative impact on their firms due to their misinterpretation by shareholders.

III. Summary and Conclusions

The results of this survey suggest that two major reasons underlying the current proliferation of common stock repurchases (a good investment of excess cash and use in employee bonus or stock option plans) are similar to other periods of repurchase growth. A relative shift in emphasis of other motives has occurred since the 1960s. That is, the use of treasury stock for acquisitions, stock dividends and splits, and conversions is no longer of primary importance.

Repurchases also seem to be viewed from a different perspective. During the 1960s stock repurchases were viewed largely as a financing decision, whereas today reacquisitions are seen more as an investment decision. Instead of borrowing money to repurchase stock in order to achieve an optimal capital structure, firms are more reluctant to borrow to repurchase their stock and view stock repurchase as having a harmful effect on the firm's capital structure.

Much of the theory underlying stock repurchases is applied in practice. For example, financial managers realize that by repurchasing stock, fewer shares will remain outstanding and earnings per remaining share will likely increase. An increase in earnings per share may also result in a higher market price per share. Thus, under certain conditions, e.g., low stock prices and excess cash, a firm may contribute to maximization of wealth of its shareholders through stock repurchases.

Some gaps between the theory and practice of common stock buybacks do exist. The most pronounced discrepancy is the notion that stock repurchases are an alternative to dividends. The managers surveyed disagree with the idea that stock repurchases may be viewed as a substitute for paying cash dividends.

In summary, although many of the same reasons based on financial theory for stock repurchases are reiterated by the financial managers surveyed, some shifts appear to exist in the relative importance of these reasons. Although the underlying reasons for the gap between theory and practice regarding stock repurchases as an alternative for dividends are not fully explained by the questionnaire, the results of this survey do provide a basis for understanding the current rationale of financial managers for repurchasing and not repurchasing their own stock.

References

1. Douglas V. Austin. "Treasury Stock Reacquisition by American Corporations: 1961–67," *Financial Executive* (May 1969), pp. 41–53.

2. Harold Bierman, Jr. and Richard West. "The Acquisition of Common Stock by the Corporate Issuer," *Journal of Finance* (December 1966), pp. 687–696.

3. "Borrowing to Buy Back Your Stock," *Business Week* (April 9, 1979), pp. 107–108.

4. Eugene F. Brigham. "The Profitability of a Firm's Repurchase of its Own Common Stock," *California Management Review* (Winter 1964), pp. 69–75.

5. Charles D. Ellis. "Repurchase Stock to Revitalize Equity," *Harvard Business Review* (July-August 1965), pp. 119–128.

6. Edwin Elton and Martin Gruber. "The Effect of Share Repurchase on the Value of the Firm," *Journal of Finance* (March 1968), pp. 135–149.

7. Joseph E. Finnerty. "Corporate Stock Issue and Repurchase," *Financial Management* (Autumn 1975), pp. 62–66.

8. Leo A. Guthart. "Why Companies Are Buying Back Their Own Stock," *Financial Analysts Journal* (March-April 1967), pp. 105–110.

9. Haim Levy and Marshall Sarnat. *Capital Investment and Financing Decisions*. London: Prentice-Hall International, Inc., (1978).

10. Anna Merjos. "Well-Timed Repurchases," *Barron's* (January 8, 1979), pp. 11–12, 14.

11. Franco Modigliani and Richard A. Cohn. "Inflation, Rational Valuation and the Market," *Financial Analysts Journal* (March-April 1979), pp. 24–44.

12. "Repurchasing Gets 'A New Lease on Life,'" *Business Week* (April 4, 1977), pp. 101.

13. Marvin Rosenberg and Allan Young. "Firms Repurchasing Stock: Financial Security Market, and Operating Characteristics," *University of Michigan Business Review* (May 1978), pp. 17–22.

14. *Standard & Poor's Statistical Service*, "Security Price Index Record," New York: Standard & Poor's Corporation, (1980), p. 104.

15. Samuel S. Stewart, Jr. "Should a Corporation Repurchase Its Own Stock?" *Journal of Finance* (June 1976), pp. 911–921.

16. "Stock Repurchase Plans Benefit Investors," *The Outlook,* Standard & Poor's Corporation (May 7, 1979), pp. 729–780.

17. J. Fred Weston and Eugene F. Brigham. *Managerial Finance*, 6th ed. Hinsdale, Ill.: The Dryden Press, (1978), pp. 804–808.

18. Donald H. Woods and Eugene F. Brigham, "Stockholder Distribution Decisions: Share Repurchase or Dividends?" *Journal of Financial and Quantitative Analysis* (March 1966), pp. 15–28.

19. Allan Young. "The Performance of Common Stocks Subsequent to Repurchase," *Financial Analysts Journal* (October 1967), pp. 117–121.

20. "Tender Offers That Nobody Opposes," *Forbes* (July 15, 1977), p. 26.

21. "The Monthly Report of Changes in Treasury Stock," *New York Stock Exchange* (December 23, 1977; May 25, 1979).

22. Herbert Weintraub and Douglas V. Austin. "Treasury Stock Reacquisition: 1971–73," *Financial Executive* (August 1974), pp. 28–35.

Questions

1. Identify several reasons that might explain why corporations repurchase shares of their common stock.

2. What are the two primary reasons given by managers for the repurchase of common stock?

3. Explain why managers might view the repurchase of common stock as a dividend decision, a financing decision, or an investment decision.

4. Would you expect corporations to increase their repurchases of shares of common stock when the value of Standard and Poor's 500 Index is high? Explain.

PART VII
SPECIAL TOPICS

How to Negotiate a Term Loan

Jasper H. Arnold III

Despite the proliferation of services available to finance ongoing opera-tions, the fundamental source of capital for all companies remains banks. And negotiations with banks always boil down to a contract between those who have the money and those who need it. Most growing companies need to seek external financing at some point, and a very common form of this financing is the bank term loan. These loans often carry with them restrictive covenants that can unduly hamper manage-ment and increase the risk of a default.

Unfortunately, for many managers these negotiations are pitted with more uncertainties and difficulties than other types of contracts. The responsibility weighs heavily on a small company manager who may lack financial expertise, especially if the company's future is uncertain. An officer in a more financially sophisticated corporation may understand the process—but not know how to best protect the diverse interests of one part of the company from the demands of the others.

Talks with participants on both sides of the loan process, coupled with his own banking experience, give the author a knowledgeable perspective on how to turn the process around to the company's advantage. His advice for the manager is to plan a negotiating strategy. By learning to think like a banker, you will be better able to obtain a loan agreement that meets your needs without putting a stranglehold on your business.

At the time of this writing, Jasper H. Arnold III was senior vice president and manager of the credit department at First City National Bank of Houston.

Author's note: Bankers' restrictions are imposed via a formal, written loan agreement, which typically contains two distinct types of covenants, affirmative and negative. I review both, as well as the structure of a typical agreement, in the *Appendix*. Throughout the article, I deal solely with negative covenants, since they are the most restrictive and vigorously debated.

Financial managers responsible for negotiating term loans from commercial banks often feel confronted by a stone wall—the banker's restrictions (*restrictive covenants*) on the company to ensure repayment. While the ultimate objectives are easily understood (getting the least expensive funds under the fewest restrictions), achieving them is not. Since the first cave man loaned a spear to a friend only to have it returned the next day broken into little pieces, lenders have been cautious in dealing with borrowers. Moreover, lenders know they have a certain power over borrowers and have turned it into a mystique. Unlike the case in other contract negotiations, many borrowers feel they have few, if any, cards to play—that is, they have to take most of what the banker decides to dish out.

After years of participating in the loan negotiation process, I have found it not as one-sided as it appears. The banker does *not* always win; savvy companies realize that, as in every other aspect of the business, success depends on negotiating strategy.

To help companies devise an effective negotiating strategy, I studied 50 requests for term loans made at eight New York and regional banks. The study, a review of the borrower's financial statements and the final loan agreements, confirms that managers winding up with the best (least restrictive) loan package:

■   Learn to think like the banker and identify the bank's objectives.

■   Meet the banker's objectives in making the loan with the least damage to their own position.

■   Set a list of priorities on the restrictions wanted by the banker, so that they can give in on one or two of them without hindering the company's strategy.

■   Influence the banker to relax or withdraw noncrucial restrictions.

Inside the Banker's Head

First, let's look at the two sides in this contest. At the outset the bank's perspective is built on an objective and subjective analysis of the borrowing company's financial position. The analysis rests on that well-established tenet—permanent asset needs should be financed with permanent capital. When permanent capital takes the form of long-term debt, the lender wants to find out how healthy the borrower's long-term earning power is. So the bank asks for financial information as a start—historical financial statements (typically five years) as well as a forecast of your company's income statement, balance sheet, and the sources and uses of funds statements for each year.

The bank's principal and interest will be returned from the future stream of earnings before interest and taxes (EBIT). (Normally, a bank calculates EBIT as *sales* less *cost of sales* less *selling, general, and administrative expenses*.) Consequently, the bank wants to learn the extent of business risk—in other words, how much the future EBIT stream could vary. Another important element is understanding the borrower's industry—both the company's strengths and weaknesses and its overall strategy. (While EBIT is available to cover interest expense, principal payments, not being tax deductible, must be paid out of the net income stream. Moreover, annual principal payments cannot be made out of "cash flow" [net income + depreciation] unless the borrower can forego replacing depreciated fixed assets.)

Banks consider some lines of business inherently risky and this will influence the analysis, but the financial forecast becomes the primary basis on which the banker quizzes the manager to determine the degree of business risk. The banker also uses the forecast to establish how restrictive the loan will be.

Bankers also put considerable emphasis on the company's historical earnings record as an indicator of business risk. Wide fluctuations in profits or net losses—or consistently thin profit margins—usually lead to an assessment of high business risk.

After the EBIT stream, the company's balance sheet is the most important financial indicator because the assets are the bank's secondary source of repayment if earnings are not adequate to repay the loan. Therefore, the assessment of balance sheet strength or weakness hinges on the extent to which the banker thinks the loan is recoverable if assets must be sold.

Judgment is largely based on a few key ratios. For example, the current ratio or net working capital position represents the amount of liquid assets the company has available to repay debts. The banker also investigates fixed asset liquidity, important in the event of financial distress or bankruptcy.

Another key balance sheet variable is the company's margin of safety (i.e., the extent to which it is leveraged). To a banker, a company with a total liabilities-to-equity ratio of 1 to 1 can suffer a 50% deterioration in asset value and still repay a loan. If leverage is at a 3-to-1 ratio, however, creditors can only tolerate a 25% shrinkage in asset value. Moreover, since the size of annual principal and interest payments increases as leverage rises, the greater the leverage the greater the chance EBIT will not cover these payments.

The Making of Restrictions

Bankers use these simple financial indicators to determine the scope and severity of the restrictions placed on a potential borrower. The five possible types of restrictions include cash flow control, strategy control, the default "trigger," balance sheet maintenance, and asset preservation.

Cash Flow Control

The first source of restrictions comes directly from an analysis of cash flow. A company may want to build its assets so rapidly or pay such excessive dividends that the banker questions whether the EBIT stream will be sufficient to service the loan. In this case, repayment must come from a refinancing by another creditor or an equity sale. If the bank is confident that the company's earnings record and balance sheet will be strong enough to permit refinancing, it will not seek to control the company's cash flow. However, even when refinancing appears possible, bankers will usually limit excessive dividends and stock repurchases to preserve the company's equity base.

Strategy Control

The lender may try to control future strategy if he or she believes that the company's resources are ill-matched with the opportunities and risks present in the environment — or when a particular strategy requires an imprudent degree of leverage or illiquidity. Resulting covenants either prohibit managers from implementing the strategy or force them to modify it. In such cases, bankers usually want to reduce the total amount of money invested in a particular product market or spread the investment out over a longer time period, either by limiting capital expenditures and acquisitions or by writing in a debt-to-equity test.

The Infamous Trigger

One of the most feared aspects of restrictions is the bank's right to call the loan, or trigger a default. The readiness of the trigger depends on the strength of the balance sheet and the degree of business risk — that is, the potential variability in EBIT. Losses erode company assets by reducing the net working capital and the equity base. In that event (or possibly if profitability declines), the banker wants the right to call the entire loan for repayment before deterioration advances. If the company cannot repay the loan, the bank has legal recourse on the assets.

Banks, however, seldom pull the dreaded trigger. Such action usually means bankruptcy for the company, adverse publicity for the bank, and a time-consuming, costly legal proceeding for both parties. In most cases, if the restrictions trigger a default the loan is not called; instead, this imminent possibility forces the borrower to return to the bargaining table. The banker then wants a proposal for corrective action. In return for continuing the loan, the bank can boost the interest-rate, demand collateral as compensation for the risk or else rewrite the covenants.

Balance Sheet Maintenance

A company can harm its balance sheet by excessive leveraging or by financing fixed assets with short-term loans, both of which reduce its net working-capital position and liquidity. To keep the borrower from wantonly employing short-term credit, lenders impose a current ratio and/or net working-capital minimum. Also included is a debt-to-equity limit or even a prohibition on additional borrowings.

Asset Preservation

Because bankers regard assets as the ultimate source of repayment, they do not want to see a significant portion sold or pledged to other creditors.

Examples of the Versatility of Covenants

Debt-equity ratio

Limits the ability of management to leverage the company.

Restricts expansion of assets in traditional or new markets if this expansion must be financed with debt.

Limits dividend payments.

Triggers a default in the event of losses.

Current ratio or minimum net working capital

Keeps management from borrowing short term to finance long-term assets.

Limits dividend payments, capital expenditures, and investments because such cash outflows are a use of working capital in the flow-of-funds sense.

Triggers a default in the event of losses because losses are a use of working capital.

Net worth minimum

Causes a default if losses occur.

Restricts dividend payments.

Interest coverage ratio

Causes a default if losses occur.

Limits the ability of management to leverage the company.

Capital expenditure restrictions

Conserves cash within the company.

Keeps the borrower from expanding in particular markets or product lines.

So, unless the loan is secured, lenders will write in a limit on the extent to which companies can pledge assets (a "negative pledge clause").

Even if the company can put up sufficient collateral, the bank will restrict the sale of assets to forestall disposal for less than their value or for securities that could prove worthless. The bank will place limits on asset sales or require that any sale be made at fair market value in cash and that the proceeds be used to reduce the loan or to acquire replacement assets.

How the Restrictions Are Set

Using this general information, you can see how to chart your initial negotiating strategy. In the *Exhibit,* I illustrate the minimum objectives the banker must achieve, depending on the degree of a particular company's business risk and balance sheet strength. Six principal rules of loan negotiation hold:

The banker will always require certain balance sheet standards. At a minimum, management will be unable to leverage assets too highly or use excessive short-term liabilities to finance long-term assets.

There will always be a trigger. Despite the fact that the banker will probably never call the loan, the presence of a trigger gives the bank the power to take over the company's assets as a result of poor earnings performance.

Assets will be preserved. No banker wants to see the assets of a company sold — or pledged to another creditor.

Restrictions on cash flow vary. Bankers feel comfortable when companies with good prospects and healthy balance sheets can call on outside capital to service debt. Yet they are concerned lest management authorize excessive dividends or buy back large amounts of stock, so they include a very loose limit on dividends or rely on a debt-to-equity or a net working-capital test for control. A company with a weak balance sheet or high business risk will encounter demands to ensure that most of the cash it generates is used for repayment instead of dividends or capital expenditures.

Tightness of restrictions depends on the level of business risk and strength of the balance sheet. "Tightness" is the degree to which the balance sheet and income statement tests track existing and forecast levels. The tighter the covenant, the more restrictive the control on management's freedom to pay cash out, leverage the company, or incur losses.

Strategy control applies across the board. With a company having a high degree of business risk and a weak balance sheet, the bank will try to restrain strategic movement that it deems inappropriate. More credit-worthy candidates will suffer fewer restrictions if the banker does not like the corporate strategy but will be faced with more sensitive triggers that can be quickly set off if the strategy fails.

Exhibit   **Determinants of the Objectives and Tightness of Restrictive Covenants**

| **Covenant Objectives** | 1
Cash Flow Control
2
Strategy Control
3
Trigger | 4
Balance Sheet Maintenance
5
Asset Preservation |

Quadrant 4 **Moderate Covenants** Relevant Objectives: 1, 3, 4, and 5	**Low Business Risk** ↑	**Quadrant 1** **Loose Covenants** Relevant Objectives: 1, 3, 4, and 5 but limited to controlling excessive dividend payments or stock repurchases
← **Weak Balance Sheet**		**Strong Balance Sheet** →
Relevant Objectives: 1, 3, 4, and 5 **Tight Covenants** **Quadrant 3**	**High Business Risk** ↓	Relevant Objectives: 1, 3, 4, and 5 **Moderate Covenants** **Quadrant 2**

Note: If the banker believes that the borrower intends to pursue an inappropriate strategy, he will make the covenants restrictive — possibly, in the case of Quadrant 3 borrowers, even prohibiting or modifying the strategy.

Some examples of different negotiations help illustrate the various possibilities.

An oil field pump manufacturer (Quadrant II) wanted a five-year term loan of several million dollars to double the size of its manufacturing facility and to provide working capital to expand sales. The company had been plagued with low profit margins, inventory control problems, and operating inefficiencies. To retain market share, however, the expansion was necessary even though the added production and sales capacity might exacerbate the problems.

The banker thought the balance sheet was reasonably strong. To maintain that strength, he set a long-term debt-equity limit and a current ratio minimum. Since the borrower's strategy exposed it to much business risk, however, the banker wanted a quick default triggered if losses occurred. So he set a minimum net worth covenant that increased every year and closely tracked the forecast levels. The banker also thought that the company's ultimate profitability was too uncertain for him to risk refinancing as a source of required principal payments, so he imposed capital expenditure, investment, and dividend restrictions. The bank included a negative pledge clause and a prohibition on asset sales of more than $1 million in any fiscal year.

Most of the successful companies in Quadrant I were members of the *Fortune* "1000" industrials. The lenders were willing to let these companies do as they pleased if balance sheet ratios remained within certain bounds and profits did not drop. Therefore, they set debt-to-equity maximums and current ratio or working capital restrictions well outside of the forecast levels. These covenants, taken together with either a net worth minimum or a coverage test, also provided a trigger. Negative pledge clauses were always used and asset sales were limited.

A regional chain of steak houses wanted financing to open up several new restaurants within one year in a distant market where it was unknown. The expansion, which would more than double the chain's size, required high leveraging, and management wanted to expand at a time when some of the new restaurants had not yet realized satisfactory profits. Further, restaurant business assets are viewed as highly illiquid if sold under distress conditions. Thus, the bank saw a rapid growth strategy as too risky — and set restrictions to slow growth.

A moderate debt-to-equity ratio would curtail expansion until the existing restaurants generated enough new equity to support the borrowings necessary to open the new units. This test simultaneously ensured holding the company's leverage to a satisfactory level. Unwilling to rely on a refinancing for repayment and determined to control the company's cash, the banker prohibited dividends and long-term investments. The creditor used a debt-to-equity test as a trigger if losses occurred and added a cash-flow-coverage ratio. The loan agreement did not restrict the company's extension of collateral to other creditors, but it did restrict excessive asset sales.

Forge Your Own Strategy

You can use the model in the *Exhibit* to determine what will influence the banker in your particular case and what restrictions the banker is likely to impose. Keep in mind the following guidelines:

1.   Consider your earnings history over the past five years. Losses, consistently low profit margins, or very volatile earnings usually indicate a great degree of business risk.

2.   Ask yourself whether the variables that determine EBIT (e.g., raw material costs, sales volume, product price, foreign exchange rates) will change over the life of the loan and cause severe declines in earnings.

3.   After taking into account the loan, look at the existing and forecast balance sheet ratios such as the debt-to-equity ratio and the current

ratio. Do they indicate an illiquid or highly leveraged condition? (If a company's forecast is based on assumptions that are overgenerous in view of historical results, a banker will frequently draw up a forecast with more conservative assumptions. Try it yourself. In that case, can the debt be serviced? What happens to the leverage and liquidity ratios?)

4.   Considering the types of assets the company owns, the net working capital level, and the margin of safety for creditors (leverage), could the bank get repayment if the company's assets were liquidated? If the answer is yes, then yours is a strong-balance-sheet company. If the answer is no or maybe, then yours is a weak-balance-sheet company.

Supplement this analysis by questioning the banker before negotiations start. First ask about the bank's preliminary judgments on the balance sheet, historical earnings performance, and the business risk of the company. Then inquire about the soundness of your proposed strategies.

Be careful. Probe responses and always read between the lines. Following initial conversations, make sure the banker receives any additional information necessary about the company—its products, markets, and strategy.

Once you have a good idea as to the banker's objectives, evaluate each possible restriction. To do this properly, you must understand how the more popular restrictive covenants are used and how they can simultaneously accomplish one or more objectives. The ruled insert gives a good example of their versatility.

For example, the current ratio and minimum net-working-capital tests give the bank a broad range of control. They simultaneously provide a trigger, control cash flow, and maintain the balance sheet. These covenants, particularly the current ratio minimum, are the most often violated—simply because almost every financial event or managerial action affects the company's working capital.

Identify Costly Restrictions

During negotiations the manager must try to minimize the impact of restrictions that might unduly hamper management or easily trigger a violation before the company's financial situation has seriously deteriorated. The most useful tool to determine whether restrictions are too tight is your financial forecast. For example, suppose the bank wants to impose a long-term debt-equity limit of .75 to 1, and you forecast that next year's profit will be $3 million; long-term debt, $15 million; and equity, $21 million. You can figure that a drop greater than $1 million in anticipated net income would cause a default (.75 = $15 million/X; X = $20 million; necessary decline in net income = $21 million − $20 million, or $1 million). In light of that margin, you must decide how likely such earnings performance is.

A Basic Negotiating Posture

At the outset, the banker will try to impose as many tight restrictions as possible, especially if yours is a small company or one that has traditionally dealt with one bank. Address each proposed restriction individually and push for its elimination, or at least its relaxation, by using an appropriate mix of the following arguments:

- Management needs strategic flexibility to avoid default.

- Even if the restriction is dropped, the banker will still achieve the objectives with the remaining covenants.

- A strong balance sheet shows that company assets provide a secure, secondary source of repayment if earnings deteriorate.

- A strong earnings outlook means the bank can tolerate a weaker balance sheet. Large payouts of cash are acceptable since strong future earnings make it possible to service the bank debt by refinancing.

- The banker can tolerate large payouts of cash or other managerial actions because, if earnings deteriorate, a trigger covenant will be violated and the bank can then demand tighter covenants that closely control management.

Watch out for unnecessarily tight dividend restrictions or capital expenditure limits. You can have them dropped or relaxed if your balance sheet is strong enough or if you can point to a low amount of business risk. To the extent that you can, stress: (1) your high margin of safety (low leverage), the liquidity of the balance sheet (high current ratio), and the availability of your assets as a secondary source of repayment even if earnings are used for something else; and/or (2) that your strong earnings will permit a refinancing if they are used for something other than debt servicing.

A borrower with a strong balance sheet and a low level of business risk can usually convince the banker that a very loose dividend restriction (e.g., "cumulative dividends and stock repurchases shall not exceed 45% of cumulative net income") is acceptable. Or you can maintain that the debt-to-equity ratio and the current ratio (or net working capital minimum) adequately protect the bank from excessive payouts of the company's equity.

If you are not so fortunate, try to make trade-offs among covenants. For example, bankers will reduce controls on cash flow if you agree to an easily released trigger. If you start losing money, the trigger will cause a default and allow the banker to demand a tightening in the controls to stop the cash drain.

Eliminate Duplication

The smart manager will insist that the banker can achieve many objectives through a single covenant. For example, the debt-equity ratio restriction can control management's use of leverage and also serve as the yardstick for a trigger if the company incurs losses.

If the banker proposes a net worth minimum as a trigger and a debt-equity ratio as a brake on leverage, the manager can argue for elimination of the trigger because the debt-equity ratio is a sufficient control. The banker may counter by maintaining that he wants to safeguard loss control directly, but the borrower may at least get the restrictions relaxed somewhat.

Relax the Trigger

When a trigger is too restrictive, you may be able to show that even though future earnings might be less than planned, this would not necessarily reflect a fundamental or long-lasting deterioration in the company's earning power. In the previous example (where more than a $1 million fall in net income, from the forecast of $3 million to less than $2 million, would have violated the .75-to-1 long-term debt-equity limit), you might argue that such a profit decline could be caused by temporary factors beyond your control, such as bad weather or strikes. Or make the point that an exact forecast is impossible and you need a wide enough margin for error to properly test decisions.

You will have better luck with this appeal if you show that your company's assets will still provide an assured, secondary source of repayment if the banker relaxes the covenant from .75 to 1 to, say, 1 to 1. Prospects for strong earnings also may help you bargain for more flexibility on the use of debt financing.

Dealing with Strategy Control

A strategy restriction often leads corporate executives to seek a more "enlightened" bank. Unfortunately, if one bank thinks this kind of control necessary, usually most others will agree.

Rather than shopping around, find out why the banker objects to a strategy; then point out your thinking behind it and the importance of flexibility. After all, success here should guarantee future earnings power. Then agree to other restrictions—for example, a tight trigger that allows the bank to put a stop to the strategy if it results in losses. If, after considerable discussion, the bank officer continues to regard the plan as inappropriate, consider financing from a source less averse to risk than a commercial bank.

A Competing Note . . .

Some *Fortune* "1000" companies shop for the best terms by requesting several banks to bid on a loan. They instruct bidders to quote the interest rate, the compensating balance arrangement, the repayment provisions, and a set of restrictive covenants. Such a procedure — or even the *threat* of it — influences some banks to propose more acceptable terms.

I do not suggest that all companies, particularly smaller ones, use this technique. Before negotiating a term loan, however, you should obtain some information on the types of covenants that might be demanded either by visiting the financial officers in companies that have recently raised bank debt or by talking with lending officers to get a feel for the types of covenants that might be required. Armed with this knowledge, you can mention the requirements of other banks when the potential lender is unduly restrictive.

. . . and a Concluding One

Covenants set at the time a loan is negotiated that allow you free rein still may prove restrictive in light of future opportunities. However, compliance can be — and nearly always is — waived or the covenant amended if the bank's review of a project shows it to be strategically appropriate without drastically altering the risk picture.

Appendix   **The Typical Bank Loan Agreement**

Bank loan agreements contain a *representation and warranties section* normally stipulating that the borrower:	The *affirmative covenants section,* considered "bollerplate covenants," includes promises that the borrower will:	The *negative covenants section* stipulates any number of the following promises that the borrower will not:	
Is properly incorporated.	Submit annual, audited financial statements.	Permit some type of debt-to-equity ratio (e.g., total liabilities-to-equity or long-term debt-to-equity) to exceed a specified maximum.	Pledge its assets to another creditor (a variation is to pledge its assets unless the bank is equally secured by the assets).
Has the power and authority to enter into the loan agreement and the promissory note.	Submit periodic (usually quarterly or monthly) unaudited, interim financial statements.		
Is current on its taxes.			Merge with or acquire another company (a variation is to merge with or acquire another company unless the borrower is the surviving company and no violation of a covenant would result).
Is not the subject of any litigation except as disclosed.	Submit periodic certificates signed by an officer of the company stating whether the company is in compliance with the loan agreement.	Permit the interest coverage ratio (EBIT/interest expense) to be less than a specified minimum. (Other coverage tests are also used; *cash flow coverage: net income + depreciation/ current maturities*	
Has good title to its assets.			
Has not pledged any of its assets except as disclosed.	Maintain its corporate		Sell its assets

Appendix The Typical Bank Loan Agreement

Bank loan agreements contain a *representation and warranties section* normally stipulating that the borrower:	The *affirmative covenants section,* considered "bollerplate covenants," includes promises that the borrower will:	The *negative covenants section* stipulates any number of the following promises that the borrower will not:	
Is not in violation of any other credit agreement. Has made full disclosure of its financial condition in its most recently submitted financial statements.	existence. Maintain adequate insurance. Maintain its corporate assets in good condition. Pay all taxes unless contested in good faith.	of long-term debt shall be no less than a specified minimum.) Permit additional borrowings. Permit guarantees of third-party obligations to exceed a specified dollar amount. Permit the current ratio to fall to less than a specified minimum. Permit net working capital to fall to less than a specified minimum. Permit annual capital expenditures to exceed specified dollar amounts. Permit dividend payments and stock repurchases to exceed a specified cumulative or annual dollar amount.	(except inventory in the ordinary course of business and obsolete or fully depreciated equipment), unless the money received is used to retire the bank loan or to buy replacement assets. Permit investments (such as the purchase of common stock or bonds of other companies), loans, or advances to exceed a specific dollar amount outstanding.
	Occasionally a banker will tailor a restriction. For example, one institution recently prohibited an agricultural commodities trader from incurring a loss that exceeded a certain amount on closing out all long and short positions.	Loan agreements also list *events of default,* including failure to pay principal or interest when due, failure to comply with an affirmative covenant after notice of the violation has been given by the bank, violation of a negative covenant, discovery that a representation or warranty was incorrect, a default in the payment of money owed to another lender, and bankruptcy of the company.	The *remedies section* states that should a default occur, the lender may declare the entire principal of the note, together with accrued interest, immediately due and payable.

Questions

1.   What is a term loan?

2.   Define each of the following parts of a typical term-loan agreement:
     a.   Affirmative covenants
     b.   Negative covenants
     c.   Representation and warranties
     d.   Events of default
     e.   Remedies

3.   Assume that you are a corporate loan officer at a commercial bank. Describe the covenant(s) that you would impose as a condition for a term loan to protect the bank in each of the following events:
     a.   Net working capital becomes dangerously low.
     b.   Company profit becomes dangerously low.
     c.   Increased debt dramatically increases financial risk.
     d.   Expansion into new product lines dramatically increases business risk.

4.   Assume that you are the Chief Financial Officer of a company planning to apply for a five-year term loan of $1 million. Describe the information that you will supply to the corporate loan officer.

The Evaluation of Lease Financing Opportunities

Lawrence D. Schall

Leasing is interesting both because of its popularity as a financing technique and because it involves complicated managerial finance issues. Billions of dollars in new assets are leased each year and virtually anything of size that can be bought can also be leased. As a conceptual problem, leasing's allure lies in its complexity, since the decision to lease or buy involves both a financing decision (buy and finance with equity or debt, or lease and let the lessor finance the acquisition) and an investment decision (as to whether the asset should be acquired at all). A sound lease-or-buy analytic framework can be highly complex. It can also be highly rewarding, since errors in making the lease-or-buy choice can cost a company dearly.

I. Leasing in "Perfect Markets"

We begin with an asset user who must decide whether to purchase or lease an asset in a very simple world, a world we will refer to as "perfect markets." The "perfect markets" exercise provides a general, albeit simplified, framework that also applies in actual ("imperfect") markets. We will find that, in perfect markets, leasing produces no benefits and asset users are indifferent between leasing and purchasing assets.[1]

Perfect markets (as the term is used here) satisfy the following conditions:

Excerpted from Lawrence D. Schall, "The Evaluation of Lease Financing Opportunities," *Midland Corporate Finance Journal* (Spring 1985): 48–65. Excerpted with permission.

At the time of this writing, Lawrence D. Schall was Professor of Finance and Business Economics at the University of Washington's Graduate School of Business Administration.

[1] For a more complete presentation of the arguments presented here, see Lewellen, Long and McConnell (1976) and Miller and Upton (1976).

- Information is costlessly available to everyone; there are no costs or delays in enforcing contracts or in monitoring compliance with contractual provisions; and markets are competitive and there are no transaction costs (for example, there are no brokerage fees in conducting leasing or other transactions).

- Everyone assigns the same probabilities to future events. For example, everyone might agree that a particular building erected in 1985 will have a value in 1987 of between $10 million and $15 million, with equal probability for all values between $10 million and $15 million.

- Personal taxes do not affect the business decisions of a particular firm (because they do not exist or, if they do exist, because they are unbiased).

- All firms (including lessees and lessors) have the same tax rate, are charged the same purchase price for any particular asset, depreciate any given asset in the same way, and obtain the same market price in selling any given asset.

For simplicity only, assume that the lessee and lessor are both all-equity financed. The after-tax rental income each period received by the lessor equals $(1 - \text{tax rate})$ times the lease rental. For example, if the lessor's tax rate is 40 percent and the annual lease rental is $10,000, the annual after-tax lease rental is $6,000. Let PV[ ] signify the present value of the term in the brackets. The present value of the lessor's income from the asset is therefore:

(1)   PV[lessor's after-tax income] = PV[$(1 - \text{tax rate})$(lease rental)]

Equation (1) is the stream of after-tax lease rentals stated in today's dollars. For example, if the annual after-tax lease rental were $6,000 beginning one year from now and continuing for five years, and if the discount rate (interest rate) used to compute the present value were 10 percent, the present value of the lessor's after-tax rental income would be $22,749. This present value equals the 10 percent present value factor for five years (3.79081) times the $6,000 after-tax rental.

The present value of the lessor's cost of purchasing the asset equals the initial purchase price minus the investment tax credit minus the present value of the tax savings from depreciating the asset, minus the present value of the after-tax salvage value at the end of the asset's useful life.[2] That is,

(2)   PV[lessor's after-tax purchase cost] = purchase
price − ITC − PV[depreciation tax savings] − PV[after-tax salvage value]

---

[2] We are assuming for simplicity that the tax savings from the investment tax credit are received when the asset is acquired. In actuality, the tax savings occur over the year of acquisition or, if the credit is carried forward, in future years.

Under the above perfect markets assumptions, competition among lessors will drive down lease rentals to a level at which lessors earn only a fair (competitive) rate of return on the capital they have invested in the asset. At this level, lease rentals will also be such that the present value of the after-tax lease rental income to the lessor (equation (1)) just equals the present value of the cost to the lessor of buying the asset (equation (2)). That is, given the forces of competition in the leasing market,

(3)   PV[lessor's after-tax income] = PV[lessor's after-tax purchase cost]

Now let's adopt the perspective of the user of the asset, the potential lessee. In deciding whether to lease or buy the asset, the user will have to compare the present value of the after-tax lease cost with the present value of the after-tax purchase cost. The after-tax lease cost each period equals (1 − tax rate) times the lease rental; and because the lessor and the lessee have the same tax rates (by the fourth perfect markets assumption), the after-tax cost to the lessee must equal the after-tax rental income to the lessor. For example, if the annual lease rental were $10,000, and the user (lessee) had a 40% tax rate, the annual after-tax rental cost to the lessee would be $6,000. It follows that the present value of the after-tax lease cost to the lessee is the right-hand side of equation (1).[3] Thus,

(4)   PV[user's after-tax lease cost] = PV[lessor's after-tax income]

We are assuming that the lessee and the lessor have the same purchase price, investment tax credit, depreciation tax savings, and estimated salvage value for the asset. Therefore, the after-tax purchase cost of the asset to the user is the same as for the lessor, which is the amount shown in equation (2); thus,

(5)   PV[user's after-tax purchase cost] = PV[lessor's after-tax purchase cost]

Setting equations (3), (4) and (5) side by side, we see that

(6)   PV[user's after-tax lease cost] = PV[user's after-tax purchase cost]

Equation (6) states that, for the user of the asset, the present value of the cost of leasing the asset equals the present value of the cost of purchasing the asset. This means that the user is indifferent between leasing and purchasing.

The above result is very important because it says that leasing does not produce gains if no "imperfections" exist in the marketplace. It also illustrates interrelations between markets. Both the lessor and the user can buy the asset in the asset market, and the two can establish a lease market in which the lessor passes on the cost of purchase to the lessee in the form of a lease rental. Under the above assumptions, the user incurs the same present value of costs whether it purchases the asset directly or

---

[3] In perfect markets, everyone uses the same discount rate to compute the present value of any particular cash flow stream. Therefore, the lessor and lessee use the same discount rate to value the after-tax lease rental.

pays the cost in the form of lease rental fees to the lessor (the present value of which equals the after-tax purchase cost of the asset to the lessor). In this world, the lessor is simply an intermediary who is willing to tie up capital in an asset and earn a fair return on that capital. The user can either lease from the lessor and pay that fair return to the lessor, or the user can tie up its own capital and incur the same capital cost (the interest lost on the dollars invested in the asset). The cost to the user is the same in either case.

II. Leasing in Actual Markets

Missing from the simplified world we just examined are factors often referred to by financial theorists as "imperfections." These include differential income tax rates, sales taxes, transaction costs, information costs, and contract enforcement and monitoring costs. In imperfect markets, leasing or purchasing an asset may be preferred in a particular instance. Below we discuss the primary considerations that affect the lease-or-buy decision in actual "imperfect" markets.[4]

Taxes

Differences between the tax rates of lessors and asset users can make leasing the preferred alternative for the user. For example, if the user is an airline with no taxable income and no use for the investment tax credit or depreciation tax shelters on a new airplane, the airline may be able to benefit by leasing the plane from a lessor who can take the depreciation and investment credit, and who will pass on the tax savings to the airline in the form of a lower lease rental. The tax advantage of letting the lessor use the tax shelters is at least in part offset (and possibly more than offset) by the added taxes that must be paid because the zero tax bracket airline lessee gets no tax benefit from deducting the lease rental, whereas the lessor must pay taxes on the rental income received. For example, if the user-lessee has a zero tax bracket and the lessor has a 40% tax bracket, a $10,000 lease payment from the lessee to the lessor is an after-tax cost to the lessee of $10,000 but produces an after-tax income to the lessor of only $6,000; the transfer of funds from the lessee to the lessor in the form of a lease rental means that the government gains $4,000 in taxes. Compensating for this tax disadvantage are the investment tax credit and depreciation tax savings received by the lessor which, given that the user has a zero tax bracket, could not be obtained by the user if the asset were purchased by the user.[5]

---

[4] For an overview of the firm and asset characteristics and market factors that influence the decision to lease, see Smith and Wakeman (1985).

[5] See Brealey and Young (1980), Franks and Hodges (1978), and Miller and Upton (1976) for a discussion of various tax considerations in leasing.

Any tax benefits from leasing will be reflected in the lease-or-buy analysis performed by the lessee.

Asset Value Risk

The owner of an asset will be concerned about the asset's future market value if future sale of the asset is a possibility. This asset value risk can be shifted (for a price) to a lessor who owns the asset and charges a rental for its use. Leasing can also increase the risk faced by a lessee. A lease can expose the lessee to the risk of paying a lease rental on an asset that is no longer useful to the lessee. To avoid this risk the lease contract can include a cancellation clause (at the option of the lessee) or a provision allowing the lessee to sublease the asset.

The fundamental issue here is risk-sharing. Leasing gives the user the opportunity to shift some or all of the ownership risks to the lessor. Generally, the better the position assumed by the lessee, the worse the position assumed by the lessor and the higher the lease rental. For example, the right to sublease or the right to cancel the lease are both, all else equal, an advantage to the lessee and a disadvantage to the lessor—for which the lessor will charge a fee. Similarly, an option allowing the lessee to purchase the leased asset is better for the lessee and worse for the lessor than no option at all (assuming an option price that is not so high that the lessee would never exercise the option). The lessor will charge for such an option. Depending on the circumstances, the lessee may be willing to pay the added charge.

Note that the user may want to shift ownership risk to the lessor even if the lessee and lessor assign identical probabilities to potential future values of the asset (that is, even if they have the same expectations about the future). The lessee may be trying to minimize cash flow uncertainty.[6] A fixed lease rental may provide the user with greater certainty of the dollar cost of the asset than would ownership of the asset (e.g., because of uncertainty about the asset's future abandonment value).[7]

---

[6] With the presence of imperfections (e.g., potential financial distress costs) or corporate taxes, there may be a benefit to the company from reducing the uncertainty of its cash flow. For example, if large legal costs and significant disruptions of the company's operations result from financial distress (inability to service liabilities), there may be benefits from reducing the likelihood of financial distress by making the cash flow more predictable. Also, owners of small businesses may wish to lease rather than purchase some assets in order to reduce investment in the company and thereby achieve a higher degree of wealth diversification (on this, see Fama and Jensen (1983)).

[7] After the user has employed the asset, the user must find a market for the asset if it was purchased or must return the asset to the lessor if it was leased. If the lessor can more readily find a market for the asset than could the user, there may be an advantage to leasing. However, this advantage disappears if there are dealers in used assets (to whom the user could sell the asset) who are as able as the lessor in finding a market for the asset.

Transaction Costs and Sales Taxes

Leasing is an easy way to obtain the services of an asset with minimal uncertainty about the dollar cost (since the lease rental is fixed and the salvage value risk is assumed by the lessor). An alternative to leasing that is economically equivalent (except for tax effects) is purchase of the asset with a simultaneous arrangement to sell the asset at some future date at a currently specified price. One advantage of leasing over such a purchase-saleback agreement is that leasing may involve lower legal costs and lower state sales taxes. Leasing does not entail the legal costs and sales taxes associated with transferring title twice, initially to the user and later from the user to the other buyer.

Specialized Assets and Negotiation Costs

Sometimes assets are designed specifically for the needs of a particular user and thus have greater value to that user than to anyone else. If the asset is leased, and at the end of the lease term the asset is worth more to the lessee than to other potential users, there will be a bargaining problem for the lessor and the lessee as to the level of the rental when and if the lease is renewed. The lessor will want to charge what the asset is worth to the lessee, and the lessee will want to pay only what the lessor could get elsewhere. Negotiating the renewal agreement can be costly, and this cost can be avoided if the user simply purchases the asset in the first place. Negotiating costs in this case favor purchase of the asset by the user.[8]

Asset Maintenance and Contracting Costs

If it were costless to determine the condition of an asset (no inspection costs, etc.) and to negotiate and enforce contracts (no costs in arranging the contract and ensuring compliance by the parties), in competitive asset markets the incentives to maintain an asset would be the same whether the asset were owned or leased by the user. A lessor could detect and charge the lessee for wear and damage. Anyone later leasing or buying the used asset from the lessor (if the user leased the asset) or from the user (if the user purchased the asset) would be able to assess the asset's condition and would pay an amount reflecting that assessment. The asset would thus be used and maintained in the most economically efficient way, thereby maximizing benefits less costs.

In practice, however, asset damage is often difficult to detect until some time after the damage has occurred; and contracting involves significant negotiation and enforcement costs. These "imperfections" imply that the net benefits from an asset may depend on which contractual arrangement is adopted (for example, on whether the asset is leased or

---

[8] On the incentives to lease or purchase specialized assets, see Klein, Crawford and Alchian (1978).

purchased by the user). And in competitive markets, as we have observed, there is an incentive to use the contractual form which generates the greatest net benefits.

Purchase of an asset by the user may be the most economical way to ensure its efficient use. Suppose, for example, that an owner-user of the asset would employ it to the end of its useful life, but that a lease of the asset would be for a term less than the asset's useful life (i.e., at the end of the lease, the user would have to renegotiate with the lessor or obtain an asset somewhere else). Suppose also that internal damage to the asset during the lease period is unlikely to be fully detectable at the end of the lease period, but that such damage will affect the long-run productivity of the asset. Finally, assume that the maintenance to prevent the damage can be economically provided only by the user (e.g., if the maintenance takes the form of care in using the asset). The asset would likely be better maintained if the user purchased rather than leased it. This is because any loss due to damage is borne in effect by a user-owner; but a user-lessee is not charged for the specific amount of damage it has caused.[9]

Under different circumstances, leasing may be more efficient. Consider, for example, the case of a lessor who leases an asset on a short-term basis (e.g., a three-month lease period on an asset with several years' useful life). This lessor has an incentive to invest in maintenance which increases the asset's long-run productivity. In a competitive lease market, the net gain from this maintenance (increased long-run rentals less maintenance expenditures) will be reflected in the lease rental charged users. On the other hand, a short-term user (e.g., one who needs the asset for only three months) has no incentive to invest in such maintenance whether the user leases the asset or buys and resells it (at the end of three months). The asset will thus be better maintained with leasing than with purchase and resale by the user.[10]

We have made several interrelated points. First, the nature of the contractual arrangements (e.g., lease or purchase) can affect the level of maintenance since incentives to maintain an asset depend on those arrangements. Second, costs are involved in establishing and enforcing contracts, and these costs are relevant in selecting the most economical

[9] The lessor will charge a lease rental which, on average, covers the cost of undetectable damage regardless of the maintenance undertaken by the lessee. Therefore, the average cost of undermaintenance is borne by the lessee. For details on the assumptions and analysis relating to this point, see Alchian and Demsetz (1972) and Flath (1980).

[10] We are here referring to a particular type of maintenance. We assume the following: maintenance can be provided as economically by the lessor as by the user; the level of maintenance during the use period (e.g., three months) is not apparent at the end of the use period and there is no costless way to prove (to someone who did not do the maintenance) or guarantee what the maintenance was; and benefits from such maintenance do not occur until after the use period. Under these conditions, a lessor has an incentive to provide maintenance but a user does not. If the user buys and resells the asset, the party buying the used asset will assume no maintenance and will pay the initial user a price reflecting this; with lease by the user, the lessor will assume no maintenance by the user and will charge a lease rental reflecting this. For further discussion, see Flath (1980).

legal relationships among parties. Third, in a competitive market, asset users ultimately benefit from use of those contractual arrangements which provide the greatest net economic benefits (where net benefits include the returns from better maintenance less the costs, including contracting costs, of providing the maintenance). In competitive markets, we can expect these economically efficient contracts to arise.

Restrictions on the Firm

Lenders and lessors (to a smaller extent) often impose restrictions on the firm as a condition for extending credit. These restrictions can include such things as limits on dividends, executive salaries, capital expenditures and further company borrowing, or required minimum levels of working capital and net worth. Such restrictions reduce a creditor's or lessor's exposure to the risk of non-payment. This means that a lender or lessor who imposes no constraints on the firm will generally charge more than one that does impose constraints.

In a given situation, it may or may not be advantageous to the asset user to avoid the restrictions, for example, by leasing from a lessor who would impose fewer restrictions than would a lender financing a purchase. The choice has to be made on a case-by-case basis. The decision as to whether to lease or to buy and borrow will depend on how the restrictions affect the firm and on the relative costs of lease and debt financing.[11]

Lessor Market Power and the Incentive to Lease

If a manufacturer can affect the price of its product (i.e., if it is in a market that is not perfectly competitive), leasing can provide a way to increase profits through price discrimination. This may motivate the manufacturer to lease as well as sell its product to customers. If the demand for the asset by potential buyers differs from the demand by potential lessees, profits are maximized if one price is charged buyers and another, implicit, price is charged lessees. It can also be shown that under certain conditions a lessor's profits can be increased through price discrimination if the lease rental charged depends on the intensity of asset usage by the lessees.[12]

Capital Expenditure Controls

In some organizations—especially government agencies—restrictions are placed on the level of capital expenditures (i.e., asset purchases) but

---

[11] On the provisions commonly included in lease agreements, see Crawford, Harper and McConnell (1981), Smith and Wakeman (1985), and Sorensen and Johnson (1977).

[12] On alternative contractual arrangements and price discrimination, see Burnstein (1960) and Liebowitz (1983).

not on the level of lease rental expense incurred. In such a case, if the capital budget limit has been reached, leasing may be the only way of obtaining an asset. Clearly, in a rational system, lease proposals will be reviewed just as carefully as capital expenditure proposals, and any limits on capital expenditures will apply both to the purchase and to the lease of assets. Under such a system, leasing will not provide an escape from capital outlay controls.

Compensation Contracts

Under some compensation contracts bonuses depend on the rate of return on invested capital. This can provide an incentive to the manager to lease if the asset base on which the return on capital is calculated includes owned assets but not leased assets. Leasing would mean a smaller denominator in the return on capital formula but often without a proportionally smaller numerator (if the lease rental is competitive). This presumably unintended incentive to lease — one which, at least, has no obvious benefits to stockholders — can be removed by including the value of leased assets in the invested capital base.[13]

Two Myths: Cash and Borrowing Capacity Advantages of Leasing

We have all heard that "leasing conserves cash." So does borrowing, however. Leasing involves lower current cash outlays only in situations in which a company can lease an asset but cannot obtain similar levels of financing from other sources. Leasing and borrowing are both ways of financing assets with someone else's money, and both require that the money be paid back (whether in the form of lease rental payments or loan repayments).

One might counter that, although one can borrow rather than lease, leasing has the advantage of producing a stronger balance sheet. With borrowing, a liability appears on the balance sheet and this reduces the ability to borrow further; no such debt appears with leasing, and borrowing capacity is thereby preserved. This argument overlooks the fact that audited financial statements report all significant lease obligations, whether among liabilities on the balance sheet (if the lease is a "capital lease" under accounting principles) or in a footnote to the financial statements. Knowledgeable creditors view lease obligations as fixed claims similar to debt, and take significant leases into account when reviewing a prospective borrower.[14]

---

[13] On alternative contracting arrangements and incentives, see Smith and Watts (1982).

[14] There is some evidence that many lenders ignore noncapitalized leases (those not appearing as liabilities on the balance sheet); see Abdel-Khalik (1981). For any given asset a noncapitalized lease generally imposes a smaller economic burden (liability) than would a capitalized lease.

III. Summary

Under ideal conditions referred to by economists as "perfect markets," asset users are indifferent between purchasing and leasing assets because the after-tax cost to the user is the same for the two methods of acquisition. Under actual conditions, however, leasing may provide advantages, such as tax savings, a better firm cash flow risk level (risk can be passed on to the lessor for a fee), lower transaction costs, better asset maintenance, less onerous restrictions on the firm than with borrowing, and the avoidance of capital expenditure controls. Leasing can also be used by a lessor as a way of increasing profits through price discrimination.

The argument that leasing conserves cash is valid only if the company cannot obtain similar financing by borrowing to finance asset purchases. Also dubious is the notion that leasing provides asset financing without disclosure of any fixed financial obligations by the lessee. Audited financial statements disclose significant lease obligations, and lenders generally inquire whether a potential borrower has any such obligations outstanding.

References

Abdel-Khalik, A.R., "The Economic Effects on Lessees of F.A.S.B. Statement No. 13 Accounting for Leases," Stanford: FASB, 1981.

Alchian, Armen A. and Harold Demsetz, "Production Information Costs, and Economic Organization," *American Economic Review,* 62, no. 5 (December 1972): pp. 777–795.

Ang, James and Pamela P. Peterson, "The Leasing Puzzle," *Journal of Finance,* 39, no. 4 (September 1984): pp. 1055–1066.

Bowman, R.G., "The Debt Equivalence of Leases: An Empirical Investigation," *Accounting Review,* 55 (April 1980): pp. 237–253.

Brealey, Richard and C.M. Young, "Debt, Taxes, and Leasing—A Note," *Journal of Finance,* 35, no. 5 (December 1980): pp. 1245–1250.

Brealey, Richard and Stewart Myers, *Principles of Corporate Finance,* New York: McGraw-Hill, 1984.

Burnstein, M.L., "The Economics of Tie-In Sales," *Review of Economics and Statistics,* 42, no. 1 (February 1960): pp. 68–73.

Copeland, Thomas E. and J. Fred Weston, "A Note on the Evaluation of Cancelable Operating Leases," *Financial Management,* 11 (Summer 1982): pp. 68–72.

Copeland, Thomas E. and J. Fred Weston, *Financial Theory and Corporate Policy,* Addison Wesley, 1983.

Crawford, Peggy J., Charles P. Harper and John J. McConnell, "Further Evidence on the Terms of Financial Leases," *Financial Management,* 10 (Autumn 1981): pp. 7–14.

Fama, Eugene F. and Michael C. Jensen, "Agency Problems and Residual Claims," *Journal of Law and Economics*, 26 (1983): pp. 327–349.

Flath, David, "The Economics of Short-Term Leasing," *Economic Inquiry*, 18 (April 1980): pp. 247–259.

Franks, Julian R. and Stewart D. Hodges, "Valuation of Financial Lease Contracts," *Journal of Finance*, 33, no. 2 (May 1978): pp. 657–672.

Haley, Charles W. and Lawrence D. Schall, "Problems with the Concept of the Cost of Capital," *Journal of Financial and Quantitative Analysis*, 13, no. 4 (December 1978): pp. 847–870.

Kim, E. Han, Wilbur G. Lewellen and John J. McConnell, "Sale-and-Leaseback Agreements and Enterprise Valuation," *Journal of Financial and Quantitative Analysis*, 13 (December 1978): pp. 871–884.

Klein, Benjamin, Robert G. Crawford and Armen A. Alchian, "Vertical Integration, Appropriate Rents, and the Competitive Contracting Process," *Journal of Law and Economics* 21, no. 2 (October 1978): pp. 297–326.

Lewellen, Wilbur G., Michael S. Long and John J. McConnell, "Asset Leasing in Competitive Capital Markets," *Journal of Finance*, no. 3 (June 1976): pp. 787–798.

Liebowitz, Stanley J., "Tie-In Sales and Price Discrimination," *Economic Inquiry*, 21 (July 1983): pp. 387–399.

McConnell, John J. and James S. Schallheim, "Valuation of Asset Leasing Contracts," *Journal of Financial Economics*, 12 (August 1983): pp. 237–261.

Miller, Merton H. and Charles W. Upton, "Leasing, Buying and the Cost of Capital Services," *Journal of Finance*, 31, no. 3 (June 1976): pp. 761–786.

Myers, Stewart C., "Interactions of Corporate Financing and Investment Decisions — Implications for Capital Budgeting," *Journal of Finance*, 29, no. 1 (March 1974): pp. 1–25.

Myers, Stewart C., David A. Dill and Alberto J. Bautista, "Valuation of Financial Lease Contracts," *Journal of Finance*, 31, no. 3 (June 1976): pp. 799–820.

Robichek, Alexander A. and James C. Van Horne, "Abandonment Value and Capital Budgeting," *Journal of Finance*, 22 (December 1967): pp. 417–429.

Schall, Lawrence D., "The Lease-or-Buy and Asset Acquisition Decisions," *Journal of Finance*, 29, no. 4 (September 1974): pp. 1203–1214.

Schall, Lawrence D. and Gary L. Sundem, "The Investment Tax Credit and Leasing Industry," *Journal of Accounting and Public Policy*, 1, no. 2 (Winter 1982): pp. 83–94.

Smith, Clifford W. and L. Macdonald Wakeman, "Determinants of Corporate Leasing Policy." *Journal of Finance* (forthcoming).

Smith, Clifford and Ross Watts, "Incentive and Tax Effects of U.S. Executive Compensation Plans," *Australian Journal of Management*, 7 (1982): pp. 139–157.

Sorensen, Ivar W. and Ramon E. Johnson, "Equipment Financial Leasing Practices and Costs: An Empirical Study," *Financial Management* (Spring 1977): pp. 33–40.

Questions

1.   What does the author mean by the term *perfect markets?*

2.   FM, Inc. pays an annual lease payment of $15,000. The company's marginal tax bracket is 34 percent. Calculate the tax shield created by the lease payment. Also calculate the company's after-tax cost of the lease payment. Show the relationship between the company's before- and after-tax cost and the tax shield.

3.   ". . . leasing does not produce gains if no *imperfections* exist in the marketplace." Explain why this statement is true.

4.   In the real world of actual markets, leasing arrangements have the potential for producing financial gains for lessees. Explain the role of each of the following factors in producing these gains:
     a. Taxes
     b. Asset value risk
     c. Asset maintenance and contracting costs

5.   Does leasing conserve the cash and borrowing capacity of lessees? Explain.

44
Mergers and Takeovers — The Value of Predators' Information
Mack Ott and G.J. Santoni

*If $150 is the proper "free market" value of a share of CBS, isn't there
something fundamentally wrong with a system that values a share at
barely half that unless some buccaneer comes along?*

—Michael Kinsley

Skepticism about the efficiency of capital markets cause people to
be uneasy about corporate mergers and acquisitions.[1] In many cases
corporate takeovers have been criticized for stripping management, labor
and owners of career, livelihood and wealth.[2] Even the jargon that is used
to describe this method of changing corporate ownership is notable for its
value-laden terms (see "The Language of Corporate Takeovers"). It
creates the impression, perhaps deliberately so, of innocence on the part
of the target — e.g., maiden, defense, white knight — and evil on the part
of the buyer — e.g., raider, stripper, pirate.

Why is all of this brouhaha being raised now? Is the rate or size of
corporate takeovers much larger in the 1980s than in the past and, if so,
why? Are takeovers harmful — to the efficient operation of targeted firms,
to stockholders' wealth, or to third parties? This article addresses each of
these questions.

Mack Ott and G.J. Santoni, "Mergers and Takeovers — The Value of Predators' Information," *Review* (Federal Reserve Bank of St. Louis, December 1985): 16–28.

At the time of this writing, Mack Ott and G.J. Santoni were senior economists at the Federal
Reserve Bank of St. Louis. James C. Poletti provided research assistance.

[1] Kinsley's statement contrasts with the conventional view of economists and financial
analysts that stock markets are "efficient" in the sense that asset prices reflect all publicly
available information. Changes in individual asset prices, therefore, are caused by changes
in information. See, Fama, Fisher, Jensen and Roll (1969); Jensen (1983), (1984); and Jensen
and Ruback (1983).

[2] See Grossman (1985), Lipton (1985), Saddler (1985), Sloan (1985), Werner (1985); for
examples of legislative or regulatory proposals, see Rep. Leach on "Talking Takeovers"
(1985), Domenici (1985), Rohatyn (1985) and Martin (1985).

The Language of Corporate Takeovers

Crown Jewel: The most valued asset held by an acquisition target; divestiture of this asset is frequently a sufficient defense to dissuade takeover.

Fair Price Amendment: Requires super majority approval of non-uniform, or two-tier, takeover bids not approved by the board of directors; can be avoided by a uniform bid for less than all outstanding shares (subject to prorationing under federal law if the offer is oversubscribed).

Going Private: The purchase of publicly owned stock of a company by the existing or another competing management group; the company is delisted and public trading in the stock ceases.

Golden Parachutes: The provisions in the employment contracts of top-level managers that provide for severance pay or other compensation should they lose their job as a result of a takeover.

Greenmail: The premium paid by a targeted company to a raider in exchange for his shares of the targeted company.

Leveraged Buyout: The purchase of publicly owned stock of a company by the existing management with a portion of the purchase price financed by outside investors; the company is delisted and public trading in the stock ceases.

Lockup Defense: Gives a friendly party (see *White Knight*) the right to purchase assets of a firm, in particular the crown jewel, thus dissuading a takeover attempt.

Maiden: A term sometimes used to refer to the company at which the takeover is directed (*target*).

Poison Pill: Gives stockholders other than those involved in a hostile takeover the right to purchase securities at a very favorable price in the event of a takeover.

Proxy Contest: The solicitation of stockholder votes generally for the purpose of electing a slate of directors in competition with the current directors.

Raider: The person(s) or corporation attempting the takeover.

Shark Repellents: Antitakeover corporate charter amendments such as staggered terms for directors, super-majority requirement for approving merger, or mandate that bidders pay the same price for all shares in a buyout.

Standstill Agreement: A contract in which a raider or firm agrees to limit its holdings in the target firm and not attempt a takeover.

Stripper: A successful raider who, once the target is acquired, sells off some of the assets of the target company.

Target: The company at which the takeover attempt is directed.

Targeted Repurchase: A repurchase of common stock from an individual holder or a tender repurchase that excludes an individual holder; the former is the most frequent form of greenmail, while the latter is a common defensive tactic.

Tender Offer: An offer made directly to shareholders to buy some or all of their shares for a specified price during a specified time.

Two-Tier Offer: A takeover offer that provides a cash price for sufficient shares to obtain control of the corporation, then a lower non-cash (securities) price for the remaining shares.

White Knight: A merger partner solicited by management of a target who offers an alternative merger plan to that offered by the raider which protects the target company from the attempted takeover.

Mergers and Acquisitions — A Historical Perspective

Economic historians identify three major merger waves from 1893 to 1970.[3]

(1) 1893–1904 — horizontal mergers for monopoly following the Sherman Antitrust Act of 1890, which outlawed collusion, but not mergers; ended by the Supreme Court's *Northern Trust* decision in 1904 which "made it clear that this avenue to monopoly was also closed by the antitrust laws."[4]

(2) 1926–30 — horizontal mergers resulting in oligopolies in which a few large firms dominated an industry; ended by collapse of securities markets associated with the Depression.

(3) mid-1950s–1970 — conglomerate mergers in which corporations diversified their activities through mergers; driven by the Celler-Kefauver Merger Act (1950) which "had a strongly adverse effect upon horizontal mergers" and the financial theory of diversification;

[3] Simic (1984), pp. 2–3; Greer (1980), pp. 142–46.
[4] Stigler (1968), p. 100.

the merger wave ended in 1970 with the decline in the stock market, which eroded the equity base for the leveraged purchases.[5]

Some have suggested a fourth major wave in the 1980s, perhaps beginning at the end of the 1970s.[6] Yet, as can be seen in chart 1, the overall rate of U.S. mergers and acquisitions per 10,000 firms peaked in 1969 at 25. From 1969 to 1975, it declined to slightly less than 10 and has remained there.

An alternative measure of merger and acquisition activity is its share as a percentage of the total value of common and preferred stock listed on U.S. exchanges. While this measure also declined sharply at the end of the 1960s, after a trough in 1975, it increased from less than 2 percent to nearly 8 percent in 1984.[7] For the four years of available data, chart 1 also shows the mergers of listed firms in relation to the value of listed stock; as can be seen, it follows the pattern of total mergers. Consequently, while this latest merger wave is not as widespread as was the conglomerate merger wave in terms of the rate per 10,000 firms, it is notable for the number of very large transactions.

Deregulation and the Current Merger Wave

There are basically two explanations that economists and other analysts have offered for the current wave of mergers: (1) the removal of the U.S. Justice Department's antitrust rules against vertical mergers in 1982 and the relaxing of rules against horizontal mergers in 1984; (2) the deregulation of specific industries since 1978.[8]

Antitrust

In 1982, the U.S. Justice Department repealed restrictions against vertical mergers, that is, between suppliers and customers. Summarizing this policy, Assistant Attorney General William F. Baxter asserted that "mergers are never troublesome except insofar as they give rise to horizontal problems."[9] In the same year, constraints on horizontal mergers — mergers between competitors — also were relaxed.

Nonetheless, the standard measure of concentration by which the Justice Department assessed the monopoly power in potential mergers continued to be criticized by economists as inefficiently restrictive:

[5] Stigler, p. 270.

[6] Simic, p. 3; Jensen (1984), p. 109.

[7] The figures for the first half of 1985 imply a similar rate for 1985; see *Acquisition/ Divestiture Weekly*, p. 2095.

[8] Council of Economic Advisers (1985), pp. 192–95.

[9] Quoted in Stillman (1983), p. 225.

Chart 1   Merger and Acquisition Activity

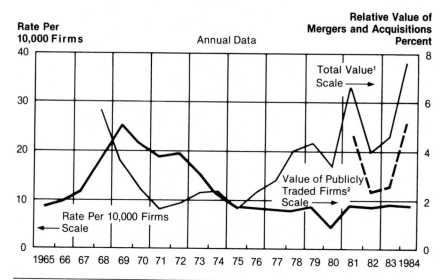

Rate Per 10,000 Firms   Annual Data   **Relative Value of Mergers and Acquisitions Percent**

[1] Ratio of the dollar value of *total* mergers and acquisitions to the total dollar value of common and preferred stock of all publicly traded domestic firms.

[2] Ratio of the dollar value of mergers and acquisitions of *publicly traded firms* to the total value of common and preferred stock of all publicly traded domestic firms.

Sources: W.T. Grimm and Company and U.S. Securities and Exchange Commission.

But while horizontal mergers have the clearest anticompetitive potential, there are also potential efficiency gains from such mergers that the new antimerger policy may sacrifice. In addition to the obvious possibility of complementarities in production and distribution, managers in the same industry may have a comparative advantage at identifying mismanaged firms. By foreclosing these managers from the market for corporate control, an anti-horizontal merger policy may impair efficient allocation of managerial talent and, perhaps more importantly, weaken significantly the incentive of incumbent managers to maximize the value of their firms.[10]

Consistent with this view, the Justice Department further relaxed its restrictions on horizontal mergers in June 1984. The Department's new test for anticompetitive effects takes into account the market shares of all significant competitors, including foreign sellers.[11] Moreover, the new

[10] Stillman, p. 226.

[11] This new test employs the Herfindahl-Hirschman Index of market concentration which is calculated by summing the squares of the individual market shares of all of the firms (domestic and foreign) included in the market. Unlike the four-firm concentration ratio previously used, the new test reflects both the distribution of the market shares of the top four firms and the composition of the market outside these firms.

guidelines consider merger-related efficiencies as a positive criterion that may counterbalance a rise in market concentration. Finally, the new guidelines "permit failing divisions to be sold to direct competitors if the units face liquidation in the near future and a noncompetitive acquirer can't be found." [12]

Industry-Specific Deregulation[13]

Beginning in the late 1970s, a sequence of changes loosened restrictions in a number of industries. The Natural Gas Policy Act of 1978 lessened restrictions on the setting of well-head gas prices and set in motion their phaseout for most natural gas by 1984; crude oil prices were deregulated by an executive order in 1981.

The Depository Institutions Deregulation and Monetary Control Act of 1980 and the Depository Institutions Act of 1982 made banking and finance more competitive. These acts deregulated interest rates on deposits and allowed thrifts to offer checking accounts, money market accounts and consumer loans. In addition, decisions by the Comptroller of the Currency (1982) and Federal Reserve Board (1983) permit banks to engage in some insurance activities and to own discount security brokerages. Finally, the Supreme Court has upheld the constitutionality of regional interstate banking pacts, which permit combinations of banks in member states.

The transportation industry was changed more fundamentally by deregulation than any industrial group beginning with the Airline Deregulation Act of 1978. Deregulation of railroad, trucking and household movers followed in 1980. These acts reduced entry restrictions in these industries and made it easier to change prices and routes.

Beginning in 1982, a sequence of Federal Communications Commission decisions eased ownership transfers in the broadcasting industry. In addition, rules were relaxed on children's programming in 1983 and public service or local programming in 1984. Time and frequency restrictions on commercials were eliminated in 1984. In December of that year, the commission replaced its 7-7-7 rule with a 12-12-12 rule—allowing a single corporation to own as many as 12 TV, 12 FM, and 12 AM stations as long as the combined audience reached is less than 25 percent of all television viewers and radio listeners.

---

[12] Simic, p. 125. In addition, he notes that divestitures have amounted to between one-third and one-half of corporate acquisitions during the last 10 years (p. 78). Thus, the relaxed antitrust policy has led to greater specialization, a movement exactly opposite to the conglomerate merger wave of the 1960s; see Toy (1985).

[13] Details on these deregulatory acts and decisions are contained in the following sources: for the oil and gas industry, Executive Order 12287 (1981), pp. B1–B2; for banking and financial services, Grotton (1981), vol. V, pp. 261–65, also Fischer, et al (1985) and Garcia (1983); for the insurance and insurance agency industries, Felgran (1985), pp. 34–49; for the transportation industry, Grotton, vol. V, pp. 311–13, 331–34, 336–39; for the broadcasting industry, Wilke et al (1985) and Saddler.

Mergers and Acquisitions, 1981–84

The 1985 *Economic Report of the President* points out that "these recently deregulated industries [banking, finance, insurance, transportation, brokerage and investment] accounted for about 25 percent of all merger and acquisition activity between 1981 and 1983."[14] Table 1 shows that deregulated industries continued to dominate the merger and acquisition totals through 1984. Moreover, divestiture sales by conglomerates reflect a general move away from diversification and toward specialization, a consequence of relaxed antitrust constraints.[15] Thus, eight of the 10 industrial groupings in table 1 reflect some form of deregulation. During 1981–84, these industries accounted for 58.2 percent of the value of all reported mergers and acquisitions.

Objections to Mergers and Acquisitions

The recent objections to corporate mergers and acquisitions encompass three fundamental complaints. Some have claimed that mergers are "totally nonproductive."[16] Others have claimed that stockholders are harmed.[17] Still others have argued that there are significant third-party effects — such as employment losses, higher interest rates or reduced research activity.[18]

Are Mergers and Takeovers Unproductive?

Mergers and takeovers are simply a change in the corporation's ownership. Because these transactions are voluntary, they occur only if the buyer and the seller expect to profit from the transaction. The buyer

[14] Council of Economic Advisers (1985), pp. 194–95.

[15] In particular, sales of divisions by conglomerate corporations first rose to prominence in 1982, then doubled in 1984, the two years of significant antitrust changes discussed above. For more detail regarding the divestiture side of recent mergers and acquisitions, see Toy; also Council of Economic Advisers, p. 195.

[16] Lipton; see also Werner, and Sloan. Jensen (1984) quotes the New York investment banker Felix Rohatyn as asserting: "All this frenzy may be good for investment bankers now, but it's not good for the country or investment bankers in the long run."

[17] For examples, see Lipton, Minard (1985), p. 41, and Sloan, p. 137. Sloan provides evidence that purports to show that a target's shareholders are often better off when takeovers are unsuccessful (p. 139):

> We studied 39 cases in which companies successfully resisted hostile tenders. In 17 cases, the value of the target's stock at year-end 1984 exceeded what a shareholder would have if the offer had succeeded and the proceeds had been reinvested in the S&P's 500 Index. (Where a company defeated one offer but was later bought, our calculations run through the acquisition date.)

However, if the corporations that were taken over in subsequent attempts (28 of the 39) are excluded from the analysis, the average annual yield to stockholders of the 11 resisting corporations was negative, −3.2 percent.

[18] See Lipton and "Talking Takeovers."

Table 1   **Value of Merger and Acquisition Transactions by Industry, 1981–84 (dollar figures in millions)**

Industry	1981	1982	1983
Oil and Gas	$22,921.6	$ 9,165.5	$12,075.8
Banking, Finance and Real Estate	4,204.4	5,605.3	13,628.3
Insurance	7,862.5	5,717.8	2,966.1
Food Processing	3,800.0	3,075.2	1,163.6
Conglomerate	809.4	3,973.6	2,745.1
Mining and Minerals	10,850.6	355.2	2,946.2
Retail	1,844.4	1,948.1	1,489.0
Transportation	475.3	1,074.4	5,254.6
Leisure and Entertainment	2,150.4	1,082.1	1,797.4
Broadcasting	1,060.1	787.2	3,747.1
Other	26,638.9	20,970.1	25,267.3
Total	$82,617.6	$53,754.5	$73,080.5

Source: Simic, Tomislava, ed. *Mergerstat Review*, (W.T. Grimm and Company, 1984), p. 41.

believes that the firm's assets can be used to generate a greater return than they are producing under the current owners. Consequently, the buyer will offer to purchase the firm at a price high enough to induce the current owners to sell (the seller's reservation price), but low enough not to exceed the expected value of the firm to the buyer under his ownership (the buyer's reservation price).[19]

Buyers and sellers value the firm differently (have different reservation prices) because they have different expectations about the stream of earnings that can be produced with the corporate assets. In part, these expectations depend upon the information that people have about current opportunities as well as forthcoming events that will affect the demand for the corporations' product or its cost of production.

Such information is neither uniformly distributed across individuals nor weighted with the same subjective likelihood about its validity or usefulness. Consequently, people will have different reservation prices for the same firm. In fact, if everyone had the same reservation price, there would be no inducement to trade.

---

[19] A reservation price is the capitalized value of the future stream of earnings that the buyer (seller) *expects* the firm to generate. Generally, the capitalized value of an expected future receipt is calculated by dividing the expected future receipt by the discount factor $(1 + r)^t$, where r is the market annual rate of interest and t is the number of years in the future until the income will be received. In the case of an asset that generates a stream of receipts, summing all such discounted future receipts gives the present value of the asset, V:

$$V = \frac{S_1}{(1 + r)} + \frac{S_2}{(1 + r)^2} + \frac{S_3}{(1 + r)^3} + \frac{S_4}{(1 + r)^4} + \frac{S_5}{(1 + r)^5} + \cdots + \frac{S_n}{(1 + r)^n} + \cdots$$

If the annual receipt is expected to be constant and perpetual, the above equation reduces to $V = s/r$.

1984	1981–84	Percent of total	Cumulative percentage
$ 42,981.8	$ 87,144.7	26.3%	26.3%
5,846.3	29,284.3	8.8	35.1
3,005.9	19,552.3	5.9	41.0
7,094.8	15,133.6	4.6	45.6
6,982.9	14,511.0	4.4	49.9
346.7	14,498.7	4.4	54.3
6,673.2	11,954.7	3.6	57.9
1,251.8	8,056.1	2.4	60.3
2,580.7	7,610.6	2.3	62.6
1,917.9	7,512.3	2.3	64.9
43,541.7	116,418.0	35.1	100.0
$122,223.7	$331,676.3	100.0%	

Thus, information is the key to understanding merger or takeover activity.[20] in some cases, this information may concern the "crown jewel," that is, a particular asset of the firm that the bidder believes could be employed more profitably in some other use. The bidder may plan to gain control of the firm and strip off (liquidate) the asset.[21] On the other hand, this information may be a plan to reduce the firm's cost of production or to change its product line.[22]

Capitalizing on the bidder's information requires a plan to reorganize the corporation. Only in this way can the bidder obtain the expected increase in the value of the firm. In essence, the bidder's information can be thought of as a way to make the firm more productive or efficient.[23] The increase in productivity or efficiency can arise from one

[20] Indeed, Kinsley quotes James Tobin as offering this explanation: "Takeover mania is testimony to the failure of the market on this fundamental-valuation criterion. . . . Takeovers serve a useful function if they bring prices closer to fundamental values." The market price in an efficient market incorporates all publicly available (and some private) information; Tobin's indictment notwithstanding, the market's nonincorporation of all private information (prior to someone revealing it) cannot be classified as failure.

[21] For example, Crown Zellerbach's timber holdings appeared to be the "jewel" in James Goldsmith's plan for the firm. In the case of Trans World Airlines, it was the PARS reservation system and the overseas air routes.

[22] An example of reduced production cost is Carl Icahn's renegotiation of TWA's labor contracts. It is estimated that, had these renegotiated contracts been in place during the past year, TWA would have reported a $70 million profit rather than a $56 million loss; see Burrough and Zieman (1985).

[23] The analysis in this paper assumes that the rise in the value is not due to obtaining monopoly power through merger. All mergers of publicly traded corporations are subject to Justice Department review to determine possible anticompetitive effects; mergers found to imply anticompetitive conditions are either enjoined or the corporations are compelled to divest those subsidiaries resulting in the anticompetitive condition. Conversely, research into recent mergers blocked by the Justice Department suggests that, if anything, antitrust review has been too strict, not too lax; see Stillman.

of three sources. First, the reorganization may permit greater output from the existing resources with no change in output prices. Second, the reorganization may exploit a change in regulatory constraints in the form of production or permitted market share. Third, the reorganization may permit a greater value of output because the current management has not responded appropriately to a change in relative prices.

Whichever the source, the fact that the bidder offers to purchase the firm at a price attractive to the current owners can be explained by an increase in the target firm's profitability under the planned reorganization. Moreover, by observing the movements of stock prices during and after takeover attempts, the hypothesis of expected increased profitability under reorganization can be tested. If it is valid, there should be significant differences between the price movements of firms that are taken over and those that successfully resist takeovers.

Table 2 is a summary of a number of individual studies that examine the effect of takeovers on stock prices. The data are abnormal percentage changes in stock prices for both targets and bidders involved in corporate takeovers. Abnormal changes are those that exceed general movements in stock prices. The data are broken down by the type of takeover technique employed (tender offer, merger, proxy contest) and by the success of the takeover attempt.

The individual studies summarized differ in terms of the period over which the returns are measured. For successful tender offers, the period was roughly one month before to one month after the offer. For successful mergers, the price change was measured from about one month before the offer to the offer date. For unsuccessful takeovers, the measurement period runs from about one month before the offer through the announcement that the offer had been terminated.

The data indicate a statistically significant increase in the stock prices of targets when the takeover was successful.[24] The above discussion suggests that the rise in capital value can be explained by an increase in the firm's future stream of profits that investors expect to result from its reorganization by the bidder. Rudely stated, the rise in value is *not* simply the result of a speculative craze induced by the knowledge that an outside bidder is attempting to gain control of the firm. The latter explanation is lurking in Kinsley's critique.

Fortunately, there is some evidence that helps discriminate between the two alternative explanations. First, in a proxy contest, there is no

---

[24] Each of the individual studies summarized in table 2 found statistically significant positive abnormal returns. See Jensen and Ruback (1983), pp. 7–16. Furthermore, Bradley, Desai, and Kim (1983), one of the studies summarized in table 2, conduct a detailed study of unsuccessful tender offers, segmented into those targets that did and did not receive offers during the subsequent five years. They found that the cumulative average abnormal return for the targets that received subsequent offers is 57.19% (t = 10.39). In contrast, the average abnormal return over the same period for targets that did not receive subsequent offers is an insignificant −3.53% (t = −0.36); this return includes the announcement effects.

Table 2 **Abnormal Percentage Stock Price Changes Associated with Attempted Corporate Takeovers**

Takeover technique	Successful		Unsuccessful	
	Target	**Bidders**	**Target**	**Bidders**
Tender offers	30%	4%	−3%	−1%
Mergers	20	0	−3	−5
Proxy contests	8	N.A.	8	N.A.

Source: Jensen, Michael, and Richard S. Ruback, *Journal of Financial Economics*, (April 1983), pp. 7–8.

Note: Abnormal price changes are price changes adjusted to eliminate the effects of marketwide price changes.

outside bidder to start a "speculative" snowball. Rather, a proxy contest is an internal takeover attempt by some of the existing stockholders. An alternative slate of directors is proposed and its proponents attempt to oust the existing board. Yet successful proxy contests result in a statistically significant abnormal return for the firm (see table 2).[25] Second, in contrast to unsuccessful mergers and tender offers, which leave the stock prices of targets statistically unchanged, unsuccessful proxy contests result in statistically significant positive abnormal returns.

These contrasting results are important because they illuminate the role played by information in changing the stock price. In the case of an outside takeover attempt, the bidder has every incentive to keep his special information or reorganization plan secret so that he may acquire the stock cheaply. Consequently, if the target is not taken over (either initially or in subsequent attempts), the price of the stock returns to its original level since other investors have learned nothing in the process (see footnote 24). In contrast, in a proxy contest, the cost to the instigators of revealing their special information is lower. Since they own substantial shares of the firm they are less likely to be concerned about acquiring additional shares and revealing their plan may aid in obtaining support from other stockholders. Thus, the special information is more likely to be revealed in proxy contests, and it is this information that raises the firm's present value even though the contest may not have succeeded in ousting the existing board.

Are Stockholders Harmed by Mergers and Takeovers?

The evidence reviewed above shows that the values of target firms rise in takeover attempts, implying that owners of targeted firms experience wealth gains in the event of a successful takeover. On these grounds, it is difficult to claim, as some have, that existing owners are harmed by

[25] See Jensen and Ruback, p. 8.

successful takeovers. Nor does it appear to be the case that the owners of targeted firms are harmed by unsuccessful takeovers (the small negative abnormal returns earned by targets in unsuccessful tender offers and mergers are not statistically significant). Targets of unsuccessful proxy contests earn significantly positive abnormal returns. While this evidence is inconsistent with shareholder harm, some have criticized takeovers on other grounds. These are considered below.

Two-Tier Offers.   Since mergers and takeover attempts are aimed at acquiring corporate control, the bidder frequently offers a higher price, in cash, for shares necessary to obtain a majority holding, then a lower price, in securities, for the remaining shares. Some allege that this two-tier offer is an attempt to frighten shareholders into tendering their shares rather than holding on for a possibly higher-valued offer later. Yet, even if this were true, the value of the stock will rise relative to its pre-takeover level so the issue is the distribution of the gain among shareholders, not of harm.[26]

Management Self-Interest and Golden Parachutes.   Management will seek the highest bid for the firm's shares if their wealth depends heavily on this effort. Generally this is the case; most of top management's compensation is in equity terms, not cash salary.[27] Moreover, the so-called golden parachute may be thought of as a guarantee that management will be rewarded for obtaining a high bid (one that is acceptable to the owners). Its purpose is to assure that management will not impede the auction.

Corporate Charter Changes — Shark Repellents.   If takeover attempts were harmful to shareholder interests, changes in corporate charters that make takeovers more difficult should raise the share prices of firms passing these amendments. A recent study by the Securities and Ex-

---

[26] Council of Economic Advisers (1985), pp. 204–05:

In addition, two-tier tender offers can be desirable for target stockholders and managements. SEC data show that two-tier offers are used in friendly takeovers about as often as they are used in hostile takeover attempts. There are at least two reasons that target stockholders could prefer a two-tier bid. If a two-tier offer is properly structured, target stockholders who accept securities in the back end of the transaction may be able to defer tax due on the appreciated value of their shares. In addition, the acquirer may find that it is easier to finance the transaction by issuing securities for the back end than by borrowing funds from banks or through other financing mechanisms. If these savings induce the bidder to offer a higher blended premium, then the two-tier offer can also be beneficial for the target's stockholders.

[27] Lewellen (1971) found that after-tax executive compensation for large U.S. manufacturing firms for both chief executives and the top five executives was primarily from (1) stock-based remuneration, (2) dividend income, and (3) capital gains, with (4) fixed dollar remuneration being relatively minor in comparison. In particular, over the period 1954–63 the average annual ratio of $[(1) + (2) + (3)]/(4)$ ranged from 2.123 to 7.973 for chief executives and from 1.753 to 8.669 for the top five executives in large U.S. manufacturing corporations (Lewellen, pp. 89–90). Moreover, these executives, on average, had large stock holdings in their own corporations — $341,437 to $3,033,896 during 1954–63 — and were not active sellers (Lewellen, p. 79).

change Commission, however, finds a statistically significant 3.0 percent decline in the average price of 162 corporations passing certain kinds of antitakeover amendments.[28]

Role of Institutions and Other Fiduciaries.   A final piece of evidence suggesting that takeovers do not harm shareholders is the voting behavior of institutional holders and other trustees. The SEC study just cited found that "institutional stockholdings are lower on average for firms proposing the most harmful amendments." That is, the institutional holdings of stock were smaller in corporations proposing antitakeover restrictions than in corporations that had not proposed such restrictions.[29]

Recently, administrators of pension fund investments have begun to favor rather than oppose the auction process entailed in a takeover attempt. In particular, California's state treasurer, Jesse Unruh, has formed a Council of Institutional Investors (CII) to combat antitakeover abuses, which he views as depriving the institutional funds of profitable opportunities.[30] As CII co-chairman Harrison Goldin, New York City comptroller, put it, "Should Mr. Pickens, Mr. Icahn, the Bass brothers or others care to hold an open auction for any of the stocks held by my pension funds, I would not want to restrain them."[31]

Furthermore, fiduciaries opposing takeover bids have been held liable for the loss of stock value:

. . . *a judge ruled that trustees who helped Grumman Corp. frustrate a takeover bid by LTV Corp. in 1981 were personally liable for damages because they didn't act in the best interests of family beneficiaries for whom they held Grumman stock in trust.*[32]

Third-Party Effects

Critics of the recent wave of mergers and takeovers frequently allege that they have "third-party" effects that damage the economy, individuals or regions in ways not measured by changes in corporate value or stockholder returns.[33] To a certain extent, this is true but such costs typically accompany innovations:

---

[28] Jarrell, Poulsen, and Davidson (1985). The study distinguishes between "fair price amendments" (requiring super majority shareholder approval in the case of a two-tier offer) and other shark repellants—classified boards, authorization of blank-check preferred stock, and super majority amendments for approval of *any* merger or tender offer regardless of whether it is a two-tier offer. The fair price amendments had no effect on stock prices while the others lowered stock prices significantly.

[29] Jarrell, Poulsen, and Davidson (1985), pp. 44–46.

[30] Smith (1984).

[31] Makin (1985), p. 212.

[32] Stewart and Waldholz (1985), p. 13.

[33] The "lost jobs" argument has been raised by Rep. Leach; in "Talking Takeovers"; the "financial destabilizing" argument by Rohatyn (1985), Domenici, Lipton, and President Hartley of Unocal Corp in Minard (1985); the "shortened planning horizon" by Lipton (1985), Hartley, and Leach.

For example, innovations that increase standards of living in the long run initially produce changes that reduce the welfare of some individuals, at least in the short run. The development of efficient truck and air transport harmed the railroads and their workers; the rise of television hurt the radio industry. New and more efficient production, distribution, or organizational technology often imposes similar short-term costs.

The adoption of new technologies following takeovers enhances the overall real standard of living but reduces the wealth of those individuals with large investments in older technologies. Not surprisingly, such individuals and companies, their unions, communities, and political representatives will lobby to limit or prohibit takeovers that might result in new technologies. When successful, such politics reduce the nation's standard of living and its standing in international competition.[34]

Labor Displacement.   The argument that employment is lowered by mergers and takeovers appears to be based on the belief that plant closings and consolidations inevitably follow and that labor demand must therefore decline.[35] However, if output expands as a result of the reorganization, wages as well as the number of jobs may increase. Even when employment cutbacks are associated with mergers and takeovers, such effects apparently have been overcome by other forces: Payroll employment growth during the current expansion has been at a 3.68 percent rate (November 1982–October 1985) compared with a 3.39 percent rate during economic expansions over the 1970–81 period.[36]

Adverse Effects on Capital Markets.   One allegation frequently made about the impact of takeovers on capital markets is that the extra demand for credit to finance takeovers raises interest rates and crowds out productive investment. This critique is specious. Takeovers and mergers are productive (in that asset values rise). Any crowding out that occurs is of less productive investment. Moreover, the funds obtained by the bidders are transferred to the sellers who can reinvest them. Consequently, there is no reason to expect interest rates to change.[37]

Neglect of Long-Term Planning.   Several critics have argued that take-over threats force management to concentrate on projects that raise

---

[34] Jensen (1984), p. 114.

[35] In some cases, wage, salary and benefit schedules exceeding labor productivity may be the cause of low corporate value. The potential for reorganization through a takeover and an increase in efficiency would then entail either a reduction in wages or a reduction in labor use. In the TWA takeover, it was the former (see footnote 22); in the AMF takeover by Minstar Corp., it was the latter. See Ehrlich (1985).

[36] Payroll employment growth rates during each of the preceding economic expansions of the 1970–81 period were as follows: 3.48 percent during November 1970–November 1973; 3.62 percent during March 1975–January 1980; 2.00 percent during July 1980–July 1981.

[37] See Martin, p. 2.

earnings in the near term at the cost of long-range planning, in particular, research and development. For example, the chairman of Carter-Hawley-Hale department stores said that takeover activity causes management to "take the short-term view and to neglect what builds long-term values."[38] This implies a serious inefficiency in capital markets, since capital values are expected *future* returns discounted to the present.

This short-term focus is said to be imposed by institutional shareholders who view current earnings as more important than capital appreciation; evidence, however, demonstrates the opposite. Jarrell and Lehn of the SEC found that institutional investors tended to prefer higher rather than lower research and investment expenditures. More to the point, they found that, of the 217 firms that were takeover targets during 1981–84, 160 reported that research and development expenditures were "not material," while the remaining 57 had research and development expenditure rates less than half the averages in their respective industries.

Finally, Jarrell and Lehn also found significant announcement effects attending new research and development projects:

Our study examined the net-of-market stock price reaction to 62 Wall Street Journal *announcements between 1973–1983 that firms were embarking on new R&D projects. These tests show that, on average, the stock prices of these firms increased (1% to 2%) in the period immediately following the publication of these stories.*[39]

Thus, the market appears to reward rather than punish the long-term view; takeovers are most frequent in firms that have ignored the long term. As Joseph observes: "If you take the best-run companies, they typically make long-term commitments, and they sell at decent multiples. IBM is not a target. ITT is a target, because it hasn't managed its businesses very well. So ITT is complaining that it can't plan long term because of the sharks."[40]

Conclusion

We have examined three criticisms of corporate takeovers: 1) that mergers and takeovers are unproductive, 2) that stockholders are harmed, 3) that third parties are harmed. Both theory and evidence suggest that resource values rise and, consequently, stockholders generally benefit from takeover activity. Both are consistent with the proposition that takeovers are expected to result in a more efficient use of the target's assets. As with any economic change, third-party effects probably exist. Negative employment effects, higher interest rates or neglect of long-term planning, however, do not seem to be caused by merger and takeover

[38] Work and Peterson (1985), p. 51; see also Drucker (1984), Lipton, Rohatyn, and Sloan.
[39] Jarrell and Lehn (1985).
[40] Sloan, p. 139.

activity. These potential third-party effects do not appear to be important and do not establish a case for additional contraints on corporate ownership transfers. Since takeovers contribute to the efficient working of capital markets, policy or legislative initiatives to impede takeovers should bear the burden of proving the harm they propose to ameliorate.

References

The Acquisition and Divestiture Weekly Report. Quality Services, October 7, 1985.

Bradley, Michael, Anand Desai, and E. Han Kim. "The Rationale Behind Interfirm Tender Offers: Information or Synergy?" *Journal of Financial Economics* (April 1983), pp. 183–206.

Burrough, Brian, and Mark Zieman. "Investor Icahn Lifts TWA Stake to 40.6% And Is Said to Be Purchasing More Shares," *Wall Street Journal,* August 7, 1985.

Council of Economic Advisers. *Economic Report of the President* (U.S. Government Printing Office, 1985), chapter 6.

Domenici, Pete V. "Fools and Their Takeover Bonds," *Wall Street Journal,* May 14, 1985.

Drucker, Peter F. "Taming the Corporate Takeover," *Wall Street Journal,* October 30, 1984.

Ehrlich, Elizabeth. "Behind the AMF Takeover: From Highflier to Sitting Duck," *Business Week* (August 12, 1985), p. 50–51.

Executive Order 12287, 1981, United States Code, Congressional and Administration News.

Fama, Eugene F., Larry Fisher, Michael C. Jensen, and Richard Roll. "The Adjustment of Stock Prices to New Information," *International Economic Review* (1969, No. 10), pp. 1–21.

Felgran, Steven D. "Banks As Insurance Agencies: Legal Constraints and Competitive Advances," *New England Economic Review* (September/October 1985), pp. 34–49.

Fischer, Thomas G., William H. Gram, George G. Kaufman, and Larry R. Mote. "The Securities Activities of Commercial Banks: A Legal and Economic Analysis," Federal Reserve Bank of Chicago, Staff Memoranda SM-85-2, 1985.

Garcia, Gilian. "Financial Deregulation: Historical Perspective and Impact of the Garn-St Germain Depository Institutions Act of 1982," Federal Reserve Bank of Chicago, Staff Study 83-2, 1983.

Greer, Douglas F. *Industrial Organization and Public Policy* (MacMillan Publishing Co., 1980).

Grossman, Harry I. Letter to Editor, *Wall Street Journal,* April 14, 1985.

Grotton, Martha V. *Congress and the Nation* (Congressional Quarterly, Inc., 1983), vol. 5.

Hirshleifer, Jack. *Price Theory and Applications* (Prentice Hall, 1976).

Jarrell, Gregg, and Kenneth Lehn. "Takeovers Don't Crimp Long-Term Planning," *Wall Street Journal,* May 1, 1985.

Jarrell, Gregg, Annette Poulsen, and Lynn Davidson. "Shark Repellants and Stock Prices: The Effects of Antitakeover Amendments Since 1980," Office of the Chief Economist, Securities and Exchange Commisssion, July 1985.

Jensen, Michael C., ed. "Symposium on the Market for Corporate Control: The Scientific Evidence," *Journal of Financial Economics* (April 1983).

————. "Takeover: Folklore vs. Science," *Harvard Business Review* (November-December 1984), pp. 109–21.

Jensen, Michael C., and Richard S. Ruback. "The Market for Corporate Control: The Scientific Evidence," *Journal of Financial Economics* (April 1983), pp. 5–50.

Kinsley, Michael. "You Won't Find An Efficient Market on Wall Street," *Wall Street Journal,* July 18, 1985.

Lewellen, Wilbur G. *The Ownership Income of Management* (Columbia University Press, 1971).

Lipton, Martin. "Takeover Abuses Mortgage the Future," *Wall Street Journal,* May 4, 1985.

Makin, Claire. "Is the Takeover Game Becoming Too One-Sided?" *Institutional Investor* (May 1985), pp. 207–22.

Martin, Preston. Statement to Subcommittee on Oversight and Select Revenue Measures of U.S. House Ways and Means Committee, April 16, 1985, (B.I.S. Press Review, No. 88).

Minard, Lawrence. "Millions for Defense Not One Cent for Tribute," *Forbes* (April 8, 1985), pp. 40–46.

Rohatyn, Felix G. "Junk Bonds and Other Securities Swill," *Wall Street Journal,* April 18, 1985.

Saddler, Jeanne. "Storer Dissidents' Bid for Board Control Clears Hurdle in 3–2 Decision by FCC," *Wall Street Journal,* December 4, 1985.

Simic, Tomislava, ed. *Mergerstat Review* (W.T. Grimm and Company, 1984).

Sloan, Allen. "Why Is No One Safe?" *Forbes* (March 11, 1985), pp. 134–40.

Smith, Randall. "California Official Moves to Organize Pension Funds to Combat Greenmail," *Wall Street Journal,* July 26, 1984.

Stewart, James B., and Michael Waldholz. "How Richardson-Vicks Fell Prey to Takeovers Despite Family's Grip," *Wall Street Journal,* October 30, 1985.

Stigler, George J. *The Organization of Industry* (Richard D. Irwin, Inc., 1968).

Stillman, Robert. "Examining Antitrust Policy Towards Horizontal Mergers," *Journal of Financial Economics* (April 1983), pp. 225–40.

"Talking Takeovers." *McNeil-Lehrer News Hour,* Transcript 2518 (May 22, 1985), pp. 3–8.

Toy, Stewart. "Splitting Up, the Other Side of Merger Mania," *Business Week* (July 1, 1985), pp. 50–55.

U.S. Securities and Exchange Commission. *Fiftieth Annual Report, 1984* (GPO, 1984), p. 112.

Werner, Jesse. Letter to Editor, *Wall Street Journal,* April 16, 1985.

Wilke, John, Mark N. Vamos, and Mark Maremont. "Has the FCC Gone Too Far?" *Business Week* (August 5, 1985), pp. 48–54.

Work, Clemens P., and Sarah Peterson. "The Raider Barons: Boon or Bane for Business?" *U.S. News and World Report* (April 8, 1985), pp. 51–54.

Questions

1. Define the italicized terms: The *maiden's* defense began with the threat to sell the *crown jewel*. Perhaps the *raider* would lose interest if the maiden's primary asset were *stripped*. Alas, the raider persisted. A *standstill agreement* was out of the question; the raider was too hostile. *Shark repellents* would at least slow down the raider. Rejecting a *poison pill* and *greenmail,* the maiden guilefully designed a *golden parachute* and befriended a *white knight.*

2. What are horizontal mergers? Vertical mergers? Conglomerate mergers?

3. What explanations have been offered for the merger wave of the 1980s?

4. According to Michael Kinsley, "If $150 is the proper *free market* value of a share of CBS, isn't there something fundamentally wrong with a system that values a share at barely half that unless some buccaneer comes along?" Provide an argument to persuade Mr. Kinsley that nothing is wrong.

5. Are stockholders of the target company harmed in tender offers and mergers? What evidence supports your answer?

6. Why do stockholders of the bidding company earn little or no abnormal returns in tender offers and mergers?

7. Harrison Goldin, New York City Comptroller, stated: "Should Mr. Pickens, Mr. Icahn, the Bass brothers or others care to hold an open auction for any of the stocks held by my pension funds, I would not want to restrain them." Explain the point being made by Mr. Goldin.

8. MFAB, Inc. is a metal fabricating company with five plants located in three midwestern states. The company manufactures brackets, braces, and duct work. More than 500 employees work in each of MFAB's plants. Greenville Metal, a southeastern company, has agreed to acquire MFAB, Inc. for $35 million. To justify the price, Greenville Metal will have to close MFAB's Ohio plant, which produces the same products as Greenville Metal's North Carolina plant. The plant closing will cause 550 employees to lose their jobs. In your opinion, should Greenville Metal be prevented from acquiring MFAB, Inc. and closing the Ohio plant? Defend your answer.

The Takeover Controversy: The Restructuring of Corporate America

Michael C. Jensen

Delivered at the Town Hall of California,
Los Angeles, California, March 17, 1987

Corporate America is being restructured at a rapid pace. This restructuring is being accomplished through a variety of transactions in the market for corporate control and through voluntary actions of managers as they rationalize and refocus the firms they lead. These events take the form of hostile takeovers, voluntary mergers, leveraged buyouts, stockholder buyouts, spinoffs, split-ups, divestitures, asset sales, and liquidations.

In the last two years merger and acquisition activity has run at the rate of $180 billion in over 3,000 transactions per year. Last year over 1,200 of these transactions valued at over $45 billion were divestitures— sales of divisions by many of our largest corporations. This explains why these control transactions have not increased the concentration of economic power in large corporations.

Restructurings are frequently wrenching events in the lives of those linked to the involved organizations—the managers, employees, suppliers, customers and residents of surrounding communities. Restructurings usually involve transfers of ownership and major organizational changes (such as shifts in corporate strategy) to meet new competition or market conditions, increased use of debt, and a flurry of recontracting with managers, employees, suppliers and customers. This activity sometimes results in expansion of resources devoted to certain areas and at other times in contractions involving plant closing, layoff of top-level and middle managers, staff and production workers, and reduced compensation.

Change due to corporate restructuring requires people and communities associated with the organization to adjust the ways they live, work

Michael C. Jensen, "The Takeover Controversy," *Vital Speeches of the Day*, Vol. 53, No. 14 (May 1, 1987): 426–429. Reprinted with permission.

At the time of this writing, Michael C. Jensen was Professor of Business Administration at Harvard Business School and LaClare Professor of Finance and Business Administration and Director of the Managerial Economics Research Center.

and do business. It is not surprising, therefore, that this change is creating controversy and that those who stand to lose are demanding that something be done to stop the process. Shareholders in restructured corporations are clear-cut winners; the restructurings generate increases in total market value of approximately 50 percent, with some over 100 percent. SEC estimates indicate gains to target-firm shareholders in tender offers alone of over $40 billion in the 1981 to May 1985 period. While no one has yet tallied the gains from mergers, hostile acquisitions, and voluntary and involuntary restructurings from 1980 to the present, it is likely to be in the hundreds of billions of dollars. The corporate control market generates these gains by loosening control over vast amounts of resources and enabling them to move more quickly to their highest-valued use. This is a healthy market in operation, on both the takeover side and the divestiture side, and it is playing a healthy role in moving the American economy from its former reliance on auto production and manufacturing to its modern emphasis on services.

Those threatened by the changes that restructuring brings about argue that corporate restructuring is damaging the American economy and that the value restructuring creates does not come from increased efficiency and productivity. They argue that this activity pressures executives to manage for the short-term and that the gains from lower tax payments, broken contracts with managers, employees and others, and mistakes in valuation by inefficient capital markets are the source of increased corporate values. Thus, the benefits are illusory and the costs are real, and therefore takeover activity should be restricted.

There have been more than two dozen bills introduced in Washington to restrict takeovers in the last two years. The Business Roundtable, a collection of CEO's of the 200 largest corporations, has pushed hard for restrictions.

The market for corporate control is best viewed as a major component of the managerial labor market. It is the arena in which alternative management teams compete for the rights to manage corporate resources. Understanding this is crucial to understanding much of the rhetoric about the effects of hostile takeovers.

Managers formerly protected from competition for their jobs by antitrust and financing constraints that prevented takeover of the nation's largest corporations are now facing a more demanding environment and a more uncertain future. The data indicate that, within three years of an acquisition, roughly half of the top level managers of acquired corporations are gone. Interestingly this percentage does not differ between voluntary and hostile acquisitions. It is not surprising that many executives of large corporations would like relief from this new competition for their job, but restricting the corporate control market is not the efficient way to handle the problems caused by their increased job uncertainty.

Takeovers generally occur because changing technology or market conditions mean a major restructuring of corporate assets is required, but in some cases takeovers occur because incumbent managers are incompetent. In other cases takeovers occur when managers launch diversification programs — code words for building empires at shareholders' expense. When the internal processes for change in large corporations are too slow, costly and clumsy to efficiently accomplish the required restructuring or change in managers, the capital market, through the market for corporate control, is bringing about substantial changes in corporate strategy.

Takeovers are particularly important in bringing about efficiencies when exit from an activity is required. The oil industry is a good example of the control market as an instrument of change in such a situation. It is particularly hard for managers in an industry that must shrink to deal with the fact that some firms in the industry have to go out of business. This is often cheaper to accomplish through merger and the orderly liquidation of marginal assets of the combined firms than by slow death in a competitive struggle in an industry with overcapacity. The end of such a process often occurs in the bankruptcy courts with high losses and unnecessary destruction of valuable parts of organizations that could be used productively by others.

In short, the external takeover market serves as a court of last resort that plays an important role in: 1) generating organizational change, 2) motivating the efficient utilization of resources, and 3) protecting shareholders when the corporation's internal controls and board-level control mechanisms are slow, clumsy, or break down entirely. The market does not, however, operate without cost.

If assets are to move to their most highly valued use, acquirers must be able to sell off assets to those who can use them more productively. Therefore, divestitures are a critical element in the functioning of the corporate control market and it is important to avoid inhibiting them.

Divested plants and assets do not disappear, they are reallocated. Sometimes they continue to be used in similar ways in the same industry, and in other cases they are used in very different ways and in different industries. But in both cases they are moving to uses that their new owners are betting are more productive. This is beneficial to society. We're all familiar with old warehouses that have been reallocated from their original use to popular shopping areas. The change, however, can cause some people to lose their jobs even though others gain jobs.

In fact, the best evidence available indicates that wages and employment grow faster following acquisitions than would otherwise be expected. How can this be true when the impression given in the media is so different? When reporting on the employment effects of takeovers, it is as if the news media only reported on the 100 warehousemen who were displaced in a conversion to a shopping center, and ignored the thousands of new workers employed in the newly opened center.

Finally, the takeover and divestiture markets provide a private market constraint against bigness for its own sake. The potential gains available to those who correctly perceive that a firm can be purchased for less than the value realizable from the sale of its components provide an incentive for entrepreneurs to search out such opportunities and to capitalize on them by reorganizing such firms into smaller entities. That is exactly what is taking place with Beatrice Foods, which was taken private last year in the largest leveraged buyout in history. New management is reorganizing the divisions into more focused businesses and selling them off as leaner, more competitive entities.

The mere possibility of such takeovers also motivates managers to avoid putting together uneconomic conglomerates and to break up those that currently exist. This is happening at ITT, United Technologies, CBS, and Litton.

Recently, the defensive reaction of many firms to avoid unwanted takeover has led to policy changes similar to the proposed actions of the potential acquirer. Examples of this are the reorganizations that are occurring in the oil industry (Diamond International is the most recent), the sale of "crown jewels," and divestitures brought on by the desire to liquidate large debt positions incurred to buy back stock or to make other payments to stockholders. Unfortunately, the basic economic sense of these transactions is often lost in a blur of emotional rhetoric and controversy.

More than a dozen separate forces drive takeover activity, including such factors as deregulation, synergies, economies of scale and scope, taxes, managerial incompetence, empire building and the increasing globalization of U.S. markets. But one factor has been largely ignored despite its important role in acquisitions and restructurings over the last decade. Its roots lie in an inherent conflict between managers and stockholders: the conflict over the payout of free cash flow.

Free cash flow is cash in excess of that required to fund all of a firm's projects which promise to earn more than the cost of capital. Such free cash flow must be paid out to shareholders if the firm is to be efficient.

The problem is how to motivate managers to disgorge cash to investors rather than wasting it on organizational inefficiencies or low-return projects. Sometimes this waste can be large. In the oil industry, for example, it has amounted to tens of billions of dollars since the late 1970s.

Managers are generally reluctant to pay out resources to share-holders because it reduces their power and subjects them to the monitoring of the capital markets that occurs when they must obtain new capital. Managers also have incentives to over-retain funds for growth because their compensation is positively related to growth. Moreover, the tendency of firms to reward middle managers through promotion rather than year-to-year bonuses also creates a strong organizational bias toward growth to supply the new management positions that such promotion-based reward systems require.

Managers with substantial free cash flow can increase dividends or repurchase stock and thereby pay out current cash that would otherwise be invested in low-return projects or wasted. However, this leaves managers with control over the use of future free cash flows. Promised cash payout in the form of a "permanent" increase in the dividend is weak because future dividends can be reduced at the will of management.

Debt has important control effects in reducing the agency costs of free cash flow. Buying back stock with newly created debt enables managers to effectively bond their promise to pay out future cash flows in a way that cannot be accomplished by simple dividend increases. Through such debt creation, managers give shareholder-recipients of the debt the right to take the firm into bankruptcy court if they do not maintain their promise to make the interest and principal payments.

Debt for stock exchanges reduce the waste associated with free cash flow by reducing the cash available for spending at the discretion of managers. Debt also creates organizational incentives to motivate managers and to give them the crisis—the threat of bankruptcy—to help overcome the normal organizational resistance to retrenchment which the payout of free cash flow often requires; programs must be cancelled, careers must change, and layoffs are frequently required. Debt for stock exchanges also create tax advantages at the corporate and personal levels.

The control effects of debt are not as important for rapidly growing organizations that have large and highly profitable investment projects but no free cash flow. Such organizations have a surplus of desirable investment opportunities and will experience the monitoring of the capital markets when they raise new funds.

The control effects of debt are more important in organizations which generate large cash flows but have low growth prospects and even more important in organizations which must shrink. In these organizations the pressure to waste cash flows by investing them in uneconomic projects is most serious.

The takeover activity in the oil industry is a good example of this phenomenon.

Radical changes in the energy market since 1973 simultaneously generated large increases in free cash flow and required a major shrinking of the petroleum industry. In this environment, the waste of free cash flow was large, and the takeover market played a critical role in reducing it.

Following the 10-fold increase in crude oil prices, the consumption of oil and expected future increases in oil prices fell. Real interest rates and exploration and development costs also increased so that the optimal level of capacity in the industry fell. By the late 1970s, the industry had substantial excess capacity in crude reserves, refining, and distribution. At the same time, cash flows were huge. For example, in 1984 the ten largest oil companies generated cash flows of $48.5 billion, 28 percent of the total cash flow of the top 200 firms.

Consistent with free cash flow theory, management did not pay out the excess resources to shareholders. Instead, the industry continued to spend heavily on exploration and development activity even though average pre-tax returns were low. Bernard Picchi of Salomon Bros. estimated them to be substantially below 10 percent. They also launched unsuccessful diversification programs to invest funds outside the industry—programs that led to seven of the worst mergers of the decade according to *Fortune* magazine. These purchases of other companies, however, generated social benefits because the resources were paid out to target-firm shareholders rather than wasted on uneconomic drilling programs.

In this way mergers in the oil industry, motivated largely by T. Boone Pickens, have led to large increases in debt, payouts of large amounts of capital to shareholders (albeit target shareholders), reduced expenditures on wasteful drilling programs and reduced capacity in refining and distribution. When Chevron acquired Gulf for $13.2 billion in cash in 1984, the oil industry was instantly smaller by $13.2 billion. The benefits have been huge. The acquisition of Gulf in 1984 led to gains of $6 billion for Gulf shareholders and $2.8 billion for Chevron shareholders. Total gains in the Chevron/Gulf, Texaco/Getty and Du Pont/Conoco takeovers alone were more than $17 billion. More is possible.

Actual takeover is not necessary to induce the required retrenchment and return of resources to shareholders.

- The Phillips restructuring, brought about by threat of takeover, resulted in a $1.2 billion (20 percent) gain in its market value. It repurchased 53 percent of its stock for $4.5 billion in debt, raised its dividend 25 percent, cut capital spending and initiated a program to sell $2 billion of assets.

- Unocal's defense in the Mesa tender offer battle resulted in a $2.2 billion (35 percent) gain to shareholders. It paid out 52 percent of its equity by repurchasing stock with a $4.2 billion debt issue. The Unocal defense, incidentally, caused its shareholders to lose the $1.1 billion higher Mesa offer.

- Arco's voluntary restructuring resulted in a $3.2 billion (30 percent) gain in market value. It involves a 35 percent to 40 percent cut in exploration and development expenditures, repurchase of 25 percent of its stock for $4 billion, a 33 percent increase in its dividend, withdrawal from gasoline marketing and refining east of the Mississippi, and a 13 percent reduction in its workforce.

- Diamond-Shamrock's reorganization announcement in July 1985 is further support for the theory because its market value fell 2 percent on the announcement day (and continued falling). Its restructuring involved **reducing** cash dividends by 76¢/sh (−43 percent), creating a master limited partnership (MLP) to hold 35 percent of its North American production, paying 90¢/sh annual dividend in partnership shares, repurchasing 6 percent of its shares for $200 million, selling 12 percent of its MLP to the public, and **increasing** expenditures on oil and gas exploration by $100 million/year.

Many said at the time of these takeovers that the companies would be ruined by the large debt increases. That has obviously not happened even though oil prices dropped by more than 50 percent, a non-trivial recession in the industry. In fact recent analysts' reports tout the substantial debt reductions achieved by Chevron and Phillips. They forecast that Unocal will substantially reduce its debt by 1989 even without asset sales. The doomsayers have been wrong and Pickens and Icahn have thus far been correct in saying the firms could be more efficient and could support more debt.

In summary, the theory predicts that value-increasing takeovers occur in response to breakdowns of internal control processes in firms with substantial free cash flow and organizational policies (including diversification programs) that are wasting resources. It predicts hostile takeovers, large increases in leverage, dismantlement of conglomerate empires which lack economies of scale or focus to give them economic purpose and much controversy as current managers object to loss of their jobs or the changes in organizational policies forced on them by threat of a takeover. The CBS and Union Carbide restructuring to avoid takeover are also good examples.

Free cash flow theory also predicts which mergers and takeovers are more likely to destroy, rather than to create, value; it shows how takeovers are both evidence of the conflicts of interest between shareholders and managers and a response to the problem.

Acquisitions are one way managers spend cash instead of paying it out to shareholders. Therefore, the theory implies managers of firms with unused borrowing power and large free cash flows are more likely to undertake low-benefit or even value-destroying mergers. Diversification programs generally fit this category, and the theory predicts they will generate lower total gains.

Acquisitions made with cash, or securities other than stock, involve payout of resources to (target) shareholders, and this can create net benefits even if the merger generates operating inefficiencies. Recall that repurchasing stock is one way to resolve free cash flow problems, and it makes no difference whose shares are repurchased (your own or your neighbor's) as long as no negative productivity effects are generated. The benefits come when managers buy back the stock of the target firm and therefore do not waste the free cash flow on unprofitable internal investments.

Thus, acquisitions can be both a symptom of the conflicts between shareholders and managers over free cash flow, and a solution to those conflicts.

Unproductive mergers are more likely to occur in industries with large cash flows whose economics dictate that exit occur. Such firms are more likely to launch wasteful diversification programs such as occurred in the oil industry. The tobacco and forest products industries also fit this description. Tobacco firms face declining demand due to changing smoking habits but generate large free cash flow and have been involved in major acquisitions recently. Acquisitions and restructurings have been solving excess capacity problems in forest products also. The CBS debt for stock restructuring also fits the theory.

The debt created in a hostile takeover (or takeover defense) of a firm suffering severe agency costs of free cash flow need not be permanent. Indeed, sometimes it is desirable to "overleverage" such a firm. In these situations, levering the firm so highly that it cannot continue to exist in its old form generates benefits. It creates the crisis to motivate cuts in expansion programs and the sale of those divisions which are more valuable outside the firm. The proceeds are used to reduce debt to a more normal or permanent level. This process results in a complete rethinking of the organization's strategy and its structure. When successful, a much leaner and competitive organization results. Beatrice seems to be a good example of this phenomenon.

It is important to recognize that new restrictions on takeover activity imposed by state regulations in the recent past and the prospective new federal restrictions that are likely to result from the current antagonism created by the insider trading scandals will prevent realization of the productive gains from acquisitions and reorganizations that would otherwise occur.

One of the major imperfections in current regulations of takeover activity is the SEC 13d disclosure requirements.

It has become popular to argue there is too much takeover activity. Yet the opposite is most likely true because of free riding problems caused by the current regulations that require disclosure of holdings and intentions of the purchaser in SEC 13d reports. These reports must be filed within 10 days of acquisition of 5 percent or more of a company's shares and must disclose the number of shares owned, the identity of the owner, and the purpose of the acquisition of the shares. Current rules allow the acquiring firm to buy as many additional shares as it can in the 10-day window between the time the 5 percent filing barrier is reached and the time of filing. This allows buyers to acquire shares that average about 10 percent of the target firm.

Since market prices adjust to the expected value of the takeover bid quickly after the 13d announcement, the acquirer's profits are made almost entirely on the difference between the price paid for the shares purchased prior to the filing of the 13d and their value after the acquisition. This forced disclosure of valuable private information is equivalent to an antipatent law. It denies private rights in valuable privately produced information, by requiring that value to be given away to others. It drives a wedge between the private benefits earned by the acquirer and the total social benefit of the acquisition; the acquirer pays 100 percent of the acquisition costs and, on the average, captures less than 10 percent of the benefits. The remaining benefits go to the other shareholders.

Boone Pickens, for example, has contributed well in excess of $10 billion in gains to the shareholders of companies that he has attempted to take over, while making about $750 million for the shareholders of Mesa Petroleum.

Consider an acquisition that promises total expected gains of $100 million. If the acquirer expects to capture only $10 million of this amount if the bid is successful, the bid will occur only if the legal, investment banking and other costs (including the required risk premium) are less than $10 million. All acquisitions that are expected to cost more than this will not be made, and shareholders and society are thus denied the benefits of those reorganizations. If the costs, for example, are expected to be $15 million, the bid will not occur and the $85 million benefit will not be realized. The solution to this problem is to abolish the SEC 13d reporting requirements or to increase significantly the trigger point from the current 5 percent level. There is considerable pressure, however, from those who wish to handicap the entrepreneurial activities of takeover specialists to tighten the 13d reporting requirements rather than loosen them.

In conclusion, I want to emphasize the fact that many of our largest corporations have become too large and too complicated to be efficient. The pressures created by the competition for top-level jobs in the corporate control market are having very healthy effects on corporate America. The restructurings that are now occurring are simplifying these organizations and bringing managers closer to the shareholders, closer to production workers, and closer to consumers. The result is a more productive and competitive economy. It would be a shame to stop this progress by the unwise and hasty legislation that is now being proposed by entrenched managers and other parties who stand personally to lose from these improvements.

Questions

1.   In what ways is corporate America being restructured?

2.   "SEC estimates indicate gains to target firm shareholders in tender offers alone of over $40 billion in the 1981 to May 1985 period." Who paid the $40 billion premium to the target firm shareholders? What are the possible reasons that they were willing to pay such a large premium?

3.   Andrew C. Sigler, president of the Business Roundtable, comments as follows on the recent wave of mergers and acquisitions: "It is nothing but a grubby asset play. They are acquiring the greatest accumulation of wealth of all time — greater than the Rockefellers or the Rothchilds — they are doing it by snapping it out of companies, thus damaging the capability of the economic system to perform." Do you think the author (Michael C. Jensen) would agree with Mr. Sigler's charge? Do you agree with his charge? Explain.

4.   In what way is the market for corporate control a major component of the managerial labor market?

5.   Corporate takeovers have led to the substantial restructuring of several corporations. Moreover, just the threat of takeover often

Resisting Takeovers Isn't Always Bad

Robert Jennings and Michael Mazzeo

Contrary to popular belief, management's resistance to takeovers actually may be in the best interests of stockholders. When management plays hard to get, the result may be a better offer—or another suitor.

The 1980s, it seems, are destined to become known as the decade of corporate consolidation in the United States. Although the decade is only sixty percent over, the number of mergers and their dollar value are both setting records.

Many public forums have questioned, on both social and economic grounds, the merits of this takeover frenzy. Even more controversial than the mergers themselves, it seems, is the reaction of the management of target firms. No longer is management content to be passive or to put up minimal resistance in the face of an unwelcome takeover attempt. Indeed, the responses of target managements have become as imaginative as the methods used by the would-be acquirers. These so-called "antitakeover" tactics have received nearly universal condemnation from government regulatory bodies, the popular financial press, and some academic publications. One such article, in a recent issue of this journal, included the following statement in its conclusions:

Shark repellents, poison pills, greenmail, white knights, and golden parachutes are among the most troubling antitakeover tactics. It seems clear that none is in the interest of the stockholder.[1]

As with any controversial subject, however, there are two sides to the story. This article will present the other side: the economic arguments and the empirical evidence which indicate that some management resis-

Robert Jennings and Michael Mazzeo, "Resisting Takeovers Isn't Always Bad," reprinted from *Business Horizons* (March/April 1986): 56–60. Copyright 1986 by the Foundation for the School of Business of Indiana University. Used with permission.

At the time of this writing, Robert Jennings was an associate professor of finance and Michael Mazzeo was an assistant professor of finance, both at Indiana University.

[1] I. Kesner and D. Dalton, "Antitakeover Tactics: Management 42, Stockholders 0," *Business Horizons,* September-October 1985: 25.

tance may be beneficial to shareholders.[2] We will discuss the benefits of management resistance and the logic behind a few common defensive techniques.

Benefits of Management Resistance

Why is there so much criticism when managements resist takeovers? At the most general level, criticism is based on empirical studies that find a negative return to the target shareholders when negotiated (friendly) merger activities, voluntarily undertaken by two management teams, are unsuccessful.[3] These studies examine the cumulative return from the period of time just prior to the first public announcement of the proposed merger through the announcement of the cancellation. Results range from a total return of −9.02 percent to +3.68 percent, with an average of −2.88 percent. In unsuccessful mergers, therefore, stockholders in target firms lose on the average about three percent of the firm value. In none of the cases is the estimate statistically significant; in other words, the variability in firm returns is so great that we cannot state with any confidence that the observed return is different from zero.

But looking at the returns only through the termination date can be misleading, as one study found.[4] When examining tender offers, the target cumulative return remains large *even after the unsuccessful termination of the offer*. The total return from six months prior to the offer through six months after the offer is nearly +36 percent, *even though the offer was unsuccessful*. Given the market reaction to negotiated mergers, this is a curious finding. The answer to this seeming anomaly emerges when firms are divided into two groups:

- Those targets eventually acquired by some *other* bidder; and
- Those targets who are not acquired.

At the end of a two-year period after the initial offer, those firms that were subsequently acquired had earned an *additional* 20 percent return *above* the initial 36 percent. Those firms that had *not* been acquired gave

---

[2] Many of the arguments and much of the empirical evidence synthesized here are mentioned in two excellent review articles: M. Jensen, "Takeovers: Folklore and Science," *Harvard Business Review,* November-December 1984: 109–21; and M. Jensen and R. Ruback, "The Market for Corporate Control: The Scientific Evidence," *Journal of Financial Economics,* April 1983: 5–50.

[3] Throughout, returns are measured net of the normal (or expected) level of return, leaving only the excess (unexpected) risk-adjusted component. Examples of such findings are P. Asquith, "Merger Bids, Uncertainty, and Stockholder Returns," *Journal of Financial Economics,* April 1983: 51–84; P. Dodd, "Merger Proposals, Management Discretion, and Stockholder Wealth," *Journal of Financial Economics,* June 1980: 105–38; and P. Weir, "The Costs of Antimerger Lawsuits: Evidence from the Stock Market," *Journal of Financial Economics,* April 1983: 207–24.

[4] See M. Bradley, A. Desai, and E. Kim, "The Rationale Behind Interfirm Tender Offers: Information or Synergy?" *Journal of Financial Economics,* April 1983: 183–206.

back the entire 36 percent return earned during the initial tender offer. In firms where the acquisition initially failed but subsequently succeeded, shareholders earned a total return of 56 percent. Those earnings compare favorably to the 30 percent return earned by the target shareholders of all successful tender offers.[5] Thus, resisting an initial offer may pay off handsomely for target shareholders.

These empirical results suggest that some form of resistance by management may be desirable. Playing "hard-to-get" may influence the initial suitor to increase the bid, or it may permit time for other competing bids to be submitted. According to one study, opposed tender offers generate about a 21 percent greater return for target shareholders than do those where management offers no opposition.[6] In another study the return for the target shareholders of single bid offers averaged 27 percent; multiple bid offers provided a 43 percent return to target owners.[7] A rule decreeing passivity by target managements may be best for shareholders in some cases. But if permitting a target to resist is necessary to stimulate competition, then resistance may be the superior strategy.[8] The market for takeovers appears to be competitive in the sense that unsuccessful bidders cannot raise their bids without generating negative returns for their shareholders.[9]

Breaking Out of Prison: A Case Study

But why must the managements of the target firms get involved? The answer lies in the fact that management is in a better position than the diverse owners of modern corporations to coordinate negotiations that may result in a larger stockholder return. Consider the following scenario.[10]

Firm A has 100 shares of stock outstanding with a total current market value of $950—or $9.50 per share. A $50 gain in combined value can be realized through a merger with Firm B. The exact source of the gain is immaterial; as an example, it could be cost savings from efficiency of scale. Assume Firm B makes a two-tiered tender offer: it will purchase

---

[5] See M. Bradley, "Interfirm Tender Offers and the Market for Corporate Control," *Journal of Business,* October 1980: 345–76; and P. Dodd and R. Ruback, "Tender Offers and the Market for Corporate Control," *Journal of Financial Economics,* September 1977: 351–74.

[6] D. Krummer and R. Hoffmeister, "Valuation Consequences of Cash Tender Offers," *Journal of Finance,* May 1978: 505–16.

[7] M. Bradley, A. Desai, and E. Kim, "Determinants of the Wealth Effects of Corporate Acquisition," Working paper, University of Michigan, August 1984.

[8] See D. Baron, "Tender Offers and Management Resistance," *Journal of Finance,* May 1983: 331–42.

[9] R. Ruback, "Assessing Competition in the Market for Corporate Acquisitions," *Journal of Financial Economics,* April 1983: 141–54.

[10] First outlined in Jensen and Ruback (note 2): 31–32.

51 of A's shares at $12 a share and the remaining 49 shares for $7 per share. The average price is $9.55 per share. Suppose no other offers are forthcoming. Will B's offer be successful? The answer is yes. Each shareholder will tender to get the average price of $9.55 per share rather than risk the possibility of being one of the minority shareholders not tendering and receiving only $7 per share.[11]

In this example the target firm shareholder gets $5 of the $50 gain, and the bidder firm shareholder receives $45. Is this a competitive distribution of the gain? Possibly not.

The shareholders of Firm A are caught in a classic "prisoner's dilemma."[12] As individuals, they are acting rationally by selling at a very low premium. Collectively, however, they may regret their action. In fact, the bidding firm intentionally may structure the takeover offer with an extreme difference between the front-end offer ($12 in the example) and the back-end offer ($7). The severe treatment of the nontendering target shareholders in a successful takeover magnifies the prisoner's dilemma and helps ensure the success of the offer. Without some form of resistance or outside competition, the bidder may offer less than the "true" value for the target in an attempt to capture most (or all) of the gains.

If, instead of acting on an individual basis, the shareholders act as a group, they may be able to get a more favorable division of the synergistic gain. Allowing management to negotiate for the shareholders may be an efficient collective bargaining arrangement, which can nullify the prisoner's dilemma problem. In other words, shareholders may benefit from some resistance by management.

This resistance may convince Firm B to raise its bid. Or it may give Firm C time to make a higher bid. In fact, the possibility of resistance may make B's initial bid competitive. Lengthening the tender offer process redistributes gains to favor target shareholders.[13]

Generally speaking, therefore, some resistance of acquisition offers by management may be in the stockholders' best interest.

Resistance Tactics

In recent years, target managements have devised many different tactics in an effort to resist or defeat proposed mergers. Several of these tactics can benefit shareholders.

[11] In fact, B could reduce its bid until the average price per share paid is just above the current market price. If B tries to capture the entire gain by offering only $9.50, any firm could match the offer.

[12] R. Luce and H. Raffia, *Games and Decisions* (New York: Wiley, 1957): 95–97.

[13] See Bradley, Desai, and Kim (note 7).

Shark Repellents

"Shark repellent" is a generic name given to changes in the corporate charter or operating policy that make takeovers more difficult. One such ploy is to change the state of incorporation to one (Delaware, for example) that places fewer limits on the actions of management. In effect, when management's hands are not tied by regulation, it is better able to resist or defeat proposed takeovers.

By reincorporating in such states, management implicitly alters its contract with the shareholders. If the shareholders are hurt by such actions, a decline in stock price could be anticipated once management's intentions become known. Yet study of the stock price movements reveals that just the opposite occurs.[14] In the two years prior to announcing the reincorporation, shareholders of these firms averaged returns of 30 percent, and they experienced a small positive gain in the month the reincorporation was announced. This evidence is inconsistent with the hypothesis that reincorporation is detrimental to the best interests of the shareholders.

"Antitakeover" Amendments

A second tactic by management is to add "antitakeover" amendments to corporate charters. These maneuvers include:
- Super-majority rules;
- Staggered terms for the board of directors;
- Elimination of mandatory retirement; and
- Fair price provisions.

These amendments are intended to make a takeover more difficult and more costly.

If "antitakeover" amendments are injurious to stockholders, stock prices should fall when the plans are made public. Two studies in this area fail to find any significant returns (either positive or negative) to the stockholders in the period when such amendments are announced.[15] In fact, there appears to be significantly negative returns to stockholders when such amendments are *removed*. Neither result is consistent with the notion that shareholders are being hurt by management's actions.

[14] See P. Dodd and R. Leftwich, "The Market for Corporate Charters: 'Unhealthy Competition' versus Federal Regulation," *Journal of Business*, July 1980: 259–83.

[15] See H. DeAngelo and E. Rice, "Antitakeover Charter Amendments and Stockholder Wealth," *Journal of Financial Economics*, April 1983: 329–60; and S. Linn and J. McConnell, "An Empirical Investigation of the Impact of 'Antitakeover' Amendments on Common Stock Prices," *Journal of Financial Economics*, April 1983: 361–400.

Litigation

Another common "antitakeover" maneuver employed by target management is to undertake some litigious action. A recent study finds that, in more than one-third of the takeover contests involving New York or American Stock Exchange firms since 1962, target-instigated litigation has occurred.[16] In addition, the evidence indicates that most of the legal decisions rule against the target.

Given the costs of litigation, it seems that allowing target management to litigate usually would not be in the best interests of the stockholders. The empirical evidence indicates that takeover targets experience a negative return of about one-half of one percent when their management announces legal action. However, those target firms that ultimately are acquired (about 80 percent of those litigating) gain, on the average, about a one percent return prior to the completion of the merger. This gain results from additional bids that occur after the lawsuit is announced. Firms that litigate are more likely to receive higher bids. Despite the costs of litigation and the initial negative return associated with litigation, these higher bids ultimately enhance shareholder wealth.

Golden Parachutes

One of the most hotly debated tactics used by target management to increase the cost of acquisitions is the golden parachute. Managers with this clause in their compensation contracts are guaranteed a substantial sum of money if they do not remain in their jobs after a change in control of the corporation. In some cases the change in control itself triggers the payment. A golden parachute is considered an "antitakeover" device because the acquiring firm is required to make large payments to the target management if the acquisition is successful.

Critics argue that a golden parachute provides top managers with a substantial bonus for doing merely what they are already paid to do—look out for the interests of stockholders. Supporters argue that golden parachutes may have a favorable influence on management's reaction to takeover bids.

These arguments rely in part on the presumption that most top managers have a considerable investment in firm-specific human capital. That is, they have performed tasks that were essential to the well-being of the target firm but generally will not be rewarded by the labor market. An example might be charity appearances in the firm's name or involvement in community groups. These activities increase goodwill toward the firm, but they do little to help the individual's value in the labor market.

There are a variety of circumstances in which the current management loses when a firm is taken over by another company. The manager's

---

[16] See G. Jarrell, "The Wealth Effects of Litigation by Targets: Do Interests Diverge in a Merger?" *Journal of Law and Economics,* April 1983: 151–77.

existing contract intentionally may have paid less than his or her marginal product in the early career stages with the explicit (or implicit) agreement to pay above marginal product in the late career stages. Or the target firm may have a bonus system that will not reward the manager on the basis of the market price of the stock. In these cases, the manager may be hesitant to relinquish control of the firm. She or he realizes that, in the likely case of merger-related unemployment, the next labor contract negotiated may not be so lucrative.

Since the golden parachute reduces the potential loss to the manager from a takeover, it may help lessen the manager's preference for control of the firm, and it may reduce the tendency to fight a favorable offer. According to this point of view, shareholders are helped by having golden parachute agreements in place. Empirical evidence indicates a small (about 3 percent), but significant, *positive* return to the shareholder when a golden parachute is enacted.[17] The evidence suggests that shareholders are helped by the existence of these contractual obligations.

In summary, management's resistance to takeover attempts is not necessarily unfavorable to stockholders. If the manager uses defensive measures as a technique to increase the bid to a competitive level, the shareholder benefits. This does not mean that managers are altruistic and ignore their own interests. In deciding how aggressively to fight the merger, they do consider how the proposed merger will affect their wealth.[18]

When Resistance Is Unhealthy

It is possible, of course, to have "too much" of a good thing. While measures that increase the manager's bargaining position do not seem to harm the stockholders, any action that directly eliminates the possibility of a pending takeover does hurt the owners. For example, consider targeted share repurchases and standstill agreements.

Targeted Share Repurchase.   In a targeted share repurchase (a potential "greenmail" situation), the firm repurchases at a premium over market price the shares accumulated by one person or by a few individuals. (The "greenmail" terminology comes from the idea that management is paying the individuals who have acquired the shares to give up any further takeover-related activity.) Empirical evidence indicates that the shareholders suffer a negative return (from −3 percent to −2 percent) in this

---

[17] See R. Lambert and D. Larcker, "Golden Parachutes, Executive Decision-Making and Shareholder Wealth," *Journal of Accounting and Economics,* June 1985: 179–203.

[18] R. Walking and M. Long, "Agency Theory, Managerial Welfare, and Takeover Bid Resistance," *Rand Journal of Economics,* Spring 1984: 54–68.

activity.[19] The negative return for targeted share purchase is even more surprising given the evidence that stockholders benefit by nontargeted share repurchases.[20]

Standstill Agreements.   Standstill agreements are contracts between a firm and a potential bidder in which the bidder voluntarily agrees to quit accumulating shares. These agreements usually are made after some party has acquired a significant position in the firm and acts as if it plans to acquire more. Evidence from the capital markets indicates a fairly substantial negative return to shareholders when standstill agreements are announced.[21]

What lesson can be learned from examining the tactics target managements use to fight takeovers? Stockholders are not harmed—and may be helped—by tactics that create additional negotiating power for future, potential takeovers. But when management actions apparently are designed to eliminate a takeover by a specific (potential) bidder, then shareholders may be harmed. Even the defeat of a specific takeover proposal may not be contrary to the stockholders' long-run interests, however, if additional offers at more favorable terms are forthcoming.

Furthermore, we cannot conclude that every unsuccessful merger is the fault of target management. In a recent study that the authors made of negotiated mergers, about one-third of the cancellations that could be attributed to a single party were attributed to the bidder. Even mergers that fail because of the actions of target management are not necessarily evidence that management is acting in its own self-interest. Target management conceivably could have had the interests of shareholders in mind and believed—mistakenly—that a higher bid would be forthcoming. Just because it may be difficult to distinguish errors in judgment from managerial conflicts of interest, it seems unreasonable to assume arbitrarily the latter.

"Antitakeover" tactics do not deserve the blanket condemnation they receive in the popular press. Although arguments can be made against measures that enable management to resist takeover offers more effectively, equally persuasive arguments support the enactment of such measures. The stock market shows that stockholders do not always believe that management's actions are contrary to their own best inter-

---

[19] See L. Dann and H. DeAngelo, "Standstill Agreements, Privately Negotiated Stock Repurchases, and the Market for Corporate Control," *Journal of Financial Economics,* April 1983: 275–300; and M. Bradley and L. Wakeman, "The Wealth Effects of Targeted Share Repurchases," *Journal of Financial Economics,* April 1983: 301–29.

[20] See L. Dann, "Common Stock Repurchases: An Analysis of Returns to Bondholders and Stockholders," *Journal of Financial Economics,* June 1981: 113–38; and T. Vermaelen, "Common Stock Repurchases and Market Signalling: An Empirical Study," *Journal of Financial Economics,* June 1981: 139–83.

[21] See Dann and DeAngelo (note 19): 275–300.

ests. The point to be made is that the issue is still unresolved. In this game of "antitakeover" tactics, the score (if there is a contest at all) is not nearly so lopsided as some have suggested.

Questions

1.   Describe the returns earned by shareholders of target companies under the following circumstances:

    a.   Unsuccessful attempts by friendly management teams to merge two companies.

    b.   Unsuccessful tender offers.

    c.   Unsuccessful tender offer, but target company is eventually acquired by another bidder.

    d.   Successful tender offers.

    e.   Successful tender offers with one bidder.

    f.   Successful tender offers with multiple bidders.

2.   Why may it be in the target shareholders best interest for management to offer some resistance to takeover attempts?

3.   Describe the following tactics for resisting corporate takeovers: (a) shark repellents, (b) golden parachutes, (c) greenmail, and (d) standstill agreements.

4.   "Empirical evidence indicates a small (about 3 percent), but significant, *positive* return to the shareholder when a golden parachute is enacted." If you were a shareholder, would you be pleased to learn that golden parachutes had been given to top management? Explain.

A Guide to Foreign Exchange Markets

K. Alec Chrystal

The economics of the free world are becoming increasingly interdependent. U.S. exports now amount to almost 10 percent of Gross National Product. For both Britain and Canada, the figure currently exceeds 25 percent. Imports are about the same size. Trade of this magnitude would not be possible without the ability to buy and sell currencies. Currencies must be bought and sold because the acceptable means of payment in other countries is not the U.S. dollar. As a result, importers, exporters, travel agents, tourists and many others with overseas business must change dollars into foreign currency and/or the reverse.

The trading of currencies takes place in foreign exchange markets whose major function is to facilitate international trade and investment. Foreign exchange markets, however, are shrouded in mystery. One reason for this is that a considerable amount of foreign exchange market activity does not appear to be related directly to the needs of international trade and investment.

The purpose of this paper is to explain how these markets work.[1] The basics of foreign exchange will first be described. This will be followed by a discussion of some of the more important activities of market participants. Finally, there will be an introduction to the analysis of a new feature of exchange markets — currency options. The concern of this paper is with the structure and mechanics of foreign exchange markets, not with the determinants of exchange rates themselves.

K. Alec Chrystal, "A Guide to Foreign Exchange Markets," *Review* (Federal Reserve Bank of St. Louis, March 1984): 5–18.

At the time of this writing, K. Alec Chrystal, professor of economics-elect, University of Sheffield, England, was a visiting scholar at the Federal Reserve Bank of St. Louis. Leslie Bailis Koppel provided research assistance. The author wishes to thank Joseph Hempen, Centerre Bank, St. Louis, for his advice on this paper.

[1] For further discussion of foreign exchange markets in the United States, see Kubarych (1983). See also Dufey and Giddy (1978) and McKinnon (1979).

Table 1   Foreign Exchange Rate Quotations

Foreign Exchange
Wednesday, September 7, 1983
The New York foreign exchange selling rates below apply to trading among banks in amounts of $1 million and more, as quoted at 3 p.m. Eastern time by Bankers Trust Co. Retail transactions provide fewer units of foreign currency per dollar.

Country	U.S. $ equiv.		Currency per U.S. $	
	Wed.	Tues.	Wed.	Tues.
Argentina (Peso)	.09652	.09652	10.36	10.36
Australia (Dollar)	.8772	.8777	1.1340	1.1393
Austria (Schilling)	.05296	.0560	18.88	17.84
Belgium (Franc)				
Commercial rate	.01851	.01855	54.01	53.90
Financial rate	.01844	.01846	54.21	54.15
Brazil (Cruzeiro)	.001459	.00149	685.	671.00
Britain (Pound)	1.4910	1.5000	.6707	.6666
30-Day Forward	1.4915	1.5004	.6704	.6664
90-Day Forward	1.4930	1.5010	.6697	.6662
180-Day Forward	1.4952	1.5028	.6688	.6654
Canada (Dollar)	.8120	.8123	1.2315	1.2310
30-Day Forward	.8125	.8128	1.2307	1.2303
90-Day Forward	.8134	.8137	1.2293	1.2289
180-Day Forward	.8145	.8147	1.2277	1.2274
Chile (Official rate)	.01246	.01246	80.21	80.21
China (Yuan)	.50499	.50489	1.9802	1.9806
Columbia (Peso)	.01228	.01228	81.4	81.40
Denmark (Krone)	.10362	.10405	9.65	9.6100
Ecuador (Sucre)				
Official rate	.02082	.02082	48.03	48.03
Floating rate	.010917	.010917	91.60	91.60
Finland (Markka)	.17424	.17485	5.7390	5.7190
France (Franc)	.1238	.1238	8.0750	8.0750
30-Day Forward	.1235	.1230	8.0955	8.1300
90-Day Forward	.1224	.1223	8.1695	8.1725
180-Day Forward	.1203	.1202	8.3100	8.3150
Greece (Drachma)	.01075	.01078	93.	92.70
Hong Kong (Dollar)	.1297	.13089	7.71	7.6400
India (Rupee)	.0980	.0980	10.20	10.20
Indonesia (Rupiah)	.001015	.001015	985.	985.
Ireland (Punt)	1.1715	1.1775	.8536	.8493
Israel (Shekel)	.0173	.0173	57.80	57.80
Italy (Lira)	.000624	.0006255	1602.	1598.50

continued

The Basics of Foreign Exchange Markets

There is an almost bewildering variety of foreign exchange markets. Spot markets and forward markets abound in a number of currencies. In addition, there are diverse prices quoted for these currencies. This section attempts to bring order to this seeming disarray.

Country	U.S. $ equiv.		Currency per U.S. $	
	Wed.	Tues.	Wed.	Tues.
Japan (Yen)	.004072	.004067	245.55	245.85
30-Day Forward	.004083	.004079	244.88	245.15
90-Day Forward	.004107	.004102	243.48	243.75
180-Day Forward	.004147	.004142	241.10	241.39
Lebanon (Pound)	.20618	.20618	4.85	4.85
Malaysia (Ringgit)	.42462	.42489	2.3550	2.3535
Mexico (Peso)				
Floating rate	.00665	.00666	150.25	150.00
Netherlands (Guilder)	.33288	.3333	3.0040	3.000
New Zealand (Dollar)	.6497	.6505	1.5397	1.5327
Norway (Krone)	.13368	.1340	7.48	7.4625
Pakistan (Rupee)	.07518	.07518	13.30	13.30
Peru (Sol)	.0005105	.0005105	1958.89	1958.89
Philippines (Peso)	.09085	.09085	11.007	11.007
Portugal (Escudo)	.00804	.00807	124.35	123.90
Saudi Arabia (Riyal)	.28735	.28735	3.48	3.48
Singapore (Dollar)	.46609	.4664	2.1455	2.1440
South Africa (Rand)	.8870	.8900	1.1273	1.1236
South Korea (Won)	.001285	.001285	778.20	778.20
Spain (Peseta)	.00655	.00658	152.60	151.90
Sweden (Krona)	.12635	.12666	7.9140	7.8950
Switzerland (Franc)	.4596	.4591	2.1755	2.1780
30-Day Forward	.4619	.4615	216.46	2.1666
90-Day Forward	.4662	.4657	2.1449	2.1470
180-Day Forward	.4728	.4723	2.1150	2.1172
Taiwan (Dollar)	.02489	.02489	40.17	40.17
Thailand (Baht)	.043459	.043459	23.01	23.01
Uruguay (New Peso)				
Financial	.02798	.02798	35.73	35.73
Venezuela (Bolivar)				
Official rate	.23256	.23256	4.30	4.30
Floating rate	.07194	.07272	13.90	13.75
W. Germany (Mark)	.3726	.3726	2.6835	2.6835
30-Day Forward	.3740	.3741	2.6731	2.6728
90-Day Forward	.3767	.3768	2.6540	2.6538
180-Day Forward	.3808	.3808	2.6260	2.6259
SDR	1.04637	1.04903	.955685	.953625

Special Drawing Rights are based on exchange rates for the U.S., West German, British, French and Japanese currencies. Source: International Monetary Fund.

z—Not quoted.

Source: *The Wall Street Journal,* September 8, 1983.

Spot, Forward, Bid, Ask

Virtually every major newspaper, such as the *Wall Street Journal* or the *London Financial Times,* prints a daily list of exchange rates. These are expressed either as the number of units of a particular currency that exchange for one U.S. dollar or as the number of U.S. dollars that exchange for one unit of a particular currency. Sometimes both are listed side by side (see Table 1).

Table 1 Foreign Exchange Rate Quotations (continued)

Sept 7	The Dollar Spot and Forward					
	Day's spread	Close	One month	% p.a.	Three months	% p.a.
UK†	1.4860–1.4975	1.4910–1.4920	0.02–0.07c dis	-0.36	0.17–0.22dis	-0.52
Ireland†	1.1665–1.1720	1.1710–1.1720	0.36–0.30c pm	3.39	0.88–0.78 pm	2.84
Canada	1.2305–1.2320	1.2310–1.2315	0.09–0.06c pm	0.73	0.24–0.21 pm	0.73
Nethlnd.	3.0050–3.0150	3.0050–3.0070	1.12–1.02c pm	4.26	3.00–2.90 pm	3.92
Belgium	54.06–54.20	54.06–54.08	7–6c pm	1.44	14–11 pm	0.92
Denmark	9.6400–9.6800	9.6400–9.6450	2–2½ore dis	-2.79	par–½dis	-0.10
W. Ger.	2.6850–2.6980	2.6865–2.6875	1.07–1.02pf pm	4.66	3.00–2.95 pm	4.42
Portugal	124.20–125.00	124.40–124.70	115–290c dis	-19.51	330–790dis	-17.98
Spain	152.40–152.70	152.50–152.60	170–220c dis	-15.33	675–775dis	-18.99
Italy	1604–1608	1605–1606	10–10½lire dis	-7.65	29½–31 dis	-7.53
Norway	7.4730–7.4940	7.4730–7.4780	1.90–2.20ore dis	-3.29	5.90–6.20ds	-3.23
France	8.0775–8.1225	8.0825–8.0875	2.02–2.12c dis	-3.07	9.65–9.85ds	-4.81
Sweden	7.9120–7.9265	7.9120–7.9170	0.90–1.10ore dis	-1.51	2.25–2.45ds	-1.19
Japan	245.50–246.50	245.65–245.75	0.69–0.64y pm	3.24	2.11–2.03 pm	3.36
Austria	18.89–18.95½	18.89–18.90	7.50–6.70gro pm	4.50	21.00–18.50 pm	4.17
Switz.	2.1770–2.1875	2.1800–2.1810	1.10–1.05c pm	5.91	3.10–3.05 pm	5.63

† UK and Ireland are quoted in U.S. currency. Forward premiums and discounts apply to the U.S. dollar and not to the individual currency.

Belgian rate is for convertible francs. Financial franc 54.40–54.45.

Source: *London Financial Times*, September 8, 1983.

For major currencies, up to four different prices typically will be quoted. One is the "spot" price. The others may be "30 days forward," "90 days forward," and "180 days forward." These may be expressed either in "European Terms" (such as number of $ per £ or in "American Terms" (such as number of £ per $). (See the glossary for further explanation).

The spot price is what you must pay to buy currencies for immediate delivery (two working days in the interbank market; over the counter, if you buy bank notes or travelers checks). The forward prices for each currency are what you will have to pay if you sign a contract today to buy that currency on a specific future date (30 days from now,etc.). In this market, you pay for the currency when the contract matures.

Why would anyone buy and sell foreign currency forward? There are some major advantages from having such opportunities available. For example, an exporter who has receipts of foreign currency due at some future date can sell those funds forward now, thereby avoiding all risks associated with subsequent adverse exchange rate changes. Similarly, an importer who will have to pay for a shipment of goods in foreign currency in, say, three months can buy the foreign exchange forward and, again, avoid having to bear the exchange rate risk.

The exchange rates quoted in the financial press (for example, those in table 1) are not the ones individuals would get at a local bank. Unless otherwise specified, the published prices refer to those quoted by banks to other banks for currency deals in excess of $1 million. Even these prices will vary somewhat depending upon whether the bank buys or sells. The difference between the buying and selling price is sometimes known as the "bid-ask spread." The spread partly reflects the banks' costs and profit margins in transactions; however, major banks make their profits more from capital gains than from the spread.[2]

The market for bank notes and travelers checks is quite separate from the interbank foreign exchange market. For smaller currency exchanges, such as an individual going on vacation abroad might make, the spread is greater than in the interbank market. This presumably reflects the larger average costs—including the exchange rate risks that banks face by holding bank notes in denominations too small to be sold in the interbank market—associated with these smaller exchanges. As a result, individuals generally pay a higher price for foreign exchange than those quoted in the newspapers.

An example of the range of spot exchange rates available is presented in Table 2, which shows prices for deutschemarks and sterling quoted within a one-hour period on November 28, 1983. There are two important points to notice. First, all except those in the first line are prices quoted in the interbank, or wholesale, market for transactions in excess of $1 million. The sterling prices have a bid-ask spread of only 0.1 cent (which is only about 0.07 percent of the price, or $7 on $10,000). On DM,

---

[2] Notice the *Wall Street Journal* quotes only a bank selling price at a particular time. The *Financial Times* quotes the bid-ask spread and the range over the day.

Table 2   Dollar Price of Deutschemarks and Sterling at Various Banks

	Deutschemark	Sterling
	Buy Sell	Buy Sell
Retail		
Local (St. Louis) banks (avg.)	.3572–.3844	1.4225–1.5025
Wholesale		
New York banks	.3681–.3683	1.4570–1.4580
European banks (high)	.3694–.3696	1.4573–1.4583
European banks (low)	.3677–.3678	1.4610–1.4620
Bankers trust	.3681	1.4588

Note: These prices were all quoted on November 28, 1983, between 2:00 p.m. and 2:45 p.m. (Central Standard Time). Prices for local banks were acquired by telephoning for their price on a $10,000 transaction. The prices quoted were reference rates and not the final price they would offer on a firm transaction. Figure for Bankers Trust is that given in the *Wall Street Journal,* November 29, 1983, as priced at 2:00 p.m. (Central Standard Time) on November 28, 1983. Other prices were taken from the Telerate information system at 2:35 p.m. New York prices were the latest available (Morgan and Citibank, respectively). European prices were the last prices quoted before close of trading in Europe by various banks. Deutschemark prices were actually quoted in American terms. The sell prices above have been rounded up. The difference between buy and sell prices for DM in the interbank market actually worked out at $0.00015.

the spread per dollars worth works out to be about half that on sterling ($4 on $10,000).[3]

Second, the prices quoted by local banks for small, or retail, transactions, which serve only as a guide and do not necessarily represent prices on actual deals, involve a much larger bid-ask spread. These retail spreads vary from bank to bank, but are related to (and larger than) the interbank rates. In some cases, they may be of the order of 4 cents or less on sterling, though the prices quoted in St. Louis involved average spreads of 8 cents on sterling. The latter represents a spread of about 5½ percent (about $550 per $10,000 transaction). The equivalent spread for DM was 7 percent ($700 per $10,000 transaction).

The spread on forward transactions will usually be wider than on spot, especially for longer maturities. For interbank trade, the closing spread on one and three months forward sterling on September 8, 1983, was .15 cents, while the spot spread was .10 cents. This is shown in the top line of the *Financial Times* report in table 1. Of course, like the spot spread, the forward spread varies with time of day and market conditions. At times it may be as low as .02 cents. No information is available for the size of spread on the forward prices typically offered on small transactions, since the retail market on forward transactions is very small.

---

[3] In practice, the spread will vary during the day, depending upon market conditions. For example, the sterling spread may be as little as 0.01 cents at times and on average is about 0.05 cents. Spreads generally will be larger on less widely traded currencies.

How Does "The" Foreign Exchange Market Operate?

It is generally not possible to go to a specific building and "see" the market where prices of foreign exchange are determined. With few exceptions, the vast bulk of foreign exchange business is done over the telephone between specialist divisions of major banks. Foreign exchange dealers in each bank usually operate from one room; each dealer has several telephones and is surrounded by video screens and news tapes. Typically, each dealer specializes in one or a small number of markets (such as sterling/dollar or deutschemark/dollar). Trades are conducted with other dealers who represent banks around the world. These dealers typically deal regularly with one another and are thus able to make firm commitments by word of mouth.

Only the head or regional offices of the larger banks actively deal in foreign exchange. The largest of these banks are known as "market makers" since they stand ready to buy or sell any of the major currencies on a more or less continuous basis. Unusually large transactions, however, will only be accomodated by market makers on more favorable terms. In such cases, foreign exchange brokers may be used as middlemen to find a taker or takers for the deal. Brokers (of which there are four major firms and a handful of smaller ones) do not trade on their own account, but specialize in setting up large foreign exchange transactions in return for a commission (typically 0.03 cents or less on the sterling spread). In April 1983, 56 percent of spot transactions by value involving banks in the United States were channeled through brokers.[4] If all interbank transactions are included, the figure rises to 59 percent.

Most small banks and local offices of major banks do not deal directly in the interbank foreign exchange market. Rather they typically will have a credit line with a large bank or their head office. Transactions will thus involve an extra step (see figure 1). The customer deals with a local bank, which in turn deals with a major bank or head office. The interbank foreign exchange market exists between the major banks either directly or indirectly via a broker.

Futures and Option Markets for Foreign Exchange

Until very recently, the interbank market was the only channel through which foreign exchange transactions took place. The past decade has produced major innovations in foreign exchange trading. On May 16, 1972, the International Money Market (IMM) opened under the auspices of the Chicago Mercantile Exchange. One novel feature of the IMM is that it provides a trading floor on which deals are struck by brokers face to face, rather than over telephone lines. The most significant difference

---

[4] See Federal Reserve Bank of New York (1983).

Figure 1   **Structure of Foreign Exchange Markets**

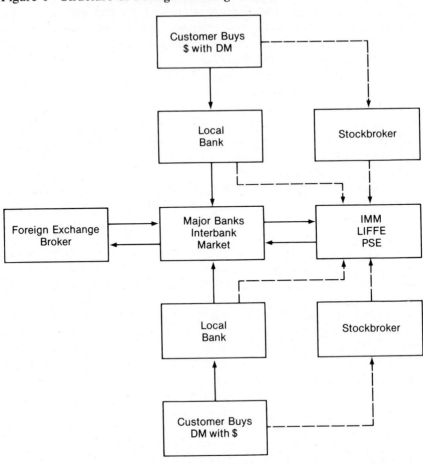

Note: The International Money Market (IMM) Chicago trades foreign exchange futures and DM futures options. The London International Financial Futures Exchange (LIFFE) trades foreign exchange futures. The Philadelphia Stock Exchange (PSE) trades foreign currency options.

between the IMM and the interbank market, however, is that trading on the IMM is in futures contracts for foreign exchange, the typical business being contracts for delivery on the third Wednesday of March, June, September or December. Activity at the IMM has expanded greatly since its opening. For example, during 1972, 144,336 contracts were traded; the figure for 1981 was 6,121,932.

There is an important distinction between "forward" transactions and "futures" contracts. The former are individual agreements between two parties, say, a bank and customer. The latter is a contract traded on an organized market of a standard size and settlement date, which is resalable at the market price up to the close of trading in the contract. These organized markets are discussed more fully below.

While the major banks conduct foreign exchange deals in large denominations, the IMM trading is done in contracts of standard size which are fairly small. Examples of the standard contracts at present are £25,000; DM125,000; Canadian $100,000. These are actually smaller today than in the early days of the IMM.

Further, unlike prices on the interbank market, price movements in any single day are subject to specific limits at the IMM. For example, for sterling futures, prices are not allowed to vary more than $.0500 away from the previous day's settlement price; this limit is expanded if it is reached in the same direction for two successive days. The limit does not apply on the last day a contract is traded.

Unlike the interbank market, parties to a foreign exchange contract at the IMM typically do not know each other. Default risk, however, is minor because contracts are guaranteed by the exchange itself. To minimize the cost of this guarantee, the exchange insists upon "margin requirements" to cover fluctuations in the value of a contract. This means that an individual or firm buying a futures contract would, in effect, place a deposit equal to about 4 percent of the value of the contract.[5]

Perhaps the major limitation of the IMM from the point of view of importers or exporters is that contracts cover only eight currencies — those of Britain, Canada, West Germany, Switzerland, Japan, Mexico, France and the Netherlands — and they are specified in standard sizes for particular dates. Only by chance will these conform exactly to the needs of importers and exporters. Large firms and financial institutions will find the market useful, however, if they have a fairly continuous stream of payments and receipts in the traded foreign currencies. Although contracts have a specified standard date, they offer a fairly flexible method of avoiding exchange rate risk because they are marketable continuously.

A major economic advantage of the IMM for nonbank customers is its low transaction cost. Though the brokerage cost of a contract will vary, a "round trip" (that is, one buy and one sell) costs as little as $15. This is only .04 percent of the value of a sterling contract and less for some of the larger contracts. Of course, such costs are high compared with the interbank market, where the brokerage cost on DM 1 million would be about $6.25 (the equivalent-valued eight futures contracts would cost $60 in brokerage, taking $7.50 per single deal). They are low, however, compared with those in the retail market, where the spread may involve a cost of up to 2.5 percent or 3 percent per transaction.

A market similar to the IMM, the London International Financial Futures Exchange (LIFFE), opened in September 1982. On LIFFE, futures are traded in sterling, deutschemarks, Swiss francs and yen in identical bundles to those sold on the IMM. In its first year, the foreign exchange business of LIFFE did not take off in a big way. The major

---

[5] A bank may also insist upon some minimum deposit to cover a forward contract, though there is no firm rule.

provider of exchange rate risk coverage for business continues to be the bank network. Less than 5 percent of such cover is provided by markets such as IMM and LIFFE at present.

An entirely new feature of foreign exchange markets that has arisen in the 1980s is the existence of option markets.[6] The Philadelphia Exchange was the first to introduce foreign exchange options. These are in five currencies (deutschemark, sterling, Swiss franc, yen and Canadian dollar). Trades are conducted in standard bundles half the size of the IMM futures contracts. The IMM introduced an options market in German marks on January 24, 1984; this market trades options on futures contracts whereas the Philadelphia options are for spot currencies.

Futures and options prices for foreign exchange are published daily in the financial press. Table 3 shows prices for February 14, 1984, as displayed in the *Wall Street Journal* on the following day. Futures prices on the IMM are presented for five currencies (left-hand column). There are five contracts quoted for each currency: March, June, September, December and March 1985. For each contract, opening and last settlement (settle) prices, the range over the day, the change from the previous day, the range over the life of the contract and the number of contracts outstanding with the exchange (open interest) are listed.

Consider the March and June DM futures. March futures opened at $.3653 per mark and closed at $.3706 per mark. June opened at $.3698 per mark and closed at $.3746 per mark. Turn now to the Chicago Mercantile Exchange (IMM) futures options (center column). These are options on the futures contracts just discussed (see inset for explanation of options). Thus, the line labeled "Futures" lists the settle prices of the March and June futures as above.

Let us look at the call options. These are rights to buy DM futures at specified prices—the strike price. For example, take the call option at strike price 35. This means that one can purchase an option to buy DM 125,000 March futures up to the March settlement date for $.3500 per mark. This option will cost 2.05 cents per mark, or $2,562.50, plus brokerage fees. The June option to buy June futures DM at $.3500 per mark will cost 2.46 cents per mark, or $3,075.00, plus brokerage fees. The March call option at strike price $.3900 per mark costs only 0.01 cents per mark or $12.50. These price differences indicate that the market expects the dollar price of the mark to exceed $.3500, but not to rise substantially above $.3900.

Notice that when you exercise a futures call option you buy the relevant futures contract but only fulfill that futures contract at maturity. In contrast, the Philadelphia foreign currency options (right column) are options to buy foreign exchange (spot) itself rather than futures. So, when a call option is exercised, foreign currency is obtained immediately.

The only difference in presentation of the currency option prices as compared with the futures options is that, in the former, the spot

---

[6] For a discussion of options in commodities, see Belongia (1983).

Table 3   Futures and Options Markets

Futures Prices

Tuesday, February 14, 1984
Open Interest Reflects Previous Trading Day.

	Open	High	Low	Settle	Change	Lifetime High	Low	Open Interest
BRITISH POUND (IMM) — 25,000 pounds; $ per pound								
Mar	1.4150	1.4400	1.4150	1.4370 +	.0170	1.6010	1.3930	17,694
June	1.4175	1.4435	1.4175	1.4395 +	.0170	1.5520	1.3950	3,251
Sept	1.4285	1.4410	1.4220	1.4410 +	.0160	1.5240	1.3980	157
Dec	1.4280	1.4435	1.4245	1.4435 +	.0160	1.4650	1.3990	75
Mar85	1.4280	1.4460	1.4270	1.4470 +	.0170	1.4625	1.4000	65

Est vol 10,651; vol Mon 1,987; open int 21,242 + 78

	Open	High	Low	Settle	Change	Lifetime High	Low	Open Interest
CANADIAN DOLLAR (IMM) — 100,000 dlrs.; $ per Can $								
Mar	.8010	.8024	.8010	.8020	. . . .	.8169	.7979	4,033
June	.8014	.8029	.8013	.8023	. . . .	.8168	.7983	740
Sept	. . . .	. . . .		.8026	. . . .	.8147	.7988	312
Dec	.8021	.8031	.8021	.8029	. . . .	.8040	.8021	152
Mar85	.8035	.8035	.8035	.8032	. . . .	.8035	.8023	50

Est vol 1,087; vol Mon 535; open int 5,287, −103.

	Open	High	Low	Settle	Change	Lifetime High	Low	Open Interest
JAPANESE YEN (IMM) 12.5 million yen; $ per yen (.00)								
Mar	.4276	.4297	.4276	.4294 +	.0011	.4396	.4125	25,730
June	.4315	.4337	.4312	.4334 +	.0011	.4435	.4180	3,908
Sept	.4354	.4375	.4354	.4374 +	.0012	.4450	.4354	974
Dec	.4416	.4420	.4400	.4415 +	.0012	.4493	.4395	271

Est vol 9,133; vol Mon 3,306; open int 30,883, +534.

	Open	High	Low	Settle	Change	Lifetime High	Low	Open Interest
SWISS FRANC (IMM) — 125,000 francs; $ per franc								
Mar	.4495	.4556	.4486	.4549 +	.0047	.5230	.4470	24,164
June	.4564	.4629	.4557	.4622 +	.0051	.5045	.4536	3,165
Sept	.4632	.4692	.4632	.4688 +	.0052	.5020	.4598	153
Dec	.4705	.4780	.4705	.4747 +	.0049	.4880	.4665	71
Mar85	. . . .	. . . .		.4830 +	.0050	.4840	.4755	5

Est vol 30,610; vol Mon 8,466; open int 27,558, +296.

	Open	High	Low	Settle	Change	Lifetime High	Low	Open Interest
W. GERMAN MARK (IMM)—125,000 marks; $ per mark								
Mar	.3653	.3713	.3650	.3706 +	.0036	.4100	.3537	30,974
June	.3698	.3754	.3688	.3746 +	.0037	.4002	.3568	4,911
Sept	.3743	.3790	.3743	.3780 +	.0034	.4030	.3602	362
Dec	.3780	.3825	.3780	.3825 +	.0043	.3825	.3640	204
Mar85	. . . .	. . . .		.3838 +	.0035	.3699	.3699	1

Est vol 30,248; vol Mon 9,045; open int 36,452, +680.

exchange rate is listed for comparison rather than the futures price. Thus, on the Philadelphia exchange, call options on March DM 62,500 at strike price $.3500 per mark cost 1.99 cents per mark or $1,243.75, plus brokerage. Brokerage fees here would be of the same order as on the IMM, about $16 per transaction round trip, per contract.

Table 3   Futures and Options Markets

Futures Options
Chicago Mercantile Exchange
W. GERMAN MARK—125,000 marks; cents per mark

Strike Price	Calls—Settle Mar	Calls—Settle Jun	Puts—Settle Mar	Puts—Settle Jun
34	. . . .	. . . .	0.01	0.01
35	2.05	2.46	0.01	0.09
36	1.11	1.66	0.06	0.25
37	0.38	1.00	0.33	0.57
38	0.10	0.54	1.00	1.02
39	0.01	0.27	. . . .	. . . .
Futures	.3706	.3746	. . . .	. . . .

Estimated total vol. 2,187.
Calls: Mon vol. 180: open int. 2,416.
Puts: Mon vol. 73: open int. 1,841.

Table 3   Futures and Options Markets

Foreign Currency Options
Philadelphia Exchange

Option & Strike Underlying Price		Calls—Last Mar	Jun	Sep	Puts—Last Mar	Jun	Sep
12,500 British Pounds–cents per unit.							
BPound	140	3.40	r	5.70	0.40	1.85	r
143.00	.145	0.70	2.40	r	3.40	r	r
50,000 Canadian Dollars–cents per unit.							
CDollar	. .80	r	r	0.68	r	r	r
62,500 West German Marks–cents per unit.							
DMark	. .34	2.67	r	r	r	r	r
36.88	. . .35	1.99	2.18	r	r	r	r
36.88	. . .36	1.04	1.59	r	0.05	0.35	r
36.88	. . .37	0.38	1.00	r	0.37	0.56	r
36.88	. . .38	0.10	0.62	0.85	r	r	r
36.88	. . .39	r	0.28	s	r	r	s
36.88	. . .40	0.01	0.11	s	r	r	s
6,250,000 Japanese Yen–100ths of a cent per unit.							
JYen	. . .42	0.95	1.49	2.04	r	r	r
42.75	. . .43	0.30	0.90	r	0.50	0.60	r
42.75	. . .44	0.04	0.45	0.99	r	r	r
62,500 Swiss Francs–cents per unit.							
SFranc	. .44	r	r	3.15	r	0.24	r
45.18	. . .45	0.65	r	r	0.26	r	r
45.18	. . .46	0.28	1.09	1.82	r	1.00	r
45.18	. . .47	0.06	r	r	r	r	r
45.18	. . .48	0.02	0.28	r	r	r	r

Total call vol. 2,271   Call open int. 37,349
Total put vol.   799   Put open int. 26,173
r—Not traded. s—No option offered. o—Old.
Last is premium (purchase price).

Source: *The Wall Street Journal*, February 15, 1984.

We have seen that there are several different markets for foreign exchange — spot, forward, futures, options on spot, options on futures. The channels through which these markets are formed are, however, fairly straightforward (see figure 1). The main channel is the interbank network, though for large interbank transactions, foreign exchange brokers may be used as middlemen.

Foreign Exchange Market Activities

Much foreign exchange market trading does not appear to be related to the simple basic purpose of allowing businesses to buy or sell foreign currency in order, say, to sell or purchase goods overseas. It is certainly easy to see the usefulness of the large range of foreign exchange transactions available through the interbank and organized markets (spot, forward, futures, options) to facilitate trade between nations. It is also clear that there is a useful role for foreign exchange brokers in helping to "make" the interbank market. There are several other activities, however, in foreign exchange markets that are less well understood and whose relevance is less obvious to people interested in understanding what these markets accomplish.

Foreign Exchange Options

An option is a contract specifying the right to buy or sell — in this case foreign exchange — within a specific period (American option) or at a specific date (European option). A call option confers the right to buy. A put option confers the right to sell. Since each of these options must have a buyer and a seller, there are four possible ways of trading a single option: buy a call, sell a call, buy a put, sell a put.

The buyer of an option has the right to undertake the contract specified but may choose not to do so if it turns out to be unprofitable. The seller of the option *must* fulfill the contract if the buyer desires. Clearly, the buyer must pay the seller some premium (the option price) for this privilege. An option that would be profitable to exercise at the current exchange rate is said to be "in the money." The price at which it is exercised is the "exercise" or "strike" price.

Consider a call option on £1000 (although options of this size are not presently available on organized exchanges, it is used to present a simple illustration of the principles involved). Suppose this costs $0.03 per pound or $30 and the exercise price is $1.50 per pound. The option expires in three months.

This means that the buyer has paid $30 for the right to buy
£1000 with dollars at a price of $1.50 per pound any time in the
next three months. If the current spot price of sterling is, say,
$1.45, the option is "out of the money" because sterling can be
bought cheaper on the spot market. However, if the spot price
were to rise to, say, $1.55, the option would be in the money. If
sold at that time, the option buyer would get a $50 return
(1000×$0.05), which would more than cover the cost of the
option ($50−$30=$20 profit). In contrast, a put option at the
same terms would be in the money at the current spot price of
$1.45, but out of the money at $1.55.

Figure 2 presents a diagrammatic illustration of how the
profitability of an option depends upon the relationship between the exercise price and the current spot price.[1] Figure 2a
illustrates the profit available from buying a call option at
exercise price A. At spot exchange rate A and anything lower,
the option will not be exercised so the loss will equal the price
of the option. At a spot exchange rate above a, the option is
sufficiently in the money to more than cover its cost. Between
A and a, the option is in the money but not by enough to cover
cost. The profit from *selling* a call could be illustrated by
reversing the + and − signs in figure 2a, or by flipping the
profit line above the horizontal axis.

Figure 2b illustrates the profit from buying a put option.
At spot exchange rates below a, the option with exercise price
A will show a profit.

Figure 2c illustrates the profit from a simultaneous purchase of a put and call at the same exercise price. This

---

[1] The pricing of options has been the subject of a large theoretical literature
with a major contribution being made by Black and Scholes (1973). The
Black-Scholes formula has been modified for foreign exchange options by
Garman and Kohlhagen (1983) [see also Giddy (1983)], but the Black-Scholes
formula is complex and beyond the scope of the present paper.

One simple relationship which is of interest may be called "option price
parity." This arises because arbitrage will ensure that the difference between a
call option price (per unit) and a put option price (per unit) at the same exercise
price will be equal to the present value of the difference between the exercise
price and the forward exchange rate at maturity of the options (if the options
are marketable, it will also hold for any date to maturity). The relationship may
be expressed:

$$C - P = \frac{F - E}{1 + r}$$

when C and P are the call and put option prices at exercise price E. F is the
forward exchange rate and r is the interest rate per period of the contracts.
This arises because the simultaneous buying of a call and selling of a put is
equivalent to buying currency forward at price E. The forward contract,
however, would be paid for at the end of the period, whereas the options are
transacted at the beginning. Hence, the forward contract has to be discounted
back to the present.

Figure 2   **Profit from Options**

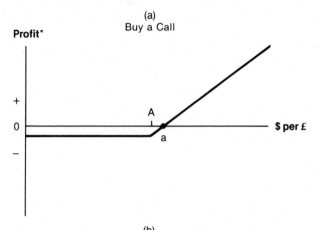

(a)
Buy a Call

Profit*

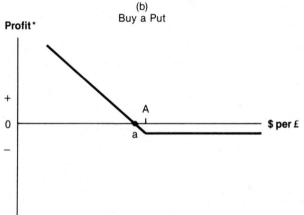

(b)
Buy a Put

Profit*

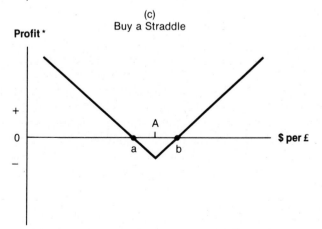

(c)
Buy a Straddle

Profit*

*Profit form exercise of option at current spot exchange rate.

* Profit from exercise of option at current spot exchange rate.

combination will show a profit at exercise price A if the spot price goes *either* above b or below a. It is known as a "straddle." The straddle is of special interest because it makes clear the role of options as a hedge against risk. The price of a straddle can be regarded as the market valuation of the variability of the exchange rate. That is, the buyer of the straddle will show a profit if the spot price moves from some central value (the exercise price) by more than plus or minus some known percentage. The seller of the straddle accepts that risk for a lump sum. More complicated "multiple strategies" are also possible.[2]

[2] See Giddy (1983).

Two major classes of activity will be discussed. First, the existence of a large number of foreign exchange markets in many locations creates opportunities to profit from "arbitrage." Second, there is implicitly a market in (foreign exchange) risk bearing. Those who wish to avoid foreign exchange risk (at a price) may do so. Those who accept the risk in expectation of profits are known as "speculators."

Triangular Arbitrage

Triangular arbitrage is the process that ensures that all exchange rates are mutually consistent. If, for example, one U.S. dollar exchanges for one Canadian dollar, and one Canadian dollar exchanges for one British pound, then the U.S. dollar-pound exchange rate should be one pound for one dollar. If it differs, then there is an opportunity for profit making. To see why this is so, suppose that you could purchase two U.S. dollars with one British pound. By first buying C$1 with U.S.$1, then purchasing £1 with C$1, and finally buying U.S.$2 with £1, you could double your money immediately. Clearly this opportunity will not last for long since it involves making large profits with certainty. The process of triangular arbitrage is exactly that of finding and exploiting profitable opportunities in such exchange rate inconsistencies. As a result of triangular arbitrage, such inconsistencies will be eliminated rapidly. Cross rates, however, will only be roughly consistent given the bid-ask spread associated with transaction costs.

In the past, the possibility of making profits from triangular arbitrage was greater as a result of the practice of expressing exchange rates in American terms in the United States and in European terms elsewhere. The adoption of standard practice has reduced the likelihood of inconsistencies.[7] Also, in recent years, such opportunities for profit making have been greatly reduced by high-speed, computerized information systems and the increased sophistication of the banks operating in the market.

Arbitrage of a slightly different kind results from price differences in different locations. This is "space" arbitrage. For example, if sterling were cheaper in London than in New York, it would be profitable to buy in London and sell in New York. Similarly, if prices in the interbank market differed from those at the IMM, it would be profitable to arbitrage between them. As a result of this activity, prices in different locations will be brought broadly into line.

Interest Arbitrage

Interest arbitrage is slightly different in nature from triangular or space arbitrage; however, the basic motive of finding and exploiting profitable opportunities still applies. There is no reason why interest rates denominated in different currencies should be equal. Interest rates are the cost of borrowing or the return to lending for a specific period of time. The relative price (exchange rate) of money may change over time so that the comparison of, say, a U.S. and a British interest rate requires some allowance for expected exchange rate changes. Thus, it will be not at all unusual to find interest rates denominated in dollars and interest rates denominated in, say, pounds being somewhat different. However, real returns on assets of similar quality should be the same if the exchange rate risk is covered or hedged in the forward market. Were this not true, it would be possible to borrow in one currency and lend in another at a profit with no exchange risk.

Suppose we lend one dollar for a year in the United States at an interest rate of r_{us}. The amount accumulated at the end of the year per dollar lent will be $1+r_{us}$ (capital plus interest). If, instead of making dollar loans, we converted them into pounds and lent them in the United Kingdom at the rate r_{uk}, the amount of pounds we would have for each original dollar at the end of the year would be $S(1+r_{uk})$, where S is the spot exchange rate (in pounds per dollar) at the beginning of the period. At the outset, it is not known if $1+r_{us}$ dollars is going to be worth more than $S(1+r_{uk})$ pounds in a year's time because the spot exchange rate in a year's time is unknown. This uncertainty can be avoided by selling the pounds forward into dollars. Then the relative value of the two loans would no longer depend on what subsequently happens to the spot exchange rate. By doing this, we end up with $S_{/F}(1+r_{uk})$ dollars per original dollar invested. This is known as the "covered," or hedged, return on pounds.

---

[7] All except U.K. and Irish exchange rates are expressed in American terms. Futures and options contracts are expressed in European terms.

Since the covered return in our example is denominated in dollars, it can reasonably be compared with the U.S. interest rate. If these returns are very different, investors will move funds where the return is highest on a covered basis. This process is interest arbitrage. It is assumed that the assets involved are equally safe and, because the returns are covered, all exchange risk is avoided. Of course, if funds do move in large volume between assets or between financial centers, then interest rates and the exchange rates (spot and forward) will change in predictable ways. Funds will continue to flow between countries until there is no extra profit to be made from interest arbitrage. This will occur when the returns on both dollar- and sterling-denominated assets are equal, that is, when

(1) $(1+r_{us}) = S/F(1+r_{uk})$.

This result is known as covered interest parity. It holds more or less exactly, subject only to a margin due to transaction costs, so long as the appropriate dollar and sterling interest rates are compared.[8]

Speculation

Arbitrage in the foreign exchange markets involves little or no risk since transactions can be completed rapidly. An alternative source of profit is available from outguessing other market participants as to what future exchange rates will be. This is called speculation. Although any foreign exchange transaction that is not entirely hedged forward has a speculative element, only deliberate speculation for profit is discussed here.

Until recently, the main foreign exchange speculators were the foreign exchange departments of banks, with a lesser role being played by portfolio managers of other financial institutions and international corporations. The IMM, however, has made it much easier for individuals and smaller businesses to speculate. A high proportion of IMM transactions appears to be speculative in the sense that only about 5 percent of contracts lead to ultimate delivery of foreign exchange. This means that most of the activity involves the buying and selling of a contract *at different times* and possibly different prices prior to maturity. It is possible, however, that buying and selling of contracts before maturity would arise out of a strategy to reduce risk. So it is not possible to say that all such activity is speculative.

Speculation is important for the efficient working of foreign exchange markets. It is a form of arbitrage that occurs across time rather

---

[8] Since there are many different interest rates, it obviously cannot hold for all of them. Where (1) does hold is if the interest rates chosen are eurocurrency deposit rates of the same duration. In other words, if for r_{us} we take, say, the three-month eurodollar deposit rate in Paris and for r_{uk} we take the three-month eurosterling deposit rate in Paris, then (1) will hold just about exactly. Indeed, if we took the interest rate and exchange rate quotes all from the same bank, it would be remarkable if (1) did not hold. Otherwise the bank would be offering to pay you to borrow from it and lend straight back! That is, the price of borrowing would be less than the covered return on lending. A margin between borrowing and lending rates, of course, will make this even less likely so that in reality you would lose.

than across space or between markets at the same time. Just as arbitrage increases the efficiency of markets by keeping prices consistent, so speculation increases the efficiency of forward, futures and options markets by keeping those markets liquid. Those who wish to avoid foreign exchange risk may thereby do so in a well-developed market. Without speculators, risk avoidance in foreign exchange markets would be more difficult and, in many cases, impossible.[9]

Covered Interest Parity: An Example

The following interest rate and exchange rate quotations are taken from the *London Financial Times* of September 8, 1983 (table 1).

Closing Exchange Rate: dollars per pound	Spot	3-Month Forward
	1.4910–1.4920	.17–.22 discount

Interest Rates: 3-Month Offer Rate	Eurosterling	Eurodollar
	$9^{13}/_{16}$	$10^{1}/_{4}$

The interest rate on the three-month eurodollar deposit is a little higher (.7 percent) than that on an eurosterling deposit. If the exhange rate remains unchanged, it would be better to hold dollars; if the exchange rate falls, the eurosterling deposit would be preferable. Suppose you decide to cover the exchange risk by selling the dollars forward into pounds. Let us compare the return to holding a sterling deposit with the return to holding a dollar deposit sold forward into sterling (assuming that you start with sterling).

Two important points need to be clarified about the above data. First, the interest rates are annualized so they are not what would actually be earned over a three-month period. For example, the three-month rate equivalent to an annual rate of $10^{1}/_{4}$ percent is 2.47 percent.

Second, the forward exchange rates need some explanation. The dollar is at a discount against sterling. This means the forward dollar buys less sterling. So we have to *add* the discount onto the spot price to get the forward price (because the price is the number of dollars per pound, not the reverse).

---

[9] This is not to say that all speculative activity is necessarily beneficial.

Notice also that the discount is measured in fractions of a cent, not fractions of a dollar! So the bid-ask spread on the forward rate would be 1.4927−1.4942.

Now let us see if we would do better to invest in a three-month eurosterling deposit or a three-month eurodollar deposit where the dollars to be received were sold forward into sterling. The return per £100 invested in eurosterling is £2.369 (annual interest rate of $9^{13}\!/_{16}$), whereas the return on a covered eurodollar deposit is

$$£2.251 = (100 \times \frac{1.4910}{1.4942} \, 1.0247) - 100.$$

Thus, we could not make a profit out of covered interest arbitrage. Despite the fact that dollar interest rates are higher, the discount on forward dollars in the forward market means they buy fewer forward pounds. As a result, there is no benefit to the operation. Transaction costs for most individuals would be even greater than those above as they would face a larger bid-ask spread than that quoted on the interbank market.

Consequently, there is no benefit for the typical investor from making a covered or hedged eurocurrency deposit. The return will be at least as high on a deposit in the currency in which you start and wish to end up. That is, if you have dollars and wish to end up with dollars, make a eurodollar deposit. If you have sterling and wish to end up with sterling, make a eurosterling deposit. If you have sterling and wish to end up in dollars, there is likely to be little or no difference between holding a eurosterling deposit sold forward into dollars or buying dollars spot and holding a eurodollar deposit. Of course, if you hold an "uncovered" deposit and exchange rates subsequently change, the result will be very different.

Risk Reduction

Speculation clearly involves a shifting of risk from one party to another. For example, if a bank buys forward foreign exchange from a customer, it increases its exposure to risk while the customer reduces his. However, there is not a fixed amount of risk that has to be "shared out." Some strategies may involve a net reduction of risk all around.

As a general rule, financial institutions (or other firms), operating in a variety of currencies, will try to minimize the risk of losses due to unexpected exchange rate changes. One simple way to do this is to ensure that assets and liabilities denominated in each operating currency are equal. This is known as "matching." For example, a bank that sells sterling forward to a customer may simultaneously buy sterling forward. In this event, the bank is exposed to zero exchange rate risk.

Banks often use "swaps" to close gaps in the maturity structure of their assets and liabilities in a currency. This involves the simultaneous purchase and sale of a currency for *different* maturity dates. In April 1983, 33 percent of U.S. banks' foreign exchange turnover involved swaps as compared with 63 percent spot contracts and only 4 percent outright forward contracts.[10]

Suppose a bank has sold DM to a customer three months forward and bought the same amount of DM from a different customer six months forward. There are two ways in which the bank could achieve zero foreign exchange risk exposure. It could either undertake two separate offsetting forward transactions, or it could set up a single swap with another bank that has the opposite mismatch of dollar-DM flows whereby it receives DM in exchange for dollars in three months and receives back dollars in exchange for DM in six months. Once the swap is set up, the bank's net profits are protected against subsequent changes in spot exchange rates during the next six months.

Within the limits imposed by the nature of the contracts, a similar effect can be achieved by an appropriate portfolio of futures contracts on the IMM. Thus, a bank would buy and sell futures contracts so as to match closely its forward commitments to customers. In reality, banks will use a combination of methods to reduce foreign exchange risk.

Markets that permit banks, firms and individuals to hedge foreign exchange risk are essential in times of fluctuating exchange rates. This is especially important for banks if they are to be able to provide efficient foreign exchange services for their customers. In the absence of markets that permit foreign exchange risk hedging, the cost and uncertainty of international transactions would be greatly increased, and international specialization and trade would be greatly reduced.

Conclusion

The foreign exchange markets are complex and, for the outsider, hard to comprehend. The primary function of these markets is straightforward. It is to facilitate international transactions related to trade, travel or investment. Foreign exchange markets can now accommodate a large range of current and forward transactions.

Given the variability of exchange rates, it is important for banks and firms operating in foreign currencies to be able to reduce exchange rate risk whenever possible. Some risk reduction is achieved by interbank swaps, but some is also taken up by speculation. Arbitrage and speculation both increase the efficiency of spot and forward foreign exchange

[10] See Federal Reserve Bank of New York (1983).

Why Is the Dollar the "Money" of Foreign Exchange Markets?

One interesting aspect of the organization of the foreign exchange markets is that the "money" used in these markets is generally the U.S. dollar. This is generally true for spot markets and universally true for forward markets. "Cross-markets" between many currencies are very thin, and future cross markets are virtually nonexistent. For example, the bulk of foreign exchange trading between £s and cruzeiro will involve dollar-£ and dollar-cruzeiro transactions instead of direct £-cruzeiro trading. The only exception to this is the transactions involving the major Organization for Economic Cooperation and Development (OECD) currencies, especially within Europe. Of the $702.5 billion turnover in foreign exchange reported by U.S. banks in April 1983, only $1.5 billion did not involve U.S. dollars.

There are two explanations for this special role of the dollar in foreign exchange markets. Both rely upon the fact that transaction costs are likely to be lower if the dollar is used as a medium. Krugman shows that the clearing of foreign exchange markets requires some "intermediary" currency.[1] Even if every country is in payments balance vis-a-vis the rest of the world, it will not necessarily be in bilateral balance with each other country. Because some currency has to be used to cover this residual finance, it is natural to choose the currency that has the lowest transaction costs. Chrystal shows there are economic reasons why cross-markets between many currencies do not exist.[2] It typically will be easier and cheaper to set up a deal in two steps via the dollar than in a single step (cruzeiro-dollar, dollar-drachma rather than cruzeiro-drachma). This is because these cross-markets, if they existed, would be fairly thin and hence relatively costly for such transactions. The two markets with the dollar, on the other hand, are well developed.

These analyses refer to the role of the dollar in the interbank market. In the development of the trading places such as the IMM in Chicago and LIFFE in London to date, it is also true that all currency futures are traded against the dollar.

---

[1] See Krugman (1980).

[2] See Chrystal (1982).

markets and have enabled foreign exchange markets to achieve a high level of efficiency. Without the successful operation of these markets, the obstacles to international trade and investment would be substantial and the world would be a poorer place.

Glossary

American option—an option that can be exercised any time up to maturity.

American terms—an exchange rate expressed as number of currency units per dollar.

arbitrage—the simultaneous purchase and sale of currency in separate markets for a profit arising from a price discrepancy between the markets.

bid-ask spread—the difference between the buying (bid) and selling (ask) price.

covered interest arbitrage—buying a country's currency spot, investing for a period, and selling the proceeds forward in order to make a net profit due to the higher interest rate in that country. This act involves ''hedging'' because it guarantees a covered return without risk. The opportunities to profit in this way seldom arise because covered interest differentials are normally close to zero.

covered interest parity—the gap between interest rates in foreign and domestic currencies will be matched by the forward exchange rate differential, such that the ''covered'' interest rate differential will be close to zero.

eurodollar deposits—bank deposits, generally bearing interest and made for a specific time period, that are denominated in dollars but are in banks outside the United States. Similarly, eurosterling deposits would be denominated in sterling but outside the United Kingdom.

European option—an option that can be exercised only on a specified date.

European terms—an exchange rate expressed as number of dollars per currency unit.

floating exchange rate—an exchange rate that is allowed to adjust freely to the supply of and demand for foreign exchange.

foreign exchange speculation—the act of taking a net position in a foreign currency with the intention of making a profit from exchange rate changes.

forward exchange rate—the price of foreign currency for delivery at a future date agreed to by a contract today.

futures market—a market in which contracts are traded to buy or sell a standard amount of currency in the future at a particular price.

hedging—or covering exchange risk, means that foreign currency is sold forward into local currency so that its value is not affected by subsequent exchange rate changes. Say an exporter knows he will be paid £10,000 in two months. He can wait until he gets the money and convert it into dollars at whatever the spot rate turns out to be. This outcome is uncertain as the spot rate may change. Alternatively, he can sell £10,000 two months forward at today's two-month forward price. Suppose this is $1.5 per £. In two months, he will receive £10,000, fulfill his forward contract and receive $15,000. This export contract has been hedged or covered in the forward market.

matching—equating assets and liabilities denominated in each currency so that losses due to foreign exchange rate changes are minimized.

options market—a market in which contracts are traded that gives a purchaser the right but no obligation to buy (call) or to sell (put) a currency in the future at a given price.

spot exchange rate—the price paid to exchange currencies for immediate delivery (two business days in the interbank market, or over the counter in the retail and travelers check market).

swap—the simultaneous purchase and sale of a currency for different maturity dates that closes the gaps in the maturity structure of assets and liabilities in a currency.

References

Belongia, Michael T. "Commodity Options: A New Risk Management Tool for Agriculture Markets," this *Review* (June/July 1983), pp. 5–15.

Black, Fisher, and Myron Scholes. "The Pricing of Options and Corporate Liabilities," *Journal of Political Economy* (May/June 1973), pp. 637–54.

Chrystal, K. Alec. "On the Theory of International Money" (paper presented to U.K. International Economics Study Group Conference, September 1982, Sussex, England). Forthcoming in J. Black and G.S. Dorrance, eds., *Problems of International Finance* (London: Macmillan, 1984).

Dufey, Gunter, and Ian H. Giddy. *The International Money Market* (Prentice-Hall, 1978).

Federal Reserve Bank of New York. "Summary of Results of U.S. Foreign Exchange Market Turnover Survey Conducted in April 1983" (September 8, 1983).

Garman, Mark B., and Steven W. Kohlhagen. "Foreign Currency Option Values," *Journal of International Money and Finance* (December 1983), pp. 231–37.

Giddy, Ian H. "Foreign Exchange Options," *Journal of Futures Markets* (Summer 1983), pp. 143–66.

Krugman, Paul. "Vehicle Currencies and the Structure of International Exchange," *Journal of Money, Credit and Banking* (August 1980), pp. 513–26.

Kubarych, Roger M. *Foreign Exchange Markets in the United States.* (Federal Reserve Bank of New York, 1983).

McKinnon, Ronald I. *Money in International Exchange: The Convertible Currency System* (Oxford University Press, 1979).

Questions

1. What are foreign exchange markets?

2. Describe each of the following three foreign exchange markets: spot market, forward market, and futures market.

3. In European terms, what was the spot rate of French francs on September 7, 1983? What was the spot rate in American terms?

4. What is the currency unit of each of the following countries: Thailand, Malaysia, Ireland, Ecuador, and Israel?

5.   What is the currency unit of each of the following countries: Taiwan, Singapore, New Zealand, Hong Kong, Canada, Australia, and the United States? Why is the United States *not* listed like other countries in foreign exchange rate quotations?

6.   Say that you plan to travel in Canada and you look in the *Wall Street Journal* to discover the price of the Canadian dollar. What is the relationship between the price that you will actually pay and the price quoted in the *Wall Street Journal?* Explain the reason for this difference.

7.   Interpret the quotations on the West German mark that appeared in the *Wall Street Journal,* February 15, 1984 (see Table 3):
      a. June futures contract for 125,000 marks.
      b. June futures option (call and put) for 125,000 marks, with a strike price of $0.35 per mark.
      c. June option (call and put) on 62,500 marks, with a strike price of $0.35 per mark.

8.   Define triangular arbitrage and space arbitrage.

9.   Assume that you are considering the following two investment strategies:
      Strategy S: Make a 3-month eurosterling deposit and earn 2.7 percent for the period.
      Strategy D: Make a 3-month eurodollar deposit and earn 3.0 percent for the period; immediately sell the dollars forward into pounds sterling. The spot rate is $1.50 per pound, and the 3-month forward rate is $1.53 per pound.
      Which investment strategy should you select? Support your answer with calculations.

Some Aspects of Japanese Corporate Finance

James E. Hodder and Adrian E. Tschoegl

I. Introduction

In this paper, we attempt to blend economic theory with an understanding of the historical context and regulation of Japanese financial markets, particularly during the 1950s and 1960s. The historical and regulatory context is critical since it represents the framework within which the economic forces operated. That is, we are interested in examining how a particular structure, characterized by controlled interest rates, segmentation of markets and functions, and limited entry, gave rise in understandable ways to distinctive corporate financial practices.

There have been a number of recent publications that attempt to describe and explain the Japanese corporate financial system.[1] Perhaps the most discussed topics are the relatively high degree of financial leverage for the "typical" Japanese firm and the predominance of bank financing for the external funding of large corporations. There also has been discussion of such apparent peculiarities in the equity markets as the issue of shares at a par value of 50 yen when their market value is 1,000 yen or more, as well as the extensive cross holdings of shares between corporations. The role of a firm's "main bank" as not only lender and financial advisor, but, in some cases, exercising management control, also has received attention.

Before we address these issues, we wish to make two points. First, the structure of the Japanese financial system changed radically after World War II as a consequence of legislation introduced by the Occupation Authorities and the need to rebuild. For example, with respect to

James E. Hodder and Adrian E. Tschoegl, "Some Aspects of Japanese Corporate Finance," *Journal of Financial and Quantitative Analysis* (June 1985) Vol. 20, No. 2: 173–191. Reprinted with permission.

At the time of this writing, James E. Hodder was affiliated with Stanford University and Adrian E. Tschoegl was affiliated with the University of Michigan.

The authors would like to thank John G. McDonald, Tom Roehl, and Toshiharu Takahashi for their helpful comments on previous drafts.

[1] See, for example, [13], [8], [39], [22], [23], and [16].

high debt to equity ratios and heavy dependence on bank loans, Naka-mura [26] cites evidence that equity comprised 67 percent of gross capital (total assets) for manufacturing industries in 1935. In a related vein, Kurosawa [22] provides figures that external funding by Japanese corporations during the 1931–1936 period was only 4 percent from bank loans, with 96 percent through stocks and industrial bonds.

Second, the Japanese financial system has been evolving continuously since the war. Thus, to speak of "traditional" practices, even if one restricts the term to the postwar era, is to freeze a stylization of a much more complex reality.

In Section II, we begin by describing the debt markets, both bond and bank, and endeavor to explain firms' apparent preference for the latter. Section III discusses some characteristics of the equity market, dividend practice, and par value issues. Section IV addresses the economic rationale for a highly levered capital structure in light of current financial theory, as well as the historic and regulatory context in Japan. Section V focuses on the main bank phenomenon. Section VI examines our findings in light of the substantial deregulation of Japanese financial markets since 1970 and the slower economic growth since the "oil shock" of 1973 and provides some concluding comments.

II. Debt Markets

The vast majority of borrowing by major Japanese corporations is from private financial institutions (banks and insurance companies) rather than through bonds or commercial paper (see Table 1).

The Japanese bond market is dominated by government issues (including local and government guaranteed), which comprise roughly 75 percent of the outstanding amount. Corporate bonds (including convertibles) account for only around 6.5 percent of the total outstanding bonds of nonfinancial corporations. During 1980–1983, nonconvertible corporate bonds were less than 5 percent of total public bond offerings. Of that small fraction, three-quarters were issued by electric power companies. If we set aside the electric power companies as something of a special case and exclude convertibles on the grounds that they are primarily an equity-raising mechanism, then bonds all but disappear from the balance sheets of large Japanese industrial corporations.

A key reason for the post-World War II preponderance of bank over bond debt was the government's policy of keeping bond interest rates low. As a result, there was little public demand for bonds. In fact, after the oil shock of 1973–1974, the city banks were required to buy government bonds at par. The government essentially preempted the bond market for itself, plus public corporations, the railways, and utilities. Furthermore, corporate bond issues have been strictly controlled by a group composed of underwriters and those banks that act as agents for bond issues. Because bonds are discountable at the Bank of Japan,

Table 1   **Net Supply of Industrial Funds by Source (Percentage)**

Year	Sale of Stocks & Shares	Industrial Bonds	Borrowing from Private Financial Institutions	Borrowing from Gov't. Institutions
1950	6.2	8.5	72.6	12.7
1955	14.1	3.9	68.9	13.0
1960	16.1	5.2	71.2	7.5
1965	5.3	4.4	81.4	8.9
1970	7.9	2.8	81.2	8.0
1972	5.7	1.8	86.8	5.7
1973	5.4	3.6	82.8	8.1
1974	5.8	3.3	79.6	11.3
1975	6.6	6.7	74.9	11.8
1976	4.8	3.6	80.2	11.4
1977	7.1	4.5	75.2	13.2
1978	8.0	5.2	73.0	13.8
1979	8.5	5.7	69.3	16.5
1980	7.4	2.9	77.0	12.7
1981	9.1	4.5	72.8	13.6
1982	8.9	2.8	78.1	10.2

Source: The Bank of Japan, *Economic Statistics Annual.*

there was a further reason to insure that issued bonds were of high quality. In fact, the Bank of Japan and the Ministry of Finance monitored and occasionally exercised control over the selection of corporations qualified to issue bonds, the issuing terms, and even the total monthly amount of new issues [15].

Of the corporate bonds that were issued, a proportion ended up in the portfolios of the major banks. These could afford to hold the bonds of their loan customers because they would use compensating balances to raise the effective rate [34].

There were several other legal and institutional restrictions on the ability of corporations to issue domestic debt, which also inhibited development of the corporate bond market. The Commercial Code prohibited corporations from issuing bonds in excess of stated capital and reserve funds [15]. Until 1979, Japanese corporate bonds were all issued on a secured basis, typically with the main bank acting as trustee. The issuing criteria for unsecured bonds are rather stringent, but are less so for convertibles than for straight debt. These rules are being relaxed somewhat, but the requirements as of December 1983 still make issuing unsecured bonds difficult for all but the largest and most credit-worthy companies [19]. Apparently the restrictions under the Commercial Code were eased recently at a time when corporations were reducing their debt (and hence were less dependent on the goodwill of their banks) and when monetary conditions were easier [15]. Nevertheless, the rationing of corporate access to the bond market remains an important explanatory factor in the development of Japanese corporate financial policy [31].

A second reason for the preponderance of bank over bond debt has to do with the relative newness of Japanese companies after World War II. The Occupation Authorities broke up the pre-war zaibatsu (holding companies), dismissed all the senior management, largely dispossessed the original owners, and redistributed the shares fairly widely. These measures, together with the physical destruction of the war, insured that the companies that emerged, while carrying old names, were, to a significant degree, new organizations.

Diamond [11], [12] argues that new companies that do not yet have a reputation will prefer to issue their debt via intermediaries rather than in arms-length markets. They find it cheaper to purchase the delegated monitoring services of intermediaries than to pay a premium in bond markets for the fact that lenders cannot adequately observe and control the borrowers' decisions. Thus, not only were firms rationed out of the bond markets, but, at least in the early years, they might have encountered reputational difficulties when seeking bond financing.

The debt markets in Japan are highly segmented, both from international markets and internally. This isolation of the Japanese markets from the international ones was an important factor in sustaining the repression of the domestic ones. Within each segment domestically, the number of actors is limited and there has been little or no entry since the early 1950s. As we discuss in Section V, this structure has had important consequences for the control of lending risks.

Until recently, the ability of Japanese firms to borrow from foreign lenders was heavily regulated. Prior to the amended Foreign Exchange and Foreign Trade Control Law of 1980, overseas borrowing by Japanese residents required prior approval by the Ministry of Finance (MOF). Although a few large corporations received approval for foreign bond issues in the 1960s, such issues were a negligible aggregate funding source until the mid-1970s.

Similarly, the access of foreign banks to the Japanese markets was strictly controlled. A few foreign banks reestablished branches after the war, but further entry was essentially precluded until approximately 1969.[2] Even now, the relative position of foreign banks is very small. At the end of 1983, they accounted for only about 3 percent of total bank lending in Japan. For all practical purposes, foreign sources provided negligible debt or equity capital during the rapid growth phase (1950–1973) of Japanese industry.

Domestically, the number of major lenders to large businesses is also limited. Excluding the government agencies, there are the 13 City Banks, 3 Long-Term Credit Banks, and 7 Trust Banks as well as the large life insurance companies. Among the 21 domestic life insurance compa-

---

[2] See [30] for a discussion of this situation.

nies at the end of 1980, the top three (Nippon, Dai-Ichi, and Sumitomo) controlled 50 percent of total assets while the top eight controlled 82 percent. The nonlife insurance companies also lend to large business but are not a significant fraction of the total. The 63 Regional Banks generally focus on loans to smaller firms and individuals. Regional Banks represented 28 percent of bank loans outstanding at the end of 1983; however, given the focus of their lending, they should be a much smaller fraction of total lending to large corporations—perhaps 10 percent of the total. In summary, perhaps 90 percent or more of private lending to large industrial firms is controlled by 25 to 30 institutions.

In practice, the number of key lending institutions has been even smaller than the 25 to 30 indicated above. Realistically, the top 6 to 8 City Banks plus the Industrial Bank of Japan (a long-term credit bank) and, to some extent, the Long-Term Credit Bank of Japan have largely controlled lending to major corporations in Japan.[3]

This group of major banks and insurance companies is informally interconnected. Their senior executives know each other, many went to school together and a number are former MOF officials. They have offices within blocks of each other in central Tokyo and socialize at, for example, the Banker's Club. In some cases, several institutions belong to the same keiretsu (a group of firms with extensive business relations and cross-shareholdings)—for example, Sumitomo Bank, Sumitomo Trust and Banking, and Sumitomo Mutual Life are all members of the Sumitomo keiretsu. The high degree of contact facilitates coordination of lending policies, especially in financial distress situations.

This coordination does not imply a noncompetitive environment. The relationship between the banks is relatively complex and involves intense competition [32], but this occurs within accepted bounds. In examining the behavior of Canadian banks, Breton and Wintrobe [7] point out that "moral suasion" (i.e., window guidance) can also be viewed as a mutually advantageous exchange between the central bank and the commercial banks. That is, the latter cooperate with the regulator not just out of fear of administrative or legislative sanctions, but also because the central bank offers a quid pro quo of information and other services that facilitate collusion among the banks. Thus, the banks cooperate to maintain a system that places bounds on competition.

As a final point under this section, a substantial fraction of firm borrowing is short term and tends to be concentrated within a few large banks. Indeed, short-term borrowing actually exceeds long-term borrowing, both of which are substantially larger than borrowing via bonds. This is largely explained by the traditional practice among Japanese banks of making short-term loans and then continuously renewing ("rolling over") those loans effectively to provide longer term financing. Although

---

[3] This is, of course, subject to the views of MOF and the Bank of Japan, which exerted considerable and sometimes detailed influence over major lenders.

the maturity structure has been lengthening, as of March 1983, only 34 percent of the outstanding loans from the City, Regional, and Trust Banks had maturities greater than one year. The exceptions to this practice are the three Long-Term Credit Banks with 79 percent of their loans having maturities of over one year.

This pattern is a consequence of regulatory requirements. The City, Trust, and Regional Banks are not permitted to issue medium- and long-term liabilities. The regulatory authorities therefore require them to limit the nominal maturities of their loans. By contrast, the Long-Term Credit Banks may issue debentures, and correspondingly make longer term loans. This loan maturity structure has important implications for the main bank relationship (see Section V).

III. Equity Market

The Tokyo Stock Exchange is both large and active — second only to New York in terms of both total market value and value of shares traded annually. In 1983, the value of shares traded on the Tokyo exchange represented 48.8 percent of the total market value. However, one should treat share values and price appreciation figures with caution since trading has, in effect, been restricted to a relatively small fraction of the potentially available shares.

Table 2 gives a breakdown of ownership in 1983 for all companies listed on any of the eight Japanese stock exchanges. Of particular interest are the heavy institutional holdings (72 percent of total shares and 73.7 percent of market value). There also have been pronounced trends in the composition of share ownership, with the holdings of private domestic institutions increasing more or less continuously from 28.1 percent of total shares in 1950 to the current 66.7 percent. Over the same period, individual holdings declined from 69.1 to 28 percent. Among domestic institutions, holdings by financial institutions increased from 9.9 to 37.7

Table 2   **1983 Share Ownership by Type of Investor, All Listed Companies**

	Percentage of Listed Shares	Percentage of Market Value
Gov't. and Local Gov't.	0.2	0.3
Financial Institutions	37.7	37.0
Investment Trusts	1.2	1.6
Securities Companies	1.8	1.7
Business Corporations	26.0	25.4
Individuals & Others	28.0	26.3
Foreigners	5.1	7.6

Source: *Tokyo Stock Exchange Fact Book 1984.*

percent of total shares, while nonfinancial corporations increased their shares from 5.6 to 26.0 percent. In contrast, holdings by security companies fell from 12.6 in 1950 to the current, relatively insignificant, 1.8 percent. Investment trusts (similar to U.S. mutual funds) are not currently a major factor in the market and were negligible in 1950; however, they were much more significant in the early 1960s. Foreigners (almost entirely institutions) have been investors in Japanese securities for years. Their holdings have recently surged, more than doubling since 1980.

The major security holders in Japan basically hold shares to maintain or enhance business relationships and do very little trading. Among financial institutions, the major shareholders are banks and insurance companies, with each holding 17.6 percent of total listed shares. Although these institutions collectively hold over 35 percent of listed shares, they were involved in only 3.7 percent of the stock transactions (Tokyo, Osaka, and Nagoya exchanges) during 1983. Business corporations were somewhat more active, but still engaged in only 7 percent of stock transactions. Thus, the major institutional holders (banks, insurance companies, and nonfinancial business corporations) collectively held 61.2 percent of listed shares, but engaged in only 10.7 percent of trades. By contrast, member security firms, individuals, and foreigners accounted for 81.5 percent of trading, despite holding less than 35 percent of the listed shares. If we exclude trades by member security firms acting as dealers (23.9 percent of the total), individuals and foreigners accounted for 75.7 percent of remaining trades. Thus, we get a rather clear picture of an economy where over 60 percent of listed shares are held by institutions that do very little trading.

Most of the institutional shareholding is intra- rather than inter-group in nature [27]. The resultant cross-holding acts as a barrier to hostile takeovers and mergers by ensuring that a blocking percentage is in friendly hands. The two great waves of stock interchanges occurred in the early 1950s and early 1970s. In the first period, the keiretsu emerged from the remains of the pre-war zaibatsu. The second wave followed the 1971 liberalization of capital flows into Japan when managements feared acquisition by foreign firms.

Traditionally, large Japanese firms have paid dividends based on the par value of their stock (usually 50 yen per share). Indeed, there is a widely held view that annual dividends should be at least 10 percent of par value (5 yen per share for most companies). This view is strongly reinforced by listing criteria for the Tokyo Stock Exchange that virtually mandate a minimum annual cash dividend of 5 yen per share. Firms can be demoted from the First to Second Section of the exchange or even delisted entirely for failure to pay cash dividends; however, the delisting criteria are relatively lenient and happen only after five consecutive years of no cash dividends.[4]

---

[4] See [19] or [37] for other listing criteria.

As a consequence of the above, dividends of at least 10 percent of par are paid, except under dire circumstances. Indeed, failure to pay such a dividend is taken as a strong signal of serious financial difficulties. On the other hand, firms have not generally increased dividends as a fraction of par value despite increases in earned income and market prices for their shares. Thus, average dividends per share for First Section stocks that paid dividends fluctuated between 6.88 and 5.92 yen per share from 1960 through 1983. During the same period, the TSE Stock Price Index increased approximately sevenfold, with the result that average dividend yields have declined to approximately 1 percent of the average share price.

Individual shareholders prefer capital gains to dividends because of an asymmetric tax treatment.[5] Firms, too, prefer to minimize dividends because of investment needs (see Section IV) and because of the relatively more favorable corporate tax treatment of interest payments.

The purchase of stocks with low dividend yields, however, creates a problem for most Japanese institutional shareholders. Banks have cash flow requirements for payment of interest to depositors. Insurance companies face restrictions on declaring policy dividends (currently around 7.5 percent) without adequate reported income and they are generally not allowed to treat capital gains (even when realized) as income. Most nonfinancial corporations are, at least partially, financing their shareholding by loans with associated interest payments. Thus, we have a set of institutional shareholders who need substantial dividend yields, but traditionally follow policies of buying and holding shares to enhance business relations with the firms issuing those shares. Consequently, the purchase of low yielding market issues squeezes these institutions' ability to meet other commitments.[6]

Prior to 1969–1970, virtually all new issues were rights offerings to existing shareholders at par, with unsubscribed shares offered to the public at market prices. From 1956–1968, the amount raised at market

---

[5] Capital gains are free of income tax, depending on the size and number of transactions. Dividends are taxed at both the corporate and individual levels, but the corporate tax rate on earnings paid out as dividends is lower than the rate on retained earnings [3].

[6] Many of the above institutions apparently objected to the issue of shares at market when they started taking place in the late 1960s and early 1970s. The result was a compromise in which issuing firms agreed to return a portion of the premium (between the issue price and par) to their shareholders in the form of subsequent gratis stock issues. Coupled with the traditional dividend practice, this had the effect of raising dividend yields over time, relative to the issue price.

Accounts vary regarding how much of this premium was to be returned. Kurosawa [22] states that it was all to be returned within a ten-year period with 20 percent before the next stock issue. Currently published guidelines confirm the 20 percent return before issuing stock again, but suggest that the firm is not obliged to return the other 80 percent. This requirement is also applied to stock issued in connection with conversions of convertible bonds. In practice, most firms seem to be observing the 20 percent guideline, but some are not (particularly with overseas convertible issues). There also seems to be heavy and increasing pressure to eliminate the requirement. Probably the initial concept was 100 percent return of premium, but this has deteriorated over time.

Table 3   New Share Issues by TSE Listed Companies, 1979–1981

	Million Shares	Percent of Total
Market Issue	4,902	17
Rights Offering	8,655	29
Private Placement	505	2
Conversions	6,568	22
Gratis Issue	8,390	28
Stock Dividends	101	0
Mergers	539	2
TOTAL	29,660	100

Source: Tokyo Stock Exchange, *Annual Statistics Report.*

prices was less than 5 percent of total funds raised domestically on new equity issued by listed companies. The first completely public issue at a market price apparently took place in January 1969.[7] Since then, market price issues have become very important, accounting for approximately three-quarters of new equity funds raised from 1980–1983. Rights offerings still account for approximately 20 percent of new equity funds, with the remainder coming through private placements that are frequently priced at substantial discounts from market.

One possible interpretation of par value issues is that this practice was basically a mechanism for increasing total dividend payments to shareholders. With a 5 yen per share dividend commitment, a rights issue at less than market effectively increases dividend yield on total shareholdings. However, stock splits (which were legal and not uncommon) or simply announcing a higher dividend per share have the same effects, without the expense of registration statements, etc. Thus, it seems that these par value issues were at least partially for the purpose of raising additional equity funds.

Although market issues now dominate in terms of funds raised, they are a much smaller fraction of new shares issued, as seen in Table 3. Rights offerings and private placements account for almost twice as many new shares as market issues. Conversions of convertible bonds as well as gratis issues were both considerably greater than market issues. Thus, in terms of voting power, market issues have not been much of a factor. Even if we add conversions to market issues, the total for 1979–1981 represents only 5.2 percent of listed shares for TSE firms in 1981. Furthermore, existing shareholders are buying most of the market issues and convertibles.

---

[7] The company was Nihon Gakki, a musical instruments maker. By market price issues we mean underwritten public offerings or the granting of subscription rights to a selected person or persons. Unlike par-value issues, the price of the new shares is based on the current market price of the outstanding equity [19], though the new shares may be sold at a slight discount.

It's clear that conversions of convertible bonds are becoming a substantial source of additional equity. Since the late 1970s, the annual market value of new convertible bond issues has generally exceeded that for public offerings of new equity. From 1978–1983, convertible issues totaled 6.4 trillion yen of which 63 percent was issued in overseas markets (primarily Europe). During the same period, public offerings amounted to 5.1 trillion yen, including a 548 billion yen equivalent in foreign markets.

When issuing these bonds, the conversion price is set quite close to the market price for the firm's shares — the current guideline is a 5 percent premium. As a consequence, the vast majority of these bonds are converted. In some cases, this occurs very rapidly — e.g., 85 percent conversion within six months of issue. Thus, the issue of convertibles by Japanese firms can be largely viewed as an equity raising mechanism (at least in the long run).

IV. Leverage

In this section, we focus on the generally higher debt to equity ratios in Japan. The data in Table 4 represent the aggregate balance sheet for all nonfinancial companies listed on the Tokyo Stock Exchange in 1983. Although the fraction of shareholders' equity (22 percent) has increased in recent years, it is still quite low by U.S. standards.

The aggregate figures on leverage in Table 4 conceal extremes in both directions. There are companies, such as Matsushita or Toyota, that have relatively little debt and massive financial resources, including billions of dollars in cash and marketable securities. At the other extreme are companies, such as Maruzen Oil, that had large losses in 1981 and 1982, resulting in a negative book value.

Accounting differences as well as the enormous appreciation in market values of book assets (particularly land and securities) have raised questions about reported debt/equity ratios for Japanese firms. Some authors have even suggested that the apparent disparity between Japanese and U.S. practice may be largely a reporting artifact [21] and, at the very least, is greatly exaggerated [10]. For example, Aoki [1] attempts to adjust for a variety of possible distortions using aggregate numbers for all nonfinancial corporations listed on the Tokyo Stock Exchange. His results indicate that adjusted equity values for 1981 represent about 40 percent of total assets for a typical firm, roughly twice the reported figure.[8] Thus, the financial leverage of an average large Japanese firm may be substantially less than popularly supposed. Nevertheless, 60 percent debt is still a lot of borrowing on average, particularly since reported

---

[8] Aoki adjusted for the undervaluation of real estate and securities that were carried at historic cost and par, respectively, for certain pension reserves and for trade credit. These results are also consistent with those from confidential studies by the Japanese government and various securities firms, as summarized in [8].

Table 4   **Balance Sheets of All Nonfinancial Corporations Listed on the Tokyo Stock Exchange in 1983**

	Trillion Yen	Percentage of Total
Assets:		
Current Assets	110.3	67.0
Fixed Assets	54.3	33.0
Deferred Assets	0.1	0
Total Assets	164.7	100.0
Liabilities:		
Notes and Accounts Payable (Trade Payables)	38.2	23.2
Short-Term Borrowing	30.5	18.5
Bonds	5.6	3.4
Long-Term Borrowing	21.3	12.9
Other Liabilities	32.7	19.9
Total Liabilities	128.3	77.9
Shareholders' Equity	36.3	22.0
Total Liabilities and Shareholders' Equity	164.7	100.0

Source: *Tokyo Stock Exchange Fact Book 1984.*

equity to asset ratios have been increasing since the mid-1970s. There are also numerous firms that are much more highly levered than average and would have equity to total asset percentages of perhaps 10 to 20 percent even after a variety of adjustments.

Clearly, it has been possible to operate a major firm in Japan on a much more highly levered basis than would be generally acceptable to lenders in the United States. Given that the bond market was not a meaningful financial option for most Japanese firms during the postwar period, the question of the preference for bank borrowing over equity still remains. We advance two complementary explanations for the apparent preference for debt funding.[9] The first is a static argument based on regulated and apparently below-market interest rates [34] plus an internal capital market role by corporate groups. The second, and more novel, explanation is a dynamic theory that relates corporate financing prefer-ences to investment opportunities.

[9] Our explanations concern firms' demands for equity capital. Toshiharu Takahashi has suggested an explanation based on the supply of equity capital. His argument is that the supply of funds was limited because: (a) foreigners could not buy Japanese shares; (b) the ultimate institutional holders, banks and insurance companies, had a limited demand; and (c) individuals tended to prefer to hold their savings in the form of bank deposits because the securities companies did not seek out investors and because of a fear of insider trading and stock price manipulation.

Our first explanation rests on the fact that Japan has been characterized until recently by an elaborate system of interest rate controls and
credit allocations ([5], p. 13). The government imposed its own system of
ceilings on loan and deposit rates, which was later replaced by voluntary
ceilings based on negotiations among the Federation of Bankers' Association, the Ministry of Finance, and the Bank of Japan. The government's
apparent intention was to keep down the cost of capital to Japanese
business firms in order to promote economic development and improve
their competitive position in world markets.[10] The ceilings were, therefore, generally below equilibrium rates. To keep loan rates low, deposit
rates were also restrained. When interest rates are not free to balance loan
supply and demand, credit rationing (i.e., quantitative allocation) is
inevitable.

One can exaggerate the rigidity of the loan rate ceilings. Some loans
(small or long-term ones) were not regulated. The Japanese banks often
required heavy compensating balances and fees that raised the effective
interest rate. Had the compensating balances not usually earned interest,
the amounts held presumably would have been lower. Finally, the rate
controls were not always observed. Nevertheless, the ceilings were
sufficiently binding to provide an impetus for the formation of ties
between banks and firms. The effect was even more pronounced during
the recurring periods of tight money [35]. Under these circumstances,
banks rationed their loans on the basis of stable borrower-lender relations
as well as on the size and financial health of the firm. This provided a
strong incentive for firms to develop and maintain close bank relations.

Banks also had incentives to develop and maintain good customers.
First, the Bank of Japan allowed the city banks to have high ratios of
loans to deposits, which has come to be known as the "over-loan"
phenomenon. The city banks augmented their deposits by borrowing from
the provincial banks and from the Bank of Japan through the rediscount
window at concessionary rates. The latter has provided between 1 and
12 percent of the city banks' total capital, and has averaged about 7 percent for the 1968–1975 period ([8], p. 143). The allocation of "over-loan"
credit depended on the amount of loans the banks had made in previous
periods. Second, Caves and Uekusa ([9], p. 82) provide evidence that
group firms made higher average payments for borrowed capital than did
independent companies.

In addition to its interest rate policies, in the 1950s and early 1960s,
the government attempted to channel funds. One of the Bank of Japan's
(BOJ) most important tools was what has come to be known as window

---

[10] This does not mean that rates of return in Japan were below world levels. They may have
been above world rates and thus capital controls were necessary to keep foreign funds from
flowing into Japan [34]. In the late 1970s, the evidence is that differences between interest
rates in Japan and the unregulated Euro-yen rates on similar securities is slight [28].
Furthermore, Baldwin [3] presents evidence indicating that in the period 1960–1980, the
effective cost of capital in Japan was probably very close to that in the United States.

guidance. This involved direct, frequent contact between the BOJ and the commercial banks, with the former setting bank-by-bank quotas on loans to customers. In addition to limiting total bank credit, the BOJ directed the banks' sectoral allocations in general, and sometimes, in considerable detail. These policies also encouraged the formation of inter-firm relationships in which the credit allocation could be modified through intra-group reallocation.

Both interest rate suppression and credit allocation would have encouraged higher leverage among major firms. First, those large, stable, and favored firms that had access to below free market rates had an incentive to borrow. They would have done so until, at the margin, the interest savings equalled the additional cost shareholders faced because of the increased risk. Furthermore, the recurring periods of tight money gave firms an incentive to borrow up to their credit limits, even if they had no current need for the full amount.

Second, credit allocation by the government through the banks pushed the capital market into the large firms. That is, one can think of large firms as part industrial or trading firm and part bank. It is clear that Japanese firms engage in extensive intermediation. Trade credit is a much larger proportion of the assets of the nonfinancial sector in Japan than it is in the United States [32]. Thus, we get the following stylized picture of financial intermediation. The government channeled low-cost funds to the major banks, directly and indirectly. These, in turn, lent the funds to large companies with whom they were affiliated, who proceeded to borrow heavily. The large companies, including the trading companies, then lent the funds to their subsidiaries, affiliates, and suppliers. Thus, as Aoki [1] and Bronte ([8], p. 9) point out, netting out trade payables and receivables to remove the effect of the companies' banking role causes the apparent leverage to decline.

Our second, dynamic, explanation of leverage relates directly to what Myers [24] has called the "Pecking Order Theory" of capital structure. This theory suggests that managers have asymmetric information regarding the firm's investment opportunities that is difficult to convey in a believable manner to potential investors. New investors believe that management may be trying to exploit them for the benefit of "old" shareholders and consequently tend to undervalue new shares issued to finance favorable investment opportunities. In the model of Myers and Majluf [25], this leads to a pecking order in which internal financing is preferred, with low risk debt as a second choice. Only as debt becomes relatively risky does it become potentially desirable to issue equity. It may instead be desirable to forego the investment project, unless its NPV is sufficiently high to offset the undervaluation of new equity.[11]

---

[11] Recent empirical evidence for the United States suggests that the announcement of a new equity issue reduces the value of previously outstanding shares by 30 percent of the value of the issue [2].

From the early 1950s until the mid-1970s, major Japanese firms were growing at generally rapid rates. Kurosawa [22] provides estimates that total assets for such firms grew at an average annual rate of 15.6 percent from 1955–1974. During that same period, these firms had annual operating profits before interest or taxes that averaged 9.4 percent of assets. If these firms had been all equity financed and paid no dividends, their after-tax earnings would have financed roughly a 4.7 percent growth rate, less than one-third of the rate that actually occurred. Furthermore, they were both highly levered and paying substantial dividends.

Although dividend yield is low relative to market price (slightly over 1 percent on average with 88 percent of listed securities in 1983 having yields below 2.5 percent), it represents a substantial payout rate relative to earnings (38 percent on average, in 1983). Consequently, firms had enormous external funding requirements in order to finance their rapid growth.

Even at par value, rights issues during the 1950s were capable of raising total sums comparable in real terms to more recent market issues. For example, from 1959–1960, listed firms raised 224.8 billion yen annually through equity issues (94 percent via rights offerings). In the 1976–1980 period, listed firms raised 842 billion yen annually or 3.75 times the earlier figure (26 percent was via rights offerings). However, the Consumer Price Index increased an average of 3.85 times between these periods. Thus, listed firms actually raised less in real terms during the later period, although there were over twice as many listed companies.

The per share dividend commitment means that dividend cash flow requirements for a par value issue exceed (perhaps substantially) those on a market price issue. Thus, they do not appear, at first glance, to be an efficient way to raise capital. In the context of the Myers and Majluf model, however, rights issues make a great deal of sense because they avoid the problem of potential exploitation of new shareholders.

V. The Main Bank Lending System

While firms had a clear incentive to borrow, lending to highly levered firms would seem extremely risky from the banks' perspective. What evolved in Japan was a set of clever mechanisms for reducing lending risks, allowing continued borrowing up to seemingly extraordinary debt to equity ratios.

A point worth mentioning is the consequence of the banks' legal right to own shares. The limit currently is 10 percent of a firm's outstanding shares, falling to 5 percent after 1987. A firm's bank is far more likely to own shares in the firm than are its nonmain bank lenders. In many cases, the legal ceiling is nonbinding. However, the fact that they can and do hold shares reduces the lending risks the Japanese banks face. By being both creditor and stockholder, the banks make themselves indifferent to any attempt to make the firm more risky than anticipated by creditors and, in this way, to transfer wealth from them to shareholders. However, this is not enough to explain the Japanese banks' ability to support debt. The key factor is the main bank relationship.

Typically, each major industrial borrower had one of the top eight to ten banks acting as its main bank. The relationship between a firm and its main bank tends to be both long term and very close, with the bank being privy to extensive and confidential information on the firm's operations as well as its medium and long-range plans. Consequently, the main bank's loan evaluation was typically accepted with little question by other lenders.

The intensity of the main bank relationship appears to be largely a function of the indebtedness and consequent need for bank support by the client firm.[12] At one extreme, the main banks of cash-rich companies such as Matsushita or Toyota primarily benefit from corporate deposits as well as foreign exchange and fee-generating transactions. There is apparently relatively little flow of confidential information.

For heavy borrowers, there are extensive formal and informal contacts between the firm and its main bank at a variety of levels. In addition to providing a substantial fraction of the firm's borrowed funds, the main bank acts as a financial advisor as well as an agent on other loans and such bond issues as do occur. The bank has considerable influence and, in some cases, veto power over capital spending plans. In the extreme, a firm in financial difficulties may suddenly find several of its top executives replaced by bank personnel.

The main bank has enormous power. It can refuse to rollover short-term loans. Assuming other short-term lenders follow suit, the firm is more-or-less instantly insolvent. Also, Japanese banks have "rights to take assets, seize collateral or offset holdings to counter possible losses in the event of a threatened insolvency even though there is no literal default."[13] These rights are part of a set of General Business Conditions based on the General Banking Agreement (1948), which are the same for all Japanese banks and must be accepted by client firms in order to establish a borrowing relationship. These General Business Conditions effectively replace the variety of loan covenants prevalent in the United States while giving Japanese banks more flexibility and power.

The other side of the main bank's role is an implicit guarantee to other lenders. The main bank is providing a monitoring function for itself and those other lenders. It has much better information and the other lenders rely on its evaluation. They also typically expect the main bank to absorb a disproportionate share of loan losses in the event of a client

---

[12] This statement is based on the first author's interviews with bankers, financial managers, and consultants in Japan in 1983 and 1984.

[13] [30], p. 60.

bankruptcy.[14] Consequently, it has both a responsibility and a strong incentive to act on behalf of not only itself, but also other lenders.

There are several striking examples that illustrate these aspects of the main banking relationship. When Ataka (a large trading company) went bankrupt in 1977, its two main banks took almost all the losses. Sumitomo Bank wrote off 106 billion yen, while Kyowa Bank lost 46 billion yen. According to Prindl [30], foreign creditors of Ataka lost nothing, although their loans were basically unsecured.[15]

In the case of Toyo Kogyo (Mazda), Sumitomo Bank orchestrated a rescue effort. In late 1974, the bank sent several of its own executives to top positions at Toyo Kogyo, called a meeting of the firm's lenders, and announced that it would stand behind the automaker, in effect, guaranteeing the other lenders' loans. It also announced that Sumitomo Trust (Toyo Kogyo's second largest lender and a member of the Sumitomo Group) would provide any necessary new loans. According to Pascale and Rohlen [29], not one of the other 71 lenders called a loan or refused to rollover existing credits.

In order for the main bank system to work well, there needs to be a small number of major lenders with considerable confidence in each other. Minor lenders can be repaid, if necessary, to eliminate disagreements, so they are not a major factor in the viability of the system. However, as the number of major lenders enlarges, the system becomes unwieldy and starts to break down. We have only to look at the LDC debt reschedulings to see the difficulties in coordinating the views of a large number of lenders. Thus, the restriction of foreign borrowing and the concentration of Japanese lenders were crucial in the development of a main bank lending system.

Another significant factor was the relatively minor use of corporate bonds. Bondholders would potentially have to agree to the main bank's actions (or be repaid). If large amounts of a firm's debt were held by individual bondholders, this could prove problematic. However, the banks were generally in a position to discourage or veto bond issues, particularly by major borrowers, which includes the vast majority of Japanese firms. Furthermore, and in part as a consequence, the amounts of outstanding bonds are relatively small and mostly held by financial institutions.

The other critical feature of this system is confidence that the main bank will carry out its responsibilities and not abuse its position with respect to both the other lenders and the client firm. As in a variety of other markets, it appears the enforcement mechanism here is reputation. Any failure reduces a bank's ability to get other independent firms as

---

[14] Wallich and Wallich ([38], p. 273) describe the situation as follows: "It is taken for granted that the main bank assumes a special responsibility with respect to the borrower. In an emergency other creditors therefore can expect their claims to effectively though not legally outrank those of the main bank."

[15] Prindl was General Manager of Morgan Guaranty's Tokyo office at the time.

customers and will cause customers already in a main bank relationship to reduce or transfer their dependence. Regulatory limits on lending to each customer have resulted in a situation in which even the main bank seldom provides more than 30 percent of a firm's loans. This makes it easier for nongroup companies to switch their allegiance in a market where all the banks are constrained to offer otherwise virtually identical services.

In summary, the main bank lending system allowed sufficient monitoring and control by the main bank to overcome most of the agency problems associated with lending.[16] There were efficiencies in that one bank did the monitoring, which minimized associated costs. The level of monitoring also seems to have been an increasing function of the firm's debt level — a monitoring cost versus risk reduction tradeoff. This system appears to be capable of dramatically reducing deadweight losses in financial distress situations. The main bank can make a liquidation or rescue decision and take control rather smoothly without resorting to time-consuming bankruptcy procedures and litigation of asset claims. In addition to saving possible legal costs, it is clear that the ability to reorganize with minimum disruption to customer, supplier, and employee relations is quite valuable.

VI. Concluding Remarks

Since roughly 1970, there has been a dramatic and continuing relaxation of both formal and informal government controls over Japanese financial markets. Obviously, this can have substantial implications for Japanese corporate finance.

The phased deregulation of interest rates will permit the introduction of new instruments, such as commercial paper and bankers' acceptances, and the growth of demand for bonds. At the same time, there are now many firms that are sufficiently well established that they could and would wish to dispense with intermediaries and instead borrow directly. Because of the importance of legal and regulatory strictures, the rate at which the shift takes place will depend on a complex political process involving the Ministry of Finance, the Bank of Japan, banks, securities firms, and borrowers and investors.

To the degree that the existence of new, free market rate instruments undermines the traditional low-interest rate policy, they remove a major cause of high corporate leverage. First, as rates throughout the economy become market-determined, firms have a reduced incentive to substitute cheap debt for equity. Second, as rates come to equilibrate supply and demand, credit rationing will be reduced, removing the need or opportunity for nonfinancial firms to assume as great a role in financial intermediation.

---

[16] See [6] for a review of the literature on such problems.

In addition, several studies document a substantial increase in earnings volatility as well as a somewhat lower return on assets for Japanese firms since 1974.[17] This shift in the business environment increased the probability of financial distress for Japanese firms generally and resulted in considerable pressure for reduced leverage. The main bank system is good at dealing with financial distress occurring relatively independently across numerous firms. However, what happened was a systematic risk increase across most of the economy. Consequently, the position of main banks was weakened and the motivation for borrowers to reduce their leverage was substantial. In fact, the degree of leverage has been decreasing in recent years perhaps, in part, for this reason and, in part, due to a decreased rate of growth of assets.

In contrast with earlier rapid growth rates, the rate of growth in total assets of major manufacturing firms dropped to an average of 6.4 percent annually during 1974–1982. This allowed relatively greater internal funding and less reliance on debt. When coupled with new equity issues and conversions, the result was roughly a 40 percent increase in equity relative to total assets during 1977–1983.

Since 1974–1975, interest rate deregulation and slower economic growth have acted in the same direction in reducing corporate leverage. Intuition would suggest that the latter has had the greatest effect, partially because the former process is still in its early stages.

As indicated earlier, a critical feature of the main banking system is a small number of lenders who can be counted on to fulfill their obligations. Opening the Japanese markets to foreign lenders as well as allowing firms to borrow abroad seriously undermines the system. Not only is the number of potential lenders large, but their actions are difficult for a main bank to control. Aside from coordination problems and generally differing perspectives, reputational threats regarding the Japanese market are apt to be much less effective with foreign lenders. Indeed, recent major bankruptcies such as Riccar and J. Osawa seem to have occurred because of a breakdown in the main bank lending system.[18] In both cases, borrowing from foreign lenders appears to have precluded effective main bank control.

The crucial question for the continuance of the existing system is whether a main bank can induce client firms to limit their borrowing from nontraditional sources. A little bit of nontraditional borrowing is not a major problem since it can be repaid, if necessary. But significant borrowings from a highly diversified group of lenders essentially inhibit the main bank's ability to intervene effectively. Main banks can probably enforce borrowing restrictions on small or financially weak firms. Large and financially strong firms do not really need the main bank system to support their borrowing and may turn more to bond markets. However, if

---

[17] For example, see [22] or [23].

[18] For an interesting account of the Osawa failure, see [17].

these firms get into financial difficulties in the future with large diversified borrowings, rescue operations may be much more difficult than in the past.

Two important observations emerge from an examination of the characteristics of Japanese corporate finance in the post-World War II era. The first is that the suppression of external markets does not necessarily mean the disappearance of their functions. Instead, the location of the allocation function may shift, as it appears to have done in the Japanese case, to internal capital markets within economic groups of firms and to the firms themselves. In fact, it is possible that these internal markets contributed to economic development by mitigating bureaucratic credit allocation errors.

The second observation has to do with the responsiveness and congruence of institutions. That is, incentives for high leverage were accompanied in Japan by the development of institutions, such as the main bank relationship, that could accommodate them. This again suggests the sociologists' paradigm of "unexpected consequences." That is, one cannot change one part of a system without it having far-reaching consequences. Thus, deregulation will have many consequences, only some of which are visible now.

References

[1] Aoki, M., ed., *The Economic Analysis of the Japanese Firm*. New York, Amsterdam: NorthHolland, (1984), Chapter 1.

[2] Asquith, P., and D.W. Mullins. "Equity Issues and Stock Price Dilution," *Journal of Financial Economics* (forthcoming).

[3] Baldwin, Carliss Y. "The Capital Factor: Competing for Capital in a Global Environment." In *Competition in Global Industries,* Michael A. Porter, ed. Boston: Harvard Business School (1985).

[4] Bank of Japan. *Economic Statistics Annual* (various years).

[5] Bank of Japan, Economic Research Department. *The Japanese Financial System* (1978).

[6] Barnea, A.; R.A. Haugen; and L.W. Senbet. "Market Imperfections, Agency Problems and Capital Structure: A Review." *Financial Management,* Vol. 10 (Summer, 1981), pp. 7–22.

[7] Breton, Albert, and Ronald Wintrobe. "A Theory of 'Moral Susasion'." *Canadian Journal of Economics,* Vol. 11 (1978), pp. 210–219.

[8] Bronte, S. *Japanese Finance: Markets and Institutions*. London: Euromoney Publications (1982).

[9] Caves, Richard E., and Masu Uekusa. *Industrial Organization in Japan*. Washington, D.C.: The Brookings Institution (1976).

[10] Choi, F.D.S.; S.K. Min; S.O. Nam; H. Hino; J. Ujie; and A. Stonehill. "Analyzing Foreign Financial Statements: Use and Misuse of Ratio Analysis." *Journal of International Business Studies,* Vol. 14 (1983), pp. 113–131.

[11] Diamond, D.W. "Financial Intermediation and Delegated Monitoring." *Review of Economic Studies* (1984).

[12] ———. "Reputation Acquisition in Debt Markets." Unpublished Paper, University of Chicago (1984).

[13] Elston, C.D. "The Financing of Japanese Industry." *Bank of England Quarterly Bulletin* (1981), pp. 510–518.

[14] Federation of Bankers Associations of Japan. *Banking System in Japan 1982.*

[15] Goto, Takeshi, "Bond Market: Current Situation and Legal Aspects." In *Lectures on Japanese Securities Regulation.* Tokyo: Japan Securities Research Institute (1980).

[16] International Business Information, Inc. "Recent Trends in Japanese Corporate Finance." Report prepared by International Business Information, Inc., Tokyo (1983).

[17] International Business Information, Inc. "J. Osawa & Co., Ltd.: An Assessment of What Went Wrong." Report prepared by International Business Information, Inc., Tokyo (March 1984).

[18] *Japan Company Handbook: First Section Firms.* Tokyo: Toyo Keizai Shinposha (1984).

[19] Japan Securities Research Institute. *Securities Markets in Japan 1984.*

[20] Jensen, M.C., and W.H. Meckling. "Theory of the Firm: Managerial Behavior, Agency Costs and Ownership Structure." *Journal of Financial Economics,* Vol. 3 (October 1976), pp. 305–360.

[21] Kuroda, Iwao, and Yoshiharu Oritani. "A Reexamination of the Unique Features of Japan's Corporate Financial Structure." *Japanese Economic Studies,* Vol. 8 (Summer 1980), pp. 82–117.

[22] Kurosawa, Yoshitaka. "Corporate Financing in Capital Markets." Mimeo, Research Institute of Capital Formation, The Japan Development Bank (1981).

[23] Kurosawa, Y., and T. Wakasugi. "Business Risk, Dividend Policy and Policy for Capital Structure." Staff Paper, Research Institute of Capital Formation, The Japan Development Bank (August 1984).

[24] Myers, S.C. "The Capital Structure Puzzle." *Journal of Finance,* Vol. 39 (July 1984), pp. 575–592.

[25] Myers, S.C., and N. Majluf. "Corporate Financing and Investment Decisions When Firms Have Information Investors Do Not Have." *Journal of Financial Economics* (1984), pp. 187–221.

[26] Nakamura, T. *The Postwar Japanese Economy: Its Development and Structure.* Tokyo: University of Tokyo Press (1981).

[27] Okumura, Hiroshi. "Interfirm Relations in an Enterprise Group: The Case of Mitubishi. *Japanese Economic Studies* (1982), pp. 53–82.

[28] Otani, Ichiro, and Siddarth Tiwari. "Capital Controls and Interest Rate Parity: The Japanese Experience, 1978–81." *IMF Staff Papers,* Vol. 28 (December 1981), pp. 793–815.

[29] Pascale, R.T., and T.P. Rohlen. "The Mazda Turnaround." *Journal of Japanese Studies,* Vol. 9 (1983), pp. 219–263.

[30] Prindl, A.R. *Japanese Finance: A Guide to Banking in Japan.* New York: John Wiley & Sons (1981).

[31] Royama, Shoichi. "The Japanese Financial System: Past, Present and Future." *Japanese Economic Studies* (Winter 1983–84), pp. 3–31.

[32] Sakakibara, Eisuke, and Robert A. Feldman. "The Japanese Financial System in Comparative Perspective." *Journal of Comparative Economics,* Vol. 7 (March 1983), pp. 1–24.

[33] Sakakibara, E., and A. Kondoh. "Study on the Internationalization of Tokyo's Money Markets." JCIF Policy Study Series, No. 1, Japan Center for International Finance (1984).

[34] Suzuki, Yoshio. *Money and Banking in Contemporary Japan.* New Haven, CT: Yale University Press (1980).

[35] Teranishi, Juro. "A Model of the Relationship Between Regulated and Unregulated Financial Markets: Credit Rationing in the Japanese Context." *Hitotsubashi Journal of Economics* (February 1982), pp. 25–43.

[36] Tokyo Stock Exchange. *Annual Statistics Report* (various years).

[37] Tokyo Stock Exchange. *Tokyo Stock Exchange Fact Book 1984.*

[38] Wallich, H.C., and M.I. Wallich. "Banking and Finance." In *Asia's New Giant,* Hugh Patrick and Henry Rosovsky, eds., Washington, DC: Brookings Institute (1976).

[39] Wright, R.W., and S. Suzuki. "Capital Structure and Financial Risk in Japanese Companies." *Proceedings of the Academy of International Business Conference: Asia-Pacific Dimensions of International Business* (1979), pp. 367–375.

Questions

1. For the 1950–1982 period, describe the funding sources of Japanese corporations.

2. Why do Japanese corporations use bank debt more than bond debt?

3. The following questions relate to the Japanese equity market:
    a. How many stock exchanges does Japan have?
    b. True or false: Individuals are the principal owners of common stock. Explain.
    c. True or false: The Tokyo Stock Exchange requires listed companies to pay cash dividends.
    d. Do dividend yields tend to be larger in Japan than in the United States?
    e. What effect does taxation have on individual shareholder preferences for capital gains and dividends?
    f. What are the ways in which corporations issue new shares of common stock?

4. Based on book values in 1983, Japanese corporations listed on the Tokyo Stock Exchange appear to be highly leveraged. The ratio of

owner equity to total assets is only 22 percent. What factors cause distortion in this ratio?

5. Provide an explanation of the dominance of debt over equity in Japanese corporations.

6. "While firms had a clear incentive to borrow, lending to highly levered firms would seem extremely risky from the banks' perspective." Why are Japanese banks willing to lend to highly levered Japanese corporations?

INTERPRETING BIBLICAL TEXTS

The Gospels, Fred B. Craddock
New Testament Apocalyptic, Paul S. Minear
The Pentateuch, Lloyd R. Bailey, Sr.
The Prophets, James M. Ward
Wisdom Literature and Psalms, Roland E. Murphy
Deuteronomic History, Terence E. Fretheim
The Pauline Letters,
Leander E. Keck and Victor Paul Furnish
Old Testament Apocalyptic, Paul D. Hanson

INTERPRETING BIBLICAL TEXTS

The Prophets

James M. Ward

LLOYD R. BAILEY, SR.
and
VICTOR P. FURNISH, EDITORS

ABINGDON PRESS　　　NASHVILLE

THE PROPHETS

Copyright © 1982 by Abingdon

Third Printing 1989

Library of Congress Cataloging in Publication Data

WARD, JAMES MERRILL, 1928-
    The Prophets.
    (Interpreting Biblical texts)
    Bibliography: p.
    1. Bible. O.T. Prophets—Criticism, interpretation, etc. 2. Prophets.
    I. Title. II. Series.
    BS1505.2.W37   224'.06   81-20575   AACR2

ISBN 0-687-34370-4 (pbk.)

MANUFACTURED BY THE PARTHENON PRESS AT
NASHVILLE, TENNESSEE, UNITED STATES OF AMERICA

INTERPRETING BIBLICAL TEXTS:
Editors' Foreword

The volumes in this series have been planned for those who are convinced that the Bible has a meaning for our life today, and who wish to enhance their skills as interpreters of the biblical texts. Such interpreters must necessarily engage themselves in two closely related tasks: (1) determining as much as possible about the original meaning of the various biblical writings, and (2) determining in what respect these texts are still meaningful today. The objective of the present series is to keep both of these tasks carefully in view, and to provide assistance in relating the one to the other.

Because of this overall objective it would be wrong to regard the individual volumes in this series as commentaries, as homiletical expositions of selected texts, or as abstract discussions of "the hermeneutical problem." Rather, they have been written in order to identify and illustrate what is involved in relating the meaning of the biblical texts in their own times and places to their meaning in ours. Biblical commentaries and other technical reference works sometimes focus exclusively on the first, paying little or no attention to the second. On the other hand, many attempts to expound the contemporary "relevance" of biblical themes or passages pay scant attention to the intentions of the texts themselves. And although one of the standard topics of "hermeneutics" is how a text's original meaning relates to its present meaning, such discussions often employ highly technical philosophical language and proceed with little reference to concrete examples. By way of contrast, the present volumes are written in language that will be understood by scholars, clergy and laypersons alike, and they deal with concrete texts, actual problems of interpretation, and practical procedures for moving from "then" to "now."

Each contributor to this series is committed to three basic tasks: (1) a description of the salient features of the particular type of biblical literature or section of the canon assigned; (2) the identification and explanation of the basic assumptions that guide the analysis and explication of those materials; and (3) the discussion of possible contemporary meanings of representative texts, in view of the specified assumptions with which the interpreter approaches them. Considerations that should be borne in mind by the interpreter in reflecting upon contemporary meanings of these texts are introduced by the sign ● and are accentuated with a different size of type.

The assumptions which are brought to biblical interpretation may vary from one author to the next, and will undoubtedly vary from those of many readers. Nonetheless, we believe that the present series, by illustrating how careful interpreters carry out their tasks, will encourage readers to be more reflective about the way they interpret the Bible.

Lloyd R. Bailey, Sr.
Duke Divinity School

Victor Paul Furnish
Perkins School of Theology
Southern Methodist University

CONTENTS

I. INTRODUCTION

Our subject is the Prophets: the books of Isaiah, Jeremiah, Ezekiel, and the Twelve (Minor) Prophets. The task of interpreting these books is fascinating and important. It is also formidable. It is important because of the central place occupied by the Prophets in the canon of the Bible and in Christian proclamation. It is formidable because of the size and complexity of the books themselves. The fascination in working with the books of the prophets is due to the rhetorical variety and power of their oracles and the intensity of their engagement with their people and with God.

The Prophets constitute fully one-fourth of the OT. Their length alone makes it difficult to provide a guide to their interpretation in one brief book. Moreover, the difficulty is compounded by the diversity of the material and the absence of explicit aids to understanding in the text itself. In spite of the superficial appearance of rational order and continuity in parts of the prophetic corpus, much of it is a loose, even haphazard, arrangement of oracles, laments, visions, sayings, narratives, prayers, and other kinds of writing. The shape and extent of the literary units vary greatly and are often difficult to determine.

Indications of date, historical setting, audience, and purpose are infrequent, and the authorship of many sections is unknown.

Nevertheless, the Prophets command our attention. Quite apart from the intrinsic literary merits of the prophetic books, which are sufficient to justify the attention of modern readers, their theological importance requires the attention of responsible ministers and students of the Bible. The books of the prophets are more explicit theologically than other parts of the OT, so they lend themselves more directly to religious discourse. Furthermore, the dominant forms of prophetic speech are closer to those of the modern preacher than most of the rest of the Bible is. The oracles of the ancient prophets can serve to some extent as models for preaching, and they provide a rich resource of thematic material for this purpose.

The writings of the Bible are not uniformly authoritative for the Christian witness of faith, and they have not been employed equally in the life of the church. Among the writings of the OT, the Prophets have occupied a place of special regard. This was true already in the earliest church, and it has continued to be true down to the present time. The Prophets are quoted and alluded to hundreds of times in the NT. Of the other OT books, only the Psalms, Genesis, Exodus, and Deuteronomy show comparable usage. The primary focus of the NT writers' interest in the Prophets is in the messianic prophecies, but there are many other elements of the prophetic message that informed their understanding and influenced their proclamation. They cited the messianic prophecies because they believed them to be fulfilled in Jesus' life, death, and resurrection. They cited other passages from the Prophets for a variety of reasons, but all of these rooted in the conviction that God had spoken through the prophets and that this word was as true and lively for them as for the first hearers. God's word was rich and varied, but what it communicated most of all was the knowledge of God and of God's relationship with people. The Scriptures were addressed to them, and in the Scriptures, especially in the Pentateuch and the Prophets, they found the disclosure of God's love, God's righteousness, God's purpose for humanity, the faith and obedience God required, the meaning of life and suffering and death, the characteristics of the true family of God, and the identity of God's Messiah.

A well-informed, intellectually open modern reader cannot read the Bible as the word of God as directly and simply as the early church did. We know things about the Bible and ask questions about it that earlier Christians and Jews did not know or think to ask. The expansion of knowledge about ancient literature, history, and religion that has occurred since the Enlightenment has led to an understanding of the origin and development of the biblical writings, and of the communities that produced them, which calls into question the naive conviction that God speaks to us directly and consistently in the Bible. We are only too aware of the inconsistencies in the biblical witness, the intellectual and cultural limitations of the biblical writers, and the fragmentary and disjointed character of the surviving biblical documents. It is impossible for us today to see the word of God simply, fully, and uniformly in every page of the Bible. If we wish to find the word of God there, we must seek it within, through, and behind the words of the Bible and not merely in them.

Not all students of the Bible are interested in finding the word of God in, or through, the Bible. Some are interested in it primarily for esthetic or historical reasons. For example, one of my fellow students in graduate school wrote his M.A. thesis on the militia in the OT, in order to learn whether it might serve as a model for modern Israeli military science. He was an atheist and had no interest whatever in the Bible as the word of God.

The purpose of this present book is to seek the word of God in the writings of the prophets. More specifically, it is to reflect upon the principles, assumptions, and convictions that are operating in my mind as I try to interpret prophetic writings as bearers of the word of God for me. It is hoped that by observing this, readers will be helped to reflect more adequately upon the

underlying principles and convictions that govern their own
reading of the Prophets and control their efforts to interpret
these writings in the midst of contemporary religious communities. We will not do this reflecting abstractly, but in the act of
interpreting particular biblical texts. The principles of interpretation are not to be learned in advance and then applied to
specific texts. They are to be learned—and revised—in the very
process of studying specific texts. More usually, they are not
made explicit in the act of interpreting, nor is the interpreter
always conscious of them.

Our task, then, is twofold. It is to interpret selected prophetic
texts in order to see whether and to what extent we may discern
the word of God in them, and to examine the assumptions and
convictions that affect the way we deal with these texts and the
conclusions we reach in interpreting them.

If examining methods and presuppositions were the sole aim
of this book, it would not matter which texts we selected from
the corpus assigned to us, so long as we chose ones that
provided ample opportunity to exhibit our methods and
presuppositions. This is not our sole aim, however. We wish
also to interpret texts that contain prominent themes of the
books of the prophets. It is important, not only to know *how* to
interpret the words of the prophets and to recognize what we
are doing when we engage in this interpretation, but also to
know *what* the prophets were most concerned to say and what
this message might mean to us.

We will not examine *all* the principles, assumptions, and
convictions that underlie and control our interpretation of the
chosen texts. For one thing, we may fail to recognize some of
them, at least some of the time. A few may remain unconscious,
even in the face of our best efforts to become self-conscious
about them. For another thing, some may be too trivial or too
obvious to warrant discussion. Others may be recurrent in our
working but not require repetition in our discussion. For these
and other reasons, including limitations of space, our treatment
of assumptions will not be exhaustive in every section of the

exposition. However, we hope it may be full enough to serve the stated purpose of this series.

Similarly, our exposition of the themes of the prophetic message must be selective also. Here, the limitation of space is decisive. Nevertheless, we shall try to give a fair representation of the major themes of the Prophets, using texts that have been especially important in Christian usage through the ages. Many of these texts are contained in the Ecumenical Lectionary, so widely used today in Christian worship and study.

The exposition is organized into four chapters. In the first we will consider texts relating to the call, commission, and ministry of Isaiah, Amos, Jeremiah, Ezekiel, and the Servant of Yahweh (in Isaiah 40–55). In addition to discussing the theological implications of these texts generally, we will ponder their possible bearing on an understanding of ministry today.

In the next chapter we will deal with the theme of worship and idolatry. Jeremiah, Hosea, Ezekiel, and Second Isaiah will provide the major texts. The formal worship of God in the sanctuary will figure in the discussion, but worship in a broader sense will be considered also.

In chap. 4 we will turn to the righteousness of God. Most of the contents of the books of the prophets could be discussed under this heading. The issues raised or implied by the selected texts include the justice of God, God's covenant with Israel, the day of wrath, punishment and forgiveness, individual responsibility and the righteousness of God, God and the foreign nations, providence and history, the prosperity of the wicked, and the new covenant. The texts come mainly from Isaiah, Jeremiah, and Ezekiel.

Finally, we will take up the theme of God and the gods. God is the subject of everything considered in the other chapters, so one may wonder what remains to be said in a separate chapter on this topic. The aim will be, not to repeat or summarize what is said in the preceding discussion, but to interpret two specific texts in which the identity of God is the explicit focus of concern. These texts are Isaiah 40 and Ezekiel 34.

Some Basic Assumptions About Nature and History

I have several principles—basic convictions—that should be made clear at the outset, because they affect everything I do in biblical interpretation. Indeed, I believe they are essential to any effort to appropriate the message of the Bible in our own lives.

The first of these convictions is that nature, both in its human and nonhuman aspects, is essentially the same today as it was in biblical times. The face of our planet has changed somewhat, a number of animal species have become extinct, and human beings have devised new ways of using and consuming natural resources. Thus, many new things have happened to and upon the earth. However, it is the same earth—the same, basic physical environment, operating in the same ways—that it was three thousand years ago. Human nature is also essentially the same now as it was then. In other words, there has been fundamental continuity for humankind and for its physical environment from biblical times to our own era.

A corollary—and this is our second basic conviction—is that physical events that can happen in nature (human and nonhuman) in one age can happen in another, but those that cannot happen in one cannot happen in another. Thus, if an iron axhead cannot float in water in our time, one could not have floated in Elisha's time; so the account in 2 Kgs 6:1-7 is a legend.

New things emerge in nature that were not there before, but their emergence results from the same natural processes that have always been at work. Thus, a volcano can appear where none was before, but it will be created by the same processes that produced volcanoes in earlier times.

Historical events are a different matter. Since each individual human being is unique, the interactions of human beings are infinite in their variety. What emerges from these interactions is a constantly changing aggregation of institutions, associations, happenings, movements, and communications. And all of this is unpredictable and uncontrollable. Nevertheless, the kinds of interaction among human beings, and the psychological concomitants of these interactions, are similar today to what they were in biblical times. Our material culture and our technology have changed drastically in three thousand years, but people are essentially the same today as they were in ancient Israel.

The third basic assumption—and it is closely related to the others—is that human beings are related to God in the same way today as in biblical times. The language used to describe this relationship may change, but the relationship itself is the same. In itself it is not static, but dynamic and multifaceted—a living, personal relationship. However, what the biblical writers experienced in relation to God we may experience also, and what we experience many of them experienced. Not all of us have the same experiences they had, but anything they experienced we may experience also. Conversely, anything we experience they might have experienced, too.

If these assumptions are not correct, then I do not see how we can make any sense of the Bible for ourselves. If human existence in the biblical world were essentially different from ours, and if God interacted with people differently in that time, then we could not know what their existence was, and we could not share their knowledge of God. In that case we could not appropriate what they said about God in any relevant or effective way.

The Authority of the Old Testament

The Bible is an indispensable source of the knowledge of God. The understanding of God expressed in it is decisive for Christian faith. The witness of faith in the OT is decisive for Jewish faith also, but it would be presumptuous of me to speak about this. Jews and Christians have much in common in their religious and moral understanding. There is little difference between the Jewish and Christian expositions of the OT that I

have read over the years. The laws of the Pentateuch are still
authoritative for conservative Jews, but Christian interpreters
do not uniformly share that conviction. On the other hand,
Christians believe Jesus of Nazareth to be the Messiah
promised in the OT, and Jews do not share that conviction.
Otherwise, it is difficult to distinguish Christian from Jewish
exegesis of the OT. There is much variety among Jewish works,
as there is among Christian, but the differences cut across the
two traditions rather than following them. There are fundamentalist scholars on both sides and historically critical scholars
on both sides. Fundamentalist interpretations sound much
alike whether they are Jewish or Christian and so do historically
critical interpretations. Seldom can one tell whether a work is
written by a Jew or a Christian merely from what is said about
the OT. Therefore, I would be surprised if there were much
written here that would be unacceptable to Jewish readers
solely because of incompatibility with Jewish faith. As a
Christian I believe the norm for faith to be the NT witness of
faith in Jesus Christ. For me this is the ultimate standard of
truth about God and about the meaning and goal of human life.
However, the NT witness presupposes the OT witness. Most of
the categories of NT thought are drawn from the OT, so the NT
would be incomprehensible without it. Therefore, Christians
and Jews hold much more in common in their understanding of
the OT than they hold separately.

The biblical witness of faith in God is decisive for my faith.
Any profession of the knowledge of God, unsupported by the
central witness of the Bible, is, I believe, untrue. The Bible is
indispensable for Christian understanding; however, the
biblical witness is not uniform in all its parts. Convictions stated
in one place are sometimes contrary to those expressed
elsewhere. The Bible is not only the vehicle of the word of God.
It is also the record of Israel's experience. Israel learned much
about God during the course of her history and was forced to
unlearn much as well. Part of the story of this development is
contained in the OT. Clearly, our responsibility is to read the

story as an account of changing perceptions of God and not as a uniform, unchanging witness that is binding for us.

Some readers of the Bible regard it as the infallible word of God, accurate and true in all its parts and on every level of meaning. This view is often called the literal view of the Bible. However, I prefer not to use the term in this way. The opposite to "literal" is "figurative," or "allegorical." The whole thrust of modern biblical scholarship is to understand and interpret the Bible literally, that is, to ascertain the meaning of the words in the way they were intended by the writers. The alternative to this is to reinterpret them figuratively, allegorically, or "spiritually." The latter is a highly subjective endeavor, widespread in previous eras, but largely rejected by scholars of all faiths since the Reformation. What we should ascertain now is the literal meaning of the words. Whether we regard the literal sense as the word of God is another matter.

The so-called literalist view of the Bible identifies the word of God with *all* the words of the biblical text. Thus, it regards all the words as authoritative for faith. The assumption underlying this view is that unless everything the Bible says is true, nothing can be trusted. If one doubts the accuracy or truth of anything in the text, where does the doubting stop? If anything is questionable, isn't everything questionable?

The answer to this question is yes. Everything *is* questionable. That is to say, every individual statement made in the Bible is subject to examination in the light of the total biblical witness of faith, the experience of the community of believers through the centuries, accumulated human knowledge, and our own reason and experience. When this examination is made, many statements in the Bible are found to be inaccurate or wrong or theologically unacceptable. But the central witness of faith in God is not lost. Indeed, it becomes clearer. The Bible contains reliable testimony to the truth about God, humanity, life, the meaning of history, moral responsibility, and the nature of community, among other things. This witness can be discerned by an earnest seeker. And the discernment will be enhanced, not impeded, by a rigorous scrutiny of the words of the biblical text. What modern scholars call the historical-critical method is not a roadblock to faith in God, but is an aid to such faith. The biblical witness of faith undergirds the kind of fearless criticism involved in the use of this method. Indeed, for me, as for many others, faith in God *requires* this kind of criticism. I do not accept the biblical witness of faith *in spite* of the results of historical-critical study, but, in part, *because* of them. For me, belief in the inerrancy of the Bible is incompatible with the knowledge of God proclaimed in the Bible. Historical criticism of the Bible is not a retreat from faith but a necessary consequence of it. Nothing essential to faith can be lost by it, while much that is unessential, or even detrimental, to faith can be identified by it. I believe it to be an essential means of knowledge, including the knowledge of God. Not all believers need to employ it, or even be aware of it. However, the Christian community as a whole cannot bear true witness without it.

Everything in the Bible is a human statement and reflects, in different ways and varying degrees, the limitations of human understanding and knowledge. There is no single statement in the Bible that can be accepted as true simply because it is contained there—not even statements about God. Everything must be examined and weighed by our reason, in the light of our accumulated knowledge and experience, and in the light of the central biblical witness of faith. None of us can do this adequately alone. It is a shared responsibility, and we fulfill it in continual dialogue with one another.

Biblical statements about the origin and working of our physical environment and our bodies are subject to correction in the light of advancing knowledge. For example, we know that disease is caused by germs and other organic factors, and not by demons or curses; therefore, we must reject many biblical statements in this area. Even if we allow room for a "demonic" element in disease (i.e., psychogenic disorders), there is still much in the Bible about human illness that has to be rejected as wrong.

Again, we know the earth is not flat but spherical, and that it is not circled daily by the sun but rotates on its own axis and orbits around the sun. Therefore, we must correct what the Bible says about these matters. Indeed, in every area of natural science the Bible is subject to correction in the light of accumulated human knowledge and practiced reason.

In the area of history the situation is similar, yet different. The biblical writers' knowledge of history was extremely limited. Their sources were fragmentary and often legendary. They did not have sufficient information available to give a reliable account of the past, and they did not keep sufficient records of current events to provide adequate sources for subsequent writers. Therefore, every historical statement in the Bible is subject to correction in the light of fuller knowledge. The problem here is that we do not have adequate independent sources to do much correcting. Thus, our situation here is very different from that in the physical sciences. Nevertheless, we should adopt the same approach to the Bible in both areas. Because we know how limited and inaccurate the biblical writers' knowledge of science and history was, we cannot accept *any* biblical statement in these areas uncritically. It is not a case of trusting the accuracy and validity of what is said unless there is good reason to reject it. Rather it is a case of *not* accepting anything said unless there is good reason to do so. The Bible is simply not authoritative in matters of science or history. In these realms it is subject to the same standards of criticism that apply to any other writings. Little of biblical science has survived the advancement of knowledge. However, much of biblical history has proved to be usable. The OT is a good source for the history of ancient Israel, but still it must be used critically.

The authority of the Bible for faith lies entirely in the area of faith, that is the knowledge of God. The biblical witness of faith is discernible to anyone who takes the trouble to study the Bible carefully, with an open mind, and with the help of other earnest students, including biblical scholars and theologians. This witness is discernible to anyone. However, there are dimensions of it that require faith in order to be truly understood. The knowledge of God is not purely intellectual, although it involves the intellect completely. It is also experiential; it engages the heart and will as well as the intellect. One cannot fully understand the knowledge of God about which the Bible speaks unless one shares in this knowledge personally, that is, unless one has faith. And the final test of the truth of the biblical witness of faith is faith itself, both in the individual person and in the community of believers.

Inspiration

The question of the inspiration of the Bible is finally the same as that of its authority. If we ask whether the Bible *itself* is inspired, it is the same thing as asking whether it is authoritative. Is it the word of God? Is it true? All the same issues and considerations are involved whether we are concerned with the Bible's authority or with its inspiration.

To ask whether the *writers* of the Bible were inspired is a different question. However, we find in the end that there are no objective tests of literary inspiration other than the writings themselves; therefore we are forced back where we began, asking whether the biblical writings are inspired. There is no evidence that the processes of perception or communication of the biblical writers were different from those of other people. Their inspiration, to the extent that they were inspired, consisted solely in the content of their communication. We call them inspired because their communications are inspiring (beautiful, true, moving, edifying).

In biblical times dreams and visions were sometimes thought to be better sources of knowledge about God, or the future, than the ordinary waking mind. However, there is considerable doubt about this belief expressed in the Bible, too. And *we* know that the contents of dreams and visions are subject to the same canons of reliability as other forms of information. Truth can be perceived in dreams or visions or in any other mental state. There are many different kinds of truth. Whether a communication is true (or beautiful) cannot be decided on the basis of the mental process that produced it or the mental state in which it was produced. It can only be decided on other grounds. It is the *content* of the communication that determines whether it is true, or "inspired," not the source. Exactly the same thing is true of all communications. An inspired artist or writer or composer is one who produces inspired works of art, literature, or music. There is no way of locating the cause of the inspiration or analyzing the process. The mental processes of the creators are the same as those of other people. Why some produce beautiful or inspiring or edifying works and others do not is a mystery beyond human knowing. It simply happens. But, in any case, to say that a work is inspired is to say that it is true, in whatever way one means this term. In regard to the Bible, to say that its writings are true is to say that they are authoritative for faith. Thus, the inspiration and authority of the Bible are one and the same. The Bible is inspired to the same extent that it is authoritative. How far that is we have already discussed.

The Books of the Prophets

Literary context does affect the meaning of a text; therefore, we must take account of an entire book or the prophetic books as we try to interpret representative passages within them. The more we know about the origin and purpose of the books, their shape and component parts, the social settings in which they were produced, the better we may understand an individual text. Frequently we can also be helped by studying a text in relation to others of a similar type, in the same book or in other books. Some questions of context and literary relationship will be raised in the course of our treatment of individual texts and do not need to be mentioned here. Others, however, especially those of a more general kind, may be reviewed more appropriately here, before we begin the interpretation of specific texts.

My purpose is not to survey the entire prophetic literature and all the attendant questions of authorship, date, composition, and historical background, as well as the present state of scholarly discussion. Such surveys are readily available in Bible dictionaries, introductions, and commentaries (see the Aids for the Interpreter), and it would be a misuse of space to duplicate them here. However, it seems only fair to the reader to say something about the view of the prophetic books that informs the judgments made in the remainder of this book.

All four of the books of the prophets—Isaiah, Jeremiah, Ezekiel, and The Twelve—are composite works. Each is highly diverse in the kinds of material it contains and in authorship and date of composition. Large portions of these books were composed by anonymous writers. With the exception of Jeremiah, even the writers whose names we know remain effectively anonymous, since we know little or nothing about them as persons. This literary situation is frustrating to us. We would like to know who wrote what parts of these books, what their literary and theological intentions were, who their audience was, and so forth. Only in a few instances does the Bible provide this information.

Two principal responses have been made to this literary situation in the prophetic canon. Some students (scholars) have tried to supply the missing information by subjecting the texts to rigorous literary analysis and drawing inferences from the results. Other readers have denied that a problem exists. This second group of interpreters accepts the biblical statements of authorship as correct. Thus, Isaiah wrote the Book of Isaiah, Jeremiah wrote the Book of Jeremiah, and so forth. This view is held naively by many readers of the Bible who are unaware of critical scholarship. It is held dogmatically by others who are acquainted with critical scholarship but reject it for theological reasons. Believing in the inerrancy of the Bible, they accept the attributions of authorship in the books themselves and find various ways of explaining away any alleged evidence to the contrary. It matters a great deal to them whether the prophetic books were actually written by the men to whom they are attributed. The assumption underlying this view of the Prophets is that the writings would lose their authority if the attributions of authorship were incorrect. We have already commented on this belief above.

Ironically, a similar assumption underlies much critical scholarship. Many scholars who accept the historical-critical method of biblical study have regarded the portions of the prophetic books which can be attributed to the prophets themselves as "authentic" and those which cannot, as "inauthentic." The tacit assumption was that a text had greater worth if the author were known than if it were anonymous. To put it another way, the prophets whose names are given in the Bible were assumed to be better prophets than the writers whose names were not. Fortunately, this assumption has been widely exposed to scrutiny in recent years and rejected by many scholars. Nevertheless, it is so pervasive in the work of earlier generations of scholars that it is difficult to eradicate. It requires conscious effort to resist, especially by those of us who were schooled in it.

The conviction which I hold in this matter, together with many other readers of the Bible, is that the worth of a writing is not determined by who wrote it. The ultimate value of a text is intrinsic. The same thing is true of works of art or musical compositions. A bad painting by a good artist is still a bad painting, though it may have commercial value merely because of the reputation of the painter. A good painting by an unknown artist is no less good because the artist is unknown, and it would be no better if it were found to be by a great artist. In the case of the biblical literature, we need not be anxious to prove who the author of a text was before we can take it seriously as a true and lively word. Great texts are great, whoever wrote them. Each text should be judged on its own merits.

We need not be anxious theologically (or esthetically) over questions of authorship, but we may properly be interested in them. Where the Bible provides information about the authorship, audience, and historical setting of the prophetic writings, we should make use of this information in trying to determine their original meaning. Where the Bible is silent about such matters we should be cautious about any conclusions we draw. In either case we may legitimately reflect upon the meaning of the text for our own times.

According to a widespread judgment of modern biblical scholars, the prophets meant their words for a particular audience in a particular place and time, and we can understand the meaning of their words and judge their truth only in relation to their original historical setting. Their words are not directly relevant to other audiences. They have value for modern readers only as sources for understanding the history of ancient Israel. Any illumination we might derive from them for our own lives is accidental.

Many readers of the Bible hold an opposite view to this one. For them the biblical texts are a vehicle by which the word of God is communicated to faithful people in every age. It does not matter so much what the original writer intended or who the audience was. What matters is that these texts were preserved as the Holy Scriptures for the perennial guidance of the people of God. The process by which they were preserved and canonized is also not important. It is only important that they are in the canon of the Bible, that they are authoritative for faith, and that they yield inspiration and direction to those who read them with submissive hearts and open minds.

There are merits in both of these views. The first is correct in trying to determine the original meaning of the texts as the writers seem to have intended them. Many of the prophetic writings indicate that they were in fact meant for particular audiences. We will understand them better if we know who these audiences were and their historical circumstances. However, words can have meaning beyond the knowledge or intention of the author. Of course, if we take this approach, there is always a danger that we will read into them meanings that are purely subjective. On the other hand, it is very difficult to define objective limits to the possible meanings inherent in a text. Perhaps the best safeguard against subjective or arbitrary interpretation is not a set of criteria defined in advance but a continuing conversation among interpreters. If one can convince others of the plausibility of an interpretation, then it is not purely subjective.

The Book of Isaiah is the third longest (after the Psalms and Jeremiah) in the OT. It is more diverse in content and historical background than the other two so-called major prophets (Jeremiah and Ezekiel), and it is nearly equal in this regard to the Book of the Twelve Prophets. Its contents span a period of approximately two and one-half centuries (from ca. 740 B.C. to sometime after 500 B.C.). Many of the materials in chaps. 1–11, 13–23, and 28–32 appear to have derived from the prophet Isaiah, who was active in Jerusalem from ca. 740 B.C. until sometime after 701. According to an allusion in 8:16 to a binding-up of his testimony among his disciples, he himself was responsible for the beginning of the literary process that produced the complex collection we call the Book of Isaiah. Most of the remaining material in the book appears to derive from anonymous writers of the seventh and sixth centuries B.C., especially the sixth century. Chaps. 40–55 constitute a highly unified group of lyrical prophetic poems, written shortly before the fall of the Empire of Babylon to Cyrus the Great of Persia (539 B.C.). For lack of a better alternative, the writer of these poems is commonly referred to as the Second Isaiah. Chaps. 56–66 reflect conflicting religious perspectives from the early years of the second temple of Jerusalem (after 520 B.C.). Some of the poems in this section resemble those of the Second Isaiah (notably chaps. 60–62). Chaps. 40–55 are set against the background of the dispersion of the Jewish people, while chaps.

56–66 reflect the restoration of the cultic community of Jerusalem. These two groups of writings, together with the eighth century oracles of Isaiah, constitute the largest blocks of material in the book. Other, smaller blocks include chaps. 24–27, a group of eschatological poems from the fifth-third centuries B.C., and chaps. 36–39, an emended excerpt from 2 Kgs 18:13–20:19.

This vast collection of diverse writings has been arranged according to a threefold, topical scheme: (1) oracles of judgment concerning Jerusalem and Judah (chaps. 1–12); (2) oracles of judgment concerning foreign nations (chaps. 13–23); and (3) oracles of restoration and fulfillment (chaps. 24–66). This same scheme has been followed in the final edition of the books of Jeremiah and Ezekiel. It is impossible to determine whether all three books were arranged in this way at the same time, or whether one provided the model for the other two.

Almost nothing is known about the other contributors to the book. For all practical purposes, then, it comes to us as anonymous prophetic literature.

The Book of the Twelve Prophets is not unlike the Book of Isaiah in its diversity of literary types and its range of dates of origin. Most of the books of Amos and Hosea concern the northern Kingdom of Israel during its last quarter-century (ca. 750–725 B.C.). The oldest material in the Book of Micah deals with the southern Kingdom of Judah at about the same time, although many of the promises of hope in this book appear to be from a later time. Zephaniah, Nahum, and Habakkuk come from the end of the following (seventh) century. Joel, Obadiah, Jonah, Haggai, Zechariah, and Malachi are from the late sixth and fifth centuries, in part perhaps later. Little or nothing is known about any of these prophets, or about the circumstances of the writing or transmission of their works. The dominant theme of the collection is the pronouncement of God's judgment upon Israel and Judah. However, there are sections dealing with foreign nations (e.g., Amos 1–2, Obadiah, and Nahum). There are also many parts concerned with the future hope of the people of God (e.g., Hosea 14; Amos 9:11-15; Micah 4; Zechariah 9–14; and Malachi 3).

The Book of Jeremiah contains considerable information about the career of the prophet. He is unique in this respect among the OT prophets. Indeed, Jeremiah is the best known individual in the whole of the OT. The prose narratives and speeches in Jeremiah 26–45 contain a rich and detailed record of the prophet's life during the reigns of Jehoiakim and Zedekiah of Judah (ca. 609–586 B.C.). His call to prophesy is dated in the thirteenth year of King Josiah (1:1; ca. 626 B.C.). In about 605 B.C. he had recorded on a scroll the oracles he had composed up to that time (36:1-3). Many of the oracles now contained in chaps. 1–23 may have been on that scroll, though there is no certainty about this. None of the extant oracles can be placed with certainty in the time between Jeremiah's call (ca. 626 B.C.) and the time of the first dated material in the book (26:1; cf. 7:1; ca. 609 B.C.), however, it is possible that some of the oracles in the book may have come from this early period of the prophet's life.

In its canonical form the book has been arranged according to the threefold topical scheme which is also evident in the books of Isaiah and Ezekiel: (1) oracles of judgment concerning Judah and Jerusalem (1:1–25:13); (2) oracles of judgment against foreign nations (25:14-38 and chaps. 46–51; the Greek OT places these chapters together at the center of the book; this arrangement seems to antedate that of the Hebrew Bible); (3) prophecies of restoration for Israel and Judah (chaps. 26–45). Each of these sections contains materials of various dates, and they are not arranged in chronological order.

The editorial arrangement of materials in these three groups partly obscures one of the most distinctive literary features of the Book of Jeremiah. This is a combining of poetic oracles and prose narratives that is unique among the books of the prophets. The book is approximately half poetry and half prose. By contrast, the Book of Isaiah is almost entirely poetry, and the Book of Ezekiel, almost entirely prose. As a composer of poetic oracles, especially oracles of divine judgment, Jeremiah stands in the tradition of Amos, Hosea, Isaiah, and Micah, the great prophets of the eight century B.C. However, he seems to have been responsible, either directly or through disciples, for the development of a prophetic prose style, which is reflected not only in the biographical narratives and sermons of the Book of Jeremiah, but also in portions of the books of Deuteronomy and Kings.

It is uncertain exactly how much of the present Book of Jeremiah derives from the prophet himself, or from his scribe Baruch (36:4; and 45:1-5), but it is unlikely that any of it is more than one generation removed from these two men. Thus, whereas the books of Isaiah and The Twelve Prophets exhibit prophetic traditions spanning 250 years, the tradition represented by the Book of Jeremiah spans only 50 years (from the end of the seventh to the middle of the sixth century B.C.). Despite the relative brevity of this span, the writers of the Book of Jeremiah addressed two quite different historical situations during that half-century. The first situation was essentially the same as that in which Amos, Hosea, Micah, and Isaiah worked a century earlier. These prophets spoke to a people who were settled in their own land, governed by native rulers, and served by long-established religious institutions. The activity of the prophets was characterized above all by moral confrontation with the leaders of Israel and Judah, who were wielders of economic and political power, and could affect the course of the nation's life and the social conditions of its people. The Kingdom of Israel was destroyed by Assyria and absorbed into its empire in 722 B.C. However, the Kingdom of Judah survived until the beginning of the sixth century. During the first half of his career Jeremiah prophesied to a society whose political and religious institutions, geographical and economic circumstances, were fundamentally the same as those which prevailed during the careers of the other preexilic prophets. Everything changed half-way through Jeremiah's life. Jerusalem was subjugated and then destroyed, and the leadership of the nation was exiled. From 597 on Jeremiah addressed a disempowered and exiled people. Thus Jeremiah was a prophet of transition, with one foot in the monarchy and the other in the Exile. Ezekiel and Second Isaiah, who were the only great prophetic figures after Jeremiah, spoke entirely within an exilic situation (although Ezekiel, who was among those deported from Jerusalem in 597 B.C., did concern himself with the fate of Jerusalem and its temple until the time of their destruction).

The Book of Ezekiel shows us a different world from that of the preexilic prophets. As a result of his deportation to Babylon, Ezekiel was removed from the social setting that had called forth the oracles of earlier prophets. The people among whom Ezekiel found himself were powerless exiles. They were deprived of the institutions and responsibilities of a sovereign nation.

This changed situation is reflected in both the content and the form of Ezekiel's writings. The concise, poetic oracles which dominate the books of the preexilic prophets are gone, and in their place are expansive prose discourses, allegories, and visionary narratives. Much discursive prose is found also in the Book of Jeremiah, but the literary situation there is quite different from that in the Book of Ezekiel. In Jeremiah the prose stands alongside large collections of oracles in traditional poetic form, from which it is easily distinguishable, formally and substantively. Most of the poetry can be attributed to Jeremiah, while the prose must (I believe) be attributed to his disciples. The Book of Ezekiel, on the other hand, is almost all prose (the only major exception is a series of oracles concerning foreign nations in chaps. 27–32). There is no group of poetic oracles concerning Israel. Several scholarly efforts have been made to separate out a core of poetic sayings from the prose, but these efforts have failed to convince other scholars. The unity of thought and style in the book is too great. We are forced to view Ezekiel himself as a writer of prose, even though we cannot be sure exactly how much of the book comes from the prophet himself and how much from disciples or later redactors. The work of the latter consists largely of expansions of Ezekiel's narratives and discourses. Therefore, it is much more difficult to distinguish the various strata in the book than it is in the Book of Jeremiah.

The Book of Ezekiel is arranged in the threefold grouping with which we are already familiar: (1) words of judgment concerning the house of Israel (chaps. 1–24), (2) words of judgment concerning foreign nations (chaps. 25–32), and (3) words of promise concerning the house of Israel (chaps. 33–48). Chaps. 40–48 constitute a great blueprint for a restored, theocratic nation in Judah, centering on the temple of Jerusalem.

Many parts of the book are dated, using as a point of reference the first deportation of Judah. These dates range from soon after 597 (1:1) to about 571 B.C. (29:17). Thus, the book is thoroughly exilic in date.

The OT provides little explicit information about the literary process that produced it. Among the books of the prophets only one passage does this. It is Jeremiah 36. According to this account Jeremiah engaged Baruch, son of Neriah, to record on a scroll at his dictation the words of God that he had spoken "against Israel and Judah and all the nations" from the time of his call until that day, which was in the fourth year of King Jehoiakim (ca. 605 B.C.) He did this because he was debarred from prophesying in the temple of Jerusalem (36:5). Once the prophet's words were written down, Baruch read them in the temple (v 10). Eventually the scroll reached King Jehoiakim, who burned it column by column as it was read to him (vv 20-26). Therefore, Jeremiah dictated his oracles a second time to Baruch (vv 27-32). The text says nothing about the ultimate fate of this second scroll. However, modern scholars assume that it survived to become the nucleus around which the Book of Jeremiah grew.

It would be going too far to build a whole history of the prophetic literature upon this one narrative. Nevertheless, it seems reasonable to suppose that Jeremiah's experience was typical of the preexilic prophets. Isa 8:16-20 indicates that the prophet Isaiah also recorded his words as testimony for a later time, when he was frustrated in his efforts to communicate with the royal court of Judah and influence its actions (7:1–8:15). We know that Amos received a similar rebuff from the national leaders of Israel (7:10-17), although in this case the Bible does not say explicitly that he recorded his oracles as a result. Thus there is not much evidence to go on, but what there is is suggestive.

The prophetic movement in Israel emerged into the clear light of history in the time of Saul and David. Saul, who had some sort of encounter with a group of ecstatic prophets early in his career (1 Sam 10:5-13; 19:23-24), consulted prophets on the eve of his battle with the Philistines at Gilboa in an unsuccessful effort to divine the outcome of the battle (1 Sam 28:5-6). Then, according to the narrative, he resorted to a medium at Endor, who conjured up the spirit of the dead Samuel, by which he was warned of his impending defeat (vv 8-19). The picture of Samuel is somewhat confused in the OT. However, he was remembered in some circles in Israel as a forceful prophet. The rebuke of Saul contained in the passage we have just cited suggests as much. In the reign of David, which followed, we see the prophet Nathan exercising a similar function as a moral critic of the king (2 Sam 12:1-15). In this instance, when Nathan rebuked David for his adultery with Bathsheba and his murder of her husband Uriah, David accepted the prophetic judgment. However, later prophets did not fare so well as the critics of kings. The stories of Elijah and his contemporary Micaiah depict conflict with the royal house of Israel (1 Kgs 19:1-3; 22:1-28). Elisha was able to influence the course of affairs in the Kingdom of Israel, but only by participating in a bloody coup d'etat (2 Kgs 9:1-10). Our point here, however, is not to rehearse the entire history of relations between the prophets and kings of Israel, but merely to point to some of the narratives in the books of Samuel and Kings that illustrate the nature of the prophetic office during the preexilic period. The prophets seem to have been primarily the counselors and critics of kings and other leaders of Israelite society. Their word appears to have been delivered orally for specific occasions, either upon the request of a king or in response to a turn of affairs which in the prophet's judgment called for comment. The books of Samuel and Kings provide no information about the origin or development of a written prophetic literature. The only OT evidence of this process is contained in the book of the prophets themselves, and all of it except Jeremiah 36 and Isa 8:16-17 is inferential. Therefore any attempt to reconstruct the history of the literary process is conjectural.

The collections of writings of the preexilic prophets consist largely of brief poetic oracles suitable for oral delivery. With Jeremiah a new development takes place, namely, the creation of a discursive prose style, which constitutes approximately half of the book. Since Jeremiah did not himself write down his oracles (Jeremiah 36), we may suppose it was not he who was responsible for the creation of the new prose forms. It was probably Baruch or someone like him. We do not know precisely for whom the biographical narratives and sermonic discourses in the Book of Jeremiah were composed. However, the Book of Ezekiel, which is made up even more of lengthy prose discourses, mentions Ezekiel's communicating with Judean exiles in Babylonia, or with elders of the exiles (3:15; 8:1; 11:25; 14:1; 20:1). It does not say whether the materials collected into the book were composed for the use of the elders; however, it is not unreasonable to suppose that the forms exhibited here were developed in response to this new situation in which the prophet found himself. If this supposition is correct, it helps explain the shift in literary style, observable first in the Book of Jeremiah, from poetic oracles to prose sermonic discourses. The discursive, didactic style would have been more appropriate to the kind of intimate, sustained relationship between prophet and people referred to in the Book of Ezekiel.

The writings collected in Isaiah 40–66 are poetry. In this they are closer to the oracles of the preexilic prophets than to the prose narratives of Ezekiel and Jeremiah. However, these poems have been fashioned into larger literary compositions quite different from the oracles of the preexilic prophets. They seem to have been composed initially in written form for use with a new audience in the radically changed circumstances of the Exile. However, the information about this audience is indirect and ambiguous (e.g., it is unclear where the poems were written), whereas the Book of Ezekiel contains explicit notices about Ezekiel's location and audience.

For further discussion of the literary and historical aspects of the books of the prophets, readers are referred to the works cited in the Aids for the Interpreter.

II. THE CALL AND RESPONSE
OF THE PROPHET

Among the most interesting and theologically important passages in the prophetic books is a series of texts dealing with the call and commission of the prophets and the effect of these experiences in their lives. These are the only texts in the prophetic corpus that illuminate directly the prophets' understanding of their own relation to God. Thus they help us to see what it meant personally to be a prophet. Since there are prophetic dimensions in the ministry of the church in every age, a study of these texts may be helpful to those who wish to share this ministry. We may ask what bearing the role and experience of the biblical prophet may have upon the religious experience and ministerial calling of persons in the church today.

The experiences related in these passages contain elements specific to prophets, but they also contain elements that are universal, or potentially universal, in God's encounter with people. The Psalms are the principal writings in the OT that reflect the interior religious life. Some prophetic writings also do this, and the texts we will be considering here are the ones that do it most directly. These texts also contain a number of themes that occur in the oracles of the prophets, thus providing a kind of theological framework for the prophetic proclamation, and so they furnish a good starting point for our examination.

We will begin with the account of the call and commission of the prophet Isaiah in 6:1-13. This will lead us to consider, more briefly, the similar accounts in Amos 7:10-17, Jer 1:4-10, and Ezek 1:1–2:15.

The second part of the chapter will focus on Jer 20:7-18. This passage is one of the complaints (or laments) of Jeremiah. The others are 11:18–12:6; 15:10-21; 17:14-18; and 18:18-23. These five texts represent a continued dialogue between the prophet and God about the purpose of his vocation in the light of the persecution he suffered for his work. These texts are unique in the prophetic canon.

Next we will consider another kind of text relating to the role and activity of a prophet, namely, the prophetic sign, or symbolic action. These brief narrative passages raise further questions about the form of prophetic ministry and the relation of person to office in this calling. Finally, we will examine Isa 52:13–53:12, the famous poem on the suffering servant of Yahweh. This is the climactic word of the OT about the calling and experience of a prophet.

The Call of Isaiah (Isaiah 6)

The best-known prophetic call-narrative has been a rich resource to commentators and preachers alike. It is vivid in its imagery, compelling in its dramatic development, and eloquent in its oracular climax. And it is so familiar and so powerful, it seems to preach—and interpret—itself. Therefore, it is a good text with which to begin. The reader will have enough familiarity with it to be able to follow readily, looking over my shoulder as I work with the text, and enough familiarity also to use critical judgment in assessing the interpretive moves that are made.

We need to do three things: first, determine what the passage actually says; second, reflect on its meaning in the Book of Isaiah; and third, interpret its meaning for us. In order to do the third adequately, we must do the first and second.

A fourth inquiry might also illuminate our interpretation, but it is not indispensable. This is to study what other interpreters have said about the text, either in the past or in recent times. If we did this thoroughly for Isaiah 6, the results would be voluminous. Some of them would be helpful while others would be historical curiosities. One possible benefit would be to discover whether the interpretation we regard as correct— perhaps take for granted, even to the disdain of contrary views—is a parochial one or is one that has received general assent. General, traditional assent does not guarantee the correctness of an interpretation, but parochialism surely calls an interpretation into question. Although it will not be our task to inquire into the history of interpretation, one should be ready to do this generally, with the aid of the commentaries, when this kind of help is needed in one's exegetical work.

Turning now to our first task, we ask what the text says. This assignment may seem too obvious to merit mention. Nevertheless, it must be done; and one should never assume that one knows what the text says until adequate homework has been done. I once heard a sermon on John 21:15-19 where Jesus asks Peter three times whether he loves him, and each time, after Peter assures him that he does, Jesus admonishes him to feed his sheep. The preacher asserted that the three words for love in Jesus' three questions were *eros, philia,* and *agape,* or sensual, fraternal, and divine love. This preacher had not done his homework! The passage does use *philia* and *agape* (in their verbal forms), but it uses them interchangeably. *Eros* is never mentioned, here or anywhere else in the NT. So the sermon misinterpreted the text. In this example the preacher would have had to consult a Greek NT, or a commentary on it, to determine whether the text could support his interpretation. He failed to do this; therefore his sermon was false. In some instances, it may not be necessary to determine what the original Greek, or Hebrew, says in order to proceed with one's interpretation. But, the least one can do is study several modern English versions of the Bible to be sure that one's interpretation is not based upon a dubious or eccentric reading. If all the reliable modern versions agree on the translation, one is relatively safe to proceed. If they disagree in substance (slight differences in phrasing or the choice of synonyms are unimportant), one should investigate further to find out why they disagree, and which of them is more likely to be correct (on which versions to use, see the Aids for the Interpreter). The first practical rule of biblical interpretation is, Never trust your favorite English Bible—uncritically!

Let us turn then to the text of Isaiah 6. In a rapid reading the nine major recent English versions seem very much alike. This is not surprising, for translators tend to be conservative about departing from the traditional wording of texts hallowed by usage, and ours is such a text. Nevertheless, closer scrutiny of the recent versions discloses some significant differences among them. I want to go through these in some detail as a case exercise. This is an integral part of exegesis and an indispensable basis for interpretation. I will not do a detailed review of all the recent versions for each text discussed in this book, but I want to do it once at the beginning to illustrate the process.

The nine versions constituting our translation-panel are, in chronological order, The Complete Bible, An American Translation (CBAT); the Revised Standard Version (RSV); the New American Standard Bible (NASB); The Jerusalem Bible (JB); The New English Bible (NEB); The New American Bible (NAB); Today's English Version (TEV); A New Translation of the Holy Scriptures According to the Masoretic Text, Second Section: The Prophets (NJV); and the New International Version (NIV). (An explanation of the grounds for including these versions in the panel, and excluding others, is given in the Aids for the Interpreter.)

In this exercise, and elsewhere, I will use the RSV as the base text; first, because it is the modern version most widely available to American readers; second, it is the English version with the best claim to ecumenical authorization; and third, it is unsurpassed among recent versions, all things considered.

In Isaiah 6, CBAT differs little from RSV. It places the last sentence of v 13 in brackets, thus suggesting that this is an editorial addition to the original text (NEB, NAB, and TEV do likewise). This is a question of critical interpretation, not of translation. You will not be able to resolve it merely by consulting the English versions, but will need help from the commentaries.

NASB also agrees almost entirely with RSV, though it has "temple" instead of "house" in v 4 and "repent" instead of "turn" in v 10. JB, TEV, and NIV also read "temple" in v 4, although the other five members of our panel read "house." Nothing major is at stake here, since we know from v 1 that the house meant in this passage is a temple (or sanctuary), as all nine versions indicate. Nevertheless, a check of the Hebrew text or the commentators would show that "house" is the literal translation of the original Hebrew word (beth), and "temple" is an interpretation. "Repent" in v 10 is not wrong (NJV also has it), but it does have a different nuance from "turn" which the other versions have. "Turn" is more general than "repent." Repenting is a particular sort of turning. The Hebrew word (shub) often connotes repentance; however, "turn" is a more literal translation. Thus, in both of the instances of minor variation in NASB it is evident that the translation involves interpretation.

The wording of JB is quite different from RSV. This should not surprise us, for, like the five versions in our panel which were published after it, JB makes no effort to preserve the literary tradition of the Authorized (King James) Version. Therefore we can expect each of these newer versions to have its own distinctive sound. Judging the sound and the other specific literary qualities of the versions is important in deciding which translation to read in public worship. However, it is not important in studying the meaning of the text. Most of the variations among recent translations are stylistic and not substantive.

In JB we encounter for the first time the use of the name *Yahweh*. The other translations use the euphemism "Lord" (in small capitals) to represent the original Hebrew name *yhwh*. Thus JB is the only version in our panel which follows the original Hebrew text literally (only the consonants of the name are contained in the extant Hebrew manuscripts, but it was probably vocalized "Yahweh"). Of course, this is not a translation of the Hebrew, but a transliteration. Deciding what practice to follow in this case is not a question of translation, nor is it really a matter of interpretation. Rather, it is a matter of liturgical tradition and religious sensibility, that is, habit and taste.

There are a few other significant variations in JB. It reads "be our messenger" in v 8, instead of "go for us"; "be converted" instead of "turn" in v 10; and "stripped" instead of "burned again" in v 13. The first of these variations is minor, since it is clear from the passage as a whole that the purpose of the going is to deliver a message. The second variation is perhaps not insignificant. At least the change to the passive voice contains a nuance that is not in the other versions. The third variation cited changes the image considerably. In the other versions it is of a stump that remains standing after a tree is felled and is to be burned out. This image is lost in JB.

JB does not have brackets around the last sentence of v 13, as several of the other recent versions do. However, it has a footnote explaining that this sentence is absent from the Greek (meaning the ancient Greek, or Septuagint) version of the OT. Here we have passed out of the realm of translation into that of textual criticism. Whether this sentence is indeed absent from the Greek OT is debatable (my own opinion is that the Greek OT presupposes the existence of this sentence in the Hebrew text from which the Greek translators were working), but the

⌐rpreter of the English Bible must turn to the critical commentaries for help in this case.

The sense of NAB is almost identical to that of RSV. The one difference that catches our attention is "purged" instead of "forgive" in v 7. Comparison with the rest of the panel yields the following result: CBAT, NASB, and TEV agree with RSV in translating "forgiven"; however, JB and NJV read "purged," while NEB has "wiped away," and NIV "atoned for." Thus all the most recent translations except TEV use a word with a ritual connotation. This is in keeping with the context. Therefore, even without a knowledge of Hebrew one could decide on the appropriateness of one of these alternative readings. (The Hebrew word means first of all "to cover over" or "make expiation," and to forgive is a secondary or derivative sense of the word.)

The next three versions, NEB, TEV, and NJV, present more serious problems to the interpreter than most of the ones we have been considering. NEB alters the sense of the passage at two points, vv 10 and 13. The other eight versions understand v 10 as an imperative. Thus the RSV:

> Make the heart of this people fat,
>   and their ears heavy,
>   and shut their eyes;
> lest they see with their eyes,
>   and hear with their ears,
> and understand with their hearts,
>   and turn and be healed.

According to this translation, the hardening of the people's hearts is the deliberate purpose of the prophet's commission. However, the situation is quite different according to NEB. It translates:

> This people's wits are dulled,
>   their ears are deafened, and their eyes blinded,

> so that they cannot see with their eyes
> nor listen with their ears
> nor understand with their wits,
> so that they may turn and be healed.

This rendition changes the prophet's role in the transaction between God and the people. This translation should be more palatable to those readers of the Bible who regard the purpose of prophecy as bringing about repentance, and who are therefore offended by the idea that Isaiah might have understood his mission as exactly the opposite of this. However, all the other versions support the alternative translation, so one must be cautious in accepting that of NEB.

The second major difference in NEB comes in the final sentence of the chapter, v 13*b*. The whole verse reads:

> Even if a tenth part of its people remain there,
> they too will be exterminated
>   [like an oak or a terebinth,
> a sacred pole thrown out from its place in a hill-shrine.]

In this rendition, the word of hope which stands at the end of the passage in the other translations disappears (RSV: "The holy seed is its stump").

I believe there is only one responsible course to follow here for the English reader who does not know Hebrew. It is to trust the majority of the modern translations, which is overwhelming in this case. Readers may assume that the NEB committee had *something* to go on to support their translation; however, unless the readers have the linguistic tools to assess the translation, they would be irresponsible to take the translation of NEB as the probable sense of the text, in the face of the overwhelming weight of contrary opinion on the part of the other modern versions.

TEV is a special case. In reading our passage through in this version we sense a greater degree of freedom. The entire wording is fresh and original. Rereading it, we see possibilities in the text which we had not seen before. However, a close comparison of the wording of TEV with that of the other versions has to evoke questions in our minds about the legitimacy of this version. Two examples should make the point. In v 5 TEV reads "There is no hope for me!" instead of "Woe is me!" At the end of v 13 it reads "(The stump represents a new beginning for God's people)." Neither of these is translation. Both are interpretation. Already, then, after studying just one major passage in the recent English versions, our suspicions should be aroused over the reliability of TEV for a close reading of the text. Its freshness and fluidity are attractive, and it certainly makes the passage easier to read than some other versions. But we have to wonder whether it makes it too easy.

Finally, in this last group, we come to NJV. Our attention is arrested in the very first line of the passage by the wording "my Lord" where all the other versions have "the Lord." This is appealing, because it makes the reference personal. Is it legitimate? One cannot be sure on the basis of the English text alone. It is clear that the Hebrew word in question is not *yhwh,* for if it were, "Lord" would be in small capitals, in this version as in the others. So it must be some other Hebrew term. This is as far as we can go without consulting the commentators and/or the Hebrew text. When we do this, we find that the Hebrew word is *'adonay* and that this term, very common in the Hebrew Bible, sometimes means "the Lord" and sometimes means "my Lord." Which is meant in a given instance is a matter of judgment, based primarily upon the context. Therefore, we may conclude that NJV's is a justifiable translation. I expect most readers will welcome this discovery. The second difference to command our attention in NJV occurs in v 3, where it reads "His presence fills all the earth!" instead of the usual "The whole earth is full of his glory." Once again we are forced to go to the commentaries to adjudicate this difference in translation. But even before we do this we can be led to reflect afresh on this familiar line. Is "presence" the deeper connotation of the term? Is "glory" merely the verbal and pictorial symbol of the indescribable presence of God?

In v 10 we encounter another substantial variant in NJV. It reads "Lest . . . it . . . repent and save itself," where the other versions read "Turn and be healed." This difference is substantial, exegetically and theologically. The text as it has been translated traditionally poses a serious theological problem to many readers. They find it difficult to believe that a prophet of God should wish to prevent people from being healed, and they are scandalized at the notion that this should be God's own sentiment. The scandal is eliminated if we follow NJV, for it is entirely conceivable that a prophet, or the God whom he represents, should wish to prevent people from trying to save themselves, on the ground that salvation comes only from God. What can the English reader make of this difference in translation? Our usual rule is to trust the majority when the vote is very one-sided. In the present case the vote of our panel is eight to one! Unfortunately, however, the vote is misleading this time. "Heal itself" is a literal rendering of the Hebrew text. This does not necessarily make the passive "be healed" wrong, but it certainly does support the legitimacy of the reflexive translation of NJV. However, there is no way that readers without Hebrew can know this, unless they happen to find a commentary that explains it. Otherwise they are helpless in the face of a difference in the versions that has significant implications for the theological interpretation of the text. One is led inevitably to the conclusion—and similar circumstances are repeated again and again in the OT—that every interpreter of the Bible should learn Hebrew! It is not necessary to become expert, but if one is not to be kept at the mercy of the English versions, one must learn enough Hebrew to be able to use a Hebrew-English lexicon and to check the text of the Hebrew Bible when one encounters major differences among the English translations.

The last variant for us to discuss in NJV occurs in v 13. By this time the reader may be confused by the variety of renderings of this difficult verse. NJV adds to the confusion. It reads, "but while a tenth part yet remains in it, it shall repent. It shall be ravaged like the terebinth and the oak, of which stumps are left even when they are felled: its stump shall be a holy seed." Much of this is familiar by now. However, the first sentence may be puzzling. Where did "it shall repent" come from, and what does the verse mean if this is the correct translation?

There is not much that English readers can do at this point, except perhaps wait for a new critical commentary that will explain this new translation in NJV. Most readers, therefore, will probably disregard this novel rendering and rely upon the old familiar one, which seems the most responsible course of action. The facts of the case, textually, are these: the Hebrew text has three verbs in immediate succession. The first means "to do again" or "to turn" (or "repent"), the second means "to be," and the third means "to burn." If one takes the three verbs together as parts of a single clause, then the traditional translation "it shall be burned again" or literally, "it shall again be for burning" is correct. However, if one takes the first verb as part of a sentence with the preceding words, and the second and third verbs as parts of a second sentence with the following words, then the translation adopted by NJV is correct. The textual issue is simply how to punctuate the verse. The Masoretic punctuation supports the former translation; however, this punctuation goes back only to the middle ages, and it is possible that the intention of the original writer was what NJV has taken it to be. The upshot is that, even if one is working with the Hebrew text, one is forced out of the realm of translation, where the problem is insoluble, and into the realm of interpretation. In this realm, NJV creates a serious exegetical problem. According to this translation, the prophet is commanded by God to dull the people's mind, lest it repent and save itself (v 10); but then, when he asks how long this shall go on, he is told that there will be widespread desolation and that when there is a tenth part left, it shall repent and then be ravaged (vv 11-13). Thus on the one hand, the prophet is supposed to prevent the people from repenting in order to save itself, but on the other, he is supposed to expect that a tenth (of the people, presumably) will in fact repent but be destroyed nevertheless. This is confusing. There are various ways one might try to explain away the difficulty, of course, but it is reasonable to ask whether we should even try to do so. The difficulty is created by the translation. If v 13 is translated in accordance with the Masoretic punctuation, that is, in the way all the other modern versions do, this particular problem does not arise at all. Thus the course to follow seems clear to me.

After struggling through the problems inherent in some of the recent English translations, the reader may have a sense of relief to discover that our last version, NIV, agrees almost entirely with RSV!

This completes our review of the major, recent English versions of Isaiah 6. It may have become tedious, and at some points it was certainly frustrating. I can almost hear readers asking, "Isn't there a simpler way to do this?" There is only one responsible answer, and it is no. Albert Einstein once said that he always made his difficult mathematical writings as simple as possible and no more! Greater simplification would mean misrepresentation. So it is with biblical interpretation. The textual problems are there whether we like it or not, and responsible interpreters have no choice but to acknowledge them and do the best they can.

When we have gone as far as we can in determining what our text says, we are ready to reflect about its meaning in the Book of Isaiah and its meaning for us.

The *meaning* of a passage in its original literary setting is not necessarily different from what it *says*. It is not as if the writer said one thing, but meant something else. On the contrary, we should begin by assuming that the writer meant what he said, and that his chosen words conveyed his intended meaning. However, in order to decide what meaning the text might have for us, it may be necessary to probe beyond or behind what is said into its implications.

Some biblical texts address us directly. Prov 15:1 is an example: "A soft tongue turns away wrath, but a harsh word stirs up anger." We do not need to know anything about the writer of these words (including his theology), or about their literary history, in order to determine their meaning for us. We need only to ask whether they are true. Have we found what they say to be true of our experience? Is this something we might find useful to remember?

Other biblical texts address us only indirectly, if at all. In these cases, we must ask about the presuppositions or implications of the words in order to know whether they have any meaning for us. So it is with Isaiah 6.

According to the text, the prophet saw a vision of God, enthroned like a king and surrounded by angelic beings. His first reaction was to sense his own uncleanness and that of his people. But next he felt himself to be forgiven and purged of his guilt; and then he accepted the invitation to be God's spokesman. Isaiah's commission was to harden the hearts of the people as part of the process of God's judgment upon them, until all of them had passed through the fire. When this was done there would be a possibility of new life in the land.

The vision is dated in the year that King Uzziah died, but we are not told here or elsewhere in the book whether the vision marked Isaiah's initial call to prophecy. Nevertheless, since the purport of his commission conforms to the heavy weight of divine judgment expressed in the surrounding oracles, we may conclude that it was a decisive moment in the formation of his self-understanding as a prophet and in his knowledge of God.

● Visions are intense human experiences which have happened to men and women in many lands and cultures throughout history, and they still occur today. Like all other human experiences, they are conditioned by the culture and society in which the subject lives. However, cultural conditioning does not invalidate the vision. There is no unmediated knowledge of God. Perception of the presence or providence of God does not always, or even usually, take clear visionary form in the mind of the one who senses this presence or this leading. Sometimes, however, it does, and whether or not the experience itself has the form of a vision, any description of the experience is likely to use images rooted in ordinary human life. Thus any verbal expression of an inward perception of the power or leading of the Divine, will be anthropomorphic, in one degree or another. Some expressions will be highly concrete and pictorial, like this vision of Isaiah's, and others will be more vague and ethereal. The authenticity of the experience as an encounter with the Divine cannot be determined simply on the basis of the accompanying images which are formed in the subject's mind. This can only be determined on the basis of the theological and ethical content of the subject's interpretation of the experience. The effect of a deeply moving religious experience upon the understanding, the attitudes, and the behavior of the subject provides the only possible measure of its authenticity as an *experience* of God. With respect to the authenticity of the *report* of a religious experience, that is, whether the experience reported actually took place in the consciousness of the reporter, cannot be determined by anyone else. We can do nothing but take the person's word that it happened.

We are curious to know more about Isaiah's vision. What was he doing when it took place? Was he awake or asleep? Was he in the temple? Had he had such an experience before? None of these questions can be answered. We cannot even know whether the prophet actually saw a vision as clear and vivid as the one described in the report. In short, we know nothing about the personal circumstances surrounding the experience and nothing about its psychological dimensions. We have only the report. As a result we cannot use the biblical record of Isaiah's vision to test the validity of the visionary experiences of other persons, past or present. Since we know nothing about Isaiah's visionary experience, but a great deal about the visionary experiences of other persons, we have to draw our conclusions about Isaiah's experience by comparing his report with those of other visions whose psychological concomitants are known. Thus the direction of movement in our interpretation is not only from the text to our own situation. It is first of all from the better-known experience of other visionaries to the lesser-known experience of Isaiah, and *then* to our own situation. Therefore, if we wish to ask whether it is possible for someone today to perceive the presence and leading of God in the way Isaiah did, we cannot answer the question merely by examining the biblical text and our own personal exerience. We know that the kind of experience Isaiah reported has occurred in the lives of other persons, both in the past and in the present day, because many others have reported such experiences of their own. According to the accounts in the OT, Ezekiel was more of a visionary than Isaiah. We will be studying two of his visions later, one (Ezekiel 1–3) in this chapter and the other (Ezekiel 8–11) in the next. We will have more to say about the nature of these prophetic visions then.

When we turn to the content of Isaiah's report of his vision, we find a compact religious drama, rich in its theological statements. The impression of God's transcendent holiness and sovereignty dominates the vision. Isaiah is overwhelmed by a sense of his own lostness and uncleanness and that of his people. Yet, while Isaiah experiences God as unapproachable, the seraphim declare that the glory (or presence, NJV) of the Holy One fills the whole earth.

This earth, which is filled with the glory of God, can become desolate because of sinful people (vv 11-13a). And yet, the desolation may be the prelude to a new beginning, "a holy seed" (v 13b). God endures through the desolation. The glory of God, which fills the earth, remains though nations fall, and is present for those who, like the seraphim, have eyes to see. Amid the passing of kings ("In the year that King Uzziah died, I saw the Lord," v 1) and kingdoms, God is still enthroned, in and beyond the world.

When the Holy God asks for a messenger to speak to the sinful people, Isaiah responds. As a necessary preparation for his mission, Isaiah's unclean lips are purified—by burning!—

and his sin is forgiven. The forgiveness is not merited by Isaiah. It is an unbidden gift.

His message is a hard one. He is to proclaim the people's moral blindness and hardness of heart; and the proclamation will only increase the blindness and hardness, until the people are beyond reformation and fall under the burning judgment of God. Will this burning be final destruction, or will it, like the burning of Isaiah's lips, be a purgation leading to a new beginning? The last word of the text suggests the latter. The painful gift given to the prophet will also be experienced by the remnant of the people.

What meaning can this text have for us? How, if at all, do we move from an ancient prophet's vision of God to our own situation? Are there aspects of Isaiah's vision that can aid our perception of reality or stimulate our awareness of the holy or guide our moral judgment?

● First of all, we must be clear about the elements of Isaiah's vision relative to his own time and place and which therefore may have nothing at all to do with our own. He spoke about the people of Judah in the eighth century B.C. as a people of unclean lips and heedless minds who were going to be devastated in their land and deported from it, partly as a consequence of their response to his prophesying. As it turned out, he was largely correct in his prophecy, although it took longer to come to pass than he seems to have expected. There may be parallels to Judah's national experience, but we cannot take Isaiah's vision as applying to any other nation than his own. It may alert us to look for parallels, however, and thus to examine more carefully the dynamics of social history.

Other historically conditioned elements of the narrative are the image of the heavenly court of God and that of a ritual purgation. These images are projections of monarchial rule and ritual practice as Isaiah knew them in Judah, and they do not reflect our own political and religious consciousness. If we are to identify at all with Isaiah, then we must demythologize the image of God as king and translate the act of expiation into more general terms.

What elements of the narrative can be generalized to illuminate our experience? There are several, though they must be taken as suggestive and not absolute, as invitations to reflect upon our own existence and not as self-evident principles of human life. And none of this will make much sense except to readers who share, or are disposed to share, faith in God as the primal source of all things and the ultimate arbiter of human destiny. With this attitude of faith, we may be able to put ourselves in Isaiah's place and relate his experience to our own. At least we can ask whether anything in his experience or understanding corresponds to ours or helps to clarify it or appeals to us as credible in the light of our understanding.

By reporting his vision as the basis of his commission, Isaiah affirmed the abiding presence and power of God amid and beyond the world. God ruled the course of history, called prophetic messengers, and forgave sin. One humbled oneself in awe and unworthiness before God, but responded in confidence to the assurance of God's forgiveness and in obedience to the urgency of God's command. This can make sense to persons of faith in any age, although a specific call to prophecy may be discerned only by a few.

The commission and prophecy in Isa 6:1-13 were meant for Judah in Isaiah's time. Yet its affirmation that new life may come to people as a result of desolation or, to put it in theological terms, that judgment can be a means of grace, is one that recurs often in the Bible and may be taken as a fundamental tenet of biblical faith. This affirmation has universal relevance.

The hope for Israel, according to Isaiah, lay on the far side of physical and social disaster. It involved stripping away all material supports, false gods, and political illusions. This was a hard road to renewal. We may ask whether the road to renewal for a community or a society always involves some sort of agony. Societies do not repent as individuals do, for the structures necessary to maintain them are so pervasive and complex that they resist change by deliberate effort. Real change often requires an inward crisis or outward calamity to provide sufficient impetus for it to occur.

Isaiah's call was apparently a unique moment in his life, a single inner experience so intense and vivid that it shaped the subsequent course of his life. He affirmed that God's glory, which is the symbol of God's presence, filled the whole earth, and yet he sensed the presence of God and its significance for him in a distinctive way in a single moment. Such experiences are not uncommon, although they are not universal, among the religious heirs of Israel.

Isaiah's willing, unhesitating response to God's call, "Here am I! Send me," is used frequently in the church as a model of obedience for faithful people, especially potential ministers. This use is not illegitimate, provided that it is qualified. Taken by itself and represented as the definitive model of religious or ministerial calling, it can be inhibiting to those whose sense of calling is uncertain or gradual in its development. The narrative of Isaiah's call should be set alongside those of other prophetic calls in order to give a fuller picture of such experiences. Jeremiah's call, e.g., was in marked contrast to Isaiah's. Jeremiah resisted his call and suffered persistent self-doubt in trying to follow it. We will study the report of his call below. Any use of such texts as models of behavior for persons today should be cautious and balanced.

In Isaiah's vision, God is king. The image is regal and masculine. Imagery of this sort permeates the Bible.

● The ways in which we imagine God are always conditioned by our culture. Isaiah's culture was patriarchal and monarchial. However, our culture is neither patriarchal nor monarchial, and we know that we must use other metaphors in thinking and speaking about God.

The Call of Amos (Amos 7)

One biblical passage frequently throws light upon another. This is true whether we are studying individual words and phrases or larger units of the text. There are several other accounts of calls to prophesy in the books of the prophets, and it is edifying to examine them together with that of Isaiah's call. The earliest of these narratives is Amos 7:10-17. Amos was a contemporary of Isaiah. Although he lived in the vicinity of Tekoa, in Judah, he prophesied in the northern Kingdom of Israel during the prosperous and outwardly successful reign of King Jeroboam II. As far as we can tell from the internal evidence of his writings (which is all we have to go on), his public activity as a prophet was confined to the years of Jeroboam and did not extend into the time of troubles that marked the following decades. Isaiah's ministry, on the other hand, spanned both the time of tranquility and the time of troubles (the period ca. 735 to 700 B.C.).

As always, our first task in interpreting a text is to determine what it says. Therefore we should read it with care in the recent English versions. Readers may protest that this is a tedious way to read the Bible, and of course it is. However, we are not merely reading the Bible, but trying to interpret it. When one is reading the Bible for the main story line or for overall impressions, it is sufficient to read any one of the standard versions. Then as one moves to an ever more rigorous and detailed reading, where the homiletical, didactic, or theological use of the text depends upon a careful determination of its proper wording, one increases the intensity of study, including a more thorough consultation of the available versions. Thus one might adopt a three-stage strategy for reading the text. The first stage would be simply to read any of one's favorite versions. The second would be to read the two, three, or perhaps four versions which continued use has shown to be the most satisfactory. The third would be to consult the entire panel of recent versions, whether it be the nine I have selected or a larger group of the interpreter's own choosing.

At this time it is not necessary to go through the entire process of examining the nine versions of Amos 7:10-17. Instead, I will merely call attention to two lines in vv 12 and 14 whose translation affects our understanding of Amos' prophetic call.

First of all, let us set the stage. Amos has been prophesying in Bethel, the site of the royal sanctuary of the northern kingdom, that is, the Israelite rival to the primary Judean sanctuary in Jerusalem. The priest Amaziah considers Amos' prophesying to be destructive of public morale, and therefore a threat to the integrity of the kingdom. He warns the king about Amos and expels the prophet from the royal sanctuary, and ostensibly from the city and the kingdom. The charges he levels at the prophet and the prophet's reply have been the basis of a considerable modern discussion concerning the nature of the prophetic office. Therefore, we do well to consider these lines with care.

The issue in v 12 is whether Amaziah regarded Amos as a professional prophet, that is, as one who earned his living by prophesying. The issue in v 14 is whether Amos regarded himself as a prophet at all.

The most literal translation of v 12 is that of NASB: "Then Amaziah said to Amos, 'Go, you seer, flee away to the land of Judah, and there eat bread and there do your prophesying!'" In other recent versions, the sense of the line is shifted. One shift is made by rendering the line, "Earn your bread (or living) there and prophesy there" (JV, NEB, NIV, and NJV). A further shift occurs when it is rendered, "Earn your bread (or living) by prophesying there" (CBAT, NAB). TEV goes even further: "Do your preaching there. Let *them* pay you for it."

Now, Amaziah's accusing Amos of being a professional prophet would not make it so. Nevertheless, if the accusation is there in the text, it is something with which interpreters must reckon; but if it is not, they need not do so. My own judgment is that the best translation here is a literal one. There is a genuine ambiguity in the original Hebrew line. Therefore, it is the responsibility of the translator to let the ambiguity stand. The freer modern translations remove this ambiguity. This is particularly true of TEV, which here as elsewhere is more paraphrase than translation.

What should interpreters do who do not know Hebrew? In

situations like this one should trust the more literal translations, namely, RSV and NASB. The translators of NASB in particular have made it their consistent purpose to hue as closely to the Hebrew wording as correct English will allow. As a result, NASB is the best English "pony" to the Hebrew text among recent versions (in this it follows its predecessor, the American Standard Version of 1901; another older version that is generally a good guide to the literal wording of the Hebrew text is *The Holy Scriptures According to the Masoretic Text,* of the Jewish Publication Society, 1917).

The issue in v 14 is whether Amos' reply is to be taken in the present or the past tense: "I am/was no prophet." Properly speaking, there are no tenses in Hebrew, so one must decide on the basis of the context whether the temporal reference intended is present or past. RSV, CBAT, NEB, NASB, and NJV understand it to be present in this case, while JV, NAB, and NIV regard it as past. If the tense is present, then Amos seems to be saying that he is not a prophet at all in the usual sense of the word, but merely a layman (a shepherd, as it happened) who was called by God to prophesy on this occasion. However, if the tense of the verb is past, then Amos appears to be saying that although he has become a prophet, he had not been one until God called him from his former work for this particular occasion. In either case, Amos is making two important points in response to Amaziah's effort to keep him from prophesying in Bethel. The first is that he is doing this prophesying because of a special commission from God and not because it is something he does habitually. The second point is that God has sent him to prophesy to the Israelite people, and on the basis of this authority he is prophesying in Bethel. The implication is that neither Amaziah nor his king, Jeroboam, has the right to prohibit him from prophesying.

The question of Amos' professionalism cannot be answered with certainty, in the face of the ambiguities in the wording of the Hebrew text. Nevertheless, regardless of the way one prefers to translate vv 12 and 14, Amos' account of his call depicts him as a layman, an amateur, who suddenly found himself prophesying in the principal temple-city of the Kingdom of Israel, because of a powerful sense of religious obligation. The narrative of his confrontation with Amaziah makes a further point. It indicates the kind of reception a prophet of God was likely to receive from the leaders of the religious and political community.

Isaiah realized in receiving his commission that his prophetic words would fall on deaf ears, and would even deepen the deafness. However, the Book of Isaiah does not say that he himself was suppressed or persecuted. In the case of Amos we see that his words were taken quite seriously, indeed that they were regarded as a threat to the security of the kingdom, and that as a result, his prophetic activity was suppressed.

Unlike Isaiah, Amos did not report a visionary call to prophecy. In the two narratives of prophetic calls which we are about to examine, we will see that one was visionary (Ezekiel's) and one was not (Jeremiah's).

The report of Amos' call is not as rich theologically as Isaiah 6. Nevertheless, several features of this narrative are suggestive as we ponder the meaning of prophetic ministry in the church today. Amos' message was one of moral criticism of the leaders of Israelite society and government, and a prophecy of dire consequences for their behavior at the hand of God. This message was viewed as a conspiracy, that is, as a threat to the status quo. In an age like ours, when people doubt the power of a prophetic word, this text in Amos serves to caution us not to underestimate the power of such a word.

There were ministers of God on both sides of the debate at Bethel. The priest Amaziah doubtless understood himself to be doing his work faithfully when he rejected Amos from the temple and the city. Of course, Amaziah was a member of the political and ecclesiastical establishment. Therefore, he was less objective and less free than Amos to discern a genuine word of God in the message of social criticism.

Regardless of the way we translate vv 12 and 14, it seems

evident that Amos was not a religious professional and had not been trained in prophesying. His call was spontaneous and his ministry was for a particular occasion. Ordained ministers in the church today occupy offices that are closer in function to that of the priest Amaziah than to that of the prophet Amos. This then raises the question whether it is possible or even desirable to combine the two functions into one. My own conviction is that both are indispensable to the vitality and authenticity of the church's ministry. It is less important who performs them that that they be performed. However, if the ordained clergy do not speak the prophetic word, it is unlikely in most congregations that it will be spoken.

The Call of Jeremiah (Jeremiah 1)

Though biographical information about most of the OT prophets is scant or nonexistent, in Jeremiah's case the biographical information contained in the book is so copious, a volume the size of this one could be devoted to it. Therefore we are being highly selective when we confine ourselves to the account of Jeremiah's call in 1:4-19 and to one of his complaints (20:7-18).

When we take our usual first step in interpretation, which is to compare the standard translations of the passage, we find no serious problems with the text. There is almost complete agreement among the modern versions. The account of the call in Jer 1:4-10 is followed by two brief sign-narratives, describing experiences of Jeremiah that serve to confirm his sense of prophetic calling (the almond branch, 1:11-12, and the boiling pot, 1:13-19). One notable variation in translation appears in NEB in the statement of God's promise of support to the prophet as he discharges his commission. NEB reads, "I am with you and will keep you safe" (v 8). The rest of the versions translate, "I am with you to deliver you." The promise in NEB is more comfortable than the other, for being assured of deliverance does not preclude one's having to endure suffering and danger. The translation of the majority here turns out to be the better one in the light of Jeremiah's unfolding experience, and it is also a more literal rendering of the Hebrew word.

One other noteworthy English variant, this one supportable, appears in the sign-narrative accompanying the account of the call. The word play contained in the Hebrew of vv 11-12 is captured nicely by JB ("Watchful Tree") and NAB ("watching tree"). Some of the other versions explain the Hebrew pun in a footnote; however, these two manage to duplicate it in the translation.

Jeremiah's experience of being called to a prophetic career was apparently not visionary as Isaiah's. It is reported as a dialogue between the prophet and God. However, we cannot tell whether there actually were auditory elements in his experience or whether this is merely the form used to describe the emergence of his sense of divine vocation. Jeremiah did not step forward and volunteer readily for the commission as God's messenger as Isaiah did. Indeed, Jeremiah was a very reluctant prophet. We receive the impression that he felt compelled against his own will to follow this arduous and thankless career. This impression is confirmed by Jeremiah's complaints, as we shall see.

A major difference between Jeremiah's vocation and Amos' is that Jeremiah believed his whole life from birth to have been fashioned by God for service as a prophet, while Amos' report of his calling points to a brief interlude in an otherwise nonprophetic life.

We cannot be sure whether Jeremiah was a layman or a cultic functionary. Jer 1:1 places him among the priests of Anathoth, but it is not clear from this reference whether he himself was a priest or only his father Hilkiah. Since the office was hereditary, they may have both been priests. If so, this fact would distinguish Jeremiah from Amos, who was not a cultic functionary. Thus it appears that a prophetic calling could come to people in ancient Israel in widely differing circumstances and could occupy them in various ways for various lengths of time.

Apparently any faithful Israelite might be called to prophesy. If this was true in ancient Israel, is it also true in the church today?

According to the report of his call, Jeremiah's message was to contain words of both judgment and renewal (1:10). The element of hope is more explicit here than in Isaiah's call. Some interpreters have argued that this difference in the call-narratives reflects a difference in the message of the two prophets, namely, that Isaiah's was entirely a proclamation of national doom, while Jeremiah's combined prophecies of destruction and of reconstruction. A judgment on this issue is linked to the problem of the authorship of the oracles in the Book of Isaiah. In its canonical form, it intermixes oracles of doom with oracles of renewal, even within chaps. 1–11, which are generally regarded as the section most likely to contain the original oracles of the eighth-century prophet Isaiah. (Isa 2:2-4; 4:2-6; 9:2-7; 11:1-16 are all oracles of hope, while the rest of the materials in chaps. 1–11 are oracles of judgment.) Those who regard Isaiah's commission as entirely negative, and Isa 6:13b to be a secondary gloss, are also likely to regard the oracles of hope in chaps. 1–11 as not from Isaiah himself. On the other hand, critics are more inclined to attribute the words of hope in the Book of Jeremiah to the prophet himself and to see both doom and restoration belonging in the original account of Jeremiah's call. This view may be correct; however, it should be observed that the narrative of Jeremiah's call was as subject to modification by later editors as the narrative of Isaiah's call.

These considerations relate to the literary, or redactional, history of these two prophetic books. Now I want to consider an issue of another sort, which is involved in our interpretation of the calls of Isaiah and Jeremiah. This consideration is theological.

- • Prophets are not only channels through whom the word of God is communicated to the people, but are themselves members of the people of God. They have similar needs and aspirations to those of other people. They are subject to the same temptations.

They are equally finite and sinful. Therefore, the judging and saving word of God is addressed as much to them as to others. Furthermore, the presence of God the prophets perceive, and the knowledge of God they attain, must be similar to the perception and knowledge available to every other human being. In the end there can be no radical discontinuity between the prophet's experience of God and that of other people to whom the word of God is addressed. If prophets know the presence of God as sustaining power and forgiving love, then this same knowledge is available to the people to whom they are called to minister.

The path to renewal may be quite different for a whole community from that for an individual, but it is questionable whether the purpose of God can be essentially different in the two cases. Therefore, any adequate exposition of the relationship of God and Israel would have to offer the possibility of forgiveness, reconciliation, and renewal. This does not mean that such a possibility must be explicit in every prophetic oracle. On the contrary, some prophetic oracles may be entirely accusatory and judgmental. Many such oracles appear in the Book of Isaiah and the other books of the prophets. However, oracles of judgment are rooted in a faith where hope is always implicit, if the experience of God is as it is described in Isaiah 6 and Jeremiah 1. A prophet could hardly perceive the presence of God as sustaining and redeeming for himself, and deny the availability of this resource to those whom he addressed. No message grounded properly in such experiences could be merely condemnatory. In the end it would have to be redemptive.

This means that whoever was responsible for the positive elements in the commissions of Isaiah and Jeremiah (Isa 6:13*b* and Jer 1:10*b*), and in the collections of oracles that bear their names, understood the prophetic experience and the prophetic word correctly. For the purposes of the church's proclamation, it does not matter greatly whether those who were responsible were the prophets themselves or others. However, I see no adequate reason, on the basis of a critical reading of the prophetic literary tradition, not to conclude that the initial responsibility lay with the prophets themselves. There are probably secondary elements among the words of hope in the books of Isaiah and Jeremiah, just as there are secondary elements among the words of judgment. However, this is not a sufficient ground for denying all the words of hope to the prophets themselves.

Ezekiel's Inaugural Vision (Ezekiel 1)

In Ezekiel's call to prophecy the visionary elements are expanded to the extreme. The account of his call extends from Ezek 1:2 through 3:15. The vision is dated in the fifth year of the exile of King Jehoiachin of Judah (ca. 593 B.C.). A second vision, which occurred about a year later, is described in Ezek 8:1–11:25. These are supreme prophetic visions. The image in Ezekiel 1 of God enthroned and surrounded by winged creatures is clearly reminiscent of Isaiah's vision, indeed, we may wonder whether Ezekiel's vision was influenced by the Isaian tradition. However, it is probably sufficient to observe that both visions reflect the symbolism of the temple at Jerusalem, and it is probably the knowledge of that sanctuary and the habit of worshiping there that gave rise to the two visions, independently of one another. Ezekiel is identified as a priest (1:3), and this identification accords well with the priestly preoccupations that pervade the book, especially preoccupation with the temple.

Examination of the modern English version reveals no significant problems with the translation of this passage. Therefore, we may move at once to our reflections upon it. The narrative goes on at some length and in considerable detail to describe the winged creatures and the appearance of the glory of God, before any transaction takes place between God and the prophet. Ezekiel is overwhelmed by the stupendous sight and falls upon his face to the ground. Then he hears the voice of God addressing him. The spirit sets him upon his feet, and he receives his commission.

There is no experience of personal atonement in Ezekiel's

vision, corresponding to Isaiah's. He is simply lifted to his feet and told to go and speak to the Israelites. He is told not to be afraid of them, whether they heed him or not; but unlike Jeremiah, he is not told that the basis of his assurance is in the sustaining presence of God. He is not to fear the people, simply because they are not fearful. He is told in effect, "Don't be afraid of them. They are just a bunch of rebels!"

Not much is said about the content of his message. It is not until a hand appears in the vision, holding a scroll, that any clue is provided (2:10). The scroll contains "words of lamentation and mourning and woe" (RSV). Ezekiel's reaction to this is strange. Instead of the repulsion Isaiah felt to his commission (Isa 6:11), Ezekiel eats the scroll (in the vision, of course), and it tastes as sweet as honey to him (3:3). However, by the time the vision has ended, the prophet is left bitter in spirit, and he sits overwhelmed among his fellow exiles for seven days (3:14-15).

There is no reference to the Spirit of God in the calls of Isaiah, Amos, or Jeremiah. In Ezekiel's vision, however, the spirit is a prominent figure. It is not identified explicitly as the Spirit of God, although the implication is that it manifests the power of God. Thus the relation of the Spirit to God is not completely clear. The words addressed to the prophet come unmistakably from God, but the spirit has a kind of independence from God. Nevertheless, the function of the spirit seems to be entirely to prepare Ezekiel for his prophetic mission. Although the experience of his call is deeply ecstatic, so deep in fact that he remains overwhelmed emotionally for seven days, the significance of the experience does not lie in the ecstasy itself but in the commission to the people that issues from it. True religion, according to the biblical witness, is always communal, even though it is deeply personal. Moments in the religious life may be intensely emotional, even ecstatic, but they are always to be appropriated for the good of the people of God. They are not merely to be enjoyed in private.

Although Ezekiel's vision is as graphic as one can be, a

careful reading of the narrative shows that he understood the visual elements of the experience to be nothing more than pointers to the reality of God. God's being transcends human comprehension, and no image formed in the human mind can do more than hint at God's relation to human beings and the rest of creation. This is true of images formed in the waking mind and also of images seen in a dream or vision. This recognition of the incomprehensibility of God is implicit in Ezekiel's vision. Notice the care with which the manifestation of God's glory is described (1:26-28). The figure seated upon a throne is not that of a human being. It is nothing more than the likeness of the appearance of a human being (v 26). Thus what he sees is two steps removed from a human being. At the conclusion of the description the prophet wrote, "Such was the appearance of the likeness of the glory of the Lord" (RSV). The last word in the Hebrew text, of course, is "Yahweh." But it is not Yahweh whom the prophet sees. It is only the glory of Yahweh. And yet it is not the glory of Yahweh, nor is it even the likeness of the glory of Yahweh. It is nothing more than the appearance of the likeness of the glory of Yahweh! There is anthropomorphism here. However, the prophet has exercised great care in reporting the vision, so as not to violate his awareness of the transcendence of God.

It is interesting to observe how the prophet's ministry to the people of Israel is narrowly circumscribed. All he has to do is speak the word he is given. He is not to worry about how they respond. That is not his responsibility. He simply utters the word, nothing more, nothing less. There is no sense of pastoral identification with the people in this commission. The prophet's relationship to them is cool and distant, almost mechanical. There is no indication that he shares their situation morally or that he stands with them as one to whom the word of God is addressed. He is merely the transmitter of a message from God to the Israelite people.

In both Isaiah 6 and Ezekiel 1–3 it is acknowledged that the prophetic words will be delivered to a heedless audience. There is a difference, though, in the two acknowledgments. For Isaiah the blindness of the people was so complete that they were incapable of understanding his message and responding to it positively. They lacked genuine freedom of the will. For Ezekiel, however, the people's failure was more a stubborn willfulness than a psychological incapacity. They were capable of making the right choice, but they would probably not do so because they were so rebellious. In this respect Ezekiel was the most rationalistic of the OT prophets. He seems not to have acknowledged the bondage to which the human will is subject.

The call of Ezekiel contains many of the same theological and ethical implications as the other texts we have discussed, and these need not be reviewed. However, there are several other observations to be made here. Ezekiel was a priest who was called to prophesy. Since he was among the Judean exiles deported from Jerusalem in 598 B.C., he was separated from the legitimate Yahwistic sanctuary and was not able to function as a priest during the period reflected in the book. In other words, he did not combine priestly and prophetic functions into a single ministry. These occupied successive, rather than simultaneous, stages of his career. Nevertheless, by training and temperament Ezekiel was a priest. This did not prevent his becoming a prophet, even though his priestly theology and priestly sensibilities affected the way he perceived and proclaimed the word of God. One of the principal points to be drawn from a study of these and related prophetic texts is that the prophetic role is compatible with a wide variety of personal temperaments, professions, and circumstances. It is a ministry that belongs to the whole people of God, and at any given moment in that people's history the responsibility to fulfill it may fall upon anyone.

Moses as the Prototype of the Prophets (Exodus 3)

Let us look briefly at a text in Exodus that is closely related to the prophetic call-narrative we have been discussing. Exodus 3 is the account of Moses' encounter with God via the burning bush at Horeb (or Sinai), the mountain of God.

It is impossible to date this text. It is part of the major narrative stratum of the Pentateuch frequently identified as the JE narrative (the narrative formed out of the combination of the J, or Yahwist, and E, or Elohist, traditions). Although the tradition that lies behind it may go back in part to the time of Moses himself, the present form of the narrative gives an idealized picture of Moses as a prophet of God. It seems to reflect a knowledge of the prophetic office as it was exercised in the eighth and seventh centuries B.C. by such people as Isaiah and Jeremiah. The picture of Moses' call and commission is a kind of synthesis of the prophetic calls described elsewhere in the OT. As is the case in the other call-narratives, the encounter with the Holy God is an intense experience emotionally. This is symbolized in the present account by the strange phenomenon of the burning bush. Moses expresses reverence before the awful presence of God by the removal of his shoes. We have seen that Isaiah cried, "Woe is me!" and Ezekiel fell stunned to the ground. Like Jeremiah, Moses here protests his inability to undertake the heavy commission that God gives him, but his protestation is turned aside by the assurance that God will be with him and will sustain him in the undertaking. Inspired by the encounter and emboldened by the promise of God's presence, Moses becomes God's messenger to the people of Israel.

The picture of Moses contained in the narrative of the Pentateuch combines a number of roles, or offices, ordinarily separate in Israel in historical times: prophet, priest, judge (i.e., legal arbiter), and chieftain (the precursor of the king in Israel). Thus Moses is made the prototype of the ideal Israelite leader. He is a kind of father to the family of God, or shepherd of God's flock. By providing this composite figure in the Pentateuch, the creators of the OT canon have legitimized these forms of leadership for the people of God, the covenantal community. This seems to imply that these are the normal functions of the pastoral office, whether they be exercised separately or in combination. The figure of Moses, then, serves as a kind of flexible, multifaceted model for the ministry of the people of God in any age. Exactly how and by whom these facets are to be embodied, whether by men or women, amateurs or professionals, ordained or lay, has to be determined in the context of changing needs and shifting circumstances.

The Cost of Prophetic Ministry:
Jeremiah's Complaints (Jeremiah 20)

Thus far we have been considering prophetic call-narratives. In their present form, they may have been influenced by the prophets' experience subsequent to the call; by and large, however, we must take them as reflections of the call-experience itself. Our next text is of a different sort. It is one of the so-called complaints of Jeremiah, and it deals with prophetic ministry in mid-course. It is interesting not only because of its place in the biblical tradition, but because the kind of experience it embodies can occur in the lives of the prophets in all ages.

There are five complaints of Jeremiah (sometimes dubbed his confessions). They are Jer 11:18–12:6; 15:10-21; 17:14-18; 18:18-23; and 20:7-18. We will concentrate upon the last of the five. Before turning to the text and interpretation of this passage we need to say something about the origin of these complaints and their place in the Book of Jeremiah.

These complaints are similar, in both form and content, to the individual complaint psalms of the Psalter. Scholars have raised the question whether there is any literary dependency between the two sets of complaints, and various answers have been given. Earlier in this century, when biblical critics were inclined to regard the Psalms as one of the latest segments of the OT, there were some who supposed that Jeremiah was the original creator of this type of material and that the complaints in the Psalms were influenced by his example. In more recent times the dominant scholarly judgment is that the main forms of the Psalms were created in the early monarchial period, if not earlier. If this judgment is correct, then it is more likely that Jeremiah's complaints were influenced by the Psalter forms than vice versa. A few scholars have suggested that in content as well as form Jeremiah's complaints derived from the older complaint psalms. It has even been suggested that Jeremiah was a priest who composed these poems for use in the rituals of the temple, and that they are not personal reflections of his own life as a prophet. This last theory, however, has been rejected by the majority of scholars, who believe the complaints reflect the prophet's own struggles, even though the literary forms and some of the language has been influenced by psalms familiar to Jeremiah in the temple. Whatever the origin of these complaints, they are presented as the personal commentary of the prophet upon the interior course of his life.

Like most of the other Israelite prophets, Jeremiah's words went largely unheeded by his contemporaries, and he was persecuted for threatening the Judean kingdom with destruction at the hand of God. The earliest dated account of the ill treatment is contained in Jeremiah 26, which recounts an incident when Jeremiah was preaching in the temple. A longer version of the sermon is given in chap. 7. His address was taken as a direct attack upon the temple establishment by the prophets and priests who were the professional staff of the temple. On this occasion Jeremiah's life was protected by some of the lay leaders of the Jerusalemite community, princes of Judah (26:10-19). This incident is dated at the beginning of the reign of King Jehoiakim (ca. 609 B.C.). Later, when Jeremiah's oracles of judgment threatened, not only the temple and the religious establishment, but also the city of Jerusalem and the Kingdom of Judah itself, the princes abandoned their former virtue, and Jeremiah's safety was in constant jeopardy at their hands (37:11-15; 38:1-28). These narratives provide a general background to the complaints, which among other things decry a plot against his life (11:18-23). However, we are not able to place the complaints chronologically, either within the stages of Jeremiah's career as a prophet or among the known events of the history of Judah in his time. It would help us to interpret these laments (not to be confused with the Book of Lamentations) if we could date them more precisely. Do they reflect Jeremiah's struggle with his calling at an early time in his career, when he was not yet sure of himself and was less able to endure the persecution? Do they perhaps reflect doubt and anxiety that recurred over a longer period of time, even throughout his life? Unfortunately, these questions cannot be answered on the basis of the information in the Book of Jeremiah.

The uncertainty concerning which time in Jeremiah's life is reflected in these complaints arises in part from lack of information about his activities prior to the reign of Jehoiakim (609–598 B.C.). Although the prophet's call is dated in the thirteenth year of the reign of King Josiah (ca. 626 B.C.; 1:2, 36:2), none of the oracles is dated during his reign. Therefore, we cannot be sure how extensive a public career the prophet may have had during the remainder of Josiah's reign. The earliest dated prophetic materials are placed at the beginning of the reign of Jehoiakim, i.e., 609 B.C. (26:1). There are numerous references to the reigns of Jehoiakim, Jehoiachin, and Zedekiah (609–586 B.C.). We know that the public ridicule and persecution of Jeremiah extended throughout this period. However, since we do not know whether his public ministry actually began with the reign of Jehoiakim or much earlier in the reign of Josiah, we have a very uncertain background upon which to project Jeremiah's complaints.

The main point of interest to us would be in knowing whether Jeremiah eventually attained a sense of inner security and confidence in God, after an initial period of doubt and inward suffering brought about by his public rejection, or whether the doubt and anguish he experienced persisted throughout his life. Either outcome would be intelligible to us, and either would be useful in illuminating similar experiences in the lives of later servants of the word of God. However, we simply do not know which conclusion is the right one.

A plausible setting for the complaint contained in 20:7-18 has been provided by the editorial placement of this passage immediately after 20:1-6. According to this latter narrative, Jeremiah was beaten and put in stocks on the order of Pashhur, chief officer in the temple of Jerusalem, for prophesying the destruction of the city. This event probably took place prior to 605 B.C., for Jeremiah was forbidden to appear in the temple after that time (36:5, 9), and the prophecy that led to Pashhur's order was delivered in the temple (19:14). The complaint that follows is the last of the complaints of Jeremiah, in their canonical order. However, we do not know whether this corresponds to their chronological order; therefore, the juxtaposition of 19:1–20:6 and 20:7-18 does not provide a sufficient clue for dating of the complaints. Though the incident narrated provides a plausible occasion for the complaint immediately following, we cannot be certain that the two were linked so closely in Jeremiah's experience. Since we do not know the order of composition of the complaints, it is impossible to trace any psychological or theological development in them.

These observations do not empty the complaints of meaning, they merely set the limits within which we must interpret that meaning. I believe the complaints express Jeremiah's struggle to understand his calling as a prophet of God and to understand and accept the suffering he experienced as a result of obedience to this call. To say more than this, however, is to speculate in the absence of any real evidence.

Let us look now more closely at the fifth complaint (20:7-18). Four themes stand out. First, the prophet asserts that Yahweh has seduced him, and he has allowed himself to be seduced (v 7). Second, he says that proclaiming Yahweh's word is the cause of ridicule and persecution when he speaks, and inner turmoil when he keeps silent. Third, the prophet pleads with God for the punishment of his opponents, and he expresses certainty over their eventual downfall, on the basis of confidence in God's justice. Fourth, he curses his own life.

The seduction to which Jeremiah refers is apparently his very calling as a prophet. According to the report of his call (1:4-9) Jeremiah understood it to be under the support and protection of God. Therefore, the persecution he experienced in fulfilling his prophetic vocation appeared to him to be a breach of God's promise. The suffering involved both humiliation in the face of ridicule and physical pain and anxiety at the threat of death.

There are several references in other complaints to the faithful service the prophet had rendered in obedience to his call (15:10-11, 16-18; 17:16-17; 18:20) and to the persecution he had suffered as a result of this obedience (11:18-19; 12:6; 17:15). These themes are not echoed in the individual complaints of the Psalter. There are frequent lamentations there over the sufferings of the righteous, and particularly the sufferings endured for God's sake. Appeals to God to effect justice are a prominent feature of the individual complaint psalms, and the plea to punish the workers of iniquity occurs frequently. However, the specific complaint over suffering for speaking the word of God does not occur among these psalms. Furthermore, the charge that God had deceived the prophet is distinctive of Jeremiah's complaint.

The fourth major theme of Jeremiah's complaint is the curse of his own life, a theme unique in the prophetic literature. Its only parallel in the entire OT is in the third chapter of Job, which many scholars regard as dependent upon Jeremiah 20. Since there are no parallels to this curse in the Psalter, we have no literary models to help us decide whether Jeremiah's curse is an integral part of the preceding complaint or an independent literary unit. The woe expressed in the second complaint (15:10: "Woe is me, my mother, that you bore me . . .") is related to the curse in chap. 20, although the latter extends the motif to the limit, cursing the prophet's very life. Thus we see that here Jeremiah gathers up themes found in the other four complaints; however, the intemperate accusation of God that begins the fifth complaint and the despairing condemnation of his life that concludes it, distinguish this complaint from the others. Here the prophet's anguish reaches its depth.

There are several features of the other four complaints that do not appear in this one. One is specific reference to the identity of his opponents (11:21-23 and 12:6). Another is the expression of general theological perplexity over the prosperity of the wicked (12:1-2). Still another is the plea for God's healing (17:14). Finally, there is God's reply to the prophet's complaint (12:5 and 15:19-21). Thus the fifth complaint is not a mere repetition of the other four. It shares several themes with them, but it omits some they contain, and it includes some they lack. This variety in form and substance among the complaints of Jeremiah suggests that they do indeed reflect his personal experience and his struggle of faith.

There are three variants in the modern English translations of this passage that bear mentioning here. Several versions translate the second verb in v 7 reflexively ("and I let myself be seduced," CBAT, JB, NAB). This represents Jeremiah as blaming both God and himself for his deception. The implication is that although Jeremiah had sensed God's call as a persistent leading from the time of his birth (1:4), finally he had made the decision himself to accept the call. It was not a predetermined destiny that he was powerless to resist, but a vocation he was free to choose.

Three versions (JB, NEB, and NJV) translate v 9 in the past tense, "I used to say, 'I will not think about him. . . .'" (JB). This makes Jeremiah's anguish when not prophesying an occurrence in the past rather than an ongoing experience.

The third variant to note here comes in the final line of the complaint (v 18). RSV reads, "Why did I come forth from the womb to see toil and sorrow, and spend my days in shame?" Five other recent versions translate the last clause, "end my days in shame" (JB, NEB, NAB, TEV, NIV; cf. NJV: "spend all my days in shame"). This second alternative connotes an irreversibility and finality that are missing in the other translations. The Hebrew word readily supports the translation, "end my days." Indeed, it may even require it (the verb *kalah* means "to come to an end," "be finished," "be consumed").

What shall we make of this remarkable text? First of all, one is struck by the writer's fearless candor in expressing his pain and resentment toward God, a resentment mixed with deep perplexity over his calling and its cost in ostracism and persecution. The complaint is an excellent example of what today we call "being honest," i.e., giving free expression to one's feelings. If acknowledging one's feelings and trying to deal openly with them helps one to be a more mature and responsible person, with healthier, more constructive human relationships, then we can only applaud the candor of one who does this. However, dealing constructively with one's feelings, including those of anger, hatred, jealousy, and vengefulness, does not mean that one must give frequent reports to others on the state of one's emotions. Jeremiah confessed publicly to the extent that he recorded these complaints along with his oracles. However, judging from the picture of him in the biographical narratives, he was not known publicly as a complainer or an exhibitor of his personal feelings. His complaints are addressed to God; therefore, they must be seen first of all as episodes in his own inner life. They were made public only secondarily. We do not know in how wide a circle they were known, although my own guess is that it was initially only a small one including his friends and disciples, perhaps only Baruch, his emanuensis and biographer (see Jeremiah 36).

Jeremiah's complaints are not the only OT texts that exhibit candor in dialogue with God. The individual complaints in the Psalter are similar documents. As a model of piety these materials provide a correction to the habits of suppression and denial that often characterize the handling of doubt and anger by religious people. We tend to believe that such sentiments are incompatible with true faith and, therefore, we suppress them. However, they do not disappear, but persist in the subconscious mind, often diminishing our self-regard and inhibiting constructive personal relations. The psalmists and Jeremiah confessed their fears, doubts, and hostilities to God, even when they believed God to be responsible for them! In my judgment they provide an appropriate example for modern readers. The alternative to fearless honesty is fearful dishonesty. Self-deception can be destructive in the long run, whatever it may accomplish at first.

Religious doubt frequently centers upon uncertainty concerning the existence of God or the reality of God's involvement in one's life. However, these were not Jeremiah's problems. For him God was only too real and too fully involved in his life! The problem for Jeremiah was that he perceived God as a kind of monster who deliberately misled him into a vocation that brought nothing but humiliation, persecution, and pain. His problem was not the fear that God was powerless to affect the circumstances in his life, but the recognition that God had the power to determine those circumstances, and did so to Jeremiah's detriment. He could not understand why fidelity in the service of God yielded no personal satisfaction or blessing, but only sacrifice of all the comforts and joys of ordinary human existence. Twice in his complaints Jeremiah gave voice to what he believed God said in response to his pleading. The first time it was an admonition to prepare for still harder service (12:5), and the second time it was counsel to give up self-pity and rededicate himself in service to the word (15:19-21). This divine summons to a renewal of his obedience was matched on another occasion by Jeremiah's own plea for healing (17:14). These passages indicate Jeremiah's awareness of his limited understanding and his need to put his destructive feelings and doubts in a larger perspective.

Jeremiah's cursing his own life is not something we should take lightly, on the ground that he did not really mean it. It should be accepted just as it is, as an expression of genuine despair. At the time when it was uttered the prophet saw life as nothing but pain—no blessing, no joy, no fellowship with others. The loss of fellowship is the extreme curse. In part this loss was inflicted upon Jeremiah by those who rejected him, but partly it was a self-sacrifice made freely in obedience to his calling (15:17-18). This word from a complaint is reinforced by the biographical narrative in 16:1-5. This passage relates Jeremiah's decision to forego marriage and the ordinary comforts of family, as well as other kinds of human association, because of the disjointed times in which he lived, and as a way of symbolizing that disjointedness in his own life. To Jeremiah it was an age of wrath, and he allowed the symptoms of wrath to show in his own person and life as a part of his prophetic witness.

Jeremiah's example of self-sacrifice, particularly the sacrifice of fellowship among the people of God, is an interesting one for the modern believer to ponder. One can understand a short-term sacrifice of this sort for the sake of a long-term goal. However, in Jeremiah's case the sacrifice lasted to the end of his life. Thus for him there was no final personal satisfaction to be gained by his sacrifice, nor did he have the consolation of belief in an afterlife. Such belief was not part of Yahwistic faith at that time. Thus Jeremiah was not motivated by confidence in eventual personal fulfillment for himself, but only by radical obedience to the word of God.

The Servant of Yahweh (Isaiah 53)

Jeremiah's suffering as a man was a living-out of the story of Israel in his time. He himself experienced the deprivations of the age of wrath that was to come for the Kingdom of Judah. Thus the prophet's personal experience was a kind of incarnation of the judgment he proclaimed. This embodiment of the word of God in the life of the messenger is carried a step farther in the example of the servant of Yahweh in Isaiah 40–55. In the figure of the servant the conception of prophetic ministry in the OT reaches its highest development.

As an introduction to the discussion, I want to deal briefly with some sign-narratives in the books of the prophets. The prophetic actions described in these narratives are similar to the story of the servant of Yahweh in that the action of the prophet is a dramatic embodiment of the word that is proclaimed. In addition to publishing oracles, the OT prophets performed symbolic actions embodying aspects of their message. These symbolic actions took various forms, the most common reported in the OT being the momentary dramatization of a single word, usually a word of divine judgment. Ezekiel 4 and 5 describe a series of such dramatic actions performed by the prophet Ezekiel. They symbolized the impending destruction of Jerusalem. Jeremiah also performed several such signs (Jer 18:1-11; 19:1-13; 27:1-11; 51:59-64). The meaning of these symbolic actions was not self-evident. Each of them required some explanatory word from the prophet before they could convey the intended message. However, once understood, they provided a vivid, concrete reminder of the word the prophet wished to convey.

Some of the prophet's symbolic actions extended over a considerable period of time. Isaiah, e.g., is said to have gone half naked in public for three years as a warning of the future defeat of Egypt and Ethiopia (chap. 20). Hosea married a prostitute to symbolize the relationship between God and Israel (Hos 1:2). Jeremiah remained unmarried in order to symbolize the abnormality of the times (Jer 16:1-4).

Another lasting prophetic symbol was the naming of prophets' children. Isaiah named two of his children symbolically (Isa 7:3 and 7:1-4; Immanuel, in 7:14, may have been a third). Hosea gave such names to three of his children (Hos 1:4, 6, 9).

In most instances, it appears that the prophet actually performed the action reported in the narrative. However, in a few cases it is not clear whether this happened or not. An example is Jeremiah's burying of a linen loincloth in a riverbank (chap. 13). The long distance the prophet traversed in the dramatization, and the length of time between the two parts suggest that the incident was a parable told by the prophet rather than an action that he performed. Ezekiel's eating of the scroll in his vision (2:9–3:3) was the same sort of sign. It is not something that took place before the eyes of his audience, since it occurred only in his vision. It was only his telling about it that made it available to his audience. So it was with Jeremiah and the linen loincloth. Even if he actually journeyed the hundreds of miles from Jerusalem to the river Euphrates, as is indicated by the narrative, the journey could not be observed by his Judean audience. The point of the action could be evident to them only in the telling about it. Thus the narrative of the loincloth was really a parable and not a dramatized sign.

The unity of word and deed in these symbolic actions of the prophets is similar to the Christian church's understanding of the unity of word and deed in the life and ministry of Jesus. The OT does not represent the prophet as himself an incarnation of the word of God, in the way the church came to understand Jesus. However, the prophets' lives were bound up with the word in various ways. In some of the prophetic actions reported, the association between word and deed was brief and superficial. Here the prophet's behavior was nothing more than the public dramatization of an oracle. However, in other instances the link between the word and the life of the prophet was much more substantive. The principal example is Hosea's marriage. The most important relationship in Hosea's life became a lasting symbol of his message. His children, too, with their prophetic names, were incarnations of the prophetic word.

The symbolic action that comes closest to presenting the prophet as representative of the word he declares is Hosea's redemption and remarriage of his wife described in Hosea 3. Here the word of God's redemption of Israel is embodied in Hosea's redemption of his own wife. Thus he exemplifies in his treatment of Gomer the attitude and activity he believed God would make manifest in his relationship with Israel. The behavior of Hosea toward Gomer was only one episode in his life, albeit an important one. The whole of the prophet's life is not presented as an embodiment of the word of God. Thus when the church declared Jesus of Nazareth to be the word of God incarnate, it went well beyond anything suggested in the OT concerning the prophets. Nevertheless, some of the acts of the prophets are formative for the NT picture of Jesus as the Christ.

We turn now to the figure of the servant of Yahweh as he is presented in Isa 52:13–53:12.

The identity of the servant and the nature and scope of his mission are among the most controversial issues in OT interpretation. There is a vast scholarly literature dealing with these questions, and we cannot deal extensively with them here. Nor can we survey the numerous problems of translation presented by the Hebrew text, or assess all the variants among the modern English versions. Nevertheless, I want to include it in this discussion, for several reasons. The passage exercised a powerful influence upon the writers of the NT as they interpreted the meaning of the life and death of Jesus; and from their time until our own it has figured prominently in Christian theology and preaching. It is included in almost all Christian lectionaries, including the current Ecumenical Lectionary. Therefore, it is very likely to fall within the exegetical responsibility of preachers and teachers of the Bible.

> • Since there are so many affinities between the servant of Yahweh in Isaiah 40–55 and Jesus of Nazareth in the NT, the Christian interpreter of this passage must take special pains to understand it within its own literary and historical context and avoid jumping at once to the NT parallel to find out what the text "really means." Texts can mean something to later readers that they did not mean to the writer or the initial readers, and it is quite legitimate for Christian readers to view this passage in Isaiah in the context of the NT witness. However, there is much to be learned by examining it first within the OT context.

I have already stated the major conclusions concerning the literary composition and historical setting of Isaiah 40–55. I regard the four so-called servant songs (42:1-4; 49:1-6; 50:4-9; 52:13–53:12) as integral parts of the book. One must take account of what is said about the servant outside these passages (e.g., 42:18-20; 44:1-2) as well as within them. The servant is Israel, God's light to the nations (49:6; 42:6). However, the historical Israel only partially fulfilled the mission God intended for it. This tension between commission and performance is reflected in the poems of Second Isaiah. Thus at times, and especially in the four servant songs, the picture of the servant is that of the ideal that Israel is meant to follow. At other times the writer refers to the actual Israel as the servant of God, and then the flawed character of Israel's service is acknowledged (e.g., 42:18-19). Or, the writer speaks of the servant as having a mission to Israel itself (49:6), because there are always many who fail to understand or perform the service that is meant for them. When the writer refers to the servant as an individual, he is personifying the mission of the people in an ideal, or representative, figure. This understanding of the servant makes the most sense, in my judgment, out of all that has been said about this figure.

The mission of the servant is prophetic. He is to bring justice to the nations and *torah* (divine law or instruction) to the remote parts of the world (42:1, 4). He is to enlighten the blind and free the captive (42:7). Thus the mission combines word and action, instruction and justice, enlightenment and liberation.

There are important similarities between the picture of the servant and the experience of Jeremiah. The servant was called before his birth (Isa 49:5), as Jeremiah believed he was (Jer 1:5). Like Jeremiah, he sometimes wondered whether he had toiled in vain, but he remained convinced fundamentally that his call and his reward were with Yahweh (42:4). Although he was persecuted, he found support and strength from God in his distress (50:7). Also, his mission, like Jeremiah's, was to affect nations and not merely Israel (42:6, cf. Jer 1:10). These are some of the more evident similarities between the two prophetic figures, and they make it clear that Second Isaiah's understanding of the prophetic office was in direct continuity with Jeremiah's.

Our designated text (Isa 52:13–53:12) is rich theologically. Its important implications for understanding the mission of the people of God command our attention and yet the passage is used so frequently in Christian preaching and teaching that it is too familiar. For this reason, it is difficult to avoid hackneyed comments or to say something that might catch the attention of an audience. Familiarity makes the greatest texts of the Bible difficult to teach or preach.

Close scrutiny of this prophetic poem reveals numerous difficulties in translation and interpretation, especially in matters of detail. Indeed, there are many more variants in this passage among recent English versions than in any of the others we have discussed—too many to be listed, let alone discussed. Furthermore, in many places, our usual reliance upon the majority of the modern translations leaves us uncertain about what the text really says. The footnotes and annotations in the English versions do not help much, nor do the commentaries. The divergence among the commentators on significant points is as great as that among the translators. What, then, is the practicing interpreter to do?

In a situation like this interpreters must take responsibility themselves for formulating a coherent interpretation, and for a text as long, complex, and important as our Isaiah passage this entails some hard work. However, the rewards are considerable, for one gains deeper insight into the meaning. One also gains a kind of independent authority in speaking about it that cannot be achieved in any other way. Thus our rationale for including this passage among the representative prophetic texts is partly to lead readers into an exegetical assignment where they must learn to be on their own.

What impresses me first of all in reading the passage is the sharp contrast between the meaning and value of the servant's life in the eyes of the world and its significance in the eyes of God. The servant has none of the beauty, wealth, or power people desire to make them happy and successful (52:14–53:3). Furthermore, the servant's life is filled with suffering and failure. He suffers the fate of criminals and outcasts (53:7-8), and those who see his misery and ignominy regard them as justly deserved punishments from God (53:4). However, God declares the servant to be righteous, his life to be the fulfillment of the divine purpose for him, and his ultimate vindication and reward to be assured (52:13; 53:11-12).

It is also remarkable that, although the servant is rejected, persecuted, and condemned, he is the source of ultimate blessing to the very people who treat him this way. Thus, the servant does not deserve the sufferings that come to him at the hands of the people, and the people do not deserve the salvation that comes to them through the mediation of the servant. Neither destiny is fair by ordinary standards of justice.

Another striking feature of the servant's life is his nonresistance to the treatment he receives. He uses no force to resist, but quietly accepts what happens to him.

The people declare that the sufferings borne by the servant were their own (53:4), as were the sins for which he was afflicted (53:5, 6). They assert further that his affliction brings them wholeness and healing (53:5). Correspondingly, God declares that his servant is responsible for making many righteous (v 11). In what sense are the servant's sufferings those of the people, and for which of their sins is he being punished? How does he bring about their justification? It would help us to answer these questions if we could first of all identify those who are speaking in vv 1-9 and the many to whom God refers in v 11.

It seems to me that the speakers of 53:1-9 are the many nations and kings referred to in the preceding verse (52:15). Vis-á-vis these many nations, the servant must be Israel, as he is identified elsewhere in the book (44:1; 45:4; 49:3). Therefore, the sufferings borne by the servant are those experienced by

Israel, and it is these that should have been borne by the
nations. When we ask what specific sufferings Israel experienced in place of the nations, and what sins the nations
committed for which Israel was afflicted, our text does not
provide the answers. We must turn to the context of the passage
in the book as a whole.

How the servant brings about the justification of many is also
not explained in the text. The poet has God declare it to be so;
however, he says nothing of how it comes about. We are forced
to supply our own answer, hoping that our interpretation will
not do violence to the text, even though it cannot claim its
explicit support.

It seems to me that this passage makes the best sense if we
understand the servant as one who declares the truth about God
and the justification of the many as the appropriation of that
truth. The clue to this interpretation is found in 53:11: "By his
knowledge shall the righteous one, my servant, make many to
be accounted righteous" (RSV). The servant's knowledge is
knowledge of God, and the justification (or the being-
accounted righteous) of the many is their attainment of this
knowledge.

The text does not tell us what the servant does, what his
vocation is, how he lives, or what his values, activities, and
associations are. It also tells us nothing about his religious
understanding, his theology, his faith. We must learn about
these elsewhere in Isaiah 40–55, by studying all the passages
dealing with the servant. He is described as God's messenger
and witness (42:1-7; 49:5-6; 50:4). The message is everything
about God and God's purpose of salvation expounded in Isaiah
40–55. It is not stated in Isaiah 53 that this is the case,
nonetheless, I will try to show that it is implied in the overall
development of thought.

Isaiah 40–55 is a theological unity. Whatever may have been
the history of composition of the individual poems, they have
been fashioned into a single proclamation, a remarkable
witness of faith in God.

The principal theological motifs of the book are stated in chap. 40, which serves as an introduction to the work as a whole and which we will be examining later in detail. For our present purposes, only one point needs to be made: In the unfolding drama of salvation announced to Israel in its time of exile, an indispensable responsibility must be fulfilled by God's witnesses. Without them, there will be no understanding of the mighty acts of salvation that are transpiring in the people's experience. Indeed, since understanding is an essential ingredient of the acts themselves, the drama of salvation will not occur without it. Word and event are inseparable in the activities of God.

When Moses asked how he would know that God was present with him as he undertook to deliver the Israelites from bondage in Egypt, God replied, "But I will be with you; and this shall be the sign for you, that I have sent you: when you have brought forth the people out of Egypt, you shall serve God upon this mountain" (Exod 3:12). The saving presence of God is manifest in the historical event of deliverance and in the reflective act of worship. The act of worship bears witness to God and his word: faith in the God who has been revealed in the past (the God of the ancestors) and in the God of the future (whose promises provide goal and substance to the unfolding journey of the people). All this is signified in the revelation and recollection of the name of God, which is made to Moses as part of his prophetic commission (Exod 3:13-18).

Word and event, then, are inseparable. The saving event does not and cannot occur apart from the word that clarifies it as an act of God. The word, which calls for faith, precedes the saving event as promise and commission, and it follows the saving event as confession and act of praise. Without the prophetic witness of faith there can be no history of the people of God, since faith is the source and goal of the people's participation in the events that constitute their history. The people are not puppets manipulated unconsciously in a mock drama, but free persons whose acceptance of and participation in the providential destiny offered by God is necessary for that destiny to be unfolded. Faith in God precedes the saving event, thus the motive for leaving Egypt and going to the wilderness is precisely to worship God (Exod 3:18). Although Moses presents this motive to the pharaoh of Egypt as a momentary observance, an act that will require only a week's absence from Egypt, his actual intention is to leave with his fellow Israelites permanently. This is the true motive of the journey. It is to worship God.

Faith also follows the saving event, celebrates it, makes sense of it. Within the overarching purpose of God the escape of the Israelites from Egypt is completed when they worship upon the mountain from which Moses was sent to their deliverance. This act of worship also is an essential ingredient in the saving event, for without it the purpose of the journey would remain unfulfilled.

So it is with the new event of salvation that Second Isaiah proclaims. What this salvation will be is the subject of the entire series of poems that constitute the book. It includes releasing the Israelite exiles from oppression and breaking the tyrannical rule of Babylon. Furthermore, it involves proclamation of faith in the one God, Yahweh, creator of the heavens and the earth and redeemer of all people. It also involves repudiation of all forms of idolatry. It means beholding the glory of Yahweh in the drama of salvation (40:5), and it means joining in the universal celebration of God, which is the goal of the drama (chap. 55).

The prophetic witness is indispensable to the saving activity of God. Without it, the presence of God is not known within the life of the people, and the hand of God is not discerned in the course of their history. Therefore, already at the very beginning of Isaiah 40–55 there is a summons to the "herald of good tidings" to announce what God is doing (40:9). The servant of Yahweh is introduced to us at the end of the second major section of the book (41:1–42:4). Here faith in the God of Israel is contrasted with the idolatrous understanding of the nations, and the servant is exhibited as the one who, empowered by the Spirit of God, establishes justice and *torah* in the earth (42:1-4). Subsequent references to the servant make his prophetic vocation abundantly clear (43:10-13; 44:1-8; 49:1-6; 50:4-9). In some of these passages the servant is depicted as the individual model of the prophetic office, a kind of ideal figure, and in some of them the servant represents the actual people of Israel, who are called to bear witness to God.

The paradox of the prophetic vocation is that in proclaiming the knowledge of God the prophet comes to know God (43:10; 50:4). The knowledge of God is intellectual, of course, in that it involves understanding the ways of God and being able to communicate this understanding to others. However, it is more than intellectual. It involves the heart and the will as well as the mind. It is thus fully personal or experiential. It is a living, dynamic awareness of God and of oneself as a creature of God. The knowledge of God is attained partly by attending to the witness of others, i.e., to the prophetic tradition from Abraham and Moses to the present generation, but it is fully attained only by allowing it to become the ground and guide of one's whole existence. Thus word and life must finally be one. This unity is manifested in the story of Jeremiah, and it is also manifested in the story of the servant of Yahweh. In their lives, prophetic vocation and personal experience become indistinguishable.

The knowledge of God is the basis of health and wholeness; therefore, when the speakers in the fourth servant song affirm that the servant's afflictions have brought about their wholeness and health (53:5), it is not his afflictions alone that have done this, but rather the knowledge of God which is the basis of his entire life and for which he has been willing to suffer martyrdom. Merely being beaten and killed could not have brought about the well-being of those who knew him or observed him. It was the knowledge of God to which he bore witness and in which he lived that was the only possible basis of the people's health and wholeness. Righteousness, i.e., right living in relationship with God and other people, is grounded in and guided by the knowledge of God. Therefore, when God declares that his servant has made many to be accounted righteous through his knowledge, this can only be the knowledge of God.

Since the servant's prophetic vocation, which is identical with his life, is wholly dedicated to bearing witness to God and to the unfolding drama of salvation, the fulfillment of the servant's life and vocation is the acceptance by those to whom he is sent of his message and their appropriation of the faith that is grounded in it. Thus, when the people make the confession contained in this climactic servant song (53:1-9), the exaltation of the prophet that God promises (52:13; 53:11-12) is accomplished.

This interpretation of Isa 52:13–53:12 does not depend upon an exact determination of the original meaning of 53:8-9. It is debated by biblical scholars whether these verses describe the actual death of the servant or merely point to his being led up to the point of death. My own opinion is that the verses refer to his death, because of the clause "he was cut off out of the land of the living" (53:8), a phrase, which in Jer 11:19 must mean to be killed. Since other scholars consider the passage to be ambiguous, I would not wish to press the point of the servant's death. Whether he died or was merely brought up to the point of death, in faithfulness to his prophetic calling, is not important to the central message of the text. It may be important to Christian interpreters of the OT, who are concerned to draw the parallel between the experience of the servant and that of Jesus. However, I do not believe that a resolution of this issue is necessary to grasp the sense of the passage in its OT context.

● Second Isaiah depicted the prophetic vocation of Israel as he understood it in the sixth century B.C. In doing this he made reference to circumstances in Israel's life in that time, as well as to historic developments among contemporary world powers. These features of his writing are historically relative and do not bear directly upon the circumstances of the people of God or the nations of the world in other times. However, the knowledge of God which he proclaimed to Israel, and which he summoned Israel to proclaim to others, is true in every age. We will be dealing more fully with the content of this faith, as it is presented in other portions of Isaiah 40–55, in subsequent chapters. Our primary concern here has been to relate the life and mission of the servant of Yahweh to the understanding of prophetic vocation which is presented in the other books of the prophets.

I have asserted that the overall interpretation of the fourth servant song presented here does not depend upon our knowing with certainty whether the writer meant to depict the servant as actually dying. Nevertheless, this is an interesting and important question and is related to two others. The first is whether the servant's triumph and vindication involve his restoration to life, and if so, how this resurrection is to be understood. The second question is What happened to bring about the transformation of the people's perspective? What brought them to an entirely different understanding of the servant from the one they had originally?

The radical change in the people's perspective does not appear to have been caused by God's ultimate vindication of the servant, insofar as the latter might be regarded as a separate event. This final vindication or triumph of the servant still lies in the future, even though it is promised by God (52:13-15; 53:10-12). However, the transformation of the people's perspective has already occurred. They confess right now their new understanding of the meaning of the servant's life (53:1-9). Therefore, this confession cannot be merely a response on their part to an outward restoration of life, health, and blessedness, that is, to an observable change in the outward conditions of the servant's existence. According to the sequence of events suggested by the text, the reversal of the servant's fortune either follows the conversion of the people or is identical with it. If the latter, then the servant's victory is an entirely spiritual or moral one. However, the poet refers to the prospect of the servant's long life (v 10) and prosperity (v 12). These should perhaps be understood literally and these outward blessings not taken merely as symbols—metaphors—of an inner, spiritual reality.

Whether the servant is depicted as being restored to life, or resurrected from the grave, depends upon whether he is described as dying. Perhaps we should think only of his coming very close to death, like the prophet Jeremiah (who was thrown into a cistern and left to die, Jer 38:1-13). On the other hand, it seems to me legitimate to infer from the language of 53:8-9 that the servant was actually killed. In either case, it is important to note that the restoration of the prophet is entirely God's work. The people have done their worst to destroy him. His deliverance from the power of death and his restoration to fullness of life come about solely by the will and power of God.

If the servant is a symbol of Israel—a kind of ideal representation of the life and witness of the people of God—and the story of the servant, a parable of Israel's story, then the servant's affliction and his restoration to life may be taken as symbolic of all sorts of concrete experiences in the historic life of Israel, and in the life of the manifold people of God.

The servant did not deserve the affliction he suffered, according to the people's confession, but they themselves did deserve to suffer in this way (53:4-5). Was his suffering vicarious, then, and if so, did it effect vicarious atonement? These have been important issues in the history of interpretation, especially among Christians, and they are valid issues for us to consider today. It seems to me that both vicarious suffering and vicarious atonement are depicted in this drama of the servant's life. However, I believe it unnecessary, and even undesirable, to interpret these terms in a mechanical or legalistic way, as has sometimes been done. What is suggested here is not the arbitrary or mechanical transfer of punishment from one person or group of persons to another, as if one's prison sentence were being served by another. Instead, we should try to understand these terms in the light of the experience of the prophets in Israel, and the experience of Israel among the nations. Not all vicarious suffering is vicariously atoning. It makes a difference how the sufferings come about and for what purpose they are endured. The servant was the prophet of God, messenger of God's word of judgment and redemption, teacher of God's *torah,* witness to the truth about God. The suffering he endured came about primarily because of his fidelity to his calling. According to ordinary standards of justice, obedience to God should be rewarded and not punished. Other people deserve suffering far more than the righteous servants of God. Indeed, others may deserve punishment doubly insofar as they are responsible for the sufferings of God's servants. These servants may be willing to suffer for their faith, partly for its own sake, and partly for the good that may come from their testimony and example. If this testimony and example bring others to an awareness of the truth about God, and thus to a truer relationship with God, then atonement—wholeness, fulfillment, righteousness, salvation—has occurred. Then the one who has made the witness to the truth, by word or example, can be said to have done so for the sake of, or on behalf of, the one whose understanding and life are affected. It is in this sense, it seems to me, that vicarious atonement is brought about by the servant of Yahweh. Regardless of whether the servant is an individual prophet like Jeremiah or a community of faithful Israelites in exile, the kind of communication and transaction symbolized in Isaiah 53 can occur.

III. WORSHIP AND IDOLATRY

Worship may be defined in both a broad and a narrow sense. In the broad sense it comprehends the whole of religion, the service of God, and thus the whole life of the worshiper. In the narrow sense it refers to the performance of ritual acts. The second meaning is intended in the title of this chapter. However, worship in the ritual sense is inseparable from worship in the larger sense, therefore the following discussion will touch repeatedly upon the relationship of the two. Similarly, idolatry can be understood in both a narrow and a broad sense, that is, as false ritual or as false way of life.

According to Gen 4:26 people began to worship God in the third generation of humankind. Then, after the flood, the first thing Noah did was build an altar for Yahweh and present burnt offerings upon it (Gen 8:20). Abraham marked the journey undertaken in response to God's call by building several altars (Gen 12:7-8). Jacob is said to have established the first sanctuary in Bethel as a memorial of his nocturnal apprehension of the divine presence in that place (Gen 28:16-19). Moses told the king of Egypt that the reason for his request to take the Israelite slaves on a journey into the wilderness was so they could worship Yahweh their God (Exod 3:18; 5:1). When Moses and the Israelites later made good their escape from Egypt into the wilderness, they did worship God there (Exod 19; 24). A large portion of the Pentateuch consists of regulations for the proper performance of the worship, and this theme is a central one in the books of Samuel and Kings, and it entirely dominates the books of Chronicles. Many, if not most, of the hymns and prayers in the Psalms were composed for worship in the Israelite sanctuary, or were modeled upon compositions used there. It is clear, therefore, that public worship was one of the central realities in the life of ancient Israel. Indeed, without it Israel would never have existed as a people. Therefore it is not surprising that sanctuaries, sacrifices, priests, and ceremonials receive considerable attention in the writings of the prophets. In this chapter we will consider one major text from each of the four great books of the prophets. These texts are Isaiah 55, Jeremiah 7, Ezekiel 8–11, and Hos 5:15–6:6 (the last representing the Book of the Twelve Prophets). In addition several other texts will be treated briefly. Although united by a common theme, these texts differ greatly from one another in form, style, and imagery. They also come from a wide range of periods in the life of Israel, beginning with Hos 5:15–6:6 from the eighth century, and concluding with Isaiah 55 from the sixth century B.C. Thus our representative texts span the prophetic corpus, both literarily and historically, in relation to the theme of worship and idolatry.

Jeremiah's Temple Speech (Jeremiah 7)

This chapter contains a brief sermon (vv 1-15) delivered by Jeremiah in the court of the temple at the beginning of the reign of King Jehoiakim. A narrative report of the event is contained in chap. 26. This sermon is the first dated public utterance of Jeremiah in the book. It is uncertain how much public activity Jeremiah engaged in before this time. Although chap. 1 dates his call seventeen years earlier during the reign of King Josiah, none of the extant materials are dated during this period, and there are insufficient internal clues among the undated oracles to supply the missing picture with any certainty. However, the prose narratives provide a fairly detailed chronicle of the prophet's life from the beginning of Jehoiakim's reign in 609 B.C. to the governorship of Gedaliah, sometime after 586 B.C. The famous scroll that Jeremiah dictated to Baruch is dated four years after the temple address (i.e., 605 B.C.; Jeremiah 36). The bulk of the oracles contained in the scroll may have been composed during this four-year period; however, it may have contained oracles dating from the reign of Josiah also.

It is uncertain whether Jeremiah prophesied publicly during the reign of Josiah; it is also quite uncertain how he evaluated the reform that Josiah carried out about 621 B.C. (2 Kings 22–23). This issue has been debated by biblical scholars, and no consensus has emerged. On the one hand, we may presume that Jeremiah approved the removal of idolatrous images and practices from the Israelite cult (2 Kgs 23:4-14), as well as the renewal of the covenant with Yahweh (23:1-3, 21-25). On the other hand, it is difficult to believe he would have approved the slaughter of the priests in the former Kingdom of Israel (23:20). It is certain, according to Jeremiah 7 and 26, that he rejected the superstitious regard for the temple that he found among the people of Judah at the end of Josiah's reign. This superstition must have been abetted by Josiah's reform, for the reform made this temple the only legitimate sanctuary in the kingdom.

An additional factor in the Judean regard for the temple and Jerusalem was the tradition concerning their deliverance from the Assyrian siege in 701 B.C. This tradition had grown to legendary proportions, until it was believed that Yahweh had delivered Jerusalem miraculously from the hand of the Assyrians because of the presence of the sanctuary there (Isa 36:1–37:38, esp. 37:36). Whatever may actually have happened to bring Sennacherib's siege to an end (2 Kgs 18:13-16 suggests that it occurred because of the capitulation of the Judean king Hezekiah), the people of Judah in Jeremiah's time were infected by the superstitious conviction that as long as the presence of Yahweh in the sanctuary of Jerusalem was acknowledged and the proper worship of Yahweh performed, the city, and the kingdom of which it was the capital, were secure. This is the attitude that Jeremiah addressed in his temple speech (7:1-15).

The issue raised by the temple speech was this: Under what conditions could the people of Judah continue to live in the land they had inherited from their ancestors, land long regarded as God's gift to Abraham and his descendants? Apparently many Judeans believed they would be secure in the land as long as the worship of Yahweh was maintained in the temple of Jerusalem. The temple address puts the matter differently. Mere maintenance of the sanctuary would provide them no security at all. Worshiping Yahweh at the sanctuary of Shiloh in an earlier time had not given the people of Israel any protection against the Philistines, as was only too apparent from its ruins that were still visible in Jeremiah's time (7:12-15). However, the people of Judah could expect to remain securely in their ancestral land, provided they maintained social justice and personal morality (vv 3-7). On the other hand, if they violated the moral and religious principles of Yahwism—as the prophet believed many of them were doing—they would lose possession of their land, and the temple in which they trusted would be destroyed (vv 8-15).

The professional temple personnel were scandalized by this speech (26:11), and they tried to put Jeremiah to death. Obviously, the prophet threatened their self-interest as officials of the religious establishment. However, the lay leaders of Judah, the princes (vv 16-19), saw no crime in what Jeremiah had done, and they prevented the priests and prophets from carrying out their wish. The royal officials of Judah appear in a favorable light in this narrative; however, we should remember, if we are tempted to compare the religious officials invidiously with the lay officials, that the latter proved to be equally selfish when their own interests were threatened by the prophet's prediction of the Babylonian destruction of the kingdom (37:11-16).

Before we probe the major theological issues in Jeremiah 7 we should do our familiar homework in the recent English versions. As it happens, we find only one significant variant among our panel of nine. In vv 3 and 7, where seven read "I will let you dwell/live in this place," JB and NAB translate "I will stay/remain with you in this place." A check of the commentaries will reveal that the consonantal Hebrew text will support either translation, that the vocalized Hebrew (Masoretic) text supports "let you dwell," and that the ancient versions of Aquila (Greek) and Jerome (Latin) support "dwell with you." The point is different in each case. In the first the prophet is asserting that the people will continue to live in the land of Judah if they obey the moral commandments of God. In the second he is saying that God will continue to be present in their midst if they obey the commandments. Of course, we cannot decide which translation is correct on the basis of our preference for one or the other of these propositions. Rather, we must decide which is more likely in the context of the rest of the passage. On this ground, it seems to me the preferred reading is "let you dwell in this place." The issue is not whether Yahweh will be present in the land, but whether the people of Judah will be there. Thus, when the prophet has Yahweh declare that he will drive the sinful Judeans out of his sight (v 15), as he has done previously to the inhabitants of Shiloh, the meaning is that they will be dispossessed from the land. Nevertheless, since there is an ambiguity in the text, it is probably best to consider both translations in relation to Jeremiah's prophetic argument.

The lesson usually extracted from this passage is that ritual without morality is unacceptable to God. As far as it goes, this seems to be a fair reading, provided that morality is understood both as individual uprightness and as social justice. This is a lesson taught over and over in the Bible, and it is not surprising to find it here. Nevertheless, this is not quite the same point

Jeremiah was making in his speech. He was not stressing the inseparability of morality and religion in true Yahwism. Rather he was saying that if the Kingdom of Judah relied upon the existence of the temple as the basis of its national security, while disregarding covenantal ethics, it could expect ruin. On the other hand, if the kingdom were faithful to covenantal ethics, it could expect to be preserved as a nation. This is the central issue to consider, and it poses two questions for us. First, was Jeremiah correct in his analysis of Judah's social and political situation? Second, does Jeremiah's analysis disclose a general truth about human communities that is applicable to our own time?

When we study the outward course of Judah's national history, it is evident she was a victim of the ambitions of the major powers of the ancient Near East. Located as she was in the narrow corridor between Africa and Asia, she was helpless throughout most of her history to resist control by the kings of Egypt and Mesopotamia. In the end, the only alternatives open to her were absorption into one of the great empires or vassalage. The great powers preferred to control the smaller kingdoms through vassalage, and resorted to annexation only when the vassals persisted in withholding tribute or disturbing the political and economic interests of the sovereign. King Ahaz of Judah led his kingdom into vassalage to Assyria ca. 735 B.C. (2 Kgs 16:7-18), and from that time on Judah was unable to determine her own destiny. She enjoyed a brief respite during the reign of Josiah. Assyria went into rapid decline as a world power after the death of Ashurbanapal (ca. 626 B.C.), and it was twenty years before another power was able to establish imperial control over Judah and the other petty kingdoms of western Asia. Babylonia achieved this hegemony in 605 when Nebuchadnezzar defeated Pharaoh Necho of Egypt at the battle of Carchemish on the Euphrates. During the interregnum Josiah mounted his reform, which was both religious and political. He managed briefly to reunite the central districts of the old United Kingdom of David and Solomon and to reestablish covenantal Yahwism as the sole legitimate religion. However, Josiah's dream of rejuvenating the Kingdom of David came to an end in 609 when he was killed by Pharaoh Necho at Megiddo. His son Jehoiakim enjoyed relative independence, as an ally of Egypt, until the battle of Carchemish. From that time on, Judah's destiny was determined by the neo-Babylonian monarch. At first Jehoiakim accepted vassalage, but in 598 he rebelled. The Babylonians subdued the rebellion, deported King Jehoiachin, who had succeeded Jehoiakim, together with most of the political leaders, the upper classes, and the skilled artesans to Babylonia. They set Zedekiah, the brother of Jehoiakim, on the throne of Judah as their vassal. A renewed Judean rebellion in 588 B.C. led to the final destruction of the city of Jerusalem and reduction of the Kingdom of Judah to provincial status within the empire of Babylon. This in brief was the course of national events during the life of Jeremiah.

Jeremiah's temple speech was delivered about 609, soon after the death of Josiah and the ascension of Jehoiakim. Reading Jeremiah's speech in the light of the international politics of the time, one may wonder what relevance Jeremiah's message had to Judah's national fortunes. Did the people's attitude toward the temple or their morality really affect their possession of the land or their political independence?

How shall we regard Jeremiah's contention that God would allow the people of Judah to continue in their ancestral land if they maintained their moral integrity and practiced social justice? First of all, we should acknowledge that Jeremiah viewed the course of national affairs, both Judah's and that of the other nations of the world, as under the direct control of God. Therefore, if Judah lost her political independence and her people were exiled from their land, these events occurred not so much because of the will of the Babylonian king, but because of the will of God. But if God willed this or that political fortune for the people, the decision would not be capricious. It would be a manifestation of righteous divine governance in their life, and this would be a response to their moral deserving. Thus, any major fortune in the life of Judah would be interpreted by Jeremiah and those who shared his prophetic faith as a blessing or punishment bestowed by God.

Was Jeremiah correct? The answer is both yes and no. It seems to me that the leaders of the Kingdom of Judah deserved the subjugation and exile that came to them at the hands of the Babylonians, though primarily because of their political folly. The state of morality and social justice within Judah had less to do with their political independence and continued possession of the land than their international politics. Nevertheless, these realms were not really separable. The political decisions made by the rulers of Judah were partly expressions of the moral and religious values they held and the quality of the social relations they shared. A leadership that indulged itself in a self-serving, magical view of religious ritual, and disregarded social justice and personal morality, was likely to make short-sighted, self-serving decisions in the realm of international politics. Thus, there is a sense in which the outward fortunes of the kingdom were the fruits of its religious consciousness and moral behavior.

• If we wish to apply the kind of ethical analysis Jeremiah made in ancient Judah to the circumstances of a modern nation, we must acknowledge the greater complexity of modern social and political life. What happens in national and world history today is the product of so many factors that it is almost impossible to comprehend what takes place, let alone control it. Simple moral explanations of the actions of nations and communities seem to have little place in our world. There are so many people, groups, and nations caught up in intricate networks of economic, political, scientific, technological, and cultural relationships; it is a wonder any sort of order and coherence is maintained in human affairs. Governments with the greatest concern for social justice may have the least power to effect it, and the well-being of nations may have more to do with the accidents of history and the possession of natural resources than with the religious life or morality of their citizens.

Nevertheless, prophetic statements like Jeremiah 7 continue to merit our interest and consideration. They tell us again and again to acknowledge the moral dimension in communal and national life, the importance of social justice for all members of the human community, the futility of all forms of magic and superstition, and the essential qualities of obedience to God. The religious convictions and moral behavior of a people have definite consequences for the life of their nation, even though it is impossible to trace them precisely. In this sense Jeremiah's analysis of the religious situation of his day has relevance in any age.

The subjects of worship and idolatry are treated not only in the temple speech, which constitutes the opening portion of chap. 7, but also in several other literary units that make up this chapter. Two of these (vv 16-20 and vv 29-34) contain comments on certain idolatrous religious practices current in Jeremiah's time, and a third (vv 21-28) refers to Israelite worship in patriarchal times. We will not discuss all these passages in detail here. However, the juxtaposition of these texts to the account of the temple speech suggests a question about the proper content of worship in Israel that deserves our consideration. In the third section (7:21-28) it is asserted that Yahweh had not commanded Israel's ancestors to offer sacrifices to him, but had required only that they follow in the way of life in which he guided them. This statement suggests that Jeremiah condemned the entire system of sacrifices, and thus called into question the whole content of temple ritual, which centered in the sacrifices. Furthermore, by placing Jeremiah's temple speech alongside passages concerned with the worship of alien gods (vv 16-21 and 29-34), the editors of the book seem to imply that the rituals of the temple were idolatrous. So we may ask whether the burden of these texts is the rejection of sacrifice, and the rites and ceremonies built around it.

We will leave the Book of Jeremiah for a time with the question of his view of the sacrificial system unanswered, and turn to another passage in the books of the prophets where this issue is raised quite explicitly.

Mercy and Not Sacrifice (Hosea 6)

This text from Hosea contains the famous statement, "I desire mercy, not sacrifice; the knowledge of God rather than burnt offerings" (v 6). Many a modern reader of the Bible has taken this assertion, which we have quoted here in the traditional King James Version, as the true prophetic estimate of Israel's sacrificial system, or of any ritualistic religion. Along with Micah 6:7-8, this word of Hosea has been used to set the prophetic against the priestly tradition in the OT. It has also been used by Protestant Christians as a warrant for criticizing Roman Catholic sacramentalism. It certainly puts the question of the validity of sacrificial ritual very sharply and therefore provides a useful focus for our reflection about the shape and substance of worship.

The Book of Hosea provides no definite clue to the specific historical setting of this passage. When in the preceding oracle Hosea pronounces the judgment of God upon the kingdoms of Israel and Judah for engaging in warfare with one another, he seems to be alluding to the events surrounding the Syro-Ephraimitic invasion of Judah (ca. 735 B.C.; cf. 2 Kgs 16:5; Isa 7:1). This oracle ends with Yahweh's declaring that he will tear both kingdoms like a lion and return to his lair with the prey, until they confess their guilt and seek God instead of territorial aggrandizement. What follows next in chap. 6 is a confession by the people. Thus, the theme of confession provides a link between the two passages (5:15 and 6:1). It is not clear whether this is an editorial, catchword association or whether the two passages were meant by the prophet to form a unity. This ambiguity is reflected in the modern English versions. Some of them regard 6:1ff. as a continuation of 5:15 (CBAT, NAB, RSV), while others distinguish them as two separate passages (NASV, NEB, TEV, NJV, NIV, JB).

It seems likely that 6:1-6 is a separate oracle. In 5:15 Yahweh declares that he is going to wait for Israel and Judah to return to him, and the clear implication is that this means a return in genuine repentance and earnest confession. However, the confession of the people quoted in 6:1-3 is spurned by Yahweh as an ephemeral act of devotion (vv 4-6). Therefore, I do not see how we can take this confession as the kind of return referred to in 5:15. In any case, 6:1-6 can stand on its own as a prophetic commentary on the meaning of worship.

The people's confession expresses the heart of biblical faith: God is certainly present among them, and their fulfillment (healing, wholeness, vitality) comes about by living in the full acknowledgment of this presence. God had declared to Moses and to Jeremiah, among others, "I will be with you" (Exod 3:12; Jer 1:8). This presence was a reality not only for the prophet, but also for the whole people of God. The reality of God's presence that Moses perceived in the incident of the burning bush (Exodus 3) was the same as that perceived by the people at Mount Sinai (Exodus 19; 24). However, the moment of intense awareness of God differed from the rest of life only in its concentration. The experiences at the burning bush and the mountain pointed to the continuing presence of God, and the memory of them served as reminders of this presence. The awareness could be concentrated anew whenever the people assembled in corporate worship. The rituals of the sanctuary were the vehicles for recollection and celebration of the sustaining and saving presence of God. It was a distortion of Israel's faith to regard the sanctuary as the only place where one could enter into the presence of God, or to regard the traditional sacrificial rites as the necessary and sufficient means of appropriating the blessing of the God who was present. However, it was easy for people in Israel to slip into such misunderstandings, just as it is possible for people today to think of the worship of God as confined to sacred times, places, and rituals.

The people's confession, which Hosea records in 6:1-3, is in itself a fully appropriate expression of the relationship of God with his people, according to the prophetic faith. The prophet's objection to this confession, expressed in vv 4-6, is not over the intrinsic meaning of the statement, but over the people's inconstancy of devotion. Everything they said about God was true. Fullness of life was indeed to be found in his presence, and this presence was as available as any of the common phenomena of nature (v 3). But the God who provided fullness of life required steadfast devotion. This meant not only periodic public worship, but daily obedience to his righteous demands. Loyal devotion to God in all of life was so important that in comparison performance of sacrificial ritual was not important at all (v 6). This did not mean that sacrificial ritual was entirely unacceptable, but it did relegate it to relative unimportance as a means of communication and encounter between the people and God. It certainly made ritual an unacceptable *substitute* for steadfast devotion.

The term we have rendered "steadfast devotion" is the Hebrew word *hesed,* and it occurs twice here. In v 4 Yahweh declares that Israel's *hesed* is like a morning cloud or dew that disappears quickly, and in v 6 he makes the declaration "I desire *hesed* and not sacrifice, the knowledge of God rather than burnt offerings." In the modern versions the word is translated variously, "life," "mercy," "piety," "loyalty," "constant love," "goodness," or "steadfast love." It connotes both love, as strong affection, and steadfast loyalty; thus, it is lasting devotion. It is the kind of inward disposition and outward commitment that characterize family relationships at their best. It involves the heart, the mind, and the will, and it is expressed in deeds of love and service.

It is significant that the prophet placed *hesed* in poetic parallelism with the knowledge of God (v 6). The two are not synonymous, but they are closely related. We are reminded of the servant's knowledge in Isa 53:11, as the means by which many are brought into right relationship with God. This right relationship is characterized above all by *hesed.* The two terms

Hosea uses in this line express the two dimensions of faith: awareness of the reality of God and obedience.

Hosea's estimate of Israel's worship was largely negative. His words may fall short of utter rejection of sacrificial ritual as a valid means of corporate worship, but they certainly express grave doubt about it. Therefore, it is not surprising to find no mention of it in Hosea's prophecy of the future conditions of Israel's relation to God. He speaks of a ritual of words alone, without sacrifice (14:2).

This passage at the end of Hosea presents an important model for worship even though it is a brief one. The prophet is speaking about the age to come, after the destruction of the Kingdom of Israel. In the new age, when God would renew the covenant with his people and reestablish them in the land of promise (2:14-23; 11:10-12), their worship would involve confession of sin, petition for forgiveness, and disavowal of idolatry, both political and cultic (14:2-3). This is not a complete prescription for worship, but it is a significant beginning.

Hos 6:1-6 is not linked to the history of Israel in the same way as Jer 7:1-15. It contains a critique of worship that is applicable to all religious communities. It also expresses an understanding of the content and purpose of worship that can serve as a model in other ages.

The Temple and the Glory of God (Ezekiel 8–11)

In Ezekiel 8–11, we return from Hosea's Kingdom of Israel in the eighth century B.C. to Jeremiah's Kingdom of Judah in the sixth century. Ezekiel and Jeremiah were contemporaries, though neither mentions the other. These chapters contain the second of Ezekiel's great visions (we have already examined the first in chaps. 1–3). The second vision presents a remarkable portrayal of idolatrous worship in the temple of Jerusalem, and it expresses the sensibility of a devout priest concerning the meaning of worship.

Ezekiel's vision of the temple took place ca. 592 B.C. (i.e., the sixth year of the exile of King Jehoiachin; 8:11), or about fifteen months after his first vision (1:2). He was in his home in Babylonia among the elders of the Jewish exiles when he experienced this vivid vision of idolatry in the sanctuary and of Yahweh's response in wrath.

As we would expect, Ezekiel's experience has been the subject of a considerable scholarly discussion, which has focused upon the question of how he obtained information about the rituals in Jerusalem. Some have argued that the vision was a genuine clairvoyant experience in which the prophet observed activities occurring five hundred miles away. Others have argued that Ezekiel made one or more trips back to Jerusalem after his initial deportation. Still others have concluded that he received reports of travelers from Jerusalem. A few have interpreted his journeying to Jerusalem as an experience of levitation.

My own view is that the experience was entirely visionary and that all the images were drawn from Ezekiel's own memory, supplemented perhaps by reports from travelers. We cannot determine to what extent his vision reflects actual rites and images used in the temple. King Josiah purged it of alien cult objects and practices in 621 (2 Kgs 23:4-7), and the accounts of the reigns of the subsequent kings of Judah in 2 Kings and 2 Chronicles say nothing about a reintroduction of idolatrous practices during the time the temple remained standing. On the basis of so little evidence, it seems best to regard Ezekiel's vision as a dreamlike amalgam of images and memories acquired in various times and places, including perhaps the pre-Josian temple, the post-Josian temple, and other sanctuaries frequented by Jews in Babylonia. Indeed, it is not necessary to take all the images contained in Ezekiel's vision as direct reflections of things he had seen in the Jerusalem temple. There may be purely imaginative features in this picture, in keeping with the character of dreams and visions. Someone who regarded the worship in the Jerusalem temple as idolatrous, as Jeremiah did, e.g. (Jeremiah 7), might have a dream or vision in which the temple appeared to be filled with images and rituals that actually had no place there. These would merely be the dreaming/visionary mind's way of depicting something that was not itself visible, or at least not visible in the same form. The dream/vision is not so much a photographic representation of the external world as observed or remembered, as it is a semiconscious dramatization of the dreamer/visionary's response to and interpretation of the world. One's *evaluation* of reality dominates one's dreams. The emotional element of dreams is usually high. The feelings expressed in them may be exaggerated projections of feelings experienced in waking life. Thus Ezekiel's vision may be regarded as an expression of his own interpretation of Judean worship and his intense emotional reaction to it.

The best way to account for the narrative in Ezekiel 8–11, it seems to me, is to consider it the report of an actual vision. However, as the account comes to us it presents a highly coherent and consistent drama, unfolding logically from beginning to end. Few dreams and visions are like this, and for this reason I believe we must conclude that the vision was reshaped when it was recorded. So what we have before us is a conscious, literary re-creation of what was seen in a vision. Some interpreters have regarded these chapters as entirely the product of literary imagination without any basis in visionary experience. However, there is no objective reason for denying that Ezekiel was a visionary, as the book reports; and it is entirely plausible to regard this narrative as a consciously polished version of a semiconscious, psychic experience. In any case, the principal responsibility of the interpreter is to perceive what is said, and implied, in the text; and to this task we now turn.

This bizarre, but remarkable, narrative unmistakably conveys the utter seriousness with which Ezekiel regarded the public worship of God. He treats it as a life or death matter. The horror with which he regarded idolatry is a measure of his awe before the majesty and holiness of God. True worship means life, idolatry means death, and the vision symbolizes this in two ways. First, the idolatry drives the glory of Yahweh away from the sanctuary, and second, the agents of death move into the city and slaughter the idolators. Significantly, they begin at the temple and work outward. The temple is the center of life, and the power of life and blessing moves out from the worship of God in the sanctuary to permeate all of the community's experience. Similarly, when worship is corrupted and falsified, it becomes the source of death—morally and spiritually—which works outward from the center to undermine and destroy the life of the community.

The picture of God's ordering the slaughter of every idolatrous man, woman, and child in Jerusalem is offensive to our eyes. Could God be so bloodthirsty? Where is the compassion and forgiveness other OT writers found in God? However, before we dismiss Ezekiel's picture as incompatible with faith in a loving, redeeming God, we should set the vision in its psychological and historical context.

Ezekiel's vision reflects the conviction that idolatry was destroying the Kingdom of Judah. He was outraged at this, and his anger was reflected in his vision. In the circumstances this was understandable. As a priest he had devoted his entire life to the public worship of God, and he had seen this worship used as an instrument of royal politics and self-interest. Judah was only a few steps away from national ruin, and for Ezekiel this destruction was the consequence of folly and idolatry within the kingdom. Judah and Jerusalem were about to die. Ezekiel had no doubt about this, and he interpreted this death as the outward manifestation of an inner corruption that had begun much earlier in Judah's life and progressed to fatal proportions.

● Modern readers may view the collapse of the nation as the final result of a long moral, social, and political process. However, the prophet Ezekiel viewed the destruction as an act of God, the divine punishment of a wicked and incorrigible nation. Ezekiel's picture of God's relation to the life of Judah is a highly anthropomorphic one. We may prefer to put the matter in nonanthropomorphic terms. However, if we believe God to be Lord of history, then we must find some way of accounting for the fall of Judah in relation to this divine sovereignty. We may be disinclined to interpret the destruction of Judah as simply and solely a punishment of God, as Jeremiah and Ezekiel did, but we may nevertheless be able to discern some moral coherence between the political policies and way of life of the Kingdom of Judah, on the one hand, and the kingdom's fate on the other.

Ezekiel's vision of the temple and the glory of God is a memorable essay on the presence and power of God. The fundamental promise of God to his people was "I will be with you" (Exod 3:12). How was this presence known? How should the people respond to it? What function did the sanctuary have in the recognition and appropriation of this presence? These are questions raised by Ezekiel's vision, and they are central to the understanding of every religious community.

People in the biblical world, and in other times and places, experienced certain places as holy, i.e., they sensed them as invested with extraordinary power. This power was potentially beneficial, but it could also be dangerous if it were treated inappropriately. Priesthoods, sanctuaries, liturgical calendars, laws of sacrifice, rules of access and proscription, prayers and incantations were all devised and maintained in order to manage the extraordinary power available in the holy place and to channel it into various forms of blessing.

Few of Israel's rituals and few of her holy places were distinctively Israelite, or Yahwistic. Much of her cultic life was indistinguishable from that of the surrounding peoples. Much of the ritual of the altar was the legacy of pre-Israelite times, and its original purpose or rationale had long been forgotten. Thus, they are unexplained in the biblical tradition. Most of this legacy seemed compatible with Yahwistic faith, in the minds of those who shaped the pentateuchal tradition. However, a few features of popular religious practice, such as the use of plastic images to represent the deity and the ritual dramas based upon polytheistic deification of the forces of nature, with their mythology of divine warfare, sexual procreation, and sensual seasonal rituals, were intolerable to Yahwistic faith. However, some of the seasonal festivals were demythologized and reinterpreted as responses to the blessings of God in history and nature. An elaborate system of animal sacrifices, common to most popular religion, was retained.

Ritual played a far greater part in the life of ancient people than it does in ours. Modern Western people regard nature as autonomous and self-regulating, and they regard history solely as a process of human interaction. There is no room in the modern view for superhuman or supernatural forces. To be sure, the forces and processes of nature transcend human power and understanding, but our means of dealing with the limitations of our power and knowledge is to develop new technology and promote science. Ritual means of controlling or placating powers greater than ourselves are obsolete.

International relations are another area in which ancient people resorted routinely to divine aid, but which for us are a matter of purely human (or secular) concern. In the next chapter we will discuss the oracles concerning foreign nations that comprise a substantial portion of the books of the prophets. We will see in these oracles how Israel's prophets understood the role of the divine in her international politics. To a considerable extent they desacralized and deritualized politics, just as they desacralized many other areas of human activity. In this respect our modern perspective on nature and history has been deeply influenced by prophetic teaching, and their critique of ritual, and the theology infusing it, was a potent factor. A major difference between the prophets' perspective and that of many modern people is that the prophets' critique of ritual and their desacralization of nature were called forth by their faith in God, whereas the modern perspective is often a mere secularism in which faith in God plays no part. In modern secular perspective the powers that make up people's environment and shape their destiny are entirely natural and human; in ancient perspective they were largely divine. Thus, the choice for ancient Israelites, as they tried to relate to powers greater than themselves, was not between God and no God, but between God and other gods. Every aspect of life was believed to be permeated by divine power or subject to the will of divine beings. Therefore, one had constantly to deal with these powers in some appropriate way, so ritualism was a way of life for everyone. Changes of the seasons, months, and days were marked by private and public rituals. No major enterprise was undertaken without first seeking divine blessing or attempting to ascertain the outcome in relation to the will of the gods. Every turn of fortune, both good and ill, required an appropriate ritual response. Responses to good fortune were meant to preserve it, while responses to ill fortune were meant to reverse it. Sanctuaries, priests, and seers were ubiquitous, for they were thought indispensable to survival.

When King Josiah centralized public worship in Israel, destroying every sanctuary except the temple in Jerusalem, and prohibiting even the legitimate priests of Yahweh from performing rituals anywhere but in this one national sanctuary, he went squarely against the grain of all ancient life and culture, including that of the people of Israel. The project was doomed to failure. Popular faith conflicted too much with the theology behind the reform, and the need for ritual in daily life was too great.

When Ezekiel envisioned the departure of the glory of Yahweh from the temple and city of Jerusalem (10:18-22; 11:22-25), he foresaw for the people of Jerusalem a religious situation that had already come to pass for other Israelite communities during Josiah's reign. This was the experience of being denied access to the ritual presence of Yahweh. In their minds the power of blessing had been removed from their midst and from their control. Ezekiel foresaw this process carried to its conclusion, where the entire people of Israel would be deprived of the tabernacaling glory of God.

In his vision Ezekiel saw the people of Jerusalem practicing a variety of idolatrous rites (8:5-17) and saw that these idolatries were the cause of God's punishment of the people. The punishment was two-fold: the slaughter of the idolators themselves and the removal of the glory of God from the temple. In reporting this vision to the elders of Israel, Ezekiel not only described his own moral and emotional response to the religious situation in Jerusalem, but he also provided a parable of the story of Israel and Yahweh.

Ezekiel's vision lends itself to several possible interpretations. One might analyze it, like any other vision or dream, as a reflection of Ezekiel's own feelings, experiences, and perceptions. It certainly manifests the horror a devout priest of Yahweh would feel toward popular religious idolatry in Judah, and the rage these practices would provoke in him. Though correct as far as it goes, such an analysis would not be sufficient, for Ezekiel's report of the vision was presented as a prophetic statement with regard to the inner corruption and outward destruction of the temple and the city of Jerusalem. It may originally have been a prophecy of their final destruction, but it was also an interpretation of the cause of that destruction. Beyond its personal meaning for Ezekiel and its historic meaning for the people of Judah, the vision ought to be provocative to congregations in the present. It serves as a kind of negative image against which to measure the religious situation within our communities, or at least to raise significant questions concerning the moral and religious condition of our own sanctuaries, whatever they may be. What idolatries in our own religious practice, or in the practice of our nation, capture us in the way the people of Judah were captured? What are the moral and social consequences? Is anyone immune from these consequences? Is anyone innocent of the idolatry? Are there any remedies? Can the redemptive power of God break through before it is too late? Are worship and idolatry matters

of life and death in our time as they were in Ezekiel's? Was this
visionary prophet a fanatic or a realist? How does the glory of
God manifest itself? What is the relation of the glory to the
presence and power of God? How should the people respond to
the presence, and how may they rightly appropriate the power?
Isaiah saw the glory of God as filling the whole earth (6:3),
while Ezekiel located the glory primarily in the sanctuary.
Perhaps we must perceive the glory of God in both realms
before we can do so in either. Indeed, Isaiah's vision suggests
this to be true, for the affirmation that God's glory fills the
whole earth is made by those who stand in the presence of God
in the sanctuary.

Seeking God in Exile (Jeremiah 29)

For ancient Israel, seeking God meant primarily going to a
sanctuary and engaging in a private or public ritual. Although
the Holy might manifest itself anywhere at any time, this
happened most frequently and predictably in conjunction with
acts of worship performed at places and in ways hallowed by
ancient usage and made familiar by long habit. The experience
of the Holy is a sign of the presence of God, or at least of the
conscious recognition of his presence. The Holy One whose
presence is acknowledged in the act of worship is the source of
blessing, but sensing the presence of the Holy One, i.e., the
experience of encounter itself, is also a blessing. Indeed, it may
be the supreme blessing. Thus for the writers of psalms 42 and
137, to be denied participation in worship in accustomed places
and traditional ways was to be denied the primary source of
happiness and peace. For a faithful Judean, exile from
Jerusalem and the temple meant separation from the sanctify-
ing presence of God. In Ezekiel's vision the glory of God left
the temple and the city, but this did not signify that the
glory—or the presence it symbolized—would be subsequently
manifest in the places of Israel's exile. It would not be manifest
at all, at least not in any way that would make blessing available

to the people. According to the prophet, Yahweh's glory would return when the city of Jerusalem and its temple were restored and purified (43:1-7). This prophecy is part of the larger picture of the future establishment of a theocratic kingdom which occupies Ezekiel 40–48. It is not certain whether these chapters embody Ezekiel's own hope or were composed by a later, anonymous writer. However, as the book stands now, the vision of the future return of Yahweh's glory parallels the vision of its present departure. There is no indication elsewhere in the book that the glory, and all it signifies, are to be manifest and available to the remnant of Israel in the time between the times.

The glory of Yahweh and the presence of Yahweh are not identical, but they are closely related. God is present everywhere, sustaining all creation. The glory of God is also everywhere, to those who have eyes to see. The glory is a manifestation of the presence which provides the conditions of existence, always and everywhere. The presence is the source of vitality, strength, wisdom, love, blessing. These are available to everyone, everywhere, always. However, many in ancient Israel did not understand this. For them God—the God of the fathers, the God of the covenant, the God they had known—was present and accessible primarily, if not exclusively, in the land of Israel, in the city of David, in the temple of Jerusalem. Even the Book of Ezekiel, with its visions of the departure and return of the glory of Yahweh, implies that the effective presence of God is tied to a properly functioning and purified holy place. God is Lord of all nations and peoples, but God's saving presence, the special power of the blessing, is made available through the worship of Yahweh in Yahweh's chosen place. Nor is this conviction merely an ancient or priestly phenomenon, it is the conviction of many religious people today. For them the forms of worship have changed, but the fundamental understanding of the means of access to the saving power of God has not.

Jeremiah had a correcting word to say about such an understanding in a letter he sent from Jerusalem to Judean exiles in Babylon sometime after the first deportation in 597 B.C. The text is Jer 29:1-14. There is nothing like this letter anywhere else in the prophetic corpus. This alone would mark it as a special prophetic text. However, its chief importance lies in its content. The historical setting is clearly described in the introduction (29:1-3). Prophets like Hananiah in Jerusalem, and others among the exiles in Babylon, were predicting a speedy restoration to their homeland and the removal of the yoke of Babylonian rule (27:16–28:16). Jeremiah disputed this and insisted that the nation would sink deeper into subjugation and that the time of captivity would be very long. This conflict in prophetic judgment is the subject of chaps. 27–29, which constitute a small booklet within the larger Jeremianic collection.

The course of events confirmed Jeremiah's prophecy of a long captivity. This may be one reason why these words were preserved. However, fulfillment alone does not establish the value of a prophetic word; it is the substance that matters most. The enduring word that emerged from Jeremiah's dispute with the other prophet is contained in this letter, and it is one of his most important contributions to the prophetic witness of faith.

Jeremiah's counsel to the exiles was threefold: First, they could expect to spend the rest of their lives in Babylon, so they should seek their welfare and happiness there. Second, they should seek the welfare of the people among whom they were living, because their own well-being was inseparable from that of the people among whom they lived. Third, they should seek God right where they were, and not long to return to Jerusalem, for God was accessible wherever they happened to be.

These were radical words in Judea in the sixth century B.C. The kingdom was in process of being destroyed. The royal line of David, which Judeans had believed would last forever (2 Samuel 7), was threatened with annihilation. The people's possession of the land of promise had already been drastically reduced and stood in final jeopardy. The very survival of the people of the covenant was in serious doubt. In the face of this enormous national trauma and a totally uncertain future, Jeremiah calmly delivered his advice. There are two questions to be answered here.

The first is raised by Jeremiah's instruction to the exiles to marry (v 6). Did he intend this to mean marriage with non-Israelites? The letter does not say. Does this silence imply that intermarriage was acceptable to Jeremiah? Naturally, we cannot be certain, but Jeremiah's instruction does not preclude intermarriage, and therefore, it may be legitimate to infer that this possibility was within the purview of his prophetic teaching. The issue is important for it concerns the openness of the covenantal community and the conditions of membership within it.

We do not have space to discuss the history of this issue in ancient Israel, and the literary evidence is fragmentary and difficult to interpret. All we can do here is call attention to this important question posed by Jeremiah's letter to the exiles. The issue is not merely historical, it confronts every religious community. Who may belong to the religious group? What are the conditions of membership? How should the religious community interact with the world around it? Should it be self-protective and exclusive? Should it be passively open to those who seek membership? Should it be aggressive in the recruitment of new participants? These questions came to occupy Judaism in the years after Jeremiah. His letter to the exiles does not anticipate them, let alone provide solutions for them. However, the liberal spirit that animates it suggests openness to the world rather than parochialism.

The second question arises over the time indicated in Jer 29:12-13. Several versions translate v 12 in such a way that the seeking and finding of God in Babylon are placed at the end of the period of exile, on the eve of restoration to the land of Judah. "Then when you call to me, and come to plead with me I will listen to you" (JB; cf. CBAT, NASV, TEV, NIV, and RSV). Others, however, render the verse so that it makes the time of reference indeterminate, saying in effect, "Whenever

you call to me and come to plead with me, I will listen to you"
(cf. NEB, NAB, and NJV). The Hebrew conjunction is the
multipurpose *waw,* which can mean many things, depending
upon the context. The second, indefinite, temporal reference
seems to be meant here. Had the writer wished to place the
exiles' seeking and finding God specifically in the time of
restoration, and not before, he could have done so without any
ambiguity by using one of the common Hebrew words for
"then" or "at that time." However, the writer left the
statement indefinite. It seems to me, therefore, that we may
understand Jeremiah's word to be that whenever and wherever
they sought God with all their hearts, God would be found by
them, would hear their prayers, and would respond to their
deepest needs. If this is indeed what vv 12-13 say, then the
meaning for faithful people in all generations is clear.

Jeremiah's counsel to the exiles to seek the welfare of the
people in the cities where they found themselves is unambi-
guously stated, and this too is a radical word, not only for
Jeremiah's contemporaries, but for people in all times and
places. It goes against our natural instincts, our cultural
conditioning, and our personal preferences. The implications
for our religious, social, and political attitudes and behavior are
extensive and profound.

We began this chapter with a discussion of Jer 7:1-15. In that
famous speech, delivered in the temple of Jerusalem, the
prophet warned the Judean worshipers against a superstitious
trust in the temple as a guarantee of the protection and support
of God. He also suggested that divine blessing was linked to the
people's righteousness. In defining the behavior acceptable to
God, he referred to several of the Ten Commandments (7:9)
and to the ancient ideal of protection for the resident alien, the
orphan, and the widow (v 6). He placed the fulfillment of these
moral goals above ritual performance as a response to the
claims of God.

Other oracles in the books of the prophets are devastating in
their criticism of Israel's worship. Among these are Isa 1:10-17;

Amos 5:21-27; and Hos 5:1-7; 10:1-8. Some of these words appear to constitute a total rejection of ritual as a legitimate service of God. Some biblical scholars have understood them in this way and have set the prophetic tradition of the OT over against the priestly as incompatible rivals. Other scholars have rejected this interpretation of the oracles, arguing that the prophets rejected, not ritual itself, but ritualism unaccompanied by zeal for social justice and moral integrity. Others have concluded that the prophets rejected the ancient system of animal sacrifice. In this view, other forms of worship, e.g., singing, praying, and professing the saving acts of God, were acceptable to the prophets. In these last two interpretations, what seems to be a radical rejection of worship in the prophetic oracles is regarded as a rhetorical exaggeration. Presumably, this exaggeration is rooted in passionate indignation over ritual abuses, and its purpose is to create the strongest possible impression upon the hearers. The interpretation dominating biblical criticism today is that the prophets condemned ritual abuses as well as ritualism unaccompanied by righteousness.

● Whether or not this view is correct, the prophetic criticism of worship is pertinent to religious life in the twentieth century. The prophetic word challenges believers in all generations to consider seriously what they are doing in public worship and personal devotion. The prophetic words probe, challenge, provoke, and stimulate greater self-awareness and greater responsibility on the part of religious people. The questions raised are relevant to every worshiping congregation. Although the forms of worship today differ in many respects from those of ancient Israel, the reasons why people worship, and their experiences in doing so, are similar. There is continuity between Israel's worship and our own. Our worship is subject to many of the same abuses the prophets criticized, and Israel's worship had many of the same strengths that can be recognized in present-day worship. Indeed, most of these strengths are a legacy from ancient Israel.

Prophetic teaching concerning the worship of God reaches its climax in the great concluding poem of Isaiah 40–55. This poem

114   The Prophets

comprises the whole of Isaiah 55. Here is a lyrical prophecy of
the eschatological celebration of the presence and word of God.
No ordinary sanctuary is mentioned, for the worshipers are
"everyone who thirsts," that is, all humanity.

In the introduction to his proclamation of the new age of
salvation, the writer of Isaiah 40–55 emphasized the word of
God, which would stand forever amid everything transient and
human (40:6-8), and the glory of God, which would ultimately
be made manifest to all humanity (v 5). In the concluding scene
of the drama of salvation, the writer lays stress upon the word of
God (55:10-11). The glory is not mentioned explicitly;
however, it is implicit in the entire scene. The glory symbolizes
the presence and power of God, and these are to be found by
those who heed the prophet's injunction to "seek the Lord" (v 6).

In the eschatological banquet, which culminates not only all
institutions of worship, but all of life itself, Israel's special
knowledge of God becomes the common blessing of all nations
(vv 4-5). In this way the purpose of creation is fulfilled, so that
the very mountains, hills, and trees can be said to take part in
the acknowledgement of the Creator (v 12). The satisfaction of
the deepest human needs and the fulfillment of life are free gifts
of God (vv 1-2). They cannot be earned. However, moral
earnestness is a part of any true response to the grace of God.
Repentance and acceptance of God's forgiveness characterize
those who know and seek the Lord (vv 6-7). Thus the ethical
teaching of the prophetic forerunners of this anonymous exilic
writer is taken up into his lyric evocation of the culmination of
the story of God and Israel.

IV. THE RIGHTEOUSNESS OF GOD

Most of the prophetic writings could be treated under the heading we have chosen for this chapter. The theme comprehends the proclamation of God's judgment on both the individual and the nation and the affirmation of God's righteous demand—the righteousness of human beings in response to the righteousness of God. It also includes the mercy of God and the corresponding requirement of mercy and compassion in people. Both justice and mercy are aspects of the righteousness of God, and this righteousness is grounded in love. The entire story of God and Israel may be told and interpreted under this heading. In order to explicate the theme fully as it appears in the books of the prophets we would have to give a full account of these books, which, of course, is not possible here. We must be highly selective of the kinds of writing and of the themes contained in them, and so we have chosen: Jer 11:1-13 (covenant, judgment, idolatry); Isa 2:12-22 (the day of wrath); Ezekiel 18 (individual responsibility—punishment and forgiveness); Isa 10:5-21 (Assyria as the instrument of God's punishment of Israel); Isa 19:16-26 (the conversion of Egypt and Assyria to faith in God); Hosea 2 (the story of God and

115

Israel); Jer 12:1-3 (the problem of prosperity of the wicked); Isa
11:1-9 (the righteous ruler, the vicegerent of God); and Jer
31:31-34 (the new covenant). Most of the themes of prophetic
teaching are contained in these passages: history and eschatol-
ogy, the providence of God, the rule of God, social justice,
individual morality and retribution, covenant, the wrath of
God, the love of God, wealth and poverty, power and
weakness, order and freedom, international justice and peace,
blessing and affliction, suffering and death, sin and repentance.
We will begin with the sermon on the covenant in Jeremiah 11,
and conclude with the famous prophecy of the new covenant in
Jeremiah 31.

Jeremiah and the Covenant (Jeremiah 11)

The covenant speech in Jer 11:1-13 is one of a substantial
number of sermonic discourses in prose which make up one of
the principal strata of the book. The literary style, as well as the
theological emphases, are similar to those of the great sermonic
introduction to the book of Deuteronomy (chaps. 5–11).
Jeremiah 11, like the other prose sermons in the book, may
reflect an oracle originally delivered by Jeremiah; however, in
its present form it appears to be a product of a group of
anonymous exilic and postexilic writers who composed or
edited much of the material in the books of Deuteronomy,
1 and 2 Kings, and parts of Joshua, Judges, and 1 and 2 Samuel.
The teaching of this so-called Deuteronomic (or Deuterono-
mistic) school has close affinities with the message of the
preexilic prophets. However, the covenant plays a more
explicit role in this literature than in the oracles of the prophets.
Moreover, a much smaller number of theological motifs is
contained in this material, and they are treated in a much more
uniform manner. The style is didactic and repetitive, material
appropriate for use in teaching or preaching. It seems
reasonable to surmise that it was developed among congregations of Jewish exiles after the destruction of the monarchy.

These sermons lack the rich imagery and rhetorical power of the poetic oracles of the prophets. Few of the lines are truly memorable, and the theology tends to be simplistic and legalistic. In this regard it stands in tension with other prophetic writings. Nevertheless, these prose sermons deserve our attention for they represent a new form of religious literature which is the direct forerunner of the modern sermon. All preachers today stand in debt to the Deuteronomic writers of the sixth century. In addition to their value for understanding the history of OT literature and religion, the prose sermons of Jeremiah have a continuing didactic value for modern congregations.

The message of Jer 11:1-13 is straightforward. God entered into covenant with Israel at the time of their deliverance from slavery in Egypt. This covenant required Israel to obey the commandments of God, and in return God renewed the promise to give them the land of Canaan, which had originally been promised to their ancestors. Despite perennial warnings, Israel refused to be obedient. Therefore, a series of curses, contained in the covenant, were put into effect, but this failed to bring about Israel's obedience. As a result the supreme curse would fall upon Israel, namely, dispossession of the land of promise. This would be a punishment long deserved.

There are other prose sermons in the Book of Jeremiah (e.g., 7:1–8:6; 18:1-12; 21:1-10; 25:1-11; 34:8-22; 35:1-19; and 44:1-14), and their message is similar. It is uncertain whether these sermons were written originally for a preexilic audience or an exilic one. Since the theology of these passages is in essential agreement with that of the poetic oracles many scholars regard them as Jeremiah's, though actually written by his scribe Baruch. Other scholars believe they were written later for Jews in exile by an anonymous disciple or disciples of Jeremiah. They base this conviction on the differences in style and theological emphasis between the prose sermons and the poetic oracles.

Interpreters should take account of both of these possibilities. Addressed to a preexilic audience, the sermons would seem to have been intended to elicit repentance and amendment of life. Addressed to an exilic audience, they would have served well to justify the fall of Judah as a righteous act of God and to warn the exiles not to repeat the sins of the past. We know that these and the other writings in the book were collected and transmitted in the exile, since they tell the story of Jeremiah up to that time. Therefore, whether or not they were first intended for a preexilic audience, they were intended eventually for the exiles and other survivors of the fall of Judah. For these people the sermons, as well as other portions of the book, would have helped strengthen their faith by explaining the fall as a manifestation of God's justice rather than a defeat of God's power by the gods of a foreign nation. They would also have encouraged the exiles to order their lives so as to avoid a similar punishment in the future.

A rapid reading of the recent English versions shows no serious problems of translation in Jer 11:1-13. This text is clear, expansive prose in which the meaning lies open, on the surface, as it were. It is quite different from the compact, subtly nuanced poetry of some oracles in the book.

● Using the message of this text in the setting of modern life is not so straightforward as translating the ancient Hebrew into modern English. There are pitfalls along the way. Modern interpreters should move slowly in trying to formulate general religious truths from this text, because it deals concretely with the history of a particular people. In this passage the writer declared to the people of Judah that they would be dispossessed from their land because of their perennial and incorrigible disobedience to God's commandments. This is not the formulation of a universal moral truth, but an analysis of their distinctive history. Is there then a general truth lying beneath the surface that we can uncover and appropriate for the instruction in our own time?

The temptation for interpreters in the United States is to apply the prophetic analysis to their own nation. There is a long and pervasive tradition in American culture that this is the promised land of the modern era and that the American nation is the new Israel of God. There must be some analogy between the experience of ancient Israel and the experience of the United States, or this conviction could not have arisen and persisted so long. Nevertheless, the differences between the two nations are far greater than the similarities. Indeed, socially, politically, economically, and technologically the United States is totally unlike ancient Israel, which was a small, homogeneous nation with an agricultural and pastoral economy, little military power and no capacity to influence the cultures and nations of the ancient world. The contrast with the United States is obvious. Again, in Israel no distinction was made among the religious, social, and political orders. Separation of church and state—even the *idea* of separation of church and state—was inconceivable, and so was the notion of individual religious liberty. In the light of these innumerable differences, we should be cautious about drawing parallels between Israel's religious situation and our own.

We have suggested that the audience for whom Jer 11:1-13 was ultimately intended was the survivors of the fall of Judah and that its purpose was to strengthen their faith in God's righteous providence and encourage them to learn from the experience of preexilic Israel. If this analysis is correct then it may help us to appropriate Jeremiah's covenant-speech for ourselves. Perhaps we should place ourselves with the Judean exiles and ask, What are the consequences for our faith and for our understanding of the nature of religious community of the fall of Judah, as this event was interpreted by the prophets. Perhaps a lesson to be drawn is that the people of the covenant are not to be identified with a national state. Perhaps the mistake of the ancient Israelite community was trying to become like the nations, possessing territory with definable boundaries and being ruled by a king. Perhaps now the effort to become like the nations was at an end, and, in the providence of God, Israel was meant to understand herself in different terms. Should we not then, as heirs of the biblical tradition, identify our covenantal community, not with Israel under the monarchy, but with Israel in exile? If the covenantal community is to be distinguished from all political entities—and this, it seems to me, is the outcome of prophetic teaching—then we should observe this distinction in proclaiming the demands of God and interpreting the fortunes of the various communities to which we belong.

The Day of Wrath (Isaiah 2)

We move from pedestrian prose to the exalted poetry of Isa 2:6-22. There are a few minor problems of translation in this passage, but they do not affect the meaning of the whole. The issue in choosing among recent versions of this text is not how to deal with the minor textual uncertainties but how to convey the dramatic force of the poetry. In my judgment, CBAT and RSV do this very well, NASB does it poorly, and TEV not at all. TEV renders the passage as prose! It also paraphrases here, as elsewhere, and thus blunts the impact of this magnificent poem. The other versions are adequate poetically but are not equal to RSV and CBAT. For example, the Hebrew of vv 12-16 uses the preposition "against" ten times, creating a mounting staccato effect that is devastating. RSV and CBAT capture this effect, but NEB and NIV lose it by translating the preposition as "for" instead of "against." Again, v 22 is very important in the development of the mood of the poem. After the fury of what goes before, there is a lull, and then comes the single line of the conclusion: "Turn away from man / in whose nostrils is breath, / for of what account is he?" (RSV). CBAT is equally good in capturing the effect of this conclusion, but the other versions are less successful.

A high percentage of the oracles of the preexilic prophets contain accusations of human evil and announcements of divine judgment. Indeed, there are so many oracles of judgment in the books of the prophets that they blend together when read

rapidly, and the impression they create obscures other features
of the literature. To be appreciated fully, the oracles should be
read slowly, a few at a time. Many of them, like Isa 2:6-22, merit
reading again and again. They should be read aloud for the
poetry to have its full effect. But interpretations of masterful
poems pale beside the originals, and there is no substitute for
the poem itself. Isaiah 2 is not so much a text from which to
extract theological ideas as a work of art to be perceived.

The poem is all about human arrogance. It depicts the
vainglorious pride of human beings, trying to master the world
and control their destinies by their own wisdom and power.
Their efforts include both politics and religion. In the end,
however, they are all futile. Such mastery and control are
simply not given to humankind. They belong only to God. Here
we see the awe which Isaiah experienced before God in his
inaugural vision (Isaiah 6) translated into a picture of terror
before the wrath of God. For Isaiah, God was first of all the
transcendent, Holy One, before whom one falls in reverence
and humility. Therefore pride and idolatry, which characterize
much human behavior, are totally at odds with the fundamental
conditions of human existence before God. The inevitable
outcome of all human efforts to achieve autonomy and mastery
of the world is humiliation and destruction. This is not a pretty
picture, but it is unforgettable.

Isaiah's poem is undated, and therefore we cannot place it in
relation to any of the specific historical events of his time. We
do not know, e.g., whether he composed it in a time of peace,
prosperity, and political strength for the nation of Judah, or in a
time of adversity, or even disaster. Probably it doesn't matter.

• This poem is not merely a commentary on the affairs of
particular people in a particular time and place. It can serve as a
commentary on all human behavior. The pretentions and
idolatries of Judah alluded to in this poem can be matched by
similar attitudes and activities in the lives of people in all times and
places. Nor should we think of Isaiah's awesome picture of the

wrath of God as pointing to the end of history, the eschaton, the final judgment. This is not an apocalpytic vision of the age to come, but a prophetic account of the present age. This is what happens to the proud! However, we miss Isaiah's point if we take his poem merely as a description of what happens in human history. His point is that this is what *ought* to happen! This is what the arrogance and idolatry of human beings deserve. The reasons we deserve it, of course, is that in behaving this way we usurp the power and authority of God. Isaiah was not merely describing the course of history realistically; he was interpreting it theologically. Only in the light of faith in a sovereign God could one condemn human pride as Isaiah did in this oracle. If "man is the measure of all things," a judgment like Isaiah's is unreasonable and unfair. It is only on the basis of faith in God that such a statement makes sense.

This oracle is easy to apply to our own times. Isaiah's picture of the destructive consequences of human pride and idolatry has been fulfilled more terribly in our century than in any other in human history. The challenge of this passage to the modern reader is not in deciding whether this is really what happens in human life, but in judging whether the faith in God to which it points is true.

Individual Responsibility and Reward (Ezekiel 18)

We turn next to an entirely different kind of text. This prophetic treatise (Ezekiel 18), which is not an oracle in the conventional sense, is wholly concerned with individual retribution. Do individual human beings get what they deserve from the hand of God, and are they free at a given moment to earn their own reward or punishment?

Ezekiel's essay was provoked by a popular complaint that the current generation in Israel was suffering because of the sins of their fathers. The complaint was expressed in a proverb: "The fathers have eaten sour grapes, and the children's teeth are set on edge" (v 2). The same proverb is quoted in Jer 31:29, so it seems to have been repeated widely during and after the period of Judah's national demise. Since there is no indication of literary dependence between Jeremiah and Ezekiel at this point, we may assume that each writer heard the proverb himself and made his own response to it. Jeremiah's response is very brief. It is that in the time to come the people will not repeat the proverb, for then individuals will be punished for their own sins and not for those of their fathers. In making this assertion Jeremiah seems to concede that in his own age the children were indeed suffering for the sins of the parents. Whether he was right about this, and whether the same thing is true of people in other times and places, are issues to which we shall return, but first we will consider Ezekiel's response to the proverb.

He said it wasn't true! To make his point as clear as possible he told a parable about three men, father, son, and grandson. The first is a righteous man, and as a consequence of his righteousness he lives (vv 5-9). This man's son does not live up to his father's standards, but commits evil. As a result he dies (vv 10-13). However, the second man's son avoids the evil of his father and is entirely righteous, like his grandfather. As a result he lives (vv 14-17). The second man is not granted life automatically because his father was a righteous man; rather, because he himself is wicked, he dies. However, the third man does not die because of his father's wickedness, but because of his own righteousness he lives. Thus, contrary to the popular proverb, one generation does not suffer because of the sins of another, nor is one generation rewarded because of the virtues of another. There is no carryover of reward and punishment from one generation to the next. Each generation—each individual—lives or dies as a result of its own righteousness or iniquity. But this is not all.

Not only is one's living or dying not determined by the behavior of the father, but it is not even determined irrevocably by one's own previous behavior. If a wicked man turns from his wickedness and lives righteously, he will live (vv 21-23), and if a righteous man turns from his virtue and sins, he will die (v 24).

Is this analysis universally correct? Children really do suffer for the sins of their parents. The attitudes and behavior of one generation deeply affect the lives of the next generation, and, to a diminishing extent, the generations after that. When the attitudes are widespread, and especially if they are institutionalized in the structures of society, their effects may persist for centuries. Both in families and in societies, it is an empirical fact that when the fathers eat sour grapes the children's teeth are set on edge. Since Ezekiel 18 denies this, must we then reject it as a rationalistic fantasy of an unreal world?

There are two principal clues to guide our understanding and appreciation of this text, one external, and the other internal. The external clue is the proverb which the prophet quotes, and the internal one is the recurring reference to living and dying within the treatise itself.

The proverb, "The fathers have eaten sour grapes and the children's teeth are set on edge," excused Ezekiel's generation of responsibility for the fall of Judah and blamed previous generations. Ezekiel's treatise can be taken as an effort to counteract this attitude of irresponsibility. Understood in this way, his response is something we can affirm. The moral lethargy reflected in the proverb was a deterrent to the recovery of the Jewish community from the effects of the fall of Judah, and it was incompatible with prophetic teaching. Ezekiel's response to the proverb was, in effect, to tell the generation of the Exile that whether they lived or died depended upon themselves and not upon the legacy they had received from the past. Ezekiel did not suggest in his essay what forms the exiles' life might take, or what the limits and conditions of their social and economic achievements might be. He did not promise them complete mastery over their destiny, nor did he deny the existence of continuing problems resulting from the fall of the Kingdom of Judah. He told his contemporaries simply—and this is the internal clue to our appreciation—that upright people "live" and wicked people "die." Thus he invited his hearers to choose between life and death.

Life and death are not defined in this parabolic essay. The silence of the text in this regard means that, on the one hand, we can only speculate about the sense Ezekiel intended these terms to have, and, on the other hand, we are free to attach our own sense to them, in the light of our own knowledge of life and of the broader biblical witness of faith. Ezekiel's parable of the three generations invites us to engage in this kind of reflection.

Living and dying in this passage cannot be merely physical. If this were the case, it would be impossible for a wicked man to turn from evil and live (vv 21-22), for he would already have died as a result of his wickedness (vv 10-13). If one can die as a result of one's wickedness and then turn from that wickedness and live, then the living and dying are not simply physical, they must be something more—or less—than these. "To live" here must signify a range of positive experiences, conditions, and relationships, and "to die" must signify a corresponding range of negative possibilities. These possibilities need not be merely "spiritual," in the usual sense of that term. They might also be tangible. For example, they might include health and disease or prosperity and poverty. However, they would certainly include inward possibilities—mental, psychological, emotional, spiritual.

Ezekiel presented his parable as the word of God. Throughout, it is God who speaks. Thus, what the prophet was discussing first of all was God's reaction to righteousness and wickedness, rather than the tangible consequences of the two. He was declaring that in the sight of God the upright person lives and the evil person dies. This does not mean that such living and dying take place only in the sight of God, independently of the outward course of life. Ultimately, the two realms must be the same. However, to assert that something is right or wrong in the sight of God is to make a declaration concerning its intrinsic worth, apart from its outward appearance. If the assertions made in Ezekiel 18 are taken in this way, they are reasonable when judged in relation to actual human experience.

● The subject of Jeremiah 11 was Israel's covenant. The subject of Ezekiel 18 is "a man." What is said about the first may not be applicable to people in other times and places. However, what is said about the second would appear to be applicable to anyone, regardless of time and place. The covenant is an aspect of the life of a particular nation during a particular period of its history. The facts of that case, and the truths that might be deduced from them, may have little or no bearing upon modern life. In order to apply the teaching to our own situation, we would need to establish the factors common to our situation and Israel's. The responsiblity of the interpreter is different in the case of Ezekiel 18. Here the writer presents a theory concerning individual moral retribution that is not tied to the history of Israel or the distinctive features of the nation's corporate life. As stated, the text appears to apply to every human life. Therefore the modern interpreter is justified in asking whether and to what extent the theory provides a true account of human experience, without first having to establish the cultural links between the writer's setting and our own. Upon close examination we may find in the writer's treatment of the subject evidence of cultural conditioning. We may conclude that there are specifically Israelite features in the language, imagery, or presuppositions of the text. We will certainly notice that the examples of righteous and wicked behavior are based upon the moral standards of the Israelite covenant, esp. the Ten Commandments. Nevertheless, the text is not merely about what happens to Israelites, but what happens to human beings.

If Ezekiel was trying to combat defeatism among his exilic contemporaries, as we have suggested, his treatise on individual retribution has considerable cogency. It minimizes the influence that one's ancestors have upon one's own life, and in this respect, it simplifies human experience. Still, it makes several points worthy of consideration. It declares that one's future is never completely blocked by the legacy of the past—that, in the providence of God, there are always possibilities of new beginning. One really can make a fresh start. It also declares that one is not responsible for the sins and failures of one's parents, nor for their virtues and achievements. One "lives" or "dies," in the sense that really matters, as a result of one's own life-enhancing or life-destroying deeds. According to Ezekiel, things work out this way because this is the way God wills human existence to be. However, if he has described human affairs accurately—if this is the way life really is—then one does not have to share Ezekiel's faith in God in order to agree with his analysis of the human situation. One can disagree with him over the reason why life is this way, and still agree with him in his description of it.

On the other hand, if the life and death about which Ezekiel is speaking are religious, or spiritual, either wholly or in part, then one would not be able to agree with his analysis, or appropriate it meaningfully into one's own life, without sharing his faith. If the reward of virtue is knowing that one is righteous and acceptable in God's sight, and the punishment of iniquity is knowing that one is sinful and unacceptable in God's sight, then attaining such knowledge is impossible apart from an active faith in God. This appears to be the ultimate implication of the essay. We could translate this affirmation into nontheological terms, by asserting that righteousness is its own reward and wickedness its own punishment, but we would lose an important dimension of Ezekiel's statement in doing so. This would be to equate God with the moral order, or the laws of human behavior. However, the God whom Ezekiel talks about and presupposes in all his writings is personal, and not merely an aspect of the natural order.

The Prosperity of the Wicked (Jeremiah 12)

According to Ezekiel 18, the righteous live and the wicked die. According to the next text we are to consider, Jer 12:1-3, the wicked often prosper. What shall we make of this contrary assertion?

Jer 12:1-3 stands in the middle of one of the prophet's complaints (11:18–12:6). These verses state the general theological problem suggested by the attempted murder of a man of God: Why do the wicked prosper? Jeremiah had given up all private interests in order to dedicate himself completely to God's cause. Although his proclamation contained severe moral criticism of the people of Judah and warnings of national calamity, it was ultimately directed at the people's good. Therefore, the violent response he received from them perplexed him and led him to doubt the justice of God. Are human affairs ordered by a righteous providence when the godly suffer persecution and the godless thrive? This question is asked repeatedly in the OT. It is the theme of Psalm 73, e.g., and it is one of the dominant motifs of the Book of Job. The prophet Habakkuk was another who joined Jeremiah in his complaint to God (Hab 1:1-4). The answer given by the psalmist is that the wicked eventually receive their just punishment, even though they seem to prosper in the short run. Jeremiah, Habakkuk, and the writer of the Book of Job do not propose any theoretical solution to the problem. The practical solution that Jeremiah adopted himself was to turn from his questioning of God and redouble his efforts as a prophet (Jer 12:5; 15:19-21). The absence of a theoretical answer sets a limit to our responsibility as interpreters. We have before us a major theological question and no answer.

Jer 12:1-6 resembles Jer 31:29-30 (the proverb about the sour grapes) in posing a profound theological question and providing no theoretical answer. To the charge that children suffer for the sins of their parents (31:29), a charge that challenges the justice of God, the only answer is that it will not always be so (v 30). Similarly, when the question arises in Jeremiah's mind concerning the prosperity of the wicked (12:1), he does not formulate a theoretical answer. His response is not theological but practical. He carries on his prophetic ministry, perplexed by the mystery of God's providence, but not immobilized by it.

No guidelines are laid down in the books of the prophets to help us resolve the problems that arise when we place texts like Jer 12:1-3 and Ezekiel 18 side by side. The questions and the contradiction in perspectives they seem to exhibit must be dealt with according to canons of understanding that lie outside the prophetic works themselves. Two principal solutions to the problem of the prosperity of the wicked have been proposed by interpreters of the Bible. The first is to deny that the wicked really prosper, at least in the sense that matters most, namely, psychological and spiritual well-being. This answer to the question may be supported by an appeal to Ezekiel 18, if living and dying there mean inward states of being rather than material conditions. The second principal solution is to project the resolution of the problem into a future time. We have already referred to Psalm 73 where the writer affirms that the wicked will eventually receive their punishment. The implication is that this will take place within their lifetime. Other biblical writers, and a great many later Jews and Christians, expected the final working out of justice to occur in a future age or an afterlife. These ideas, however, carry us beyond the immediate tasks of interpreting prophetic texts.

God and Israel (Hosea 2)

The OT prophets believed that all the kingdoms of the earth were subject to the righteous rule of God. They gave primary attention to the nation of Israel, but they published many oracles concerning foreign nations as well. Each of the four major collections of prophetic writings contains a substantial body of material dealing with foreign nations. There are large blocks of oracles concerning foreign nations in Isaiah, Jeremiah, and Ezekiel (Isaiah 13–23; Jeremiah 46–51; and Ezekiel 25–32), and several parts of The Book of the Twelve Prophets as well (Amos 1:3–2:5; Joel 3:1–21; Obadiah; Jonah;

Nahum; Zeph 2:4-7; Zech 9:1-8, 14:1-21). In addition there are innumerable allusions and brief oracular statements concerning foreign nations scattered throughout the books of the prophets. This is a considerable body of literature. Obviously, it had an important place in the prophetic tradition and in the formation of the biblical canon. Nevertheless, it is almost totally neglected in modern teaching of the Bible.

This modern neglect of the oracles concerning non-Israelite nations is not entirely undeserved. Compared to the oracles concerning Israel, they are monotonous and two-dimensional. Many of them ring the changes on a single theme: sooner or later in the justice of God, the nations will be punished for their pride, their idolatry, and their oppression of weaker peoples. This is an important theme of prophetic theology, but it becomes tedious when repeated over and over again. Furthermore, there is little if anything among these oracles that is edifying to individual persons concerning their relationship to God or concerning other important issues in their lives. On the other hand, they do merit some attention, if for no other reason than that they raise for us the important theological question about the rule of God in world history.

In our discussion we will consider briefly two oracles concerning foreign nations from the Book of Isaiah (10:5-21 and 19:16-25). First, however, we will examine Hosea 2, which presents a theological interpretation of Israel's history.

Here is one of the most interesting passages in the prophetic canon, and it is one of the most important theologically. In it the prophet interprets the history of Israel as a marriage between God and the covenant people. The marriage began when God led Israel out of slavery in Egypt and brought her into the land of Canaan (vv 14-15). The fruits of this land, which supported her life, were gifts of God. However, she did not remain faithful to God, but pursued "lovers." These were the deities of Canaan. Devotion to a religion of nature undermined her faith and corrupted her morality. These consequences are referred to only metaphorically in chap. 2; however, they are catalogued in detail in the oracles in chaps. 4–13. Israel interpreted the fruits of the earth as gifts of the gods of the earth (v 5) and proved to be incorrigible in her apostasy. Therefore, Yahweh would devastate the land and exile Israel from it, not only as a punishment, but also as a disciplinary measure aimed at bringing about her repentance and a renewal of her fidelity to the true God (vv 10-17). Once this had taken place God would renew the marriage covenant with Israel, restore her to the land she required as the basis of life, and fulfill her corporate life in righteousness (vv 18-23).

A similar interpretation of Israel's history is made in Hosea 11. However, there the metaphor used to symbolize God's relationship with Israel is that of parent and child, rather than husband and wife. The marriage metaphor is used again in Hosea's report of his call to prophesy (1:2-3), and in the narrative about his redemption of his profligate wife (3:1-5). Thus, the two family metaphors—marriage and parenthood—are central to Hosea's proclamation.

There are many details that we would want to examine here if we were doing a thorough exegesis of the chapter. We would want to determine as far as possible what historical events are alluded to, and how these allusions relate to what we know about the history of Israel from other sources. We would find that the picture presented here conforms to the broad outline of the story of Israel contained in the Pentateuch and Former Prophets (Joshua to 2 Kings). However, the real significance of Hosea 2 lies, not in its recounting of the history of Israel, but in the theological interpretation of this history. The first question for the interpreter to ask, then, is whether Hosea's allegory of Israel as the wife of Yahweh is a valid representation of Israel's experience.

There are two ways to affirm Hosea's interpretation of Israel's history. The first involves a merely historical judgment, while the second requires a judgment of faith. As historians of culture we can evaluate the place of religion in Israel's life. If Israel came into being, as the biblical sources indicate, as a people defined by a religious covenant, then the quality of her life and her existence as a nation were bound up with the strength and integrity of the religious commitment of her people. The structures of Israel's corporate life, the self-understanding of individual Israelites, the quality of human relations within Israelite society, the economic and political values of the people, in short, the whole of Israelite life and culture, was an expression of her faith in God. When her faith was eroded by religious syncretism or idolatry, her social unity and moral strength were undermined, and she became vulnerable to deliberate or unwitting assimilation by other nations.

If Israel came into being as the people of Yahweh, then she could not surrender her faith in Yahweh, and the understanding of human existence that was rooted in that faith, without becoming a different sort of people or ceasing to be a people at all. If this is what Hosea was saying, we can accept his analysis as historically accurate. Moreover, our acceptance does not require us to share his faith. However, when we ask whether Hosea's story of Israel is true theologically, we cannot answer the question on the basis of historical considerations alone. To interpret the creation of the Israelite nation and its settlement of the land of Canaan as blessings of God, and the dissolution of the nation as a punishment of God, is an act of faith, not of historiography. Furthermore, there is no way to move by rational argument from historiography to faith. One can perceive the hand of God in history only because of prior conviction.

Why did Hosea tell the story of Israel as an allegory of an adulterous wife? Surely it could not have been because the ingredients of Israel's history suggested it. It must have been because of the nature of Hosea's own religious experience. His knowledge of God must have been such that he found it appropriate to talk about the relationship of Israel to God as that of a wife to her husband (or in the case of chap. 11, that of a child to its parent). This does not mean that Hosea's knowledge of God was unique in Israel, or that he was the first to speak about the relationship to God in personal terms. On the contrary, God is represented as personal in all the OT traditions, and the relationship of God to human beings is spoken of everywhere in metaphors drawn from social institutions and social relations, e.g., judge, king, warrior, shepherd, teacher, and parent. Hosea did not invent this kind of language about God. What he did was to give a new emphasis to the familial metaphors of marriage and parenthood by creating the allegorical poems of chaps. 2 and 11, and by performing the prophetic acts with his wife and children that are reported in chaps. 1 and 3.

The images of God as husband and parent, so unforgettably embodied by Hosea in his allegories, connote a wider scope and greater depth in the divine-human relationship than any other metaphors employed in the OT. The range of involvement and the limit of responsibility between king and subject, judge and petitioner, captain and soldier, or teacher and pupil, e.g., are relatively narrow, and the depth of feeling between them is correspondingly shallow. By contrast, the range of involvement and responsibility in a husband-wife or parent-child relationship is unlimited, and the depth of feeling is extreme. Furthermore, these relationships are lifelong, whereas the others are usually transient or sporadic. Thus the images drawn from the family comprehend the whole of life throughout its length. For this reason they are superior theologically to images taken from other kinds of social relationship.

When we move from the situation of Hosea in the eighth century B.C. to our own, it is difficult to translate his analysis of Israel's history into one that applies to our own nation or to other modern communities. Taken as a whole, the story of ancient Israel is unique. It is not at all like our story, however we may define ourselves sociologically. But the metaphors of marriage and parenthood are transferrable to our own experience, with all that these metaphors imply about the relationship of human beings to God.

• The metaphor of marriage used in chap. 2 casts God in a masculine role. In this respect Hosea's language is characteristic of the OT generally, where language about God was conditioned by Israel's patriarchal society and her male-dominated culture. Hosea 11 is somewhat different, however. Although we may presume that Hosea was thinking paternally when he composed this oracle, the imagery he actually employed is not distinctively so. It applies as well to mothers, and thus it seems legitimate to refer to God as parent rather than father when interpreting this passage, and this usage is certainly more adequate theologically in our own time. Modern readers who insist upon viewing the figure of God in Hosea 11 as a father should at least take note of the loving tenderness which characterizes God there, an attribute our culture has been inclined to associate more with mothers. Hosea 11 is one of many passages in the Bible in which feelings and activities that many modern people tend to attribute to women are attributed to God.

God and Other Nations (Isaiah 10 and 19)

Hosea's theology of history was confined to the history of Israel, and there are no oracles concerning foreign nations. Other nations are alluded to, but primarily as powers that Israel depended upon to compensate for its own weakness (e.g., 5:13 and 7:8-11). However, there are a few references to foreign nations as instruments of God's judgment against Israel (7:16; 9:3, 6; 10:6; 11:5). In other books of the prophets there are extended oracles and groups of oracles concerning foreign nations. We have chosen just two of these to include in the present discussion. One of them concerns God's judgment against a foreign nation, and the second concerns God's redemption of foreign nations. The texts are Isa 10:5-21 and Isa 19:16-25.

"Woe Assyria, the rod of my anger, the staff of my fury!" Thus begins Isaiah's famous oracle. It is a literary masterpiece and a brilliant theological statement. Heretofore in this book we have paid little attention to the literary features of the passages. However, the literary form of the present text is so elegant and contributes so to the discernment of its message that it deserves comment. In vv 5 and 6 God declares that Assyria is the instrument of his punishment of a godless nation (Israel is to be understood). V 7 declares that Assyria's purpose in this enterprise is quite different from God's. It is not to punish, but to destroy. Vv 8-11 quote the vainglorious boasting of the Assyrian conqueror. V 12, which stands at the center of the oracle, is in prose. It affirms the twofold purpose of God, first to punish Mount Zion and Jerusalem, and then to punish Assyria. Vv 13-14 resume the poetic development of the oracle; they return to the theme of Assyria's pride, shown in the conquest of nations. V 15 asks the question whether an axe can vaunt itself above its wielder. Finally, vv 16-19 describe the devastation which God will bring upon Assyria. The seven segments of the oracle contain, respectively, the following number of poetic lines (in Hebrew): 3, 2, 6 (brief prose interlude), 6, 2, and 6. The form is chiastic. The prose statement of the twofold purpose of God at the center of the composition is preceded and followed by the two six-line exhibitions of the pride of Assyria. These in turn are flanked by two-line references to the contradiction between Assyria's purpose and God's. Then, on the outside of this structure, at the beginning and end of the oracle, are two announcements of God's wrath. The first is against Israel and the second against Assyria. The second is twice as long as the first, befitting the climactic section of the composition. If the reader will mark the sections of the poem with penciled brackets in the margins of a Bible in the way I have indicated, this finely articulated form will become evident. The seven elements are vv 5-6, 7, 8-11, 12, 13-14, 15, and 16-19.

Clearly, Isaiah believed God was the Lord of Assyria as well as Israel. Furthermore, his oracle implies that God was Lord of all the nations of the earth. This point becomes explicit when we read the other oracles concerning foreign nations in the Book of Isaiah (chaps. 13–23). In Isaiah's theological perspective the conquest of Israel by Assyria constituted a just punishment by

God for Israel's godlessness. The specific content of her wickedness is not spelled out in the present text, but it is expounded by Isaiah in his other oracles. The point here is that God's justice toward the nation is executed in the interactions of nations. In this case the judgment of God is executed by a nation whose own understanding of history is quite different from Isaiah's. It is thus the unknowing instrument of God's righteousness. The prophet, viewing international affairs in the perspective of faith, discerns the justice of God at work there. The participants in these affairs may not see this dimension at all.

The next assertion is that Assyria, the mighty conqueror, will eventually receive the same punishment for its pround defiance of God as it had mediated to Israel. God is no respecter of nations. The means of Assyria's punishment would be the same as Israel's, namely, conquest by another nation. To this extent the judgment of God is observed within the processes of history. Secular historians viewing the same events might discern a causal coherence in the interactions of nations, but they would not attribute it to the working of a transcendent, divine justice. The prophet, viewing this interaction through the eyes of faith, sees within it the providence of God.

Before asking whether this prophetic perception can illuminate our own understanding of history, we will turn to a different sort of oracle concerning non-Israelite nations. Most of the oracles on foreign nations in the OT pronounce God's judgment against arrogance and oppression, and, like Isa 10:5-21, envision the working out of God's justice through the conflicts of nations and the rise and fall of rulers. Some of them manifest an internationalist perspective that transcends national zeal and sectarian prejudice. The best example of this kind of oracle is Amos 1–2. Many others exhibit Israelite nationalism, e.g., Ezek 25:1-7. A few prophetic writers looked beyond the horizon of their own national interests and imagined the operation of a creative providence among the nations. The most notable of these was the author of Isaiah

40–55, whose constructive vision was truly worldwide. Another was the anonymous writer of the brief but remarkable word in Isa 19:23-25. This text stands in the midst of a series of oracles of judgment against Egypt (chaps. 19–20). The conviction and sentiment expressed in this prophecy are astonishing to find in any ancient writing. "In that day Israel will be the third with Egypt and Assyria, a blessing in the midst of the earth, whom the Lord of Hosts has blessed, saying, 'Blessed be Egypt my people, and Assyria the work of my hands, and Israel my heritage'" (vv 24-25). Assyria and Egypt were the upper and lower millstones between which Israel was ground throughout most of her history. For an Israelite prophet to compose these lines required extraordinary cultural transcendence. The passage contains no statement of the theological ground for the writer's prophecy. However, it must have been rooted in faith in the universal sovereignty of God and the will of God to create a harmonious community of nations in the world. The oracle preceding this one, which could be from the same writer, prophesies the conversion of the Egyptians to the worship of Yahweh, and thus suggests that a common devotion to the one Lord would provide the bond uniting the peoples into a single community.

Can these ancient texts have any meaning for us, other than as sources for the history of ideas? This is a difficult question. The dream of international harmony expressed in Isa 19:23-25 is an ideal that has persisted through the centuries and has had widespread currency in our time. However, the actualities of history, esp. the twentieth century, make it appear little more than an ideal. Nevertheless, the spirit that animates this ideal can affect attitudes and behavior powerfully, esp. among small groups, but also among nations. The prophetic conviction that tyrannical, rapacious powers will eventually fall is still credible today. We know that tyranny and oppression, among nations, groups, and individuals, often last a long time, and that there is seldom a perfect correlation between what is deserved and what is received. The OT prophets knew these things, too, but they were not deterred by this knowledge from proclaiming the righteousness of God.

The Righteous Ruler and the New Covenant
(Isaiah 11 and Jeremiah 31)

The prophetic oracles concerning foreign nations deal with what we might call the gross justice of God as it is implemented through the interactions of nations within the historical process. This is a gross rather than a precise justice because of the freedom that human beings have to shape their destiny, and because of the host of fortuitous circumstances affecting the course of history. Many righteous acts go unrewarded and many evil acts unpunished. Many noble efforts in behalf of human rights are thwarted, while many unjust social systems persist for generations. In these and other ways, justice is frustrated. The fulfillment of the righteous purposes of God among the nations, as these are conceived in prophetic theology, remains incomplete from generation to generation. Consequently, the prophetic interpretation of history includes the promise of a future fulfillment of the righteousness of God. This promise takes many forms. Jeremiah 33 (which seems unlikely to have been written by Jeremiah himself) prophesies the restoration of the Judean monarchy in the land of Canaan. The great blueprint for the future people of God in Ezekiel 40–48 describes a theocratic government and a society controlled by priests, in place of the traditional monarchy. Other prophetic texts contain a more ecumenical vision of the future. We have already referred to one of these, Isa 19:23-25. The greatest of them all is Isaiah 40–55, which prophesies the unfolding of God's purpose for the nations in a single world empire, ruled in righteousness by God's anointed leader and taught by the prophetic servants of the Lord (45:1-25 and 49:1-13, et al.). A full exposition of the prophetic teaching concerning the righteousness of God would have to take account of these and other texts. Such an exposition is beyond the scope of this book, but our discussion would be deficient if it omitted all consideration of a motif we have not yet mentioned. It has to do with the fulfillment of God's righteous purpose through the mediation of righteous people.

The achievement of justice and the other values that enhance life in community requires righteous rulers and righteous people. Isa 11:1-9 presents a picture of the righteous ruler who promotes the good of his people, and Jer 31:31-34 describes a good people. These two texts have no literary relationship to one another and are the work of different writers. The first is thought by many biblical scholars to be the work of the eighth-century Isaiah. However, some regard it as the work of an anonymous writer of a later time, perhaps during the Exile in the sixth century. The text from Jeremiah is attributed by most commentators to Jeremiah himself; however, it has much in common with the prose traditions of the Book of Jeremiah, which are primarily the work of the prophet's followers. Therefore it too may be from an anonymous exilic hand. I have chosen these two passages with which to conclude the present chapter, not because of any literary or historical relation between them, but because they express so well the two elements of prophetic thought just stated, viz., that the achievement of justice in society requires righteous rulers and righteous people.

Isa 11:1-9, a familiar messianic passage, is one of several passages concerning the Israelite king. The royal office was considered sacred in ancient Israel, and a special ritual of anointing consecrated the king for the service of God. Monarchy is almost always hereditary and in ancient Judah the hereditary principle became firmly established in the dynasty of David. The Davidic claim to sole legitimacy was supported by a tradition of divine election, which was expressed in the oracle of Nathan in 2 Samuel 7. This tradition was celebrated in Judean worship (Psalm 89), and it helped to secure the Davidic line in the Kingdom of Judah until the destruction of Jerusalem in 586 B.C. (e.g., 1 Kgs 8:16-19).

Isaiah 11 may reflect the influence of the royal liturgies that were celebrated in the temple of Jerusalem. The substance of these liturgies may be traced in the royal psalms, which probably arose in this setting (Ps 2, 18, 20, 21, 45, 72, 89, 101, 110, 132, 144). There is no evidence in the book that Isaiah challenged the dynastic principle itself or the tradition of God's election of the line of David. However, he was severely critical of the contemporary Judean king, Ahaz, for his conduct of national affairs (chaps. 7 and 8), and it is against the background of this criticism that we may view the portrait of the ideal Davidic ruler in chap. 11. It should be read together with the companion oracle 9:1-7, which describes a future deliverance of the people of God from oppression, the renewal of sovereignty for the Davidic king, and the establishment of peace. All this would take place through the power of God (v 7). The oracle in chap. 11 deals with the characteristics of the future king and the manner of his rule. Thus it describes the internal qualities of government by the vicegerent of God, whereas chap. 9 depicts the outward manifestations of the establishment of sovereignty by the anointed Davidic king (the "Messiah").

The oracle in 11:1-9 is framed as the promise of a future king, and we may accept it as a genuine prophecy in this sense. Therefore it is legitimate for interpreters of the Bible to ask whether and in what way this prophecy was fulfilled. Christians, beginning at least as early as Paul (Rom 15:12), have regarded Jesus Christ as the fulfillment, although they acknowledge that the promised age of peace and harmony has not yet been realized. Jews regard both the promise of an age of peace and promise of a messianic ruler as unfulfilled.

This oracle is a messianic prophecy, but it is also a model of the ideal ruler, and as such can serve as a guide and stimulus to rulers in the present age, even though no actual ruler could achieve that standard perfectly and permanently. Self-interest and finitude inevitably affect every government, and the conflicting demands of the people who are governed preclude the achievement of perfect justice or permanent harmony.

Nevertheless, rulers sharing the religious convictions of an Isaiah can learn from this model and rule more justly as a consequence.

In this oracle, the foundation of just rule is faith in God. It is the knowledge and fear of Yahweh from which the other qualities flow (11:2). This faith is not perfunctory or peripheral—something required traditionally by the office— but the central reality of the ruler's life. He delights in it! (v 3). The Spirit of God is manifested first of all in the protection of the rights of the weak and the poor and in the restraint of evil (v 4). However, this justice is not achieved through the ordinary use of violence, or the threat of violence, but by the intrinsic authority of the king's word. For such authority to be truly operative it requires the consent of the governed. This means there must be a people whose life and values are rooted in faith in God and who are willing to be subjects of a ruler whose administration is built upon this foundation.

The famous new-covenant text in Jer 31:31-34 is the prophecy of a future event, and it bears many similarities to Isa 11:1-9. It may be regarded by Christian interpreters as having been fulfilled in the creation of the Christian community through the life, death, and resurrection of Jesus of Nazareth. It may also function as a model of covenantal obedience in any age, quite apart from its association with the Christian proclamation. The obedience to God that characterizes the people of the New Covenant arises from personal knowledge of God, i.e., from faith, and fulfillment of covenantal law is achieved, not by external constraint, but by willing compliance arising out of the disposition of the heart. Here is a prophetic promise of forgiveness of iniquity offered by God, which is the only effective way to break the power of guilt. The statement that there will be no need for religious instruction, for everyone will already have attained the knowledge of God (v 34), points forward to the ultimate fulfillment of the people's existence in faith. It is not a simple description of any actual human community, though the promise of the oracle was partially fulfilled in the life of the Jewish community in the generations following Jeremiah's pronouncement. Although the promise contains the statement of an ideal that eludes total achievement by any people in history, it is an ideal that can be partially achieved in a community of faith. In this sense the oracle can serve as a model for existing religious communities as well as a promise of the future fulfillment of the purposes of God.

The righteousness of God is manifested in the fulfillment of creation. It is positive, life-supporting, enabling, nurturing, disciplining, and caring. It is not punitive or destructive. It elicits righteousness from the creatures and thus fulfills itself and them. This positive goal of the activity of God is suggested eloquently in the two prophecies from the books of Isaiah and Jeremiah.

V. "WHO IS LIKE GOD?"

Each of the passages we have discussed expresses or presupposes an understanding of God and God's relationship to the world, and so they might well have been included in the present chapter. By the same token, the two texts to be studied here (Isaiah 40 and Ezekiel 34) could have been treated appropriately in the preceding chapter, for they speak about God's activity as the righteous Lord of creation. We will consider them separately in order to focus attention upon the question of the nature of God. The first is the introductory poem to the great work of the Second Isaiah, and the second is Ezekiel's prophecy of the Good Shepherd. Both come from the exilic period.

No abstract doctrine of God is stated in the OT. There is no systematic or philosophical discussion of the nature or attributes of God and no argument for the existence of God against those who might question it. There was no secular atheism among the peoples of the ancient world, and many of the questions that arise in modern minds concerning the existence of and nature of God did not occur to ancient minds. The existence of invisible, superhuman, personal powers and their active involvement in the human environment were taken for granted by everyone. These were the immemorial assumptions that permeated people's perception of the world and their thoughts and feelings about their relation to it. Divine power and will were at work everywhere, and everything depended upon them. All of life, both corporate and individual, was lived in awareness of such forces and was punctuated by ritual acts, again both corporate and individual, aimed at attaining fuller comprehension and control of these powers and responding more appropriately to them. The most religious people in modern Western society would appear to be irreligious if compared with ordinary people in the biblical world. The imaginations of ancient people were filled with gods, spirits, and demons, and their lives were regulated at every turn by rituals predicated upon the demands, promises, or threats of these beings. Atheism for most ancient people was simply inconceivable, and so was life without regular worship of the gods.

Throughout the history of ancient Israel there was a profound struggle between the religions of the environing peoples and Israel's faith in Yahweh. Both involved an understanding of reality in which the Divine played a central part. The difference lay in their conceptions of the Divine. One was polytheistic and involved the deification of powers in nature (earth, sky, rain, sun, sea, etc.). It also involved an interpretation of the processes of nature according to the analogy of animal procreation. Things came to be and were renewed in the world as a result of the sexual mating of gods and goddesses, and much of the ritual practice of religion was intended to support this regeneration and respond to it suitably. Individual deities were imagined in human or animal form and were symbolized accordingly. The processes of nature and the structures of society were described in myths, and these provided the intellectual background for the performance of ritual and were sometimes dramatized in the rituals themselves. Offerings to the gods were often magical, in the sense that they were meant to coerce or purchase the favor and intervention of the gods, and the omission of offerings and other ritual acts from the routine of human life would place the whole human enterprise in jeopardy. Good and ill fortune were determined, battles were won and lost, kings rose and fell, crops flourished or failed, people lived and died by the will of the gods. Sometimes the gods acted arbitrarily, but sometimes they acted in response to human behavior, including the performance or omission of worship. Disease and health were controlled by the gods, although disease was often interpreted as possession by demonic powers. Healing, therefore, was sought through propitiation of the gods or exorcism of the demons. The cycle of the seasons was celebrated, and the fertility of crops and flocks was supported by rituals designed to assure the favor of the gods and assist in the regulation of the natural processes. Kings ruled by the will of the gods, and kingship itself was established on the earth as a mirror of divine rule. The rituals that accompanied the birth and enthronement of kings and the major events of their reigns were profoundly religious matters. In these and many other ways, the life of ancient people was founded upon and permeated by an intense and active polytheism.

Israelite Yahwism contended with this understanding and way of life throughout its history. We can obtain a rough idea of this struggle from the OT. However, the account is incomplete and biased for it oversimplifies the picture of the rival religion as well as the account of the conflict between the two faiths. As a result we cannot determine accurately who in Israel at various stages in its history shared the faith expressed in the OT itself. The OT is the final literary product of the history of Yahwism, and through it we receive fragmentary glimpses of its earlier developments, but we do not know with certainty what the persons mentioned in the OT story believed or exactly how they practiced their religion, except for the prophets, whose own writings are incorporated in the canonical OT. We can be certain only about the faith of the writers of the OT, and most of them are anonymous. We can only speculate about the faith of

oracles from the preexilic period are short, staccato, slashing, and critical, and place the speaker in confrontation with the audience. In contrast, the poems of Second Isaiah "speak to the heart" (v 2) of the hearer, appealing and encouraging, and placing the speaker in sympathetic relation to the audience. This requires repetition and persuasion, the creation of a mood, the stirring of feelings. This poem is not so much a text to be used as the starting point of a sermon, it is a sermon. Yet, how much more stirring and memorable than the discursive prose sermons in the Book of Jeremiah!

The poem is positive from beginning to end. It opens with an admonition to the messengers of God to comfort his people, and it ends with the affirmation that those who wait upon, or trust in, the Lord will be sustained. Thus the mood of this opening section conforms entirely to that of the joyful, exuberant closing passage, Isaiah 55, which we discussed earlier. Every line of the poem merits careful reflection. However, we will make only a few comments upon some of the salient features.

The initial injunction to comfort the people of God and declare his pardon for all their iniquities is followed immediately by another command to prepare the way of God in the wilderness, so that his glory may be beheld by all flesh (vv 3-5). Thus, the word of comfort is reinforced by the assurance of the imminent coming of God. Then this second word gives way to the third, in which the transience of all humanity is contrasted with the permanence of the word of God (vv 6-8). Thus, the three opening themes of the work are, first, comfort and forgiveness, second, the impending appearance of God's glory as the sign of his presence, and third, the everlasting reliability of God's word amidst an evanescent humanity. In sum, God's comfort, God's glory, God's word.

The next section of the chapter (vv 9-17) has three segments parallel in content to the three we have just considered. The first affirms that God is coming, with his reward and recompense before him, to be the shepherd of the flock (vv

9-11). The second speaks about who God is (vv 12-14), and the third contrasts the insignificance of the nations with the grandeur of God (vv 15-17).

The third section of the poem (vv 18-31) has two principal segments. In the first, which opens with the question, "To whom then would you liken God?" elaborates upon the theme introduced in the second division about the absurdity and futility of idols (vv 18-24). This segment closes by asserting that God brings the rulers of the earth to nothing, thus echoing the concluding comment in the second division of the poem (vv 23-24, cf. v 15). The final segment of the third division, which concludes the entire poem, brings us back to the opening theme, viz., the word of comfort and assurance to the people of God. It asks, "Why do you say, O Jacob, and speak, O Israel, 'My way is hid from the Lord . . . ?'" (v 27) and goes on to reply to this question. The message is addressed to discouraged Israelites who have given up on God. Here the practical goal of the proclamation is reached, and the reason for the repeated contrast between human finitude and divine transcendence becomes clear. The discouraged Israelites are to take heart, place their confidence in the unsearchable power of God, and allow themselves to be revived and strengthened in their way (vv 27-31). "They who wait upon the Lord . . . shall walk and not faint." This is the goal of the prophecy.

The fall of the Kingdom of Judah, the destruction of Jerusalem, and the exile of the nation's leaders appeared to many to demonstrate the ineffectiveness of Yahweh, the God of Israel, and caused them to turn to the worship of other gods, esp. the gods of the conquering Babylonians (Jer 44:15-30). Isaiah 40–55 responds to the despair underlying this behavior and the inadequacy of the idolatries to which the people have turned. The prophet's treatment of the theme of idolatry is introduced only briefly in chap. 40 and is expanded in subsequent poems. In contrast to the various idolatries, which deify objects and forces within nature, the conception of God presented by Second Isaiah places the entire natural order within the comprehension and power of God. This picture of Yahweh as sovereign creator of all things makes explicit an element in Israel's faith that is only implicit in some other OT writings. Genesis 1, the Book of Job, and some of the Psalms, are OT texts that definitely express this concept, and they may be roughly contemporary with Second Isaiah. Here in Isaiah 40 the implications of the prophetic faith in one God are made evident. There is but one God, and this God is both sustainer of Israel and creator of the heavens and the earth.

The understanding of God as creator of the natural order is linked with that of God as sovereign over the historical order. Nations are subject to this sovereignty, just as the stars are. It manifests itself in both the humbling of the mighty (v 23) and the empowering of the weary (vv 29-31). Creation and providence are thus united in the activity of the one God. Although the prophet expressed this faith in a new way, he insisted that he was proclaiming to Israel what they had been told from the beginning, what indeed should have been understood from the foundations of the earth (v 21). Here and elsewhere Second Isaiah shows how the new message he is proclaiming is rooted in the old witness of Israel's faith.

The coming revelation of God's glory, which is announced at the beginning of the poem, is an event described only symbolically in chap. 40, in the image of the leveling out of valleys and hills to prepare a processional highway for the appearance of God (v 4). In subsequent chaps. this event is described in concrete historical terms. Indeed, the entire collection of Second Isaiah's poems is an elaboration of this theme. The whole community of nations will be involved in this vast historical development. It will include the conquest of Babylon by Cyrus and the creation of a great world empire (cf., e.g., chap. 45). It will also involve the dissemination of God's *torah* and the establishment of God's justice (42:4) by Israel, the servant of Yahweh. And it will include the release of exiled Israelite captives and the restoration of the city of Jerusalem as the focal point of the witness to God and his saving purpose (e.g., 40:9; 48:20; 49:8-18). Thus, although the major themes of the work are stated in chap. 40, it is only an introduction to the rich exposition in chaps. 41–55.

The understanding of God expressed in Isaiah 40 is clear and coherent. However, in the actual experience of human beings, in both ancient and modern times, this faith is not held by everyone, nor is it easily attained. The prophet himself was aware of this, for he observed that witnesses of God come to understand the God whom they proclaim in the very process of bearing witness (43:10 and 50:4). The teacher learns by teaching, and the messengers of God come to full understanding by proclaiming the word to others. The role of the witnesses, who form an ever-widening circle from Jerusalem to the ends of the earth, is indicated already in the introductory poem (vv 3, 6), and it occupies a central place in the subsequent chapters.

The message of Isaiah 40–55 was the announcement of a drama of salvation, which the prophet believed to be unfolding in his own time, and it was a summons to his fellow Israelites to play their proper part in this drama. Before discussing the outcome of this proclamation and its possible relevance to the life of a modern reader, let us turn to Ezekiel 34.

The Good Shepherd (Ezekiel 34)

Ezekiel 34 is an allegory of the history of Israel under the monarchy, and a prophecy of the future restoration of the nation. There are many historical allusions that we would have to probe in a thorough exegesis. However, we are only considering it here because of what it says about God, and so we will not follow the other exegetical paths suggested in the text.

Earlier we examined several other passages from the Book of Ezekiel that represent God as the punitive judge of idolators in Jerusalem (8:16, 9:11) and as the guarantor of a strict, retributive justice in the lives of individual persons (chap. 18). It comes as something of a surprise, therefore, to see the wrathful executioner and impersonal judge displaced by a shepherd eager to rescue, protect, and provision his flock. The metaphor of the shepherd implies many of the qualities suggested by the metaphors of husband and parent in Hosea 2 and 11. The shepherd-image is less satisfactory than the images drawn from family relationships, since human beings are symbolized much more adequately as children or brides than as sheep. Nevertheless, from the side of the shepherd/husband/ parent there are common dimensions of commitment and affection that are connoted by all of these metaphors. It is noteworthy that the image of God as the Good Shepherd, which received its classic formulation in Ezekiel 34, became one of the most popular images in later Jewish and Christian piety and iconography.

Ezekiel's allegory of the shepherds and the Good Shepherd says much about his understanding of God and his understanding of the function of kingship. For him, kings are clearly meant to be servants of God and God's people, in contrast to what the kings of Israel had made of the institution. Several interesting points emerge in his treatment of God as the Good Shepherd. Perhaps the most important is the statement that God actively searches for the lost sheep, rescuing, gathering, and feeding them. This is not a dispassionate judge, but an impassioned savior. The goal of God's activity in the lives of people is to seek the lost, gather the strayed, heal the crippled, and empower the weak. This is also the proper goal of the servants of God, according to Ezekiel.

The shepherd "watches over" the strong as well as the weak (v 16, reading *Smr* with the Greek, Syriac, and Vulgate, and RSV, CBAT, JB, and NEB). It would make little sense to "destroy" them (*Smd,* MT), even though the shepherd may have to judge some of them (vv 17-22). God shepherds the entire flock.

In Ezekiel's prophecy the Davidic monarchy is to be reestablished in Israel (vv 23, 24), and his conception of that future life is conservative, in the sense that it projects the preexilic form of the nation. Second Isaiah does not do this with respect to the Davidic monarchy, but instead envisions Israel's role as that of prophet and teacher within a world empire ruled by a non-Israelite king. What actually happened in the postexilic era was much closer to Second Isaiah's vision than to Ezekiel's. However, the principal emphasis of Ezekiel 34 is not upon the restoration of the Davidic monarchy. This event is only one aspect of the unfolding purpose of God. The ultimate goal of the drama is to bring people to the knowledge of God. The making of a new covenant, the provision of natural blessings, the freeing of slaves, the establishment of peace and security, all serve one purpose: "And they shall know that I, the Lord their God, am with them, and that they, the house of Israel, are my people, says the Lord God" (v 31). Living in the knowledge of God is the goal of the entire process of human history and divine providence.

We return now to the questions we asked above concerning the outcome of the promises made in Isaiah 40 and Ezekiel 34 and their meaning for modern readers.

Both passages anticipate events that are to take place at some time in the future, when God will be present, will act decisively, and will be acknowledged as God. Were these anticipations actualized, and if so, in what way? If not, are they still to be realized, or were the prophets wrong? In either case, what meaning can their prophecies have for modern readers?

Clearly, when Second Isaiah speaks about God's appearing in glory (40:5), he is not speaking of an appearance visible to eyes of flesh, even though he asserts that "all flesh" shall behold the appearance. The God who "measured the waters in the hollow of his hand" (v 12) is not visible to human eyes in any circumstances. The glory of God, whose manifestation the writer prophesies, can be seen only with eyes of faith. It is the same glory that "filled the whole earth" according to the First Isaiah's inaugural vision (6:3). Just as the glory which fills the whole earth was already visible in Isaiah's time to those who had eyes to see, so the glory which Second Isaiah prophesied would be manifest only to those who had faith. However, in that event all humanity would have been brought to faith, so all would behold the glory. The eyes of faith and the eyes of unfaith observe exactly the same phenomena, but the one regards them as manifestations of God's power and wisdom, while the other sees only what they appear to be.

If the future appearance of God in glory anticipated in Isaiah 40 is not essentially different from the presence of God which could be known in the present, then we would not have to posit "a new heaven and a new earth" as the precondition of fulfillment. Both Isaiah 40 and Ezekiel 34 seem to be speaking about the not-too-distant future. Indeed, the events heralded by Second Isaiah are already beginning to take place in his own time. In chap. 34 Ezekiel is anticipating a time somewhat farther into the future, though not necessarily more than a few generations. His hope of a restoration of the Israelite nation might reasonably have been expected to be fulfilled in that length of time. The next question, then, is whether the expectations of these two writers were actually realized in subsequent years.

Specific aspects of the two prophecies were not fulfilled. The Davidic dynasty was not restored to power as Ezekiel had expected, and the creation of a unified world empire with Jerusalem as the spiritual center was not achieved. However, some of the hopes of our two writers were fulfilled significantly. Babylon was conquered by Cyrus, who did establish a more just and humane policy toward subject peoples. Jewish exiles were permitted to return to their homeland. Jerusalem was rebuilt, and the temple of Yahweh reestablished. New forms of social organization, worship, and education were developed among Jewish communities. The people of the covenant increased enormously in numbers, and they became one of the most creative peoples of the ancient world. The institution of the synagogue took form in the postexilic era, and it has persisted to the present day as a fundamental institution of Judaism. The Hebrew Bible was given its canonical form in those centuries also, and ultimately became the Holy Scriptures for millions of Jews and Christians. These are the principal ways in which the glory of God appeared to those who had eyes to see.

> • As we have observed many times before, the OT writers were not concerned to formulate general truths about God or humanity, but spoke primarily about their own times and people and the ways of God as they perceived them in Israel's experience. Therefore, many of the biblical texts do not lend themselves simply to religious instruction for modern readers, and it is difficult to move directly from Isaiah 40 and Ezekiel 34 to our own situation. They are concerned, after all, with the conditions and prospects of Israel in the sixth century B.C. One of our responsibilities as interpreters of the Bible is to acknowledge the time-bound features of these texts and not try to force them to speak to us in ways they were not meant to do. Nevertheless, there are elements in them which can illuminate our understanding of God.

God is the savior in Isaiah 40 and Ezekiel 34. This is the understanding of God that dominates the story of Israel in the Pentateuch and the Psalms, and it reappears again and again in the Prophets. Christians are often unaware of this, or disregard it. It is common for Christians to exalt the NT at the expense of the OT, by contrasting the NT message of salvation with "the OT message of judgment." However, this is an inadequate interpretation of the Bible. There is judgment in both testaments, but both are founded on faith in God as creator and redeemer. The story of Israel is a story of salvation. The prophecy of salvation in Isaiah 40 and Ezekiel 34 is a renewal of God's promise to Abraham (Genesis 12) and to Moses (Exodus 3), and it is the message that unites the OT, as well as the NT.

The primary relevance of these two texts (and the others we have discussed) for modern readers lies in this understanding of God as creator and savior. The basic meaning of these texts was what they said to Judean exiles 2500 years ago about their situation, their prospects, and their faith. Their meaning for us is twofold. We can see the witness of faith in God as it worked in ancient Israel, and we can reaffirm that faith ourselves. The fruits of God's word are always appropriate to the time in which it is spoken, and they may not be the same in every age. And yet, it is the same God whose word is spoken. Knowledge of the prophets' faith in God, which found expression in their writings but which even more undergirded them, is the principal meaning of these texts for us.

AIDS FOR THE INTERPRETER

Translation

Interpreters without Hebrew should make use of all the help available in recent English translations to determine the meaning of the text. Translations by individuals are less authoritative than the ones listed here, all of which are by qualified teams. Avoid *The Living Bible,* which is not a translation and cannot be trusted to represent the Bible's meaning. Most of the versions listed are evaluated in detail in Lloyd Bailey, ed., *The Word of God* (Atlanta: John Knox Press, 1982). Use them all.

The Complete Bible, An American Translation. Chicago: University of Chicago Press, 1939.

Good News Bible, Today's English Version. New York: American Bible Society, 1976.

The Holy Bible, New International Version. Grand Rapids: Zondervan Bible Publishers, 1978.

The Jerusalem Bible. New York: Doubleday & Co., 1966.

The New American Bible. New York: P. J. Kenedy & Sons, 1970.

New American Standard Bible. La Habra, Calif.: Lockman Foundation, 1963.

The New English Bible with the Apocrypha, Oxford Study Edition. New York: Oxford University Press, 1976.

The New Oxford Annotated Bible with the Apocrypha, Revised Standard Version. New York: Oxford University Press, 1973.

A New Translation of the Holy Scriptures According to the Masoretic Text (New Jewish Version). Philadelphia: Jewish Publication Society of America, 1962, 1978.

Be sure to buy the annotated editions of the RSV, NEB, and JB.

Reference and Commentary

A complete concordance is essential. Those of Robert Young *(Analytical Concordance to the Bible)* and James Strong *(Exhaustive Concordance of the Bible)* are based on the King James Version. However, they provide access to the Hebrew and Greek words behind the English. They will be superseded by C. Morrison, *An Analytical Concordance to the RSV.* The NT section was published in 1979, and the OT section is in preparation.

The Interpreter's Dictionary of the Bible (5 vols. Nashville: Abingdon Press, 1962, 1976) is invaluable.

The treatments of the prophets in *The Interpreter's Bible,* vols. 5 and 6 (Nashville: Abingdon Press, 1956) are generally good and often excellent. The Old Testament Library (Philadelphia: The Westminster Press) is solid, too: Otto Kaiser, *Isaiah 1–12* (1972), *Isaiah 13–39* (1974); Claus Westermann, *Isaiah 40–66* (1969); Walter Eichrodt, *Ezekiel* (1970); James L. Mays, *Hosea* (1969), *Amos* (1969), *Micah* (1976). The *New International Commentary on the Old Testament* (Grand Rapids: Eerdmans Publishing Co.) has good volumes so far by Leslie C. Allen on *Joel, Obadiah, Jonah, Micah* (1976); and by J. A. Thompson on *Jeremiah* (1980). The commentaries in the series Hermeneia (Philadelphia: Fortress Press) are thorough and technical: Hans Walter Wolff, *Hosea* (1974), *Joel and Amos* (1977); Walter Zimmerli, *Ezekiel* (vol. 1, 1978, vol. 2 in preparation).

Interpretation

There are not many profound works in English on the theology of the Prophets. Gerhard von Rad, *The Message of the Prophets* (New York: Harper & Row, 1962, 1975; this is part of vol. 2 of his *Old Testament Theology*) is perhaps the best in print. Martin Buber, *The Prophetic Faith* (New York: The Macmillan Co., 1949) is excellent, but out of print. Look for a used copy. Abraham Herschel, *The Prophets* (New York: Harper & Row, 1962) is valuable, too.

The best, thorough book on the whole phenomenon of prophecy is Johannes Lindblom, *Prophecy in Ancient Israel* (Oxford: Basil Blackwell, 1962).

Good books on individual prophetic books are: William L. Holladay, *Isaiah: Scroll of a Prophetic Heritage* (Grand Rapids: Eerdmans Publishing Co., 1978), and Hans Walter Wolff, *Micah the Prophet* (Philadelphia: Fortress Press, 1981).

The series of paperbacks for preachers (and others), Knox Preaching Guides (Atlanta: John Knox Press), emphasizes the meaning of the biblical books for today. All the Prophets will be treated, beginning with *Amos and Hosea* (1981), by James M. Ward.

Another paperback series, Proclamation Commentaries (Philadelphia: Fortress Press) is also useful, though it confines itself largely to the original meaning of the text. Volumes available so far on the Prophets are: Bernhard W. Anderson, *The Eighth Century Prophets* (1978), James L. Mays, *Ezekiel, Second Isaiah* (1978), and Elizabeth Achtemeier, *Deuteronomy, Jeremiah* (1978).